INTRODUCTION TO

HOMELAND SECURITY

SECOND EDITION

POLICY, ORGANIZATION, AND ADMINISTRATION

Willard M. Oliver, PhD
Sam Houston State University

Nancy E. Marion, PhD
Associate Chair of the Department of Political Science, University of Akron

Joshua B. Hill, PhD
Assistant Professor, The University of Southern Mississippi

JONES & BARTLETT
LEARNING

World Headquarters
Jones & Bartlett Learning
5 Wall Street
Burlington, MA 01803
978-443-5000
info@jblearning.com
www.jblearning.com

Jones & Bartlett Learning books and products are available through most bookstores and online booksellers. To contact Jones & Bartlett Learning directly, call 800-832-0034, fax 978-443-8000, or visit our website, www.jblearning.com.

Substantial discounts on bulk quantities of Jones & Bartlett Learning publications are available to corporations, professional associations, and other qualified organizations. For details and specific discount information, contact the special sales department at Jones & Bartlett Learning via the above contact information or send an email to specialsales@jblearning.com.

26712-9

Production Credits
VP, Product Management: Amanda Martin
Director of Product Management: Laura Pagluica
Product Specialist: Audrey Schwinn
Product Assistant: Melissa Duffy
Product Coordinator: Paula-Yuan Gregory
Project Specialist: Kelly Sylvester
Digital Project Specialist: Angela Dooley
Marketing Manager: Suzy Balk
Manufacturing and Inventory Control Supervisor: Amy Bacus
Composition: Exela Technologies
Project Management: Exela Technologies
Cover Design: Kristin E. Parker
Senior Media Development Editor: Shannon Sheehan
Rights Specialist: John Rusk
Printing and Binding: LSC Communications
Cover Printing: LSC Communications

Cover Image (Title Page): © Jackie Niam/iStock/Getty Images; Courtesy of Ozzy Trevino, U.S. Customs and Border Protection; © Photographer is my life/Getty Images; Courtesy of Ozzy Trevino, U.S. Customs and Border Protection; Courtesy of Donna Burton, U.S. Customs and Border Protection; Courtesy of Staff Sgt. Elvis Umanzor, U.S. Army; Courtesy of Mass Communication Specialist Seaman Gregory M. Wilhelmi, U.S. Navy; Courtesy of Mass Communication Specialist 3rd Class Kaitlyn E. Eads, U.S. Navy; Courtesy of Shawn Moore, U.S. Customs and Border Protection; Courtesy of Master Sgt. Mark C. Olsen, U.S. Air National Guard; Courtesy of Airman 1st Class Tristan D. Viglianco, U.S. Air Force; © Peter Kim/Shutterstock; Courtesy of Will Adams, U.S. Customs and Border Protection; Courtesy of Jeannie Mooney, FEMA; Courtesy of Ozzy Trevino, U.S. Customs and Border Protection; Courtesy of Ozzy Trevino, U.S. Customs and Border Protection.

Library of Congress Cataloging-in-Publication Data
Names: Oliver, Willard M., author. | Marion, Nancy E., author. | Hill, Joshua B., author.
Title: Introduction to homeland security : policy, organization, and administration / Willard M. Oliver, Nancy E. Marion, and Joshua B. Hill.
Description: Second edition. | Burlington, MA : Jones & Bartlett Learning, [2021] | Summary: "Suitable for undergraduate students entering the field of Homeland Security and for Criminal Justice students, Introduction to Homeland Security: Policy, Organization, and Administration, Second Edition, is a comprehensive, accessible text designed for students seeking a thorough overview of the policies, administrations, and organizations that fall under Homeland Security"–Provided by publisher.
Identifiers: LCCN 2019021081 | ISBN 9781284154634 (paperback)
Subjects: LCSH: United States. Department of Homeland Security. | National security–United States. | Internal security–United States. | Terrorism–United States–Prevention.
Classification: LCC HV6432.4 .O45 2021 | DDC 363.340973–dc23
LC record available at https://lccn.loc.gov/2019021081

6048

Printed in the United States of America

25 24 23 22 21   10 9 8 7 6 5 4 3

Dedication

To Danger!

Brief Contents

Contents

About the Authors

Willard M. Oliver is professor of criminal justice in the College of Criminal Justice at Sam Houston State University, Huntsville, Texas. He holds a PhD and MA in political science from West Virginia University and an MS and BS in criminal justice from Radford University, Radford, Virginia. His research interests include both police and national crime policy, of which homeland security is the intersection of both. He is a retired Major from the U.S. Army Military Police Corps, a decorated veteran of the Persian Gulf War, and a former police officer from the Washington, DC, metropolitan area. Oliver is an avid marathon runner and resides with his family in Huntsville, Texas.

Nancy E. Marion is professor of political science and associate chair of the Department of Political Science at the University of Akron, Akron, Ohio. She holds a PhD and MA in political science from the State University of New York, an MS in criminal justice from American University, and a BS in administration of justice from Pennsylvania State University. She is the author of numerous peer-reviewed journal articles and books, including *The Public Policy of Crime and Criminal Justice*. Her research interests center around the interplay of politics and criminal justice/homeland security policy. Most recently, she was awarded a research grant from the Canadian government to study border security issues and the "intermestic" nature of homeland security policies.

Joshua B. Hill is an assistant professor of Homeland Security and Terrorism at Tiffin University in Tiffin, Ohio. He holds a PhD in criminal justice, an MA in criminology and criminal justice from Sam Houston State University, Huntsville, Texas, and a BA in international relations from the University of Central Florida, in Orlando. His research interests include terrorism, international policing, and research methods. He has prior experience as a project manager with a non-governmental organization (NGO), the Institute for the Study of Violent Groups (ISVG), focusing on open-source collection of terrorist information. Most recently, he published an article examining terrorism culpability in the *Journal of Defense Modeling and Simulation*.

Reviewers

The authors and publisher wish to thank the following reviewers for their valuable input in the development of this text:

George Ackerman

Robert Jay Alley
Blue Ridge Community College

Captain David M. Allender
Indianapolis Metropolitan Police Department

Edward T. Croissant
Tampa Police Department

Dustin A. Dorough
Brandman University

Camille Gibson
Prairie View A&M University

Christopher J. Granto
St. John's University

John Halbrook
Des Moines Area Community College

Sean Joiner
Augusta Technical College

Curtis Jones
Mississippi College

Daniel J. Klenow
North Dakota State University

F. Wayne Laney, Jr.
Rowan-Cabarrus Community College

Keith Gregory Logan
Kutztown University of Pennsylvania

Felix G. Mangual
University of Central Florida

Christopher Martinez
Montclair State University

John M. McCullough
South Hills School of Business and Technology

Anna Marie Pavy
Campbellsville University

Mitchel P. Roth
Sam Houston State University

Jeffrey P. Rush
Austin Peay State University

Jeffrey R. Ryan
Jacksonville State University

Jon Whitmar
Ivy Tech Community College

Wojtek M. Wolfe
Rutgers University

Dominic D. Yin
City College of San Francisco

Introduction

On September 11, 2001, when al Qaeda terrorists hijacked four planes and purposefully flew two of them into the World Trade Towers in New York City, one into the Pentagon in Arlington, Virginia, with the fourth crashing in Pennsylvania only because of the bravery of its passengers—America's world changed forever. Ushered in were both a new era and a new phrase in our vocabulary: *Homeland Security*. Despite the long hunt for the head of al Qaeda, Osama bin Laden, and his eventual death at the hands of Navy Seal Team VI, the threat to America's homeland continues. As is evidenced by the over 50 terrorist attacks that have been thwarted since 9/11 and several successful attacks including the Boston Marathon bombing on April 15, 2013, America must remain ever vigilant and continue to work toward protecting the homeland.

In the immediate aftermath of 9/11, there was a call for an Office of Homeland Security in the White House, which eventually became the Department of Homeland Security (DHS). While the DHS is not the sole protector of America's homeland today, it has become the central player focused on the growing homeland security machinery for modern day civil defense. Yet, despite the strong federal nature of the DHS, most of the first-line responders—police, fire, and EMS—are local personnel, many from the criminal justice system. The primary methods for responding to future terrorist attacks and natural disasters, such as the Incident Command System, are all focused on these local responders. Thus, homeland security is, in many ways, an administrative and organizational response to both potential and real threats.

Homeland security has also grown in strength as an area of policy, which can be seen in the growth of oversight by all three branches of government—executive, legislative, and judiciary. The president manages the bureaucracy of homeland security, Congress the funding for and laws associated with it, and the Courts keep both in check for the constitutionality around the trade-off of more security versus less personal freedom. As a result of this ongoing policy activity, homeland security has also quickly become an area of academic study. It is for all of these reasons that this book was written.

We felt that it was important to take a broad view—to include all of the various ideas, policies, and methods for addressing terrorist attacks and natural disasters—to provide a clear picture of what "homeland security" means in today's America. In order to present this picture realistically, we felt that it was important to highlight homeland security policy, organization, and administration, as currently found in the field, study, and practice of homeland security. Thus, we have tried to incorporate the many perspectives of homeland security through our varied backgrounds and areas of expertise, including the administrative and organizational approaches (Oliver), the public policy perspectives (Marion), and the many aspects of terrorism and security (Hill).

Toward that end, this book is organized into 15 chapters, which lead the student of homeland security from the beginning to contemporary America.

The book starts with a prologue detailing the tragic events of September 11, 2001, as a reminder of why we have created the field of homeland security in the first place. It then details the history of homeland security (Chapter 1), for although the term *homeland security* did not come about until 9/11, it was rooted in past concepts of civil defense and emergency management. The book then strives to define the concept of homeland security (Chapter 2) from its many and varied perspectives, particularly how it has developed conceptually, administratively, and organizationally over the past 12 years. The book then moves to discuss the two major concerns of homeland security, terrorism and natural disasters (Chapter 3).

This introduction to homeland security then proceeds to discuss how it developed in the aftermath of 9/11 (Chapter 4), and then describes its current status as a central federal organization—the Department of Homeland Security (Chapter 5). Chapter 6 moves beyond the federal bureaucracy to focus on the broader community. Chapter 7 looks at how this community, through anti-terrorism and counter-terrorism measures, works to address the terrorism side of homeland security.

The book then presents the National Strategy for Homeland Security (Chapter 8), the particular threats it attempts to address (Chapter 9), and how the homeland security cycle progresses (Chapter 10). In Chapter 11, it then looks at the local response mechanisms of the National Incident Management System (NIMS) and the Incident Command System (ICS).

The text then details the political (Chapter 12) and legal (Chapter 13) issues surrounding homeland security, and then deals with a wide array of issues that have evolved over the last 12 years, including communications and technology issues (Chapter 14), domain security issues (sea, land, and air, in Chapter 15), and then briefly discusses the future of homeland security in America (also Chapter 15).

New to the *Second Edition*

Ever since homeland security policy, organization, and administration, came into existence post 9/11, it has been in a rapid state of growth and change. One only has to note the differences in homeland security during the Bush, Obama, and Trump administrations to understand how policy has differed among presidential administrations, how homeland security organizations have changed and grown, and how administrators have come and gone, while administration itself has become more complex. A new edition was necessary simply to keep up with the changes. One simple example of the administrative heads of the federal Department of Homeland Security (DHS) should demonstrate just how much has changed between editions. When the first edition was published, Janet Napolitano was the Secretary of Homeland Security. Since then, Jeh Johnson was appointed the fourth secretary by Obama and John F. Kelly the fifth and Kirstjen Nielsen the sixth secretary by President Trump. Therefore, much of the second edition consists of changes to the book that keep up with the many changes in homeland security.

In addition to just updates, there are also other changes to the text. Some of these are behind the scenes, often in the endnotes. When the first edition was published, there was still a lot of speculation or anecdotal information, but as we get further along in seeing homeland security implemented, we now have many scholarly studies of homeland security that have been released and they often confirm what we know; however, in other cases, they alter our knowledge of homeland security. The addition of these many studies can be found in this second edition. Still further, we are very grateful to our many reviewers of the first edition who offered suggestions and recommended that we not neglect certain omissions from the first edition. For instance, in the first edition, in an attempt to keep the homeland security history brief, the text made no mention of the Stafford Disaster Relief and Emergency Assistance Act. Several of our reviewers pointed out that this was far too important to leave out of any discussion regarding emergency management and we agreed. So, material that we may have omitted from the first edition has been added to the second edition. And, finally, as hard as we tried to avoid making any minor mistakes, nevertheless, some cropped up in the first edition that have now been fixed in the second edition. Again, we thank the reviewers for their close reviews of the first edition. Still, any such mistakes found in the second edition are still those of the authors, but we thank those second edition reviewers for taking the time to ensure that no such mistakes were present in the new edition.

The Student Experience

The second edition of *Introduction to Homeland Security* was designed with numerous features to create an engaging learning environment for students and enhance their experience with this text.

Chapter Objectives: The learning objectives are listed at the beginning of each chapter. Emphasis is placed on active, rather than passive, learning. It is hoped that the reader gains knowledge of how to apply the concepts and material and does not simply retain information temporarily with plans to regurgitate it. The learning objectives concentrate on the acquisition of knowledge and the foundations needed to understand, compare, contrast, define, explain, predict, estimate, evaluate, plan, and apply.

Chapter Outlines: The chapter's framework is clearly laid out to help students plan their reading and study.

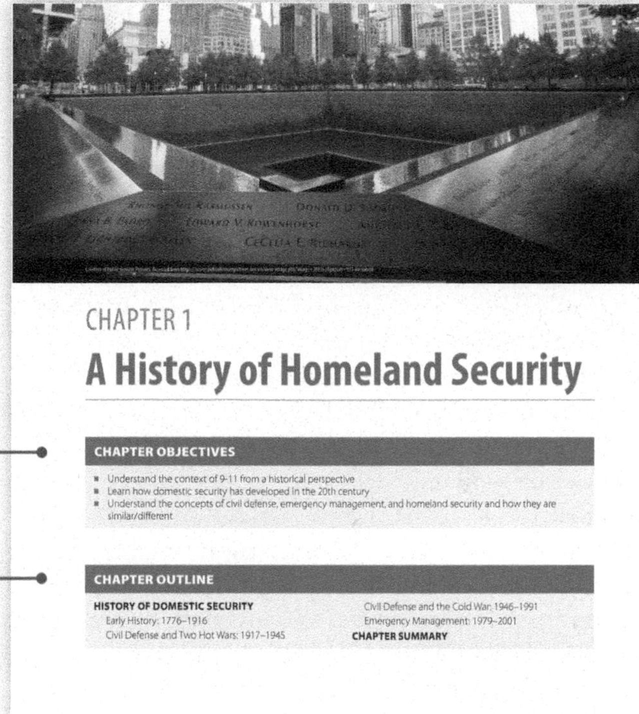

CHAPTER 1

A History of Homeland Security

CHAPTER OBJECTIVES

- Understand the context of 9-11 from a historical perspective
- Learn how domestic security has developed in the 20th century
- Understand the concepts of civil defense, emergency management, and homeland security and how they are similar/different

CHAPTER OUTLINE

HISTORY OF DOMESTIC SECURITY
Early History: 1776–1916
Civil Defense and Two Hot Wars: 1917–1945
Civil Defense and the Cold War: 1946–1991
Emergency Management: 1979–2001
CHAPTER SUMMARY

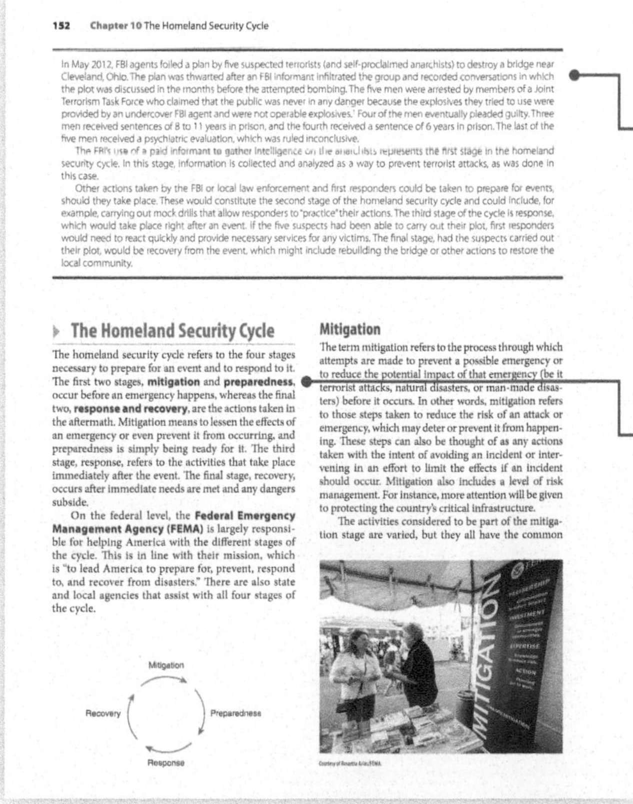

152 Chapter 10 The Homeland Security Cycle

In May 2012, FBI agents foiled a plan by five suspected terrorists (and self-proclaimed anarchists) to destroy a bridge near Cleveland, Ohio. The plan was thwarted after an FBI informant infiltrated the group and recorded conversations in which the plot was discussed in the months before the attempted bombing. The five men were arrested by members of a Joint Terrorism Task Force who claimed that the public was never in any danger because the explosives they tried to use were provided by an undercover FBI agent and were not operable explosives.[1] Four of the men eventually pleaded guilty. Three men received sentences of 8 to 11 years in prison, and the fourth received a sentence of 6 years in prison. The last of the five men received a psychiatric evaluation, which was ruled inconclusive.

The FBI's use of a paid informant to gather intelligence on the anarchists represents the first stage in the homeland security cycle. In this stage, information is collected and analyzed as a way to prevent terrorist attacks, as was done in this case.

Other actions taken by the FBI or local law enforcement and first responders could be taken to prepare for events, should they take place. These would constitute the second stage of the homeland security cycle and could include, for example, carrying out mock drills that allow responders to "practice" their actions. The third stage of the cycle is response, which would take place right after an event. If the five suspects had been able to carry out their plot, first responders would need to react quickly and provide necessary services for any victims. The final stage, had the suspects carried out their plot, would be recovery from the event, which might include rebuilding the bridge or other actions to restore the local community.

The Homeland Security Cycle

The homeland security cycle refers to the four stages necessary to prepare for an event and to respond to it. The first two stages, **mitigation** and **preparedness**, occur before an emergency happens, whereas the final two, **response and recovery**, are the actions taken in the aftermath. Mitigation means to lessen the effects of an emergency or even prevent it from occurring, and preparedness is simply being ready for it. The third stage, response, refers to the activities that take place immediately after the event. The final stage, recovery, occurs after immediate needs are met and any dangers subside.

On the federal level, the **Federal Emergency Management Agency (FEMA)** is largely responsible for helping America with the different stages of the cycle. This is in line with their mission, which is "to lead America to prepare for, prevent, respond to, and recover from disasters." There are also state and local agencies that assist with all four stages of the cycle.

Mitigation

The term mitigation refers to the process through which attempts are made to prevent a possible emergency or to reduce the potential impact of that emergency (be it terrorist attacks, natural disasters, or man-made disasters) before it occurs. In other words, mitigation refers to those steps taken to reduce the risk of an attack or emergency, which may deter or prevent it from happening. These steps can also be thought of as any actions taken with the intent of avoiding an incident or intervening in an effort to limit the effects if an incident should occur. Mitigation also includes a level of risk management. For instance, more attention will be given to protecting the country's critical infrastructure.

The activities considered to be part of the mitigation stage are varied, but they all have the common

Chapter Opening Vignettes: Each chapter begins with a real-world vignette that conceptualizes topics using actual scenarios.

Key Terms: Key terms are highlighted in bold within the chapters and defined in a glossary at the back of the book.

Featured Boxes: Most chapters contain boxes providing greater depth on special historic and contemporary topics relating to homeland security. For example, Box 9.2 details a comprehensive timeline of the presence of nuclear weapons in North Korea.

Chapter Summaries: Each chapter concludes with several paragraphs detailing the key concepts addressed in the chapter.

Topics for Discussion and Review: Topics for discussion and review are provided for student self-study options and for use by instructors who are developing written assignments and examinations.

Suggested Readings: Suggested Readings list of outside supplementary readings to enhance the understanding of homeland security concepts and topics.

References: At the end of each chapter, the reader will find the scholarly references that were used to assemble the information contained within the chapters, which will provide the reader with suggested readings pertaining to the key areas addressed within the chapter.

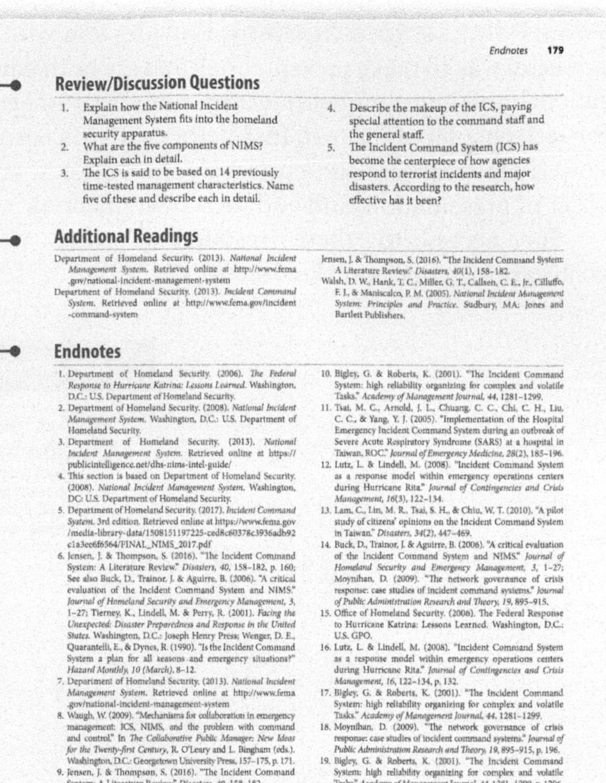

Endnotes 179

Review/Discussion Questions

1. Explain how the National Incident Management System fits into the homeland security apparatus.
2. What are the five components of NIMS? Explain each in detail.
3. The ICS is said to be based on 14 previously time-tested management characteristics. Name five of these and describe each in detail.
4. Describe the makeup of the ICS, paying special attention to the command staff and the general staff.
5. The Incident Command System (ICS) has become the centerpiece of how agencies respond to terrorist incidents and major disasters. According to the research, how effective has it been?

Additional Readings

Department of Homeland Security. (2013). *National Incident Management System*. Retrieved online at http://www.fema.gov/national-incident-management-system

Department of Homeland Security. (2013). *Incident Command System*. Retrieved online at http://www.fema.gov/incident-command-system

Jensen, J. & Thompson, S. (2016). "The Incident Command System: A Literature Review." *Disasters, 40*(1), 158–182.

Walsh, D. W., Hank, T. C., Miller, G. T., Callsen, C. E., Jr., Cilluffo, F. J., & Maniscalco, P. M. (2005). *National Incident Management System: Principles and Practice*. Sudbury, MA: Jones and Bartlett Publishers.

Endnotes

1. Department of Homeland Security. (2006). *The Federal Response to Hurricane Katrina: Lessons Learned*. Washington, D.C.: U.S. Department of Homeland Security.
2. Department of Homeland Security. (2008). *National Incident Management System*. Washington, D.C.: U.S. Department of Homeland Security.
3. Department of Homeland Security. (2013). *National Incident Management System*. Retrieved online at https://publicintelligence.net/dhs-nims-intel-guide/
4. This section is based on Department of Homeland Security. (2008). *National Incident Management System*. Washington, DC: U.S. Department of Homeland Security.
5. Department of Homeland Security. (2017). *Incident Command System*. 3rd edition. Retrieved online at https://www.fema.gov/media-library-data/1508151197225-ced8c60378c3936adb92c1a3ee6f6564/FINAL_NIMS_2017.pdf
6. Jensen, J. & Thompson, S. (2016). "The Incident Command System: A Literature Review." *Disasters, 40*, 158–182, p. 160; See also Buck, D., Trainor, J. & Aguirre, B. (2006). "A critical evaluation of the Incident Command System and NIMS." *Journal of Homeland Security and Emergency Management, 3*, 1–27; Tierney, K., Lindell, M. & Perry, R. (2001). *Facing the Unexpected: Disaster Preparedness and Response in the United States*. Washington, D.C.: Joseph Henry Press; Wenger, D. E., Quarantelli, E., & Dynes, R. (1990). "Is the Incident Command System a plan for all seasons and emergency situations?" *Hazard Monthly, 10 (March)*, 8–12.
7. Department of Homeland Security. (2013). *National Incident Management System*. Retrieved online at http://www.fema.gov/national-incident-management-system
8. Waugh, W. (2009). "Mechanisms for collaboration in emergency management: ICS, NIMS, and the problem with command and control." In *The Collaborative Public Manager: New Ideas for the Twenty-first Century*, R. O'Leary and L. Bingham (eds.). Washington, D.C.: Georgetown University Press, 157–175, p. 171.
9. Jensen, J. & Thompson, S. (2016). "The Incident Command System: A Literature Review." *Disasters, 40*, 158–182.
10. Bigley, G. & Roberts, K. (2001). "The Incident Command System: high reliability organizing for complex and volatile Tasks." *Academy of Management Journal, 44*, 1281–1299.
11. Tsai, M. C., Arnold, J. L., Chuang, C. C., Chi, C. H., Liu, C. C., & Yang, Y. J. (2005). "Implementation of the Hospital Emergency Incident Command System during an outbreak of Severe Acute Respiratory Syndrome (SARS) at a hospital in Taiwan, ROC." *Journal of Emergency Medicine, 28*(2), 185–196.
12. Lutz, L. & Lindell, M. (2008). "Incident Command System as a response model within emergency operations centers during Hurricane Rita." *Journal of Contingencies and Crisis Management, 16*(3), 122–134.
13. Lam, C., Lin, M. R., Tsai, S. H., & Chiu, W. T. (2010). "A pilot study of citizens' opinions on the Incident Command System in Taiwan." *Disasters, 34*(2), 447–469.
14. Buck, D., Trainor, J. & Aguirre, B. (2006). "A critical evaluation of the Incident Command System and NIMS." *Journal of Homeland Security and Emergency Management, 3*, 1–27; Moynihan, D. (2009). "The network governance of crisis response: case studies of incident command systems." *Journal of Public Administration Research and Theory, 19*, 895–915.
15. Office of Homeland Security. (2006). The Federal Response to Hurricane Katrina: Lessons Learned. Washington, D.C.: U.S. GPO.
16. Lutz, L. & Lindell, M. (2008). "Incident Command System as a response model within emergency operations centers during Hurricane Rita." *Journal of Contingencies and Crisis Management, 16*, 122–134, p. 132.
17. Bigley, G. & Roberts, K. (2001). "The Incident Command System: high reliability organizing for complex and volatile Tasks." *Academy of Management Journal, 44*, 1281–1299.
18. Moynihan, D. (2009). "The network governance of crisis response: case studies of incident command systems." *Journal of Public Administration Research and Theory, 19*, 895–915, p. 196.
19. Bigley, G. & Roberts, K. (2001). "The Incident Command System: high reliability organizing for complex and volatile Tasks." *Academy of Management Journal, 44*, 1281–1299, p. 1296.

Teaching Tools

Test Bank: Allows you to originate tailor-made classroom tests and quizzes quickly and easily by selecting, editing, organizing, and printing a test along with an answer key that includes page references to the text.

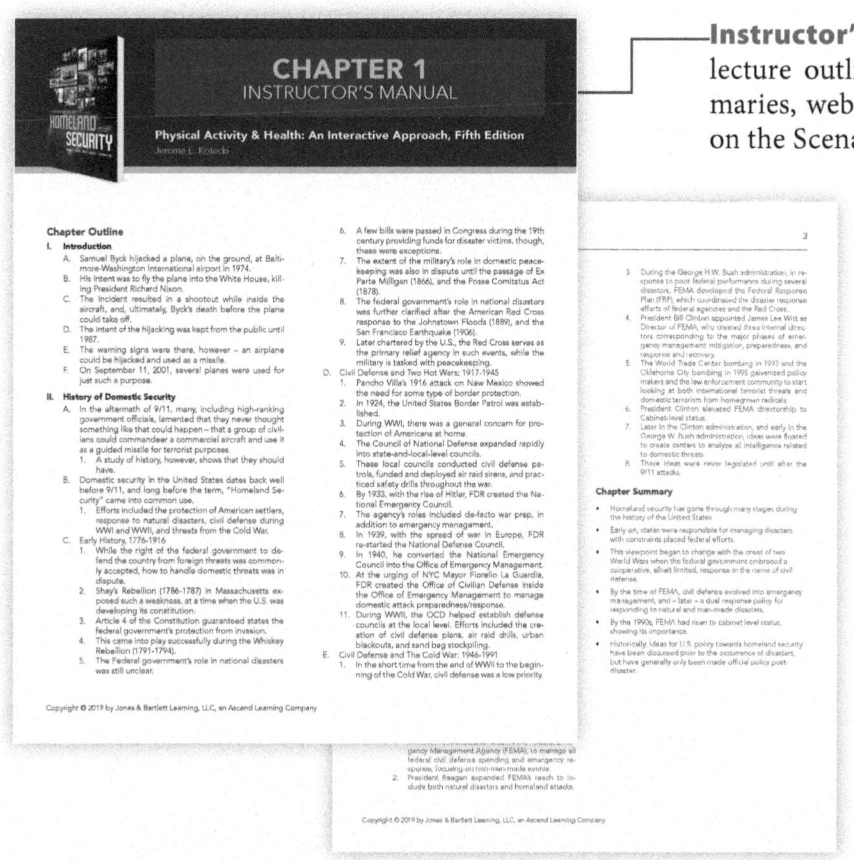

CHAPTER 1
INSTRUCTOR'S MANUAL

Physical Activity & Health: An Interactive Approach, Fifth Edition
Jerome E. Kotecki

Chapter Outline

I. **Introduction**
   A. Samuel Byck hijacked a plane, on the ground, at Baltimore-Washington International airport in 1974.
   B. His intent was to fly the plane into the White House, killing President Richard Nixon.
   C. The incident resulted in a shootout while inside the aircraft, and, ultimately, Byck's death before the plane could take off.
   D. The intent of the hijacking was kept from the public until 1987.
   E. The warning signs were there, however – an airplane could be hijacked and used as a missile.
   F. On September 11, 2001, several planes were used for just such a purpose.

II. **History of Domestic Security**
   A. In the aftermath of 9/11, many, including high-ranking government officials, lamented that they never thought something like that could happen – that a group of civilians could commandeer a commercial aircraft and use it as a guided missile for terrorist purposes.
      1. A study of history, however, shows that they should have.
   B. Domestic security in the United States dates back well before 9/11, and long before the term, "Homeland Security" came into common use.
      1. Efforts included the protection of American settlers, response to natural disasters, civil defense during WWI and WWII, and threats from the Cold War.
   C. Early History, 1776-1916
      1. While the right of the federal government to defend the country from foreign threats was commonly accepted, how to handle domestic threats was in dispute.
      2. Shay's Rebellion (1786-1787) in Massachusetts exposed such a weakness, at a time when the U.S. was developing its constitution.
      3. Article 4 of the Constitution guaranteed states the federal government's protection from invasion.
      4. This came into play successfully during the Whiskey Rebellion (1791-1794).
      5. The Federal government's role in national disasters was still unclear.
      6. A few bills were passed in Congress during the 19th century providing funds for disaster victims, though, these were exceptions.
      7. The extent of the military's role in domestic peacekeeping was also in dispute until the passage of Ex Parte Milligan (1866), and the Posse Comitatus Act (1878).
      8. The federal government's role in national disasters was further clarified after the American Red Cross response to the Johnstown Floods (1889), and the San Francisco Earthquake (1906).
      9. Later chartered by the U.S., the Red Cross serves as the primary relief agency in such events, while the military is tasked with peacekeeping.
   D. Civil Defense and Two Hot Wars: 1917-1945
      1. Pancho Villa's 1916 attack on New Mexico showed the need for some type of border protection.
      2. In 1924, the United States Border Patrol was established.
      3. During WWI, there was a general concern for protection of Americans at home.
      4. The Council of National Defense expanded rapidly into state-and-local-level councils.
      5. These local councils conducted civil defense patrols, funded and deployed air raid sirens, and practiced safety drills throughout the war.
      6. By 1933, with the rise of Hitler, FDR created the National Emergency Council.
      7. The agency's roles included de-facto war prep, in addition to emergency management.
      8. In 1939, with the spread of war in Europe, FDR re-started the National Defense Council.
      9. In 1940, he converted the National Emergency Council into the Office of Emergency Management.
      10. At the urging of NYC Mayor Fiorello La Guardia, FDR created the Office of Civilian Defense inside the Office of Emergency Management to manage domestic attack preparedness/response.
      11. During WWII, the OCD helped establish defense councils at the local level. Efforts included the creation of civil defense plans, air raid drills, urban blackouts, and sand bag stockpiling.
   E. Civil Defense and The Cold War: 1946-1991
      1. In the short time from the end of WWII to the beginning of the Cold War, civil defense was a low priority.

gency Management Agency (FEMA), to manage all federal civil defense spending and emergency response, focusing on non-man-made events.
2. President Reagan expanded FEMA's reach to include both natural disasters and homeland attacks.

3

3. During the George H.W. Bush administration, in response to poor federal performance during several disasters, FEMA developed the Federal Response Plan (FRP), which coordinated the disaster response efforts of federal agencies and the Red Cross.
4. President Bill Clinton appointed James Lee Witt as Director of FEMA, who created three internal directors corresponding to the major phases of emergency management: mitigation, preparedness, and response and recovery.
5. The World Trade Center bombing in 1993 and the Oklahoma City bombing in 1995 galvanized policy makers and the law enforcement community to start looking at both international terrorist threats and domestic terrorism from homegrown radicals.
6. President Clinton elevated FEMA directorship to Cabinet-level status.
7. Later in the Clinton administration, and early in the George W. Bush administration, ideas were floated to create centers to analyze all intelligence related to domestic threats.
8. These ideas were never legislated until after the 9/11 attacks.

Chapter Summary

- Homeland security has gone through many stages during the history of the United States.
- Early on, states were responsible for managing disasters with constraints placed federal efforts.
- This viewpoint began to change with the onset of two World Wars when the federal government embraced a cooperative, albeit limited, response in the name of civil defense.
- By the time of FEMA, civil defense evolved into emergency management, and – later – a dual response policy for responding to natural and man-made disasters.
- By the 1990s, FEMA had risen to cabinet level status, showing its importance.
- Historically, ideas for U.S. policy towards homeland security have been discussed prior to the occurrence of disasters, but have generally only been made official policy post-disaster.

Instructor's Manual: Includes complete chapter lecture outlines, learning objectives, chapter summaries, weblinks, suggested assignments, and notes on the Scenarios in the text.

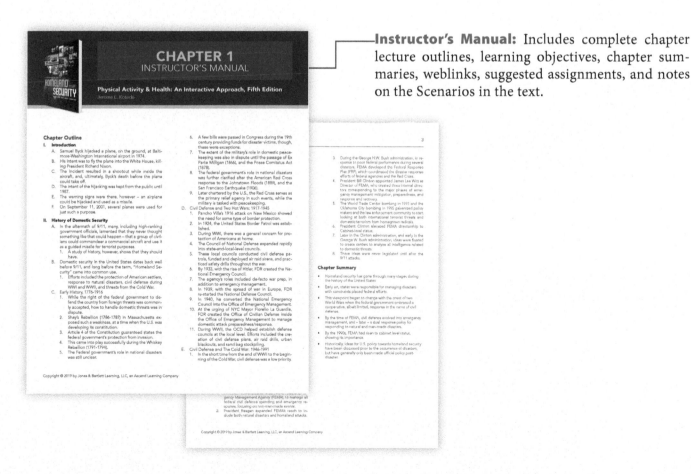

PowerPoint Lecture Outlines: Provides you with a powerful way to make presentations that are both educational and engaging with lecture notes and images for each chapter of the text. Instructors with Microsoft PowerPoint software can customize the outlines, art, order of presentation, and add their own material.

For access to these resources, please visit go.jblearning.com/homelandsecurity2e

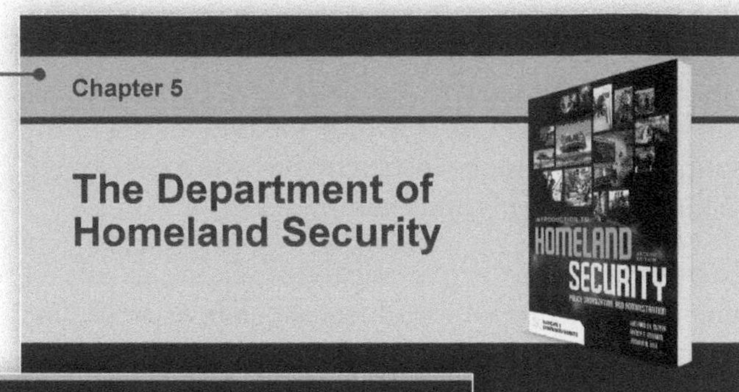

Prologue

September 11, 2001

Tuesday, September 11, 2001, dawned temperate and nearly cloudless in the eastern United States.[1] Millions of men and women readied themselves for work. Some made their way to the Twin Towers, the signature structures of the World Trade Center complex in New York City. Others went to Arlington, Virginia, to the Pentagon. Across the Potomac River, the United States Congress was back in session. At the other end of Pennsylvania Avenue, people began to line up for a White House tour. In Sarasota, Florida, President George W. Bush went for an early morning run.

For those heading to an airport, weather conditions could not have been better for a safe and pleasant journey. Among the travelers were Mohamed Atta and Abdul Aziz al Omari, who arrived at the airport in Portland, Maine.

Boston: American 11 and United 175

Atta and Omari boarded a 6:00 AM flight from Portland to Boston's Logan International Airport.

When he checked in for his flight to Boston, Atta was selected by a computerized prescreening system known as CAPPS (Computer Assisted Passenger Prescreening System), created to identify passengers who should be subject to special security measures. Under security rules in place at the time, the only consequence of Atta's selection by CAPPS was that his checked bags were kept off the plane until it was confirmed that he had boarded the aircraft. This did not hinder Atta's plans.

Atta and Omari arrived in Boston at 6:45 AM. Seven minutes later, Atta apparently took a call from Marwan al Shehhi, a longtime colleague who was at another terminal at Logan Airport. They spoke for 3 minutes. It would be their final conversation.

Between 6:45 and 7:40, Atta and Omari—along with Satam al Suqami, Wail al Shehri, and Waleed al Shehri—checked in and boarded American Airlines Flight 11, bound for Los Angeles. The flight was scheduled to depart at 7:45 AM.

In another Logan terminal, Shehhi, joined by Fayez Banihammad, Mohand al Shehri, Ahmed al Ghamdi, and Hamza al Ghamdi, checked in for United Airlines Flight 175, also bound for Los Angeles. A couple of Shehhi's colleagues were obviously unused to travel; according to the United ticket agent, they had trouble understanding the standard security questions, and she had to go over them slowly until they gave the routine, reassuring answers. Their flight was scheduled to depart at 8:00.

The security checkpoints through which the passengers, including Atta and his colleagues, gained access to the American 11 gate were operated by Globe Security under a contract with American Airlines. In a different terminal, the single checkpoint through which passengers for United 175 passed was controlled by United Airlines, which had contracted with Huntleigh USA to perform the screening.

In passing through these checkpoints, each of the hijackers would have been screened by a walk-through metal detector calibrated to detect items with a minimum metal content of a .22-caliber handgun. Anyone who might have set off that detector would have been screened with a hand wand—a procedure requiring the screener to identify the metal item or items that caused the alarm. In addition, an x-ray machine would have screened the hijackers' carry-on belongings. The screening was in place to identify and confiscate weapons and other items prohibited from being carried onto a commercial flight. None of the checkpoint supervisors recalled the hijackers or reported anything suspicious regarding their screening.

While Atta had been selected by CAPPS in Portland, three members of his hijacking team—Suqami, Wail al Shehri, and Waleed al Shehri—were selected in Boston. Their selection affected only the handling of their checked bags, not their screening at the checkpoint. All five men cleared the checkpoint and made their way to the gate for American 11. Atta, Omari, and Suqami took their seats in first class (seats 8D, 8G, and 10B, respectively). The Shehri brothers had adjacent seats in row 2 (Wail in 2A, Waleed in 2B), in the first-class cabin. They boarded American 11 between 7:31 and 7:40. The aircraft pushed back from the gate at 7:40.

Shehhi and his team, none of whom had been selected by CAPPS, boarded United 175 between 7:23 and 7:28 (Banihammad in 2A, Shehri in 2B, Shehhi in 6C, Hamza al Ghamdi in 9C, and Ahmed al Ghamdi in 9D). Their aircraft pushed back from the gate just before 8:00.

Washington Dulles: American 77

Hundreds of miles southwest of Boston at Dulles International Airport in the Virginia suburbs of Washington, D.C., five more men were preparing to take an early morning flight. At 7:15, Khalid al Mihdhar and Majed Moqed checked in at the American Airlines ticket counter for Flight 77, bound for Los Angeles. Within the next 20 minutes, they would be followed by Hani Hanjour and two brothers, Nawaf al Hazmi and Salem al Hazmi.

Hani Hanjour, Khalid al Mihdhar, and Majed Moqed were flagged by CAPPS. The Hazmi brothers were also selected for extra scrutiny by the airline's customer service representative at the check-in counter. The representative did so because one of the brothers did not have photo identification, nor could he understand English, and because the agent found both of the passengers to be suspicious. The only consequence of their selection was that their checked bags were held off the plane until it was confirmed that they had boarded the aircraft.

All five hijackers passed through the main terminal's west security screening checkpoint; United Airlines, which was the responsible air carrier, had contracted out the work to Argenbright Security. The checkpoint featured closed-circuit television that recorded all passengers, including the hijackers, as they were screened. At 7:18, Mihdhar and Moqed entered the security checkpoint.

Mihdhar and Moqed placed their carry-on bags on the belt of the x-ray machine and proceeded through the first metal detector. Both set off the alarm, and they were directed to a second metal detector. Mihdhar did not trigger the second alarm and was permitted through the checkpoint. After Moqed set it off, a screener used the hand wand on him. He passed this inspection.

About 20 minutes later, at 7:35, another passenger for Flight 77, Hani Hanjour, placed two carry-on bags on the x-ray belt in the main terminal's west checkpoint and proceeded, without alarm, through the metal detector. A short time later, Nawaf and Salem al Hazmi entered the same checkpoint. Salem al Hazmi cleared the metal detector and was permitted through; Nawaf al Hazmi set off the alarms for both the first and second metal detectors and was then hand-wanded before being cleared. In addition, his over-the-shoulder carry-on bag was swiped by an explosive trace detector and then passed. The video footage indicates that he was carrying an unidentified item in his back pocket, clipped to its rim.

When the local civil aviation security office of the Federal Aviation Administration (FAA) later investigated these security-screening operations, the screeners recalled nothing out of the ordinary. They could not recall that any of the passengers they screened were CAPPS selectees. Later, a screening expert reviewed the videotape of the hand-wanding, and he found the quality of the screener's work to have been "marginal at best." The screener should have "resolved" what set off the alarm, and in the case of both Moqed and Hazmi, it was clear that he did not.

At 7:50, Majed Moqed and Khalid al Mihdhar boarded the flight and were seated in 12A and 12B in coach. Hani Hanjour, assigned to seat 1B (first class), soon followed. The Hazmi brothers, assigned to 5E and 5F, joined Hanjour in the first-class cabin.

Newark: United 93

Between 7:03 and 7:39, Saeed al Ghamdi, Ahmed al Nami, Ahmad al Haznawi, and Ziad Jarrah checked in at Newark's United Airlines ticket counter for Flight 93, going to Los Angeles. Two checked bags, two did not. Haznawi was selected by CAPPS. His checked bag was screened for explosives and then loaded on the plane.

The four men passed through the security checkpoint, owned by United Airlines and operated under contract by Argenbright Security. Like the checkpoints in Boston, it lacked closed-circuit television surveillance so there is no documentary evidence to indicate when the hijackers passed through the checkpoint, which alarms may have been triggered, or which security procedures were administered. The FAA interviewed the screeners later; none recalled anything unusual or suspicious.

The four men boarded the plane between 7:39 and 7:48. All four had seats in the economy-class cabin; their plane had no first-class section. Jarrah was in seat 1B, closest to the cockpit; Nami was in 3C, Ghamdi in 3D, and Haznawi in 6B.

The 19 men were aboard four transcontinental flights. They were planning to hijack these planes and turn them into large guided missiles, loaded with some 11,400 gallons of jet fuel. By 8:00 AM on the morning of Tuesday, September 11, 2001, they had defeated all the security layers that America's civil aviation security system then had in place to prevent a hijacking.

The Hijacking of American 11

American Airlines Flight 11 provided nonstop service from Boston to Los Angeles. On September 11, Captain John Ogonowski and First Officer Thomas McGuinness piloted the Boeing 767, which carried its full capacity of nine flight attendants. Eighty-one passengers boarded the flight with them (including the five terrorists).

The plane took off at 7:59. Just before 8:14, it had climbed to 26,000 feet, not quite its initial assigned cruising altitude of 29,000 feet. All communications and flight profile data were normal. About this time, the "Fasten Seatbelt" sign would usually have been turned off and the flight attendants would have begun preparing for cabin service.

At that same time, American 11 had its last routine communication with the ground when it acknowledged navigational instructions from the FAA's air traffic control (ATC) center in Boston. Sixteen seconds after that transmission, ATC instructed the aircraft's pilots to climb to 35,000 feet. That message and all subsequent attempts to contact the flight were not acknowledged. From this and other evidence, we believe the hijacking began at 8:14 or shortly thereafter.

Reports from two flight attendants in the coach cabin, Betty Ong and Madeline "Amy" Sweeney, tell us most of what we know about how the hijacking happened. As it began, some of the hijackers—most likely Wail al Shehri and Waleed al Shehri, who were seated in row 2 in first class—stabbed the two unarmed flight attendants who would have been preparing for cabin service.

It is unknown exactly how the hijackers gained access to the cockpit; FAA rules required that the doors remain closed and locked during flight. Ong speculated that they had "jammed their way" into the cabin. Perhaps the terrorists stabbed the flight attendants to get a cockpit key, to force one of them to open the cockpit door, or to lure the captain or first officer out of the cockpit. Or the flight attendants may just have been in their way.

At the same time or shortly thereafter, Atta—the only terrorist on board trained to fly a jet—would have moved to the cockpit from his first-class seat, possibly accompanied by Omari. As this was happening, passenger Daniel Lewin, who was seated in the row just behind Atta and Omari, was stabbed by one of the hijackers—probably Satam al Suqami, who was seated directly behind Lewin. Lewin had served 4 years as an officer in the Israeli military. He may have made an attempt to stop the hijackers in front of him, not realizing that another was sitting behind him.

The hijackers quickly gained control and sprayed Mace, pepper spray, or some other irritant in the first-class cabin, in order to force the passengers and flight attendants toward the rear of the plane. They claimed they had a bomb.

About 5 minutes after the hijacking began, Betty Ong contacted the American Airlines Southeastern Reservations Office in Cary, North Carolina, via an AT&T airphone to report an emergency aboard the flight. This was the first of several occasions on 9/11 when flight attendants took action outside of the scope of their training, which emphasized that in a hijacking, they were to communicate with the cockpit crew. The emergency call lasted approximately 25 minutes as Ong calmly and professionally relayed information about events taking place aboard the airplane to authorities on the ground.

At 8:19, Ong reported: "The cockpit is not answering, somebody's stabbed in business class—and I think there's Mace, that we can't breathe—I don't know, I think we're getting hijacked." She then told of the stabbings of the two flight attendants.

At 8:21, one of the American employees receiving Ong's call in North Carolina, Nydia Gonzalez, alerted the American Airlines operations center in Fort Worth, Texas, reaching Craig Marquis, the manager on duty. Marquis soon realized this was an emergency and instructed the airline's dispatcher responsible for the flight to contact the cockpit. At 8:23, the dispatcher tried unsuccessfully to contact the aircraft. Six minutes later, the air traffic control specialist in American's operations center contacted the FAA's Boston Air Traffic Control Center about the flight. The center was already aware of the problem.

The Boston Center knew of the problem in part because they overheard the hijackers attempting to communicate with the passengers. Just before 8:25, the in-flight microphone was keyed and one of the hijackers said, "Nobody move. Everything will be okay. If you try to make any moves, you'll endanger yourself and the airplane. Just stay quiet." Air traffic controllers heard the transmission, and Ong did not. The hijackers probably did not know how to operate the cockpit radio communication system correctly, and thus inadvertently broadcast their message over the air traffic control channel instead of the cabin public-address channel. Also at 8:25, and again at 8:29, Amy Sweeney (flight attendant) got through to the American Flight Services Office in Boston but was cut off after she reported that someone was hurt aboard the flight. Three minutes later, Sweeney was reconnected to the office and began relaying updates to her manager, Michael Woodward.

At 8:26, Ong reported that the plane was "flying erratically." A minute later, Flight 11 turned south. American also began getting identifications of the hijackers, as Ong and then Sweeney passed on some of the seat numbers of those who had gained unauthorized access to the cockpit.

Sweeney calmly reported that the plane had been hijacked; a man in first class had his throat slashed; two flight attendants had been stabbed; one was seriously hurt and on oxygen while the other's wounds seemed minor; a doctor had been requested; the flight attendants were unable to contact the cockpit; and, there was a bomb in the cockpit. Sweeney told Woodward that she and Ong were trying to relay as much information as they could to people on the ground.

At 8:38, Ong told Gonzalez that the plane was flying erratically again. Around this time, Sweeney told Woodward that the hijackers were Middle Eastern, naming three of their seat numbers. One spoke very little English and one spoke excellent English. The hijackers had gained entry to the cockpit, and she did not know how. The aircraft was in a rapid descent.

At 8:41, Sweeney told Woodward that passengers in coach were under the impression that there was a routine medical emergency in first class. Other flight attendants were busy with various activities, such as getting medical supplies, while Ong and Sweeney were reporting the events as they unfolded.

At 8:41, in American's operations center, a colleague told Marquis that the air traffic controllers had declared Flight 11 a hijacking and "think he's [American 11] headed toward Kennedy [airport in New York City]. They're moving everybody out of the way. They seem to have him on primary radar. They seem to think that he is descending."

At 8:44, Gonzalez reported losing phone contact with Ong. At about this same time, Sweeney reported to Woodward, "Something is wrong. We are in a rapid descent . . . we are all over the place." Woodward asked Sweeney to look out the window to see if she could determine where they were. Sweeney responded: "We are flying low.

> "We are flying very, very low. We are flying way too low." Seconds later she said, "Oh my God, we are way too low." The phone call ended.
>
> At 8:46:40, American 11 crashed into the North Tower of the World Trade Center in New York City. All on board, along with an unknown number of people in the tower, were killed instantly.

The Hijacking of United 175

United Airlines Flight 175 was scheduled to depart for Los Angeles at 8:00 AM. Captain Victor Saracini and First Officer Michael Horrocks piloted the Boeing 767, which had seven flight attendants. Fifty-six passengers boarded the flight.

United 175 pushed back from its gate at 7:58 and departed Logan Airport at 8:14. By 8:33, it had reached its assigned cruising altitude of 31,000 feet. The flight attendants would have begun their cabin service.

The flight had taken off just as American 11 was being hijacked, and at 8:42, the United 175 flight crew completed their report of a "suspicious transmission" overheard from another plane (which was Flight 11) just after takeoff. This was United 175's last communication with the ground.

The hijackers attacked sometime between 8:42 and 8:46. They used knives (as reported by two passengers and a flight attendant), Mace (reported by one passenger), and the threat of a bomb (reported by the same passenger). They stabbed members of the flight crew (reported by a flight attendant and one passenger).

Both pilots had been killed (reported by one flight attendant). The eyewitness accounts came from calls made from the rear of the plane from passengers originally seated further forward in the cabin, a sign that passengers and perhaps crew had been moved to the back of the aircraft. Given similarities to American 11 in hijacker seating and in eyewitness reports of tactics and weapons, as well as the contact between the presumed team leaders, Atta and Shehhi, it is believed the tactics were similar on both flights.

The first operational evidence that something was abnormal on United 175 came at 8:47, when the aircraft changed beacon codes twice within a minute. At 8:51, the flight deviated from its assigned altitude, and a minute later, New York air traffic controllers began repeatedly and unsuccessfully trying to contact it.

At 8:52 in Easton, Connecticut, a man named Lee Hanson received a phone call from his son Peter, a passenger on United 175. His son told him: "I think they've taken over the cockpit—an attendant has been stabbed—and someone else up front may have been killed. The plane is making strange moves. Call United Airlines. Tell them it's Flight 175, Boston to LA." Lee Hanson then called the Easton Police Department and relayed what he had heard.

Also at 8:52, a male flight attendant called a United office in San Francisco, reaching Marc Policastro. The flight attendant reported that the flight had been hijacked, both pilots had been killed, a flight attendant had been stabbed, and the hijackers were probably flying the plane. The call lasted about 2 minutes, after which Policastro and a colleague tried unsuccessfully to contact the flight.

At 8:58, the flight took a heading toward New York City.

At 8:59, Flight 175 passenger Brian David Sweeney tried to call his wife, Julie. He left a message on their home answering machine that the plane had been hijacked. He then called his mother, Louise Sweeney, told her the flight had been hijacked, and added that the passengers were thinking about storming the cockpit to take control of the plane away from the hijackers.

At 9:00, Lee Hanson received a second call from his son Peter:

> It's getting bad, Dad—a stewardess was stabbed. They seem to have knives and Mace. They said they have a bomb. It's getting very bad on the plane. Passengers are throwing up and getting sick. The plane is making jerky movements. I don't think the pilot is flying the plane. I think we are going down. I think they intend to go to Chicago or someplace and fly into a building. Don't worry Dad. If it happens, it'll be very fast. My God, my God.

The call ended abruptly. Lee Hanson had heard a woman scream just before it cut off. He turned on a television, and in her home, so did Louise Sweeney. Both then saw the second aircraft hit the World Trade Center.

At 9:03:11, United Airlines Flight 175 struck the South Tower of the World Trade Center. All on board, along with an unknown number of people in the tower, were killed instantly.

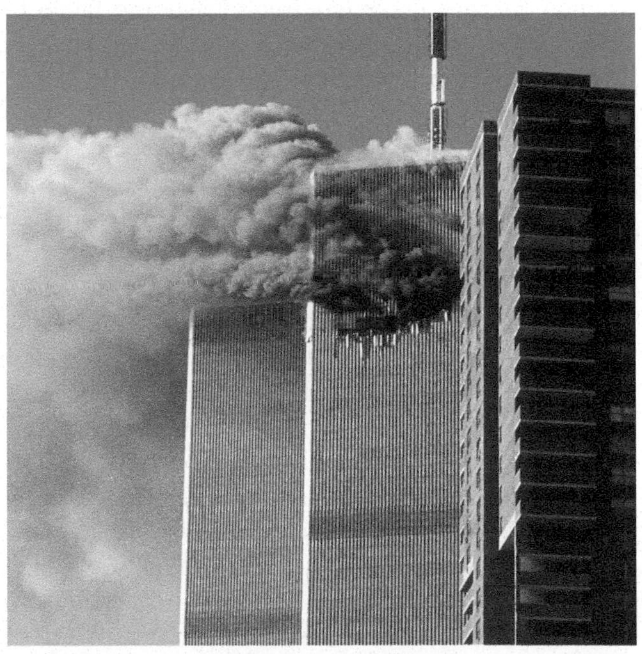

The Hijacking of American 77

American Airlines Flight 77 was scheduled to depart from Washington Dulles for Los Angeles at 8:10 AM. The aircraft was a Boeing 757 piloted by Captain

Charles F. Burlingame and First Officer David Charlebois. There were four flight attendants. The flight carried 58 passengers.

American 77 pushed back from its gate at 8:09 and took off at 8:20. At 8:46, the flight reached its assigned cruising altitude of 35,000 feet. Cabin service would have begun. At 8:51, American 77 transmitted its last routine radio communication. The hijacking began between 8:51 and 8:54. As on American 11 and United 175, the hijackers used knives (reported by one passenger) and moved all the passengers (and possibly crew) to the rear of the aircraft (reported by one flight attendant and one passenger). Unlike the earlier flights, the Flight 77 hijackers were reported by a passenger to have box cutters. Finally, a passenger reported that an announcement had been made by the "pilot" that the plane had been hijacked. Neither of the firsthand accounts mentioned any stabbings or the threat or use of either a bomb or Mace, although both witnesses began the flight in the first-class cabin.

At 8:54, the aircraft deviated from its assigned course, turning south. Two minutes later, the transponder was turned off and even primary radar contact with the aircraft was lost. The Indianapolis Air Traffic Control Center repeatedly tried and failed to contact the aircraft. American Airlines dispatchers also tried, without success.

At 9:00, American Airlines Executive Vice President Gerard Arpey learned that communications had been lost with American 77. This was now the second American aircraft in trouble. He ordered all American Airlines flights in the Northeast that had not taken off to remain on the ground. Shortly before 9:10, suspecting that American 77 had been hijacked, American headquarters concluded that the second aircraft to hit the World Trade Center might have been Flight 77. After learning that United Airlines was missing a plane, American Airlines headquarters extended their ground stop nationwide.

At 9:12, passenger Renee May called her mother, Nancy May, in Las Vegas. She said her flight was being hijacked by six individuals who had moved them to the rear of the plane. She asked her mother to alert American Airlines. Nancy May and her husband promptly did so.

At some point between 9:16 and 9:26, passenger Barbara Olson called her husband, Ted Olson, the Solicitor General of the United States. She reported that the flight had been hijacked, and the hijackers had knives and box cutters. She further indicated that the hijackers were not aware of her phone call, and that they had put all of the passengers in the back of the plane. About a minute into the conversation, the call was cut off. Solicitor General Olson tried unsuccessfully to reach Attorney General John Ashcroft.

Shortly after the first call, Barbara Olson reached her husband again. She reported that the pilot had announced that the flight had been hijacked, and she asked her husband what she should tell the captain of the flight to do. Ted Olson asked for her location and she replied that the aircraft was then flying over houses. Another passenger told her that they were traveling northeast. The Solicitor General then informed his wife of the two previous hijackings and crashes. She did not display signs of panic and did not indicate any awareness of an impending crash. At that point, the second call was cut off.

At 9:29, the autopilot on American 77 was disengaged; the aircraft was at 7,000 feet and approximately 38 miles west of the Pentagon. At 9:32, controllers at the Dulles Terminal Radar Approach Control "observed a primary radar target tracking eastbound at a high rate of speed." This was later determined to have been Flight 77.

At 9:34, Ronald Reagan Washington National Airport advised the Secret Service of an unknown aircraft heading in the direction of the White House. American 77 was then 5 miles west-southwest of the Pentagon and began a 330-degree turn. At the end of the turn, it was descending through 2,200 feet, pointed toward the Pentagon and downtown Washington. The hijacker pilot then advanced the throttles to maximum power and dove toward the Pentagon.

At 9:37, American Airlines Flight 77 crashed into the Pentagon, traveling at approximately 530 miles per hour. All on board, as well as many civilian and military personnel in the building, were killed.

The Battle for United 93

At 8:42 AM, United Airlines Flight 93 took off from Newark (New Jersey) Liberty International Airport bound for San Francisco. The aircraft was piloted by Captain Jason Dahl and First Officer Leroy Homer and there were five flight attendants. Thirty-seven passengers, including the hijackers, boarded the plane. Scheduled to depart the gate at 8:00, the Boeing 757's takeoff was delayed because of the airport's typically heavy morning traffic.

The September 11 hijackers had planned to take flights scheduled to depart at 7:45 (American 11), 8:00 (United 175 and United 93), and 8:10 (American 77). Three of the flights had actually taken off within 10 to 15 minutes of their planned departure times. United 93 would ordinarily have taken off about 15 minutes after pulling away from the gate. When it left the ground at 8:42, the flight was running more than 25 minutes late.

As United 93 left Newark, the flight's crew members were unaware of the hijacking of American 11. Around 9:00, the FAA, American, and United were facing the staggering realization of apparent multiple hijackings. At 9:03, they would see another aircraft strike the World Trade Center. Crisis managers at the FAA and the airlines did not yet act to warn other aircraft. At the same time, Boston Center realized that a message transmitted just before 8:25 by the hijacker pilot of American 11 included the phrase, "We have some planes."

No one at the FAA or the airlines that day had ever dealt with multiple hijackings. Such a plot had not been carried out anywhere in the world in more than 30 years and never in the United States. As news of the hijackings filtered through the FAA and the airlines, it does not seem to have occurred to their leadership that they needed to alert other aircraft in the air that they too might be at risk.

United 175 was hijacked between 8:42 and 8:46, and awareness of that hijacking began to spread after 8:51. American 77 was hijacked between 8:51 and 8:54.

By 9:00, FAA and airline officials began to comprehend that attackers were going after multiple aircraft. American Airlines' nationwide ground stop began between 9:05 and 9:10 and was followed by a United Airlines ground stop. FAA controllers at Boston Center, which had tracked the first two hijackings, requested at 9:07 that Herndon Command Center "get messages to airborne aircraft to increase security for the cockpit." There is no evidence that Herndon took such action. Boston Center immediately began speculating about other aircraft that might be in danger, leading them to worry about a transcontinental flight (Delta 1989) that, in fact, was not hijacked. At 9:19, the FAA's New England regional office called Herndon and asked that Cleveland Center advise Delta 1989 to use extra cockpit security.

Several FAA air traffic control officials later explained that it was the air carriers' responsibility to notify their planes of security problems. One senior FAA air traffic control manager said that it was simply not the FAA's place to dictate to the airlines what they should tell their pilots. The 9/11 Commission noted that such statements do not reflect an adequate appreciation of the FAA's responsibility for the safety and security of civil aviation.

The airlines bore responsibility, too. They were facing an escalating number of conflicting and, for the most part, erroneous reports about other flights, as well as a continuing lack of vital information from the FAA about the hijacked flights. The 9/11 Commission found no evidence, however, that American Airlines sent any cockpit warnings to its aircraft on 9/11. United's first decisive action to notify its airborne aircraft to take defensive action did not come until 9:19, when a United flight dispatcher, Ed Ballinger, took the initiative to begin transmitting warnings to his 16 transcontinental flights: "Beware any cockpit intrusion. Two a/c [aircraft] hit World Trade Center." One of the flights that received the warning was United 93. Because Ballinger was still responsible for his other flights as well as Flight 175, his warning message was not transmitted to Flight 93 until 9:23.

By all accounts, the first 46 minutes of Flight 93's cross country trip proceeded routinely. Radio communications from the plane were normal. Heading, speed, and altitude ran according to plan. At 9:24, Ballinger's warning to United 93 was received in the cockpit. Within 2 minutes, at 9:26, the pilot, Jason Dahl, responded with a note of puzzlement: "Ed, confirm latest mssg plz. Jason."

The hijackers attacked at 9:28. While traveling 35,000 feet above eastern Ohio, United 93 suddenly dropped 700 feet. Eleven seconds into the descent, the FAA's air traffic control center in Cleveland received the first of two radio transmissions from the aircraft. During the first broadcast, the captain or first officer could be heard declaring "Mayday!" amid the sounds of a physical struggle in the cockpit. The second radio transmission, 35 seconds later, indicated that the fight was continuing. The captain or first officer could be heard shouting: "Hey, get out of here! Get out of here! Get out of here!"

On the morning of 9/11, there were only 37 passengers on United 93—33 in addition to the 4 hijackers. This was below the norm for a Tuesday morning during the summer of 2001. But there is no evidence that the hijackers manipulated passenger levels or purchased additional seats to facilitate their operation.

The terrorists who hijacked three other commercial flights on 9/11 operated in five-man teams. They initiated their cockpit takeover within 30 minutes of takeoff. On Flight 93, however, the takeover took place 46 minutes after takeoff and there were only four hijackers. The operative likely intended to round out the team for this flight, Mohamed al Kahtani, had been refused entry by a suspicious immigration inspector at Florida's Orlando International Airport in August.

Because several passengers on United 93 described three hijackers on the plane, not four, some have wondered whether one of the hijackers had been able to use the cockpit jump seat from the outset of the flight. FAA rules allow use of this seat by documented and approved individuals, usually air carrier or FAA personnel. There is no evidence indicating that one of the hijackers, or anyone else, sat there on this flight. All of the hijackers had assigned seats in first class, and they seem to have used them. It is more likely that Jarrah, the crucial pilot-trained member of their team, remained seated and inconspicuous until after the cockpit was seized; and once inside, he would not have been visible to the passengers.

At 9:32, a hijacker, probably Jarrah, made or attempted to make the following announcement to the passengers of Flight 93: "Ladies and gentlemen: Hear the captain, please sit down keep remaining sitting. We have a bomb on board. So, sit." The flight data recorder (also recovered) indicates that Jarrah then instructed the plane's autopilot to turn the aircraft around and head east.

The cockpit voice recorder data indicates that a woman, most likely a flight attendant, was being held captive in the cockpit. She struggled with one of the hijackers who killed or otherwise silenced her.

Shortly thereafter, the passengers and flight crew began a series of calls from GTE airphones and cellular phones. These calls between family, friends, and colleagues took place until the end of the flight and provided those on the ground with firsthand accounts. They enabled the passengers to gain critical information, including the news that two aircraft had slammed into the World Trade Center.

At 9:39, the FAA's Cleveland Air Route Traffic Control Center overheard a second announcement indicating that there was a bomb on board, that the plane was returning to the airport, and that they should remain seated. While it apparently was not heard by the passengers, this announcement, like those on Flight 11 and Flight 77, was intended to deceive the passengers. Jarrah, like Atta earlier, may have inadvertently broadcast the message because he did not know how to operate the radio and the intercom. According to the 9/11 Commission, none of them had ever flown an actual airliner before.

At least two callers from the flight reported that the hijackers knew that passengers were making calls but did not seem to care. It is quite possible that Jarrah knew of the success of the assault on the World Trade Center. He could have learned of this from messages being sent by United Airlines to the cockpits of its transcontinental flights, including Flight 93, warning of cockpit intrusion and telling of the New York attacks. But even without them, he would certainly have understood that the attacks on the World Trade Center would already have unfolded, given Flight 93's tardy departure from Newark. If Jarrah did know that the passengers were making calls, it might not have occurred to him that they were certain to learn what had happened in New York, thereby defeating his attempts at deception.

At least 10 passengers and two crew members shared vital information with family, friends, colleagues, or others on the ground. All understood that the plane had been hijacked. They said the hijackers wielded knives and claimed to have a bomb. The hijackers were wearing red bandanas, and they forced the passengers to the back of the aircraft.

Callers reported that a passenger had been stabbed and that two people were lying on the floor of the cabin, injured or dead—possibly the captain and first officer. One caller reported that a flight attendant had been killed.

One of the callers from United 93 also reported that he thought the hijackers might possess a gun, but none of the other callers reported the presence of a firearm. One recipient of a call from the aircraft recounted specifically asking her caller whether the hijackers had guns. The passenger replied that he did not see one. No evidence of firearms or of their identifiable remains was found at the aircraft's crash site, and the cockpit voice recorder gives no indication of a gun being fired or mentioned at any time. We believe that if the hijackers had possessed a gun, they would have used it in the flight's last minutes as the passengers fought back.

Passengers on three flights reported the hijackers' claim of having a bomb. The FBI said they found no trace of explosives at the crash sites. One of the passengers who mentioned a bomb expressed his belief that it was not real. Lacking any evidence that the hijackers attempted to smuggle such illegal items past the security screening checkpoints, it is believed that the bombs were probably not real.

During at least five of Flight 93's passengers' phone calls, information was shared about the attacks that had occurred earlier that morning at the World Trade Center. Five calls described the intent of passengers and surviving crew members to revolt against the hijackers. According to one call, they voted on whether to rush the terrorists in an attempt to retake the plane. They decided and acted.

At 9:57, the passenger assault began. Several passengers had terminated phone calls with loved ones in order to join the revolt. One of the callers ended her message as follows: "Everyone's running up to first class. I've got to go. Bye."

The cockpit voice recorder captured the sounds of the passenger assault muffled by the intervening cockpit door. Some family members who later listened to the recording report that they could hear the voice of a loved one among the din. The 9/11 Commission could not identify the specific voices.

In response, Jarrah immediately began to roll the airplane to the left and right, attempting to knock the passengers off balance. At 9:58:57, Jarrah told another hijacker in the cockpit to block the door. Jarrah continued to roll the airplane sharply left and right, but the assault continued. At 9:59:52, Jarrah changed tactics and pitched the nose of the airplane up and down to disrupt the assault. The recorder captured the sounds of loud thumps, crashes, shouts, and breaking glasses and plates. At 10:00:03, Jarrah stabilized the airplane.

Five seconds later, Jarrah asked, "Is that it? Shall we finish it off?" A hijacker responded, "No. Not yet. When they all come, we finish it off." The sounds of fighting continued outside of the cockpit. Again, Jarrah pitched the nose of the aircraft up and down. At 10:00:26, a passenger in the background yelled, ". . . in the cockpit. If we don't, we'll die!" Sixteen seconds later, a passenger yelled, "Roll it!" Jarrah stopped the violent maneuvers at about 10:01:00 and said, "Allah is the greatest! Allah is the greatest!" He then asked another hijacker in the cockpit, "Is that it? I mean, shall we put it down?" to which the other replied, "Yes, put it in it, and pull it down."

The passengers continued their assault and at 10:02:23, a hijacker yelled, "Pull it down! Pull it down!" The hijackers remained at the controls but must have judged that the passengers were only seconds from overcoming them. The airplane headed down; the control wheel was turned hard to the right. The airplane rolled onto its back, and one of the hijackers began shouting "Allah is the greatest! Allah is the greatest!" With the sounds of the passenger counterattack continuing, the aircraft plowed into an empty field in Shanksville, Pennsylvania, at 580 miles per hour, about 20 minutes' flying time from Washington, DC.

Jarrah's objective was to crash the airliner into symbols of the American Republic, the U.S. Capitol, or the White House. He was defeated by the unarmed passengers of United 93.

Endnotes

The prologue is based on the *9/11 Commission Report*. See National Commission on Terrorist Attacks Upon the United States. (2004). *The 9/11 Commission Report: Final Report of the National Commission on Terrorist Attacks Upon the United States (Authorized Edition)*. New York, NY: W.W. Norton & Company, Inc.

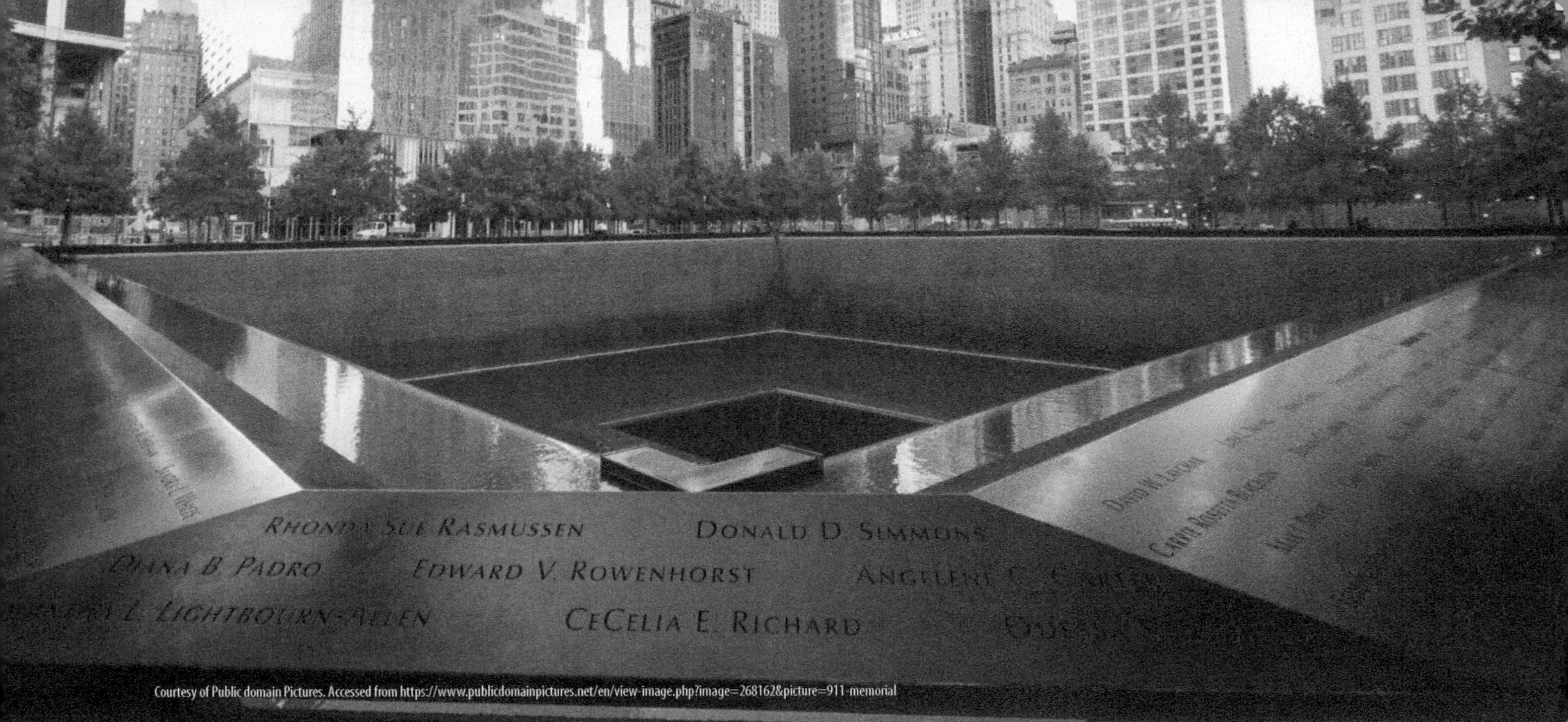

Courtesy of Public domain Pictures. Accessed from https://www.publicdomainpictures.net/en/view-image.php?image=268162&picture=911-memorial

CHAPTER 1
A History of Homeland Security

CHAPTER OBJECTIVES

- Understand the context of 9-11 from a historical perspective
- Learn how domestic security has developed in the 20th century
- Understand the concepts of civil defense, emergency management, and homeland security and how they are similar/different

CHAPTER OUTLINE

On the morning of February 22, 1974, "a burly, middle-aged man" by the name of Samuel Byck entered the Baltimore–Washington International (BWI) Airport with a briefcase in hand.[1] He walked to the front of the line at Gate C. The people in line were waiting to board Delta Flight 523 bound for Atlanta, Georgia. A security guard by the name of George Ramburg stood nearby, his back turned to the passenger line. Byck pulled a .22 caliber pistol from underneath his raincoat and fired twice into the security guard's back, killing him instantly. As Ramburg's body crumpled to the ground, people began screaming and running in all directions. Byck leaped over the security chain, ran down the boarding ramp, and boarded the airplane. Delta Flight 523 had just been hijacked, and its destination was the White House. Samuel Byck intended to use the plane as a missile, flying it into the White House, in order to assassinate President Richard M. Nixon.[2]

Samuel Byck was born on January 30, 1930, in South Philadelphia. His parents were poor, and Byck dropped out of high school in the ninth grade in order to help support the family. After a series of odd jobs, he enlisted in the U.S. Army in 1954 and was honorably discharged 2 years later. He married and had four children, but he struggled with employment, attempting to start several businesses, all of which failed. While working as a tire salesman, he applied for a Small Business Administration loan to start yet another business but was turned down. He became depressed and blamed his troubles on President Nixon.[3]

His depression led to marital troubles, which led to divorce, and finally, he ended up in a psychiatric clinic. A year later, in 1973, he began plotting to assassinate President Nixon. Byck began a series of tape recordings threatening the president, which he mailed to various public officials. The Secret Service was notified and they investigated, but after speaking with Byck's psychiatrist, they determined he was harmless. By late 1973, Byck had formulated a plan to assassinate the president. Then, on February 20, 1974, he wrote his last will and testament, writing, "I will each of my children . . . the sum of one dollar each. They have each other and they deserve each other."[4] Since he knew he would not be able to purchase a gun, he stole a .22 caliber pistol from a friend, and on the morning of February 22, 1974, he drove to BWI. Along the way, he tape recorded his complaints against President Nixon and explained that his plans were to hijack a plane, fly it into the White House, and assassinate the president. Byck even gave his mission a name: Operation Pandora's Box.

As Byck entered the plane, he fired one round inside the cabin of the plane and then entered the cockpit through the open door. He screamed at the pilot, "Fly this plane out of here!"[5] The pilot, after regaining his composure, explained that he could not roll back from the gate until the ground crew removed the wheel blocks. Byck became enraged and shot the copilot in the stomach. He then turned back to the pilot and screamed, "The next one will be in the head."[6] Byck then returned to the passenger cabin and grabbed a female passenger and dragged her into the cockpit, telling her to help the pilot fly the plane. At this point, two shots from outside of the plane exploded through the windshield, causing Byck to shove the woman out of the cockpit. He then turned back into the cockpit and fired twice. One bullet struck the already-wounded copilot in the eye, and the other entered the pilot's right shoulder.[7]

The pilot then radioed ground control: "Emergency, emergency, we're all shot . . . ah . . . can you get another pilot here to the airplane . . . ah . . . this fellow has shot us both."[8] The pilot also asked that the wheel blocks be removed so the plane could taxi away from the gate. He then passed out.

With his rage now growing, Byck grabbed another female passenger, dragged her into the cockpit, and ordered her to fly the plane. He then fired two more shots in anger: One into the copilot and another into the pilot. The woman became hysterical after seeing the two pilots shot and tried to flee the cockpit. Two more shots rang out and the cockpit windows again shattered, as two more bullets entered from outside of the plane. Byck began firing wildly at the windows, which made him more of a visible target to the snipers outside. They fired two more shots. The first one entered Byck's stomach and the second entered his chest. He fell to the floor.[9]

When Byck fell, he lost hold of his weapon. While on the floor, he frantically searched for the lost gun. He found it, sat up, and put the .22 pistol to his temple and fired. The carnage was over.

Police entered the airplane and found Byck dying. He only lived a few more minutes. They found the briefcase he had carried aboard the plane. Inside was an improvised gasoline bomb with an igniter.

The media reported on the hijacking but did not disclose Byck's intent of flying the plane into the White House to assassinate President Nixon. They wanted to avoid any potential copycats. Apparently, no one had ever thought about hijacking an airplane and using it as a missile, and it was not something anyone wanted to share.

In 1987, an FAA Report titled, *Troubled Passage: The Federal Aviation Administration During the Nixon–Ford Term 1973–1977*, revealed Byck's intent.[10] It chillingly predicted, "though Byck lacked the skill and self-control to reach his target, he had provided a chilling reminder of the potential of violence against civil aviation. Under a more relaxed security system, his suicidal rampage might have begun when the airline was aloft."[11]

Fourteen years later, on September 11, 2001, Byck's suicidal intent was realized when the four airplanes were aloft. In the wake of the attacks that day, many remarked that no one had ever thought this possible.[12]

History knows better.

History of Domestic Security

In the aftermath of September 11, 2001, a recurring lament by the media was the fact that no one had imagined that a small group of men would be able to commandeer a passenger jet and use it as a missile to target American landmarks such as the World Trade Towers, the U.S. Capitol, the Pentagon, or the White House. Even government officials made similar statements, including the acting Chairman of the Joint Chiefs of Staff at the time, Air Force General Richard Myers, who said, "You hate to admit it, but we hadn't thought about this."[13] The reality, however, as history will show, is very different. As is illustrated in the previous, short vignette, Samuel Byck had already considered the idea in 1974. While it is recognized that the reasons for Byck's attack on the passenger airline that morning were concealed for some time from the public, the concept was considered by others. Twenty years later, on September 12, 1994, Frank Eugene Corder, a 38-year-old truck driver who faced mental and financial issues and suffered from both alcohol and drug addictions, flew a Cessna 150 into the White House.[14] Although he was only successful in killing himself, it highlighted the potential threat that an aircraft could have on the American government. It is also interesting to note that 1 month prior to Corder's plane crash into the White House, bestselling author Tom Clancy released the book *Debt of Honor*, in which a plane is deliberately crashed into the U.S. Capitol during the State of the Union speech.

The type of scenario in *Debt of Honor* (in real life) is examined in this chapter along with the history of homeland security by reaching further back into American history, both before the terrorist attacks on September 11, 2001, and before the term **homeland security** entered the American lexicon. It does so to highlight the reality that homeland security was not created in a vacuum in the wake of 9-11, but rather, developed across all of American history: From the early threats to American settlers and the quandary of which level of government was responsible for responding to natural disasters, through changes wrought by two world wars and the birth of the term **civil defense**, and into the modern age when Americans saw the multi-decade Cold War come to an end, only to be replaced by terroristic threats from both rogue nations and organizations. The focus of the chapter will remain on our federalist system, assessing how the national and state governments responded to threats and then dealt with both terrorism and natural disasters prior to 9-11.

Early History: 1776–1916

The Founding Fathers had to deal with issues relating to America's defense, both foreign and domestic, from the very beginning. After declaring itself free of England, the new government was forced to deal with the British government while operating under the Articles of Confederation. After winning the Revolutionary War and settling into the new system of government, it became clear that the Articles were no longer working, and a Constitutional Convention was convened in Philadelphia in the summer of 1787. While the right of the national government to deal with foreign enemies was readily accepted by all, an issue arose over how to deal with domestic insurrections. If there are internal threats, does that fall under the purview of the states or the national government? The question was an important one for Shays' Rebellion (see **BOX 1.1**) and was still on the minds of those in attendance that summer.[15]

In 1786, the United States, still operating under the Articles of Confederation, was suffering from a monetary crisis.[16] Many farmers were grossly in debt, and more than 4,000 were forced to enter debtors' prisons until their debts could be paid. The rebellion started with petitions to the government for paper currency, lower taxes, and judicial reform. When this failed, the farmers in western Massachusetts united under the reluctant leadership of Daniel Shays, a bankrupt farmer and former captain in the Revolutionary War. Shays and his followers, many of whom were also veterans, donned their old uniforms and began marching in Massachusetts courts to prevent them from holding session and throwing more of their own into prison.

Courtesy of WPClipart. Acessed at, https://www.wpclipart.com/

BOX 1.1 George Washington on Shays' Rebellion

Letter to Henry Knox
Mount Vernon, 25th Feb. 1787

. . . On the prospect of the happy termination of this insurrection I sincerely congratulate you; hoping that good may result from the cloud of evils which threatened not only the hemisphere of Massachusetts but by spreading its baneful influence, the tranquility of the Union. Surely Shays must be either a weak man—the dupe of some characters who are yet behind the curtain—or has been deceived by his followers. Or which may yet be more likely, he did not conceive that there was energy enough in the Government to bring matters to the crisis to which they have been pushed. It is to be hoped the General Court of that State concurred in the report of the Committee that a rebellion did actually exist. This would be decisive, and the most likely means of putting the finishing stroke to the business . . .

George Washington

After 11 rebellion leaders were arrested and indicted on disorder charges, approximately 1,200 farmers went to the Springfield Court House to prevent the Massachusetts Supreme Judicial Court from holding session. These types of protests continued until January of 1787, when the protesters made their boldest move, seizing the federal arsenal in Springfield. Within 2 weeks, the governor of Massachusetts sent in the militia, some 4,000 strong, to rout the 2,000 members of Shays' Rebellion. Several were killed and some of the leadership, including Shays, were arrested. They were then tried and sentenced to death for treason. Two of these men, John Bly and Charles Rose, were hanged, but with the election of a new governor, John Hancock, the rest were granted pardons.[17]

Shays' Rebellion was not unique, but its timing is of the utmost importance. That summer in Philadelphia, members of the Constitutional Convention considered the implications of Shays' Rebellion, for it "reminded everyone attending in Philadelphia that the Confederation, as it stood, was powerless to protect itself, or any of the states, from large-scale domestic violence, and that this absence of a central power was itself a limitation on state sovereignty."[18] As a result, the framers, in Article 4, Section 4, of the U.S. Constitution, would resolve this issue by stating that "the United States shall guarantee to every State in this Union a Republican form of Government, and shall protect each of them against Invasion; and on Application of the Legislature, or the Executive (when the Legislature cannot be convened) against domestic Violence."[19] This particular article and the concerns of the Constitutional Convention did not take long to make real the problems foreseen.

Another group of farmers, this time in western Pennsylvania during President Washington's first term in office, protested the tax his administration imposed on whiskey.[20] The protests began in 1791 and reached a climax in July of 1794 when a U.S. Marshal came with warrants to arrest tax derelicts and was attacked, followed by an attack on the local tax assessor in his own home. As Pennsylvania could not get the rebellion under control, a request was made to President Washington for the national government to assist, who responded with 12,000 military soldiers. The Whiskey Rebellion quickly fell apart, but its legacy would be everlasting, for it demonstrated the centralized power of the new government to suppress not only foreign threats but also domestic threats (see **BOX 1.2**).

While the national government's role in foreign threats was primary, and against domestic threats secondary (only after the state government, which includes local government, had exhausted its capabilities), what was unclear was the government's role in responding to natural disasters. The U.S. Constitution has no clause stating that it is the role of the government to assist states in recovery from natural disasters. In fact, the 9th and 10th amendments subsume this notion, meaning that since the power is not delegated to the United States by the Constitution, it would be reserved for the states. However, because it was not prohibited, it raised a reasonable question regarding the federal government's role in helping with recovery.

BOX 1.2 Whiskey Rebellion Proclamation

By the President of the United States of America
A Proclamation, August 7, 1794

I, George Washington, President of the United States, do hereby command all persons, being insurgents, as aforesaid, and all others whom it may concern, on or before the 1st day of September next to disperse and retire peaceably to their respective abodes. And I do moreover warn all persons whomsoever against aiding, abetting, or comforting the perpetrators of the aforesaid treasonable acts; and do require all officers and other citizens, according to their respective duties and the laws of the land, to exert their utmost endeavors to prevent and suppress such dangerous proceedings.

G. Washington,
By the President, Edm. Randolf

The "Father of the Constitution" would, on several occasions, have the opportunity to address this particular issue. In 1794, while James Madison was serving in the U.S. House, Congress had appropriated $15,000 in relief for French refugees who had fled from an insurrection in Santo Domingo to both Baltimore and Philadelphia. Madison voted against the bill and noted, "I cannot undertake to lay my finger on that article of the Constitution which granted a right to Congress of expending, on objects of benevolence, the money of their constituents."[21] While this was relief being granted to foreign refugees, the question raised was whether he would offer the same response when it involved Americans. In 1803, while serving as Secretary of State, a bill came before Congress to provide relief for the victims of a major Christmas (1802) fire in Portsmouth, New Hampshire. Madison railed against the idea, and Madison's replacement in the House of Representatives, William Giles, wrote that it was not the role of Congress to "attend to what generosity and humanity require, but to what the Constitution and their duty require."[22] The legislation passed, allowing for the payment of local bonds to be delayed by 1 year.[23]

Similar resolutions would arise occasionally throughout the 19th century, but they tended to be the exception and not the rule. One particular exception, however, was the American Civil War. After America split into the Union versus the Confederacy, many people remaining in the north were southern sympathizers. Realizing the dangers to the Union of subversive activity and sabotage, President Lincoln authorized the suspension of habeas corpus, meaning that people deemed a threat to the U.S. government could be arrested and kept in jail indefinitely without a hearing. Although the constitutionality of the suspension was challenged, it was not resolved until after the war, finding in the case *Ex Parte Milligan* (1866) that neither Congress nor the president had the right under the U.S. Constitution to impose martial law and suspend habeus corpus when civilian courts were functioning.

The Civil War also generated another issue regarding the powers of the national government and states in times of insurrection. After the Civil War, during Reconstruction, when the southern states were undergoing the process of rejoining the union, the states were often patrolled by the U.S. military. In part, the issue had to do with the rise of the Ku Klux Klan and its acts of terrorism on southern blacks, but it also had to do with the national government using the military as a police force, which weighed against the U.S. Constitution.

After a compromise, the military was removed, but in order to prevent such future transgressions, the U.S. Congress passed the Posse Comitatus Act in 1878 (see **BOX 1.3**). The purpose of the act was to limit the powers of the federal government in using the military to enforce domestic law unless Article IV, Section IV of the Constitution had been invoked. This is why the military can only serve in advisory and support roles for state and local law enforcement and never in a direct law enforcement role.[24]

Between the end of the Civil War (1865) and before the U.S. entry into World War I (1917), a number of natural disasters helped to shape America's response to future events, both man-made and natural. One of the

BOX 1.3 The Posse Comitatus Act

Section 15 of chapter 263, of the Acts of the 2nd session of the 45th Congress.

Sec. 15. From and after the passage of this act it shall not be lawful to employ any part of the Army of the United States, as a posse comitatus, or otherwise, for the purpose of executing the laws, except in such cases and under such circumstances as such employment of said force may be expressly authorized by the Constitution or by act of Congress; and no money appropriated by this act shall be used to pay any of the expenses incurred in the employment of any troops in violation of this section and any person willfully violating the provisions of this section shall be deemed guilty of a misdemeanor and on conviction thereof shall be punished by fine not exceeding ten thousand dollars or imprisonment not exceeding 2 years or by both such fine and imprisonment.

BOX 1.4 American Red Cross Congressional Charter, 1905

To continue and carry on a system of national and international relief in time of peace and to apply the same in mitigating the sufferings caused by pestilence, famine, fire, floods, and other great natural calamities, and to devise and carry on measures for preventing the same.

worst disasters in American history came on May 31, 1889, with the Johnstown Flood.[25] The Johnstown Flood was the result of a catastrophic failure of a dam above Johnston, Pennsylvania, after several days of heavy rain, nearly wiping out the entire town. The estimated damages were $17 million, and 2,209 people lost their lives. In the aftermath, a relatively new organization, the American Red Cross (see **BOX 1.4**), led by its founder Clara Barton, descended upon Johnstown and handled the disaster recovery. The American Red Cross was there for 5 months.

Another major event that had a significant impact on disaster response in America was the Great San Francisco Earthquake and Fire of 1906. Initially, the local police and fire responded, but soon the military located at the Presidio military post took charge of the response in violation of Posse Comitatus. Military soldiers were directed to help fight the fires, prevent looting, provide relief, and police the streets.[26] In addition, the American Red Cross once again responded, serving alongside the army as a relief agency. In fact, as a result of the San Francisco Earthquake, the American Red Cross, now chartered by Congress, began to serve as the primary relief agency in catastrophic events, freeing the military to engage in those duties necessary to reestablish order—a symbiotic relationship that continues to this day.

Civil Defense and Two Hot Wars: 1917–1945

Prior to World War I, the United States was largely an isolationist country, protected by the vast expanse of two vast oceans. There was one occasion on American soil that raised the issue of America's defenses just prior to the war, and that was when Pancho Villa and his *Villistas* bandits crossed into the United States on March 9, 1916, and entered the town of Columbus, New Mexico.[27] They attacked the American 13th Cavalry, looted houses, and fought with civilians. Eight American soldiers and 10 civilians died, raising not only a military response but also a concern for establishing some form of civil defense along the U.S.-Mexico Border. General "Black Jack" Pershing was sent into Mexico to pursue Villa, while additional consideration was given to enhancing the mounted watchmen of the United States Immigration Service, although it was not until May 28, 1924, that this group would become the United States Border Patrol.[28]

At the time that Pancho Villa attacked the United States, the world had already been at war for several years. World War I began on July 28, 1914, and very quickly came to include all of the major empires at the time, including the German, Austro-Hungarian, Ottoman, Russian, and British empires.[29] President Woodrow Wilson took a strong noninterventionist stance, and the United States remained on the sidelines trying to broker a peace settlement. After his reelection in 1916, the sinking of seven U.S. merchant ships, and the interception of the famous Zimmerman telegram (in which Germany encouraged Mexico to join the war as an ally against the United States[30]), President Wilson asked for a declaration of war. Congress deliberated for several months but declared war on April 6, 1917. Pershing was recalled from his hunt for Pancho Villa and was established as the commander of the American Expeditionary Force (AEF). America was about to step onto the world stage.

During this time, there was concern back home about the safety of the American people. While the United States did not have to fear the aerial bombardments that European citizens now suffered, there was a perceived need to protect the general public from future attacks. In fact, consideration had already been given to this possibility. Tucked into an army appropriations bill, on August 29, 1916, the federal government established the Council of National Defense.[31] The Council was a presidential advisory board that included the Secretaries of War, Navy, Interior, Agriculture, Commerce, and Labor, and was assisted by an Advisory Committee appointed by the president. Its responsibilities included "coordinating resources and industries for national defense" and "stimulating civilian morale."[32]

When the United States declared war in 1917, the work of the council escalated. The federal government asked state governors to create their own councils in order to support the National Council's efforts. Every state responded by organizing its own state-level council of defense, and by the end of the war, 182,000 local civil defense councils had been formed across the United States. These local councils conducted civil defense patrols, funded and deployed air raid sirens, and practiced safety drills. After the war ended on November 11, 1918, the National Council switched

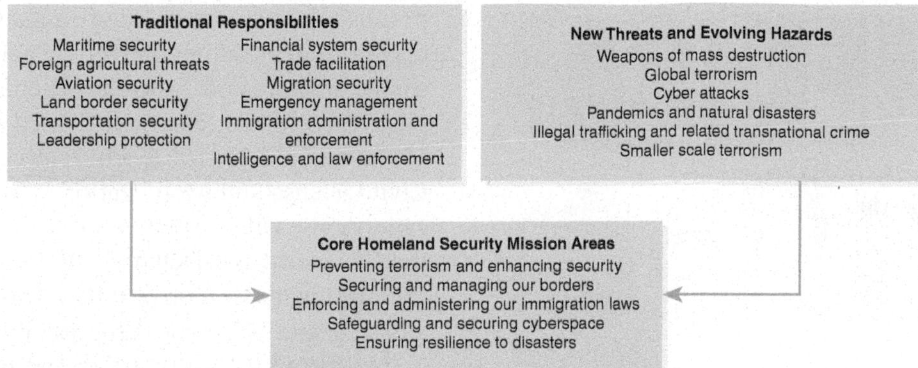

FIGURE 1.1 Flowchart of Civil Defense, Emergency Management, & Homeland Security.

Data from: Defense Civil Preparedness Agency. (1975). Significant Events in United States Civil Defense History. Washington, D.C.: Defense Civil Preparedness Agency; Homeland Security National Preparedness Task Force. (2006). Civil Defense and Homeland Security: A Short History of National Preparedness Efforts. Washington, D.C.: U.S Department of Homeland Security.

its focus to demobilization efforts until their operations were suspended in June of 1921. Although the National Council ceased operations, many of the local councils continued to operate over the next decade (see **FIGURE 1.1**.).

For that next decade, the federal government did little with regard to civil defense, but after Hitler came to power in 1933, the White House became concerned. That year, President Franklin D. Roosevelt created the National Emergency Council by executive order. The focus of the council was essentially war preparation without calling it that, and only one aspect of its mission was the coordination of emergency programs among all agencies involved in national preparedness.[33] Once World War II ignited in Europe, Roosevelt resurrected the National Defense Council in 1939, and shortly after in 1940, converted the National Emergency Council into the Office of Emergency Management.[34]

An issue of federalism quickly arose between the national government and the states. The federal funding for civil defense was only for dealing with attacks such as the bombing of civilians in Europe. The states and many of the large metropolitan cities were concerned with nonattack disaster preparedness. New York City Mayor Fiorello La Guardia wrote to Roosevelt and argued, "there is a need for a strong Federal Department to coordinate activities, and not only to coordinate but to initiate and get things done. Please bear in mind that up to this war and never in our history, has the civilian population been exposed to attack. The new technique of war has created the necessity for developing new techniques of civilian defense."[35] President Roosevelt agreed and responded with the creation of the Office of Civilian Defense (OCD) within the Office for Emergency Management, and he named Mayor La Guardia as the Director.[36] The OCD coordinated attack preparedness between the federal and state governments and established defense councils at the local level. Some of the more renowned initiatives related to the OCD included the creation of civil defense plans, air raid drills, urban blackouts, and sand bag stockpiling. As World War II came to a close in 1945, so too did the Office of Civilian Defense.

Civil Defense and the Cold War: 1946–1991

Immediately after the end of World War II, the Truman administration began bringing troops home and drawing down the military. Civil defense was no longer deemed an important issue. That was the case until the beginning of the Cold War, when the Soviet Union turned hostile toward the United States and began developing the atomic bomb. The War Department's Civil Defense Board reviewed the issue of civil defense and deemed it a local issue but did note that the majority of the necessary resources could be provided by the federal government. In 1947, Congress passed the National Security Act, which, in addition to creating the Central Intelligence Agency, created the National Security Resources Board (NSRB). The NSRB was tasked with mobilizing civilian and military support and maintaining adequate supplies for use in the event of a war, specifically a nuclear attack on the United States. Additionally, the following year, Truman created the Office of Civil Defense Planning within the newly restructured Department of Defense (also created by the National Security Act of 1947).

At this point, the Truman administration had a variety of organizations focused on civil defense, state and local governments demanding more assistance, and a public growing ever more concerned with national security. The NSRB was tasked with coming up with a plan that was finally released in 1950 and became known as the *Blue Book*.[37] The

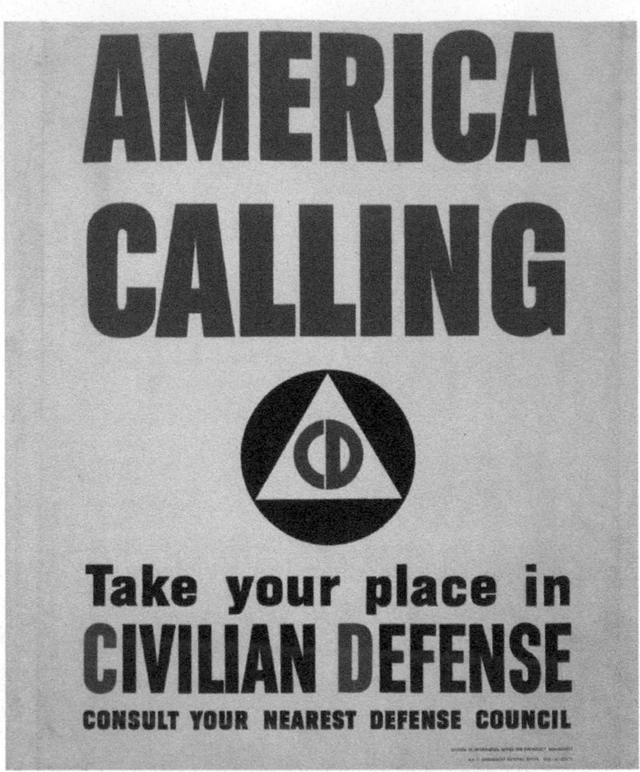
AMERICA
CALLING
CD
Take your place in
CIVILIAN DEFENSE
CONSULT YOUR NEAREST DEFENSE COUNCIL

Reproduced from America calling–Take your place in civilian defense–Consult your nearest defense council. United States, 1941. [Washington, D.C.: Government Printing Office] Retrieved from the Library of Congress, https://www.loc.gov/item/96507339/.

overall recommendation was to create one agency to deal with coordinating civil defense in America. In response, Congress enacted the Federal Civil Defense Act of 1950, which placed most of the civil defense burden on the states and created the Federal Civil Defense Administration (FCDA) as the one agency to formulate national policy to guide the states' efforts.[38] Throughout the 1950s, the FCDA led shelter-building programs, sought to improve federal and state coordination, established an attack warning system, stockpiled supplies, and started a well-known national civic education campaign, which included Bert the Turtle in "Duck and Cover."[39]

In 1953, when former World War II General Dwight D. Eisenhower was sworn in as President of the United States, the new president realized that civil defense would be an expensive venture on the part of the federal government, and so he minimized the responsibility and requested less funding for the FCDA.[40] Then, in 1958, to highlight the diminished role that the federal administration would play in Eisenhower's second term, the FCDA was downgraded to the Office of Defense and Civilian Mobilization. Then, as if to highlight the greater emphasis on *civil* defense, the name of the office was changed again to the Office of Civil Defense and Mobilization.

In 1961, when President John F. Kennedy took office, he had a different approach and embraced federal involvement in emergency planning. He proposed a "nationwide long-range program of identifying present fallout shelter capacity and providing shelter in new and existing structures."[41] To accomplish these goals, Kennedy issued Executive Order 10952 on July 20, 1961, which divided the Office of Civil Defense and Mobilization into two new organizations: The Office of Emergency Planning (OEP) and the Office of Civil Defense (OCD). OEP was part of the president's Executive Office and was tasked with advising and assisting the president in determining policy for all nonmilitary emergency preparedness, including civil defense. OCD was part of the Office of the Secretary of Defense and was tasked with overseeing the nation's civil defense program. Although the creation of fallout shelters was initiated during the Kennedy administration, adequate funding began to dwindle during the Johnson administration due to funding needs for both his Great Society programs and the Vietnam War. The importance of civil defense and emergency planning had been greatly diminished.

In 1969, President Richard M. Nixon entered office, and shortly thereafter, a series of natural disasters struck, with the most devastating coming from Hurricane Camille.[42] Nixon charged the Office of Emergency Planning to conduct a review, which released its results in 1970. As a result, several new federal agencies arose. The Office of Civil Defense would fold into the Defense Civil Preparedness Agency under the Department of Defense. This agency was responsible for a military response to natural and man-made disasters. The Office of Emergency Planning became the Office of Emergency Preparedness, which was to handle the civilian side of these events. However, a number of tasks were given to other agencies, including the Office of Science and Technology Policy, the Department of the Treasury, and the Federal Disaster Assistance Administration under Housing and Urban Development (HUD). While the decentralization of the planning did allow each agency to concentrate on its area of expertise, coordination between these agencies was lacking and there was an inordinate amount of overlap, leading to wasteful spending.[43]

One complicated issue, how and under what circumstances the federal government would assist state and local governments in the case of disaster, started to see resolution under the Nixon Administration when Congress passed the Disaster Relief Act of 1974. The act was amended in 1988 as the Robert T. Stafford Disaster Relief and Emergency Assistance Act and is commonly known as the Stafford Act. It was named for a U.S. Senator who was instrumental in its passage. The Stafford Act established the procedures by which states can apply for disaster relief from the federal government.

It did not cover all disasters, such as public health emergencies or flood control and coastal emergencies, as other acts covered these types of disasters, nor did it cover foreign disasters. It did, however, streamline the process for declaring and ending a disaster and how the federal government would provide assistance. At the time when the act was passed; however, there were more than 100 different federal agencies tasked with providing disaster relief without one necessarily being in charge. President Carter was about to change that.

Emergency Management: 1979–2001

President Jimmy Carter entered office in 1977 with the goal of reining in federal bureaucracy by making it more efficient. Carter ordered a review of civil defense agencies and programs, and the review found an enormous amount of duplication of effort and wasteful spending. The recommendation was to consolidate all civil defense spending under one agency in order to better coordinate the federal response to natural disasters. The result was Executive Order 12148, dated July 20, 1979, which created the Federal Emergency Management Agency (FEMA) as the lead agency for coordinating federal disaster relief. FEMA also absorbed a number of agencies such as the Federal Insurance Administration, the National Fire Prevention and Control Administration, and the National Weather Service Community Preparedness Program. At the time, the creation of FEMA represented the single largest consolidation of civil defense efforts in U.S. history.[44]

Although civil defense had now given way to **emergency management** under the Carter administration, the sole purpose of FEMA was to respond to natural disasters, not man-made attacks. When President Ronald Reagan entered office, he changed that and made FEMA a dual-use agency, enabling all future emergency management funds to be used for natural disasters as well as attacks on the homeland.[45] FEMA then began working toward the development of a full all-hazard preparedness plan at the federal level known as the Integrated Emergency Management System (IEMS). Despite all of the efforts by FEMA to launch this all-hazards plan, Congress would not fund the system and the idea was shelved.

After President George H.W. Bush (Bush I) took office in 1989, a number of disasters occurred that once again galvanized the emergency management community. The *Exxon Valdez* oil spill, Hurricane Hugo (which struck the Virgin Islands, Puerto Rico, and South Carolina), and the Loma Prieta earthquake (which hit southern California) all struck in 1989, and the federal response was criticized as poor. FEMA dusted off the IEMS plan and developed the Federal Response Plan (FRP) as a means of improving performance. Drawing from the Incident Command System and Incident Management System Framework, the FRP defined how 27 federal agencies and the American Red Cross would respond to the needs of state and local governments when they were overwhelmed by a disaster. The national government now had an all-hazards plan.

Just prior to the 1992 presidential election, Hurricane Andrew struck South Florida and once again highlighted the poor performance of the government in its response. As one report noted, "government at all levels was slow to comprehend the scope of the disaster."[46] Arkansas Governor Bill Clinton won the election and entered office in 1993. Clinton brought with him from Arkansas James Lee Witt, who had been the Director of Emergency Management for the State of Arkansas (see **BOX 1.5**). He was the first appointee to the position who had an emergency management background. He created three functional directorates corresponding to the major phases of emergency management: Mitigation, preparedness, and response and recovery. These three directorates were all then focused on creating and implementing an all-hazards plan.

The implementation of the plan would prove necessary for one bombing and fortuitous in the wake of a second. The first bombing was of the World Trade Center by international terrorists on February 26, 1993, and the second was of the Alfred P. Murrah Federal Building in Oklahoma City by domestic terrorists on April 19, 1995. In many ways, both of these bombings caught America—its public, media, and law enforcement community—off guard: The World Trade Center bombing, because America was shocked by such an international terrorist bombing occurring inside the United States and the Oklahoma City Bombing, because no one suspected it was a case of domestic terrorism. What both of these bombings did was to galvanize policy makers and the law enforcement community to start looking at both international terrorist threats and domestic terrorism from homegrown radicals.

At the federal level, the immediate actions of these two bombings led to President Clinton elevating the

Courtesy of Jocelyn Augustino/FEMA.

BOX 1.5 James Lee Witt Biography

James Lee Witt was born in Paris, Arkansas, in 1944, and met former President Bill Clinton in 1974. He eventually founded his own construction business in 1968, and then years later, he was elected as County Judge in Yell County. In 1988, while Bill Clinton served as Arkansas Governor, Witt was appointed as the head of the Arkansas Office of Emergency Services and he successfully reorganized that organization. After Bill Clinton was elected president in 1992, he appointed Witt to serve as the head of the Federal Emergency Management Agency (FEMA), making him the first director to have any emergency management experience. In 1996, the agency was elevated to cabinet status, giving it far more importance and visibility. Witt's reorganization of FEMA was considered highly successful because he turned a very weak agency into a strong agency by ceasing political appointments, removing excessive layers of bureaucracy, and creating an agency that was seen as responsive to the needs of the people in the wake of a disaster. Witt set the standard by which all future directors and the agency itself would be evaluated.

Courtesy of FEMA.

FEMA directorship to Cabinet-level status in order to improve the line of communication between the director and the president. What then followed was a series of Congressional hearings, commissions, and recommended policies where policymakers began to determine how best to deal with domestic preparedness and national security.

One of the more influential commissions was formed by the Clinton administration and was known formally as the Advisory Panel to Assess Domestic Response Capabilities for Terrorism Involving Weapons of Mass Destruction. Virginia Governor Jim Gilmore was appointed as the commission chair, hence the commission became known more simply as the Gilmore Commission. It developed a series of five reports to the president and Congress, starting in 1999, which made numerous recommendations, including the creation of a fusion center to integrate and analyze all intelligence pertaining to terrorism and counter-terrorism and the creation of a civil liberties oversight board. In the commission's first several years, most of the recommendations were considered, but very few were acted upon.

Another influential commission was The U.S. Commission on National Security in the 21st century, chartered by the Department of Defense and known as the Hart–Rudman Commission. It began a comprehensive re-examination of U.S. national security policies. One of the commission's recommendations was the creation of a Cabinet-level National Homeland Security Agency responsible for planning, coordinating, and integrating various U.S. government activities involved in "homeland security." The commission defined homeland security as "the protection of the territory, critical infrastructures, and citizens of the United States by federal, state, and local government entities from the threat or use of chemical, biological, radiological, nuclear, cyber, or conventional weapons by military or other means."[47] Legislation toward this end was actually introduced on March 29, 2001, but hearings continued through April of 2001 without the passage of any legislation.

Then came September 11, 2001, and the concept of emergency management in the United States would quickly give way to the concepts of homeland security.

Chapter Summary

Although the United States has always been concerned with securing the homeland, it is evident from the historical record that this effort has gone through many stages. Initially, it would appear that under the strict constructs of federalism, states were seen as being responsible for dealing with all natural disasters themselves, and that resources from the national government would only be applied when Article 4, Section 4 of the U.S. Constitution was invoked (see **BOX 1.6**).

BOX 1.6 U.S. Constitution Article 4, Section 4

The United States shall guarantee to every State in this Union a Republican Form of Government, and shall protect each of them against Invasion; and on Application of the Legislature, or of the Executive (when the Legislature cannot be convened) against domestic Violence.

Two World Wars would subtly begin to change that mindset in the first half of the 20th century, when the national government embraced a cooperative, albeit limited, response in the name of civil defense. As the United States shifted to a Cold War in the fight against communism, a more cooperative response evolved with a division between civil and military responses. In 1979, a consolidated approach under the Federal Emergency Management Agency (FEMA) saw civil defense evolve into emergency management, and eventually, a dual response policy for responding to natural and man-made disasters. As emergency management evolved in the 1990s, its elevation to Cabinet-level status marked its significant rise as a policy issue and the importance the federal government now paid to the issue.

Most of the evolution from civil defense to emergency management has been marked as a reactionary response to some natural or man-made disaster. World War I brought about civil defense. The World Trade Center and Oklahoma City bombings brought about the elevation of FEMA to a Cabinet-level agency. Yet, it should also be noted that the ideas for these changes tended to exist prior to the events; it was only after the natural or man-made disasters that these changes came about. The ultimate evidence for this is the 21st-Century Commission's ideas about creating a "Cabinet-level National Homeland Security Agency," which did not come about until after September 11, 2001.[48] And finally, it would seem that the federal government apparatus has waffled between strong centralization and consolidation, to a more decentralized and multi-agency response.

In brief, the evolution of the homeland security apparatus (also call it civil defense or emergency management) has generally resulted from disasters (natural and man-made) but was based on ideas that existed prior to these events.

Review/Discussion Questions

1. In the aftermath of September 11, 2001, it was said that no one had ever thought planes could be used as weapons. Why is this not the case?
2. Describe domestic security in the 18th and 19th centuries. Why was domestic security not so much an issue?
3. Detail the development of civil defense, especially describing the development during both World War I and World War II.
4. What is emergency management, how did it develop, and how is it different from civil defense?
5. What were the antecedents to the development of homeland security in America prior to the terrorist attacks on September 11?

Additional Readings

Defense Civil Preparedness Agency. (1975). *Significant Events in United States Civil Defense History.* Washington, DC: Defense Civil Preparedness Agency.

Homeland Security National Preparedness Task Force. (2006). *Civil Defense and Homeland Security: A Short History of National Preparedness Efforts.* Washington, DC: U.S. Department of Homeland Security.

Maxwell, Bruce. (2004). *Homeland Security: A Documentary History.* Washington, DC: CQ Press.

Endnotes

1. Melanson, P. H. & Stevens, P. D. (2002). *The Secret Service: The Hidden History of an Enigmatic Agency.* New York, NY: Carrol & Graff, p. 107.
2. Oliver, W. M. & Marion, N. E. (2010). *Killing the President: Assassinations, Attempts, and Rumored Attempts on U.S. Commanders-in-Chief.* Santa-Barbara, CA: Praeger.
3. Sifakis, C. (2001). *Encyclopedia of Assassinations.* New York, NY: Checkmark.
4. Melanson, P. H. & Stevens, P. D. (2002). *The Secret Service: The Hidden History of an Enigmatic Agency.* New York, NY: Carrol & Graff, p. 109.
5. Clarke, J. W. (1982). *American Assassins: The Darker Side of Politics.* Princeton, NJ: Princeton University Press, p. 128.
6. Clarke, J. W. (1982). *American Assassins: The Darker Side of Politics.* Princeton, NJ: Princeton University Press, p. 128.

7. Oliver, W. M. & Marion, N. E. (2010). *Killing the President: Assassinations, Attempts, and Rumored Attempts on U.S. Commanders-in-Chief.* Santa Barbara, CA: Praeger.
8. Melanson, P. H. & Stevens, P. D. (2002). *The Secret Service: The Hidden History of an Enigmatic Agency.* New York, NY: Carrol & Graff, p. 108.
9. Oliver, W. M. & Marion, N. E. (2010). *Killing the President: Assassinations, Attempts, and Rumored Attempts on U.S. Commanders-in-Chief.* Santa Barbara, CA: Praeger.
10. Preston, E. (1987). *Troubled Passage: The Federal Aviation Administration During the Nixon-Ford Term, 1973–1977.* Washington, DC: U.S. Government Printing Office.
11. Preston, E. (1987). *Troubled Passage: The Federal Aviation Administration During the Nixon-Ford Term, 1973–1977.* Washington, DC: U.S. Government Printing Office.
12. National Commission on Terrorist Attacks Upon the United States. (2004). *The 9/11 Commission Report: Final Report of the National Commission on Terrorist Attacks Upon the United States (Authorized Ed.).* New York: W.W. Norton & Company, Inc.
13. Pinkerton, J. (2002). "Our Homeland Securitizers Should Read More." *New American Foundation.* Retrieved from http://www.newamerica.net/publications/articles/2002/our_homeland_securitizers_should_read_more
14. Oliver, W. M. & Marion, N. E. (2010). *Killing the President: Assassinations, Attempts, and Rumored Attempts on U.S. Commanders-in-Chief.* Santa Barbara, CA: Praeger.
15. Szatmary, D. P. (2002). *Shays' Rebellion: The Making of an Agrarian Insurrection.* Boston: University of Massachusetts Press.
16. Oliver, W. M. & Hilgenberg, J. F., Jr. (2010). *A History of Crime and Criminal Justice in America.* 2nd ed. Durham, NC: Carolina Academic Press.
17. Richards, L. L. (2002). *Shays' Rebellion: The American Revolution's Final Battle.* Philadelphia: University of Pennsylvania Press.
18. Johnson, P. (1997). *A History of the American People.* New York: HarperCollins, p. 188.
19. Article 4, Section 4, United States Constitution.
20. Hogeland, W. (2006). *The Whiskey Rebellion.* New York: Scribner; Slaughter, T. P. (1986). *The Whiskey Rebellion: Frontier Epilogue to the American Revolution.* New York: Oxford University Press.
21. As quoted in Williams, W. E. (2006). "Constitution Day." Ideas on Liberty. Retrieved from http://econfaculty.gmu.edu/wew/articles/fee/constitution.html
22. As quoted in Williams, W. E. (2006). "Constitution Day." Ideas on Liberty. Retrieved from http://econfaculty.gmu.edu/wew/articles/fee/constitution.html
23. Sauter, M. A. & Carafano, J. J. (2012). *A Complete Guide: Homeland Security.* 2nd ed. New York: McGraw Hill.
24. Hendell, G. B. (2011). Domestic use of the armed forces to maintain law and order—*posse comitatus* pitfalls at the inauguration of the 44th president. *Publius: The Journal of Federalism, 41(2)*, 336–348.
25. The Posse Comitatus Act of 1878, Section 1385 of Title 18, United States Code.
26. McCullough, D. (1968). *The Johnstown Flood.* New York: Simon & Schuster.
27. Barker, M. E. (1998). *Three Fearful Days: San Francisco Memoirs of the 1906 Earthquake & Fire.* San Francisco, CA: Londonborn Publications; Thomas, G. & M. M. Witts. (1971); *The San Francisco Earthquake.* New York: Stein and Day.
28. Welsome, E. (2007). *The General and the Jaguar: Pershing's Hunt for Pancho Villa.* Lincoln, NE: Bison Books.
29. Bumgarner, J. B. (2006). *Federal Agents: The Growth of Federal Law Enforcement in America.* Westport, CT: Praeger Publishers.
30. Keegan, J. (2000). *The First World War.* New York: Vintage; Meyer, G. J. (2007). *A World Undone: The Story of the Great War, 1914 to 1918.* New York: A Delta Book.
31. Tuchman, B. W. (1985). *The Zimmerman Telegram.* New York: Ballantine Books.
32. Homeland Security National Preparedness Task Force. (2006). *Civil Defense and Homeland Security: A Short History of National Preparedness Efforts.* Washington, DC: U.S. Department of Homeland Security.
33. Homeland Security National Preparedness Task Force. (2006). *Civil Defense and Homeland Security: A Short History of National Preparedness Efforts.* Washington, DC: U.S. Department of Homeland Security, p. 5.
34. Homeland Security National Preparedness Task Force. (2006). *Civil Defense and Homeland Security: A Short History of National Preparedness Efforts.* Washington, DC: U.S. Department of Homeland Security.
35. Defense Civil Preparedness Agency. (1975). *Significant Events in United States Civil Defense History.* Washington, DC: Defense Civil Preparedness Agency.
36. Homeland Security National Preparedness Task Force. (2006). *Civil Defense and Homeland Security: A Short History of National Preparedness Efforts.* Washington, DC: U.S. Department of Homeland Security, p. 5.
37. Defense Civil Preparedness Agency. (1975). *Significant Events in United States Civil Defense History.* Washington, DC: Defense Civil Preparedness Agency.
38. Defense Civil Preparedness Agency. (1975). *Significant Events in United States Civil Defense History.* Washington, DC: Defense Civil Preparedness Agency; Homeland Security National Preparedness Task Force. (2006). *Civil Defense and Homeland Security: A Short History of National Preparedness Efforts.* Washington, DC: U.S Department of Homeland Security.
39. Kerr, T. (1983). *Civil Defense in the U.S.: Bandaid for a Holocaust.* Denver, CO: Westview Press.
40. Homeland Security National Preparedness Task Force. (2006). *Civil Defense and Homeland Security: A Short History of National Preparedness Efforts.* Washington, DC: U.S. Department of Homeland Security. See Duck and Cover (1951). Available online at http://archive.org/details/DuckandC1951
41. Homeland Security National Preparedness Task Force. (2006). *Civil Defense and Homeland Security: A Short History of National Preparedness Efforts.* Washington, DC: U.S. Department of Homeland Security.
42. Homeland Security National Preparedness Task Force. (2006). *Civil Defense and Homeland Security: A Short History of National Preparedness Efforts.* Washington, DC: U.S. Department of Homeland Security, p. 12.
43. Hearn, P. D. (2004). *Hurricane Camille: Monster Storm of the Gulf Coast.* Jackson, MS: University of Mississippi Press.
44. Lanouette, W. (1978). "The Best Civil Defense May Be the Best–Or Worst–Offense." *The National Journal*, September 9.
45. Homeland Security National Preparedness Task Force. (2006). *Civil Defense and Homeland Security: A Short History of National Preparedness Efforts.* Washington, DC: U.S. Department of Homeland Security.

46. Blanchard, B. W. (1986). "American Civil Defense 1945-1984: The Evolution of Programs and Policies." *Federal Emergency Management Agency Monograph Series, 2*, 1–29.
47. Homeland Security National Preparedness Task Force. (2006). *Civil Defense and Homeland Security: A Short History of National Preparedness Efforts.* Washington, DC: U.S. Department of Homeland Security, p. 22.
48. Homeland Security National Preparedness Task Force. (2006). *Civil Defense and Homeland Security: A Short History of National Preparedness Efforts.* Washington, DC: U.S. Department of Homeland Security, p. 24.

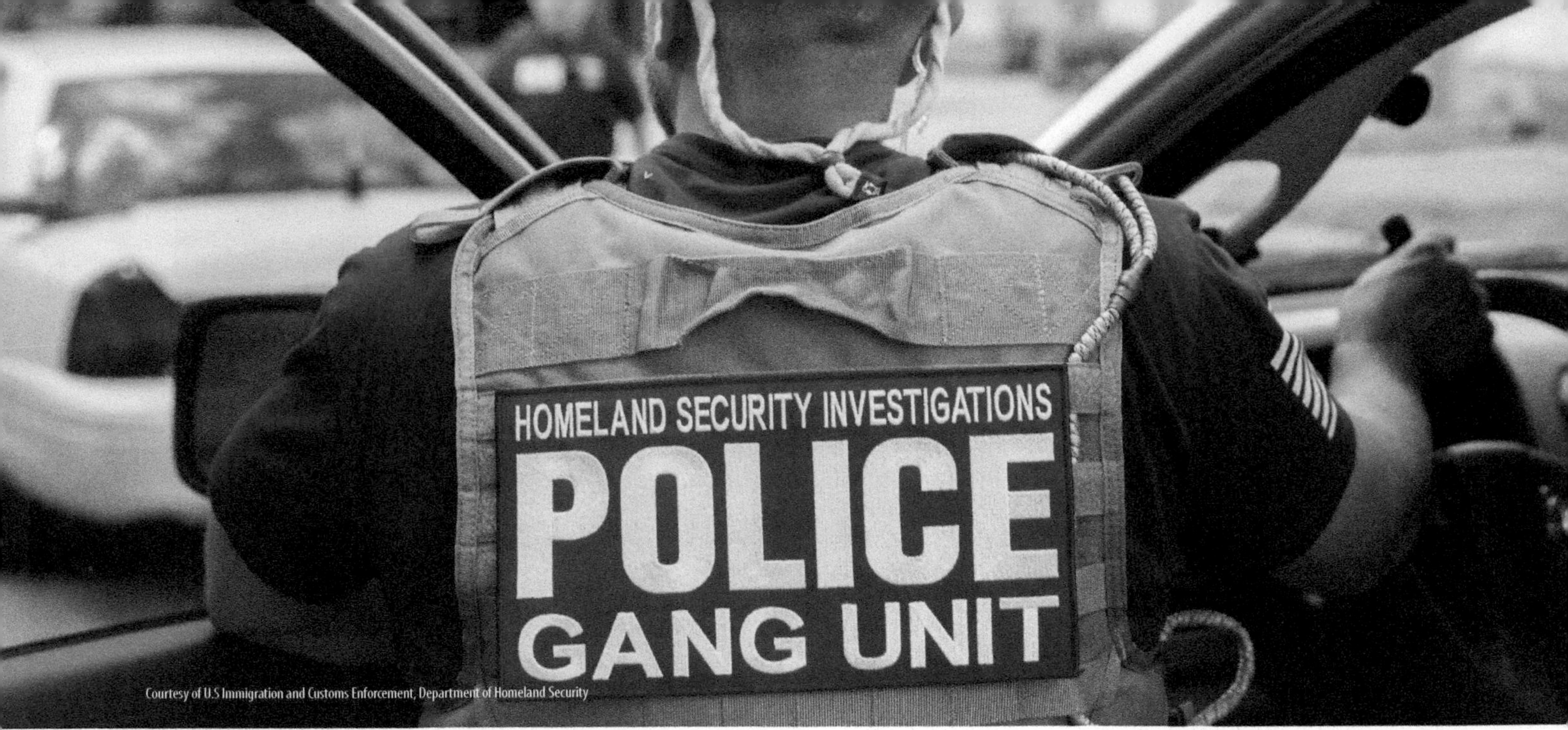

Courtesy of U.S Immigration and Customs Enforcement, Department of Homeland Security

CHAPTER 2

Homeland Security Defined

CHAPTER OBJECTIVES

- To understand that there is no commonly accepted definition of homeland security and why this is the case
- To understand common themes of homeland security as found through the homeland security bureaucracy, concepts, strategy, mission, goals, and areas of emphasis
- To consider the importance of having an acceptably shared definition of homeland security

CHAPTER OUTLINE

Dawn broke cold and brisk as coffee pots began to percolate and people stirred to life that January morning in the northern Virginia suburbs. Soon, the traffic was as heavy as ever in Fairfax and neighboring Arlington County, as people made their way down side streets and highways on their way to work. Police officers responded to a variety of traffic fender-benders, moving them off to the side of the road in order to keep the flow of traffic from backing up on the main arteries into the nation's capital, Washington, D.C. With each passing minute, traffic became heavier and heavier.

One location that always backed up was Dolley Madison Boulevard, Route 123, heading eastbound toward the George Washington Parkway, the "G.W." in local parlance. At what appeared to be a typical traffic intersection, cars began backing up in the two left-turn lanes, waiting for the light to turn red. The road they were waiting to turn left onto appeared to lead into just another northern Virginia suburb. Only, it was not a suburb at all. Nor was it typical. It was the entrance to the headquarters of the Central Intelligence Agency (CIA).

Reproduced from Highsmith, C. M., photographer. Aerial view of the CIA Headquarters, Langley, Virginia. Langley United States Virginia, None. [Between 1980 and 2006] [Photograph] Retrieved from the Library of Congress, https://www.loc.gov/item/2011632954/.

It was January 25, 1993. The time was approximately 8:00 am.

In one of the left-hand turn lanes was a brown 1970s Datsun station wagon, waiting behind several other vehicles stopped at the light.[1] The two turn lanes behind the Datsun were full, and the left travel lane was also backed up with people waiting to turn left into CIA headquarters. Suddenly, the door of the Datsun opened and a man in his late 20s exited the vehicle. He was short in stature with olive skin and a thick mustache. As he exited the vehicle, he pulled an AK-47 semi-automatic rifle from the car and began walking down the median strip. He raised the AK-47 and began firing shots into the cars stopped behind him, aiming toward the drivers. He fired eight rounds as he walked along the median, ultimately hitting five men: Frank Darling, Lansing Bennett, Nicholas Starr, Calvin Morgan, and Stephen Williams.[2]

As the shooter reached a certain point on the median, he stopped, turned, and began walking back. As he reached the first car he had fired into, the one immediately behind his car, he raised the AK-47 and shot Frank Darling in the head two more times. He then climbed back into the driver's seat of the Datsun and proceeded to drive east toward the G.W. Parkway, then headed south into Arlington County.

A police officer in Arlington County heard two tones on his radio and was told to check his on-board computer for an important message.[3] The screen read that there was a shooting at the CIA headquarters, several people were injured from an AK-47, and the suspect was heading toward the G.W. Parkway. He began making his way toward the parkway as it followed along the Potomac River, heading south to George Washington's Mount Vernon. As he traveled the G.W. Parkway, he was asked to be on the lookout for a 1970s model station wagon. He started to drive into one of the many parks along the Parkway but was called to Arlington Hospital to guard one of the shooting victims who had been transported there by ambulance.

It turns out that the suspect was one Aimal Kasi, born in Pakistan in the mid-1960s, who had entered the United States in 1991.[4] He stayed in Reston, Virginia, with a friend and found work as a courier, driving by the entrance to the CIA almost every day. He knew that all of the people turning left at the intersection worked for the CIA, so he purchased the AK-47 and began planning his attack.

After the shooting, he drove to a nearby park and waited for about an hour and a half. As no one approached his car, he traveled back to Reston, hid the weapon under a sofa and left the house. He purchased lunch at McDonald's, checked into a hotel, and watched the news about his attack. He then flew home to Pakistan the following morning.[5]

Two of the shooting victims, Frank Darling and Lansing Bennett, died from their wounds. The other three survived. A joint investigation between the Federal Bureau of Investigation (FBI) and local police was launched, and Kasi was eventually identified as the shooter.[6] He was listed on the FBI's Most Wanted Fugitives[7] list. The search turned international as it was discovered that Kasi had returned to Pakistan (see **BOX 2.1**). Eventually, a source identified his whereabouts; he was captured and smuggled back into the United States. He was placed on trial, found guilty of murder, and executed on November 4, 2002.[8]

BOX 2.1 What Happened After the CIA Shooting?

At the time of the shootings, U.S. officials knew nothing of Kasi's identity or affiliations. Authorities identified Kasi as the shooter several days later, after his roommate filed a missing person's report with local police. Soon after, the FBI placed Kasi on their Most Wanted List, while the State Department posted a $2 million reward for his capture; it was later increased to $3.5 million. Yet, for 4 years, various plans to locate, track, and capture Kasi failed.

As the years passed, Kasi assumed that the United States had forgotten about him, and he began leaving Afghanistan to visit friends in Pakistan. On June 15, 1997, acting on an informant's tip, a combined FBI and CIA team lured Kasi to a meeting in the Dera Ghazi Khan District of Punjab, Pakistan, to work out details of a supposed business venture involving smuggled arms and electronics. As the plan unfolded, CIA headquarters established radio contact with a Chevy Suburban containing a joint CIA–FBI team sitting outside of a Chinese restaurant and hotel where Kasi waited to meet his alleged new business partners.

The appointed 4 pm meeting time came and went, as Acting DCI George Tenet anxiously awaited word. At 4:30, according to one account, the radio cracked "Base, base, this is Red Rover. The package is aloft, the package is aloft." Kasi was in American hands. Within minutes, Tenet phoned the families of Kasi's victims.

Tenet made a public announcement of the arrest 2 days later, praising the 4-year effort—and ultimate success—of the CIA, FBI, and State Department.

The Justice Department decided that local authorities in Fairfax County should try Kasi on capital murder charges since federal law did not then provide for the death penalty for terrorist acts. In court, Kasi acknowledged his role in the shootings but pleaded not guilty. Convicted after a jury trial, Kasi received the death penalty, carried out by lethal injection at the Virginia State Penitentiary in Jarratt on November 14, 2002.

A permanent memorial to Frank Darling and Lansing Bennett was erected in May 2002 near the site of the shootings on Route 123.

Reproduced from: Central Intelligence Agency. (2013). "A Look Back... Murder at CIA's Front Gate." Retrieved online at https://www.cia.gov/news-information/featured-story-archive/murder-at-cia.html

What Is Homeland Security?

The killing of two CIA employees and the wounding of three others was the first attack in the 1990s that suggested the possibility of international terrorism coming to the United States. The case of Aimal Kasi, however, was treated as an isolated incident, and in many ways, as nothing more than a domestic crime. Although both the FBI and local police worked together to solve the case, when it was discovered that Kasi had fled back to Pakistan, the operation became a joint effort between the CIA and the FBI. He was captured and, in an early use of rendition, was brought back to the United States without going through diplomatic channels. Once he returned to the United States; however, he was tried as a criminal in a Virginia Court and charged with two counts of capital murder. Found guilty of these crimes, he was executed in Virginia's death chamber, as Virginia has, and uses, death penalty statutes.

The question that arises from this short case study is whether this was an act of terrorism (see Chapter 3 for a discussion on terrorism), and if so, was this an early example of America defending the homeland? Kasi, by all accounts, acted alone out of hatred that arose from watching CNN and seeing "Americans kill Muslims."[9] He had no accomplices, represented no terrorist group per se, and was simply driven by his personal hatred toward Americans being in the Middle East. Hence, the murders were criminal acts. However, Kasi was not born in the United States, came from a country where many people tend to foster a hatred for America, and may have grown up among many of the radical Mullahs preaching violence against Americans. Given this scenario, was this an act of terrorism?

Regardless, the following month, the United States would witness the first bombing of the World Trade Center; this time, through a conspiracy among terrorists with Al Qaeda ties. Yet, even this attack was treated more as a crime than as an act of terrorism. Interestingly, when, 2 years later, the Oklahoma City bombing was perpetrated by Americans, this act was generally considered more of an act of terrorism than the first World Trade Center bombing, albeit it was domestic terrorism, not international terrorism. The attacks on 9-11, however, brought the concept of terrorism to the forefront of the minds of most Americans. It was also this event that brought the concept of **homeland security** to life, which has left us to beg the question: What exactly is homeland security?

Bellavita, in his article about defining homeland security, noted that people often ask, "What is homeland security? Is it a program, an objective, a discipline, an agency, an administrative activity, another word for emergency management? Is it about terrorism? All hazards? Something completely different?"[10] Logan and Ramsay explained in their book on homeland security that "Although the United States was familiar with terrorism long before September 11, 2001, the term *homeland security* was not commonly used until the aftermath of the 2001 terrorist attacks on New York and Washington, D.C.," and that even though the new agency was called the Department of Homeland Security by the Bush Administration, "the lack of definition of what is meant by *homeland security* and how it related to existing civilian agencies and their missions resulted in challenges for the new department, for agencies that combined in it, and for state government counterparts."[11] Even 10 years after the September 11 attacks, Reese, in an analysis of emergency management and homeland security policy for Congress, observed that "the U.S. government does not have a single definition for 'homeland security.'"[12] This was again confirmed in 2013 in an article by Kahan and in 2015, in an article by O'Sullivan and Ramsay, both of which suggest that part of the definitional problem is distinguishing the differences between homeland security and national security.[13] Another aspect of the variation in homeland security definitions is found at the state level through research conducted by Robinson and Mallik (2015). These researchers found that there were significant differences among the 50 states. Looking at state definitions of homeland security over the years 2012 to 2013, they took two different approaches. Their first approach was to look strictly at the codified law of each state. In that method, they found that many states did not have a definition in their state code (n = 20), while others used a terrorism-only definition (n = 13) or an all-hazards definition (n = 17). Their second approach was less legalistic but was focused more on the operational definitions as found in various state-level documents. In those documents, they found a shift in how homeland security was defined for then only two states had no definition, while 14 used a terror-only definition and 34 used an all-hazards definition.[14] The authors raised the issue that states with different definitions for their codified laws versus their operational documents could potentially cause confusion, posing difficulty for not just defining homeland security but also for how homeland security is conducted.

Recognizing there is no generally accepted definitive definition of homeland security, it is important to understand that the current and varied definitions come from various sources. The first is from an historic perspective, as primarily detailed in the following text. The second is also from an historic perspective but related more to the evolution of governmental usage of the term as found in documents such as presidential directives and commission reports. A third source, and closely related to the second, is found in federal strategic documents attempting to wrestle with the definition, but in a post 9-11 environment. A fourth source comes not from abstract strategy but instead from a focus on the mission and **goals of homeland security** in this same post-9-11 world.

Finally, we can return to Bellavita's analysis, in which he argues that the definition has actually developed in eight different areas and has not yet reached a shared definition, although some of the definitions do share certain elements. It is to these four perspectives that we now turn.

Definition by Homeland Security Bureaucracy Evolution

As is detailed elsewhere in this text, civil defense arose out of fears during World War I but responsibility was largely relegated to the states. In World War II, the idea of civil defense was resurrected, and although initially under state responsibility, the states were given direction through federal coordination. During the Cold War, at least at first, civil defense became more centralized under the federal government and, more specifically, coordinated out of the White House.[15] During the Nixon administration, the move was toward a centralized, independent agency, eventually the Federal Emergency Management Agency (FEMA), with a decentralized execution. FEMA became the primary means for emergency management policies and practices throughout the 1990s. In the wake of 9-11, however, the emphasis was on a much broader federal government response in which emergency preparedness and response, essentially FEMA's role, was only a part. FEMA would then be absorbed as only one component, or directorate, under the Department of Homeland Security.

In this quick historic review, it is evident that the true nature and development of homeland security, and hence, its eventual definition, is primarily a response to cataclysmic events and an evolving bureaucratic organization to best deal with such events. World Wars I and II were events that called for a response, and civil defense was that bureaucratic response. Throughout the Cold War and a number of serious natural disasters, changes to the bureaucracy were the usual response to these events. Hence, the creation of the Department of Homeland Security (DHS)

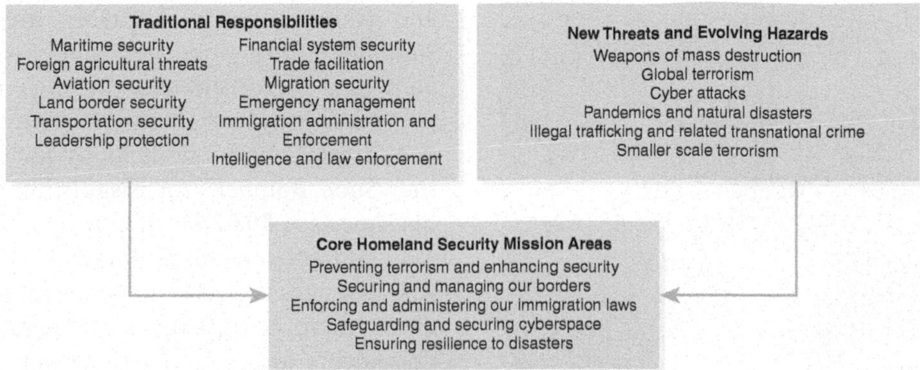

FIGURE 2.1 The Evolution of Homeland Security.

Reproduced from: U.S. Department of Homeland Security. (2010). Quadrennial Homeland Security Review Report: A Strategic Framework for a Secure Homeland. Washington, D.C.: U.S. Department of Homeland Security, p. 14. Courtesy of the DHS.

was simply a response to the events of September 11, and merely the next step in an evolutionary development of bureaucratic changes (See **FIGURE 2.1**).[16] After 9-11, "homeland security" could be loosely defined as a wider-reaching, bureaucratic response (and organization) to better prepare and respond to future terrorist attacks against the United States. Although charged to include natural disasters, early on, DHS was heavily focused on terrorist attacks. It was not until Hurricane Katrina (2005) that it came to focus also on natural disasters (as in an "all-hazard" organization).

In this sense, the term homeland security is part of an historic evolution that is embodied by the federal bureaucracy created in the wake of the various cataclysmic events. As a result, the definition would simply be the reigning bureaucracy. Today, the Department of Homeland Security defines the concept.

Definition by the Homeland Security Concept Evolution

Rather than developing as a bureaucratic reaction to events over time, the concept of homeland security can be thought of as evolving from the policy experts in the decade prior to September 11, 2001. While most Americans were not focused on the issue of terrorism in the 1990s, many government entities and researchers/think tanks were. For instance, in Presidential Directive Number 62, dated May 22, 1998, President Clinton addressed the issue of "Protection Against Unconventional Threats to the Homeland and Americans Overseas."[17] On the same day, Clinton also issued Presidential Directive Number 63, regarding Critical Infrastructure Protection, and while not using the term homeland security, discussed what could be considered the preliminary plans for a Department of Homeland Security.

In 1999, a number of interested government agencies, including defense, justice, and energy, along with the Director of FEMA, entered into a contract with the RAND Corporation's National Defense Research Institute to establish a federally funded advisory panel. It was officially known as the U.S. Congressional Advisory Panel to Assess Domestic Response Capabilities for Terrorism Involving Weapons of Mass Destruction. Informally, it was known as the Gilmore Commission, named for its chair, former Virginia Governor Jim Gilmore. In the Advisory Panel's first official report, published on December 15, 1999, it speaks of "federal funding for domestic preparedness and homeland defense programs."[18]

Another commission, which was formed the year before, was the U.S. Commission on National Security/21st Century, also known as the Hart–Rudman Task Force on Homeland Security, which was developed at the request of the Secretary of Defense William Cohen. The goal of the task force was to assess the emerging international security environment and to develop possible responses. In one document, released on February 15, 2001, the task force noted that "mass-casualty terrorism directed against the U.S. homeland was of serious and growing concern," and that "it recommends a new National Homeland Security Agency to consolidate and refine the missions of the nearly two dozen disparate departments and agencies that have a role in U.S. homeland security today."[19] The task force's recommendations actually found their way into a bill, House Resolution 1158 in the 107th Congress, titled the National Homeland Security Agency Act.[20] The bill was introduced into the House on March 21, 2001, and was referred to the committee, where it subsequently died.

In this case, the term homeland security developed not so much as a bureaucratic response to attacks or disasters but rather bureaucratic policy development within the federal government focused on changing the bureaucracy to meet future attacks. In this case, it is

Courtesy of Donna Burton, Defense Information Systems Agency.

clear that the concept of homeland security was being circulated among policy experts concerned with the issue of terrorism, and they had developed a plan for evolving the bureaucratic response to future attacks.

The only problem was that while the policy experts had identified a legitimate problem (international terrorism attacks on the United States) and they created a possible plan for dealing with this problem more effectively (the creation of the National Homeland Security Agency), they were missing serious public concern in order to galvanize the issue to force passage through Congress. That would not come until the events of September 11, 2001.

In this historic sense, the development of homeland security, and hence its definition, was placed in the hands of the federal policy makers, developing plans based on perceived problems rather than as merely a reaction to them.

Definition by Homeland Security Strategic Documents

Reese has explained that homeland security has been defined in several strategic documents post 9-11.[21] The first homeland security strategy document issued by the Bush Administration was the 2003 *National Strategy for Homeland Security*, which was revised in 2007. In 2008, the Department of Homeland Security issued *Strategic Plan—One Team, One Mission, Securing Our Homeland*. The *2007 National Strategy for Homeland Security* primarily focused on terrorism, whereas the *2008 Strategic Plan* included references to all-hazards and border security. Arguably, the *2003* and *2007 National Strategies for Homeland Security* specifically addressed terrorism, due to such incidents as the 9-11 terrorist attacks and the attempted bombing of American Airlines Flight 93, by Richard Reid, named the "Shoe Bomber" for disguising the bomb within his shoe (see **BOX 2.2**). In contrast, the *2008 Strategic Plan* addressed terrorism and all-hazards due to natural disasters such as Hurricanes Katrina and Rita in 2005. These documents were superseded by several documents, which are now considered the principal homeland security strategies.

Today, the White House and the Department of Homeland Security have advanced the homeland security strategies in the *2010 National Security Strategy*, which addresses all-hazards and is not primarily terrorism focused. DHS's strategic documents are the *2010* and *2014 Quadrennial Homeland Security Review*, the *2010 Bottom-Up Review*, and the *2012 Strategic Plan*. DHS states that these documents are

BOX 2.2 Richard Reid—"The Shoe Bomber"

Richard Reid, a British citizen and self-proclaimed follower of Osama bin Laden, boarded a plane in December of 2001, flying from Paris, France, to Miami, Florida. While in flight across the Atlantic Ocean, Reid was seen by fellow passengers lighting matches and trying to touch them to his shoe. He was subdued by a combination of passengers and flight attendants and, after an emergency landing in Boston, he was turned over to the FBI. Reid was found to have had enough explosives in his shoe to damage the plane, but he could not get the fuse to light. Reid was dubbed the "Shoe Bomber" by the media and was eventually tried and found guilty of terrorism. He is serving a term of life in prison.

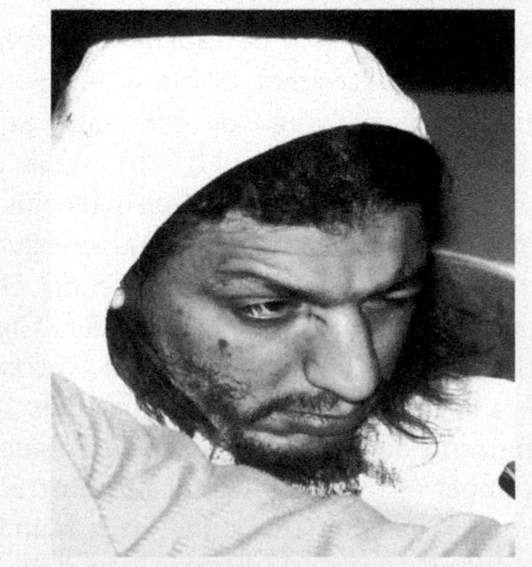

© Elise Amendola/AP/Shutterstock.

Reproduced from: Carafano, James Jay. (2007). "U.S. Thwarts 19 Terrorists Attacks Against America Since 9/11." Backgrounder. Washington, DC: The Heritage Foundation.

TABLE 2.1 Summary of Homeland Security Definitions

Document	Definition
2007 National Strategy for Homeland Security (White House)	A concerted, national effort to prevent terrorist attacks within the United States, reduce America's vulnerability to terrorism, and minimize the damage and recovery from attacks that do occur.
2008 U.S. Department of Homeland Security Strategic Plan, Fiscal Years 2008–2013 (DHS)	A unified, national effort to prevent and deter terrorist attacks, protect and respond to hazards, and secure the national borders.
2010 National Security Strategy (White House)	A seamless coordination among federal, state, and local governments to prevent, protect against, and respond to threats and natural disasters.
2010 Quadrennial Homeland Security Review (DHS)	A concerted, national effort to ensure a homeland that is safe, secure, and resilient against terrorism and other hazards where American interests, aspirations, and ways of life can thrive.
2010 Bottom-Up Review (DHS)	Preventing terrorism, responding to and recovering from natural disasters, customs enforcement and collection of customs revenue, administration of legal immigration services, safety and stewardship of the nation's waterways and marine transportation system, as well as other legacy missions of the various components of DHS.
2011 National Strategy for Counterterrorism (White House)	Defensive efforts to counter terrorist threats.
2012 Strategic Plan (DHS)	Efforts to ensure a homeland that is safe, secure, and resilient against terrorism and other hazards.
2014 Quadrennial Homeland Security Review (DHS)	Reiterates the 2010 Quadrennial Review definition, only adding "Since then, we have developed capabilities and processes to become more risk-based, more integrated, and more efficient."

Reproduced from: Reese, Shawn. (2012). "Defining Homeland Security: Analysis and Congressional Considerations." Congressional Research Service. Retrieved online at http://www.fas.org/sgp/crs/homesec/R42462.pdf

nested in the *2010 National Security Strategy.* At the national level, the *2010 National Security Strategy* not only guides DHS's homeland security activities but it also guides the homeland security missions of all federal government agencies.

TABLE 2.1 provides a summary of the various homeland security definitions along with the specific documents from which they originated. Some of the common themes that can be found among these definitions include: 1) the **homeland security enterprise** (see **BOX 2.3**), which encompasses a federal, state, local, and tribal government and private sector approach that requires coordination; 2) homeland security, which can involve securing against and responding to both hazard-specific and all-hazards threats, and: 3) homeland security activities, which do not imply total protection or complete threat reduction. Each of these documents highlights the importance of coordinating homeland security missions and activities. However, individual federal, state, local, and tribal government efforts are not identified in the documents. Homeland security, according to these documents, is preventing,

BOX 2.3 The Homeland Security "Enterprise"

The homeland security "enterprise" refers to the collective efforts and shared responsibilities of federal, state, local, tribal, territorial, nongovernmental, and private-sector partners—as well as individuals, families, and communities—to maintain critical homeland security capabilities. It connotes a broad-based community with a common interest in the safety and well-being of America and American society.

Reproduced from: U.S. Department of Homeland Security. (2010). Quadrennial Homeland Security Review Report: A Strategic Framework for a Secure Homeland. Washington, DC: U.S. Department of Homeland Security, p. 12.

responding to, and recovering from natural and man-made disasters, especially terrorist attacks, which is consistent with evolving homeland security policy after 9-11.

The focus of the definition of homeland security communicated in these strategy documents differs in two areas that may be considered substantive. Natural disasters are specifically identified as an integral part of homeland security in only four of these six documents but are not mentioned in the *2007 National Strategy for Homeland Security* and the *2011 National Strategy for Counterterrorism.*[22] Only one document—the *Bottom-Up Review*—specifically includes border and maritime security and immigration in its homeland security definition.[21] The *2012 Strategic Plan* uses the encompassing terms "other hazards" to define any threat other than terrorism.[23] These "other hazards" are obviously significant and require substantial funding.[24] An absence of consensus about the inclusion of these policy areas may result in unintended consequences for national homeland security operations. For example, not including maritime security in the homeland security definition may result in policymakers, Congress, and stakeholders inadequately addressing maritime homeland security threats, or, more specifically, being unable to prioritize federal investments in border versus intelligence activities.[25]

The varied and sometimes competing definitions in these documents indicates that there is no generally accepted and succinct **homeland security concept**.[26] Without a definitive homeland security concept, policymakers and others with homeland security responsibilities may not successfully coordinate activities well or focus on the most necessary activities. Coordination is especially essential to homeland security because of the multiple federal agencies and the state and local partners with whom they interact. Coordination may be difficult if these entities do not operate with the same understanding or set of priorities. For example, definitions that do not specifically include immigration or natural disaster response and recovery may result in homeland security stakeholders and federal entities not adequately resourcing and focusing on these activities. Additionally, an absence of a consensus definition may result in Congress funding a homeland security activity that DHS does not consider a priority. For example, Congress may appropriate funding for a counterterrorism program such as the State Homeland Security Grant Program when DHS may have identified an all-hazards grant program, such as the Emergency Management Performance Grant Program, as a priority. It is, however, possible that a consensus definition and overall concept exists among policymakers and federal entities, but that it isn't communicated in the strategic documents.

Finally, former DHS Deputy Secretary Jane Lute recently stated that homeland security "... is operation, it's transactional, it's decentralized, it's bottom-driven," and influenced by law enforcement, emergency management, and the political environment. Conversely, Lute stated that national security "... is strategic, it's centralized, it's top-driven," and influenced by the military and the intelligence community.[27] Some see in these comments an attempt by DHS to establish a homeland security definition that is more operational than strategic. If nothing else, these comments serve as a fine illustration of the difficulty of reaching a common understanding of homeland security and its associated missions.[28]

Definition by Homeland Security Mission and Goals

Another means by which to assess a common definition of homeland security is through the mission and goals of homeland security as articulated by the many sources detailed previously. These varied homeland security definitions, in numerous documents, result in the homeland security stakeholders identifying and executing varied strategic missions.[29] Homeland security stakeholders include federal departments and agencies, state and local governments, and nonprofit and nongovernmental organizations. The strategic documents specifically identify numerous homeland security missions such as terrorism prevention; response and recovery; critical infrastructure protection and resilience; federal, state, and local emergency management and preparedness; and border security. As noted earlier, none of these documents specifically task one federal entity with the overall homeland security responsibilities. **TABLE 2.2** details the various missions and goals that have been articulated by these government documents.

The federal documents all identify specific missions as essential to securing the nation. All of the documents state that the nation's populace, critical infrastructure, and key resources need protection from terrorism and natural disasters. Protection from both terrorism and natural disasters is a key strategic **homeland security mission**. Some, but not all, of the documents include missions related to border security, immigration, the economy, and general resilience. Members of Congress and congressional committees have sometimes criticized these documents.[30]

Senator Susan Collins (R-ME), at the time, a ranking member of the Committee on Homeland Security and Governmental Affairs; expressed disappointment in the *2010 Quadrennial Homeland Security*

TABLE 2.2 Summary of Homeland Security Missions and Goals

Document	Mission and Goals
2007 National Strategy for Homeland Security (White House)	■ Prevent and disrupt terrorist attacks ■ Protect the American people, critical infrastructure, and key resources ■ Respond to and recover from incidents that do occur ■ Strengthen the foundation to ensure long-term success
2008 U.S. Department of Homeland Security Strategic Plan, Fiscal Years 2008–2013 (DHS)	■ Protect the nation from dangerous people ■ Protect the nation from dangerous goods ■ Protect critical infrastructure ■ Strengthen the nation's preparedness and emergency response capabilities ■ Strengthen and unify the department's operations and management
2010 National Security Strategy (White House)	■ Strengthen national capacity ■ Ensure security and prosperity at home ■ Secure cyberspace ■ Ensure American economic prosperity
2010 Quadrennial Homeland Security Review (DHS)	■ Prevent terrorism and enhance security ■ Secure and manage our borders ■ Enforce and administer our immigration laws ■ Safeguard and secure cyberspace ■ Ensure resilience to disasters ■ Provide essential support to national and economic security
2010 Bottom-Up Review (DHS)	■ Prevent terrorism and enhance security ■ Secure and manage borders ■ Enforce and manage immigration laws ■ Safeguard and secure cyberspace ■ Ensure resilience to disasters ■ Improve departmental management and accountability
2011 National Strategy for Counterterrorism (White House)	■ Protect the American people, homeland, and American interests ■ Eliminate threats to the American people's, homeland's, and interests' physical safety ■ Counter threats to global peace and security ■ Promote and protect U.S. interests around the globe
2012 Strategic Plan (DHS)	■ Prevent terrorism and enhance security ■ Secure and manage our borders ■ Enforce and administer our immigration laws ■ Safeguard and secure cyberspace ■ Ensure resilience to disasters ■ Provide essential support to national and economic security
2014 Quadrennial Homeland Security Review (DHS)	■ Prevent terrorism and enhance security ■ Secure and manage our borders ■ Enforce and administer our immigration laws ■ Safeguard and secure cyberspace ■ Strengthen national preparedness and resilience

Review and *Bottom-Up Review* because they did not communicate priorities and stated that they did not compare favorably with the most recent *Quadrennial Defense Review*.[31] According to Collins, the *Quadrennial Defense Review* identifies national security and U.S. military priorities through a process ". . . from objectives to capabilities and activities to resources."[32] Furthermore, the *2010* and *2014 Quadrennial Homeland Security Review* missions are different from the *2007 National Strategy for Homeland Security* missions and neither identifies priorities or resources for DHS or other related federal agencies. Since the *National Strategy for Homeland Security* and both the *2010* and *2014 Quadrennial Homeland Security Review* missions are differing and varied, and because the *Quadrennial Homeland Security Review* does not specifically identify a strategic process to achieve its mission, one may assume that these documents serve solely as operational guidance (see **BOX 2.4**). Additionally, other critics have stated that the *2014 Quadrennial Review* changed little, while others found the *Bottom-Up Review* lacking in detail and failing to meet its intended purpose.[33]

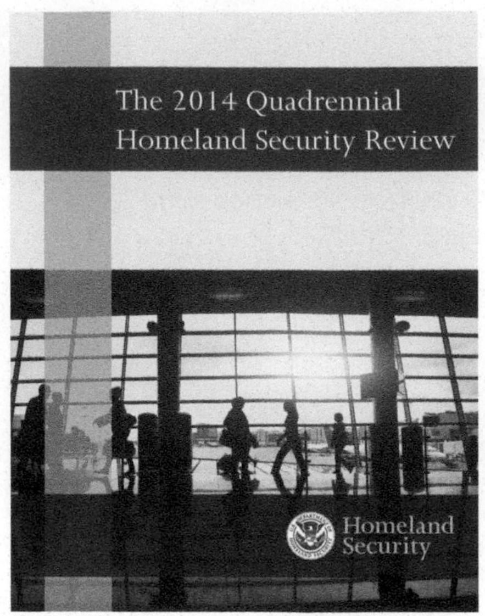

"Homeland security describes the intersection of evolving threats and hazards with traditional governmental and civic responsibilities for civil defense, emergency response, law enforcement, customs, border control, and immigration."

2014 Quadrennial Homeland Security Review

Courtesy of DHS.

BOX 2.4 The Five Missions and Goals of the U.S. Department of Homeland Security

Mission 1: Prevent Terrorism and Enhance Security

Goal 1.1: Prevent Terrorist Attacks

- Analyze, fuse, and disseminate terrorism information
- Deter and disrupt operations
- Strengthen transportation security
- Counter violent extremism

Goal 1.2: Prevent and Protect Against the Unauthorized Acquisition or Use of Chemical, Biological, Radiological, and Nuclear Materials and Capabilities

- Anticipate chemical, biological, radiological, and nuclear emerging threats
- Identify and interdict unlawful acquisition and movement of chemical, biological, radiological, and nuclear precursors and materials
- Detect, locate, and prevent the hostile use of chemical, biological, radiological, and nuclear materials and weapons

Goal 1.3: Reduce Risk to the Nation's Critical Infrastructure, Key Leadership, and Events

- Enhance security for the Nation's critical infrastructure from terrorism and criminal activity
- Protect key leaders, facilities, and national special security events

Mission 2: Secure and Manage Our Borders

Goal 2.1: Secure U.S. Air, Land, and Sea Borders and Approaches

- Prevent illegal import and entry
- Prevent illegal export and exit

Goal 2.2: Safeguard and Expedite Lawful Trade and Travel

- Safeguard key nodes, conveyances, and pathways
- Manage the risk of people and goods in transit
- Maximize compliance with U.S. trade laws and promote U.S. economic security and competitiveness

Goal 2.3: Disrupt and Dismantle Transnational Criminal Organizations and Other Illicit Actors

- Identify, investigate, disrupt, and dismantle transnational criminal organizations
- Disrupt illicit actors, activities, and pathways

Mission 3: Enforce and Administer Our Immigration Laws

Goal 3.1: Strengthen and Effectively Administer the Immigration System

- Promote lawful immigration
- Effectively administer the immigration services system
- Promote the integration of lawful immigrants into American society

Goal 3.2: Prevent Unlawful Immigration

- Prevent unlawful entry, strengthen enforcement, and reduce drivers of unlawful immigration
- Arrest, detain, and remove priority individuals, including public safety, national security, and border security threats

Mission 4: Safeguard and Secure Cyberspace

Goal 4.1: Strengthen the Security and Resilience of Critical Infrastructure

- Enhance the exchange of information and intelligence on risks to critical infrastructure and develop real-time situational awareness capabilities that ensure machine and human interpretation and visualization
- Partner with critical infrastructure owners and operators to ensure the delivery of essential services and functions
- Identify and understand interdependencies and cascading impacts among critical infrastructure systems
- Collaborate with agencies and the private sector to identify and develop effective cybersecurity policies and best practices
- Reduce vulnerabilities and promote resilient critical infrastructure design

Goal 4.2: Secure the Federal Civilian Government Information Technology Enterprise

- Coordinate government purchasing of cyber technology to enhance cost-effectiveness
- Equip civilian government networks with innovative cybersecurity tools and protections
- Ensure that government-wide policies and standards are consistently and effectively implemented and measured

Goal 4.3: Advance Law Enforcement, Incident Response, and Reporting Capabilities

- Respond to and assist in the recovery from cyber incidents
- Deter, disrupt, and investigate cybercrime.

Goal 4.4: Strengthen the Ecosystem

- Drive innovative and cost-effective security products, services, and solutions throughout the cyber ecosystem
- Conduct and transition research and development, enabling trustworthy cyber infrastructure
- Develop skilled cybersecurity professionals
- Enhance public awareness and promote cybersecurity best practices
- Advance international engagement to promote capacity building, international standards, and cooperation

Mission 5: Strengthen National Preparedness and Resilience

Goal 5.1: Enhance National Preparedness

- Empower individuals and communities to strengthen and sustain their own preparedness
- Build and sustain core capabilities nationally to prevent, protect against, mitigate, respond to, and recover from all hazards
- Assist federal entities in the establishment of effective continuity programs that are regularly updated, exercised, and improved

Goal 5.2: Mitigate Hazards and Vulnerabilities

- Promote public- and private-sector awareness and understanding of community-specific risks
- Reduce vulnerability through standards, regulations, resilient design, effective mitigation, and disaster risk reduction measures
- Prevent incidents by establishing, and ensuring compliance with standards and regulations

Goal 5.3: Ensure Effective Emergency Response

- Provide timely and accurate information
- Conduct effective, unified incident response operations
- Provide timely and appropriate disaster assistance
- Ensure effective emergency communications

Goal 5.4: Enable Rapid Recovery

- Ensure continuity and restoration of essential services and functions
- Support and enable communities to rebuild stronger, smarter, and safer

Reproduced from: U.S. Department of Homeland Security. (2014). The 2014 Quadrennial Homeland Security Review. Washington, D.C.: U.S. Department of Homeland Security.

Further congressional criticism includes an observation of the absence of a single DHS strategy. At a recent House Homeland Security Committee's Subcommittee on Oversight, Investigations, and Management hearing, Chairman Michael McCaul (R-TX) stated that ". . . DHS needs a single strategic document, which subordinate agencies can follow and make sure the strategy is effectively and efficiently implemented. This single document should conform to the National Security Strategy of the United States of America. If the agencies do not have a clearly established list of priorities, it will be difficult to complete assigned missions."[34]

Other criticism includes the Council on Foreign Relations' (CFR) discussion of the 2010 National Security Strategy (NSS). CFR states that the ". . . one thing that the NSS discussion of resilience omits, but which the Deputy National Security Adviser John Brennan has emphasized, is that despite all the homeland security precautions, there is likely to be a successful attack. When that happens, real resilience will entail a calm, deliberate response and confidence in the durability of the country's institutions."[35] In summary, as Reese has noted, "Multiple definitions, missions, and an absence of prioritization results in consequences to the nation's security."[36]

Definition by Homeland Security Areas of Emphasis

One further means of coming to a consensus on a definition of homeland security has been articulated by Naval Postgraduate School Instructor Christopher Bellavita.[37] He advances the idea that rather than focusing on historic evolution, government definitions, or homeland security missions, the best way to define homeland security is by focusing on various **areas of emphasis in homeland security**. He argues there are essentially seven areas of focus: 1) Terrorism, 2) All-Hazards, 3) Terrorism and Catastrophes, 4) Jurisdictional Hazards, 5) Meta Hazards, 6) National Security, and 7) Security *Über Alles*.[38]

In the first instance, homeland security is about terrorism, hence it is focused on the prevention of, response to, and recovery from future terrorist attacks.[39] Terrorism, in this case, is both foreign and domestic, and the mechanisms to deal with terrorism are located at the federal, state, local, and tribal levels of government, while also including the private sector. The focus on homeland security in this regard is aimed at mitigating the impact that these attacks may have on the United States.

In the second area of focus, homeland security is about all-hazards; thus, it is not limited solely to terroristic attacks, but encompasses terrorism; natural disasters such as hurricanes, floods, and earthquakes; and other issues such as border security, illegal immigration, and cyber-attacks. It is a concerted effort by national, state, local, and tribal agencies to prevent and disrupt terrorism, protect against man-made and natural disasters, and respond to and recover from such incidents.

The third area of Terrorism and Catastrophes appears to be similar to the previous two. Bellavita argues here that the Department of Homeland Security often details homeland security as either including both terrorism and natural disasters, and sometimes just terrorism. In this case, it is not just a focus on terrorism (as in area one), or on everything, but whatever the Department of Homeland Security sets as a priority, which state, local, and tribal governments tend to follow. Therefore, the focus is on what DHS sets as a priority and the other agencies then follow to prepare for, respond to, and recover from either a terrorist attack or a catastrophe.

The fourth area of focus, according to Bellavita, is Jurisdictional Hazards. In this case, the concept of homeland security is really contingent upon the jurisdiction one is talking about and the specific hazards they may face. Washington, D.C. and New York City both face unique challenges because of their size and importance to the nation; San Diego and El Paso face different issues in that they are border cities; Houston and Boston face unique challenges as major port cities; while New Orleans and Miami face the threat of hurricanes. In other words, homeland security means different things to different people based on the environment in which they live, and what is most likely to threaten the safety and security of the local citizens.

The fifth area, Meta Hazards, takes on a much larger focus. Moving beyond terrorism and natural disasters, or even such terror threats as cyber-attacks, meta hazards begin to look at threats that may affect any aspect of the American way of life. In this case, things such as the growing federal debt, global warming, or America's dependence on foreign oil, may be a cause for future threats to the United States, and thus warrant a broad homeland security response.

The sixth area sounds more confined, National Security, as when government efforts to define homeland security are solely focused on threats to our national security. The goal here is to use the instruments of national power to protect the sovereignty, territory, domestic population, and critical infrastructure of the United States against threats and aggression. In many ways, this area of focus is rooted in the development of our 20th century national security apparatus, and homeland security is the evolution from earlier concepts of civil defense, as discussed elsewhere in this text.

The last area, according to Bellavita, is what he calls Security *Über Alles*, which translates from German as being "security above all." In other words, homeland security is about protecting the United States, no matter what, even if it means curtailing American civil liberties, taking away personal freedoms, and deferring to government to have the best interest of American citizens in mind. This concept of homeland security emphasizes process over outcomes.

In the end, when asking the larger question, "What is homeland security?" Bellavita avoids answering the question, because, depending on the emphasis of the seven areas he details, one would end up with various definitions. Furthermore, it matters whether one is trying to develop a pragmatic and usable definition, an objective reality definition, or simply a coherent definition, all of which further exacerbates reaching a commonly shared definition of homeland security.

Whither a Definition?

Policymakers are faced with an extremely complex list of potential threats to security, for which they then attempt to plan. However, failure to anticipate and respond to just one of those threats may lead to significant human and financial costs.[40] Homeland security is essentially about managing risks.[41] The purpose of a strategic process is to develop missions to achieve that end. Before risk management can be accurate and effective, policymakers must coordinate and communicate. That work depends to some degree on developing a foundation of common definitions of key terms and concepts in order to ensure that stakeholders are aware of, trained for, and prepared to meet assigned missions. At the national level, there does not appear to be an attempt to align definitions and missions among disparate federal entities. DHS is, however, attempting to align its definitions and missions but does not prioritize its missions. Because of this, funding may drive priorities rather than priorities driving funding.

DHS is aligning its definitions and missions in both of the *Quadrennial Homeland Security Reviews*, the *Bottom-Up Review*, and the *2012 Strategic Plan*; however, DHS does not prioritize the missions. DHS prioritizes specific goals, objectives, activities, and specific initiatives within the missions, and prioritizes initiatives across the missions. However, there still neither exists a single national homeland security definition nor is there a prioritization of national homeland security or DHS missions.

There is no evidence in the existing homeland security strategic documents that supports the alignment and prioritization of the varied missions, nor do any of the documents convey how national, state, or local resources are to be allocated to achieve these missions. Without prioritized resource allocation to align missions, proponents of prioritization of the nation's homeland security activities and operations maintain that plans and responses may be haphazard and inconsistent.

Congress may decide to address the issues associated with **homeland security strategy**, definitions, and missions, in light of the potential for more significant events to occur similar to the 9-11 terrorist attacks and Hurricane Katrina. Many observers assert that these outstanding policy issues result from the varied definitions and missions identified in numerous national strategic documents. Additionally, they note that these documents do not consistently address risk mitigation associated with the full range of homeland security threats. From this perspective, one missing piece from these documents is a discussion of the resources and fiscal costs associated with preparing for low-risk, but high-consequence, threats.

Specifically, Congress may choose to consider a number of options to address the apparent lack of a consensus regarding definitions, missions, and priorities by requiring the development of a clearer and more comprehensive national homeland security strategy. One of these options might be a total rewrite of the national homeland security strategy. This option would be similar to the Bush Administration's issuance of national homeland security strategies in 2002 and 2007. Such a strategy could include a definitive listing of mission priorities based on an encompassing definition that not only includes DHS-specific responsibilities but also all federal department and agency responsibilities. A strategy that includes priorities could improve Congress's and other policymakers' ability to make choices between competing homeland security missions. This option would also be a departure from the current administration's practice of including national homeland security guidance in the National Security Strategy.

Another option would be to build upon the current approach by requiring the administration to develop the National Security Strategy that succinctly identifies homeland security missions and priorities. Alternatively, Congress may determine that the present course of including national homeland security guidance in the National Security Strategy is adequate and may focus strictly on DHS activities. This option would entail DHS further refining its *2018 Quadrennial Homeland Security Review* and the *2012 Strategic Plan*,

It has been argued that homeland security, at its core, is about coordination because of the disparate stakeholders and risks.[42] Many observers assert that homeland security is not only about coordination of resources and actions to counter risks; it is also about the coordination of the strategic process policymakers use in determining the risks, the stakeholders and their missions, and the prioritization of those missions.

Without a general consensus on the physical and philosophical definition and missions of homeland security, achieved through a strategic process, some believe that there will continue to be disjointed and disparate approaches to securing the nation. From this perspective, a general consensus on the homeland security concept necessarily starts with a consensus definition and an accepted list of prioritized missions that are constantly reevaluated to meet the many risks of the new paradigm that is homeland security in the 21st century.

Chapter Summary

In the aftermath of the September 11, 2001, terrorist attacks, the term "Homeland Security" entered America's lexicon. While the Office of Homeland Security stood up and was later replaced by the Department of Homeland Security, those working in the field, at all levels of government and academia, have attempted to create an acceptable definition of what homeland security encompasses. The desire is to avoid the "all things to all people" problem and to reach a shared, unified definition. However, definitions have greatly varied for a number of reasons. The first set of definitions appear to have developed based on the bureaucratic structure moving from civil defense in the early 20th century to emergency management in the late 20th century. This was then further refined in the wake of 9-11. Another set of definitions is related more directly to how quickly the homeland security response occurred after 9-11 and are rooted in the contemporary post-9-11 responses. Yet, another set of definitions draws upon strategic documents, some on the missions and goals of homeland security, while still others emphasize specific areas of focus or attention. In all, while there does not yet appear to be a consensus on the definition, there are common themes that appear throughout these varied definitions.

Review/Discussion Questions

1. Trace the origins of the term homeland security and articulate how that has affected the bureaucratic perspective in defining this term. Give consideration to the chapter review of civil defense and emergency management.
2. Provide a definition of homeland security based on homeland security concepts. Justify your definition.
3. What is the homeland security enterprise? Does it help define homeland security or does it just muddy the waters?
4. When reviewing the various homeland security strategies, missions, and goals, do these clarify our definition of homeland security?
5. Provide a definition of homeland security based on Bellavita's "areas of emphasis." Justify your definition.

Additional Readings

Bellavita, C. (2008). "Changing Homeland Security: What is Homeland Security?" *Homeland Security Affairs, 4.* Retrieved online at http://www.hsaj.org/?fullarticle=4.2.1

Reese, S. (2012). "Defining Homeland Security: Analysis and Congressional Considerations." *Congressional Research Service.* Retrieved online at http://www.fas.org/sgp/crs/homesec/R42462.pdf

Endnotes

1. Kessler, R. (2003). *The CIA at War: Inside the Secret Campaign Against Terror.* New York: St. Martin's Press.
2. *Kasi v. Commonwealth of Virginia* (1998). Record Nos. 980797, 980798, November 06, 1998. Retrieved online at http://caselaw.findlaw.com/va-supreme-court/1206379.html
3. That police officer was the lead author of this book (Oliver).
4. Kessler, R. (2003). *The CIA at War: Inside the Secret Campaign Against Terror.* New York: St. Martin's Press.
5. *Kasi v. Commonwealth of Virginia* (1998). Record Nos. 980797, 980798, November 06, 1998. Retrieved online at http://caselaw.findlaw.com/va-supreme-court/1206379.html
6. Lengel, A. (2006). "Celebrated FBI Agent Will Retire Haunted By Those Who Got Away." *The Washington Post.* Retrieved

online at http://www.washingtonpost.com/wp-dyn/content/article/2006/08/27/AR2006082700923.html

7. *Kasi v. Commonwealth of Virginia* (1998). Record Nos. 980797, 980798, November 06, 1998. Retrieved online at http://caselaw.findlaw.com/va-supreme-court/1206379.html
8. CNN Justice. (2002). "Pakistani Man Executed for CIA Killings." *CNN*. Retrieved online at http://www.cnn.com/2002/LAW/11/14/cia.killings.execution/
9. *Kasi v. Commonwealth of Virginia* (1998). Record Nos. 980797, 980798, November 06, 1998. Retrieved online at http://caselaw.findlaw.com/va-supreme-court/1206379.html
10. Bellavita, C. (2008). "Changing Homeland Security: What is Homeland Security?" *Homeland Security Affairs, 4*. Retrieved online at http://www.hsaj.org/?fullarticle=4.2.1
11. Logan, K. G. & Ramsay, J. D. (2012). *Introduction to Homeland Security*. Boulder, CO: Westview Press, pp. 24–25.
12. Reese, S. (2012). "Defining Homeland Security: Analysis and Congressional Considerations." *Congressional Research Service*. Retrieved online at http://www.fas.org/sgp/crs/homesec/R42462.pdf
13. Kahan, J. H. (2013). "What's In a Name? The Meaning of Homeland Security." *Journal of Homeland Security Education, 2*, 1-18; O'Sullivan, T. M. & Ramsay, J. (2015). "Defining and Distinguishing Homeland from National Security and Climate-Related Environmental Security, in Theory and Practice." *Homeland Security & Emergency Management, 12*, 43–66.
14. Robinson, S. E. & Mallik, N. (2015). "Varieties of Homeland Security: An Assessment of US State-level Definitions." *Journal of Homeland Security and Emergency Management, 12*(1), 67–80.
15. Hogue, H. B. & Bea, K. (2006). "Federal Emergency Management and Homeland Security Organization: Historical Developments and Legislative Options." *Congressional Research Service*. Retrieved online at http://www.fas.org/sgp/crs/homesec/RL33369.pdf
16. The 9/11 Commission presents this evolution of how counterterrorism has evolved through the adaptation (and nonadaptation) of the law enforcement community, the Federal Aviation Administration, the intelligence community, the State Department, Department of Defense, the White House, and Congress. See: National Commission on Terrorist Attacks Upon the United States. (2004). *The 9/11 Commission Report: Final Report of the National Commission on Terrorist Attacks Upon the United States (Authorized Ed.)*. New York: W.W. Norton & Company, Inc.
17. The majority of PDD 62 is a classified document, but elements of it are found through a White House Fact Sheet, dated May 22, 1998, titled "Combatting Terrorism: Presidential Decision Directive 62." Retrieved online at http://www.fas.org/irp/offdocs/pdd-62.htm
18. Advisory Panel to Assess Domestic Response Capabilities for Terrorism Involving Weapons of Mass Destruction. (1999). *Assessing the Threat*. Retrieved online at http://www.rand.org/content/dam/rand/www/external/nsrd/terrpanel/terror.pdf
19. The United States Commission on National Security/21st Century. (2001). *Road Map for National Security: Imperative for Change*. Retrieved online at http://govinfo.library.unt.edu/nssg/PhaseIIIFR.pdf
20. See H. R. 1158 (107th): National Homeland Security Agency Act. Retrieved online at http://www.govtrack.us/congress/bills/107/hr1158
21. This section is based on Reese, Shawn. (2012). "Defining Homeland Security: Analysis and Congressional Considerations." *Congressional Research Service*. Retrieved online at http://www.fas.org/sgp/crs/homesec/R42462.pdf
22. Office of the President, Homeland Security Council. (2007). *The National Homeland Security Strategy*. Washington, DC: White House; Office of the President. (2011). *National Strategy for Counterterrorism*. Washington, DC: White House.
23. U.S. Department of Homeland Security. (2010). *Bottom-Up Review*. Washington, DC: U.S. Department of Homeland Security, p. 3.
24. U.S. Department of Homeland Security. (2012). *Department of Homeland Security Strategic Plan: Fiscal Years 2012–2016*. Washington, DC: U.S. Department of Homeland Security, p. 2.
25. Reese, S. (2012). "Defining Homeland Security: Analysis and Congressional Considerations." *Congressional Research Service*. Retrieved online at http://www.fas.org/sgp/crs/homesec/R42462.pdf
26. Reese, S. (2012). "Defining Homeland Security: Analysis and Congressional Considerations." *Congressional Research Service*. Retrieved online at http://www.fas.org/sgp/crs/homesec/R42462.pdf
27. Bellavita, C. (2011). "A New Perspective on Homeland Security?" *Homeland Security Watch*. Retrieved online at http://www.hlswatch.com/2011/12/20/a-new-perspective-on-homeland-security/
28. Reese, S. (2012). "Defining Homeland Security: Analysis and Congressional Considerations." *Congressional Research Service*. Retrieved online at http://www.fas.org/sgp/crs/homesec/R42462.pdf
29. Reese, S. (2012). "Defining Homeland Security: Analysis and Congressional Considerations." *Congressional Research Service*. Retrieved online at http://www.fas.org/sgp/crs/homesec/R42462.pdf
30. Reese, S. (2012). "Defining Homeland Security: Analysis and Congressional Considerations." *Congressional Research Service*. Retrieved online at http://www.fas.org/sgp/crs/homesec/R42462.pdf
31. U.S. Congress, Senate Committee on Homeland Security and Governmental Affairs. (2011). *Charting a Path Forward: The Homeland Security Department's Quadrennial Review and Bottom-Up Review*. 111th Cong., 2nd sess., July 21, 2010.
32. U.S. Department of Defense. (2010). *Quadrennial Defense Review*. Washington, DC: U.S. Department of Defense, p. iii.
33. Petes, K. M. (2010). "DHS Bottom-Up Review is Long on Ambition, Short on Detail." *Government Executive*. Retrieved online at http://www.govexec.com/defense/2010/07/dhs-bottom-up-review-is-long-on-ambition-short-on-detail/31939/
34. U.S. Congress, House Committee on Homeland Security, Subcommittee on Oversight, Investigations, and Management. (2011). *Is DHS Effectively Implementing a Strategy to Counter Emerging Threats?* 112th Cong., 2nd sess., February 3, 2011.
35. Biddle, S., Garrett, L., & Lindsay, J. M., et al. (2010). "Obama's NSS: Promise and Pitfalls." Council on Foreign Relations. Retrieved from http://www.cfr.org/defensehomeland-security/obamas-nss-promise-pitfalls/p22240
36. Reese, S. (2012). "Defining Homeland Security: Analysis and Congressional Considerations." *Congressional Research Service*. Retrieved online at http://www.fas.org/sgp/crs/homesec/R42462.pdf
37. Bellavita, C. (2008). "Changing Homeland Security: What is Homeland Security?" *Homeland Security Affairs, 4*, 1–30. Retrieved online at http://www.hsaj.org/?fullarticle=4.2.1

38. Bellavita, C. (2008). "Changing Homeland Security: What is Homeland Security?" *Homeland Security Affairs, 4*, 1–30. Retrieved online at http://www.hsaj.org/?fullarticle=4.2.1
39. This section is based on the article: Bellavita, C. (2008). "Changing Homeland Security: What is Homeland Security?" *Homeland Security Affairs, 4*, 1–30. Retrieved online at http://www.hsaj.org/?fullarticle=4.2.1
40. Kettl, D. F. (2007). *System Under Stress: Homeland Security and American Politics*. 2nd Ed. Washington, DC: CQ Press.
41. Reese, S. (2012). "Defining Homeland Security: Analysis and Congressional Considerations." *Congressional Research Service*. Retrieved online at http://www.fas.org/sgp/crs/homesec/R42462.pdf
42. Kettl, D. F. (2007). *System Under Stress: Homeland Security and American Politics*. 2nd Ed. Washington, DC: CQ Press.

CHAPTER 3

Modern Terrorism and Natural Disasters

CHAPTER OBJECTIVES

- To understand the five mission areas of the Department of Homeland Security
- To be able to articulate the role of terrorism in the genesis of DHS and how DHS currently combats terrorism
- To understand the role of DHS in the domain of cybersecurity
- To relate why DHS understands natural disasters as one of its mission areas
- To understand how DHS functions to try to improve America's border security
- To understand how DHS can improve enforcement of immigration laws

CHAPTER OUTLINE

(continues)

CHAPTER OUTLINE (Continued)

The tornado struck quickly. It was an E5, the strongest level of tornado, and while a similar storm had struck almost 15 years earlier,[1] there were not enough storm shelters to house all of the residents. After moving through the town over the course of over 30 minutes, 24 people were dead, and entire neighborhoods were leveled.[2] Meanwhile, two explosions came seconds apart. In the immediate vicinity of the blasts, over 250 individuals had significant injuries, which required transportation to local hospitals, while more minor injuries were treated on site.[3] Building windows were blown out for nearly a block, and many of the injured required amputations.[4]

During the incidents, communication systems inexplicably went down, while, at the same time, months of online "trolling" came to a head, as groups of individuals sought to sow discord about the response to the events, with some calling the attacks a "false flag" operation and others simply calling the government inept.[5] Individuals who were not normally politically involved were suddenly engaged in a wide-ranging critique of the government's response, although many of the accounts were newly created and did not have traceable email addresses. Moreover, when the server addresses were later identified, many of them came from Russia or China, although many of the posters represented themselves as Americans.

A day after the bombing mentioned above, one of the individuals suspected was captured in the airport attempting to leave the country.[6] He was not only linked to terrorist violence but also the group involved was engaged in human trafficking at the border.[7] The "family" he was a part of had several members under indictment, and he was attempting to get to a country without an extradition treaty. One of the other members was captured after a gun fight with authorities, during which a third member was killed after a significant chase, coupled with a far-reaching manhunt.[8]

While the way the story above is woven together is imaginary, each of the events depicted has a strong basis in reality. Perhaps even more surprising than the general types of incidents we face daily as a nation is the fact that much of the response to each of the incidents above is the responsibility of a single government entity: The Department of Homeland Security (DHS). From the cyber investigations provided by Homeland Security Investigations (HSI) to checking individuals at the border by Customs and Border Protection and the U.S. Border Patrol to the recovery and response provided by the Federal Emergency Management Agency (FEMA), DHS has an amazing array of responsibilities. These responsibilities are not limited to the physical world, as DHS has the lead in regarding protecting the U.S. from cyber operations as well. Each of these responsibilities would be difficult in isolation, but when they are framed together, it is easy to see both why a single agency was necessary to develop, and why it remains essential to security in the United States today.

It is no surprise that there was a perception that the government needed to be changed after the events of September 11, 2001. The aftermath of the 9/11 attacks was the worst man-made disaster since the bombing of Pearl Harbor, over 50 years earlier. The subsequent development of the DHS represented the largest change in government structure since the development of the Department of Defense.[9] However, just 4 years after the worst terrorist attack in United States History, Hurricane Katrina demonstrated that even a major overhaul in the nation's security apparatus was insufficient to deal with all hazards. In addition to the human cost, these two events combined caused over $3.4 trillion dollars in economic damage,[10] displaced 400,000 people,[11] and had profound effects on the national psyche.[12] Additional threats to U.S. security—especially in cyberspace—have also arisen and required further changes to the nation's homeland security infrastructure. Even so, the United States remains predominately focused on the security threat that terrorism, and now cyberterrorism, represent and expends a great deal of money to avoid another 9/11-like event. This chapter covers the five mission areas of Homeland Security, which are designed not only to combat the threats of terrorism and help with natural disaster resilience but also to deal with threats in cyberspace as well as on the physical borders to the country.

The Five Mission Areas

Homeland security defines its five **mission areas** as follows:

- Prevent Terrorism and Enhance Security
- Secure and Manage Our Borders
- Enforce and Administer Our Immigration Laws
- Safeguard and Secure Cyberspace
- Ensure Resilience to Disasters[13]

While each of these areas is distinct, they work together in the context of the framework of homeland security to ensure security, resilience, and to allow for customs and exchange to function smoothly. In order to be successful in these mission areas, DHS has developed specific institutional structures to allow for necessary enforcement, while reconfiguring some earlier agencies to better fulfill those goals.

The following sections detail each of these mission areas for DHS, including background on what the mission area entails, as well as some of the structures developed to help within each. The focus here is on an overview, rather than a "deep dive" into each of the agencies responsible for carrying out these mission areas, as the agencies will be covered in greater detail in later chapters.

Prevent Terrorism and Enhance Security

While the threat from terrorism is by no means new,[14] the United States did not treat it as an existential issue until after the attacks on September 11, 2001. The new reality, faced by all Americans after 9/11 was that terrorism had come to the United States in an unprecedented way, and the response to the attacks—as well as methods to prevent future attacks—would also need to be unprecedented.

As detailed in Chapter 1, DHS was developed as a direct response to those attacks. As such, the Department has always had a significant focus on preventing terrorism on American soil, and much of the organization's infrastructure was developed specifically to deal with the threat of terrorism. However, terrorism prevention is only one element of how DHS carries out the mission area of safeguarding the United States from terrorist attacks and enhancing security. Not only do they attempt to detect and deter terrorist attacks but they also are tasked with preventing the unauthorized acquisition or possession of biological, radiological, and nuclear materials and reducing the vulnerability of critical and key infrastructure within the geographic bounds of the United States.

While the goal of preventing terrorism seems straightforward, it is often quite difficult in practice, even beyond the issue of bad actors seeking to hide their activities. While today we tend to think of terrorism in religious terms, largely as a result of the amount of emphasis placed on the terrorist organization al Qaeda after the 9/11 attacks, this has not always been the case.[15] Terrorists have a variety of motivations, ranging from religious beliefs to socio-political objectives to single issues such as animal rights or abortion. Partly because of this wide range of motivations, terrorism has been very hard to define and there remains no agreed-upon definition that spans even the agencies within the U.S. government.[16] Additionally, because the threats from terrorism come in a variety of ways—both in terms of geographic location and ideology—it requires an intense cross-government coordination effort in order to be successful.

Terrorism: The Term

Definitions of terrorism have varied widely among scholars and practitioners.[25] Definitions have been suggested from the very basic, such as, "you know it when you see it," to complex definitions put together by a committee that may be practically unworkable.[26] Even differing agencies within the U.S. government have definitions of terrorism that scarcely resemble one another. Take the definitions from the United States Federal Bureau of Investigation (FBI) and the United States Department of State. The FBI's definition is:

> "The unlawful use of force or violence against persons or property to intimidate or coerce a government, the civilian population, or any segment thereof in furtherance of political or social objectives.[27]"

Important elements in this definition include the use of force, the fact that it can be against persons or property, and that the goal is to coerce a government or civilian population for social or political reasons. Examining the Department of State's definition of terrorism: Premeditated, politically motivated violence perpetrated against noncombatant targets by subnational groups or clandestine agents.[28]

In the context of the Department of State, we see different areas of emphasis with some commonalities. Specifically, the need for premeditation, the subnational status of the attackers, and noncombatant nature of the targets represent important differences between the definitions while the violence and political nature of the attacks represent areas that are similarly covered. This same overlap and difference are also represented by the Department of Defense (DoD) definitions as well as the National Counter-Terrorism Center (NCTC).

Importantly, the definition utilized by the Department of Homeland Security (DHS) (18 USC § 2331—DEFINITIONS) for terrorism is quite broad, encompassing both domestic and international terrorism as well as defining who can be a terrorist and which acts might constitute an act of terrorism according to the agency. Of particular interest is the fact that the acts to be defined as terrorism do not necessarily need to be violent in order to be considered terrorism; they need only be considered dangerous to human life and have the other elements considered in the definition. **BOX 3.1** has a complete discussion of the DHS definition of terrorism. **BOX 3.2** discusses different types of terrorism that have arisen since the term was coined.

BOX 3.1 "Regime de la Terreur"

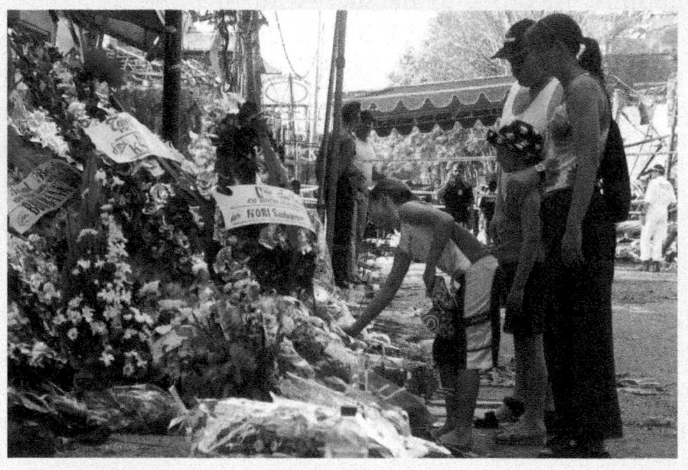

©Achmad Ibrahim/AP/Shutterstock.

Perhaps most important in terms of the development of what we consider modern terrorism is the period during the French Revolution known as the "Reign of Terror." This period of history was marked by citizen tribunals dedicated to the eradication of what was left of the aristocracy in France after the revolution.[17] These tribunals would receive secret testimony about individuals in the population who were supposedly a part of the aristocracy or supporting it. The goal, which was considered positive at first, was to create a spectacle out of the execution of those individuals found guilty in order to influence others to not support the monarchy or become counter-revolutionary.[18] This was also known as la Terreur, and those who carried it out were terrorists. It is estimated that 40,000 people were killed during the Reign of Terror.[19] Eventually, the leader of the revolution, Robespierre, was accused and executed in the same way that he oversaw so many others, by guillotine.[20] As mentioned earlier, although it was originally considered a positive term, "terrorist" eventually came to mean an excess of violence and abuse of power. Over time, it developed into the meaning of the term "terrorism" that we have today.[21]

The Reign of Terror is important insofar as it added the word "terrorism" to modern language usage. Additionally, it reinforced the political nature of terrorism, something now recognized as essential to our understanding of the concept.[22] Furthermore, because of the excesses of the revolution, the word terrorism gained a negative connotation, an aspect that remains with the word today. This negative view is partially what makes terrorism so difficult to define, as no group wishes to be labeled as a terrorist group and actively seek to change how their image is defined.[23]

In addition, like groups in other eras of terrorism, the Regime de la Terreur was successful, if only for a time. Robespierre and his compatriots were in charge of France, and despite their later ousting, it proved that terrorism could be an effective means of control. This lesson was well learned by later dictators such as Hitler, Mussolini, and Stalin, who, while not considered terrorists in the sense that we mean it today, certainly used terror to control their populations' behavior.[24]

BOX 3.2 Typologies of Terrorism

Typologies of terrorism, or ways to categorize attacks, are important to the study of terrorism as a phenomenon and specifically to homeland security. Because terrorism is an incredibly wide-ranging phenomenon, with motivations by terrorists being as diverse as saving animals to bringing about Armageddon, it is important to understand the "rationale" of a terrorist attack in order to be able to stop it and attacks like it in the future. It is important to understand that while groups usually fall primarily into one type of terrorism or another, groups can frequently be classified as more than one type (e.g., right-wing nationalist). Additionally, as is the case with most issues regarding terrorism, there is no agreed-upon typology for terrorist groups.[29] The sections following detail frequently used "types" of groups in the terrorism literature.

Domestic/International

Perhaps the most widely used typology within the context of government counter-terrorism operations is the distinction between domestic and international terrorists and terrorist groups.[30] While the difference is simple, with **international terrorism** originating from outside of the borders of the country in which the attack takes place and **domestic terrorism** originating from within the country where the attack happens, it is important because of the division of labor within the United States government. Organizations like the Federal Bureau of Investigation (FBI) are almost exclusively focused on domestic terrorism because of its limited overseas reach (although this has changed somewhat since 9-11) and organizations like the Central Intelligence Agency (CIA) are focused almost exclusively on international terrorism.[31]

Even with a generally simple distinction; however, the difference between a domestic and international terrorist attack is not always easy to determine. If an attack is carried out by citizens from within the country, but directed from outside of the country, a decision has to be made on who has primary jurisdiction, and a designation of the attack as domestic or international becomes difficult and sometimes controversial. Large attacks, particularly, such as 9-11, frequently have elements of both domestic and international terrorism involved, making investigations complex. Nevertheless, the distinction between the two remains important, both for those responsible for reacting to terrorism as well as those who study it.

Left-Wing/Right-Wing

One of the most frequently utilized typologies in the literature on terrorism is based on the historic political difference in the United States. Left-wing terrorist groups focus on the destruction of the state, with the usual justification that the state is not representative of the people and needs to be replaced with a socialist, anarchist, or communist government (or lack of government in the case of anarchists). Right-wing groups tend to be more authoritarian in nature and frequently operate in support of the government, or even argue for additional government control—particularly of groups that they believe threaten the state. The FBI still uses this terminology regularly (i.e., left-wing and right-wing) to describe terrorist organizations.[32]

Although this typology has been used frequently, especially in the context of domestic terrorism, there are limits to its relevance. While the left/right distinction is useful in the context of the United States and in some places in Western Europe, there are many places where this dichotomy does not hold. Furthermore, even in the United States, there are good reasons to believe that the distinction is more historically relevant than currently so. While there is no doubt that a political divide still exists within the United States that falls along these ideological lines, there is less terrorism that corresponds to these lines directly. In fact, more domestic terrorism appears to be stemming from a religious or nativist orientation, similar to the rest of the world during this era of modern international terrorism.

Nationalist

Nationalist terrorism is focused on the national aspirations of a group of people, usually defined along ethnic boundaries. Historically, groups such as the Palestinian Liberation Organization (PLO) and the Irish Republican Army (IRA) can be considered nationalist in orientation.[33] Even in the United States, there have been nationalist groups, particularly those organizations dedicated to the independence of Puerto Rico and groups that refuse to recognize the legitimacy of the current government. Internationally, these groups are more prominent and have had more success. National independence movements, such as the Algerian movement for independence, have even met with reasonable success in the international arena.

Single-Issue

Single-issue terrorist organizations are those organizations without a broad ideological or political agenda, but rather those that focus on a specific issue of interest to members of those groups. Anti-abortion groups that bomb clinics, while having perhaps a religious background, are only engaging in terrorism against those who they believe are responsible for abortions. Similarly, animal rights and environmental terrorists engage selectively against those who they believe harm animals or the environment. Groups like the Animal Liberation Front (ALF), Earth Liberation Front (ELF), and the Army of God (AOG) only engage those whom they believe to be in violation of their moral standards on a single issue.[34]

Like other forms of terrorism, single-issue terrorism is frequently found in association with other ideological underpinnings. As mentioned earlier, groups that bomb abortion clinics frequently have a religious motivation, and those that attack animal labs sometimes have political motivation beyond saving animals. Nevertheless, the groups that engage in this type of terrorism largely focus their violence on the individuals they feel are responsible for their specific issue of choice.

(continues)

BOX 3.2 Typologies of Terrorism *(Continued)*

Religious

Terrorist organizations that have religion as their motivation are some of the most dangerous. This is because, unlike nationalist groups for instance, they usually do not cater to a constituency. Instead, these groups and individuals feel that their primary duty is to God, and frequently, this means they are willing to go to greater lengths in terms of the amount of destruction and death that they are willing to cause. This is primarily because, while groups with a constituency must have support to achieve their goals, the religious group's goals are frequently transcendental in nature and will only be achieved through the group's actions. Additionally, those who do not support the groups are frequently considered apostates or enemies of God, and are, therefore, subject to the same treatment as those whom the group opposes.[35]

As mentioned earlier, religious groups are perhaps the primary type of organization now engaging in terrorism worldwide. This possibly accounts for the increase in the number of deaths seen post 9-11, although attacks on military and police forces in Iraq and Afghanistan have no doubt inflated that number. Even so, moving forward, it is likely that religious terrorism will remain the most frequently encountered type of terrorism and will also remain one of the most difficult to defeat.

Summary

Typologies of terrorism allow us to separate one type of group from another. This is essential for both operations against terrorists as well as research regarding terrorists and their organizations. While many of the "types" of terrorism are not mutually exclusive, distinguishing between types allows for comparison between organizations and assists with a variety of practical tasks necessary for combating terrorists. While the preceding is only a small sample of the potential types of terrorism, understanding the most frequently used types is essential to understanding both the literature on terrorism and the groups that carry it out.

So, What Is Terrorism?

Despite the differences in definitions, of which there are many, there are some common themes that arise regularly. In fact, there seem to be five generally agreed-upon attributes to attacks that are termed terrorism.[36] These are by no means universally acknowledged. However, the elements are present within most definitions of terrorism.

- Political (social or religious) motivation
- Violence or the credible threat of violence
- Subnational actors
- Instrumental in nature
- Victim/target separation

These five elements are straightforward and can be used to determine whether an event is a terrorist attack or a different form of crime. The first element, the political nature of the act of terrorism, is the most import. It is the element that most distinguishes any act of terrorism from the equivalent form of crime. Second, any act of terrorism has to be violent, or at least credibly threaten violence. With this, violence is construed broadly to include destruction to property, as in the FBI definition above, as well as in specialty legislation such as the Animal Enterprise Protection Act (AEPA). Third, acts of terrorism are carried out by subnational actors. If the actors conducting an attack were part of a nation-state, it would be an act of war, not an act of terrorism. The last two elements of terrorism, the instrumental nature of an attack and the separation of the victim and target are closely linked. Any act of terrorism must be instrumental insofar as the goal of the attack is not the violence itself, but rather a motivation to change. This is closely linked to the final element, which is victim/target separation. Specifically, while terrorists kill victims, the victims represent a means to an end: The influence on the actual target. More concretely, the terrorists kill individuals (their victims) to influence their target (whomever they wish to influence). This is quite different from murder, for instance, where the victim and target are the same individual.

In short, terrorism is a complex phenomenon encompassing a wide variety of acts and actors. Agreed-upon definitions have been hard to come by, and even within the federal government, there are important differences within definitions. Individuals who conduct terrorist attacks actively seek to change who we perceive as terrorists and frequently they are referred to in terms other than "terrorist" by the media, who wish to appear unbiased. However, despite these differences, there are five elements that make up what we generally consider terrorism: Political motivation, violence, subnational actors, instrumental nature, and victim/target separation. **BOX 3.3** on the next page discusses the definition used by DHS, which can be found in the U.S. Code.

BOX 3.3 DHS Definition of Terrorism

Definitions of terrorism are frequently complicated as they have to take into account the requirements of both the agency (or agencies) coping with it as well as the multifaceted aspects of the phenomenon itself. The Department of Homeland Security's definition is a good example of this and can serve as a paradigm for examining other government definitions.

DHS Definition

1. The term "international terrorism" means activities that:
   a. Involve violent acts or acts dangerous to human life that are a violation of the criminal laws of the United States or of any State, or that would be a criminal violation if committed within the jurisdiction of the United States or of any State;
   b. Appear to be intended:
      i. To intimidate or coerce a civilian population;
      ii. To influence the policy of a government by intimidation or coercion; or
      iii. To affect the conduct of a government by mass destruction, assassination, or kidnapping; and
   c. Occur primarily outside the territorial jurisdiction of the United States, or transcend national boundaries in terms of the means by which they are accomplished, the persons they appear intended to intimidate or coerce, or the locale in which their perpetrators operate or seek asylum;
2. The term "national of the United States" has the meaning given such term in section 101(a)(22) of the Immigration and Nationality Act;
3. The term "person" means any individual or entity capable of holding a legal or beneficial interest in property;
4. The term "act of war" means any act occurring in the course of:
   a. Declared war;
   b. Armed conflict, whether or not war has been declared, between two or more nations; or
   c. Armed conflict between military forces of any origin; and
5. The term "domestic terrorism" means activities that:
   a. Involve acts dangerous to human life that are a violation of the criminal laws of the United States or of any State;
   b. Appear to be intended:
      i. To intimidate or coerce a civilian population;
      ii. To influence the policy of a government by intimidation or coercion; or
      iii. To affect the conduct of a government by mass destruction, assassination, or kidnapping; and
   c. Occur primarily within the territorial jurisdiction of the United States.[53]

Summary

The DHS definition of terrorism is from the U.S. Code and encompasses a variety of elements that the other definitions presented in this text do not. Most interestingly, it not only provides definitions for domestic and international terrorism but it also includes elements describing who is to be considered a terrorist. In some ways, despite its length, it is a very broad definition of terrorism as it does not specify who the targets necessarily are (can be government or civilian) and does not include violence as a necessary element, only actions that are dangerous to human life. When examining other definitions of terrorism, it is instructive to consider which elements they have in common with this definition and which elements are different.

Modern Global Terrorism, U.S. Terrorist Attacks, 9/11 Attacks

Modern global terrorism is unique in the history of terrorism because of both the level of violence and the reach of the acts of terrorism.[37] Terrorists have learned how to use the media to communicate their message to an incredibly wide audience, even more so since the invention of the Internet.[38] In addition to the mass casualties and the wide reach, terrorists have become much more sophisticated in their cooperation with one another and in their use of financial networks and communication.[39] This has made combatting terrorism a much harder problem, perhaps, than it has ever been before.

While the focus of the world has been on global terrorism, it is important to note that even terrorists operating domestically have utilized these same increases in capability. The wide availability of information for creating weapons, establishing secure communications, and planning attacks have made so-called "home grown" terrorists sometimes just as threatening as global organizations with a great deal more funding and organization.[40]

US Terrorist' Attacks

While it is easy to focus on the recent events of September 11, 2001, as the "beginning" of terrorism in the United States, it is important to remember that, even well before that horrific attack, America had suffered devastating attacks from terrorists.[41] Importantly, while some of these attacks were from terrorist organizations that might be considered international, like the 1993 World Trade Center Bombing, many have been from groups that are entirely from the United States. Perhaps the most significant homegrown terrorist attack, the Oklahoma City Bombing in 1995, was carried out by an individual who most would consider at low-risk for terrorist activities, judging by today's standards.[42] Other organizations, like the Order in the 1970s; and more recently, the Unabomber, the Times Square Bomber, and the Boston Bombers (both mentioned in the vignettes that started this chapter) have also carried out successful attacks in the United States that captivated and terrorized the nation.[43]

9/11

Of course, the most significant terrorist attack of recent times is September 11. This attack, aside from being the largest single loss-of-life from a terrorist act, is also a paragon of modern terrorism.[44] Not only was it a mass-casualty event, but it took full advantage of the media, both during the attack and after, as well as targeting specific, recognizable symbols of American and Western power.[45] The attack is considered by many to be the benchmark that other terrorist organizations may try to reach and exceed.[46]

In addition to the direct loss of life and financial losses incurred, 9/11 also motivated an incredible overhaul of our national government. The creation of the Department of Homeland Security was a direct response to the 9/11 Commission Report[47] and its suggestion that poor information-sharing was, in large part, to blame for the success of the attacks. This change in government structure fundamentally changed how we view security in the United States, as well as how we combat threats such as terrorism.

Understanding Terrorism—Organization and Threat

Terrorism is a difficult problem to solve, given its wide variety of motivations, its relative ease of attack, and the wide publicity given to even unsuccessful operations.[48] Understanding how terrorism is organized, both domestically and internationally, is essential to combating the threat. One way to do this is to create a typology of terrorism, which allows academics and practitioners alike to understand the group's motivations, attack strategies, and goals, and additionally allows for comparison among groups. One of the most commonly used typologies of terrorism is also one of the simplest: Domestic versus international terrorism.[49]

International Terrorism

International terrorism, as seen in the DHS definition of terrorism taken from the U.S. Code above, is terrorism that originates partially or substantially in a jurisdiction outside of the United States. Despite the relative simplicity of the distinction between international and domestic terrorism, it is not always easy to determine whether an attack is international or domestic. At other times, such as with the Oklahoma City Bombing in 1995, determining whether an attack is domestic or international is less challenging. Making the determination is essential, however, to determining jurisdiction for the investigation. Agencies such as the CIA have much larger international reach than the FBI and take a much larger role in the context of international terrorism.

One of the important aspects of international terrorism as it relates to the United States is that the attack does not have to take place within the borders of the United States. Attacks like the Beirut Bombing, a truck bomb at the U.S. Marine Corps barracks in Beirut, Lebanon, in 1982, have targeted U.S. interests and property abroad.[50] One of al Qaeda's first large-scale attacks was against the U.S. Embassies in Kenya and Tanzania, killing citizens of those countries and U.S. citizens alike.

The threat posed by international terrorism to the United States is obviously large. This was one of the significant lessons learned from the 9/11 attacks on New York City and the Pentagon.[51] However, there have been previous instances of international terrorism, particularly those occurring against U.S. targets abroad, that have had devastating effects in terms of loss of life. Since 9/11, there has been a concerted effort to thwart international terrorist attacks that include many international partners. Thus far, these prevention efforts have been successful. However, even with the death of Osama bin Laden, there remains an international movement with significant support that will continue to attempt to attack the United States. This is clearly indicated in the 2018 Worldwide Threat Assessment, released by the Director of National Intelligence[52]:

> Sunni violent extremists—most notably ISIS and al Qaida—pose continuing terrorist threats to U.S. interests and partners worldwide, while U.S.-based homegrown violent extremists (HVEs) will remain the most prevalent Sunni violent extremist threat in the United States. Iran and its strategic partner Lebanese Hizballah also pose a persistent threat to the United States and its partners worldwide.

Domestic Terrorism

Domestic terrorism, or terrorism originating within the United States, is a continuing threat to Homeland Security.[53] While the 9/11 attacks, because of their dramatic nature, have focused attention on international terrorism, domestic terrorism has a potent history in the United States and continues to be actively carried out by various organizations and individuals within the nation, stemming from a variety of motivations. Anti-government attacks, such as the Oklahoma City Bombing in 1995; the Olympic Bombing in 1996, which was motivated by anti-abortion sentiments; and the Vail Colorado Arson that was motivated by animal rights demonstrate this variety in motivation.[54]

Domestic terrorism remains one of the principal threats to homeland security.[55] The form this threat takes is varied, including eco-terrorism and animal rights terrorism, militia extremism, anarchist extremism, white supremacy, anti-abortion terrorism, and other forms. The FBI has previously stated that they consider eco-terrorism the most threatening form of domestic terrorism and has documented over 2,000 attacks resulting in over $110 million in damages since 1979,[56] though more recent attacks like those in Orlando's Pulse club, and the attacks in San Bernardino, California have changed that dynamic.[57]

In addition to the "normal" domestic threats such as eco-terrorism and white supremacy, there is the additional problem of home-grown terrorists with religious motivations. Particularly, there is a significant threat that international organizations such as al Qaeda or the Islamic State (ISIS) may attempt to support, but not direct, domestic terrorist organizations. The National Intelligence Estimate from 2007 suggests,

> Although we have discovered only a handful of individuals in the United States with ties to al Qaida senior leadership since 9/11, we judge that al Qaida will intensify its efforts to put operatives here. . . We assess that the spread of radical—especially Salafi—Internet sites, increasingly aggressive anti-U.S. rhetoric and actions, and the growing number of radical, self-generating cells in Western countries indicate that the radical and violent segment of the West's Muslim population is expanding, including in the United States. The arrest and prosecution by U.S. law enforcement of a small number of violent Islamic extremists inside the United States—who are becoming more connected ideologically, virtually, and/or in a physical sense to the global extremist movement—points to the possibility that others may become sufficiently radicalized that they will view the use of violence here as legitimate.[58]

Though this is somewhat dated (the National Intelligence Estimates are often not public) and the actors have changed somewhat (ISIS is perhaps the more important religious terrorist organization), the underlying message remains the same.

Like 9/11 for international terrorism, many of these attacks, and particularly Oklahoma City, indicated the potential threat that domestic attacks presented for the United States and have led to wide-spread efforts of cooperation between local and federal law enforcement agencies to attempt to combat them. These efforts, though generally successful, have not been able to halt domestic terrorist activity in the United States and have not ended the threat of domestic terrorism.

Core Mission

The primary motivating factor for the development of DHS was 9/11. As such, perhaps the most important core missions—and certainly the mission that has driven the agency the most—remains defeating terrorism. This is a complex, multi-faceted mission, as the actors who are attempting to harm the United States through terrorism do not have a single ideological framework or a set method of attack. Additionally, with increases in connectivity since 2001, there has been a significant change in how terrorists are recruited, radicalized, and become operational - increasingly on social media like Facebook and Twitter. This fact makes the second element of this mission area—enhancing security—even more difficult.

In short, terrorism has been and continues to be a significant threat for the United States. Additionally, despite the large-scale efforts, particularly regarding international terrorism, there remain dedicated groups who wish to attack the US Domestically; these groups range in motivation from single issues like abortion and animal rights to home-grown religious terrorist organizations modeled on al Qaeda and ISIS. Internationally, the threat remains primarily religious in nature, with ISIS and groups inspired by them seeking large-scale attacks within the United States.

Natural and Man-Made Disasters and Hazards

Natural disasters, like terrorism, are one of the major threats that the United States experiences on a regular basis.[59] Events like Hurricane Katrina, and more recently, a series of tornadoes in the Midwest and Southeast, the 2017 Atlantic hurricane season, as well as the recent fires in California, remind us that while we face human-made threats regularly, natural hazards remain equally deadly and happen with much more frequency. As with terrorism, there are methods by which the government can mitigate the threat of, and cope with the results of, natural disasters. The sections below cover the difference between natural hazards and threats and some of the governmental responses to natural disasters when they happen at each level: national, state and local.

Hazards

Hazards, in the context of natural phenomena, are potential harms to humans or the environment caused by natural events. Hazards can be caused by hydrological, meteorological, seismic, geologic, volcanic, and mass-movement processes that occur in nature.[60] Although frequently used interchangeably with the concept of threat, the two ideas are distinct. In the United States, there is a wide variety of natural hazards including earthquakes, tornadoes, hurricanes, wild fires, floods, lightning strikes, landslides, sink holes, drought, and others. These hazards cause a tremendous amount of damage nationwide each year. Floods alone accounted for $8.4 billion dollars in damage to the economy in 2011 and were responsible for 114 deaths, and the decade leading up was more costly in terms of lives than previous decades.[61] Additionally, although not usually given as much media attention as terrorist attacks, natural hazards occur with more frequency and result in a great deal more loss-of-life than man-made hazards over time.[62]

Risks

Risks are hazards when combined with their probability of happening. For instance, while an earthquake is always a hazard, it poses little threat to states in the Southeast and is, therefore, not considered a significant risk. More concretely, risks are more contextually specific than hazards, even if they are composed of the same phenomenon. Hazard risks, therefore, are always examined within their respective locations. There are frequently hazards that pose little risk but never pose risks that do not consist of a hazard.[63]

The process of developing methods to deal with hazards, including determining the probability of the risk of a hazard, is called risk management. Risk management with regard to natural events is one of the primary responsibilities of government, and there has been a long history of risk management at all levels of government.[64] Risk management includes both qualitative and quantitative methodologies, and knowledge of the area's history of hazards and disasters is critical to risk management.

Disasters

Natural disasters are what happens when a threat comes to fruition and overwhelms the ability of a single agency to deal with it. Examples from history abound. Perhaps the most memorable natural disaster in recent memory is hurricane Katrina. This, however, was not the largest natural disaster in the history of the United States, nor even the largest hurricane. That title belongs to the Galveston Hurricane of 1900, during which 8,000 individuals died.[65] In fact, there are usually several dozen declared disasters every year. In 2011 alone, there were 99 major declared disasters, not including fire suppression authorizations or emergency declarations in the United States totaling over 80 billion dollars in damage.[66]

Different types of disasters occur with different frequency, in different locations all around the country. Floods, for instance, affect nearly every part of the nation and are one of the most costly type of disaster. Even relatively rare events, such as tsunamis, can cause huge amounts of damage, and, therefore, must be taken into account when generating response plans. Further, many disasters compound when they occur. Again taking earthquakes as an example, disasters like fires, floods, and others may happen at the same time.[67] This can easily be seen from the international example of the nuclear disaster caused by a tsunami in Japan.[68] Within this context, government has a series of responsibilities: Mitigation or the reduction of the probability of disasters happening; preparedness, or preparing for when disasters happen; response during the disaster event; and recovery, for after the disaster has passed.

Disasters in the United States

Over the course of United States' history, there have been a variety of major natural disasters, including all of the types mentioned above. Additionally, the methods by which these disasters have been addressed have changed with the rise of emergency management as a professional discipline and academic endeavor. Despite this improvement in our ability to deal with disasters when they happen, disasters continue to affect both property and life all around the nation in a variety of ways. In **BOX 3.4** below, the most frequently occurring types of disaster are examined.[69]

Core Mission

On of DHS's core missions is mitigating the effects of natural disasters when they occur. While it is not clear whether DHS, nor anyone else, can prevent natural disasters from occurring, differential responses to disasters give ample evidence that how the government helps respond to disasters matters a great deal. The response by FEMA to Hurricane Katrina, for instance, was seen largely as ineffective, while the more recent disasters, like the Camp Fire in California, have been seen as more successful. In **BOX 3.5**, we discuss a more recent failure in terms of disaster response—to Hurricane Maria.

While there are a number of government agencies involved in the context of disaster recovery and mitigation, FEMA is the primary organization within DHS that has jurisdiction. Older than DHS by far (it was established in 1979),[77] FEMA has moved from cabinet-level status (under Bill Clinton) back to an agency within DHS. However, despite its seeming decline in governmental authority, it has grown in its responsibility—particularly since 2001. The agency is not only responsible for natural disaster recovery but is also responsible for dealing with any type of fallout from chemical, biological, radiological, or nuclear disasters, either accidental or purposeful.[78]

Natural disasters are much more frequently occurring but receive less attention than terrorist attacks. This is surprising not just because of the difference

BOX 3.4 Frequently Occurring Disasters

Floods

Floods affect nearly every area of the country and can be among the most damaging types of natural disasters. While floods technically are defined as any time a significant amount of water overwhelms land that is normally dry, larger floods are not only capable of causing extensive damage but may persist for significant periods of time. Floods have a variety of causes including torrential rain, dam breaks, and frequently for large floods, hurricanes.[70] According to the Federal Emergency Management Agency's flood statistics, the most costly flood in U.S. history was caused by Hurricane Katrina in Louisiana and surrounding states and resulted in over $16 billion dollars in damage as well as at least 1,836 deaths.[71]

Wildfires

Wildfires, sometimes known as brush or forest fires, are fires that surpass the ability of local fire suppression groups to contain them. They can burn huge amounts of acreage, destroy property, and frequently result in deaths. These fires are usually caused by humans but can also be caused by lightning strikes if weather conditions are dry enough. They are becoming a more significant problem across the country as people build their homes in more wooded areas.[72]

Tornadoes

Tornadoes are frequently occurring, powerful storms that appear as rotating, funnel-shaped clouds. They are among the most destructive types of natural disasters, with winds sometimes reaching 300 miles per hour and damage trailing up to 50 miles. In the largest tornadoes, the path of destruction can reach a mile wide. Tornadoes usually develop as part of a larger storm system, but occasionally, tornadoes develop so rapidly that there is little advanced warning. Nearly every state in the country is at risk for these severe storms.[73]

Hurricanes

Hurricanes are large, powerful storms that develop in the open ocean and move into coastal areas. The Atlantic hurricane season lasts from June to November while storms in the Pacific tend to develop between May and November. These storms can be hundreds of miles wide and frequently spawn other significant weather events such as tornadoes and flooding. In order to be classified as a hurricane, wind speeds must reach a minimum sustained level of 74 miles per hour[74] but winds can reach up to 200 miles per hour in the most severe storms. Coastal communities are most at risk, but even areas far inland sometimes sustain significant damage from large hurricanes.[75]

BOX 3.5 The Response in Puerto Rico[76]

While generally unheralded, the response that FEMA provides in the context of natural disasters is essential to mitigating the effects of natural disasters. However, despite years of responses, the agency is sometimes caught off guard in its response. Such was the case with the 2017 hurricane in Puerto Rico—Hurricane Maria.

Hurricane Maria damaged over a third of Puerto Rico's homes and crippled the power grid. The massive scale of the disaster in Puerto Rico, coupled with the island's placement, made the disaster response more difficult than most. Even after 7 months of response, over 100,000 people on the island still did not have regular access to power.

While FEMA made a strong effort to support the recovery effort, the effects of an already busy hurricane season were apparent, as first response kits—including medical emergency kits—were in short supply as the storm hit. Other necessities, like tarps and even personnel, were difficult to get both because of the supplies being stretched thin by other responses as well as getting people to the island.

The response to Hurricane Maria is widely seen as a failure. In any event, the hurricane's aftermath made clear many of the difficulties of dealing with disaster response, and reminds us that there are always important lessons to be learned.

Einbender, N. 2017. "How the Response to Hurricane Maria Compared to Harvey and Irma". PBS. Retrieved on December 19, 2018 from https://www.pbs.org/wgbh/frontline/article/how-the-response-to-hurricane-maria-compared-to-harvey-and-irma/

in the number of occurrences but also because the combined monetary total of natural disasters dwarfs that of terrorism in most years. In any event, both terrorism and natural disasters require a large response effort, and many times, the recovery requires similar elements. This closely ties the two types of events together, even though their causes are distinct.

Safeguard and Secure Cyberspace

Among the many responsibilities of the DHS, there may be none more challenging than protecting and securing the nation's cyber-infrastructure and protecting us from cyber-threats. Increasing network connectivity has changed the way people live their everyday lives. With a multitude of devices now increasingly connected through the Internet of Things (IoT), individuals regularly produce information about themselves and those around them. This increase in the production of detailed personal information, not to mention financial and national security information, has meant that the types of threats that are encountered in **cyberspace** have been changing, and are likely to continue to do so.

The recent "hacking" of the election in 2016 provides an interesting example of the complexity of the topic of cybersecurity. While there is a consistent concern about votes being changed within voting machines, and indeed that remains an issue, there was little done to prevent interference on a broader, more public level. Additionally, while voting machines are not networked (in part to prevent cyber-attacks), voter registration databases are networked and could be vulnerable to attacks. While this would not directly change the results of an election, a large-scale attack could prevent a significant number of people from voting at all if, for instance, they were removed from voter rolls.

In addition to these types of attacks, the nation increasingly relies on cyber-infrastructure for any number of its necessary functions. For instance, both the New York Stock Exchange (NYSE) and the NASDAQ exchange rely on network connectivity to carry out their day-to-day operations; without it, they would stop functioning. If an incident, either an attack, or potentially the result of a disaster, interrupted this network infrastructure, the nation's financial systems would be at risk. The protection of this kind of infrastructure, then, is essential to continuing the normal operations of the government.

Importantly, cyber-threats go beyond "hacking," although that is the focus of a great deal of attention (and often misplaced[79] attention). Often, attacks involving **phishing** or other **social engineering** methods can be used to either gain illicit access to systems or to dupe others into granting permissions to bad actors. Some of these methods are detailed in **BOX 3.6** on the next page.

DHS is the agency with primary responsibility for safeguarding and securing cyberspace. Given the scope of that mission, it is an incredibly difficult task to accomplish. The scope of the problem is also not only limited to the array of types of bad actors in cyberspace but it is also complicated by the differentiated function of many different government agencies, who often have their own security responsibilities within the context of cyberspace. DHS has the responsibility of covering all of these domains and making sure that agencies are functioning together to keep people safe on the Internet.

Defining "Cyber"

Like terrorism, the definition of exactly what constitutes a cyber-threat has been somewhat troubling. While everyone agrees that "cyber" involves technology and crime, there is a degree of uncertainty to what degree these things have to be intertwined. For

BOX 3.6 Cybersecurity Issues[80]

While there is a huge number of types of cybercrime and other cyber-threats, they generally fall into one of the categories below. Each of these represent different threats to individuals and networks that are part of the nation's cyber-infrastructure and all present significant issues for national security.

An enumeration of the categories of cybercrime appears in the table below.

Crimes That Target Networks or Devices	Crimes Using Devices to Participate in Criminal Activities
Viruses	Phishing Emails
Malware	Cyberstalking
DoS Attacks	Identity Theft

In different cases, different entities can be harmed by each of the above categories. Individuals can be targeted for exploitation or whole network systems can be targeted as part of an effort to crash a system. Additionally, complex attacks can be paired with the above threats and used to take advantage in the physical world of a failed digital system.

Each of these are part of the responsibility of DHS, although often the responsibility is shared with other government agencies at multiple levels of government from local to federal. Just these limited examples give an idea of the range of threats that DHS is responsible for in the cyber realm.

Panda Security. 2018. "Types of Cybercrime". Retrieved on January 02, 2017 from, https://www.pandasecurity.com/mediacenter/panda-security/types-of-cybercrime/.

instance, if a flash drive with a virus that reads your keystrokes is placed on your computer, does it constitute a cybercrime? The answer, according to some, may depend on the method by which your keystrokes are transmitted. If it uses a network to transmit the information, it would constitute a **cybercrime**. If you retrieve the drive and then use that information, it may not because of the lack of use of networks within the theft. A broader definition would include, for instance, crimes not only using technology and networks but also computers that are used incidentally to crime. Generally speaking, when we refer to this broader range of crimes, we use the term "**technocrime**."

Core Mission

When it comes to "cyber," DHS has a variety of responsibilities included in safeguarding and securing cyberspace. The primary responsibilities, among others, include:

- Combatting cybercrime
- Securing federal networks
- Protecting critical infrastructure
- Cyber incident response

Within each of these areas of responsibility, DHS provides a variety of support services or active methods of combatting cyber-incidents. For instance, the Secret Service, Electronic Crimes Task Forces, focuses on "identifying and locating international cyber criminals connected to cyber intrusions, bank fraud, data breaches, and other computer-related crimes."[81] Similarly, both Customs and Border Protection and Immigration and Customs Enforcement also have cyber-capabilities geared toward their specific areas of responsibility, with task forces directed at detecting threats at the border or with homeland security investigations.[82] Other agencies, as part of DHS, also have response capabilities, which will be covered more in Chapters 7 and 9.

DHS's core mission to safeguard and security cyberspace is perhaps one of its broadest responsibilities. The threats faced in the cyber-domain are significant, and extremely varied, and the agencies involved span both DHS as well as the rest of the government, with organization like the Federal Bureau of Investigation also having essential roles. Increasing connectivity and access to the Internet complicate an already difficult task, and its combination with other areas of responsibility for DHS, like protecting critical infrastructure and key resources or combatting terrorism, suggest the success of this mission's import—but also its challenge.

Secure and Manage Borders

On any given day, over 1 million people enter the United States from across its borders.[83] Although the vast majority of these individuals are law abiding, a number of individuals who are either criminals or are attempting to enter the United States illegally have to be identified, isolated, and processed. Given the sheer vastness of the borders, the land borders with Canada and Mexico alone are 4,669 miles long,[84] this task is daunting. Considering both the size of the number of individuals coming across at border crossing sites, as well as the number of individuals who attempt to gain access illegally, the scope of DHS's mission is to secure and manage borders is vast.

While the mission of DHS is often focused on "security," from terrorism to cybersecurity, the mission of DHS at the borders is twofold. Not only does the agency have to make sure that the borders remain secure from threats of people who may try to enter the country but they also have to make sure that this security is done in such a way that it does not significantly impede the trade that happens between the United

States and those nations we border (and those nations that ship through border countries). This is challenging, as the nation's ports of entry and border crossings facilitate billions of dollars of trade every day. In fact, shipping from ports and across our borders constitute the majority of the ways in which we receive goods from abroad (with air freight coming in third, for which DHS is also responsible).

With this dual mission of security and trade management, DHS employs several organizations within the Department to assist with these tasks. The Customs and Border Protection (CBP) is among the most visible of these organizations, although many of their activities are not well documented in the public domain. For instance, the Container Security Initiative (CSI) examines containers bound for the United States before they're loaded onto ships at foreign ports to prevent dangerous or illicit materials from being shipped to the United States.

A key element of the security component of the border mission of DHS is the United States Border Patrol (USBP). Although recently mired in some controversy because of the migrant caravans from the Caribbean and Central America, USBP is the organization most closely associated with securing the borders with Mexico and Canada. This agency will be discussed more completely in Chapter 7.

Core Mission

When it comes to securing our border and allowing for trade is threefold, the core mission of DHS.

1. Effectively secure land, sea, and air ports of entry
2. Safeguard and streamline lawful trade and travel
3. Disrupt and dismantle transnational criminal and terrorist organizations

Each of these missions is essential to carrying out the day-to-day security of the nation. Additionally, they are linked very closely with other aspects of DHS's overall mission of securing the country within its borders. Specifically, understanding that the economy is a piece of our critical infrastructure can assist with understanding exactly why it is important to keep trade moving across the border quickly and without incident. Furthermore, without the work of organizations like CBP, carrying out the mission in the other four mission areas mentioned would be impossible.

From disrupting terrorism to facilitating trade, DHS's mission to secure the borders of the country and help manage trade is both difficult and essential to our overall security. The scope of the task is daunting, but the necessity of such a mission is undeniable—and closely tied to the other mission areas that DHS has. Additionally, understanding the centrality of the **border security** mission to other elements of DHS can help shed light on why different elements of border protection—in particular—have been controversial and politically contentious in recent years.

Enforce and Administer Our Immigration Laws

Closely related to securing the border and managing trade is the enforcement of the nation's immigration laws. While there is perhaps no other part of DHS's overall mission that has been mired in controversy recently (e.g., the Abolish Immigration and Customs Enforcement [ICE] movement), the mission to enforce immigration laws is closely tied with other mission areas of the Department. Additionally, while security has been a central component of the recent conversation regarding DHS's responsibilities in terms of immigration, administering lawful travel from foreign nationals is also a key element of what DHS does in this mission area.

Among the things that DHS is responsible for within this mission area is making sure that illicit goods and individuals who are unauthorized are investigated and processed appropriately. While this frequently means engagement with ICE, it can also pertain to issues such as human trafficking, which also falls under the purview of DHS. Specifically, agencies like ICE as well as U.S. Citizen and Immigration Services (USCIS), work together across the Homeland Security Community to help prevent and stop human trafficking. This is, of course, in addition to work that ICE, and DHS more generally, engage in to stop illicit goods like narcotics, bulk cash, and antiquities from being smuggled into the United States.

Additionally, and closely related to the abovementioned security components of this mission area, DHS also has responsibility through USCIS to ensure that those who are immigrating legally to the United States are facilitated in that process as well as checked for any security issues. The scope of this challenge is large, with over 3,000 individuals legally becoming citizens each day, in addition to those applying for asylum in the United States from abroad, background checks for incoming migrants, and even adoption issues for potential parents here in the United States.

Core Mission

The core of enforcing and administering our immigration laws falls into three broad categories.

1. Smart and effective enforcement
2. Facilitation of legal immigration
3. Combatting human smuggling

These three areas, while comprising the broad categories of DHS's mission in terms of immigration, are themselves comprised of many areas of responsibility. Through partnerships with local law enforcement to running the second largest investigative agency in the government (ICE), the immigration mission of DHS is both broad and essential to the nation's ongoing functioning.

Facilitating legal immigration as well as combatting smuggling comprise one of the key mission areas for DHS. Given that the responsibilities for investigations range from uncovering human smuggling rings to finding antiquities that have been smuggled into the United States from around the word and from vetting potential immigrants to the country to facilitating adoptions of children from abroad, it should be clear that this is one of the most varied and challenging areas that DHS is responsible for. Add to that the recent political controversies surrounding elements that deal specifically with this mission area, and it is easy to see how difficult the task of facilitating and securing the immigration process is.

Chapter Summary

The attacks on 9/11 motivated the modern change of homeland security in America and marked onc of the seminal events of the early 21st century. The attacks were as devastating as they were because of the fear generated by al Qaeda. Terrorism generally is designed to generate fear to motivate change in the individuals and groups targeted by it, and in some respects, September 11 was a success for the terrorists, as have several other attacks been since 9/11, both at home and abroad.

Natural disasters, like terrorism, can be physically and emotionally devastating. Unlike catastrophic terrorism, however, natural disasters occur with frequency, in nearly every part of the country. Wildfires and floods are the most frequent types of natural disasters in the United States, but many other types, such as hurricanes and tornadoes, also cause a significant amount of damage each year. Responses to those disasters, either terrorism-related, accidental, or manmade, are the responsibility of DHS.

In addition to these large-scale, media-intensive events, DHS is also responsible for a large number of day-to-day responsibilities that range from securing the Internet to facilitating legal immigration. These are sometimes brought to light in times of political crisis, like the recent issues surrounding election meddling and immigration. The reality is that these are important areas of security that must be dealt with on an ongoing basis. Moreover, while there are likely to be changes as administrations change in terms of policy, understanding what areas of responsibility fall to DHS is essential, as these are much less likely to change over time.

From securing the nation against terrorism and providing resilience after natural disasters to safeguarding network infrastructure and securing the borders, DHS's myriad responsibilities are far-reaching and require coordination across the entire government enterprise. The five mission areas described above, while capturing the scope of the mission of DHS, do not do justice to the significant number of programs involved in making sure those missions get carried out. Nor do they do justice to the challenges of carrying out that mission in the current political and cultural environment, which will likely continue to change in the future.

Review/Discussion Questions

1. What are the components of a definition of terrorism and why are each of them important for differentiating terrorism from crime?
2. Explain the importance of the development of terrorism across history. What elements have remained the same throughout and which have changed over time?
3. Compare and contrast the psychological explanations of terrorism to strategic explanations of terrorism. Which approach is more effective in explaining terrorism and why?
4. What is the difference between hazard and risk? Which should we use for planning purposes and why?
5. Why is there more focus on terrorism than natural disasters despite the latter's more frequent occurrence and cost?

Additional Readings

Hoffman, B. (2006). *Inside Terrorism* (2nd ed.). New York: Colombia University Press.

Sageman, M. (2004). *Understanding Terror Networks.* Philadelphia, PA: University of Pennsylvania Press.

Sloan, S. (2006). *Terrorism: The Present Threat in Context.* New York: Berg.

Endnotes

1. Agance France Press. (2013). Obama Offers Solace in Tornado-Ravaged Oklahoma. Retrieved on December 18, 2018, from https://web.archive.org/web/20130630003045/http://au.news.yahoo.com/thewest/a/-/world/17335797/obama-travels-to-tornado-ravaged-oklahoma/.
2. National Ocean and Atmospheric Association. (2018). Storm Events Database. Retrieved on December 18, 2018 from https://www.ncdc.noaa.gov/stormevents/eventdetails.jsp?id=451572.
3. Kotz, D. (2013). Injury Toll From Marathon Bombs Reduced to 264. *Boston Globe.* Retrieved on December 18, 2018 from https://www.bostonglobe.com/lifestyle/health-wellness/2013/04/23/number-injured-marathon-bombing-revised-downward/NRpaz5mmvGquP7KMA6XsIK/story.html.
4. Gates, J. D., Arabian, S., Biddinger, P., ... Yaffe, M. B. (2014). The Initial Response to the Boston Marathon Bombing: Lessons Learned to Prepare for the Next Disaster. *Annals of Surgery, 260*(6), 960–6.
5. Center for Strategic and International Studies. (2018). Significant Cyber Incidents. Retrieved on January 1, 2019, from https://www.csis.org/programs/cybersecurity-and-governance/technology-policy-program/other-projects-cybersecurity.
6. Katersky, A. (2010). Faisal Shahzad Pleads Guilty In Times Square Car Bomb Plot, Warns of More Attacks. ABC News. Retrieved on 23 March, 2019, from https://abcnews.go.com/Blotter/faisal-shahzad-pleads-guilty-times-square-car-bomb/story?id=10970094.
7. Rosenberg, E. (2016). 7 Men Accused in Sex-Trafficking Ring in U.S. and Mexico. *The New York Times.* Retrieved on January 1, 2018, from https://www.nytimes.com/2016/11/02/nyregion/7-men-accused-in-sex-trafficking-ring-in-us-and-mexico.html.
8. Carter, C. J. & Botelho, G. (2013). "Captured!!!" Boston Police Announce Marathon Bombing Suspect in Custody. *CNN.* Retrieved on December 18, 2018, from https://edition.cnn.com/2013/04/19/us/boston-area-violence.
9. Washington Post. (2010). The Department of Homeland Security. Retrieved on May 16, 2019, from https://www.washingtonpost.com/politics/homeland-security-department/gIQALxPx4O_print.html.
10. New York Times. (n.d.). One 9/11 Tally: $3.3 Trillion. Retrieved on August 15, 2012, from http://www.nytimes.com/interactive/2011/09/08/us/sept-11-reckoning/cost-graphic.html.
11. PBS Newshour. (2006). Hurricane Katrina Displaced over 400,000, report says. Retrieved on May 16, 2019, from https://www.pbs.org/newshour/arts/social_issues-jan-june06-census_06-07.
12. Silver, R. C., Holman, A., McIntosh, D. N., Poulin, M., & Gil-Rivas, V. (2002). Nationwide Longitudinal Study of Psychological Responses to September 11. *Journal of the American Medical Association, 288*(10), 1235–44.
13. DHS. (2018). Our Mission Areas. Retrieved on December 17, 2018, from https://www.dhs.gov/our-mission.
14. Hoffman, B. (2006). *Inside Terrorism* (2nd ed.). New York: Colombia University Press.
15. Sloan, S. (2006). *Terrorism: The present threat in context.* New York: Berg.
16. Hoffman, B. (2006). *Inside Terrorism* (2nd ed.). New York: Colombia University Press.
17. Hoffman, B. (2006). *Inside Terrorism* (2nd ed.). New York: Colombia University Press.
18. Hoffman, B. (2006). *Inside Terrorism* (2nd ed.). New York: Colombia University Press. Gough, H. (1998). *The Terror in the French Revolution.* New York, My: Palgrave MacMillan.
19. Gough, H. (1998). *The Terror in the French Revolution.* New York, NY: Palgrave MacMillan.
20. Hoffman, B. (2006). *Inside Terrorism* (2nd ed.). New York: Colombia University Press. Gough, H. (1998). *The Terror in the French Revolution.* New York, NY: Palgrave MacMillan.
21. Sloan, S. (2006). *Terrorism: The Present Threat in Context.* New York, Berg.
22. Hoffman, B. (2006). *Inside Terrorism* (2nd ed.). New York: Colombia University Press.
23. Norris, P, Montague, K., Just, M. (2003). *Framing Terrorism: The News Media, the Government, and the Public.* New York, NY: Routledge.
24. Hoffman, B. (2006). *Inside Terrorism* (2nd ed.). New York: Colombia University Press.
25. Hoffman, B. (2006). *Inside Terrorism* (2nd ed.). New York, NY: Colombia University Press; Sloan, S. (2006). *Terrorism: The present threat in context.* New York: Berg.
26. Sloan, S. (2006). *Terrorism: The present threat in context.* New York, NY: Berg.
27. Federal Bureau of Investigation. (2005). *Terrorism 2002-2005.* Retrieved on May 16, 2019 from https://www.fbi.gov/stats-services/publications/terrorism-2002-2005.
28. 22 U.S. Code § 2656f. Annual country reports on terrorism. Retrieved on May 16, 2019 from https://www.law.cornell.edu/uscode/text/22/2656f
29. Hoffman, B. (2006). *Inside Terrorism* (2nd ed). New York, NY: Columbia University Press.
30. Hoffman, B. (2006). *Inside Terrorism* (2nd ed). New York, NY: Columbia University Press; E.g., Crimes and Criminal Procedure 2331, 18 USC 113B (2012).
31. Hoffman, B. (2006). *Inside Terrorism* (2nd ed.). New York: Colombia University Press.
32. Jarboe, J. F. (2002). Testimony Before the House Subcommittee on Forests and Forest Health. Retrieved on August 23, 2012, from http://www.fbi.gov/news/testimony/the-threat-of-eco-terrorism.
33. Flemming, P., Stohl, M., & Schmidt, A. P. (1985). "The Theoretical Utility of Typologies of Terrorism: Lessons and Opportunities" in Stohl, M. (Ed.). *The Politics of Terrorism.* New York: CRC Press
34. Monaghan, R. (2000). "Single-Issue Terrorism: A neglected Phenomenon?" *Studies in Conflict and Terrorism, 23,* 255–265.

35. Hoffman, B. (2006). Inside Terrorism (2nd ed.). New York, NY: Columbia University Press; E.g., Crimes and Criminal Procedure 2331, 18 USC 113B (2012).
36. Sloan, S. (2006). *Terrorism: The present threat in context*. New York, NY: Berg.
37. Hoffman, B. (2006). *Inside Terrorism* (2nd ed.). New York, NY: Colombia University Press; Sloan, S. (2006). *Terrorism: The present threat in context*. New York: Berg.
38. Norris. P, Montague, K., & Just, M. (2003). *Framing terrorism. The news media, the government, and the Public*. New York, NY: Routledge.
39. Sageman, M. (2004). *Understanding Terror Networks*. Philadelphia, PA: University of Pennsylvania Press.
40. Federal Bureau of Investigation (2009). *Domestic Terrorism*. Retrieved on August 23, 2012, at http://www.fbi.gov/news/stories/2009/september/domterror_090709.
41. National Commission on Terrorist Attacks Upon the United States. (2004). *The 9/11 report*. New York, NY: St. Martin's.
42. Sloan, S. (2006). *Terrorism: The present threat in context*. New York, NY: Berg.
43. Anderson, S., & Sloan, S. (2003). *Terrorism: Assassins to Zealots*. Landham, MD: Scarecrow Press; Hoffman, B. (2006). *Inside Terrorism* (2nd ed.). New York, NY: Colombia University Press.
44. National Commission on Terrorist Attacks upon the United States. (2004). *The 9/11 report*. New York, NY: St. Martin's; Hoffman, B. (2006). *Inside Terrorism* (2nd ed.). New York, NY: Colombia University Press; Sloan, S. (2006). *Terrorism: The present threat in context*. New York: Berg; Sageman, M. (2004). *Understanding terror networks*. Philadelphia, PA: University of Pennsylvania Press.
45. Hoffman, B. (2006). *Inside Terrorism* (2nd ed.). New York, NY: Colombia University Press.
46. Hoffman, B. (2006). *Inside Terrorism* (2nd ed.). New York, NY: Colombia University Press; Sloan, S. (2006). *Terrorism: The present threat in context*. New York, NY: Berg; Sageman, M. (2004). *Understanding terror networks*. Philadelphia, PA: University of Pennsylvania Press.
47. National Commission on Terrorist Attacks upon the United States. (2004). *The 9/11 report*. New York, NY: St. Martin's.
48. Sloan, S. (2006). *Terrorism: The present threat in context*. New York, NY: Berg.
49. Federal Bureau of Investigation (2009). *Domestic Terrorism*. Retrieved on August 23, 2012 at http://www.fbi.gov/news/stories/2009/september/domterror_090709.
50. Hoffman, B. (2006). *Inside Terrorism* (2nd ed.). New York, NY: Colombia University Press.
51. National Commission on Terrorist Attacks upon the United States. (2004). *The 9/11 report*. New York, NY: St. Martin's.
52. Director of National Intelligence (2018). *Worldwide Threat Assessment of the US Intelligence Community*, p. 9. Retrieved on December 18, 2018, from https://www.dni.gov/files/documents/Newsroom/Testimonies/2018-ATA—Unclassified-SSCI.pdf.
53. Federal Bureau of Investigation (2009). *Domestic Terrorism*. Retrieved on August 23, 2012 at http://www.fbi.gov/news/stories/2009/september/domterror_090709.
54. Federal Bureau of Investigation (2009). *Domestic Terrorism*. Retrieved on August 23, 2012 at http://www.fbi.gov/news/stories/2009/september/domterror_090709.
55. Federal Bureau of Investigation (2009). *Domestic Terrorism*. Retrieved on August 23, 2012 at http://www.fbi.gov/news/stories/2009/september/domterror_090709.
56. Jarboe, J. F. (2002). Testimony before the House subcommittee on Forests and Forest Health. Retrieved on August 23, 2012 from http://www.fbi.gov/news/testimony/the-threat-of-eco-terrorism.
57. Federal Bureau of Investigation. (2012). Arkansas Man Sentenced for his Role in Firebombing Residence of Interracial Couple. Retrieved on August 23, 2012, from http://www.fbi.gov/littlerock/press-releases/2012/arkansas-man-sentenced-for-his-role-in-firebombing-residence-of-interracial-couple.
58. National Intelligence Council. (2007). *National Intelligence Estimate: The terrorist threat to the US homeland*, p. 5. Retrieved on August 27, 2012, from http://www.c-span.org/pdf/nie_071707.pdf.
59. Haddow, G. D., Bullock, J. A., and Coppola, D. P. (2011). *Introduction to Emergency Management*. Burlington, MA: Elsevier.
60. Haddow, G. D., Bullock, J. A., and Coppola, D. P. (2011). *Introduction to Emergency Management*. Burlington, MA: Elsevier.
61. Reliefweb. *Annual disaster statistical review* (2011). Retrieved on May 16, 2019 https://reliefweb.int/report/world/annual-disaster-statistical-review-2011-numbers-and-trends.
62. Haddow, G. D., Bullock, J. A., and Coppola, D. P. (2011). *Introduction to Emergency Management*. Burlington, MA: Elsevier.
63. Canadian Center for Occupational Health and Safety. (n.d.). *Hazard and Risk*. Retrieved from http://www.ccohs.ca/oshanswers/hsprograms/hazard_risk.html on March 12, 2013.
64. Haddow, G. D., Bullock, J. A., and Coppola, D. P. (2011). *Introduction to Emergency Management*. Burlington, MA: Elsevier.
65. National Oceanic and Atmospheric Administration. (n.d.). *Galveston storm of 1900*. Retrieved on March 12, 2013, from http://www.history.noaa.gov/stories_tales/cline2.html.
66. Federal Emergency Management Agency. (2012). *Disasters by year*. Retrieved on May 16, 2019 from http://www.fema.gov/disasters/grid/year.
67. Haddow, G. D., Bullock, J. A., and Coppola, D. P. (2011). *Introduction to Emergency Management*. Burlington, MA: Elsevier.
68. Demetriou, D. (2011). Japan Earthquake, Tsunami and Fukushima Nuclear Disaster: 2011 review. *The Telegraph*. Retrieved on March 12, 2013, from http://www.telegraph.co.uk/news/worldnews/asia/japan/8953574/Japan-earthquake-tsunami-and-Fukushima-nuclear-disaster-2011-review.html.
69. Haddow, G. D., Bullock, J. A., and Coppola, D. P. (2011). *Introduction to Emergency Management*. Burlington, MA: Elsevier.
70. Federal Emergency Management Agency. (2012). *Floods*. Retrieved on March 12, 2013, from http://www.ready.gov/floods.
71. National Oceanic and Atmospheric Administration. (n.d.) *Hurricane Katrina: Most Destructive Storm Ever to Hit the US*. Retrieved on March 12, 2013, from http://www.katrina.noaa.gov/.
72. Federal Emergency Management Agency. (2012). *Wildfires*. Retrieved from http://www.ready.gov/floods on March 12, 2013.
73. Federal Emergency Management Agency. (2012). *Tornadoes*. Retrieved from http://www.ready.gov/floods on March 12, 2013.

74. National Hurricane Center. (2012). *Saffir-Simpson Hurricane Wind Scale.* Retrieved on May 16, 2019 from http://www.nhc.noaa.gov/about sshws.php.
75. Federal Emergency Management Agency. (2012). *Hurricanes.* Retrieved on March 12, 2013, from http://www.ready.gov/floods.
76. Einbender, N. (2018). How the Response to Hurricane Maria Compared to Harvey and Irma. *Frontline.* Retrieved on December 19, 2018, from https://www.pbs.org/wgbh/frontline/article/how-the-response-to-hurricane-maria-compared-to-harvey-and-irma/.
77. Federal Emergency Management Agency. (2018). About the Agency. Retrieved on December 24, 2018 from https://www.fema.gov/about-agency.
78. Federal Emergency Management Agency. (2018). A New Mission: Homeland Security. Retrieved on December 19, 2018 from https://www.fema.gov/about-agency.
79. Steinmetz, K. F. (2016). *Hacked: A radical approach to hacker culture and crime.* New York, NY: NYU Press.
80. Panda Security (2018). Types of Cybercrime. Retrieved on January 02, 2017, from, https://www.pandasecurity.com/mediacenter/panda-security/types-of-cybercrime/.
81. Department of Homeland Security. (2018). Combating Cyber Crime. Retrieved on December 22, 2018, from https://www.dhs.gov/cisa/combating-cyber-crime.
82. Department of Homeland Security. (2018). Cyber Crimes Center. Retrieved on December 22, 2018, from https://www.ice.gov/cyber-crimes.
83. U.S. Customs and Border Protection. (2018). Snapshot: A Summary of CBP Facts and Figures. Retrieved on December 22, 2018, from https://www.cbp.gov/sites/default/files/assets/documents/2018-Dec/cbp-Snapshot-12102018-508.pdf.
84. Congressional Research Service. (2006). U.S. International Borders: Brief Facts. Retrieved on December 22, 2018, from https://fas.org/sgp/crs/misc/RS21729.pdf.

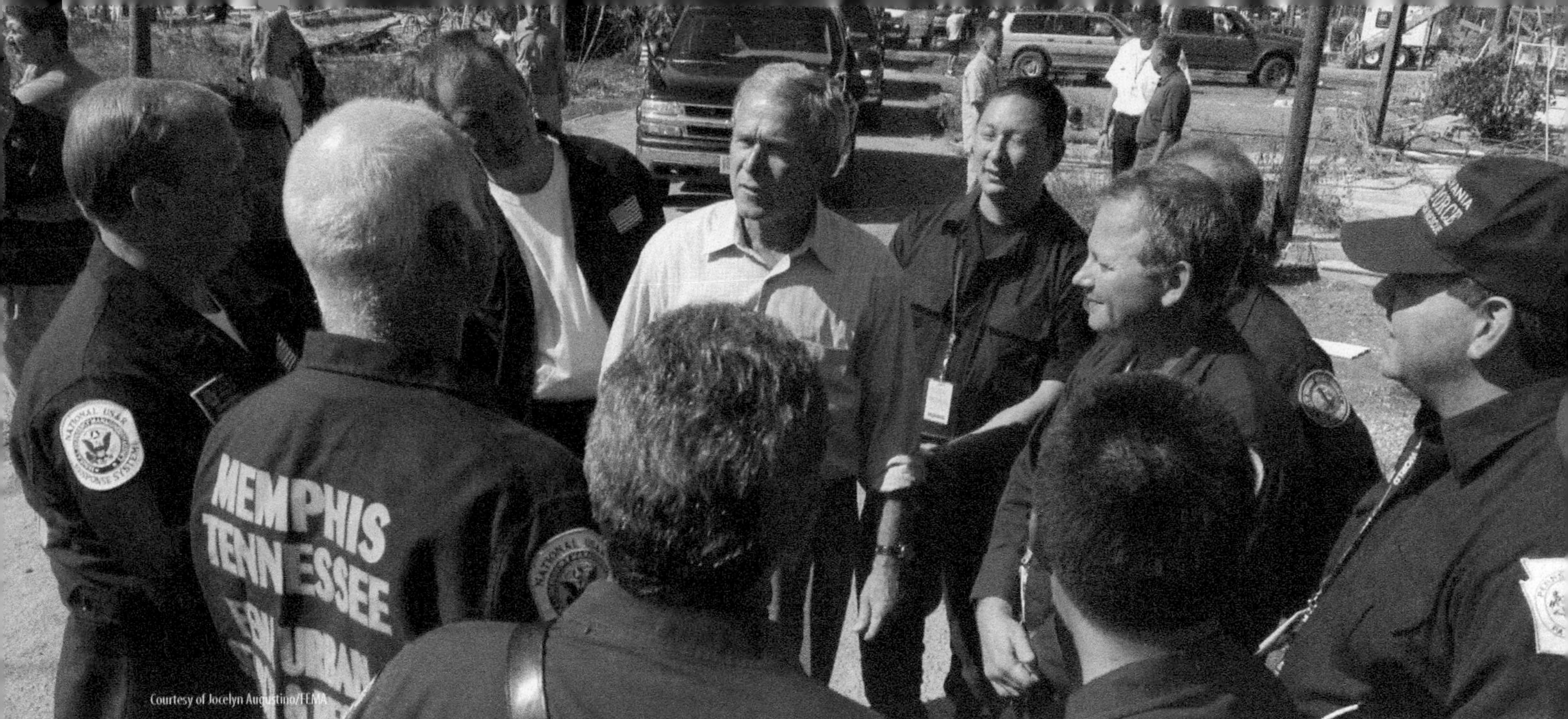

Courtesy of Jocelyn Augustino/FEMA.

CHAPTER 4

The Development of Homeland Security

CHAPTER OBJECTIVES

- Understand that the Department of Homeland Security was initially conceived of as the Office of Homeland Security within the White House/Executive branch
- Learn about the passage of the USA PATRIOT Act and the myriad laws it contained
- Comprehend that the Homeland Security Act established the Department of Homeland Security
- Understand the role of Homeland Security Presidential Directives in the implementation of homeland security in America

CHAPTER OUTLINE

OFFICE OF HOMELAND SECURITY
USA PATRIOT ACT
THE HOMELAND SECURITY ACT OF 2002
HOMELAND SECURITY PRESIDENTIAL DIRECTIVES
QUADRENNIAL HOMELAND SECURITY REVIEWS
CHAPTER SUMMARY

President George W. Bush was in Sarasota, Florida, visiting a class of children at Emma Booker Elementary School.[1] The President was seated in a classroom when, at 9:05 am, Andrew Card (Chief of Staff) whispered to him: "A second plane hit the second tower. America is under attack."[2]

Courtesy of National Archives, photo no. P7060-19A.

The President later explained that his first instinct was to project calm, not to have the country see an excited reaction from him in a moment of crisis. The press was standing behind the children; he saw their phones and pagers start to ring. The President felt that he should project strength and calm until he could better understand what was happening.

The President remained in the classroom for another 5 to 7 minutes, while the children continued reading. He then returned to a holding room shortly before 9:15, where he was briefed by staff and saw television coverage. Next, he spoke to Vice President Dick Cheney, National Security Advisor Condoleezza Rice, New York Governor George Pataki, and FBI Director Robert Mueller (who assumed the directorship on September 4, 2001). He decided to make a brief statement from the school before leaving for the airport. The Secret Service later explained that their priority was to move the President to a safer location, but they did not think it imperative to run him out the door.

Between 9:15 and 9:30, the staff was busy arranging a return to Washington, while the President consulted his senior advisers about his remarks. No one in the Bush party had any information during this time that other aircraft were hijacked or missing. Staff was in contact with the White House Situation Room, but no one was in contact with the Pentagon. The focus was on the President's statement to the nation. The only decision made during this time was to return to Washington. The President then briefly addressed the nation (see **BOX 4.1**).

The President's motorcade then departed at 9:35 and arrived at the airport between 9:42 and 9:45. During the ride, the President learned about the attack on the Pentagon. He boarded the aircraft, asked the Secret Service about the safety of his family, and called the Vice President. According to notes of the call, at about 9:45, the President told the Vice President, "Sounds like we have a minor war going on here. I heard about the Pentagon. We're at war. . .somebody's going to pay."[3]

About this time, Card, the lead Secret Service agent; the President's military aide; and the pilot were conferring on a possible destination for Air Force One. The Secret Service agent felt strongly that the situation in Washington was too unstable for the President to return there, and Card agreed. The President strongly wanted to return to Washington and only grudgingly agreed to go elsewhere. The issue was still undecided when the President conferred with the Vice President at about the time Air Force One was taking off. The Vice President recalled urging the President not to return to Washington. Air Force One departed at about 9:54 without any fixed destination. The objective was to get up in the air—as fast as possible—and then decide where to go.

BOX 4.1 Remarks in Sarasota, Florida, on the Terrorist Attack on New York City's World Trade Center, September 11, 2001

Today, we've had a national tragedy. Two airplanes have crashed into the World Trade Center in an apparent terrorist attack on our country. I have spoken to the Vice President, to the Governor of New York, to the Director of the FBI and have ordered that the full resources of the Federal Government go to help the victims and their families and to conduct a full-scale investigation to hunt down and to find those folks who committed this act.

Terrorism against our Nation will not stand.

And now if you would join me in a moment of silence.

[*A moment of silence was observed.*]

May God bless the victims, their families, and America.

Thank you very much.

Reproduced from: Bush, George W. (2001). "Remarks in Sarasota, Florida, on the Terrorist Attack on New York City's World Trade Center." Public Papers of the Presidents of the United States. Washington, D.C.: U.S. G.P.O.

In the meantime, the White House was notified that an unauthorized plane was heading toward Washington, D.C., and it was not communicating. The Vice President was rushed into the tunnels underneath the White House to a protective bunker. He stopped at one point in the tunnel where a bench, television, and phone were available. After verification of the missing plane and the attack on the Pentagon, Vice President Cheney contacted the President and advised him not to return to Washington. After the call ended, Mrs. Cheney and the Vice President moved from the tunnel to the shelter conference room.

President Bush reluctantly acceded to this advice, and at about 10:10, Air Force One changed course and began heading due west. The immediate objective was to find a safe location, not too far away, where the President could land and speak to the American people. The Secret Service was also interested in refueling the aircraft and paring down the size of the traveling party. The President's military aide, an Air Force officer, quickly researched the options and, sometime around 10:20, identified Barksdale Air Force Base, Louisiana, as an appropriate interim destination.

When Air Force One landed at Barksdale at about 11:45, personnel from the local Secret Service were still en route to the airfield. The motorcade consisted of a military police lead vehicle and a van; the proposed briefing theater had no phones or electrical outlets. Staff scrambled to prepare another room for the President's remarks. The President completed his statement, which, for security reasons, was taped and not broadcast live, and the traveling party returned to Air Force One. At 2:30 pm, the President's address was released to the nation (see **BOX 4.2**).

The next destination was discussed. Once again, the Secret Service recommended against returning to Washington, and the Vice President agreed. Offutt Air Force Base in Nebraska was chosen because of its elaborate command and control facilities, and because it could accommodate overnight lodging for 50 persons. The Secret Service wanted a place where the President could spend several days, if necessary.

Air Force One arrived at Offutt at 2:50 pm. At about 3:15, President Bush met with his principal advisers through a secure video teleconference. Rice said President Bush began the meeting with the words, "We're at war," and that Director of Central Intelligence George Tenet said the agency was still assessing who was responsible, but the early signs all pointed to Al Qaeda.[4]

The Secretary of Defense directed the nation's armed forces to Defense Condition 3, an increased state of military readiness. For the first time in history, all nonemergency civilian aircraft in the United States were grounded, stranding tens of thousands of passengers across the country. Contingency plans for the continuity of government and the evacuation of leaders had been implemented. The Pentagon had been struck; the White House or the Capitol had narrowly escaped direct attack. Extraordinary security precautions were put in place at the nation's borders and ports.

In the late afternoon, the President overruled his aides' continuing reluctance to have him return to Washington and ordered Air Force One back to Andrews Air Force Base. He was flown by helicopter to the White House, passing over the still-smoldering Pentagon. At 8:30 that evening, President Bush addressed the nation from the White House (see **BOX 4.3**). Following his speech, President Bush met again with his National Security Council, expanded to include Secretary of Transportation Norman Mineta and Joseph Allbaugh, the Director of the Federal Emergency Management Agency. Secretary of State Colin Powell, who had returned from Peru after hearing of the attacks, joined the discussion. They reviewed the day's events.

BOX 4.2 Remarks at Barksdale Air Force Base, Louisiana, on the Terrorist Attacks, September 11, 2001

Freedom itself was attacked this morning by a faceless coward, and freedom will be defended. I want to reassure the American people that the full resources of the Federal Government are working to assist local authorities to save lives and to help the victims of these attacks. Make no mistake: The United States will hunt down and punish those responsible for these cowardly acts.

I've been in regular contact with the Vice President, the Secretary of Defense, the National Security Team, and my Cabinet. We have taken all appropriate security precautions to protect the American people. Our military at home and around the world is on high-alert status, and we have taken the necessary security precautions to continue the functions of your Government.

We have been in touch with the leaders of Congress and with world leaders to assure them that we will do whatever is necessary to protect America and Americans.

I ask the American people to join me in saying a thanks for all the folks who have been fighting hard to rescue our fellow citizens and to join me in saying a prayer for the victims and their families.

The resolve of our great Nation is being tested. But make no mistake: We will show the world that we will pass this test.

God bless.

Reproduced from: Bush, George W. (2001). "Remarks at Barksdale Air Force Base, Louisiana, on the Terrorist Attacks." Public Papers of the Presidents of the United States. Washington, D.C.: U.S.

BOX 4.3 Address to the Nation on the Terrorist Attacks, September 11, 2001

Courtesy of National Archives, photo no. P7058-31A.

Good evening. Today our fellow citizens, our way of life, our very freedom came under attack in a series of deliberate and deadly terrorist acts. The victims were in airplanes or in their offices: secretaries, business men and women, military and federal workers, moms and dads, friends and neighbors. Thousands of lives were suddenly ended by evil, despicable acts of terror.

The pictures of airplanes flying into buildings, fires burning, huge structures collapsing have filled us with disbelief, terrible sadness, and a quiet, unyielding anger. These acts of mass murder were intended to frighten our Nation into chaos and retreat, but they have failed. Our country is strong.

A great people has been moved to defend a great nation. Terrorist attacks can shake the foundations of our biggest buildings, but they cannot touch the foundation of America. These acts shattered steel, but they cannot dent the steel of American resolve. America was targeted for attack because we're the brightest beacon for freedom and opportunity in the world. And no one will keep that light from shining.

Today our Nation saw evil, the very worst of human nature. And we responded with the best of America, with the daring of our rescue workers, with the caring for strangers and neighbors who came to give blood and help in any way they could.

Immediately following the first attack, I implemented our Government's emergency response plans. Our military is powerful, and it's prepared. Our emergency teams are working in New York City and Washington, D.C., to help with local rescue efforts.

Our first priority is to get help to those who have been injured and to take every precaution to protect our citizens at home and around the world from further attacks.

The functions of our Government continue without interruption. Federal agencies in Washington, which had to be evacuated today, are reopening for essential personnel tonight and will be open for business tomorrow. Our financial institutions remain strong, and the American economy will be open for business as well.

The search is underway for those who are behind these evil acts. I've directed the full resources of our intelligence and law enforcement communities to find those responsible and to bring them to justice. We will make no distinction between the terrorists who committed these acts and those who harbor them.

I appreciate so very much the Members of Congress who have joined me in strongly condemning these attacks. And on behalf of the American people, I thank the many world leaders who have called to offer their condolences and assistance.

America and our friends and allies join with all those who want peace and security in the world, and we stand together to win the war against terrorism.

Tonight I ask for your prayers for all those who grieve, for the children whose worlds have been shattered, for all whose sense of safety and security has been threatened. And I pray they will be comforted by a power greater than any of us, spoken through the ages in Psalm 23: "Even though I walk through the valley of the shadow of death, I fear no evil, for You are with me."

This is a day when all Americans from every walk of life unite in our resolve for justice and peace. America has stood down enemies before, and we will do so this time. None of us will ever forget this day. Yet, we go forward to defend freedom and all that is good and just in our world.

Thank you. Good night, and God bless America.

Reproduced from: Bush, George W. (2001). "Address to the Nation on the Terrorist Attacks." Public Papers of the Presidents of the United States. Washington, D.C.: U.S. G.P.O.

It is important to understand that President Bush and his administration now had numerous tasks to perform all at once. Among these tasks included moving America to a war footing and responding militarily to the attack; organizing federal assistance, especially to New York City; determining when civil aviation could be restored, borders and ports reopened, as well as financial markets; and to find some means of responding domestically to the attack, which would become the **Office of Homeland Security**. While there were multiple tasks at hand, each was not created in a vacuum, but in concert with each other, although when it came to reviewing domestic capabilities, a temporary "domestic consequences" group had to be developed quickly.[5]

The process of reviewing these issues during this time of crisis underscored an absence of an effective government organization dedicated to assessing domestic vulnerabilities and handling problems of protection and preparedness.

Although a number of agencies had some part of the task, none had security as its primary mission. What then developed in the months ahead were a number of responses to this deficiency. The first was the development of the Office of Homeland Security within the White House, which would assume these responsibilities. The second was the development of new tools for protection and preparedness that, within 6 weeks, became the **USA PATRIOT Act**. Third, was the implementation of a series of presidential directives to begin implementing changes in the way America protected itself against future terrorist attacks. And, finally, the even greater task of creating a **Department of Homeland Security**, a new cabinet-level bureaucracy that would deal more directly with assessing vulnerabilities and handling the problems of protection and preparedness through an aggregate of multiple agencies and various agency components. These four actions, which all followed the 9/11 attacks, occurred quite rapidly: September 20, October 26, October 29, and November 25, 2002, respectively, forming the basis for modern-day homeland security in America.

Office of Homeland Security

In the aftermath of the attacks on September 11, 2001, the following day, President Bush toured the damage at the Pentagon in Arlington, Virginia. He gave a short speech noting that, "Coming here makes me sad, on the one hand; it also makes me angry. Our country will, however, not be cowed by terrorists, by people who don't share the same values we share, by people who are willing to destroy people's lives because we embrace freedom. The nation mourns, but our government will go on; the country will function. We are on high alert for possible activity."[6] Several days later, on September 14th, Bush toured the remains of the World Trade Center site in New York City. There, he had a memorable exchange with the rescue workers. He began to speak, but an audience member yelled, "Can't hear you."[7] The President said, "I can't get any louder," and the audience laughed.[8]

He then began with his prepared speech, stating that the nation mourned the loss of thousands of lives. Several people surrounding the president shouted, "I can't hear you."[9] President Bush, in an impromptu statement, shouted back, "I can hear you. I can hear you. The rest of the world hears you. And the people who knocked these buildings down will hear from us soon!"[10] The crowd cheered and broke into a chant of "USA! USA! USA!"[11]

Courtesy of The U.S. National Archives and Records Administration.

The President returned to Washington, D.C., and worked on the development of a proper response to the attacks, both militarily and domestically. On September 20, 2001, President Bush appeared before a joint session of Congress to speak to the American people about the tragic events of 9–11 and his administration's response (see **BOX 4.4**). In this speech, Bush announced the creation of an Office of Homeland Security and he named former Pennsylvania Governor Tom Ridge as the new office's first director (see **BOX 4.5**).

In the days following the speech, President Bush and his administration crafted an Executive Order that created not only the Office of Homeland Security but also a Homeland Security Council. The Executive Order was signed on October 8, 2001, and put into motion at the beginning of what became the largest major bureaucratic restructuring of the federal government since World War II.

The mission of the Office of Homeland Security was to "develop and coordinate the implementation of a comprehensive national strategy to secure the United States from terrorist threats or attacks."[12] The functions of the office were intended to "coordinate the executive branch's efforts to detect, prepare for, prevent, protect against, respond to, and recover from terrorist attacks within the United States."[13] More specifically, the functions of the new office were spelled out in more detail under 10 areas of focus: (1) the development of a *national strategy* working with executive departments and agencies, state and local governments, as well as private entities; (2) the *detection* of terroristic threats through the collection and analysis of information; (3) *preparedness* for and mitigation of the consequences of terrorist threats and attacks; (4) *protection* of critical infrastructure; (5) *response and recovery* from terrorist attacks; (6) *incident management*; (7) *continuity of government*; (8) *public affairs*; (9) *review of legal authorities* and *development of legislative proposals*; and (10) *budget review*.

Essentially, it was intended that the new Director of Homeland Security would work as an adviser to the

BOX 4.4 Address Before a Joint Session of the Congress of the United States Proposing New Office of Homeland Security, September 20, 2001

Our Nation has been put on notice: We are not immune from attack. We will take defensive measures against terrorism to protect Americans. Today, dozens of Federal departments and agencies, as well as State and local governments, have responsibilities affecting homeland security. These efforts must be coordinated at the highest level.

So, tonight I announce the creation of a Cabinet-level position reporting directly to me, the Office of Homeland Security. And tonight I also announce a distinguished American to lead this effort to strengthen American security, a military veteran, an effective Governor, a true patriot, a trusted friend, Pennsylvania's Tom Ridge. He will lead, oversee, and coordinate a comprehensive national strategy to safeguard our country against terrorism and respond to any attacks that may come.

These measures are essential. But the only way to defeat terrorism as a threat to our way of life is to stop it, eliminate it, and destroy it where it grows. Many will be involved in this effort, from FBI agents to intelligence operatives to the reservists we have called to active duty. All deserve our thanks, and all have our prayers. And tonight, a few miles from the damaged Pentagon, I have a message for our military: Be ready. I've called the Armed Forces to alert, and there is a reason. The hour is coming when America will act, and you will make us proud . . .

Reproduced from: Bush, George W. (2001). "Address Before a Joint Session of the Congress on the United States Response to the Terrorist Attacks of September 11. September 20, 2001." Public Papers of the Presidents of the United States. Washington, D.C.: U.S. G.P.O.

President for domestic threats, much in the same way that the National Security Adviser (Dr. Condoleezza "Condi" Rice at the time) advises the President on international threats. In fact, the Chief of Staff to the President, Andrew H. Card, Jr., explained it this way: "If you take a look at what Condi Rice does so effectively, you'll get an idea what Governor Ridge will be doing just as effectively."[14]

The position of National Security Adviser had been created in 1947 in the aftermath of World War II and the beginning of the Cold War. The purpose of the position was to have one adviser to the President who worked through a council that coordinated national defense, intelligence, and diplomatic relations in order to advise on international threats to the United States. Thus, the second half of the Executive Order on the

BOX 4.5 Tom Ridge, Homeland Security Secretary, 2003–2005

On January 24, 2003, Tom Ridge became the first Secretary of the Department of Homeland Security. Ridge worked with more than 180,000 employees from combined agencies to strengthen our borders, provide for intelligence analysis and infrastructure protection, improve the use of science and technology to counter weapons of mass destruction, and to create a comprehensive response and recovery division.

Tom Ridge was sworn in as the first Director of the Office of Homeland Security in October 2001, following the tragic events of September 11. The charge to the nation's new director of homeland defense was to develop and coordinate a comprehensive national strategy to strengthen the United States against terrorist threats or attacks. In the words of President George W. Bush, he had the strength, experience, personal commitment, and authority to accomplish this critical mission. Ridge stepped down as Secretary in February 2005.

Ridge was twice elected Governor of Pennsylvania, serving from 1995 to 2001. He kept his promise to make Pennsylvania "a leader among states and a competitor among nations." Governor Ridge's aggressive technology strategy helped fuel the state's advances in the priority areas of economic development, education, health, and the environment.

Born Aug. 26, 1945, in Pittsburgh's Steel Valley, Governor Ridge was raised in a working class family in veterans' public housing in Erie. He earned a scholarship to Harvard, graduating with honors in 1967. After his first year at The Dickinson School of Law, he was drafted into the U.S. Army, where he served as an infantry staff sergeant in Vietnam, earning the Bronze Star for Valor. After returning to Pennsylvania, he earned his law degree and was in private practice before becoming assistant district attorney in Erie County. He was elected to Congress in 1982. He was the first Congressman to have served as an enlisted man in the Vietnam War, and was overwhelmingly re-elected five times.

Reproduced from: Department of Homeland Security. (2012). Tom Ridge, Homeland Security Secretary 2003–2005.

Courtesy of CPL Jose O. Mediavilla, USMC/U.S. National Archives.

Office of Homeland Security emulated the National Security Council with its own Homeland Security Council. The Director of Homeland Security would oversee this new council, being responsible for "advising and assisting the President with respect to all aspects of homeland security" and the council "shall serve as the mechanism for ensuring coordination of homeland security-related activities of executive departments and agencies and effective development and implementation of homeland security policies."[15] Director Tom Ridge and his new council, barely formed, hit the ground running and began carrying out the various charges of his new office.

On March 21, 2002, another Executive Order was issued related to the Homeland Security Council. In this case, a Senior Advisory Committee to the Homeland Security Council was created. This was a committee of 21 presidential appointees who could provide advice directly to the President and the Director of Homeland Security, and would be composed of state and local officials, academics, private-sector personnel, emergency-services personnel, and first responders. The official title of the new committee was the President's Homeland Security Advisory Council (PHSAC).[16]

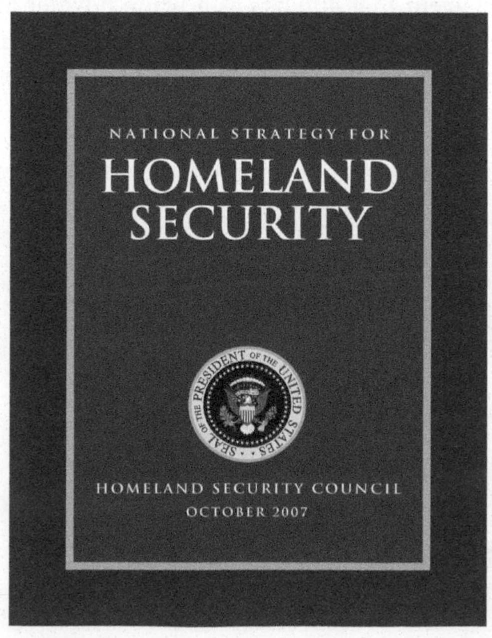

Courtesy of DHS.

The formation of the Office of Homeland Security within the White House with its Homeland Security Director and Council, as well as the Advisory Council, proved to be a very important element in the eventual development of the Department of Homeland Security. It was the first step in a very rapid process for changing the federal bureaucracy that eventually evolved into the cabinet-level Department of Homeland Security.[17] In addition, it also provided the first *National Strategy for Homeland Security*, once again emulating the National Security Council's *National Security Strategy* document. This document was important because it outlined the coordinated plan for homeland security.

USA PATRIOT Act

In the immediate aftermath of the tragedy of 9-11, the United States Congress also went to work. The gravity of the situation called for action. The debates over whether to allow certain bills to move forward, such as the Combating Terrorism Act, which gave more power to the government for investigative purposes, were over. The bills that had languished in committee or had failed passage prior to September 11, 2001, were now dusted off, introduced, and passed within hours. Congress was on a war footing, despite not yet knowing with whom, exactly, America was at war.

In the public policy literature, there are a number of scholars who can explain this phenomenon. Anthony Downs had described the "issue attention cycle" where various public problems go through a five-stage cycle.[18] The first stage is the pre-problem stage, where the policymakers, academics, and other interested experts recognize a problem, but the overall majority of Americans do not, hence the problem and its policy solution are not at the forefront of concern. The second stage is alarmed discovery and euphoric enthusiasm, where an event occurs and people instantly become concerned. The policy issue instantly moves to the forefront of people's attention. September 11 was clearly the American public's alarmed discovery of terrorism and the threat Al Qaeda posed to the United States. It is in this stage that policies are rapidly passed and a flurry of activity develops to confront the problem. Then Downs' cycle moves to the third stage, where the realization of the costs cause us to give pause, which moves us into the fourth stage, where there is a decline in public interest; and finally, to the fifth stage or "post-problem," where the issue fades to the background and only the experts give the issue any attention. In the case of the 9-11 attacks, the public became instantly concerned and there was, as Downs explains, a "euphoric enthusiasm" to pass policies to protect America.[19]

Another public policy scholar, John W. Kingdon, explains the passage of polices in more detail.[20] Kingdon argues that there are three separate factors that have to come together in order for public policy to pass. He describes these as three "streams" that flow independently of one another but which intersect at some point in order to open up a window of opportunity for passage. There is the problem stream, the solutions stream, and the political stream. The problem stream is the most basic, involving a widespread problem, one that most people would identify as a significant problem, which necessitates a governmental response. There must be a solution to the problem, generally created by those in the federal bureaucracy, private sector, or academia. These solutions are generally created by the experts in the area of concern. Finally, there is the political stream, in which both the politicians and the public are paying attention to the problem. When these three streams converge, there is a window of opportunity for the passage of new public policy.

In the case of 9-11, the terrorist attacks by Al Qaeda on American soil were clearly the problem, about which nearly all of America agreed. The political stream was also present, for the public demanded action and the politicians knew they had to respond. The solution stream then came out of largely everything that had been previously considered by stakeholders as possible solutions to the threat of terrorism but had either not reached the attention of the politicians or had simply not been passed in the U.S. House or Senate. In short, the attacks and public concern caused politicians to find any and every proposal even remotely related to protecting America against terrorism to be part of the solution—especially anything that would make investigations of terrorists easier in order to protect America against future attacks.

What happened next was a political fight that had long centered around the issue of security versus privacy.[21] On the one hand, many Democrats and the American Civil Liberties Union were concerned that if these bills were all introduced and passed, they would take away the civil liberties of many Americans, encroach upon the Fourth Amendment rights against unreasonable searches and seizures, and thus, potentially violate the Constitutional rights of Americans. On the other hand, the Republicans and many think tanks focused on anti-terrorism legislation. They were concerned that without these laws, federal law enforcement's ability to investigate terroristic threats and conduct counter-terrorism operations against potential terrorist threats would be severely limited. Members of the U.S. Senate came together and discussed what should be in the bill on September 19th, and from there, the bill began to be crafted. In reality, it was a catch-all bill; many proposals that had been previously entertained and failed plus many new proposals were all cobbled together into what became the Uniting and Strengthening America by Providing Appropriate Tools Required to Intercept and Obstruct Terrorism Act of 2001—the USA PATRIOT Act.

The Democrats realized they were in a weak position, for there was a clear need that Congress act decisively, and that it should act with solidarity. In other words, anyone who voted against the new proposal would be seen as anti-American and not overly concerned with responding to the attacks of 9-11. Democrats worked to ensure that all of the proposals that gave more authority to federal law enforcement would have court oversight. In many instances, this type of oversight was included in the bill, but in others, it was rejected as being redundant, as oversight was already granted to the courts. What hampered this political wrangling, however, turned out to be a new terroristic threat—anthrax.

One week after September 11, 2001, on September 18, someone began mailing letters containing anthrax spores to various media outlets such as ABC, CBS, and NBC News, as well as Senators Tom Daschle (D-SD) and Patrick Leahy (D-VT). Anthrax spores are a biological agent that appears as a white powder and can enter the body through inhalation, through the skin, as well as through ingestion. It causes a skin reaction and lesions and can lead to death.

BOX 4.6 Remarks on Signing the USA PATRIOT Act of 2001, October 26, 2001

We have seen the horrors terrorists can inflict. We may never know what horrors our country was spared by the diligent and determined work of our police forces, the FBI, ATF agents, Federal marshals, custom officers, Secret Service, intelligence professionals, and local law enforcement officials. Under the most trying conditions, they are serving this country with excellence and often with bravery.

They deserve our full support and every means of help that we can provide. We're dealing with terrorists who operate by highly sophisticated methods and technologies, some of which were not even available when our existing laws were written. The bill before me takes account of the new realities and dangers posed by modern terrorists. It will help law enforcement to identify, to dismantle, to disrupt, and to punish terrorists before they strike.

For example, this legislation gives law enforcement officials better tools to put an end to financial counterfeiting, smuggling, and money laundering. Secondly, it gives intelligence operations and criminal operations the chance to operate not on separate tracks but to share vital information so necessary to disrupt a terrorist attack before it occurs.

As of today, we're changing the laws governing information sharing. And as importantly, we're changing the culture of our various agencies that fight terrorism. Countering and investigating terrorist activity is the number one priority for both law enforcement and intelligence agencies. . .

This legislation is essential not only to pursuing and punishing terrorists but also preventing more atrocities in the hands of the evil ones. This Government will enforce this law with all the urgency of a nation at war. The elected branches of our Government and both political parties are united in our resolve to find and stop and punish those who would do harm to the American people.

It is now my honor to sign into law the USA PATRIOT Act of 2001.

Reproduced from: Bush, George W. (2001). "Remarks on Signing the USA PATRIOT ACT of 2001." Public Papers of the Presidents of the United States. Washington, D.C.: U.S. G.P.O.

In the case of the anthrax mailing, five people died and 17 others were infected. No one knew at the time if this was another Al Qaeda attack or an act of domestic terrorism (although one individual, Steven Hatfill, was suspected, the investigation shifted later to Bruce Ivins, who then committed suicide. No one was ever held accountable for these biological attacks). The result of the anthrax attacks, however, was to enhance the need to pass the USA PATRIOT Act. The act was introduced into the U.S. House of Representatives on October 23 and passed 357 to 66 on October 24, 2001. The following day, October 25, the Senate passed the bill 98 to 1 (Russ Feingold [D-WI] was the lone dissenter), and on October 26, 2001, President George W. Bush signed it into law (see **BOX 4.6**).

The bill, which had integrated numerous earlier proposals and several other bills that had been previously introduced into both the House and Senate, were organized around 10 titles (see **BOX 4.7**). Each of these titles consisted of numerous sections (numbering more than 1,000 in total) that detailed the new laws and modifications to previous laws. In fact, more than 15 previous acts, some dating as far back as 1934, were amended by the USA PATRIOT Act (see **BOX 4.8**). As a result, the bill was comprehensive and sweeping in scope. In order to protect against the possibility of too much power being included in the legislation, many of the act's provisions had a sunset clause, meaning that within a certain timeframe the law would no longer be on the books unless the provision was reauthorized by Congress. Most of these were set to expire on December 31, 2005.

Proponents of the USA PATRIOT Act found that it enhanced the sharing of information between intelligence and law enforcement agencies, tearing down the wall that separated them and allowing them to "connect the dots."[22] It has also been noted that the act gave investigators the same tools to go

BOX 4.7 USA PATRIOT Act (2001)—Ten Titles

Title I	Enhancing Domestic Security Against Terrorism
Title II	Surveillance Procedures
Title III	Anti-Money Laundering to Prevent Terrorism
Title IV	Border Security
Title V	Removing Obstacles to Investigating Terrorism
Title VI	Victims and Families of Victims of Terrorism
Title VII	Increased Information Sharing for Critical Infrastructure Protection
Title VIII	Terrorism Criminal Law
Title IX	Improved Intelligence
Title X	Miscellaneous

Reproduced from: P.L. 107-56, 115 Stat. 272 (2001), The Uniting and Strengthening America by Providing Appropriate Tools Required to Intercept and Obstruct Terrorism (USA PATRIOT ACT).

BOX 4.8 Federal Statutes Amended by the USA PATRIOT Act, 2001

Bank Holding Company Act of 1956 (12 USC 1841)
Communications Act of 1934 (47 USC 151)
Controlled Substances Import and Export Act (21 USC 951)
Controlled Substances Act (21 USC 826)
Electronic Communication Privacy Act of 1986 (18 USC 2510)
Fair Credit Reporting Act (15 USC 1681)
Federal Deposit Insurance Act (12 USC 1811)
Federal Wiretap Statute (18 USC 119)
Foreign Assistance Act of 1961 (22 USC 2291)
Foreign Intelligence Surveillance Act (50 USC 1805)
Intelligence Reform and Terrorism Prevention Act of 2004 (118 Stat. 3742)
National Security Act (50 USC 401)
Omnibus Crime Control and Safe Streets Act of 1968 (42 USC 3797)
Right to Financial Privacy Act of 1978 (12 USC 3401)
Violent Crime Control and Law Enforcement Act of 1994 (49 USC 46502)

Reproduced from: P.L. 107-56, 115 Stat. 272 (2001), The Uniting and Strengthening America by Providing Appropriate Tools Required to Intercept and Obstruct Terrorism (USA PATRIOT ACT).

after terrorists that it already had to go after criminals, particularly those involved in organized crime and drug trafficking, thus, allowing law enforcement to conduct investigations without tipping off terrorists. The act was also seen as updating the law to reflect not only the new threats to America but the new technologies that existed, such as cell phones and the Internet. In addition, there was much praise for the enhanced penalties for those who committed terroristic acts, allowing stiffer penalties for those who harbor terrorists, enhancing punishments for those conspiring against the government, and punishing bioterrorists. Finally, the act provided for both judicial and congressional oversight of these new laws and their enforcement to ensure that civil liberties would not be violated.

Opponents of the bill have noted that the law went too far in authorizing indefinite detentions of immigrants for purposes of investigations. They also pointed out that the ability of law enforcement to search homes and businesses without the owner's permission, or even their knowledge, went far beyond what similar legislation for organized crime and drug trafficking ever provided. Opponents also argued against the use of National Security Letters (NSLs), which allowed federal law enforcement, in the name of national security, to search telephone, cell phone, email, and financial records without a court order. Furthermore, the ability of law enforcement to request business records, cell phone logs, library records, and other financial records without even the National Security Letter was too much power and not enough protection for Americans' civil liberties. In addition, many argued that the oversight by the judiciary and Congress did not reach far enough.

Judicial challenges did surface, although these cases took time to work their way through the legal system. Several of the provisions were found unconstitutional and were struck down by federal judges, including the use of the National Security Letters to circumvent the need for court orders, as well as the warrantless searches into various records, including personal library records. Then, when the first authorization of the USA PATRIOT Act reached its first sunset period, the U.S. Congress amended the act, adding in enhanced security at seaports and new powers for the U.S. Secret Service but did not reauthorize two provisions within Title II related to roving wiretaps and access to business records, in part because of the court rulings.

There is no doubt that the USA PATRIOT Act gave federal law enforcement more power to track down, surveil, and investigate potential terrorists and terroristic threats. Yet, there is also little doubt that the ability given to the government has come at a cost of Americans' civil liberties. Any time government is given more power and authority, it encroaches upon the freedom of the people. Whether that encroachment is worth the price is an issue people continue to debate to this day.

The Homeland Security Act of 2002

Although President Bush had created the Office of Homeland Security within the White House, he initially opposed the idea of creating a cabinet-level bureaucracy. Members of the 107th Congress (2001–2002), however, wanted to create a more stable organization geared toward protecting the United States. A number of proposals were made by various members of Congress over the early months of 2002. One of those was by Senators Joseph Lieberman (D-CT) and Arlen Specter (R-PA) who introduced the Department of National Homeland Security Act of 2001 (S 1534) that would create a cabinet-level Department of National Homeland Security.

At the same time, in the U.S. House, Representative Richard K. Armey (R-TX) proposed the National

Homeland Security Act of 2002 (HR 5005). This proposal sought to establish a Department of Homeland Security, an executive department that would be headed by a Secretary who was appointed by the President with the advice and consent of the Senate. The new department would be responsible for: (1) overseeing policies for preventing terrorist attacks within the United States; (2) passing new laws that reduce the vulnerability of the United States to terrorism; (3) minimizing the damage done during a terrorist attack and assisting in the recovery from such attacks; (4) carrying out all functions of those agencies transferred to DHS; (5) ensuring that the functions of the agencies within DHS not related directly to protecting the country are not diminished; (6) ensuring that the overall economic security of the United States is not diminished by any activities related to protecting the United States; and (7) monitoring possible connections between illegal drug trafficking and terrorism.[23] Under Armey's proposal, the new department would be composed of the U.S. Customs Service, the Transportation Security Administration, the Federal Protective Service of the General Services Administration, the Federal Law Enforcement Training Center, and the Office for Domestic Preparedness within the Office of Justice Programs of the Department of Justice.[24]

The Bush administration initially resisted both proposals to develop a cabinet-level department with the responsibility of overseeing homeland security. Bush argued that the job could best be handled out of the White House Office of Homeland Security, which former Governor Tom Ridge was already at work in advancing based on President Bush's Executive Order. After Congressional support seemed to be gaining for the idea of a new department, the White House abruptly reversed its position and proposed its own plan. On June 6th, President Bush announced his proposal for a new Department of Homeland Security. In a speech before a joint session of Congress, Bush noted that "We've got to get used to the fact that they want to come again,"[25] and that "… our government must be reorganized to deal most effectively with the new threats of the 21st century."[26] Bush went on to announce a plan to create a new Cabinet-level department that would coordinate national efforts to prevent terrorism (see text of speech, **BOX 4.9**). This new department would consist of entire agencies or portions of over 40 agencies and departments that already played a role in protecting the United States.

The majority of Congressional members supported the proposal for reorganizing the federal agencies to enable the country to fight terrorism more

BOX 4.9 President Bush's Statement Proposing Department of Homeland Security

. . . So tonight I ask the Congress to join me in creating a single, permanent department with an overriding and urgent mission—securing the homeland of America and protecting the American people. Right now as many as a 100 different government agencies have some responsibilities for homeland security, and no one has final accountability. For example, the Coast Guard has several missions, from search and rescue to maritime treaty enforcement. It reports to the Transportation Department, whose primary responsibilities are roads, rails, bridges, and the airways. The Customs Service, among other duties, collects tariffs and prevents smuggling, and it is part of the Treasury Department, whose primary responsibility is fiscal policy, not security.

Tonight I propose a permanent Cabinet-level Department of Homeland Security to unite essential agencies that must work more closely together, among them, the Coast Guard, the Border Patrol, the Customs Service, Immigration officials, the Transportation Security Administration, and the Federal Emergency Management Agency. Employees of this new agency will come to work every morning knowing their most important job is to protect their fellow citizens. The Department of Homeland Security will be charged with four primary tasks. This new agency will control our borders and prevent terrorists and explosives from entering our country. It will work with state and local authorities to respond quickly and effectively to emergencies. It will bring together our best scientists to develop technologies that detect biological, chemical, and nuclear weapons, and to discover the drugs and treatments to best protect our citizens; and this new department will review intelligence and law enforcement information from all agencies of government and produce a single daily picture of threats against our homeland. Analysts will be responsible for imagining the worst and planning to counter it. The reason to create this department is not to [increase] the size of government but to increase its focus and effectiveness. The staff of this new department will be largely drawn from the agencies we are combining. By ending duplication and overlap, we will spend less on overhead and more on protecting America. This reorganization will give the good people of our government their best opportunity to succeed by organizing our resources in a way that is thorough and unified.

What I am proposing tonight is the most extensive reorganization of the federal government since the 1940s. . . .

Reproduced from: Bush, George W. (2002). "Address to the Nation on the Proposed Department of Homeland Security." Public Papers of the Presidents of the United States. Washington, D.C.: U.S. GPO.

BOX 4.10 Remarks on Signing the Homeland Security Act of 2002, November 25, 2002

The new department will analyze threats, will guard our borders and airports, protect our critical infrastructure, and coordinate the response of our nation to future emergencies. The Department of Homeland Security will focus the full resources of the American government on the safety of the American people . . . .

Dozens of agencies charged with homeland security will now be located within one Cabinet department, with the mandate and legal authority to protect our people. America will be better able to respond to any future attacks, to reduce our vulnerability and, most important, prevent the terrorists from taking innocent American lives.

The Department of Homeland Security will have nearly 170,000 employees, dedicated professionals . . . .When the Department of Homeland Security is fully operational, it will enhance the safety of our people in very practical ways. First, this new department will analyze intelligence information on terror threats collected by the CIA, the FBI, the National Security Agency, and others . . . . Second, the department will gather and focus all our efforts to face the challenge of cyberterrorism and the even worse danger of nuclear, chemical, and biological terrorism. This department will be charged with encouraging research on new technologies that can detect these threats in time to prevent an attack. Third, state and local governments will be able to turn for help and information to one federal domestic security agency, instead of more than 20 agencies that currently divide these responsibilities. This will help our local governments work in concert with the federal government for the sake of all the people of America. Fourth, the new department will bring together the agencies responsible for border, coastline, and transportation security. There will be a coordinated effort to safeguard our transportation systems and to secure the border so that we're better able to protect our citizens and welcome our friends. Fifth, the department will work with state and local officials to prepare our response to any future terrorist attack that may come. We have found that the first hours and even the first minutes after the attack can be crucial in saving lives, and our first-responders need the carefully planned and drilled strategies that will make their work effective.

Reproduced from: Bush, George W. (2002). "Remarks by the President at the Signing of H.R. 5005 the Homeland Security Act of 2002." Public Papers of the Presidents of the United States. Washington, D.C.: U.S. GPO.

effectively. Nonetheless, there was much discussion and heated deliberations about the President's proposal. On a number of occasions, proposals were put forth to bring the CIA, the FBI, and the National Security Agency (NSA) under the Department of Homeland Security, but after numerous debates and avid support against such plans, the legislation failed. Some Democrats in the House were worried that Bush's plan was inadequate and possibly even counterproductive. They thought it would only result in a larger bureaucracy without making the "parts" work together more effectively. Others argued that the Bush proposal was not "budget neutral" and would inflate the cost of doing business far beyond what the current agency structure spent on an annual basis.[27]

Ultimately, after the fall mid-term elections in 2002, there was enough support and the proposal passed Congress. The House of Representatives voted in favor 299 to 121 on November 13, 2002, and the U.S. Senate passed the bill 90 to 9 on November 19, 2002. The new Department of Homeland Security was established when President Bush signed the Homeland Security Act of 2002 on November 25, 2002 (see **BOX 4.10**).[28]

Former Pennsylvania Governor Tom Ridge, who was then serving as the Director of the Office of Homeland Security, was nominated to serve as the first Secretary of Homeland Security. Once confirmed by the U.S. Senate, he was charged with carrying out the organizational planning that ultimately joined more than 179,000 federal employees from 22 existing federal agencies (often in multiple components from one agency) to report to one single, Cabinet-level organization. The Department of Homeland Security officially opened on January 24, 2003.

Homeland Security Presidential Directives

As previously mentioned, President George W. Bush, not long after the creation of the Office of Homeland Security, created the President's Homeland Security Advisory Council and Senior Advisory Committee for Homeland Security. He did this through Executive Order 13260, which he signed on March 19, 2002.[29] This was the first of a number of presidential executive orders that Bush signed related to homeland security. The next was Executive Order 13311, pertaining to homeland security information sharing, and then another order titled Strengthening the Sharing of Terrorism Information to Protect Americans (#13356), both of which allowed intelligence agencies to share information related to potential domestic terrorism threats with other federal agencies.[30] Previously, intelligence agencies generally could not share this information with other federal agencies due to its high-level classification. Finally, Executive Order 13407, Public Alert and Warning System, created the often-ridiculed and derided color-coded warning system that signified to the U.S. public the current terrorist threat level.[31] These executive orders, which have the full force of the law, are a means by which the president can direct certain officers and agencies within the Executive branch of the government. In these instances, President Bush was directing federal agencies on new practices that they would implement, such as high-level information sharing, the creation of a Homeland Security Advisory Council, and the use of a public alert and warning system.

There is another means by which presidents can also issue directives to executive branch officers and agencies, and that is through what are known as presidential directives. These directives are a form of executive orders but are usually created through the advice and consent of a particular council. In the past, the main council for these directives has almost always been the National Security Council, and the topics have been related to national security. Bush wanted to develop the same relationship between the president and his Homeland Security Council as existed between the president and the National Security Council. Therefore, like the issuance of National Security Presidential Directives, Bush would issue **Homeland Security Presidential Directives**. During his two terms in office, President Bush issued 25 such directives (see **BOX 4.11**).

The first two Homeland Security Presidential Directives (HSPDs) were issued on October 29, 2001, and were related to the organization and operation of the Homeland Security Council (HSPD-1) and Combating Terrorism Through Immigration Policies (HSPD-2). Additional Homeland Security Presidential Directives included the management of domestic incidents (HSPD-5) and how federal agencies needed to prepare for certain emergencies (HSPD-8). These two directives, in particular, became critical to the development of the National Incident Management System (later called the National Incident Management Framework), which was focused on developing a national response to both natural disasters and terroristic attacks, and the creation of the Incident Command System (ICS) as the primary means for carrying out such responses at the federal, state, and local levels. Other Homeland Security Presidential directives were related to domestic nuclear detection (HSPD-14) and maritime security (HSPD-13). The last Bush-issued

BOX 4.11 Homeland Security Presidential Directives

HSPD-1	Organization and Operation of the Homeland Security Council Oct. 1, 2001
HSPD-2	Combating Terrorism Through Immigration Policies Oct. 1, 2001
HSPD-3	Homeland Security Advisory System Mar. 11, 2002
HSPD-4	National Strategy to Combat Weapons of Mass Destruction Dec. 11, 2002
HSPD-5	Management of Domestic Incidents Feb. 28, 2003
HSPD-6	Integration and Use of Screening Information Sep. 16, 2003
HSPD-7	Critical Infrastructure Identification, Prioritization, and Protection Dec. 17, 2003
HSPD-8	National Preparedness Dec. 17, 2003
HSPD-9	Defense of United States Agriculture and Food Feb. 3, 2004
HSPD-10	Biodefense for the 21st Century Apr. 28, 2004
HSPD-11	Comprehensive Terrorist-Related Screening Procedures Aug. 27, 2004
HSPD-12	Common ID Standard for Federal Employees/Contractors Aug. 27, 2004
HSPD-13	Maritime Security Policy Dec. 21, 2004
HSPD-14	Domestic Nuclear Detection Office Apr. 15, 2005
HSPD-15	U.S. Strategy and Policy in the War on Terror (Classified) Classified
HSPD-16	National Strategy for Aviation Security June 22, 2006
HSPD-17	Nuclear Materials Information Program Aug. 28, 2006
HSPD-18	Medical Countermeasures Against Weapons of Mass Destruction Jan. 31, 2007
HSPD-19	Combating Terrorist Use of Explosives in the United States Feb. 12, 2007
HPSD-20	National Continuity Policy Apr. 4, 2007
HSPD-21	Public Health and Medical Preparedness Oct. 18, 2007
HSPD-22	Domestic Chemical Defense Classified
HSPD-23	Cyber Security and Monitoring Jan. 8, 2008
HSPD-24	Biometrics for ID and Screening to Enhance National Security Jun. 5, 2008
HSPD-25	Arctic Region Policy Jan. 9, 2009

Reproduced from: Bush, George W. (2001-2009). Homeland Security Presidential Directives.

© Joe Marquette/AP/Shutterstock.

directive was related to security in the Arctic region (HSPD-25). Several of these HSPDs remain classified, due to the nature of the directive, but the majority are unclassified and available to the public.

Quadrennial Homeland Security Reviews

One requirement that was included in the Homeland Security Act of 2002 was the need to reevaluate the Department of Homeland Security on a routine basis. With this in mind, the law states, "in fiscal year 2009, and every 4 years thereafter, the Secretary shall conduct a review of the homeland security of the Nation."[32] The four-year review, a quadrennial review, is intended to be "a comprehensive examination of the Homeland Security strategy of the Nation, including recommendations regarding the long-term strategy and priorities of the National for Homeland Security and Guidance on the programs, assets, capabilities, budget, policies, and authorities of the Department."[33] The first quadrennial review was released in 2010, the second one in 2014, and the next review should have been released in 2018.

The quadrennial review for the Department of Homeland Security was modeled after the Defense Department's Quadrennial Defense Review, which has been considered a successful means of implementing organizational change in that department. In light of the fact that Homeland Security is a large department, it was believed that the methods by the even larger Defense Department would be workable. When the first Quadrennial Homeland Security Review (QHSR) was released in 2010, it was seen as "a concerted national effort to ensure a homeland that is safe, secure, and resilient against terrorism and other hazards where American interests, aspirations, and way of life can thrive."[34] According to Kahan's study (2015), "DHS and its federal government partners found the first QHSR helpful in providing national-level strategic guidance for executing their range of responsibilities."[35] The document was well received, but many suggestions were made for the conduct of the next review, which took place in 2014. As Kahan also explains, "The second QHSR, published in June 2014, builds upon the materials in the initial document, most importantly by providing an analytically based set of prioritized missions and associated goals for use by DHS and the entire HSE [Homeland Security Enterprise] in planning programs and policies for improving their security."[36] He does add that there was a more mixed review over the second quadrennial review, noting that many of the issues with the first review were not resolved in the second, and that the 2014 review did not elicit as much change as the first review had upon its publication.[37] There is some hope that the 2018 review will work to resolve these issues by recommending organizational changes to both the Department of Homeland Security and the entire Homeland Security Enterprise.

The strength of the quadrennial reviews is that it forces the Department of Homeland Security to reevaluate its mission and how this large bureaucracy organizes for the defense of the homeland, in the hopes of continual improvement. The greatest weakness in the quadrennial reviews, however, is that the change, so far, has focused primarily on the Department of Homeland Security and other federal-level stakeholders but has done nothing to focus on change with regard to those below the national government, including state and local agencies in the homeland security apparatus.

Chapter Summary

The terrorist attacks on September 11, 2001, called for an American response both overseas and domestically. In the immediate aftermath, to more effectively deal with future attacks as well as natural disasters, the President created the Office of Homeland Security in the White House and issued executive orders and Homeland Security Presidential Directives. The U.S. Congress passed the USA PATRIOT Act of 2001 and the Homeland Security Act of 2002, the former a wide array of laws giving federal law enforcement more investigatory powers for purposes of anti-terrorism and counter-terrorism, while the latter set in motion the creation of a new cabinet-level Department of Homeland Security. Once the new Secretary of Homeland Security, Tom Ridge, was confirmed, the new department came into existence and began consolidating all of the agencies and agency components that made up the new department. This represented the largest organizational shift in federal bureaucracy since World War II. In order to assist in directing the Department of Homeland Security, the president issued a series of policy directives, and the Homeland Security Act of 2002 required a quadrennial review, beginning in 2010, to reevaluate the department's mission and organizational practices to suggest future organizational change.

Review/Discussion Questions

1. Explain the difference between the White House/Executive Branch Office of Homeland Security and the Department of Homeland Security.
2. How was the USA PATRIOT Act, a comprehensive piece of legislation, passed so quickly in just 6 weeks? Where did all of the provisions within the bill come from?
3. What is the Homeland Security Act of 2002, how did it come about, and what did it do?
4. What is a Homeland Security Presidential Directive, how many have there been, and how have they contributed to Homeland Security in the United States?

Additional Readings

The Homeland Security Act of 2002. HR 5005; PL 107–296; 116 Stat. 2135. Retrieved online at http://www.dhs.gov/xlibrary/assets/hr_5005_enr.pdf.

National Commission on Terrorist Attacks Upon the United States. (2004). *The 9/11 Commission Report: Final Report of the National Commission on Terrorist Attacks Upon the United States (Authorized Ed.).* New York: W.W. Norton & Company, Inc.

O'Harrow, R., Jr. (2002). "Six Weeks in Autumn." *The Washington Post.* Retrieved online at http://www.washingtonpost.com/wp-dyn/content/article/2006/05/09/AR2006050900961.html.

U.S. Department of Justice. (2013). USA PATRIOT Act. Retrieved online at http://www.justice.gov/archive/ll/highlights.htm.

Endnotes

1. Portions of the introduction are based on the 9/11 Commission Report. See National Commission on Terrorist Attacks Upon the United States. (2004). *The 9/11 Commission Report: Final Report of the National Commission on Terrorist Attacks Upon the United States (Authorized Ed.).* New York: W.W. Norton & Company, Inc.
2. National Commission on Terrorist Attacks Upon the United States. (2004). *The 9/11 Commission Report: Final Report of the National Commission on Terrorist Attacks Upon the United States (Authorized Ed.).* New York: W.W. Norton & Company, Inc., p. 38.
3. National Commission on Terrorist Attacks Upon the United States. (2004). *The 9/11 Commission Report: Final Report of the National Commission on Terrorist Attacks Upon the United States (Authorized Ed.).* New York: W.W. Norton & Company, Inc., p. 39.
4. National Commission on Terrorist Attacks Upon the United States. (2004). *The 9/11 Commission Report: Final Report of the National Commission on Terrorist Attacks Upon the United States (Authorized Ed.).* New York: W.W. Norton & Company, Inc., p. 326.
5. National Commission on Terrorist Attacks Upon the United States. (2004). *The 9/11 Commission Report: Final Report of the National Commission on Terrorist Attacks Upon the United States (Authorized Ed.).* New York: W.W. Norton & Company, Inc.
6. Bush, G. W. (2001). "Remarks While Touring Damage at the Pentagon in Arlington, Virginia. September 12, 2001." *Public Papers of the Presidents of the United States.* Washington, DC: U.S. G.P.O.
7. Bush, G. W. (2001). "Remarks to Police, Firemen, and Rescue Workers at the World Trade Center Site in New York City. September 14, 2001." *Public Papers of the Presidents of the United States.* Washington, DC: U.S. G.P.O.
8. Bush, G. W. (2001). "Remarks to Police, Firemen, and Rescue Workers at the World Trade Center Site in New York City. September 14, 2001." *Public Papers of the Presidents of the United States.* Washington, DC: U.S. G.P.O.
9. Bush, G. W. (2001). "Remarks to Police, Firemen, and Rescue Workers at the World Trade Center Site in New York City. September 14, 2001." *Public Papers of the Presidents of the United States.* Washington, DC: U.S. G.P.O.
10. Bush, G. W. (2001). "Remarks to Police, Firemen, and Rescue Workers at the World Trade Center Site in New York City. September 14, 2001." *Public Papers of the Presidents of the United States.* Washington, DC: U.S. G.P.O.

11. Bush, G. W. (2001). "Remarks to Police, Firemen, and Rescue Workers at the World Trade Center Site in New York City. September 14, 2001." *Public Papers of the Presidents of the United States.* Washington, DC: U.S. G.P.O.
12. Bush, G. W. (2001). "Executive Order Establishing Office of Homeland Security. October 8, 2001." Retrieved online at http://georgewbush-whitehouse.archives.gov/news/releases/2001/10/print/20011008-2.html
13. Bush, G. W. (2001). "Executive Order Establishing Office of Homeland Security. October 8, 2001." Retrieved online at http://georgewbush-whitehouse.archives.gov/news/releases/2001/10/print/20011008-2.html
14. Becker, E. & Weiner, T. (2001). "A Nation Challenged: Homeland Security; New Office to Become a White House Agency." *New York Times*, September 28, p. A1.
15. Bush, G. W. (2001). "Executive Order Establishing Office of Homeland Security. October 8, 2001." Retrieved online at http://georgewbush-whitehouse.archives.gov/news/releases/2001/10/print/20011008-2.html
16. Bush, G. W. (2001). "Executive Order Establishing the President's Homeland Security Advisory Council and Senior Advisory Committees for Homeland Security. March 21, 2001." Retrieved online at http://georgewbush-whitehouse.archives.gov/news/releases/2002/03/20020321-9.html
17. Spencer, J., & Scardaville, M. (2002). "Federal Homeland Security Policy." The Heritage Foundation. Retrieved online at http://www.heritage.org/research/reports/2002/06/federal-homeland-security-policy
18. Downs, A. (1972). "Up and Down with Ecology: The 'Issue-Attention Cycle.'" *The Public Interest, 28*, 38–50.
19. Petersen, K. K. (2009). "Revisiting Downs' Issue-Attention Cycle: International Terrorism and U.S. Public Opinion." *Journal of Strategic Security, 2*, 1–16.
20. Kingdon, J. W. (2011). *Agendas, Alternatives, and Public Policies.* 2nd ed. Boston, MA: Longman.
21. O'Harrow, R., Jr. (2002). "Six Weeks in Autumn." *The Washington Post.* Retrieved online at http://www.washingtonpost.com/wp-dyn/content/article/2006/05/09/AR2006050900961.html
22. U.S. Department of Justice. (2012). "The USA PATRIOT Act: Preserving Life and Liberty." Retrieved online at http://www.justice.gov/archive/ll/highlights.htm, or Sauter, M. A. & Carafano, J. J. (2012). *A Complete Guide to Homeland Security.* New York, NY: McGraw Hill.
23. Congress.gov. (2002). "Bill Summary and Status: 107th Congress" http://thomas.loc.gov/cgi-bin/bdquery/z?d107:HR05005:@@@D&summ2=m&.
24. Congress.gov. (2002). "New Security Office Scrutinized" in *CQ Almanac 2001* 57th ed., 10-4-10-5. Washington, DC: Congressional Quarterly. http://library.cqpress.com/cqalmanac/cqal01-106-6372-328132.
25. Bush, G. W. (2002). "Remarks at the World Pork Expo in Des Moines, Iowa," Online by Peters, G. & Woolley, J. T. *The American Presidency Project*, http://www.presidency,ucsb.edu/ws/?pid=73027.
26. Bush, G. W. "The President's Radio Address" June 8, 2002, Online by Peters, G. & Woolley, J. T. *The American Presidency Project*, https://georgewbush-whitehouse.archives.gov/news/releases/2002/06/20020608-1.html
27. "Homeland Department Created," in *CQ Almanac 2002* 58th ed., 7-3-7-8. Washington, DC: Congressional Quarterly, 2003. http://library.cqpress.com/cqalmanac/cqal02-236-10378-664466
28. The Homeland Security Act of 2002. (2002). HR 5005; PL 107–296; 116 Stat. 2135. Retrieved online at http://www.dhs.gov/xlibrary/assets/hr_5005_enr.pdf
29. Bush, G. W. (2002). Executive Order 13260 of March 19, 2002. Establishing the President's Homeland Security Advisory Council and Senior Advisory Committee for Homeland Security. Retrieved online at http://www.fas.org/irp/offdocs/eo/eo-13260.htm.
30. Bush, G. W. (2003). Executive Order 13311 of July 29, 2003, Homeland Security Information Sharing. Retrieved online at http://www.fas.org/irp/offdocs/eo/eo-13311.htm; Bush, G. W. (2004). Executive Order 13356 of August 27, 2004, Strengthening the Sharing of Terrorism Information to Protect Americans. Retrieved online at http://www.fas.org/irp/offdocs/eo/eo-13356.htm
31. Bush, G. W. (2006). Executive Order 13407 of June 26, 2006, Public Alert and Warning System. Retrieved online at http://www.fas.org/irp/offdocs/eo/eo-13407.htm
32. U.S. Congress. (2002). *Homeland Security Act of 2002.* Retrieved online at https://legcounsel.house.gov/Comps/Homeland%20Security%20Act%20Of%202002.pdf
33. U.S. Congress. (2002). *Homeland Security Act of 2002.* Retrieved online at https://legcounsel.house.gov/Comps/Homeland%20Security%20Act%20Of%202002.pdf
34. U.S. Department of Homeland Security. (2010). *Quadrennial Homeland Security Review Report: A Strategic Framework for a Secure Homeland.* Retrieved online at https://www.dhs.gov/sites/default/files/publications/2010-qhsr-report.pdf
35. Kahan, J. (2015). "Quadrennial Homeland Security Reviews: What Value for Whom?" *Homeland Security & Emergency Management, 12*, 211–240, 213.
36. Kahan, J. (2015). "Quadrennial Homeland Security Reviews: What Value for Whom?" *Homeland Security and Emergency Management, 12*, 211–240, p. 212.
37. U.S. Department of Justice. (2014). *The 2014 Quadrennial Homeland Security Review.* Retrieved online at https://www.dhs.gov/sites/default/files/publications/2014-qhsr-final-508.pdf.

Courtesy of U.S. Department of Homeland Security

CHAPTER 5

The Department of Homeland Security

CHAPTER OBJECTIVES

- To develop an overview of the Department of Homeland Security (DHS)
- To understand the organizational structure of DHS
- To understand the missions and goals of DHS

CHAPTER OUTLINE

NEW DEPARTMENT—DHS
- Leadership
- Organization and Mission
- Budget

DHS's ROLE TODAY
- Preventing Terrorism/Enhancing Security
- Enforcement of Immigration Laws
- Security of U.S. Borders
- Protecting Cyberspace
- Preparedness, Response, and Recovery: Resilience to Disasters

CHAPTER SUMMARY

About a month after the 9-11 terrorist attacks, President George W. Bush used his power of executive order to establish the Office of Homeland Security, which would be responsible for coordinating all homeland security efforts geared toward preventing another terrorist attack similar to that of 9-11.[1] The office was given five basic responsibilities, the first of which was to work with federal, state, and local agencies to prepare for a possible terrorist event. Second, the office was to mitigate the consequences of terrorist threats and attacks. Third, personnel from the office were to coordinate efforts between federal agents and other agencies to prevent terrorist attacks within the U.S. Protecting critical infrastructure from terrorist attacks was the fourth responsibility; and the last was providing incident management, continuity of government, and the development of programs geared toward educating the public about preventing terrorism.

President Bush immediately appointed Tom Ridge, the former governor of Pennsylvania, a Vietnam Veteran, and past member of the House of Representatives, as the head of the new office. He was assigned the title of Assistant to the President for Homeland Security. According to the White House, Ridge's job would be similar to that of the National Security Advisor; he would be responsible for making policy and advising the president on homeland security measures. Joining Ridge in advising the president was a new Homeland Security Council, also created in the president's executive order. The Council was composed of representatives of the Executive branch, including the Attorney General of the United States, the Secretaries of Defense, Treasury, Agriculture, and Health and Human Services; and the directors of the FBI and the Federal Emergency Management Agency (**FEMA**).[2]

Although the **Office of Homeland Security** was a first step in creating a consistent federal policy to protect America from terrorism, many members of Congress sought a more permanent agency for overseeing homeland security policies. In 1992, Congress passed the Homeland Security Act (PL 107-296) that advanced the status of the Council to a Cabinet-level department: The **Department of Homeland Security**.

New Department—DHS

The intent of the Homeland Security Act was to realign government operations and communications into one organization by moving agencies responsible for national security into one group. The law consolidated all (or portions of) 22 existing federal agencies and departments that had some responsibility for homeland security into the new Department of Homeland Security (DHS). This was the largest reorganization of the federal government since the beginning of the Cold War.[3] Some of the more well-known agencies that were relocated into DHS included FEMA, the U.S. Coast Guard, U.S. Border Patrol, U.S. Customs Service, the Federal Protective Service, and the Transportation Security Administration (TSA).[4] Another federal agency, the Secret Service, would report directly to the Secretary of Homeland Security and retain its primary mission to protect the President and other government leaders.[5] The Immigration and Naturalization Service was split into two separate components, including an Immigration Enforcement Bureau (to protect borders and keep out illegal immigrants) and a Citizenship Bureau (to handle immigration services).[6] A list of the agencies reorganized into DHS is provided in **TABLE 5.1**.

The new Department was assigned three critical objectives, which were to (1) prevent terrorist attacks within the U.S., (2) reduce America's vulnerability to terrorism, and (3) minimize the damage from potential attacks and natural disasters.[7] Additionally, four goals were identified for the new department. The first of the goals concerned border and transportation security. As President Bush described, "We must closely monitor who is coming into and out of our country to help prevent foreign terrorists from entering our country and bringing in their instruments of terror . . . we must expedite the legal flow of people and goods on which our economy depends." In other words, the department was to find a way to prevent terrorists from entering the country, while, at the same time, allowing for trade to continue.[8] Another goal focused on emergency preparedness and response. It was important that the country prepare for possible attacks and minimize the damage if one does occur. It was also necessary to be able to recover quickly from attacks. A third DHS goal was to prepare countermeasures for possible chemical, biological, radiological, and nuclear attacks. The last goal was to increase the country's ability to collect and analyze information while protecting critical infrastructures.

The department was organized into four primary divisions. The first was Border and Transportation Security, which was composed of border control and transportation agencies. This division was given the responsibility for setting U.S. visa policy and securing U.S. borders and transportation systems. The second became the Emergency Preparedness and Response division, which included FEMA and the functions of other agencies charged with preparing for and responding to terror attacks. The third division

TABLE 5.1 Reorganization of Agencies Into DHS

New Agency	Old Agency
U.S. Customs and Border Protection	Justice and Treasury
Immigration and Customs Enforcement	Justice and Treasury
Federal Protective Service	General Services Administration
Transportation Security Administration	Transportation
Federal Law Enforcement Training Center	Treasury
Animal and Plant Health Inspection Service (Part)	Agriculture
Office for Domestic Preparedness	Justice
Federal Emergency Management Agency	None
Nuclear Incident Response Team	Energy
Domestic Emergency Support Teams	Justice
National Domestic Preparedness Office	FBI
CBRN Countermeasures Programs	Energy
Environmental Measurements Laboratory	Energy
National Biological Warfare Defense Analysis Center	Defense
Plum Island Animal Disease Center	Agriculture
Federal Computer Incident Response Center	General Services Administration
National Communications System	Defense
National Infrastructure Protection Center	Federal Bureau of Investigation (FBI)
Energy Security and Assurance Program	Energy
U.S. Coast Guard	Transportation
U.S. Secret Service	Treasury

Data from: Department of Homeland Security. (2013). "Who Joined DHS?" Retrieved online at http://www.dhs.gov/who-joined-dhs

was Science and Technology, which was composed of different programs and efforts related to science and technology and was given the task of developing countermeasures against terror attacks involving weapons of mass destruction such as chemical, biological, radiological, and nuclear. The final division was the Information Analysis and Infrastructure Protection section, which was responsible for analyzing all intelligence information on potential terrorist action against the country and for evaluating critical U.S. infrastructure for vulnerabilities to terrorism. Each division was headed by an undersecretary.[9]

Relations between the federal, state, and local governments were streamlined in the new department. A new Intergovernmental Affairs group would coordinate federal homeland security programs with state and local officials. This would give state and local officials one primary contact in the federal government for issues concerning training, equipment, planning, emergency response, or other critical needs.

The law provided for a 1-year extension for airports to install equipment to screen baggage at airports to detect explosives. It also limited the legal liability for airport screening companies and provided that noncitizen U.S. nationals could work as airport passenger and baggage screeners. Related to this were provisions to require the TSA to create a program for training commercial airline pilots to carry weapons aboard aircraft. Those pilots who volunteer will be trained, and if they achieve proficiency comparable to that for air marshals and meet other TSA requirements, they may be deputized as federal flight deck officers and then allowed to carry firearms.[10]

Leadership

Tom Ridge was named Secretary of the new Department of Homeland Security on January 24, 2003. Upon his swearing-in, he said his job is "to develop the organizational framework needed to refocus and reorganize the department's workforce to accomplish the unified mission of protecting America."[11] Following the re-election of President Bush, Ridge resigned. Admiral James Milton Loy then became the Acting Secretary of Homeland Security serving from February 1, 2005, to February 15, 2005. During this time, Bush nominated the former Commissioner of the New York City Police Department, Bernard Kerik, to replace Ridge. Kerik was forced to withdraw his nomination on December 10, citing personal reasons (he explained that he had hired an illegal immigrant as a nanny for his children). On January 11, 2005, Bush then nominated federal judge Michael Chertoff to serve as the second Homeland Security secretary. Chertoff was confirmed on February 15, 2005, by a vote of 98-0 in the U.S. Senate. He was sworn in the same day.

The third head of the Department of Homeland Security was Janet Napolitano. Nominated by President Obama, the Senate confirmed Napolitano's appointment on January 20, 2009. In order to assist in the transition, Chertoff did not resign until January 21, 2009. Napolitano established the National Terrorism Advisory System that was a two-tiered system to identify threats. This included an "imminent threat" and an "elevated threat." She also instituted the well-known "If You See Something, Say Something" campaign that encouraged all people to report suspicious activities to law enforcement. Project Global Shield, a program to prevent the theft of precursor chemicals that could be used to make explosive devices, became more established during her tenure, as did the E-Verify system to ensure that a business's workforce was legal.

When Napolitano resigned in September, 2013, former Marine Rand Beers served as Acting Secretary until December, 2013, when Jeh Johnson was nominated to serve as the Secretary by President Obama. After his nomination was approved, Johnson was sworn in as the fourth person to head the agency. Johnson, a lawyer, previously served as an assistant U.S. Attorney in New York and as the General Counsel for the Department of Defense. As the Secretary, Johnson implemented numerous management improvements within the organization.

As expected, Johnson focused a great deal of time on preventing cybersecurity and immigration. He rebuked calls to abolish Immigration and Custom Enforcement (ICE), but also faced scrutiny for separating families that were attempting to enter the United States illegally at the border. As a result, a class-action lawsuit was filed against Johnson and others for detaining the families in unsafe and unhealthy conditions. Before leaving office, and as a result of allegations of Russian involvement in the 2016 presidential elections, Johnson declared the electoral system to be part of the country's "critical infrastructure." This meant that election equipment would be considered equivalent to the country's power grid or financial sector in terms of providing protection for the polling places, equipment, and databases.

Johnson resigned from the position in January 2017. He was replaced by John F. Kelley, who served from January, 2017 until July 31, 2017. A career military officer (serving in the Marines from 1970–1972 and from 1975–2016), Kelley supported tough immigration policies proposed by the administration, including reducing the number of refugees admitted to the United States while, at the same time, increasing deportation of undocumented immigrants. In February, he ordered agents in the agency to deport every undocumented immigrant whom they identified, and then in June withdrew a policy that halted those with green cards from being deported if they were able to pass a criminal background check. He noted that a border wall along the Mexican/U.S. border would not solve the problems associated with illegal immigration. He supported the administration's travel ban attached to countries that had predominantly Muslim residents and the policy of removing children from their parents at the border.

Upon his resignation in July 2017, Elaine Duke took over as acting secretary and was in that office

BOX 5.1 Kirstjen M. Nielsen: Former Secretary of Homeland Security

Kirstjen Neilsen earned a B.S. in Foreign Service from Georgetown University and was then awarded a J.D. from the University of Virginia. In 2004, President George W. Bush asked her to be part of the White House Security Council to serve as the Special Assistant for Prevention, Preparedness, and Response. In this position, Neilson helped to develop and implement various policies regarding homeland security. She also oversaw the Office of Legislative Policy and Government Affairs, part of the Transportation Security Administration. Neilsen then became the President and General Counsel for Civitas Group, LLC, an investment firm with an emphasis on homeland security. In 2012, Neilsen founded the Sunesis Consulting firm, a consulting firm for preparedness plans regarding critical infrastructure. In 2017, President Trump asked Nielsen to serve as the Chief of Staff to John Kelly, the Secretary of DHS at the time. Upon Kelly's resignation, Trump nominated Neilsen to serve as the head of the DHS. She served in this position until her resignation on April 7, 2019. As of April 11, 2019, Kevin McAleenan is serving as the acting secretary of DHS. Before that, he served in Customs and Border Protection.

Source: Neilson, K. The White House. https://www.whitehouse.gov/people/kirstjen-nielsen/

until December 6. At that time, Kirstjen Nielsen was sworn in as the Sixth Secretary of Homeland Security (See **BOX 5.1**). She served on the White House Homeland Security Council during the Bush Administration and then as the chief of staff to John Kelley at DHS. As the head of DHS, Nielsen supported President Trump's proposal to build a wall to keep out illegal immigrants, as well as the administration's policy of separating children from their parents at the U.S. border if the parents were prosecuted for entering the country illegally. She did not support sanctuary cities[12] and supported an increased presence of military at the border.[13] Nielsen agreed with the allegation that Russians attempted to interfere in the 2016 presidential campaign in an effort to help Trump, an allegation she had previously denied knowing anything about.

Courtesy of US Department of Homeland Security.

Organization and Mission

DHS is currently the third-largest, Cabinet-level department within the federal government, trailing behind the Departments of Defense and Veteran's Affairs.[14] The agency is overseen by the Secretary of Homeland Security, who is nominated by the President and confirmed by the Senate. The Secretary is assisted by a Deputy Secretary and a chief of staff (see **FIGURE 5.2**), and the headquarters are in Washington, D.C. in a former naval facility, with many other satellite offices located throughout the city.[15]

The mission of DHS is: "With honor and integrity, we will safeguard the American people, our homeland, and our values." In general, they seek to protect the United States and its territories from terrorist attacks, man-made accidents, and natural disasters. To do this effectively, DHS was organized into different offices (see **FIGURE 5.1**). The current organization of the agency is somewhat different after various reorganizations took place to allow the agency to be more responsive to the needs of the country's security. In today's agency, the Secretary is responsible for overseeing the department's activities and assistance to state and local governments and to ensure a comprehensive approach to homeland security. Many of the offices within DHS are not well known to the public, such as Health Affairs, Legislative Affairs, or the Inspector General; other offices receive greater public attention and are easily recognized by many. These include:

- U.S. Citizenship and Immigration Services: Oversees the immigration system in the United States
- U.S. Coast Guard: Protects the maritime economy and environment and protects the country's maritime borders
- U.S. Customs and Border Protection (CBP): Protects the country from terrorists and seeks to secure trade and travel into and out of the country
- Cybersecurity and Infrastructure Agency (CISA): Seeks to protect the country's cybersecurity from online criminals
- Federal Emergency Management Agency (FEMA): Responds to and helps citizens recover from terrorist attacks and natural disasters

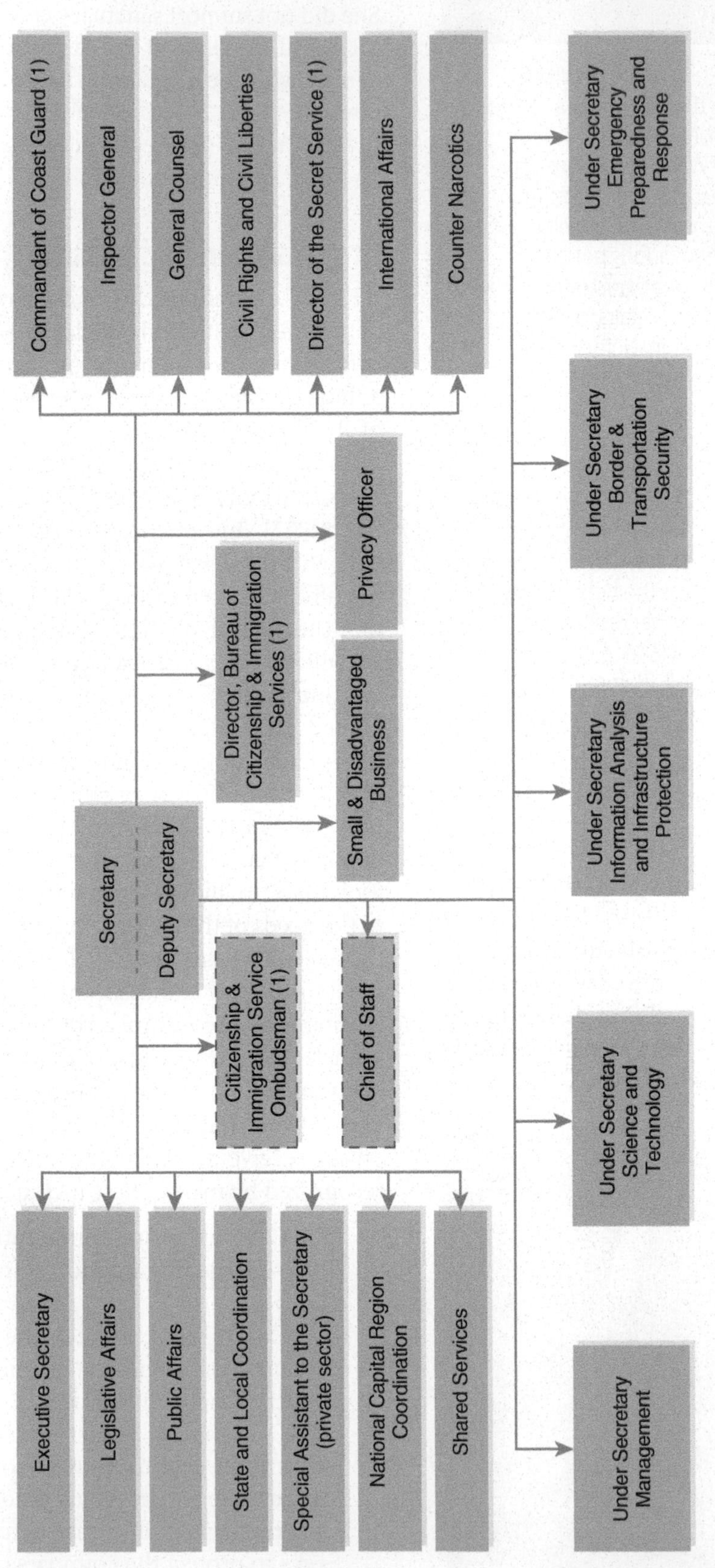

FIGURE 5.1 Department of Homeland Security: Original Organization Chart, March 2003.

Courtesy of DHS.

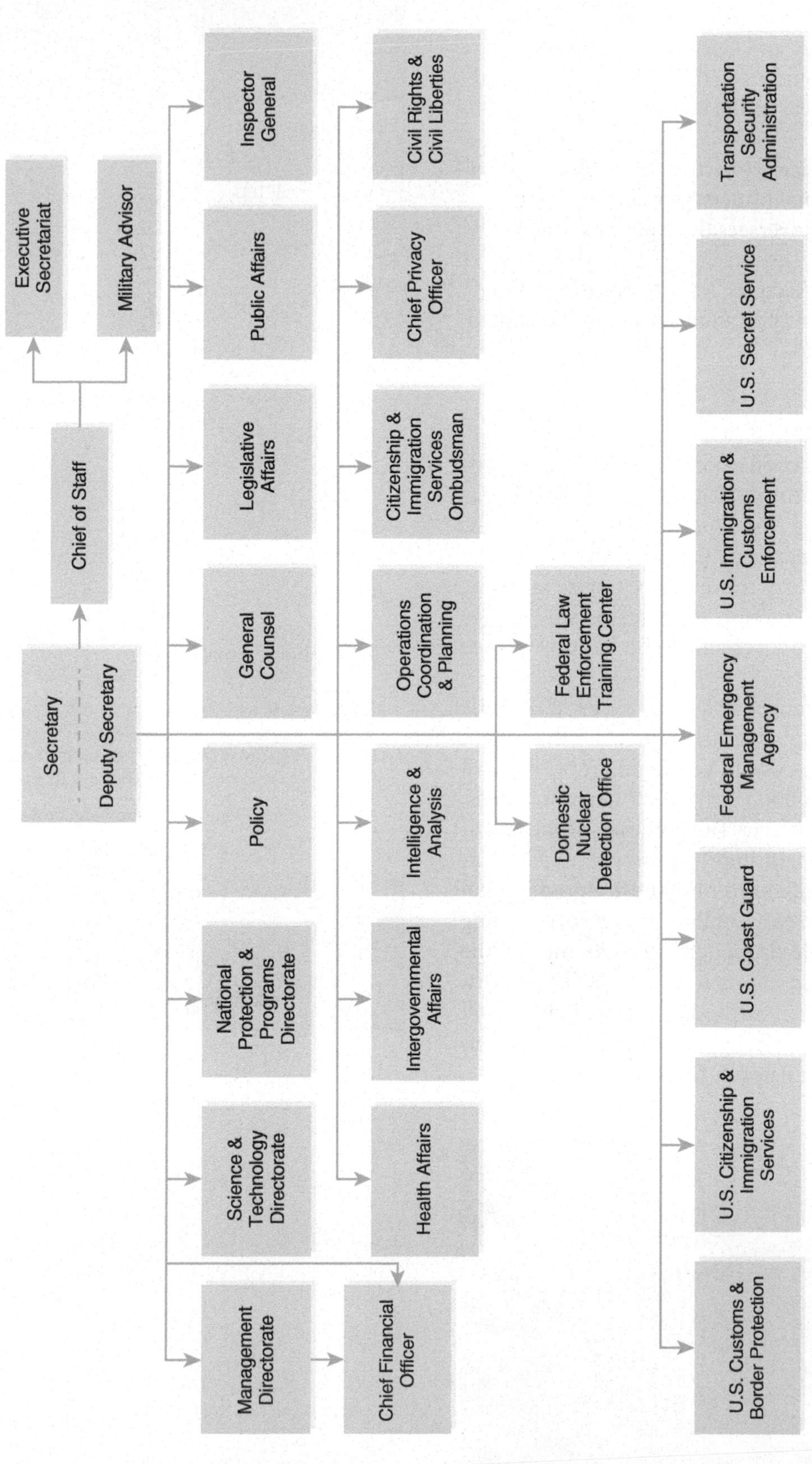

FIGURE 5.2 The Department of Homeland Security Organizational Chart.

Courtesy of the DHS. Available at, https://www.dhs.gov/organizational-chart

- Federal Law Enforcement Training Center (FLETC): Provides initial and ongoing training to those in federal law enforcement
- U.S. Immigration and Customs Enforcement (ICE): Works to improve the security of the nation in the areas of the border, trade, and immigration
- U.S. Secret Service: Protects the president and other national leaders, as well as visiting dignitaries, and oversees the country's financial structure
- Transportation Security Administration (TSA): Oversees the transportation system in the United States

Budget

In 2003, Congress passed a homeland security appropriations bill allocating $30.4 billion for fiscal year 2004. These were the first appropriations for the new department. Bush requested the money to enable the department to protect the nation's ports, airports, borders, and infrastructure from terrorism.[16] Since that time, the department's allocation has grown (See **TABLE 5.2**).

The enacted budget for fiscal year 2017 was $68,393,475. In creating the 2019 budget for the nation, President Trump requested $1.6 billion for border wall construction; $2.8 billion for 52,000 detention beds, $511.1 million to transfer and remove illegal immigrants; $223 million to improve the country's infrastructure, $210.5 million to hire and train additional border agents; and $382.1 million to support training officers at FLETC. He also sought funds to improve the Coast Guard, expand efforts to protect cybersecurity, and develop additional methods for preparedness and resilience, among other things. The budget allocations provided to DHS are listed in **TABLE 5.3**.

Courtesy of U.S. Government Accountability Office (GAO).

TABLE 5.2 Yearly Budgets for Department of Homeland Security

Year	Dollar Amount
FY 2009 Enacted	$52.7 billion
FY 2010 Enacted	$56.0 billion
FY 2011 Enacted	$54.8 billion
FY 2012 Enacted	$59.-9 billion
FY 2013	$59.2 billion
FY 2014	$60.4 billion
FY 2015	$63.5 billion
FY 2016	$65.7 billion
FY 2017	$68.4 billion
FT 2019 Presidential Request	$74.4 billion

Data from: Department of Homeland Security. (2011). "Fiscal Year 2011 Budget in Brief." Retrieved online at http://www.dhs.gov/xlibrary/assets/budget_bib_fy2011.pdf and Department of Homeland Security. (2012). "Fiscal Year 2012 Budget in Brief." Retrieved online at https://www.dhs.gov/xlibrary/assets/budget-bib-fy2012.pdf

TABLE 5.3 2013 Department of Homeland Security Budget Allocations

Organization	Percent of Budget
FEMA	22%
NPPD	5%
U.S. Secret Service	3%
U.S. Coast Guard	16%
TSA	10%
ICE	12%
Customs Border Protection	22%

Data from: Department of Homeland Security. (2013). "Fiscal Year 2013 Budget in Brief." Retrieved online at https://www.dhs.gov/xlibrary/assets/mgmt/dhs-budget-in-brief-fy2013.pdf and Department of Homeland Security. (2019). "Fiscal Year 2019 Budget in Brief." Retrieved online at https://www.dhs.gov/sites/default/files/publications/DHS%20BIB%202019.pdf

DHS's Role Today

The Department of Homeland Security has five major mission areas (see **FIGURE 5.3**):

1. Preventing Terrorism/Enhancing Security
2. Security of U.S. borders, be they land, sea, or air
3. Enforcement of our nation's immigration laws
4. Protection of cyberspace
5. Prepare in advance for and then respond quickly to any type of emergency that might occur[17]

Each of these areas is described in the following text:

Preventing Terrorism/Enhancing Security

One goal of DHS is to protect members of the public from future terrorist threats. This includes averting the acquisition and use of chemical, biological, radiological, or nuclear materials by those who seek to cause harm to others. It also means protecting the nation's infrastructure from potential attacks. DHS personnel strive to reach this goal in a multi-faceted approach that includes aviation security, cargo security, national preparedness, international cooperation, and critical infrastructure protection.

Aviation Security

One element of DHS's strategy to prevent terrorist events is aviation security. This mission area of homeland security is geared toward guaranteeing the safety of those who travel by air. One important aspect of aviation security is the Federal Air Marshal Service that helps to detect, deter, and defeat potential acts against U.S. air carriers, airports, passengers, and crews. Air marshals blend in with passengers on flights as a way to protect those on the plane. Air marshals often work with other law enforcement agencies such as the National Counterterrorism Center, the National Targeting Center, and the FBI's Joint Terrorism Task Forces.[18]

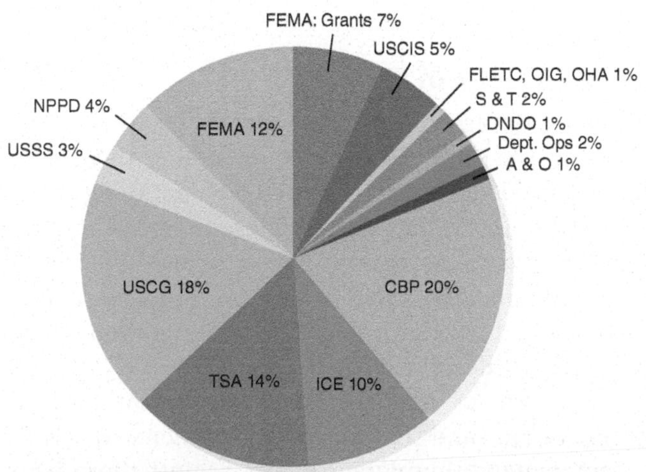

FIGURE 5.3 U. S. Department of Homeland Security.

Courtesy of DHS.

Another part of aviation security is Secure Flight, a prescreening program operated by TSA that works in conjunction with the existing Terrorism Watch List (a database of potential terrorists maintained by the government). Under the program, all airlines must provide each passenger's name as it appears on a government-issued ID, their date of birth, gender, and redress number (assigned in relation to a passenger's complaint).[19] If a passenger's name appears on the Watch list, that passenger is unable to board the plane. Other passengers may be identified as low-risk and will receive a precheck that allows them to receive minimal screening prior to boarding a plane. TSA works to keep passengers safe through screening programs in airports. TSA currently screens every passenger and every piece of luggage, both checked and carry-on bags that are taken onto commercial aircraft. Security officers are assigned to over 700 security checkpoints (located throughout the airports) and carry out nearly 7,000 baggage screenings each day (located at the airport entry point for all ticketed customers).[20]

Cargo Security

The Air Cargo Security Program helps to ensure the safety of cargo on all modes of transportation. Agents search goods at seaports, land border ports, and mail facilities in the United States and abroad. Shipments are searched for weapons, drugs, and large amounts of cash. Since October 2008, 100% of the cargo on 96% of the flights that begin in the United States is now screened. One hundred percent of international cargo that has been identified as "high-risk" is also screened. TSA also requires background checks on employees who screen cargo, those who have knowledge of how it is going to be transported, and those who actually transport the cargo.[21] Information on illegal shipments is shared amongst countries such as Brazil, Canada, and Mexico, through Program Global Shield.

Enhance National Preparedness

It is critical that the country be prepared for an event, whether it is a terrorist attack or natural disaster. This way, the damaging effects can be mitigated and deaths and injuries prevented. DHS seeks to increase the country's preparedness for a disaster by working with federal, state, and local officials. DHS provides training to leaders, agencies, medical professionals, and other stakeholders on an ongoing basis that will help to keep their communities safe and resilient. They also hold conferences to share information with others. Fusion centers, which involve officials from all levels of government, are an essential way to share critical information. If needed, communities can seek funding for equipment or programs through the Homeland Security Grant Program.

As a result of a recommendation made by the 9/11 Commission, DHS officials created the Office for State and Local Law Enforcement (OSLLE). This agency was given the responsibility of being the liaison between DHS and local, state, tribal, territorial, and campus law enforcement as they prepare for an event, and also to nongovernmental agencies. The agency not only provides information to other officials regarding activities and initiatives from DHS but also disseminates strategic information in the case of an event. The agency also provides training and funding for initiatives on those different levels.

In the case of a viable threat, the National Terrorism Advisory System was developed to communicate information pertaining to a threat to local communities. Officials will provide a summary of the threat as well as information about any actions that have been implemented to thwart the attack. Moreover, the System will suggest recommendations for action to mitigate the effects of the attack.

Local officials can also receive help from DHS through the Terrorism Prevention Partnership. DHS will provide resources to local communities that (a community is considered to be a thing; "who" is used for a person or persons) are seeking help with on-line violent extremist messages. Information for preventing such actions, as well as how to confront such behaviors, is available.

International Engagement and Cooperation

Because most acts of terrorism or threats of attack are often international in scope, DHS seeks to develop and maintain working relationships with government leaders in other countries. The Office of Policy oversees the international programs in aviation security, customs and trade regulations, efforts to counter violent extremism, and provides humanitarian support for those in need. Leaders share information and develop partnerships as a way to combat serious crimes and cooperate in investigations, when needed.

Critical Infrastructure Protection

The country's critical infrastructure refers to the assets and systems that help our country run. If they were attacked and damaged, it would have a serious, possibly debilitating effect on the country and may cause many injuries and deaths. The infrastructure includes things like the power grid, financial institutions, chemical facilities, and emergency services. Because these are vital to the everyday success of our country, it is critical that they be protected from a possible attack and be able to recover quickly in the case of a disruption or event.

Every day, officials at DHS work with owners of critical infrastructure, community officials, and governments to protect these structures. DHS officials have prepared a Protection Plan that provides information on what to do if something were to happen. DHS also provides training programs so that owners and operators of critical infrastructure know how to increase security. In addition, DHS provides resources that can be used to enhance security.

Through the Infrastructure Development and Recovery Program, DHS works with other federal, state, and local officials to plan and implement ways to improve the security of a critical infrastructure and ways to recover. They provide technical assistance such as architecture and landscaping ideas that not only can help prevent an attack but can also support following a disaster. This is often with the assistance of FEMA.

An effective way to plan and prepare for emergencies is by using tabletop exercises. Experts in DHS provide a variety of tabletop exercises to those who work in a critical infrastructure facility, allowing them to develop plans and procedures so they can respond quickly and effectively in the case of an event. The exercise can point out things such as gaps in service or ways to improve cooperation with other jurisdictions, if needed.

Enforcement of Immigration Laws

DHS is concerned with the security of all borders, while at the same time, not interrupting travel and trade. The Department is focused on identifying criminals who are in the country illegally and who may pose a threat to our nation's safety, taking measures to remove them. DHS and ICE have instituted numerous agencies and programs to oversee immigration, some of which are described here.

One agency largely responsible for this task is Immigration and Customs Enforcement, or ICE. Agents enforce immigration laws against those who are in the country illegally as well as any businesses that hire illegal workers. They do this through the

Criminal Alien Program, which seeks to find aliens who are in federal, state, and local correctional facilities and deport them. In 2003, the National Fugitive Operations Program (NFOP) was established and given the task of locating and arresting aliens in the United States. Since it began, NFOP has arrested over 350,000 illegal aliens.

The Enforcement and Removal Operations section of DHS is responsible for identifying those who are in the country illegally and seeks to remove them. This section is composed of the Air Operations Division (provides air transportation to remove individuals from the United States); the Removal Management Divisions (helps to coordinate removals by working with embassies and consulates), and the International Operations Division (agents based internationally who work with officials in those countries to coordinate removals).

At the same time, DHS has created programs to encourage employers to hire legal workers. Through a program called Mutual Agreement between Government and Employers (IMAGE), ICE agents help employers develop ways to ensure that their workers are not aliens, thereby creating a more stable workforce.

To prevent the United States from becoming a safe haven for those who have committed war crimes, torture, or other human rights violations, the Human Rights Violators and War Crimes Unit has been created. The agents investigate possible human rights violations as a way to prevent them from entering the United States. Another group, the National Gang Unit, seeks to identify those who are members of transnational gangs.

The Law Enforcement Support Center provides assistance to local, state, and federal law enforcement agencies who are dealing with aliens who are suspected of, or have been convicted of, criminal activity.

In addition to enforcing laws pertaining to immigration, ICE agents also investigate the illegal movement of both people and products (i.e., guns or counterfeit goods). One agency that does this is the Border Enforcement Security Task Force (BEST). These agents work to halt the activities of transnational criminal organizations by working with state and local law enforcement. By working cooperatively, the task force has successfully attacked trafficking in drugs, humans, cash, and counterfeit goods. They are located along the southern and northern borders, and at major seaports.

The Bulk Cash Smuggling Center investigates activities pertaining to the smuggling of large amounts of cash that will be used for money laundering operations. This is most often carried out by criminal organizations that are attempting to hide their profits from the government.

Security of U.S. Borders

A critical part of DHS's mission is to prevent illegal activity at the nation's borders while ensuring the effective policies for trade and travel. The agency largely responsible for these activities is Customs and Border Patrol. The CBP agents have modernized procedures at the border so that the goods that are brought into the country are not dangerous or harmful for consumers. They also ensure that the tax revenues from imported products are collected.

Customs and Border Patrol have identified seven trade issues that are critical for the country. They include: Agriculture; anti-dumping and countervailing duties; import safety; intellectual property rights; penalties; revenue; and textiles. Noncompliance in these areas could have a significant effect on the nation's trade and on consumers.

As a way to boost ease of trade, DHS and CBP continue to support the Trusted Traveler program. Under this system, those who travel frequently from Canada or Mexico preapprove certain travelers to enter the country quickly, without fully checking procedures that are required as a person enters the country. If they qualify, a frequent traveler can be preapproved, making it easier to bring goods into the country.

Protecting Cyberspace

The Department of Homeland Security plays an important role in countering threats against cyberspace. DHS seeks to develop ways to keep our federal networks and critical infrastructure secure by protecting against all forms of cyberattacks. In 2004, DHS created the National Cyber Security Division (NCSD), which has partnered with government, industry, and academia as well as the international community to make cybersecurity a national and shared priority.

As the Internet and technology has made the world more interconnected, cybercriminals have taken advantage of the opportunities that the Internet provides for criminal activities. DHS actively works to keep the Internet safe for all who use it. C3 was established to prevent criminal activity from being carried out by use of the Internet. The agency provides training to federal, state, and local law enforcement in investigating cybercrimes and in the recovery of digital evidence. Agents working in C3 have also been tasked with investigating those who seek to sexually abuse children via the Internet. These agents spend hours to find those who create child pornography and those who distribute or possess it. Over the years, this agency has rescued thousands of children from becoming victims of sexual predators.

The National Cybersecurity and Communications Integration Center (NCCIC) was created to share information with members of both the public and private sectors regarding cybersecurity, vulnerabilities, incidents, and recovery. Similarly, the National Infrastructure Coordinating Center also serves to share information regarding the nation's critical infrastructure. Together, these agencies open the lines of communication between DHS and other officials to security cyberspace and infrastructure.

The National Security Presidential Directive 54/Homeland Security Presidential Directive 23 established the Comprehensive National Cybersecurity Initiative (CNCI) that formalizes a series of efforts to safeguard the federal systems from cyberattacks. On the federal level, the CNCI focuses on three key areas: Establishing a defense that will reduce any vulnerabilities and prevent intrusions; Defending against all threats through use of intelligence and strengthening supply chain security; and shaping the future technological environment through research, development, and education as well as investing in technology.

As part of its role overseeing the CNCI, DHS has responsibility for ensuring the security of the nation's information technology (IT) and communications infrastructure. DHS has attempted to improve technology to prevent future attacks by hiring additional personnel for the Computer Emergency Readiness Team (US–CERT), the department's watch and warning center for the federal government's Internet infrastructure. US–CERT is charged with providing response support and defense against cyberattacks for the Federal Civil Executive Branch while providing information sharing and collaboration with state and local government, industry, and international partners.

US-CERT is working to expand the Einstein Program to all federal departments and agencies as a way of providing an early warning system to identify malicious cyber activity. The Einstein Program helps identify unusual network traffic patterns and trends that signal unauthorized network traffic so that security personnel can identify and respond to potential threats. NCSD is in the process of deploying Einstein 2.

DHS is also attempting to thwart cyber-terrorism by forming the National Cybersecurity Center that will focus on coordinating intelligence about cyber threats among the many agencies. Additionally, DHS has expanded the National Cyber Investigative Joint Task Force (NCIJTF) so that it will include representatives from many federal agencies, including the Secret Service. This organization will also aid in the coordination and information sharing on cyber threats.[22]

Recently, DHS has begun a new national campaign called "Stop. Think. Connect." aimed at increasing the public's understanding of cyber threats and empowering the public to be safer and more secure online. The main objective is to help citizens become more aware of threats and arm people with the tools needed to protect themselves and their families.[23]

Preparedness, Response, and Recovery: Resilience to Disasters

If a terrorist attack, a natural disaster, or other emergency occurs, DHS will provide a coordinated and comprehensive federal response and begin a fast and effective recovery effort. The department assumes primary responsibility for ensuring that all emergency response professionals are prepared for any situation. Their actions are based on the National Preparedness Goal, which describes the need for the nation to be active in preventing, protecting against, mitigating, responding to, and recovering from threats.

To prepare for various types of emergencies, DHS/FEMA/Citizen Corps has created a Community Preparedness Webinar Series that provides information on community preparedness topics and resources available to citizens, community organizations, and Citizen Corps Councils. These webinars are available several times each month and are free to the public.[24] FEMA also has a program known as Ready (see www.ready.gov) that involves being informed (what to do before, during, and after an emergency), making a plan (prepare, plan, and stay informed for emergencies), building a kit (build a kit for disasters and be prepared), and getting involved (find opportunities to get involved to promote community preparedness).

In the event of an emergency, FEMA is prepared to coordinate a comprehensive response that will help a community with both immediate needs (i.e., providing food and shelter for residents) and long-term goals (rebuilding critical infrastructure). They focus on individual assistance as well as public assistance. By providing individual assistance, FEMA employees will not only provide food, shelter, and clothing to victims but will also provide counseling and legal services. Public assistance can range from rebuilding roads to establishing new schools.

DHS and FEMA also have established a federal grant program to state and local governments so they can create preparedness plans through nondisaster grants. In the case of a disaster, FEMA will assist communities to recover. This will not only be done with monetary assistance but also by providing temporary housing, counseling, or unemployment. DHS and

FEMA have provided victims with billions of dollars to help them recover from disasters.

Chapter Summary

The Department of Homeland Security, formed by President Bush and Congress in the days after the terrorist attacks of 9-11, was developed to help protect the country from any more terrorist attacks. The department was formed by a reorganization and consolidation of many other federal agencies, or portions of agencies, that had some role in homeland security. Since its formation, DHS has continued to collect and analyze intelligence about terrorism as a way to understand terrorist groups and break up any potential plots against the U.S. DHS has also helped states and local governments prepare for another attack so they respond quickly if one were to happen, while also assisting state and local officials to prepare for and be able to recover from natural disasters.

Review/Discussion Questions

1. How and why was the Department of Homeland Security established?
2. What is the organizational structure of DHS?
3. What are some of the components of DHS?
4. Which agencies were transferred to DHS upon its creation?
5. Who was the first leader of DHS and who is the current Secretary?

Additional Readings

Bush, G.W. (2002). *The Department of Homeland Security.* Washington, D.C.: Office of the President.

Department of Homeland Security. (2013). *Creation of the Department of Homeland Security.* Retrieved online at http://www.dhs.gov/creation-department-homeland-security.

Department of Homeland Security. (2013). *Who Joined DHS.* Retrieved online at http://www.dhs.gov/who-joined-dhs.

Endnotes

1. Bush, G.W. (2001). Executive Order 13228: Establishing the Office of Homeland Security and the Homeland Security Council. *The American Presidency Project.* Retrieved online at https://www.presidency.ucsb.edu/documents/executive-order-13228-establishing-the-office-homeland-security-and-the-homeland-security
2. CQ Almanac. (2002). New Security Office Scrutinized. *CQ Almanac 2001* 57th ed. Retrieved online at http://library.cqpress.com/cqalmanac/cqal01-106-6372-328132
3. CQ Almanac. (2003). Homeland Department Created. *CQ Almanac 2002* 58th ed. Retrieved online at http://library.cqpress.com/cqalmanac/cqal02-236-10378-664466
4. CQ Almanac. (2003). Homeland Department Created. *CQ Almanac 2002* 58th ed. Retrieved online at http://library.cqpress.com/cqalmanac/cqal02-236-10378-664466
5. Bush, G.W. (2002). Message to the Congress Transmitting Proposed Legislation to Create the Department of Homeland Security. *The American Presidency Project.* Retrieved online at http://www.presidency,ucsb.edu/ws/?pid=64050
6. CQ Almanac. (2003). Immigration and Naturalization Service (INS) Abolished, With Border Security, Immigration Services Divided at Department of Homeland Security (DHS). *CQ Almanac 2002*, 58th ed. Retrieved online at http://library.cqpress.com/cqalmanac/cqal02-236-10366-664138
7. Bush, G.W. (2002). Memorandum on the Establishment of the Department of Homeland Security. *The American Presidency Project.* Retrieved online at https://www.presidency.ucsb.edu/documents/memorandum-the-establishment-the-department-homeland-security
8. Bush, G.W. (2002). Remarks to Federal Employees on the Proposed Department of Homeland Security. *The American Presidency Project.* Retrieved online at https://www.presidency.ucsb.edu/node/215272
9. CQ Almanac. (2003). Homeland Security Provisions. *CQ Almanac 2002* 58th ed. Retrieved online at http://library.cqpress.com/cqalmanac/cqal02-236-10378-664477
10. CQ Almanac. (2003). Homeland Security Provisions. *CQ Almanac 2002* 58th ed. Retrieved online at http://library.cqpress.com/cqalmanac/cqal02-236-10378-664477
11. Ridge, T. (2003). Homeland Security Secretary Swearing In. C-SPAN Video Library. Retrieved online at https://www.c-span.org/video/?174762-1/homeland-security-secretary-swearing

12. Dinan, S. (December 13, 2017). New Homeland Security chief: Presence of agents sows fear, urges cities to cooperate. The Washington Times. Retrieved online at https://www.washingtontimes.com/news/2017/dec/13/kirstjen-nielsen-new-dhs-chief-says-agents-cause-f/
13. Richardson, Davis. December 4, 2018. How the Migrant Caravan & a Facebook Post Saved DHS Secretary Kirstjen Nielsen's Job. Observer. Retrieved online at https://observer.com/2018/12/kirstjen-nielsen-migrant-caravan-firing-rumors/.
14. Damp, D. V. (2019). Largest Federal Departments. GovCentral. http://govcentral.monster.com/careers/articles/402-largest-federal-departments.
15. Napolitano, J. (2011). State of America's Homeland Security Address. Retrieved online at http://www.dhs.gov/ynews/speeches/sp_1296152572413.shtm.
16. Public Intelligence. (2012). The Department of Homeland Security's New HQ is an Abandoned Insane Asylum. Retrieved online at http://publicintelligence.net/the-department-of-homeland-securitys-new-hq-is-an-abandoned-insane-asylum/
17. CQ Almanac. (2004). Quick Funds for Homeland Security. *CQ Almanac 2003*, 59th ed. Retrieved online at https://library.cqpress.com/cqalmanac/login.php?requested=%2Fcqalmanac%2Fdocument.php%3Fid%3Dcqal03-835-24336-1084056
18. Napolitano, J. (2010). Remarks to Secretary Napolitano at the National Press Club. Retrieved online at http://www.dhs.gov/ynews/speeches/sp_1271433302831.shtm.
19. U.S. Department of Homeland Security. (2017). *Privacy Impact Assessment Update for Secure Flight*. Retrieved online at https://www.dhs.gov/sites/default/files/publications/pia_tsa_secureflight_18%28h%29_july2017.pdf
20. Department of Homeland Security. (2012). *Secure Flight Program*. Retrieved online at http://www.dhs.gov/files/programs/gc_1250693582433.shtm.
21. U.S. Department of Homeland Security. (2019). *Aviation Security*. Retrieved online at https://www.dhs.gov/aviation-security
22. Department of Homeland Security. (2019). *Air Cargo Program Fact Sheet*. Retrieved online at https://www.dhs.gov/publication/air-cargo-program
23. Department of Homeland Security. (2012). *Stop. Think. Connect. Campaign*. Retrieved online at http://www.dhs.gov/files/events/stop-think-connect.shtm
24. Agency, Citizen Corps. (2012). *Community Preparedness Webinar Series*. Retrieved online at https://www.fema.gov/es/media-library/assets/documents/29697

CHAPTER 6

Homeland Security Community

CHAPTER OBJECTIVES

- Learn about the agencies responsible for homeland security in the U.S. including the intelligence, defense, and security communities
- Understand the role of coordination in the intelligence community as it relates to homeland security
- Learn how the intelligence and security communities interact with the criminal justice system

CHAPTER OUTLINE

When the report by the National Commission on Terrorist Attacks upon the United States (also known as The 9/11 Commission Report) came out, it was pointed in its critique of the intelligence community. In particular, the commission stated that, while the community was theoretically prepared to deal with threats such as 9-11 presented, in practice, the community was separated by bureaucratic cultures that varied widely, had vastly different missions, and were facing a new and more complex threat from a more imaginative adversary than before.[1] This evaluation, by one of the most influential independent commissions ever appointed by the United States government, led to serious reevaluation of the structure and mission of the national intelligence apparatus.[2] Furthermore, it led to significant changes in the way that the federal level of government cooperated with the state and local levels on matters of intelligence, particularly as it pertained to homeland security.[3]

This chapter introduces the reader to the homeland security community, consisting not only of the nation's intelligence agencies, but also the security and military communities that have important roles within a homeland security paradigm. Additionally, the chapter focuses on the relationship between these organizations and local and state agencies, which also play a part in the homeland security community. Finally, it examines the role the homeland security community plays within the justice system.

Intelligence Community

The **intelligence community** in the United States is a complex one, with many organizations participating in specific capacities.[4] While most people have heard of the Central Intelligence Agency (CIA) and the National Security Agency (NSA), there are a large number of smaller agencies with more limited missions, such as the National Geospatial Intelligence Agency (NGA) that most have not heard of but that nevertheless play important roles in our national intelligence community.[5] In total, there are 16 agencies (and one administrative office) that make up the intelligence community of the United Sates, ranging across government departments as diverse as the Department of Energy and the Department of the Treasury (see **BOX 6.1**).[6] While each of the agencies in the intelligence community has a specific mission to fulfill, the cooperation between agencies and how they cooperate with local and state authorities is essential to understanding homeland security operations within the United States.

BOX 6.1 The 17 Agencies that Make Up the Intelligence Community

- Air Force Intelligence
- Army Intelligence
- Central Intelligence Agency
- Coast Guard Intelligence
- Defense Intelligence Agency
- Department of Energy
- Department of Homeland Security
- Department of State
- Department of the Treasury
- Drug Enforcement Administration
- Federal Bureau of Investigation
- Marine Corps Intelligence
- National Reconnaissance Office
- National Security Agency
- Navy Intelligence
- Office of the Director of National Intelligence
- National Geospatial-Intelligence Agency

Courtesy of CIA.

Office of the Director of National Intelligence

As provided for in the Intelligence Reform and Terrorism Prevention Act of 2004, the Director of National Intelligence (DNI) is responsible for coordinating the activities of the nation's other 16 intelligence agencies.[7] The 17th agency is the Office of the Director of National Intelligence (ODNI), which serves to support the DNI's mission. Additionally, the DNI is considered the nation's top official in relation to intelligence affairs and is responsible for advising the President's National Security Council (NSC) with regard to intelligence.[8] Perhaps most importantly, the DNI has budgetary responsibility for the majority of the nation's intelligence operations and is responsible for making sure that the national intelligence program is implemented across all of these agencies (see **FIGURE 6.1**).[9]

The ODNI was developed as a direct response to the reforms proposed by the 9/11 Commission Report, although the original proposal called for more comprehensive integration of the intelligence services under the DNI.[10] As the commission suggested, however, the DNI (originally called the National Intelligence Director [NID]) is responsible for being the Cabinet-level official in charge of national intelligence, particularly regarding homeland security.[11]

Within the ODNI, there are several missions that directly support the intelligence community. Chief among these is the National Counterterrorism Center (NCTC), which is the primary government organization responsible for integration and analysis of all intelligence that relates to terrorism, outside of domestic terrorism.[12]

In addition to their focus on terrorism, the ODNI is also in charge of the Office of Intelligence and Analysis (I&A) within the Department of Homeland Security (DHS). This is the DHS intelligence component, responsible for developing intelligence products for policymakers with regard to homeland security threats. It has a particular focus on border security and works extensively with state and local law enforcement, in addition to agencies like U.S. Customs and Border Protection Services (USBPS) within DHS.[13]

Central Intelligence Agency

The Central Intelligence Agency (CIA) is the only Cabinet-level agency for which the primary mission is intelligence.[14] Developed originally at the end of World War II and in the early Cold War years, the agency represents the most important intelligence-gathering apparatus possessed by the U.S. government.[15] The agency is not limited to intelligence regarding homeland security issues, but rather produces an extremely varied catalogue of intelligence products to support missions across the government.[16] The agency is responsible for all-source intelligence analysis, which not only uses technological means of collection (such as satellites) but also human intelligence, developed from sources sometimes operating overseas retrieving information from enemies (see **BOX 6.2**). Additionally, it has the capability of undertaking covert actions when directed to do so by the president.[17]

Office of the Director of National Intelligence Organizational Chart

Leading Intelligence Integration

Leadership

Director (DNI)

Principal Deputy Director (PDDNI)

Chief Management Officer (CMO)

Core Mission

Intelligence Integration (DDNI/II)

Assistant Deputy DNI Intelligence Integration (ADDNI/II)

Integration Management Council (IMC)	National Counterterrorism Center (NCTC)*
• National Intelligence Managers (NIMs)	National Counterproliferation Center (NCPC)*
National Intelligence Council (NIC)	National Counterintelligence Executive (NCIX)*
Mission Integration Division (MID)	**Leaders of these organizations also serve as National Intelligence Managers.*

Enablers

Policy & Strategy (P&S)	Chief Human Capital Officer (CHCO)
Partner Engagement (PE)	Chief Financial Officer (CFO)
Acquisition, Technology, & Facilities (AT&F)	Chief Information Officer (CIO)
Systems & Resource Analyses (SRA)	Information Sharing Environment (ISE)

Oversight

General Counsel (GC)	Inspector General (IG)
Civil Liberties and Privacy Office (CLPO)	IC Equal Employment Opportunity & Diversity (EEOD)
Public Affairs (PAO)	Legislative Affairs (OLA)

FIGURE 6.1 ODNI Organizational Chart.

Modified from: Office of the Director of National Intelligence. (2012). Office of Director of National Intelligence: Organizational chart. Retrieved from https://www.odni.gov/files/documents/ODNI Org Chart.pdf

BOX 6.2 The "INTs"

While people tend to refer to "intelligence" as a single entity, finalized intelligence products usually consist of a variety of types of information put into a single context. The types of information used in these products can range from the popular view of "secret" or '"covert" information to publicly accessible background information used by the public in other contexts every day. The different types of intelligence are referred to as intelligence collection disciplines and collectively are known as INTs. The different types are discussed here.

Human Intelligence (HUMINT)

Human intelligence is intelligence gathered from human sources. While this includes the popular versions of "secret" intelligence gathering from covert sources, it also includes open collection, which may come from interrogation of suspects or witness interviews. HUMINT is generally handled domestically by the FBI and internationally by the CIA.

Signals Intelligence (SIGINT)

Signals intelligence refers to any intelligence gathered from electronic transmissions. These can be transmitted from a variety of locations including ground sites, ships, or satellites. Communications intelligence (COMINT) is a subset of SIGINT when communications between two parties are intercepted. SIGINT is generally the province of the National Security Agency, although other law enforcement agencies like the FBI collect some types of SIGINT through methods like wiretapping.

Imagery Intelligence (IMINT)

Usually consisting of photographs, IMINT is one of the oldest forms of intelligence. Beginning during the Civil War, it examines a wide variety of elements, from enemy movements to geographic issues. The National Reconnaissance Office is generally responsible for developing and building the satellites most frequently used for IMINT and the National Geospatial-Intelligence Agency is responsible for processing the images collected.

Open-Source Intelligence (OSINT)

Open-source includes any information that is publicly accessible. It can range from news broadcasts on radio and television to academic papers on specific research topics of interest to the intelligence community. OSINT, unlike other forms of intelligence, is not under the specific auspices of a single agency but is instead collected by the entire intelligence community.

Despite its huge presence in the U.S. intelligence community, the CIA has a relatively small role to play with regard to homeland security because of the agency's limitations regarding American persons.[18] However, when foreign intelligence assets come to bear on domestic intelligence problems, such as terrorist organizations funded from overseas, the CIA has the ability to assist with disruption and other intelligence efforts.[19]

National Security Agency

The NSA is responsible for the nation's "signals intelligence." Signals intelligence, or SIGINT, refers to a variety of different collection methods including code-breaking, cryptanalysis, and foreign language analysis.[20] It further includes interception of messages on international telecommunications networks. Additionally, the agency is responsible for protecting the U.S. national security information systems.[21]

Military Intelligence

The intelligence apparatus of the military is one of the primary information-gathering tools of the U.S. intelligence community. The Department of Defense's (DOD's) worldwide reach, as well as its utilization of advanced intelligence-gathering technology, makes it one of the most indispensable tools for the intelligence mission of homeland security. However, much of the intelligence capacity of the military is used in support of their operations, especially in times of conflict, and the departmental independence in terms of budget and operations makes cooperation between the DOD and other intelligence agencies problematic at times.[22]

Defense Intelligence Agency

The primary intelligence agency within the DOD is the Defense Intelligence Agency (DIA). The DIA's major role is providing intelligence for the operations of the U.S. military around the world. As such, its function does not always overlap with the homeland security mission. However, within the context of homeland defense, the DIA is one of the primary intelligence agencies responsible for managing foreign military intelligence for the DOD. Additionally, given the agency's wide reach and extensive technical capacities, including drones, its role in the intelligence community's coordination is essential when dealing with the counter-terrorism mission of homeland security.[23]

Other National-Level Intelligence Agencies

Other **national-level intelligence agencies** range in function and location within the government structure. For instance, the National Reconnaissance Office (NRO), which is in charge of the nation's satellites, is housed within the Department of Defense, but it is not considered part of the DIA.[24] Similarly, the Department of State's Bureau of Intelligence and Research (INR) has the goal of analyzing information relevant to the Department of State's diplomatic mission.[25] The NGA is, like the NRO, housed within the DOD and is in charge of developing map-based intelligence solutions and other issues surrounding intelligence imagery.[26]

All of these agencies have missions that relate, some more directly than others, to the overall homeland security mission, and all of them participate in the intelligence cycle (See **BOX 6.3**). Without the coordination of these agencies under the direction of the ODNI, the nation would be less secure both in terms

BOX 6.3 The Intelligence Cycle

While generally thought of as a single step, intelligence is actually part of a process that begins with a question from lawmakers and ends with a final, finished intelligence product in those policymaker's hands. The process that different elements in the intelligence community go through to achieve a final product useful for answering the original question is called the "intelligence cycle." The intelligence cycle has five steps: Planning, collecting, processing, analyzing, and disseminating intelligence information. Each one of the steps is essential to creating a useful, complete, and correct intelligence product.

Planning and Direction

The first step in the intelligence process is tasking from a policymaker, usually in order to answer a question. Identification of what information is already known and what information needs to be collected happens during this step. Additionally, clarification is frequently required when tasking happens, and it is generally considered part of the planning and direction step in the intelligence cycle.

Collection

Once the information needed is identified, it must be collected. Collection can be overt or covert and can consist of a variety of types of information (see Box 6.1 on "the INTs"). The collection of information, from whatever sources, is generally the step in the process most identified with "intelligence."

Processing

Once the information for answering the original query is found, it needs to be put into a usable format. This consists of putting the information into a report that can be used by an analyst to interpret the information. Much of the "raw data" collected would be unusable without this step in the intelligence cycle.

Analysis and Production

After the information has been processed, it still lacks an interpretation that allows it to answer the policymaker's original question. The analysis and production stage of the intelligence cycle is the point at which the question is answered. There is an assessment of what is happening, why it is happening, and what impact the event(s) may have in the future all in light of the original question.

Dissemination

The final step of the intelligence process is taking the finished intelligence product, developed in the analysis and production step, and getting it to the policymaker who originally provided the tasking. The policymaker can then use the information to inform policy development or come back with additional tasking if more information is required.

Conclusion

While the intelligence cycle looks like a series of discrete steps taken to answer a policymaker's question, the way the process actually works is frequently more complicated. Often, steps go in reverse, and there is a collection happening to answer general, ongoing questions outside of a specific task requested. Several alternative models have been presented to this intelligence cycle, but generally, it remains the best overview of the process available.

Data from: Office of the Director of National Intelligence. (2009). National Intelligence: A consumer's guide; Johnston, J.M., and Johnston, R. (n.d.). Testing the intelligence cycle through systems modeling and simulation.

of national defense and homeland security.[27] However, given the large spread of the agencies across the federal government and the highly specialized missions of some of the agencies, coordination is a difficult task.[28]

The intelligence community in the United States has the difficult but important job of making information accessible to policymakers and operators across the government.[29] In terms of homeland security, the community is responsible for coordinating both domestic and foreign intelligence, interfacing with law enforcement intelligence, and identifying threats to the homeland with enough lead time that policymakers have the ability to act.[30] Further still, given the number of agencies and their disparate responsibilities, the job of coordinating all-source intelligence for homeland security is difficult and has not always been carried out well. The 9/11 Commission pointed this out, saying:

> ... no one [in the intelligence community] was firmly in charge of managing the case and able to draw relevant intelligence from anywhere in the government, assign responsibilities across the agencies (foreign and domestic), track progress, and quickly bring up obstacles to the level where they could be resolved.[31]

With the advent of ODNI and the increasing emphasis on coordination of effort across intelligence agencies, there has been definite improvement in our national intelligence capacity regarding homeland security.[32] However, despite this increased ability, the system remains imperfect and is still changing to meet the needs of the new security environment (see **FIGURE 6.2**).[33]

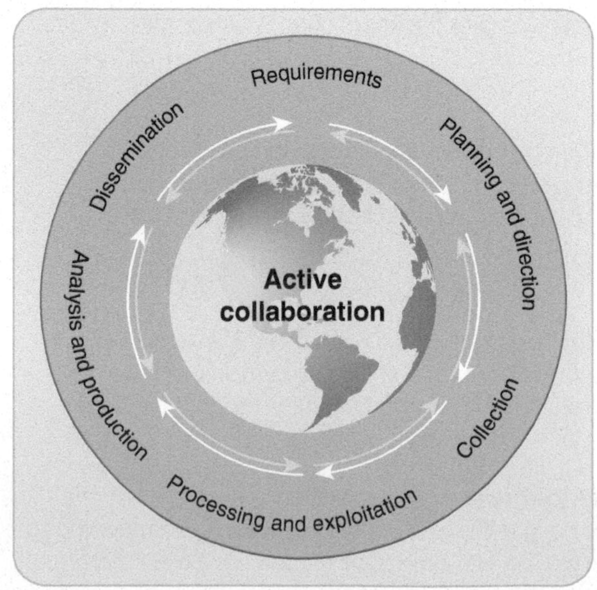

FIGURE 6.2 The Intelligence Cycle.

Modified from: Federal Bureau of Investigation. (n.d.). The intelligence cycle. Accessed at, https://archives.fbi.gov/archives/news/stories/2005/april/ia041505

Security Community

Along with the intelligence community responsible for actionable information with regard to homeland security, there is also the **security community**, consisting of federal agencies with specific homeland security-relevant missions.[34] Primary among these are the Department of Justice (DOJ) and DHS itself, although several other Cabinet-level agencies, such as the Department of the Treasury, also have important roles.[35]

Department of Justice

The DOJ is responsible for most federal law enforcement activities as well as containing the Office of the Attorney General.[36] Both of these elements are important to the homeland security goals of the United States. The DOJ is responsible for the prosecution of all federal terrorism cases, in addition to its large role in the investigation and apprehension of terrorists with domestic ties. After 9-11, DOJ came under fire for its lack of cooperation, along with other members of the U.S. intelligence community.[37] Most of this criticism was directed at the Federal Bureau of Investigation (FBI).

Federal Bureau of Investigation

In the context of homeland security, the FBI is the agency that bridges the intelligence world and the law enforcement community.[38] Although considered a full member of the intelligence community, the FBI is primarily geared toward law enforcement, with more emphasis on collecting evidence and prosecuting offenders than other agencies within the intelligence or security communities.[39] In addition to being the link between two federal-level functions, the FBI is responsible for the majority of coordination with state and local law enforcement agencies through both their participation in Joint Terrorism Task Forces (JTTFs) and normal law enforcement cooperation (see **TABLE 6.1**).[40]

Since 9-11, the FBI has taken on a much larger role in combating terrorism (see **BOX 6.4**).[41] Although always responsible for investigating and deterring acts of domestic terrorism, the 9-11 attacks caused a significant shift in agency priorities that aligned it more with other members of the homeland security and intelligence communities.[42] As such, it is the primary organization in charge of domestic homeland security law enforcement functions, with significant support from state and local agencies, particularly when responding to a specific incident. The FBI describes its mission this way:

TABLE 6.1 Anti-terrorism Task Force Participation of Local Police Departments (2010)

Basic Information Multi-agency Anti-terrorism Task Forces	
Number of Cities w/JTTFs	**104**
FBI Field Offices w/JTTF Connections	**56 (100%)**
First JTTF Established	1980 (New York City)
Participating Officers	4,000+
Participating Agencies	500 State & Local 55 Federal

Data from: Reaves, Brian A. (2010). Local Police Departments, 2007. Washington, D.C.: U.S. Department of Justice.

The FBI's top priorities are combating the threat of terrorism, counterintelligence, and cybercrime. As to counterterrorism, the FBI gives particular attention to terrorist efforts to acquire and use weapons of mass destruction . . . .The FBI must continuously adapt to trends in terrorist recruitment; financing and training; as well as terrorist's development of new explosive devices and biological and chemical agents.[43]

In addition to their homeland security functions, the FBI is also responsible for any domestic criminal activity that does not fall directly under the jurisdiction of other law enforcement agencies, as well as for crimes with which other law enforcement agencies request assistance.[44]

BOX 6.4 The FBI's Intelligence Transformation

While the FBI has always used intelligence to assist in solving criminal cases, the September 11, 2001, attacks on the World Trade Center and Pentagon brought a new emphasis on intelligence operations at the Bureau. In fact, the change that has happened since 9-11 at the FBI has been described as transformative, and the development of the Bureau's Intelligence Directorate in 2005 has been heralded as a milestone on the way to a new, "intel-driven" FBI.

Increased Intelligence Analysis

While the FBI has had intelligence analysts for many years, the agency tripled the number of analysts from 1,000 to 3,000 between the years 2001 and 2010. This is in conjunction with its efforts not only with regard to terrorism but also in its criminal cases. The increase also helps inculcate an "intelligence driven" philosophy across the Bureau, rather than confining it to its national security functions.

In conjunction with this reform, Senior Intelligence Manager Dina Corsi was quoted as saying, "IAs [intelligence analysts] could always do what was needed, but there was no system-wide program across the FBI as there is now, with formal training, standardized intelligence products, and clear-cut career paths for analysts."

Directorate of Intelligence

In 2005, the FBI created its intelligence directorate in order to assist with the transition to a more intelligence-centered FBI. The goal of the new directorate was to elevate the intelligence process in the FBI to a similar status as that of criminal investigation. The directorate, among other responsibilities, was in charge of intelligence policy within the Bureau, information technology for intelligence, and training.

The development of the FBI's Directorate of Intelligence represented, in some ways, a major departure for the organization. There has been historical resistance to the idea of a domestic intelligence agency. However, the Directorate's development marks one of the signal achievements in recent years, especially with regard to the necessity for intelligence sharing among organizations participating in the intelligence community. Indeed, data sharing is one of the main outcomes of the DI, with over 7,500 finished intelligence products shared by 2006 – and the number growing extensively since that time. The importance of the redirection on intelligence was further solidified in 2014, with the creation of the Intelligence Branch of the FBI, which combined with the Directorate of Intelligence with the Bureau Intelligence Council and the Office of Partner Engagement.

Conclusion

Although the FBI has undergone a transformation since 9/11, it remains to be seen how well this transition will work in the long term – and indeed, changes have continued to happen. Organizational change is difficult, and there are institutional norms dealing with information-sharing and the role of law enforcement in the intelligence community that will be difficult to overcome. It is likely, however, that as homeland security remains a focus—particularly the issue of terrorism—the FBI will continue to evolve into a more efficient domestic intelligence agency.

Data from: Mueller III, R.S. (2006). Testimony before the House Appropriations Subcommittee on Science, the Departments of State, Justice and Commerce and Related Agencies; Federal Bureau of Investigation. (2011). Intelligence analysts: Central to the mission; Federal Bureau of Investigation. (n.d.). Intelligence overview; MuellerÈIII, R.S.(2006). Testimony before the House Appropriations Subcommittee on Science, the Departments of State, Justice and Commerce and Related Agencies.

Courtesy of FBI.

Department of Homeland Security

Not surprisingly, given the primary goal of the agency, the Department of Homeland Security (DHS) has a large role to play in the security community as well as in the intelligence community. After the government reorganization prompted by the 9-11 attacks, several security agencies found themselves newly housed within DHS.[45]

Organizations like Customs and Border Protection and the **Border Patrol** were moved under the governance of the newly formed DHS, and new organizations were created for reasons of homeland security, such as the Transportation Security Administration (TSA).[46] Each of these agencies has an important role in homeland security.

Customs and Border Protection

Customs and Border Protection (CBP) is one of the largest security-oriented components of DHS. It is tasked with the protection of the borders from intrusion by terrorists and weapons smuggling as well as enabling legal trade and travel.[47] It must do this at the same time while enforcing a large number of governmental regulations on border crossings, including immigration and drug trafficking. This, in turn, means that CBP is constantly working with agencies like the Drug Enforcement Agency (DEA) and Immigration and Customs Enforcement (discussed next), to fulfill their homeland security mission.[48]

Immigration and Customs Enforcement

Immigration and Customs Enforcement (ICE) is the second largest investigative agency in the American government, employing over 50,000 people. It is tasked as the investigative arm of DHS and is the principal investigative unit housed within the department.[49] The agency focuses primarily on homeland security investigations, which are wide-ranging and include arms smuggling and immigration issues such as human trafficking as well as cybersecurity and other issues that affect customs.[50] It was established in 2003 through the merger of two previous agencies, the U.S. Customs Service and Immigration and Naturalization, and tasked with a primary role in the national homeland security plan.

Department of the Treasury

The Department of the Treasury is not usually considered to be an integral part of the homeland security community. However, when considering the importance of financial transactions in both funding terrorist operations, as well as tracking the terrorists themselves, it becomes clear that the role the department plays is essential. In particular, the department's Office of Intelligence and Analysis (OIA) was established to assist with tracking terrorist financing, insurgent financing, and the financing of rogue regimes around the world.

Military Community

While in most cases, the Department of Defense (DOD) is not the agency primarily responsible for homeland security, the agencies of the DOD play an important role in terms of protecting the homeland. Broadly speaking, these roles can be broken into two major components, aside from intelligence, as mentioned previously: Homeland defense and civil support.[51]

Homeland defense is the primary mission of the DOD. It provides military security for the borders of the nation, as well as through applying force at the origin of the threat, in some cases to promote deterrence, as can be seen in the invasion of Afghanistan after the September 11 attacks. Not only were the Taliban, at the time the leaders of Afghanistan, supporting Al Qaeda and Osama bin Laden but they also provided a safe haven for the organization.[52] The invasion of Afghanistan, while a projection of military power to a foreign country, was also an extension of homeland security.

The homeland defense mission, aside from retaliation, also includes preemption and defense in a more traditional sense.[53] Furthermore, it involves

Courtesy of Sgt. Brian E. Christiansen/DOD.

protection of what are considered "forward regions," which are areas outside of the continental boundaries of the United States, including territories and bases, oceans, and airspace surrounding the country. In each of these cases, the military is the only national organization with the capacity to defend against attacks and respond to the source of threats outside of the United States.[54]

USNORTHCOM

The United States Northern Command (USNORTHCOM) has a particularly important role to play regarding the homeland security of the United States.[55] It is the command of the U.S. military charged specifically with protection of the homeland. It was established as a combat command on October 2, 2002, partially in response to the attacks of September 11, 2001:

> USNORTHCOM's AOR includes air, land, and sea approaches and encompasses the continental United States, Alaska, Canada, Mexico, and the surrounding water out to approximately 500 nautical miles. It also includes the Gulf of Mexico, the Straits of Florida, and portions of the Caribbean region to include The Bahamas, Puerto Rico, and the U.S. Virgin Islands. The commander of USNORTHCOM is responsible for theater security cooperation with Canada, Mexico, and The Bahamas.[56]

In addition to their defense mission, USNORTHCOM also has the lead military role in civil support during times of disaster. While the command does not have very many permanent troops assigned, they are able to request that troops be assigned for specific missions.[57] Because of this, in order for USNORTHCOM to become involved in a disaster, it must exceed the capabilities of local, state, and federal agencies to handle it before the command will mobilize, and they will only remain involved until the event is once again able to be handled by the other levels of government.[58]

State Level

Homeland security efforts at the state level are dictated by both national policy, such as the required adoption of the National Incident Management System (NIMS) and the National Response Framework (NRF) as well as state-level concerns.[59] As a direct response to 9-11, most states that did not already have the capacity immediately began developing a homeland security capability.[60] This new capability was, in many cases, merged with the states' existing emergency management offices to create state departments of homeland security. Additionally, as major partners in cooperative efforts for homeland security, like Joint Terrorism Task Forces (JTTFs), fusion centers, as well as in training and coordination within their respective territories, state-level governments and officials play a key role in homeland security. In short, as stated by Chenowith and Clarke in their article, All Terrorism is Local, "in a federal system, national responses are only as effective as their implementation through state and local governments."[61]

Because state-level agencies are independent from DHS, different states have adopted different methods of dealing with issues surrounding homeland security. Some states have taken existing agencies and rolled them into a single state-level homeland security department. Other states have developed an additional agency that deals specifically with homeland security, and still others have simply incorporated homeland security requirements into their existing agency structure.

Local Level

Homeland security on the local level is also unique. Just as "all politics is local," so are all terrorist attacks and other disasters.[62] This presents unique challenges at the local level as the resources to deal with these events are usually inadequate. However, since the advent of federal homeland security, local governments have been able to apply for funding for homeland security-related costs to help in their preparation. Additionally, there has been a concerted effort focused on training local officers for homeland security preparedness, as well as the advent of specific homeland security-related offices, such as JTTFs and fusion centers, mentioned previously.

Standardization

One of the problems highlighted by the 9-11 attacks was the interaction between local, state, and federal first-responding organizations, and in many cases, between different local agencies with differing jurisdictions. Noting this, the 9/11 Commission Report stated:

> It is a fair inference, given the differing situations in New York City and Northern Virginia, that the problems in command, control, and communications that occurred at both sites will likely recur in any emergency of similar scale. The task looking forward is to enable first responders to respond in a coordinated manner with the greatest possible awareness of the situation.
>
> If New York and other major cities are to be prepared for future terrorist attacks, different first responder agencies within each city must be fully coordinated, just as different branches of the U.S. military are. Coordination entails a unified command that comprehensively deploys all dispatched police, fire, and other first-responder resources. The attacks on 9-11 demonstrated that even the most robust emergency response capabilities can be overwhelmed if an attack is large enough. Teamwork, collaboration and cooperation at an incident site are critical to a successful response.
>
> Preparedness in the private sector and public sector for rescue, restart, and recovery of operations should include 1) a plan for evacuation, 2) adequate communications capabilities, and 3) a plan for continuity of operations.[63]

As a direct result, President George W. Bush issued Homeland Security Presidential Directive 5 (HSPD 5, 2003),[64] which standardized the response mechanism through the National Incident Management System (NIMS), and made its adoption effectively a requirement for all federal, state, and local response efforts. NIMS will be discussed elsewhere in this text.

Fusion Centers

In addition to the standardization of response, there has been an increasing emphasis on cooperation of all levels of government, not to the exclusion of cooperation between local agencies. One of the methods by which this cooperation has been enhanced is the **fusion center**.[65] These local (or sometimes regional) centers operate with multiple jurisdictions with the express purpose of combining intelligence information and crime data to help predict and deal with terrorist events.[66] They are not part of the federal government, although they include elements of federal law enforcement. Fusion centers arose in part out of the recognition of the difficulties of sharing classified information across levels of government, and most specifically from the federal level down to the local level. Fusion centers, with their integrated staff from all levels of government, theoretically allow for this diffusion of information across the various levels of government, and thus allow for a better coordinated response to any threat.

Fusion centers are not just responsible for relaying information, however. Many centers, especially those at the state level, engage in homeland security threat analysis, based on information from local and state agencies, which can then be shared across the government and with decision-makers at all levels. The National Security Strategy of 2009 states the purpose of fusion centers clearly:

> To prevent acts of terrorism on American soil, we must enlist all of our intelligence, law enforcement, and homeland security capabilities. We will continue to integrate and leverage state and major urban area fusion centers that have the capability to share classified information; establish a nationwide framework for reporting suspicious activity; and implement an integrated approach to our counterterrorism information systems to ensure that the analysts, agents, and officers who protect us have access to all relevant intelligence throughout the government.[67]

In short, fusion centers provide local law enforcement agencies ready access to federal and state level information and agencies, to better share information and coordinate response in the case of a terrorist threat or event.[68]

Fusion centers have previously come under fire for being ineffective (see **BOX 6.5**). The Senate Permanent Subcommittee on Investigations under the Committee on Homeland Security and Governmental Affairs

BOX 6.5 Fusion Centers—From Broken to Essential

In 2012, the U.S. Senate Permanent Subcommittee on Investigations for the Committee on Homeland Security and Governmental Affairs completed a 2-year investigation of the success of fusion centers. The findings of the committee, far from seeing utility in the centers, found that they had not provided any significant information useful for counterterrorism. This finding, while contested by DHS, was a significant blow. However, rather than being eliminated, the national network of fusion centers underwent dramatic transformations with regard to everything from funding to information sharing. Below, the three criticisms, and the response to those criticisms, are detailed.

Uneven Intelligence Quality

DHS officers who participated in state and local fusion centers were found to have produced shoddy intelligence reports whose contents may have endangered civil liberties of American citizens. There were also cases, cited by the subcommittee, of finished intelligence products containing information from already-published sources. Additionally, some of the material published in these reports was unrelated to terrorist activity.

No Unique Contribution to Counterterrorism

According to the subcommittee, there was no evidence provided that the fusion centers contributed to federal counterterrorism efforts that disrupted a terrorist plot. Additionally, nearly a third of all reports were never published for use by any organization within the intelligence community, perhaps because they contained no useful information. Some of the reports that were generated were not published because DHS officials did not make a decision on whether or not to publish them in a timely manner.

Funding Problems

The subcommittee also found that DHS did not effectively monitor how funds provided by the federal government were used to strengthen federal counterterrorism efforts. Funds were used to purchase items like flat-screen TVs, sport utility vehicles, and surveillance equipment that were not directly related to the mission of the fusion centers. The subcommittee found that while these items were allowed under DHS policy, they did not help address deficiencies in the fusion centers' operations.

Response

The response from the Department of Homeland Security in terms of the criticism of fusion centers was to increase oversight and to try to demonstrate the unique intelligence capabilities that fusion centers bring to the homeland security enterprise. Since the original report in 2013, the network has generated significant contributions to the counterterrorism effort of the United States, and has also increasingly assisted with law enforcement activities related to counterterrorism—particularly dealing with issues of narcotics and organized crime. Additionally, the amount of information sharing among the agencies participating has increased dramatically, with demonstrable effects in terms of the interdiction of terrorism plots. With increasing reporting being done on the effectiveness of the fusion centers, as well as some changes internally and in funding, the fusion centers remain part of the United States's homeland security intelligence and law enforcement investigations and will remain so for the foreseeable future.

Data from: Permanent Subcommittee on Investigations. (2012). Federal Support for and Involvement in State and Local Fusion Centers. Retrieved from http://www.hsgac.senate.gov/download/report_federal-support-for-and-involvement-in-state-and-local-fusions-centers House Homeland Security Committee Majority Staff. (2017). Report: Advancing the Homeland Security Information Sharing Environment: A Review of the National Network of Fusion Centers. Retrieved from https://www.hsdl.org/?view&did=805450.

released a finding that fusion centers were largely overrated, and that little or no actionable intelligence had come from fusion centers since their inception after 2001.[69] While this finding has been disputed by some,[70] there has been an increasing push to document the effectiveness of fusion centers. This had led an annual assessment process, which has led to better outcomes for fusion centers.

When moving to a homeland security paradigm, one of the difficult transitions is the fact that while national security is obviously a national problem, events such as terrorist attacks and natural disasters are, almost by definition, local. In an article examining the nature of a federal response to local phenomenon, Chenoweth and Clarke stated,

> City security is a core national security issue, but a local responsibility; in the United States, American cities and counties control and finance the police, fire, public health, and emergency services most needed in the face of a terrorist attack.[71]

In fact, law enforcement has borne the brunt of homeland security response, particularly in the case

United States Senate
PERMANENT SUBCOMMITTEE ON INVESTIGATIONS
Committee on Homeland Security and Governmental Affairs
Carl Levin, Chairman
Tom Coburn, Ranking Minority Member

FEDERAL SUPPORT FOR AND INVOLVEMENT IN STATE AND LOCAL FUSION CENTERS

MAJORITY AND MINORITY STAFF REPORT

PERMANENT SUBCOMMITTEE ON INVESTIGATIONS

UNITED STATES SENATE

October 3, 2012

Courtesy of Homeland Security & Governmental Affairs.

of terrorism, and while there is some suggestion that policing has changed and entered an era of homeland security,[72] the research on how prepared law enforcement is remains mixed (see **TABLE 6.2**).[73] Furthermore, the preparation that has been done tends to have mirrored those steps taken at the state level, with increased emphasis on risk assessment and joint training exercises, rather than on emergency response plans or updated equipment.[74]

TABLE 6.2 Local Police Engagement in Homeland Security Activities (2017)

Activity	Percent of Departments
Intelligence Functions Assigned to Existing Unit	32
All-Hazards Plan (including terrorism)	62
Community Risk Assessment for Terrorism	55
Communications Interoperability	74
Partnerships with NGOs	59
Participation in Terrorism Task Force	38

Data from: Johnson, T. C., & Hunter, R. D. (2017). Changes in homeland security activities since 9/11: an examination of state and local law enforcement agencies' practices. *Police Practice & Research, 18*(2), 160–173.

Homeland Security Policing

A more recent development has been the advent of **homeland security policing**. This form of policing focuses many of the aspects of problem-oriented policing on the specific issue of homeland security and emphasizes that local law enforcement concentrate on homeland security, specifically terrorism prevention.[75] While it has not been adopted without controversy,[76] it has been considered by some to be the "fourth era" of policing, supplanting community-oriented policing.[77]

The focus of homeland security policing is similar, in many respects, to intelligence-led policing.[78] There is an emphasis on the SARA (Scanning, Analysis, Response and Assessment) technique, although the focus tends to be on terrorism rather than on crime. Additionally, homeland security as a policing paradigm has been criticized in that it might create significant distance between the communities that are being policed and the police themselves. This may be particularly true of minority communities that may be perceived by some as a potential source of terrorism.[79]

Regardless of whether or not homeland security becomes (or has become) the dominant paradigm of policing in the United States, there is little doubt that the change in emphasis on the national level has impacted local departments as well, in part due to potential funding opportunities via grants though these have decreased in recent years. The range of actions taken by local departments has varied, with some departments hiring more officers, some updating or writing their emergency action plans, and many increasing training.[80]

There has been a major change regarding the state and local levels of homeland security since 9-11, though it is unclear how persistent that change will remain.[81] Many state and local agencies reorganized and reoriented to focus on a homeland security mission after 9/11(see **TABLE 6.3**),[82] in some cases, supplanting agencies at both the state and local level.[83] However, through the continued standardization across jurisdictions and the use of fusion centers, there seems to be significant improvement in our national ability to deal with the complex problem of homeland security—a national problem happening at a local level (see **FIGURE 6.3**).[84] One perplexing phenomenon however,

TABLE 6.3 Preparedness Activities of Local Police Departments (2010)

Population Served	Percent of Departments That—					
	Participated in Emergency Preparedness Exercised	Increased Officer Presence at Critical Areas	Disseminated Information to Increase Citizen Preparedness	Held Community Meetings on Homeland Security	Partnered with Culturally Diverse Populations	Conducted a Public Anti-Fear Campaign
All sizes	62	36	33	26	13	4
1,00,000 or more	92	77	92	85	54	46
500,00–999,999	94	74	71	68	65	19
250,000–499,999	98	80	72	78	72	26
100,000–249,999	92	64	57	43	41	9
50,000–99,999	90	60	53	39	40	9
25,000–49,999	82	54	53	31	22	6
10,000–24,999	77	51	42	25	15	5
2,500–9,999	64	36	35	28	8	3
Under 2,500	47	23	20	21	11	2

Data from: Reaves, Brian A. (2010). Local Police Departments, 2007. Washington, D.C.: U.S. Department of Justice.

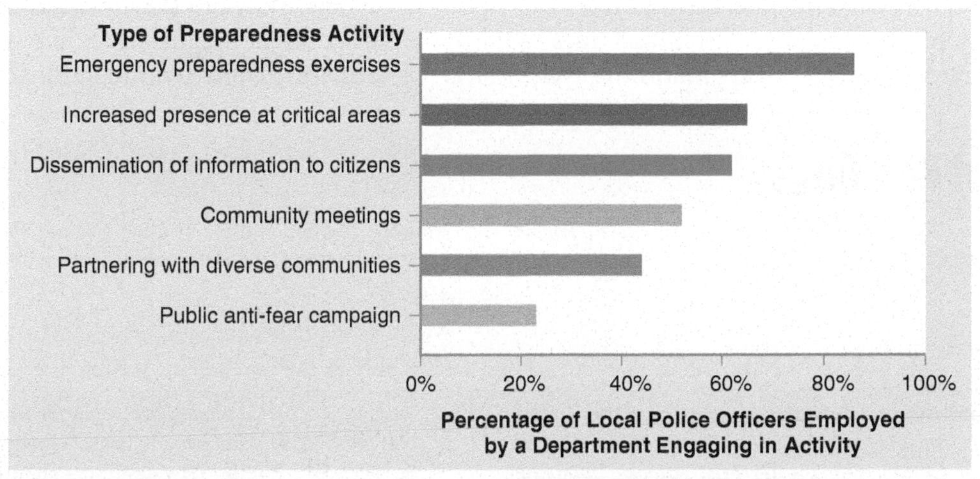

FIGURE 6.3 Local Police Officers Employed by a Department Engaging in Selected Preparedness Activities.

Data from: Johnson, T. C., & Hunter, R. D. (2017). Changes in homeland security activities since 9/11: an examination of state and local law enforcement agencies' practices. *Police Practice & Research, 18*(2), 160–173.

is the decrease in information available in more recent years, as Homeland Security has lost its novelty, much of the documentation has not been renewed, and there is a dearth of information on whether police departments remain engaged (beyond participation in JTTFs and Fusion Centers), and how much, in homeland security preparedness.[85]

Chapter Summary

There is little doubt that the homeland security community is a complex one, encompassing multiple levels of government and crossing over various areas of expertise.[86] With multiple agencies covering intelligence and security and involving all levels of government, the homeland security community has the difficult job of not only identifying and responding to threats to the homeland but of also coordinating activities among themselves to ensure our safety.[87]

With the advent of the ODNI, and the coordination that it engenders, there is now more effective communications across lines than ever before. However, at the state and local levels, the coordination remains more difficult, with mandates from higher levels of government somewhat assisting in the process, but likely insufficient by themselves. The research is inconclusive about preparation at the state and local levels for homeland security events, although there is promising improvement in several areas.

Additionally, at the local level, many jurisdictions have moved to a homeland security policing model.[88] While it appears that this has not replaced community-oriented policing as the primary policing paradigm, there is little doubt that homeland security as an ongoing concern has impacted local police significantly. With increased emphasis on training and planning, officers are almost certainly better equipped to deal with an incident than in the past, but it is by no means clear that they are well prepared.[89]

In general, because homeland security is a complex and evolving concern, there is little that is known for sure. However, with the increased coordination at all levels of government, the widespread focus on homeland security provides a direction for the various levels of government that pursued their related goals in an uncoordinated fashion previously. While communication is not perfect, there is little doubt that it has improved since 9-11. With the span of time between major attacks increasing, whether it remains a priority has yet to be seen.

Review/Discussion Questions

1. What role does collaboration play in the intelligence community, and what organization is responsible for collaboration among intelligence agencies? What makes the process difficult?
2. Describe the steps in the intelligence cycle. What is important about each step, and does the intelligence process always follow the cycle?
3. What role does the military play in the security community? Might they function as a bridge between the worlds of intelligence and law enforcement?
4. Fusion centers came under fire from the U.S. Senate. Why did they come under fire, and what might the fusion centers still be providing despite the problems identified?

Additional Readings

Lowenthal, M. M. (2005). Intelligence: *From Secrets to Policy*. Thousand Oaks, CA: CQ Press.

Sims, J. E., & Gerber, B. (Eds). (2005). *Transforming US Intelligence*. Washington, D.C.: Georgetown University Press.

Endnotes

1. National Commission on Terrorist Attacks Upon the United States. (2004). *The 9/11 Commission Report: Final Report of the National Commission on Terrorist Attacks Upon the United States (Authorized Ed.)*. New York: W.W. Norton & Company, Inc.
2. Best, R. A. (2011). *Intelligence Issues for Congress* (CRS Report No. RL33539). Retrieved from Congressional Research Service website: https://www.everycrsreport.com/files/20110413_RL33539_dfe74221276d06702b3695f0b2f083d20105282e.pdf

3. Office of the Director of National Intelligence. (2012). *About the Intelligence Community.* Retrieved from Intelligence Community website: https://www.dni.gov/index.php/what-we-do/members-of-the-ic
4. Office of the Director of National Intelligence. (2009). *An Overview of the United States Intelligence Community for the 111th Congress.* Retrieved from https://fas.org/irp/eprint/overview.pdf
5. Office of the Director of National Intelligence. (2009). *An Overview of the United States Intelligence Community for the 111th Congress.* Retrieved from https://fas.org/irp/eprint/overview.pdf
6. Office of the Director of National Intelligence. (2012). *About the Intelligence Community.* Retrieved from Intelligence Community website: https://www.dni.gov/index.php/what-we-do/members-of-the-ic
7. Intelligence Reform and Terrorism Prevention Act of 2004. Pub.S.2845, 108th Cong. (2004).
8. Office of the Director of National Intelligence. (2012). *About the Intelligence Community.* Retrieved from Intelligence Community website: https://www.dni.gov/index.php/what-we-do/members-of-the-ic
9. Best, R. A. (2011). *Intelligence Issues for Congress* (CRS Report No. RL33539). Retrieved from Congressional Research Service website: https://www.everycrsreport.com/files/20110413_RL33539_dfe74221276d06702b3695f0b2f083d20105282e.pdf
10. Best, R. A. (2011). *Intelligence Issues for Congress* (CRS Report No. RL33539). Retrieved from Congressional Research Service website: https://www.everycrsreport.com/files/20110413_RL33539_dfe74221276d06702b3695f0b2f083d20105282e.pdf; National Commission on Terrorist Attacks Upon the United States. (2004). *The 9/11 Commission Report: Final Report of the National Commission on Terrorist Attacks Upon the United States (Authorized Ed.).* New York: W.W. Norton & Company, Inc.
11. Best, R. A. (2011). *Intelligence Issues for Congress* (CRS Report No. RL33539). Retrieved from Congressional Research Service website: https://www.everycrsreport.com/files/20110413_RL33539_dfe74221276d06702b3695f0b2f083d20105282e.pdf; Office of the Director of National Intelligence. (2009). *An Overview of the United States Intelligence Community for the 111th Congress.* Retrieved from https://fas.org/irp/eprint/overview.pdf
12. Masse, T. M. (2005). *The National Counterterrorism Center: Implementation Challenges and Issues for Congress* (CRS Report No. RL32816). Retrieved from Congressional Research Service website:https://opencrs.com/document/RL32816/2005-03-16/; National Counterterrorism Center. (2012). *About the National Counterterrorism Center.* Retrieved from http://www.nctc.gov/about_us/about_nctc.html
13. Office of the Director of National Intelligence. (2013). *U.S. National Intelligence: An Overview 2013.* Retrieved from https://www.dni.gov/files/documents/USNI%202013%20Overview_web.pdf
14. Office of the Director of National Intelligence. (2009). *An Overview of the United States Intelligence Community.* Retrieved from https://fas.org/irp/eprint/overview.pdf
15. Weiner, T. (2007). *Legacy of Ashes: The History of the CIA.* New York, NY: Doubleday.
16. Office of the Director of National Intelligence. (2009). *An Overview of the United States Intelligence Community for the 111th Congress.* Retrieved from https://fas.org/irp/eprint/overview.pdf
17. Central Intelligence Agency. (2012). *CIA Vision, Mission, and Values.* Retrieved from https://www.cia.gov/about-cia/cia-vision-mission-values/index.html; Office of the Director of National Intelligence. (2009). *Overview of the Intelligence Community for the 111th Congress of the United States of America.* Retrieved from http://cstsp.aaas.org/files/overview.pdf
18. Office of the Director of National Intelligence. (2009). *An Overview of the United States Intelligence Community for the 111th Congress.* Retrieved from https://fas.org/irp/eprint/overview.pdf
19. Office of the Director of National Intelligence. (2009). *An Overview of the United States Intelligence Community for the 111th Congress.* Retrieved from https://fas.org/irp/eprint/overview.pdf; Weiner, T. (2007). *Legacy of Ashes: The History of the CIA.* New York, NY: Doubleday.
20. Aid, M. (2009). *The Secret Sentry: The Untold History of the National Security Agency.* London, UK: Bloomsbury Press; National Security Agency. (2012). *Vision.* Retrieved from http://www.nsa.gov/about/index.shtml; Office of the Director of National Intelligence. (2009). *Overview of the Intelligence Community for the 111th Congress of the United States of America.* Retrieved from http://cstsp.aaas.org/files/overview.pdf
21. Aid, M. (2009). *The Secret Sentry: The Untold History of the National Security Agency.* London, UK: Bloomsbury Press.
22. Best, R. A. (2011). *Intelligence Issues for Congress* (CRS Report No. RL33539). Retrieved from Congressional Research Service website: https://www.everycrsreport.com/files/20110413_RL33539_dfe74221276d06702b3695f0b2f083d20105282e.pdf; Knight, W. (2008). *Homeland Security: Roles and Missions for United States Northern Command* (CRS report No. RL34342). Retrieved from Federation of American Scientists website: http://www.fas.org/sgp/crs/homesec/RL34342.pdf; Office of the Director of National Intelligence. (2009). *An Overview of the United States Intelligence Community for the 111th Congress.* Retrieved from https://fas.org/irp/eprint/overview.pdf
23. Office of the Director of National Intelligence. (2009). *An Overview of the United States Intelligence Community for the 111th Congress.* Retrieved from https://fas.org/irp/eprint/overview.pdf
24. Office of the Director of National Intelligence. (2009). *An Overview of the United States Intelligence Community for the 111th Congress.* Retrieved from https://fas.org/irp/eprint/overview.pdf
25. Office of the Director of National Intelligence. (2009). *An Overview of the United States Intelligence Community for the 111th Congress.* Retrieved from https://fas.org/irp/eprint/overview.pdf
26. Office of the Director of National Intelligence. (2009). *An Overview of the United States Intelligence Community for the 111th Congress.* Retrieved from https://fas.org/irp/eprint/overview.pdf
27. Office of the Director of National Intelligence. (2009). *An Overview of the United States Intelligence Community for the 111th Congress.* Retrieved from https://fas.org/irp/eprint/overview.pdf
28. Best, R. A. (2011). *Intelligence Issues for Congress* (CRS Report No. RL33539). Retrieved from Congressional Research Service website: https://www.everycrsreport.com/files/20110413_RL33539_dfe74221276d06702b3695f0b2f083d20105282e.pdf
29. Best, R. A. (2011). *Intelligence Issues for Congress* (CRS Report No. RL33539). Retrieved from Congressional Research Service website: https://www.everycrsreport.com/files/20110413_RL33539_dfe74221276d06702b3695f0b2f083d20105282e.pdf; Office of the Director of National Intelligence. (2012). *About the Intelligence Community.* Retrieved from Intelligence Community website: https://www.dni.gov/index.php/what-we-do/members-of-the-ic
30. Office of the Director of National Intelligence. (2009). *An Overview of the United States Intelligence Community for the 111th Congress.* Retrieved from https://fas.org/irp/eprint/overview.pdf

31. National Commission on Terrorist Attacks Upon the United States. (2004). *The 9/11 Commission Report: Final Report of the National Commission on Terrorist Attacks Upon the United States (Authorized Ed.)*. New York: W.W. Norton & Company, Inc.
32. Best, R. A. (2011). *Intelligence Issues for Congress* (CRS Report No. RL33539). Retrieved from Congressional Research Service website: https://www.everycrsreport.com/files/20110413_RL33539_dfe74221276d06702b3695f0b2f083d20105282e.pdf
33. Best, R. A. (2011). *Intelligence Issues for Congress* (CRS Report No. RL33539). Retrieved from Congressional Research Service website: https://www.everycrsreport.com/files/20110413_RL33539_dfe74221276d06702b3695f0b2f083d20105282e.pdf
34. Best, R. A. (2011). *Intelligence issues for Congress* (CRS Report No. RL33539). Retrieved from Congressional Research Service website: https://www.everycrsreport.com/files/20110413_RL33539_dfe74221276d06702b3695f0b2f083d20105282e.pdf; Office of the Director of National Intelligence. (2009). *Overview of the Intelligence Community for the 111th Congress of the United States of America*. Retrieved from http://cstsp.aaas.org/files/overview.pdf
35. Office of the Director of National Intelligence. (2009). *An Overview of the United States Intelligence Community for the 111th Congress*. Retrieved from https://fas.org/irp/eprint/overview.pdf
36. Cumming, A. (2005). *Intelligence Reform Implementation at the Federal Bureau of Investigation: Issues and Options for Congress* (CRS Report No.RL33033). Retrieved from Congressional Research Service Website: https://opencrs.com/document/RL33033/2005-08-16/; Office of the Director of National Intelligence. (2009). *Overview of the Intelligence Community for the 111th Congress of the United States of America*. Retrieved from http://cstsp.aaas.org/files/overview.pdf
37. National Commission on Terrorist Attacks Upon the United States. (2004). *The 9/11 Commission Report: Final Report of the National Commission on Terrorist Attacks Upon the United States (Authorized Ed.)*. New York: W.W. Norton & Company, Inc.
38. Best, R. A. (2011). *Intelligence Issues for Congress* (CRS Report No. RL33539). Retrieved from Congressional Research Service website: https://www.everycrsreport.com/files/20110413_RL33539_dfe74221276d06702b3695f0b2f083d20105282e.pdf; Office of the Director of National Intelligence. (2009). *An Overview of the United States Intelligence Community for the 111th Congress*. Retrieved from https://fas.org/irp/eprint/overview.pdf
39. Federal Bureau of Investigation. (2019). *The Intel-driven FBI*. Retrieved from https://www.fbi.gov/investigate; Office of the Director of National Intelligence. (2009). *Overview of the Intelligence Community for the 111th Congress of the United States of America*. Retrieved from https://www.hsdl.org/?view&did=231870
40. Federal Bureau of Investigation. (2019). *The Intel-driven FBI*. Retrieved from https://www.fbi.gov/investigate
41. Federal Bureau of Investigation. (2019). *The Intel-driven FBI*. Retrieved from https://www.fbi.gov/investigate
42. Office of the Director of National Intelligence. (2009). *An Overview of the United States Intelligence Community for the 111th Congress*. Retrieved from https://fas.org/irp/eprint/overview.pdf
43. Federal Bureau of Investigation. (2019). *The Intel-driven FBI*. Retrieved from https://www.fbi.gov/investigate
44. Federal Bureau of Investigation. (2019). *The Intel-driven FBI*. Retrieved from https://www.fbi.gov/investigate
45. Office of the Director of National Intelligence. (2009). *An Overview of the United States Intelligence Community for the 111th Congress*. Retrieved from https://fas.org/irp/eprint/overview.pdf
46. Department of Homeland Security. (2018). *Border Security Overview*. Retrieved from http://www.dhs.gov/border-security-overview
47. Customs and Border Protection. (2019). *About Us*. Retrieved from https://www.cbp.gov/about
48. Office of the Director of National Intelligence. (2009). *An Overview of the United States Intelligence Community for the 111th Congress*. Retrieved from https://fas.org/irp/eprint/overview.pdf
49. Sauter, M. A. and Carafano, J. J. (2011). *Homeland Security*. New York, NY: McGraw-Hill.
50. Sauter, M. A. and Carafano, J. J. (2011). *Homeland Security*. New York, NY: McGraw-Hill.
51. Joint Chiefs of Staff. (August 2, 2009). *Joint Publication 3–26: Homeland Security*. Retrieved on 16 May, 2019 from https://www.hsdl.org/?view&did=456038.
52. National Commission on Terrorist Attacks Upon the United States. (2004). *The 9/11 Commission Report: Final Report of the National Commission on Terrorist Attacks Upon the United States (Authorized Ed.)*. New York: W.W. Norton & Company, Inc.
53. Joint Chiefs of Staff. (August 2, 2009). *Joint Publication 3–26: Homeland Security*; Knight, W. (2008). *Homeland Security: Roles and Missions for United States Northern Command* (CRS report No. RL34342). Retrieved from Federation of American Scientists website: http://www.fas.org/sgp/crs/homesec/RL34342.pdf
54. Joint Chiefs of Staff. (August 2, 2009). *Joint Publication 3*. Retrieved on May 16, 2019, from homesec/RL34342.pdf; Joint Chiefs of Staff. (August 2, 2009). Joint Publication 3_276: Homeland Defense. Retrieved on 16 May, 2019 from https://www.jcs.mil/Portals/36/Documents/Doctrine/pubs/jp3_27.pdf?ver=2018-07-09-162710-440
55. Knight, W. (2008). *Homeland Security: Roles and Missions for United States Northern Command* (CRS report No. RL34342). Retrieved from Federation of American Scientists website: http://www.fas.org/sgp/crs/homesec/RL34342.pdf
56. Knight, W. (2008). *Homeland Security: Roles and Missions for United States Northern Command* (CRS report No. RL34342). Retrieved from Federation of American Scientists website: http://www.fas.org/sgp/crs/homesec/RL34342.pdf
57. Joint Chiefs of Staff. (August 2, 2009). *Joint Publication 3–26: Homeland Security*; Knight, W. (2008). *Homeland Security: Roles and Missions for United States Northern Command* (CRS report No. RL34342). Retrieved from Federation of American Scientists website: http://www.fas.org/sgp/crs/homesec/RL34342.pdf
58. Knight, W. (2008). *Homeland Security: Roles and Missions for United States Northern Command* (CRS report No. RL34342). Retrieved from Federation of American Scientists website: http://www.fas.org/sgp/crs/homesec/RL34342.pdf
59. Department of Homeland Security. (2016). *National Response Framework*. Retrieved from https://www.fema.gov/media-library-data/1466014682982-9bcf8245ba4c60c120aa915abe74e15d/National_Response_Framework3rd.pdf
60. Chenoweth, E. & Clarke, S.E. (2010). "All Terrorism Is Local: Resources, Nested Institutions, and Governance for Urban Homeland Security in the American Federal System." *Political Research Quarterly, 63*, 495–507.

61. Chenoweth, E. & Clarke, S. E. (2010). "All Terrorism Is Local: Resources, Nested Institutions, and Governance for Urban Homeland Security in the American Federal System." *Political Research Quarterly, 63*, 495–507.
62. Chenoweth, E. & Clarke, S. E. (2010). "All Terrorism Is Local: Resources, Nested Institutions, and Governance for Urban Homeland Security in the American Federal System." *Political Research Quarterly, 63*, 495–507.
63. National Commission on Terrorist Attacks Upon the United States. (2004). *The 9/11 Commission Report: Final Report of the National Commission on Terrorist Attacks Upon the United States (Authorized Ed.)*. New York: W.W. Norton & Company, Inc. The White House. (2003). Homeland Security Presidential Directive 5. Retrieved on May 16, 2019 from https://www.dhs.gov/sites/default/files/publications/Homeland%20Security%20Presidential%20Directive%205.pdf; Monahan, T. (2010). "Homeland Security Fusion Centers." *Social Justice, 37*(2–3), 84–98.
64. The White House. (2003). Homeland Security Presidential Directive 5. Retrieved on 16 May, 2019 from https://www.dhs.gov/sites/default/files/publications/Homeland%20Security%20Presidential%20Directive%205.pdf
65. Monahan, T. (2010). Homeland Security Fusion Centers. *Social Justice, 37*(2–3), 84–98.
66. Monahan, T. (2010). Homeland Security Fusion Centers. *Social Justice, 37*(2–3), 84–98.
67. Office of the Director of National Intelligence. (August 2009). *National Security Strategy of the United States of America 2009*, p. 20. Retrieved from Office of Director of National Intelligence website: http://www.dni.gov/files/documents/Newsroom/Reports%20and%20Pubs/2009_NIS.pdf
68. The White House (2010). *National Security Strategy*. Retrieved on 16 May, 2019 from http://unipd-centrodirittiumani.it/public/docs/USA_NSS_2010.pdf
69. United States Senate Permanent Subcommittee on Investigations. (2012). *Federal Support for and Involvement in State and Local Fusion Centers*. Retrieved from http://www.hsgac.senate.gov/download/report_federal-support-for-and-involvementin-state-and-local-fusions-centers
70. O'Harrow, R., Jr. (2012). "Homeland Security 'Fusion Centers' Defended in Response to Sharply Critical Senate Report." *Washington Post*. Retrieved on May 16, 2019 from http://www.washingtonpost.com/world/national-security/fusion-centersdefendedin-response-to-senate-report/2012/10/03/58841b38-0da2-11e2-a310-2363842b7057_story.html
71. Chenoweth, E. & Clarke, S. E. (2010). "All Terrorism Is Local: Resources, Nested Institutions, and Governance for Urban Homeland Security in the American Federal System." *Political Research Quarterly, 63*, 496–507.
72. Oliver, W. M. (2006). "The Fourth Era of Policing: Homeland Security." *International Review of Law, Computers, and Technology, 20*, 49–62.
73. Giblin, M. J., Schafer, J. A., & Burruss, G. W. (2009). "Homeland Security in the Heartland: Risk, Preparedness, and Organizational Capacity." *Criminal Justice Policy Review, 20*, 274–289.
74. Giblin, M. J., Schafer, J. A., & Burruss, G. W. (2009). "Homeland Security in the Heartland: Risk, Preparedness, and Organizational Capacity." *Criminal Justice Policy Review, 20*, 274–289.
75. Chappell, A. T. & Gibson, S. A. (2009). "Community Policing and Homeland Security Policing: Friend or Foe?" *Criminal Justice Policy Review, 20*, 326–343.
76. Chappell, A. T. & Gibson, S. A. (2009). "Community Policing and Homeland Security Policing: Friend or Foe?" *Criminal Justice Policy Review, 20*, 326–343.
77. Oliver, W. M. (2006). "The Fourth Era of Policing: Homeland Security." *International Review of Law, Computers, and Technology, 20*, 49–62; Oliver, W. M. (2009). "Policing for Homeland Security: Policy and Research." *Criminal Justice Policy Review, 20*, 253–260.
78. Oliver, W. M. (2006). "The Fourth Era of Policing: Homeland Security." *International Review of Law, Computers, and Technology, 20*, 49–62.
79. Thatcher, D. (2005). "The Local Role in Homeland Security." *Law & Society Review, 39*(3), 635–676.
80. Burruss, G. W., Giblin, M. J., & Schafer, J. A. (2009). "Threatened Globally, Acting Locally: Modeling Law Enforcement Homeland Security Practices." *Justice Quarterly, 27*, 77–101.
81. Oliver, W. M. (2009). "Policing for Homeland Security: Policy and Research." *Criminal Justice Policy Review, 20*, 253–260.
82. Chenoweth, E. & Clarke, S.E. (2010). "All Terrorism Is Local: Resources, Nested Institutions, and Governance for Urban Homeland Security in the American Federal System." *Political Research Quarterly, 63*, 495–507.
83. Oliver, W. M. (2009). "Policing for Homeland Security: Policy and Research." *Criminal Justice Policy Review, 20*, 253–260.
84. Chenoweth, E. & Clarke, S. E. (2010). "All Terrorism Is Local: Resources, Nested Institutions, and Governance for Urban Homeland Security in the American Federal System." *Political Research Quarterly, 63*, 495–507.
85. Johnson, T. C., & Hunter, R. D. (2017). Changes in homeland security activities since 9/11: an examination of state and local law enforcement agencies' practices. *Police Practice & Research, 18*(2), 160–173.
86. Office of the Director of National Intelligence. (2009). *An Overview of the United States Intelligence Community for the 111th Congress*. Retrieved from https://fas.org/irp/eprint/overview.pdf
87. Office of the Director of National Intelligence. (2009). *An Overview of the United States Intelligence Community for the 111th Congress*. Retrieved from https://fas.org/irp/eprint/overview.pdf
88. Oliver, W. M. (2006). "The Fourth Era of Policing: Homeland Security." *International Review of Law, Computers, and Technology, 20*, 49–62.
89. Giblin, M. J., Schafer, J. A., & Burruss, G. W. (2009). "Homeland Security in the Heartland: Risk, Preparedness, and Organizational Capacity." *Criminal Justice Policy Review, 20*, 274–289.

CHAPTER 7

Antiterrorism and Counterterrorism

CHAPTER OBJECTIVES

- To understand the differences between counterterrorism and antiterrorism and how those differences impact efforts toward achieving homeland security
- To be able to identify the areas defined as "critical" in our nation's infrastructure and describe why critical infrastructure protection is so important to homeland security
- Identify the nine roles in the context of critical infrastructure and key resource protection and who is involved in those roles
- Identify differences and similarities in the counterterrorism approaches from pre- and post-9-11, and among different presidential administrations

CHAPTER OUTLINE

They had trained for the mission hundreds of times, and each of them had been on deployments in areas as varied as the Philippines and Iraq.[1] While their packs were heavy on their backs in the helicopter on the way to the compound, they knew that every item in them was essential and could potentially save their lives. As the helicopter arrived at its destination, there was a minor malfunction, and they had to move to Plan B. Instead of a silent assault, sliding down ropes into the courtyard of the compound, they would have to disembark and assault from outside—giving any potential bad guys time to arm themselves and resist if they realized that they were being attacked.[2]

© Mazhar Ali Khan/AP/Shutterstock.

After a controlled "hard landing" that involved striking the compound wall with the rotor of the helicopter, the members of Seal Team Six—a unit only recently recognized publicly by the government—flowed nearly silently from the downed helicopter, and another that had landed without incident, into the building owned by Arshad Khan, a Pashtun businessman from Afghanistan. Within al Qaeda; however, Khan had another name—Abu Ahmed al-Kuwaiti.[3]

Upon entering the compound, Al-Kuwaiti was the first resistance the team encountered, opening fire from behind the guesthouse door before being shot himself. The second team of commandos attacked the main building, killing al-Kuwaiti's brother and killing one of Osama bin Laden's sons, Khalid, both of whom were unarmed. In the dark of the building, assisted by night-vision goggles, the team got their first glimpse of the target: Osama bin Laden. Retreating, it was unclear whether he was retrieving a weapon or a suicide vest, and though the first shot missed as he ducked into a room, the subsequent shots to the chest and above his eye effectively achieved the goal of mission.[4]

Osama bin Laden's death was the culmination of 10 years of activity ranging from an intense intelligence-gathering effort to the training of teams like Seal Team Six. It marked, in some ways, the close of an era of U.S. history based around the identity of a single man and his attack against the country. Despite this close, however, the threat he represented—terrorism against a vulnerable target—remains an important part of America's national psyche, and the defense against it is one of the primary goals of homeland security.

The killing of Osama bin Laden represents many things to different people. One thing that most agree on, however, is that it represents a triumph of U.S. counterterrorism efforts. The ability to track down an elusive terrorist from across the globe and kill him shows not only the projection of power that the U.S. is willing to undertake to achieve its counterterrorism goals, but when combined with the lack of significant attacks against the homeland since 9-11, seems to represent a triumph of antiterrorism as well.

Fighting Terrorism

Two of the primary requirements of the homeland security mission in the United States are counterterrorism and antiterrorism. While frequently used interchangeably, and in some ways very closely tied together, **counterterrorism** and **antiterrorism** are the two elements of homeland security dedicated to protecting the United States from violent extremism.[5] Counterterrorism represents all offensive activities dedicated to tracking and eradicating terrorists both domestically and internationally. Antiterrorism, on the other hand, refers to the defensive aspects of protection from terrorism and can range from academic study to "target-hardening."[6]

Courtesy of the U.S. Immigration and Customs Enforcement/DHS.

These two elements represent nearly the entire picture of the United States' efforts at combatting terrorism. Boaz Ganor, in his book, *The Counterterrorism Puzzle*, presents the scope of counterterrorism (and antiterrorism) efforts as including several goals[7]: Eliminating terrorism, minimizing the damage caused by terrorism, and preventing the escalation of terrorism. These goals are clearly not relegated specifically to antiterrorism or counterterrorism, demonstrating the importance of understanding both topics.

In the sections following, the United States' approach to antiterrorism and counterterrorism are explored. The antiterrorism section focuses primarily on the development of antiterrorism policy post-9-11, with several important policies highlighted. It also examines closely the issue of critical infrastructure protection. The counterterrorism section details the development of counterterrorism strategy under both President George W. Bush and President Barack Obama, and the changes during the first part of the Trump administration. It details both domestic and international counterterrorism and differentiates the approaches taken by the various administrations since the 9/11 attacks.

Antiterrorism

In the American lexicon, antiterrorism is an underutilized term. Most of the focus on combating terrorism, particularly in the media, has been on the often more "kinetic" counterterrorism efforts. Even the ***National Strategy for Counterterrorism*** promulgated by the Obama administration, and those subsequent to its release, eschewed the use of the term antiterrorism.[8] However, without antiterrorism, there would be little ability to actively engage in any kind of counterterrorism effort, and if those efforts were unsuccessful, a lack of antiterrorism planning would make any attack significantly worse. The U.S. Department of Defense defines antiterrorism as "defensive measures used to reduce the vulnerability of individuals and property to terrorist acts, to include rapid containment by local military and civilian forces" (p. 19).[9] If this definition is broadly construed, antiterrorism includes a variety of elements that people do not generally consider as combating terrorism, such as efforts undertaken to understand terrorists and their motivations as well as antiterrorism policies such as the terrorism "watch list" that prevents terrorists from entering our country via air transportation. In general, antiterrorism can be broken down into two broad areas: Preventative measures and responsive measures, with preventative measures focusing on minimizing damage and responsive measures focusing on mitigation when an attack does happen.[10]

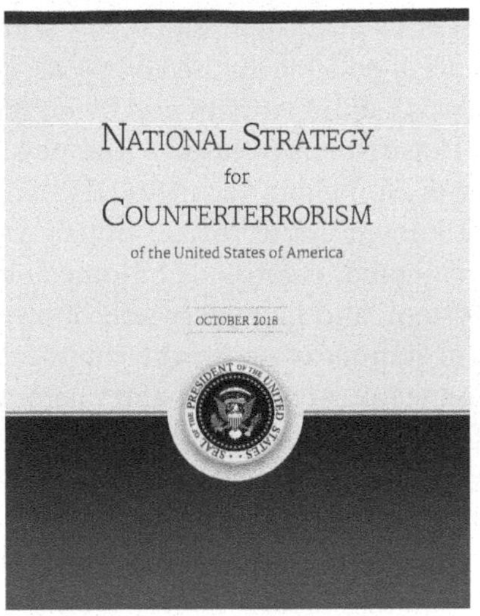

Coursty of the White House.

Not surprisingly, antiterrorism legislation changed significantly between the pre- and post-9-11 era.[11] Much of this change was in reference to the prevention of terrorist attacks. For example, Homeland Security Presidential Directive 6 (HSPD6), which was signed by President George W. Bush in 2003, established the now-familiar security screening process that the United States uses to help ensure that terrorists do not gain entry into the country by creating the Terrorism Threat Integration Center (which later became the National Counterterrorism Center) and requiring all appropriate bodies (Department of Defense, Department of State, etc.) to share all terrorist-related information with the center.[12] This was a significant adjustment to the previous screening process, which was limited to the Department of State's visa process and inspection (when appropriate) of a person by an immigration officer at the port of entry.[13]

In addition to the development of the Terrorist Screening Database (TSDB), other elements of antiterrorism legislation went into effect under the auspices of the Uniting and Strengthening America by Providing Appropriate Tools Required to Intercept and Obstruct Terrorism Act, better known as the USA PATRIOT Act.[14] While certainly controversial when it was passed, the PATRIOT Act provides law enforcement with additional antiterrorism tools that were previously either limited or nonexistent.[15] Elements such as additional methods by which to gain and use a warrant against a suspected terrorist and additional surveillance options were included in the legislation to allow for enhanced ability to seek and apprehend suspected terrorists. The PATRIOT Act was seen as a turning point for the Department of Justice's handling of terrorism, particularly regarding investigations by the FBI, in that it focused on detecting and disrupting terrorism rather than simply prosecuting terrorists.[16] In the words of then Attorney General John Ashcroft, "[we] must prevent first, prosecute second" (n.p.).[17] This is in direct opposition to the traditional, reactive model of policing focused on prosecution.

The focus on antiterrorism was by no means limited to the Department of Justice. The newly formed Department of Homeland Security (DHS) in 2002 had several well-known antiterrorism initiatives, such as the much-maligned, color-coded Homeland Security Advisory System, and many less well known, like the antiterrorism standards set for the chemical industry to protect dangerous chemicals and chemical manufacturing facilities from attack.[18] Other legislation is similarly meant to protect citizens from attack, either through strengthening potential targets or through deterring potential attackers. It is not just legislation that comprises antiterrorism, however. DHS is the lead agency in many areas of antiterrorism through its management of agencies like the U.S. Coast Guard and Immigration and Customs Enforcement, which seek not only to prevent illegal entry of immigrants but also of potential terrorists.

The most obvious examples of antiterrorism activity take place on the federal level, although antiterrorism is something that happens at all levels of government.[19] This is not only because many of the major agencies and departments that have a role are housed in the federal government but also because of the necessity for coordination across all levels of government when it comes to antiterrorism activities. In fact, the federal government's major role in the context of antiterrorism is coordination and legislation. These two areas represent the most wide-spread use of federal government authority in the context of antiterrorism.

One of the things that makes antiterrorism and counterterrorism so difficult from an organizational perspective is the fact that there is no clear delineation between antiterrorism and counterterrorism responsibilities in practice. For instance, the **National Counterterrorism Center (NCTC)** has responsibilities in areas that could be termed both counter- and antiterrorism (see **BOX 7.1**).[20] Of course, in some ways,

BOX 7.1 The NCTC's Role in Counterterrorism

The National Counterterrorism Center (NCTC) plays a unique role in the nation's counterterrorism function. Developed as a direct response to the *9/11 Commission Report's* recommendation for a single entity that is responsible for joint operational planning and joint intelligence, staffed by personnel from different intelligence agencies, the NCTC's mission is to "Lead our nation's effort to combat terrorism at home and abroad by analyzing the threat, sharing that information with our partners, and integrating all instruments of our national power to ensure unity of effort."

The NCTC's Development

NCTC originated as the Terrorism Threat Integration Center (TTIC), which was enacted by Executive Order 13354, issued by President George W. Bush in 2003. The TTIC was developed on the recommendations of the 9/11 Commission, and was meant to deal with the primary issue that the Commission saw as a problem in counterterrorism—information sharing. In 2004, the Intelligence Reform and Terrorism Prevention Act was signed, changing the TTIC's name to the NCTC. The scope of responsibility also grew to include the management of several databases.

NCTC's Operations

The operations of the NCTC can be broken down into three areas mentioned previously in the organization's mission statement. The first area, analyzing the threat, consists of NCTC's function of integrating *all* terrorist-related intelligence (save that of dealing solely with domestic terrorism) and producing finished analytic products for distribution among the intelligence community and with policymakers. The second area of responsibility, "sharing the information," is accomplished through literally collocating individuals and information. Over 30 networks are located at the NCTC, representing all of the major actors with regard to counterterrorism intelligence and activity. Finally, as part of its requirement to "integrate all instruments of national power," the NCTC conducts strategic and operational planning for counterterrorism operations across the government. This includes elements from diplomatic, financial, military, and homeland security to ensure that all parties are represented in the planning of these operations. While heavily involved in the planning process, NCTC does not participate in the execution of these operations, which remain under the auspices of the agency carrying them out.

Conclusion

The NCTC, through its unique role in the intelligence community, is one of the most tangible outcomes of the recommendations of the 9/11 Commission. The responsibilities that the agency carries out: integrating information, information sharing, and strategic and operational planning, are essential to the counterterrorism mission of homeland security. The NCTC operates under the authority of both the Homeland Security Council and the National Security Council under the direct operation of the ODNI, therefore, making it one of the most powerful intelligence-sharing platforms within the U.S. government.

Data from: National Counterterrorism Center. (n.d.). About the National Counterterrorism Center. Retrieved from http://www.nctc.gov/about_us/about_nctc.html on March 12, 2013.

Courtesy of Samantha Appleton/White House.

this blurred line is by design, with the integration of information and establishment of joint responsibility being one of the major purposes of the NCTC.[21] One place where antiterrorism is a clear focus across all levels of government is in the context of critical infrastructure protection, one of the most important aspects of antiterrorism (see **BOX 7.2**).

Critical Infrastructure Protection

A large part of the antiterrorism responsibility that falls under the rubric of the federal government is the area of **critical infrastructure and**

BOX 7.2 Critical Infrastructure Protection—The Illustrative Case of Food Security

Obviously, each element of critical infrastructure and key resource protection is essential to the nation's homeland security. Each also represents a challenge because of how intertwined the critical infrastructure is to the rest of the American economic and social system. Perhaps no element of critical infrastructure is as complex as food security. Because of this, it represents an illustrative case for the importance of CIKR protection and a framework in which to view the other areas of CIKR protection.

Food and the Nation

The nation's food supply is complex, based on a large array of distinct business and operations that bring food not only to people in the United States but around the world. The post-harvest food industry accounts for at least 12% of the nation's economy and employs at least 10% of the country's workforce. In total, when including agriculture, the food industry is responsible for 20% of the U.S. economy. Within this, there are huge subsectors including processing, storage, transportation, retail, and food service.

Complexity

Because of the large number of private entities involved in the food industry, regulation of the industry is complex. Responsibility for food safety rests primarily with two federal agencies: The U.S. Food and Drug Administration (FDA), which oversees the processing of red meat, poultry, and eggs; and the Department of Health and Human Services (HHS), which regulates virtually all other food products. Additional regulation happens at both the state and local government levels, with restaurants, institutional food service, and food retailers under local jurisdiction (primarily). However, with specific, intentional targeting of the food supply being a significant threat, other agencies such as the FBI and DHS play an important role as well.

The Threat

The threat to food safety in the United States is significant. Tommy Thompson, former Secretary of Health and Human Services, stated in 2004 that, "I, for the life of me, cannot understand why the terrorists have not attacked our food supply because it is so easy to do." Indeed, the threat of direct, purposeful contamination of the food supply is the most significant concern in food safety and security. However, other types of threats also exist, both in terms of accidental foodborne illness outbreaks and contamination by elements such as heavy metals. Both intentional and unintentional contamination are significant dangers because of the large number of consumers that products reach—with unintentional contamination reaching 300,000 people in past events.

Potential Impact

The potential impact, both in economic and human terms, of a successful attack against the nation's agriculture and food systems is massive. Not only can it directly affect people's health, but an attack could negatively affect both the nation's collective psychology as well as how well the government operates. DHS specifically recognizes these areas—psychological impact, physical heath, government functioning, and the economy—as four areas that identify what qualifies as critical infrastructure. Additionally, should an attack be successfully carried out, it would place huge burdens

(continues)

BOX 7.2 Critical Infrastructure Protection—The Illustrative Case of Food Security *(Continued)*

on those agencies responsible for mitigating the effects of such an attack, as those who fall victim may not be easily identifiable, and may also be geographically disparate.

Conclusion

Food safety is an issue that concerns every person in the United States. The complexity of the problem, the potentially massive impacts of a successful attack—both psychological and physical—and the difficult nature of dealing with an attack if one does occur, demonstrates the problems in each of the areas of critical infrastructure. The 17 areas identified by DHS as CIKR all provide fundamentally necessary elements of American life, and therefore, like food safety, must be taken seriously in the context of homeland security.

Data from: Department of Homeland Security. (2007). The Department of Homeland Security's role in food defense and critical infrastructure protection. Retrieved from http://www.oig.dhs.gov/assets/Mgmt/OIG_07-33_Feb07.pdf.

key resources (CIKR) protection.[22] Critical infrastructure protection is composed of the activities[23] meant to prevent, deter, neutralize, or mitigate the effects of a terrorist attack on the nation's critical infrastructure. Critical infrastructure itself is made up of areas considered essential to the country's continuing ability to function. Homeland Security Presidential Directive 7 identified 17 areas considered critical infrastructure[24] and DHS has identified an 18th:[25]

- Food and agriculture
- Banking and finance
- Chemical
- Commercial facilities
- Communications
- Critical manufacturing
- Dams
- Defense industrial base
- Emergency services
- Energy
- Government facilities
- Healthcare and public health
- Information technology
- National monuments and icons
- Nuclear reactors, materials, and waste
- Postal and shipping
- Transportation systems
- Water

These are the areas that have been deemed "vital to the United States that their incapacity or destruction would have a debilitating impact on our physical or economic security or public health or safety."[26] Because of this importance, ensuring the continuing operation of all of these areas is a large part of antiterrorism planning. The coordination of protection of capacities deemed to be part of critical infrastructure falls under the **National Infrastructure Protection Plan (NIPP)**.[27] The NIPP lays out which government agencies are responsible for what areas of critical infrastructure protection as well as the risk-assessment methodology to be used in identifying risks and prioritizing protection.

Because critical infrastructure protection is so essential, there are a large number of agencies involved in its implementation from the Department of Agriculture to the Department of Defense. Each of these agencies, called Sector Specific Agencies (SSA), is assigned responsibility for a specific area of critical infrastructure protection. The Environmental Protection Agency, for instance, is responsible for protection of water resources, while the DHS Infrastructure Security Division is responsible for a variety of areas like dangerous chemicals, commercial facilities, critical manufacturing, dams and nuclear power facilities, materials, and waste.[28]

Because of the nature of critical infrastructure, many, if not all, of these areas of critical infrastructure are interdependent. This means that coordination is essential in any critical infrastructure protection program, and the NIPP provides for this through several mechanisms, focusing on coordination first within CIKR sectors and then across sectors and levels of government. The level of coordination defines these coordination mechanisms. At the national level, the IP facilitates the development of the NIPP itself as well as the Sector Specific Plans (SSPs), which focus on the risk-management strategy of the different areas of CIKR protection. At the sector partnership coordination level, there are several councils that work together to create partnerships between federal, state, local, and private stakeholders so they can work together across sectors to ensure protection of critical infrastructure. Finally, regional coordination is accomplished through organizations like the Great Lakes Hazard Coalition, which consists of critical infrastructure partners from all levels of government with a regional interest, which, in this case, are partners concerned about protecting the Great Lakes region. Together, these various levels, functioning within the context of the NIPP, allow for national coordination of CIKR protection.

One of the most interesting aspects of critical infrastructure protection is the fact that over 80% of the country's critical infrastructure is privately owned. This consists of many areas that we rarely think about, from utilities in our communities to much of the cybersphere (which will be covered more in the text elsewhere). Additionally, as mentioned previously, there is no single area of government that is responsible for all of CIKR protection. The breakdown of roles is, therefore, somewhat complicated; the NIPP defines nine roles in CIKR protection:

1. **Department of Homeland Security:** DHS's primary area of responsibility is coordination. It is responsible for coordinating the overall CIKR protection efforts as well as the development of the NIPP. In addition, implementation of the NIPP and integration with other national preparedness efforts is the responsibility of DHS.
2. **Sector-specific agencies:** As mentioned previously, SSAs are responsible for implementation of the NIPP within their constituent areas. This means tailoring the overall goals of the NIPP to the sector that the agency is responsible for and making sure it fits within the overall NIPP.
3. **Other federal departments, agencies, and offices:** While some agencies or departments are responsible for a given sector of CIKR, some are not designated but still have an important role. These agencies, offices, and departments are responsible for making sure to implement their specific protection roles as designated in HSPD-7 or another relevant policy.
4. **State, local, tribal, and territorial governments:** All levels of government have an important role to play in the context of CIKR, and designing a protection program in accordance with the NIPP risk-management framework is essential to achieving overall CIKR protection as well as specific homeland security goals for these entities.
5. **Regional partners:** Regional partnerships, as mentioned previously, are designed to cross jurisdictional and sector boundaries and function within a specifically defined geographic area.
6. **Boards, commissions, authorities, councils, and other entities:** These groups perform regulatory, advisory, policy, or business oversight (depending on their specific missions) related to CIKR. They can either be single-jurisdiction or multi-jurisdiction or tend to work across sectors.
7. **Private sector owners and operators:** As such, a large part of critical infrastructure in the United States is owned by private entities, the cooperation of private sector actors is essential. Their function, in the context of CIKR, is to provide advice, recommendations, and subject matter expertise to those operating in a CIKR protection role.
8. **Homeland security advisory councils:** Homeland security advisory councils are designed to provide expertise to and recommendations for the government regarding any activities related to infrastructure protection, including any policy they are called on to evaluate.
9. **Academia and research centers:** Academia has a very important role in the context of CIKR protection. Academics and research centers provide independent analysis and evaluation of government programs, research and development, and educational programs developed to assist with CIKR protection.[29]

Antiterrorism, although often overlooked or combined in people's minds with counterterrorism, is a different and essential part of defending our country from terrorist acts. The legislation, activity, and research involved in all aspects of antiterrorism, especially critical infrastructure and key resource protection, must be there to support the overall homeland security mission of the United States. Working across regions, sectors, and disciplines, antiterrorism efforts can only succeed with significant coordination, which is one of the primary responsibilities of DHS.

Counterterrorism

Counterterrorism, particularly international counterterrorism, is one of the most visible aspects of the overall homeland security effort because of both the history of the development of modern homeland security as well as the media coverage it receives in the form of both news and entertainment. For instance, the Hollywood movie *Zero Dark Thirty* portrays the tracking and killing of Osama bin Laden. In its opening weekend, the movie grossed $24 million.[30] The news story of the killing of Osama bin Laden in 2011 was one of the most covered items over the course of that year. Similarly, *Homeland*—a series focused on domestic counterterrorism—was one of the most popular shows on television and the more recent series *Lone Survivor* also deals with the aftermath of a terrorist attack.

Given this large amount of attention, it is perhaps surprising that there are still significant questions with which the U.S. government is grappling in terms of counterterrorism. Questions about the legality of actions like drone strikes against terrorists in other countries, rendition, and lingering doubts about issues like "enhanced interrogation" and indefinite detention make the topic controversial and the difficulty of measuring success makes policy decisions difficult. It is important to consider counterterrorism from a variety of perspectives to gain an understanding of this complex function of homeland security.

Pre-September 11th Counterterrorism

As examined earlier, terrorism is not a new phenomenon and, by extension, neither is counterterrorism. However, the scope and importance placed on counterterrorism has undergone a sea change since the September 11 attacks. Prior to that event, terrorism was considered by policymakers as a threat only in the case of where it combined two other characteristics—a direct threat to the U.S. homeland and the use of weapons of mass destruction (WMDs). Scholars fared no better in predicting the threat that terrorism would become. As Martha Crenshaw suggested,

> The policy recommendations of scholars in the security studies and international relations fields typically did not cite terrorism as a major threat to American security . . . terrorism specialists tended to neglect the strategic dimensions of the issue . . . the study of terrorism was useful for a variety of things, such as understanding motivation, but it could not provide tactical warning, assess threats, or set priorities. (p. 447)[31]

However, despite the general unpreparedness of the United States for 9-11, there were those who suggested that the threat terrorism posed was significant, even without the use of weapons of mass destruction. The U.S. Commission on National Security in the 21st Century released a report in 1999 that suggested that while conventional warfare was still a significant threat, the most significant threat would be subnational groups engaging in activities like bioterrorism or, eerily, an attack on the air-traffic control system on the East Coast. The Commission's report concluded that, "together, the evidence suggests that threats to American security will be more diffuse, harder to anticipate, and more difficult to neutralize than ever before."[32]

Considered overall, there was little clear direction in counterterrorism before the 9-11 attacks. While it was on the country's security agenda, the station it occupied was low and there were few resources dedicated to terrorism outside of WMDs. This, of course, changed with the September 11 attacks, and a new focus on counterterrorism, almost to the exclusion of all other threats, developed. The following section deals with counterterrorism post-September 11.

Counterterrorism Post-9/11

Counterterrorism is unique in that it is one of the few areas that the United States that consistently operates outside of its own boundaries but still requires a domestic presence. This is functionally because the threat of terrorism, as it is popularly understood, is primarily an international phenomenon. Additionally, unlike warfare—which is handled almost solely by the Department of Defense—counterterrorism is not focused on a single adversary. Even al Qaeda and ISIS, our primary targets since September 11, 2001, are no longer considered single operational units but rather a diffuse movement of similarly minded individuals and organizations.[33] Furthermore, newer threats like ISIS have come to displace threats like al Qaeda, making the situation fluid and challenging. Complicating matters still more is the fact that there is no single agency that has sole responsibility for the United States' counterterrorism mission—roles change depending largely on the geography of the problem. Counterterrorism overseas is usually the responsibility of the CIA and Department of Defense, while domestic counterterrorism is primarily a function of the FBI and DHS.

These challenges, especially post-9-11, have led to significant changes in the way the United States handles counterterrorism. Various aspects of foreign policy, the law, and warfare have all changed in an attempt to combat what is considered one of the most pressing problems that the United States faces. However, despite these changes, there remains no grand and unified strategy in terms of combating terrorism and developing a definitive one may not even be possible. Martha Crenshaw notes that, in fact, terrorism itself is not a single entity but an aggregate of threats that we must be flexible enough to face in a variety of contexts—from international proxy wars to cyberterrorism—and the rules for each of these may be different.[34]

Counterterrorism Under President George W. Bush

Because of the widely differing threats under the one rubric of "terrorism," there have been a variety of approaches taken to combating it. The first approach post-9-11, undertaken by President George W. Bush, was the "War on Terror," which has been characterized as a "garbage pail" effort at counterterrorism.[35] This, many argue, was ineffective and may have in fact been counterproductive,[36] especially with the increasing geopolitical complexity caused by the war in Iraq, beginning in 2003. Additionally, the original focus seemed to be on state sponsors of terrorism, although the changing phrases used to describe the war over time (e.g., "the long war") indicated a broader focus.[37]

The first detailed articulation of the country's post-9-11 counterterrorism strategy came in 2002 with President George W. Bush's National Security Strategy. This, according to Bridget Nacos (a counterterrorism expert associated with Colombia University), had three primary elements that, when combined, formed what has been called the Bush Doctrine: Making the world safer and better, preemption in the face of imminent threat, and the unilateral use of force.[38]

The first of these elements, making the world better and safer, revolves around the United States' unique role as the sole remaining superpower and the belief in the superiority of a democratic system of government. The security strategy, therefore, focused on bringing elements important in American life to the rest of the world in the belief that it would assist those countries who adopted them. Democracy, free trade, and free markets were the watch-words of these efforts and the more global idea of "freedom" its banner.

The second element of the Bush Doctrine was preemption, the idea of stopping rogue states and terrorists before they became an imminent threat to the security of the United States. This is particularly relevant given the increasing number of countries with the ability to transfer knowledge of and materials for WMDs and, at the very least, provide support for terrorists. President Bush, in his commencement address to West Point in 2002, articulated this point well. The speech is significant enough to quote at length.

> For much of the last century, America's defense relied on the cold war doctrines of deterrence and containment. In some cases, those strategies still apply, but new threats also require new thinking. Deterrence—the promise of massive retaliation against nations—means nothing against shadowy terrorist networks with no nation or citizens to defend. Containment is not possible when unbalanced dictators with weapons of mass destruction can deliver those weapons on missiles or secretly provide them to terrorist allies. We cannot defend America and our friends by hoping for the best. We cannot put our faith in the word of tyrants who solemnly sign nonproliferation treaties and then systemically break them. If we wait for threats to fully materialize, we will have waited too long.
>
> Homeland defense and missile defense are part of stronger security; they're essential priorities for America. Yet, the war on terror will not be won on the defensive. We must take the battle to the enemy, disrupt his plans, and confront the worst threats before they emerge. In the world we have entered, the only path to safety is the path of action, and this Nation will act.[39]

The final element of the Bush Doctrine was the unilateral use of force, which was deemed by the administration as essential in order to adequately protect the United States. Unilateralism, in the context of the Bush administration, incorporated the notion that terrorists could be pursued wherever they went—even without the consent of the country in which they were hiding. It was, and remains, a controversial approach, in part because it may undermine multilateral efforts to stop terrorists.[40]

Counterterrorism Under President Barack Obama

Although many elements of counterterrorism remained the same from the Bush administration, the presidency of Barack Obama introduced some significant change. With regard to the Bush Doctrine, President Obama backed away significantly from the concepts of unilateralism and preemption, at least publicly, although in both cases, there have been specific instances in which they have been used. Interestingly, the most significant change was the move away from terrorism as the single threat that the United States faces in the international community. As stated by Michael Leiter, then the head of the National Counterterrorism Center, in 2009,

"Counter-terrorism is part of larger U.S. policy ... [it] rarely, if ever, should be the lead in that policy."[41]

Some of these shifts, however significant, were belied by some actions of the Obama administration, which suggest close ties between their policy and past policy under President Bush. In fact, the seminal counterterrorism act of the Obama presidency, killing Osama bin Laden, was carried out unilaterally in an (ostensibly) ally's territory.[42] Additionally, drone strikes in a variety of locations around the world, in both allied countries as well as countries more hostile to the U.S., would seem to indicate that while multilateralism is the preferred approach, the United States is willing to "go it alone" if necessary.

A second area in which the Obama administration seemingly differed from the Bush administration is in which agencies it used to address counterterrorism. President Bush tended toward using the Department of Defense as his primary agency—prosecuting wars based on the Bush Doctrine in both Afghanistan and Iraq. The Obama administration, by contrast, tended to view the CIA as its primary agency for counterterrorism internationally, with DOD in a supporting role.

This shift was reflected in the *National Strategy for Counterterrorism* released by the Obama administration in 2011 (see **BOX 7.3**). While there is mention of the military's role in counterterrorism, the focus of the document was on an approach that utilizes "every tool of American power," with an emphasis on the collective action required both within the United States' government and between our government and other nations, to succeed in countering the terrorism threat.[43]

BOX 7.3 The National Strategy for Counter-terrorism

In October of 2018, President Trump released the new *National Strategy for Counterterrorism*. This document represents the articulation of the national approach to the problem of terrorism, focusing specifically on what the administration views as the significant issues facing the country in terms of counterterrorism and the best ways to combat those problems. It additionally identifies tools that are necessary for the strategy to succeed, building both on previous strategies as well as new information. As a whole, it represents the best individual source for examining the counterterrorism efforts currently being undertaken by the government.

Structure of the Strategy

The strategy is broken down into several major parts. The first section, *The Terrorist Adversary*, examines the groups that the administration feels are most threatening when it comes to national and homeland security—notably different from the previous strategy is the focus on "radical Islamist terrorism." The next set of sections, *Prioritization and Resourcing, Pursue Terrorist Threats to Their Source, Isolate Terrorists from their Financial, Material, and Logistical sources of Support,* examine methods of dealing with the groups identified in the first source from the perspective of things the United States and its allies can do to address terrorism by combating the group. The last set of sections, *Modernize and Integrate a Broader Set of United States Tools and Authorities to Counter Terrorism and Protect the Homeland, Protect the United States Infrastructure and Enhance Preparedness, Counter Terrorist Radicalization and Recruitment,* and *Strengthen Counterterrorism Abilities of International Partners*, deal with issues of preparation at home, rather than demonstrate an active counterterrorism stance.

Overarching Goals

The overarching goals of the National Strategy are relatively straightforward, if extremely difficult to achieve. They include:

- The terrorist threat to the United States is eliminated;
- Our borders and all ports of entry into the United States are secure against terrorist threats;
- Terrorism, radical Islamist ideologies, and other violent extremist ideologies do not undermine the American way of life; and
- Foreign partners address terrorist threats so that these threats do not jeopardize the collective interests of the United States and our partners.

These goals are the foundation for America's counterterrorism activities. They represent the most important elements of counterterrorism policymaking and help to underline the important elements of any counterterrorism operations.

Conclusion

In short, the *National Strategy for Counterterrorism* is an important document in terms of understanding the counterterrorism goals for the United States. It examines both the goals that the government hopes to achieve against terrorist activity as well as some of the challenges that the country faces in achieving those goals.

It is worth noting that the current strategy differs significantly from previous strategies in both tone and approach. While the 2011 *National Strategy* was clearly as focused on defeating terrorism, there was much less talk about "America First." Additionally, while there are many threats that face the country, as acknowledged in the current strategy, the focus has shifted to be more specifically on "radical Islamist terrorism," which, while it incorporates much of what the Obama administration targeted in the Middle East as part of its strategy, also narrows the focus.

The current strategy is quite new, and the Trump administration may choose to change it over the course of their administration. Additionally, while it sets out clear goals for the country's approach to countering terrorism, it remains to be seen how the strategy will be carried out specifically in the policy decisions of the Trump administration.

Data from: The White House. (2011, 2018). National Strategy for Counterterrorism. Retrieved from http://www.whitehouse.gov/sites/default/files/counterterrorism_strategy.pdf

While it is arguable whether the Obama administration lived up to its goals in terms of the changes to the 2011 *National Strategy*, as they continued to use defense assets in places like Syria and Afghanistan, their strategy shifted the domain of focus toward more diplomatic efforts. Additionally, while much of the diplomacy was very public, different aspects of the administration's efforts focused on disruption of terrorist organizations—particularly drone strikes—were generally done without much public coverage beyond that focused on when strikes hit unintended targets.

Counterterrorism Under President Donald Trump

In October of 2018, the Trump Administration released its new *National Strategy for Counterterrorism*. The document differs significantly from previous strategies in several ways. The first, and perhaps most significant, way is the refocusing on so-called "radical Islamist terrorism," a term that was eschewed by the Obama administration because of its potentially offensive nature. Additionally, much of the language in the report is aspirational, rather than instructive. While it sets significant, and important, goals for the counterterrorism approach that the nation will take, it is unclear in many respects how these will be carried out.[44]

Outside of the *Strategy*, there have also been notable differences in the approach of the Trump administration, particularly with regard to issues on the United States/Mexico border. Specifically, the administration has regularly linked illegal border crossings to national security issues—notably terrorism. The rhetoric of the administration has reflected this difference in both its defense of its proposed border wall, as well as the general defense of what it considers necessary increases in border security—ranging from additional Border Patrol agents to increased sensor technology on the border.

Even with the new *Strategy*, it is clear that the Trump administration's approach to counterterrorism is still evolving. Notably, while President Trump has indicated in the strategy, and in public remarks, his desire for allies to take more responsibility in terms of different parts of security, including counterterrorism, recent indications in places like Turkey and Afghanistan are that the policy for how this shift in responsibility should take place is, as yet, unclear. It is likely that, as in the case of the Obama administration, much of what the Trump administration carries out will be a holdover from the post 9-11 strategy originated by President George W. Bush, but that remains to be seen.

Domestic Counterterrorism

While international counterterrorism is the purview of the federal government, domestic counterterrorism touches on every level of government. Like its international counterpart, however, there is little strategy guiding overall domestic counterterrorism in the United States, although the FBI is the lead agency. However, other federal agencies, such as the National Security Agency (which monitors signals intelligence) also play a role in domestic counterterrorism. Interestingly, the two lead agencies for international counterterrorism, the DOD and the CIA, have no role to play on the domestic front, as they are effectively barred from operating within the homeland.

Another significant difference between domestic and international counterterrorism is the fact that local agencies have a large role to play on the domestic side. They engage in monitoring of groups, ranging from right-wing white supremacist organizations to left-wing antiglobalization groups. This activity is frequently in conjunction with agencies operating at the federal level.

Given this law enforcement focus within domestic counterterrorism, much of the activity focuses on traditional law enforcement actions. Investigations into individuals and organizations attempting to engage in terrorism make up a significant part of today's domestic counterterrorism operations. As an example of the importance of these domestic investigations, in the State of America's Homeland

Security address in 2011, former Secretary of Homeland Security Janet Napolitano said,

> Historically, our domestic counterterrorism efforts were based on the belief that we faced the greatest risk from attacks planned, and carried out, by individuals coming from abroad. But the arrests of an increasing number of U.S. persons on terror-related charges in the last 2 years mean that we must move beyond this paradigm. These include Najibullah Zazi, a legal permanent resident arrested in 2009 for plotting to attack the New York City subway system; Faisal Shahzad, a naturalized U.S. citizen, who attempted to explode a car bomb in Times Square last year (see **BOX 7.4**); as well as more recent arrests in Portland, Oregon; Dallas, Texas; and here in the Washington area. One additional incident, the Pittsburgh Synagogue shooting, is covered more completely in **BOX 7.5**.
>
> Today, we operate under the premise that individuals prepared to carry out terrorist acts might already be in the country and could carry out further acts of terrorist violence with little or no warning. We must all work to gain a better understanding of the behaviors, tactics, and other indicators that could point to terrorist activity.[45]

BOX 7.4 Faisal Shahzad and the 2010 Times Square Bombing

Introduction

In 2010, one of the most high-profile terrorist bombing attempts was stopped in New York City. The perpetrator, Faisal Shahzad, had attempted to detonate an explosive-filled SUV in Times Square, but the bomb failed to detonate. The response to the incident, and subsequent investigation and arrest of Shahzad, represents an excellent example of interagency cooperation in the pursuit of counterterrorism goals.

The Bombing Incident

On May 1, 2010, a t-shirt vendor discovered an SUV parked in Times Square that was discharging smoke. The New York Police Department was notified, and one of the officers responding identified the smell of gunpowder. The bomb squad was subsequently dispatched and found an improvised explosive device in the vehicle, a Nissan Pathfinder. The bomb consisted of three propane tanks, two 5-gallon gasoline tanks, two clocks with batteries, fireworks, and a locked metal box filled with low-grade fertilizer. The bomb failed to detonate, but had it done so, it would have caused casualties, according to the NYPD investigators.

The Investigation

The investigation that led to the arrest of Faisal Shahzad unfolded very quickly. The Nissan Pathfinder used in the bombing had its vehicle identification number (VIN) vandalized, but forensic techs were able to recover the VIN. With this information, the Joint Terrorism Task Force (JTTF) traced the vehicle to Shahzad, who bought it with cash from a seller on April 24, 2010. Additionally, in the back of the SUV, the police recovered a set of keys for an Isuzu, which Shahzad drove as his normal vehicle. Also discovered early on in the investigation was Shahzad's use of a prepaid phone to call a fireworks store, as well as receive a number of calls from Pakistan. The phone stopped being used just 2 days before the bombing incident.

On May 3rd, 2010, Shahzad was arrested at John F. Kennedy International Airport in New York City attempting to board a plane to Dubai. Upon his arrest, he admitted that he had received bomb-making training in Pakistan, and that $12,500 of the money for the plot was given to him by a co-conspirator from Pakistan affiliated with the Tehrik iTaliban, itself an affiliate of al Qaeda. While much of the original investigation was done by the NYPD and the FBI, the Department of Homeland Security's U.S. Customs and Border Protection (CBP) identified him as he was trying to leave the country. Additionally, the FBI's **Joint Terrorism Task Force (JTTF)** in New York City played a significant role in the investigation.

Conclusion

While counterterrorism efforts in the United States are sometimes maligned, the Faisal Shahzad case represents an excellent example of cooperation among agencies across the homeland security spectrum. From the local investigation by NYPD officials, to the participation of national-level agencies like the FBI and CBP, agencies quickly worked to identify and apprehend a suspect. While the bombing did not harm anyone, the threat that it represented was very real, and the response of the law enforcement and intelligence agencies involved demonstrates the increased capacity of homeland security counterterrorism operations post-9-11.

Data from: *United States of America vs. Faisal Shahzad*. 10 Cr. 541. (2010). United States Department of Justice. (2010). *Faisal Shahzad pleads guilty in Manhattan Federal Court to 10 federal crimes arising from attempted car bombing in Times Square*. Retrieved from http://www.justice.gov/opa/pr/2010/June/10-ag-721.html on March 12, 2013.

BOX 7.5 The 2018 Pittsburg Synagogue Shooting

Introduction

On October 27, 2018, Robert G. Bowers entered the Tree of Life Synagogue and began shooting parishioners with an AR-15 rifle. By the time the shooting was complete, 11 people were dead, with an additional seven injured by the gunfire. It represents the single, deadliest attack on a Jewish community in the United States.

The Incident

The shooting took place during morning services at the Pittsburgh synagogue. Bowers entered the building at around 9:50 AM and began shouting religious slurs and shooting those attending to their prayers while moving throughout the building over the course of the incident. By 9:54 AM, the police had been alerted and had dispatched officers to respond and by 10 AM, offers had reached the building and attempted to respond. This led to a brief shootout, which ended after Bowers reemerged around 11 AM to surrender to police.

Relevance

While this incident was largely contained to a single individual and setting, the type of extremism it represents is growing within the United States. This, in turn, represents the difficulty of containing far-right and anti-Semitic extremism within the United States, one of the primary responsibilities of the Department of Homeland Security. While an increasing number of hate-based incidents has been recorded, the governmental response has not been as strong. Coupled with creating home-grown extremism from other ideologies, the most current set of incidents, including not only the Pittsburgh shooting mentioned above but also incidents like the pipe-bombs mailed to Democratic figures in late 2018 by Cesar Sayoc Jr. or the 2017 Charlottesville attack, demonstrate the difficulty of combating violent ideologies developed within the United States, not just those imported from abroad.[47]

Source: Goodstein, L. 2018. "There is Still So Much Evil: Growing Anti-Semitism Stuns American Jews". The New York Times. Retrieved on 23 March 2019 from https://www.nytimes.com/2018/10/29/us/anti-semitism-attacks.html.; Bradbury, S. 2018. "Timeline of Terror: A Moment-by-Moment Account of the Squirrel Hill Mass Shooting". Retrieved on 23 March from https://www.post-gazette.com/news/crime-courts/2018/10/28/TIMELINE-20-minutes-of-terror-gripped-Squirrel-Hill-during-Saturday-synagogue-attack/stories/201810280197.

Under the Trump Administration, there has been a continuation of the thinking Napolitano illustrates above. The threat, whether it be from white supremacist terrorists or so-called "home-grown" religious extremists, continues to be part of both the counterterrorism strategy put forth by the administration, although there has been a shift in emphasis away from hate groups to other forms of violent extremism.[46]

This increasing importance on the domestic side of counterterrorism, and particularly the law enforcement function that it contains, is essential to the long-term security of the nation. The efforts of both local- and state-level law enforcement have been considered the "first line" of the United States's domestic counterterrorism operations. Again, former Secretary Napolitano,

> But the homeland security enterprise extends far beyond DHS and the federal government. As I said, it requires not just a "whole of government," but a "whole of nation" approach. In some respects, local law enforcement, community groups, citizens, and the private sector play as much of a role in homeland security as the federal government. That is why I like to say that "homeland security starts with hometown security."[48]

Interestingly, the threat faced in the context of domestic terrorism is quite different from that which we face internationally, many of which have nothing to do with Islamist terrorism, which we generally associate with counterterrorism.[49] The geography of terrorism within the United States is complex, with groups differing widely in ideology—ranging from anti-government to anti-corporate—many of which share the same tactical approach. This means that, in many cases, local law enforcement or local communities are the first to notice actions or characteristics that lead to the identification of terrorism and its interdiction. Lest this just be considered idle talk, over 80% of the terrorist attacks stopped between 2001 and 2009 were originally identified by local law enforcement or community members.[50] Ways that individuals can help identify terrorism or other issues of security can be found in **TABLE 7.1**, below.

It is important to acknowledge that, while there is a difference between the efforts of domestic and international counterterrorism, many of the laws have been changed since September 11, 2001, to try and bring these two activities closer together. The "freeing up" of surveillance activities for domestic law enforcement has proven not only to be important in domestic counterterrorism but has also provided a source of controversy. The FBI has reoriented itself into a so-called "intelligence driven" organization—with a focus on stopping terrorism rather than prosecuting those who are responsible for it.[51]

TABLE 7.1 Reporting Suspicious Activity

Report Suspicious Activity	Rewards for Justice
Want to report suspicious persons or activity?	Website: www.rewardsforjustice.net, then click "Submit a Tip" E-mail: rfj@state.gov Phone: In the United States, call 1-800-US REWARDS (1-800-877-3927) **FBI** Website: https://tips.fbi.gov Phone: In the United States, call 202-324-3000 [FBI main switchboard] To find phone numbers of regional FBI offices in the United States, visit: www.fbi.gov/contact-us/field If outside of the United States and want to reach the FBI, call the nearest US Embassy or Consulate office; for phone numbers, see www.fbi.gov/contact-us/legat **CIA** Website: www.cia.gov
Think you've seen a wanted person?	To view photographs of wanted terrorists, visit these sites: www.rewardsforjustice.net www.fbi.gov/wanted/wanted_terrorists www.fbi.gov/wanted/terrorinfo
Wondering whether a business, charity, Nongovernmental Organization (NGO), or other entity has terrorist ties?	Do you want to make sure you can donate money to such an organization legally? View designated individuals and groups at these sites: Designated Foreign Terrorist Organizations https://www.state.gov/foreign-terrorist-organizations/ Individuals and entities designated under Executive Order 13224 https://www.state.gov/executive-order-13224/#state Specially Designated Nationals and Blocked Persons https://www.treasury.gov/resource-center/sanctions/SDN-List/Pages/default.aspx
Other Resources	US National Counterterrorism Center www.nctc.gov US State Department Office of the Coordinator for Counterterrorism www.state.gov/s/ct US State Department Country Reports on Terrorism www.state.gov/j/ct/rls/crt/index.htm

Modified from: National Counterterrorism Center. (2013). Counterterrorism Calendar 2013, p. 148. Retrieved from http://www.nctc.gov/site/pdfs/ct_calendar_2013.pdf on March 12, 2013.

While the federal government maintains its overall leadership role in the counterterrorism mission of homeland security,[52] there is an increasing significance to state and local law enforcement regarding domestic counterterrorism. This is largely obscured by the greater focus on international counterterrorism—particularly the pursuit of al Qaeda and the focus of the mass media on these events.

Chapter Summary

Antiterrorism and counterterrorism are the two chief elements of the homeland security mission that are often thought to be the same but, in fact, are distinctly different. Antiterrorism legislation and programs aim to keep Americans safe and to promote resiliency through reactive measures for when terrorism happens and proactive measures that attempt to stop terrorism by identifying those involved. Counterterrorism, on the other hand, seeks not only to identify and apprehend terrorists but also to counter the threat before it occurs, usually through kinetic or offensive means. Since 9-11, both antiterrorism and counterterrorism have become essential parts of the homeland security mission. They have, especially during the first George W. Bush administration, been the centerpiece of homeland security strategy, to the limited extent that an overall strategy existed. More recently, under President Barack Obama, they played a more limited, although still important, policy role and while there have been some changes under President Trump—notably regarding the language we use and the (re)emphasis on international religious terrorism—the full breadth of those changes remain to be seen.

While it is uncertain what changes the remaining time in the Trump presidency will bring in terms of antiterrorism and counterterrorism, it is unlikely that there will be a dramatic shift from the policies enacted over the past 12 years. Thus far, these have provided a high level of safety for the American homeland and are thus considered successful by most. Nearly all sources agree, however, that it is not a question of whether the United States will be attacked again, but when, and the question remains of what impact that will have on existing antiterrorism and counterterrorism policies.

Review/Discussion Questions

1. What is the difference between antiterrorism and counterterrorism, and why does the difference matter?
2. What is the NIPP, and what role does it play in antiterrorism policy in the United States?
3. What makes critical infrastructure and key resources so important? What are the areas of critical infrastructure?
4. Explain the U.S. Senate's criticism of state and local fusion centers. Is the criticism deserved?
5. What are the major elements of the *National Strategy for Counterterrorism* and how do they match up with the Obama & Trump Administration's counterterrorism actions? Do they compare with previous administrations' actions?

Additional Readings

Howard, R. D., Sawyer, R. L., & Bajema, N. E. (2009). *Terrorism and Counterterrorism: Understanding the New Security Environment* (3rd ed.). New York, NY: McGraw Hill.

The White House. (2011). *National Strategy for Counterterrorism.* Retrieved from https://www.whitehouse.gov/wp-content/uploads/2018/10/NSCT.pdf

Endnotes

1. Ownen, M. & Maurer, K. (2012). *No Easy Day: The Firsthand Account of the Mission that Killed Osama bin Laden.* New York, NY: Dutton Adult.
2. Ownen, M. & Maurer, K. (2012). *No Easy Day: The Firsthand Account of the Mission that Killed Osama bin Laden.* New York, NY: Dutton Adult.
3. Sherwell, P. (May 7, 2011). "Osama bin Laden Killed: Behind the Scenes of the Deadly Raid." *The Telegraph.* Retrieved from http://www.telegraph.co.uk/news/worldnews/al-qaeda/8500431/Osama-bin-Laden-killed-Behind-the-scenes-of-the-deadly-raid.html
4. Sherwell, P. (May 7, 2011). "Osama bin Laden Killed: Behind the Scenes of the Deadly Raid." *The Telegraph.* Retrieved from http://www.telegraph.co.uk/news/worldnews/al-qaeda/8500431/Osama-bin-Laden-killed-Behind-the-scenes-of-the-deadly-raid.html

5. Department of Defense. (2010). *Dictionary of Military and Associated Terms*. Retrieved from http://www.dtic.mil/doctrine/new_pubs/jp1_02.pdf
6. Department of Defense. (2010). *Dictionary of Military and Associated Terms*. Retrieved from http://www.dtic.mil/doctrine/new_pubs/jp1_02.pdf
7. Ganor, B. (2007). *The Counter-terrorism Puzzle*. New York, NY: Transaction Publishers.
8. The White House. (2011). *National Strategy for Counter-terrorism*. Retrieved from http://www.whitehouse.gov/sites/default/files/Counterterrorism_strategy.pdf
9. Department of Defense. (2010). *Dictionary of Military and Associated Terms*. Retrieved from http://www.dtic.mil/doctrine/new_pubs/jp1_02.pdf
10. Schneider, R. H. (2003). "American Anti-terrorism Planning and Design Strategies: Application for Florida Growth Management, Comprehensive Planning and Urban Design." *University of Florida Journal of Law & Public Policy, 15*, 129–154.
11. Conway, M. (2002). "Terrorism, the Law, and Politics as Usual: A Comparison of Anti-terrorism Legislation Before and After 9/11." *Touro Law Review, 18*, 735–781.
12. Homeland Security Presidential Directive 6. (2003). Retrieved from http://www.fas.org/irp/offdocs/nspd/hspd-6.html
13. Walther, K. A. (2012). Written testimony of Office of Policy Senior Director for Screening for the House Committee on Homeland Security, Subcommittee on Border and Maritime Security. "Eleven Years Later: Preventing Terrorists from Coming to America." Retrieved from https://www.dhs.gov/news/2012/09/11/written-testimony-us-customs-and-border-protection-house-homeland-security.
14. Uniting and Strengthening America by Providing Appropriate Tools Required to Intercept and Obstruct Terrorism Act of 2001, Pub. L. No. 107–56, 115 Stat. 272 (2001).
15. United States Department of Justice. (n.d.). *The USA PATRIOT Act: Preserving Life and Liberty*. Retrieved from http://www.justice.gov/archive/ll/what_is_the_patriot_act.pdf
16. Whitehead, J. W. & Aden, S. H. (2002). "Forfeiting 'Enduring Freedom' for 'Homeland Security': A Constitutional Analysis of the USA Patriot Act and the Justice Department's Anti-terrorism Initiatives." *American University Law Review, 51*(6), 1081–1133.
17. Homeland Defense Before the Senate Committee on the Judiciary, 107th Cong. (2001). Retrieved from http://www.justice.gov/archive/ag/testimony/2001/0925AttorneyGeneralJohnAshcroftTestimonybeforetheSenateCommitteeontheJudiciary.htm
18. Department of Homeland Security. (2007). *Chemical Facility Anti-terrorism Standards*. Retrieved from https://www.dhs.gov/cisa/chemical-facility-anti-terrorism-standards
19. Department of Justice. (2019). *Anti-Terrorism*. Retrieved on July 14, 2019, from https://www.justice.gov/usao-me/anti-terrorism.
20. Schneider, R. H. (2003). "American Anti-terrorism Planning and Design Strategies: Application for Florida Growth Management, Comprehensive Planning and Urban Design." *University of Florida Journal of Law & Public Policy, 15*, 129–1554.
21. National Counter-terrorism Center. (2009). *Strategic Intent 2009-2013*. Retrieved from http://www.nctc.gov/docs/nctc_strategic_intent.pdf
22. National Counter-terrorism Center. (2009). *Strategic Intent 2009-2013*. Retrieved from http://www.nctc.gov/docs/nctc_strategic_intent.pdf
23. Department of Homeland Security. (2009). *National Infrastructure Protection Plan: Partnering to Enhance Protection and Resiliency*. Retrieved from http://www.dhs.gov/xlibrary/assets/NIPP_Plan.pdf
24. Department of Homeland Security. (2009). *National Infrastructure Protection Plan: Partnering to Enhance Protection and Resiliency*. Retrieved from http://www.dhs.gov/xlibrary/assets/NIPP_Plan.pdf
25. Homeland Security Presidential Directive 7: *Critical infrastructure identification, prioritization, and protection*. Retrieved from http://www.dhs.gov/homeland-security-presidential-directive-7#1
26. Department of Homeland Security. (n.d.). *Critical Infrastructure Protection*. Retrieved from http://www.dhs.gov/topic/critical-infrastructure-protection
27. Department of Homeland Security. (n.d.). *Critical Infrastructure Protection*. Retrieved from http://www.dhs.gov/topic/critical-infrastructure-protection
28. Department of Homeland Security. (2009). *National Infrastructure Protection Plan: Partnering to Enhance Protection and Resiliency*. Retrieved from http://www.dhs.gov/xlibrary/assets/NIPP_Plan.pdf
29. Department of Homeland Security. (2009). *National Infrastructure Protection Plan: Partnering to Enhance Protection and Resiliency*. Retrieved from http://www.dhs.gov/xlibrary/assets/NIPP_Plan.pdf
30. Department of Homeland Security. (2009). *National Infrastructure Protection Plan: Partnering to Enhance Protection and Resiliency*. Retrieved from http://www.dhs.gov/xlibrary/assets/NIPP_Plan.pdf
31. Fritz, B. (14 January 2013). "'Zero Dark Thirty' Wins Weekend Box Office Battle." *The Los Angeles Times*. Retrieved from http://www.latimes.com/entertainment/envelope/cotown/la-et-mn-zero-dark-thirty-boxoffice-20130114,0,7161365.story.
32. Crenshaw, M. (2004). Terrorism, Strategies, and Grand Strategies. In: Howard, R. D., Sawyer, R. L., & Bajema, N. E. (2009). *Terrorism and Counter-terrorism: Understanding the New Security Environment* (3rd ed.). New York, NY: McGraw Hill.
33. U.S. Commission on National Security/21st Century. (1999). The Phase I Report on the Emerging Global Security Environment for the First Quarter of the 21st Century. Retrieved from http://www.au.af.mil/au/awc/awcgate/nssg/nwc.pdf
34. Jenkins, B. M. (2012). *New Challenges to U.S. Counter-terrorism Efforts: An Assessment of the Current Terrorist Threat*. Testimony presented before the Senate Homeland Security and Governmental Affairs Committee on July 11, 2012. Retrieved from https://www.rand.org/pubs/testimonies/CT377z1.html
35. Crenshaw, M. (2004). Terrorism, Strategies, and Grand Strategies. In: Howard, R. D., Sawyer, R. L., & Bajema, N. E. (2009). *Terrorism and Counter-terrorism: Understanding the New Security Environment* (3rd ed.). New York, NY: McGraw Hill.
36. Howard, R. D., Sawyer, R. L., & Bajema, N. E. (2009). *Terrorism and Counter-terrorism: Understanding the New Security Environment* (3rd ed.). New York, NY: McGraw Hill.
37. Scheuer, M. (2004). *Imperial Hubris: Why the West Is Losing the War on Terror*. Dulles, VA: Potomac Books.
38. Nacos, B. M. (2012). *Terrorism and Counter-terrorism* (4th ed.). New York, NY: Pearson.
39. Nacos, B. M. (2012). *Terrorism and Counter-terrorism* (4th ed.). New York, NY: Pearson.
40. Bush, G. W. "Commencement Address at the United States Military Academy in West Point, New York." The United States Military Academy, West Point, NY. 1 June 2003. Commencement Address. Retrieved from http://www.presidency.ucsb.edu/ws/index.php?pid=62730&st=America%5C%27s+defense+relied+on+the+cold+war+doctrines&st1=

41. Nacos, B. M. (2012). *Terrorism and Counter-terrorism* (4th ed.). New York, NY: Pearson.
42. Leiter, M. (2009). *Roundtable with Michael Leiter, Director of the National Counterterrorism Center*. Retrieved from http://www.aspeninstitute.org/events/2009/04/09/director-national-counterterrorism-center-michael-leiter-speaks-aspen-institute
43. Roggio, B. (2011). Pakistan Critical of 'Unilateral' Raid that Killed Osama bin Laden. Retrieved from http://www.longwarjournal.org/archives/2011/05/pakistan_expresses_d.php
44. The White House. (2011). *National Strategy for Counter-terrorism*. Retrieved from http://www.whitehouse.gov/sites/default/files/Counterterrorism_strategy.pdf
45. Byman, D. L. (2018). Takeaways from the Trump administration's new counterterrorism strategy. *Brookings Institute*. Retrieved from https://www.brookings.edu/blog/order-from-chaos/2018/10/05/takeaways-from-the-trump-administrations-new-counterterrorism-strategy/.
46. Napolitano, J. (2011). *State of America's Homeland Security Address*. Retrieved from http://www.dhs.gov/news/2011/01/27/state-americas-homeland-security-address
47. Strickler, L. (2018). Trump admin Apparently Not Renew Program to Fight Domestic Terror: Retrieved from https://www.nbcnews.com/politics/national-security/trump-admin-will-apparently-not-renew-program-fight-domestic-terror-n926361
48. Goodstein, L. (2018). "There is Still So Much Evil": Growing Anti-Semitism Stuns American Jews. *The New York Times*. Retrieved on 23 March 2019 from https://www.nytimes.com/2018/10/29/us/anti-semitism-attacks.html; Bradbury, S. (2018). Timeline of Terror: A Moment-by-Moment Account of the Squirrel Hill Mass Shooting. Retrieved on 23 March from https://www.post-gazette.com/news/crime-courts/2018/10/28/TIMELINE-20-minutes-of-terror-gripped-Squirrel-Hill-during-Saturday-synagogue-attack/stories/201810280197.
49. Napolitano, J. (2011). *State of America's Homeland Security Address*. Retrieved from http://www.dhs.gov/news/2011/01/27/state-americas-homeland-security-address
50. Jenkins, B. M. (2012). *New Challenges to U.S. Counter-terrorism Efforts: An Assessment of the Current Terrorist Threat*. Testimony Presented before the Senate Homeland Security and Governmental Affairs Committee on July 11, 2012. Retrieved from http://www.rand.org/content/dam/rand/pubs/testimonies/2012/RAND_CT377.pdf
51. Napolitano, J. (2011). *State of America's Homeland Security Address*. Retrieved from http://www.dhs.gov/news/2011/01/27/state-americas-homeland-security-address
52. Federal Bureau of Investigation. (2011). *Talking Strategy: The New Intelligence-driven FBI*. Retrieved from http://www.fbi.gov/news/stories/2010/april/sps_040210

© AB Forces News Collection/Alamy Stock Photo

CHAPTER 8

The National Strategy for Homeland Security

CHAPTER OBJECTIVES

- Understand the documents that define the government's responses to emergencies that occur in the United States
- Know the difference between the National Strategy for Homeland Security and the National Response Plan
- Comprehend the evolution of the National Strategy for Homeland Security
- Understand the roles of the federal, state, local, and tribal governments when an emergency occurs
- Recognize the importance of various planning strategies to keep the country and its citizens safe from both man-made and natural disasters

CHAPTER OUTLINE

HOMELAND SECURITY: A NATIONAL STRATEGY

- National Strategy (2002)
- National Response Plan (2004)
- National Strategy (2007)
- National Response Framework (2008)
- Strategic Plan (2012)
- Quadrennial Reports (2010, 2014)
- 2018–2022 FEMA Strategic Plan
- Department of Health and Human Services, Assistant Secretary for Preparedness and Response, Strategic Plan, 2007–2012
- Cybersecurity Strategy (May 15, 2018)

CHAPTER SUMMARY

© J Scott Applewhite/AP/Shutterstock.

Toward the end of 2002, President Bush and the Congress established a commission to investigate the attacks of September 11. The bipartisan committee, formally named the National Commission on Terrorist Attacks Upon the United States, or the 9/11 Commission, was given the task of examining the circumstances surrounding the attacks, providing an assessment of the government's response to the attacks, and making recommendations for establishing improved security policies for the future. To do this, the Commission members interviewed government officials, members of law enforcement, intelligence officers, and many others who provided their perspective of events.

The Commission completed its report in August of 2004. The details provided an account of the events leading up to the attacks and a review of why the national security apparatus failed to detect and prevent the incident. The Commission reported that several intelligence agencies had prior information about the attacks, as well as the identities of those involved, but detailed that no agency, even those at the highest level, was able to put all of the information together. They concluded that the intelligence agencies were not prepared for such a large-scale attack and that there were serious gaps between the different intelligence groups in terms of information sharing.

The report included 41 recommendations organized into three broad areas: (1) homeland security and emergency response; (2) intelligence and congressional reform; and (3) foreign policy and nonproliferation. They proposed that Congress should establish a committee to oversee homeland security, that funding to states and local governments should be based on potential targets, and that the TSA should screen all passengers, cargo, and luggage for explosives at borders and at sites of critical infrastructure. Additionally, the report noted that the government's intelligence agencies should be reorganized with one person who would oversee all national intelligence operations, and to ensure that all of the intelligence agencies shared information with each other.

Homeland Security: A National Strategy

The 9/11 Report formed the basis of further governmental action to increase the homeland's security. Immediately after the report was issued, President Bush asked his administration to create new policies that would help guide the national effort to ensure a more coordinated response should another terrorist attack occur. The plans would not only help to prevent an attack but also help minimize any damage done by an attack and then help the country recover quickly. In 2002, the White House created the **National Strategy for Homeland Security**. Two years later, the Department of Homeland Security published the **National Response Plan**. This was followed in 2007 with an update to the National Strategy, and then in 2008, with the **National Response Framework** (from DHS), a document that replaced the National Response Plan. Finally, in 2012, a new Strategic Plan was put forth by the Department of Homeland Security. Understanding the evolution of America's strategy for Homeland Security is the focus of this chapter.

National Strategy (2002)

The 2002 National Strategy was the plan developed by the White House Office of Homeland Security to set a broad agenda for protecting America's safety.[1] The plan was intended to provide guidance to, and organize the efforts of, those agencies within the federal government that play some role in homeland security. The Strategy stated goals that needed to be met, particular programs that should be implemented, and responsibilities that needed to be fulfilled in order to keep Americans safe. As President Bush wrote, the Strategy was a comprehensive plan for using America's talents and resources to enhance our protection and reduce our vulnerability to terrorist attacks. More of his introductory letter describing the Strategy is listed in **BOX 8.1**.

There were three primary objectives to the Strategy: (1) to prevent terrorist attacks within the United States; (2) reduce America's vulnerability to terrorism; and (3) minimize the damage and recovery from attacks that do occur. In addition, there were eight principles outlined in the National Strategy:

1. To require responsibility and accountability: The report designated, to the extent possible, the executive departments or agencies that would be responsible for federal homeland security initiatives.
2. To mobilize our entire society: State and local governments, private institutions, and

BOX 8.1 President Bush's Letter of Introduction for the 2002 National Strategy

"The National Strategy for Homeland Security is the product of more than 8 months of intense consultation across the U.S. My administration has talked to literally thousands of people—governors and mayors, state legislators, and members of Congress, concerned citizens and foreign leaders, professors and soldiers, firefighters and police officers, doctors and scientists, airline pilots and farmers, business leaders and civic activists, journalists and veterans, and the victims and their families. We have listened carefully. This is the national strategy, not a federal strategy. We must rally our entire society to overcome a new and very complex challenge. Homeland security is a shared responsibility. In addition to a national strategy, we need compatible, mutually supporting state, local, and private-sector strategies. Individual volunteers must channel their energy and commitment in support of the national and local strategies. My intent in publishing the National Strategy for Homeland Security is to help Americans achieve a shared cooperation in the area of homeland security for years to come. The Strategy seeks to do so by answering four basic questions:

- What is "homeland security" and what missions does it entail?
- What do we seek to accomplish, and what are the most important goals of homeland security?
- What is the federal executive branch doing now to accomplish these goals and what should it do in the future?
- What should nonfederal governments, the private sector, and citizens do to help secure the homeland?

The National Strategy for Homeland Security is a beginning. It calls for bold and necessary steps. It creates a comprehensive plan for using America's talents and resourcbes to enhance our protection and reduce our vulnerability to terrorist attacks. We have produced a comprehensive national strategy that is based on the principles of cooperation and partnership. As a result of this Strategy, firefighters will be better equipped to fight fires, police officers will be better armed to fight crime, businesses will be better able to protect their data and information systems, and scientists will be better able to fight Mother Nature's deadliest diseases. . . ."

Reproduced from: Bush, George W. (2002). Letter on the National Strategy for Homeland Security. Public Papers of the Presidents of the United States. Washington, D.C.: U.S. GPO.

the American people must all be involved in protecting the country.

3. To manage risk and allocate resources judiciously: There are a finite amount of resources for homeland security, and the strategy must identify priority programs that will receive funding.

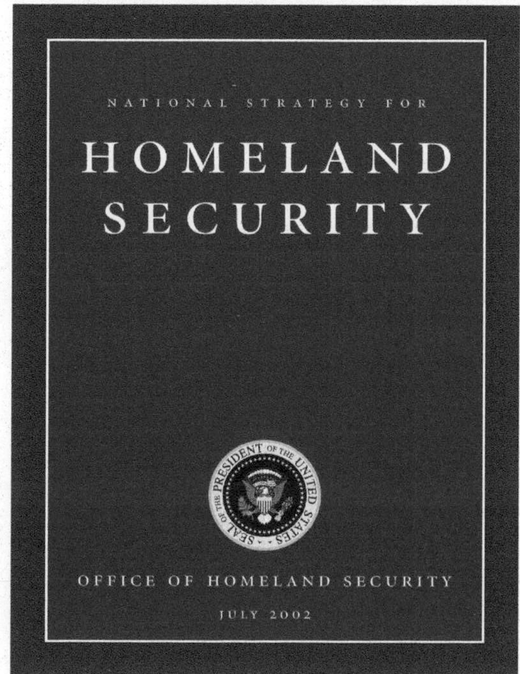

Courtesy of the DHS.

4. To seek opportunity out of adversity: It is possible to improve security while at the same time advance other important public goals or principles.
5. To foster flexibility: A flexible response to terrorism is needed because terrorists will adapt their tactics to exploit any perceived weaknesses in our defenses.
6. Measure preparedness: Every person responsible for homeland security must be accountable and their behaviors should be measured against a standard developed by the department.
7. Sustain efforts over the long term: Keeping the country safe is an ongoing, permanent task.
8. Constrain government spending: It is necessary to limit spending if possible through programs like cost-sharing arrangements with state and local governments or the private sector.[2]

The National Strategy separated homeland security functions into six mission areas, which are described in **TABLE 8.1**. The first three of the mission areas are intended to prevent terrorist attacks, and the next two are related to reducing vulnerabilities. The last mission deals with minimizing damage and recovering quickly from any attacks that do occur.

TABLE 8.1 Missions

Mission Area	Initiatives
Intelligence and Warning: "We must have an intelligence and warning system that can detect terrorist activity before it manifests itself in an attack so that proper preemptive, preventive, and protective action can be taken. The United States will take every necessary action to avoid being surprised by another terrorist attack."	1. Enhance the analytic capabilities of the FBI 2. Build new capabilities through the Information Analysis and Infrastructure Protection Division of the proposed Department of Homeland Security 3. Implement the Homeland Security Advisory System 4. Utilize dual-use analysis to prevent attacks 5. Employ "red team" techniques
Border and Transportation Security: "We must therefore promote the efficient and reliable flow of people, goods and services across borders, while preventing terrorists from using transportation conveyances or systems to deliver implements of destruction."	1. Ensure accountability in border and transportation security 2. Create "smart borders" 3. Increase the security of international shipping containers 4. Implement the Aviation and Transportation Security Act of 2001 5. Recapitalize the U.S. Coast Guard 6. Reform immigration services
Domestic Counterterrorism: "While law enforcement agencies will continue to investigate and prosecute criminal activity, they should assign priority to preventing and interdicting terrorist activity within the U.S."	1. Improve intergovernmental law enforcement coordination 2. Facilitate apprehension of potential terrorists 3. Continue ongoing investigations and prosecutions 4. Complete FBI restructuring to emphasize prevention of terrorist attacks 5. Target and attack terrorist financing 6. Track foreign terrorists and bring them to justice
Protecting Critical Infrastructure and Key Assets: "We must... improve protection of the individual pieces and interconnecting systems that make up our critical infrastructure."	1. Unify America's infrastructure protection effort in the Department of Homeland Security 2. Build and maintain a complete and accurate assessment of America's critical infrastructure and key assets 3. Enable effective partnership with state and local governments and the private sector 4. Develop a national infrastructure protection plan 5. Secure cyberspace 6. Harness the best analytic and modeling tools to develop effective, protective solutions 7. Guard America's critical infrastructure and key assets against "inside" threats 8. Partner with the international community to protect our transnational infrastructure
Defending Against Catastrophic Threats: "... the threat of terrorist attacks using chemical, biological, radiological, and nuclear weapons requires new approaches, a focused strategy, and a new organization."	1. Prevent terrorist use of nuclear weapons through better sensors and procedures 2. Detect chemical and biological materials and attacks 3. Improve chemical sensors and decontamination techniques 4. Develop broad spectrum vaccines, antimicrobials, and antidotes 5. Harness the scientific knowledge and tools to counter terrorism 6. Implement the Select Agent Program

Emergency Preparedness and Response: "An effective response to a natural disaster depends on being prepared. Therefore, we need a comprehensive national system to bring together and coordinate all necessary response assets quickly and effectively. . ."	1. Integrate separate federal response plans into a single, all-discipline incident management plan 2. Create a national incident management system 3. Improve tactical counterterrorist capabilities 4. Enable seamless communication among all responders 5. Prepare healthcare providers for catastrophic terrorism 6. Augment America's pharmaceutical and vaccine stockpiles 7. Prepare for chemical, biological, radiological, and nuclear decontamination 8. Plan for military support to civil authorities 9. Build the Citizen Corps 10. Implement the First Responder Initiative of 2003 11. Build a national training and evaluation system 12. Enhance the victim support system

Modified from: Office of Homeland Security. (2002). National Strategy for Homeland Security. Retrieved online at http://www.ncs.gov/library/policy_docs/nat_strat_hls.pdf

The National Strategy recognizes four foundations for developing a safer homeland, which refer to four of America's strengths that cut across all of the mission areas, across all levels of government, and across all sectors of our society. They include law, science and technology, information sharing and systems, and international cooperation.

The first foundation is law, which suggested new federal laws to help in the war against terror, such as the USA PATRIOT Act or the Aviation and Transportation Security Act, among others, which will enable the country to respond more quickly to terrorist activities. In the second foundation, science and technology, the need for new processes and technologies to expand the analysis of information to detect and counter potential attacks was acknowledged. Initiatives in this area include developing countermeasures for chemical, biological, radiological, and nuclear weapons, and improving the technical capabilities of first responders. New technologies will help prevent and minimize the damage from future terrorist attacks.

The third foundation was information sharing and systems. Information is vital for protecting the nation, and it was acknowledged that while information technology in the United States is the most advanced in the world, it has not adequately supported the homeland security mission. The Strategy indicated the existence of gaps in databases of federal law enforcement, immigration, and other agencies, as well as the need for all interested parties to share information. Furthermore, the majority of first responders in state and local agencies do not have compatible communications equipment.

The fourth foundation was international cooperation, something a successful homeland security initiative clearly requires. This could include creating "smart borders," identifying fraudulent travel documents, increasing the security of international shipping containers, intensifying international law enforcement cooperation, and helping foreign nations fight terrorism.[3]

In the end, many of the recommendations made in the National Strategy were based on the findings of the 9/11 Commission. The recommendations covered five broad areas: (1) cooperation, (2) information, (3) border and transportation security, (4) critical infrastructure, and (5) response (see **TABLE 8.2**).

TABLE 8.2 Implementing the National Strategy for Homeland Security

- The National Strategy for Combating Terrorism will define the U.S. war plan against international terrorism
- The National Strategy to Combat Weapons of Mass Destruction coordinates America's many efforts to deny terrorists and states the materials, technology, and expertise to make and deliver weapons of mass destruction
- The National Strategy to Secure Cyberspace will describe our initiatives to secure our information systems against deliberate, malicious disruption
- The National Money Laundering Strategy aims to undercut the illegal flows of money that support terrorism and international criminal activity
- The National Defense Strategy sets priorities for our most powerful national security instrument
- The National Drug Control Strategy lays out a comprehensive U.S. effort to combat drug smuggling and consumption

Modified from: Office of Homeland Security. (2002). National Strategy for Homeland Security. Retrieved online at http://www.ncs.gov/library/policy_docs/nat_strat_hls.pdf

1. *Cooperation*: The Strategy made it clear that it was not only federal agencies that are an essential for homeland security but that it was necessary to have a coordinated effort throughout society, including state and local governments, private companies and organizations, and individual citizens. They stressed that state and local agencies play a critical role in protecting the nation because they have the primary responsibility for funding, preparing, and operating emergency services that respond first to a terrorist attack. There is a need for states to create services that reinforce those in the federal government but not duplicate them. Instead, federal and local agencies must act as partners and work cooperatively with each other.

   The private sector (private companies) is a key partner in providing for homeland security according to the Strategy, because it has a wealth of information, new ideas, and technology that can be used to help protect the United States from terrorism. For example, pharmaceutical companies can produce vaccines to protect citizens against dangerous biological agents. It was recognized that the government must create partnerships with the private sector to increase homeland security.

   The Strategy also recognized the important role citizens play in protecting the nation. It notes that every person has a key role to play, and that every person must be willing to do their part to protect our homeland. One example is the Citizen Corps (FEMA) Community Emergency Response Team (CERT), which trains volunteers to support first responders to help victims of an attack or natural disaster. Volunteers are also used to assist law enforcement and the Medical Reserve Corps, which can help healthcare professionals during an emergency.

   The Strategy emphasized the importance of cooperation between federal, state, and local government, both horizontally and vertically, by creating complementary systems that provide essential services while at the same time avoiding duplication of services. The Strategy promised to increase collaborative efforts and coordinate services among all levels of government.

2. *Information*: The United States must be able to gather information and analyze it to successfully detect terrorist activity before enemies are able to carry out attacks. At this point in time, the government had not developed a unified, coherent method to analyze and share information that would reliably be able to predict a terrorist attack within the United States. The Strategy recognized that the United States needed to develop the means for quick and accurate threat analysis in order to disrupt and prevent future terrorist acts. It also recognized the need to continuously collect and analyze data on terrorist organizations to better them and predict their future actions. In part, this included understanding their identities, their sources of support, their motivation, goals, current and future capabilities, and vulnerabilities.
3. *Border and Transportation Security*: The security of the borders and transportation systems are vital for keeping the homeland safe. The United States shares a land border with Canada and Mexico, as well as a maritime border. Every day, people and goods enter the United States. The United States, therefore, must create a system for the safe and efficient flow of people, goods, and services across all our borders, while, at the same time, preventing terrorists from entering the country.
4. *Critical Infrastructure*: The critical infrastructure of the United States provides the essential services to its citizens, and it is vital that these are protected. They include agriculture, food, water, emergency services, the defense industrial base, information and telecommunications, energy, transportation, banking and finance, the chemical industry, and postal and shipping industry. Moreover, the nation must also protect other key assets, such as historic monuments, that, if destroyed, would not endanger any vital systems but could affect our nation's morale. In addition, some high-profile events are also part of our national identity and require special protection. The effects of a terrorist attack on our critical infrastructure could be devastating, having both immediate and long-term

consequences. Protecting our critical infrastructure and other key assets from terrorist activity will require the cooperation of all levels of government.

5. *Response*: The country must be prepared to minimize the damage of any possible attack and be able to recover quickly. To do this, we need to develop a comprehensive system that ensures that all necessary response assets can be brought together quickly and effectively. That means that many different organizations must be equipped and trained and prepared to respond to any emergency. America's first line of defense for a terrorist attack is its first responders, including police officers, firefighters, and emergency medical providers, among others. In the case of a serious emergency, the federal government can assist state and local responders. It is imperative that any gaps in the current response plans are filled.

National Response Plan (2004)

In Homeland Security Presidential Directive (HSPD) 5, President Bush ordered the Department of Homeland Security to create a National Response Plan (NRP) to align federal resources into a single, unified, all-discipline, and all-hazards approach to managing domestic emergency incidents.[4] The intent of the Plan was to reduce the "patchwork" of existing federal and local plans and replace them with a national framework that established a single, comprehensive approach to managing responses to emergencies while improving the management of these critical incidents. The objective was to create a clear and coordinated system of communication from the local level all the way to the national level in the time of an emergency.

National Response Plan

December 2004

Courtesy of DHS.

The NRP was published in 2004. It provides a range of incident management activities covering the prevention of, preparedness for, response to, and recovery from terrorism, natural disasters, and other major emergencies. It creates an overall structure that coordinates the actions of federal, state, local, and tribal organizations, nongovernmental organizations (NGOs), and private-sector groups in emergency situations so that the coordinated response can be quicker and more efficient. The plan applies to fire, rescue, emergency management, law enforcement, public works, and emergency medical services.

The NRP assumes that all levels of government, the private sector, and NGOs will take part in preventing, preparing for, responding to, and recovering from incidents of national significance. However, the NRP assumes that emergency incidents should be managed at the lowest possible jurisdictional level. This means that state or local government personnel, particularly police, fire, public health, and medical personnel, are the first to arrive and often the last to leave an incident site. Under this approach, the local executive, such as a mayor or city manager, is responsible for coordinating local resources that will be used in an emergency situation. The local executive can communicate to the public, and help people, businesses, and organizations recover from local disasters. In some cases, they may have powers to suspend local laws to establish curfews, direct evacuations, and even under some circumstances, order a quarantine, if needed. Local incident command structures (Area Command) are responsible for directing on-scene emergency management and maintaining command and control of on-scene incident operations. If the situation is serious enough, or if issues cannot be resolved at the local level, the local executive can request state or federal assistance.

A state governor is responsible for the coordination of state resources that are needed to prevent, prepare for, respond to, and recover from incidents. For example, a state governor, as the commander-in-chief of state military forces, has the ability to use, under certain conditions, police power to establish order. He or she can encourage participation in mutual aid programs and can request federal assistance if the state is unable to respond effectively.

At the regional level, the coordination is provided by a Regional Response Coordination Center (RRCC), which will oversee regional response efforts until a Joint Field Office (JFO) is established. A JFO is a temporary federal facility established locally to coordinate operational federal assistance activities to the affected jurisdiction(s) during incidents of national significance. They are multi-agency centers established locally to provide a central location for the coordination of federal, state, and local organizations that have the responsibility of responding to threats and incidents. There are various sections or departments within JFOs, including operations, planning, logistics, and finance/administration.

If needed, federal authorities will assist in coordinating the response to an attack. In that situation, the Secretary of Homeland Security will be responsible for coordinating federal operations and/or resources through the Homeland Security Operations Center. This can occur if states have requested federal assistance, if more than one federal department is substantially involved in responding to the incident, or if the Secretary has been directed by the President to take over the management responsibilities of the incident.

The Homeland Security Operations Center is the primary national center for coordinating domestic incident management operations. It combines representatives from law enforcement, national intelligence, emergency response, and the private sector to facilitate sharing of information and coordinate operations with other federal, state, local, tribal, and nongovernmental emergency operations centers (EOCs). The Homeland Security Operations Center includes officials from various federal departments, including the Departments of Agriculture, Commerce, Defense, Energy, Health and Human Services, Transportation, Veterans Affairs, the U.S. Postal Service, the Nuclear Regulatory Commission, and others.

In some cases, the Department of Justice will provide assistance. The U.S. Attorney General has the responsibility for coordinating any investigations concerning terrorist acts or terrorist threats made within U.S. boundaries or made against U.S. citizens and/or institutions overseas. After a terrorist threat or incident, the Attorney General's office will seek to identify the perpetrators and bring them to justice. During a terrorist attack, the local FBI Special Agent-in-charge will be responsible for coordinating activities with other members of the law enforcement community.

The Secretary of Defense authorizes Defense Support of Civil Authorities (DSCA) for domestic incidents as directed by the President. The Department of State coordinates response activities on the international scene. Other federal agencies may play roles as well, including the Secretary of Agriculture, administrator of the small business administration, Secretary of Commerce, Secretary of Health and Human Services, and U.S. Army Corps of Engineers.

Many other federal agencies may play a role in coordinating response to terrorist acts. For example, the Department of Homeland Security Council/National Security Council are responsible for interagency policy coordination for incident management and work together to ensure that incident management efforts are united. Moreover, the Interagency Incident Management Group (IIMG) is a federal headquarters-level multiagency group that oversees incident management. The Group is activated by the Secretary of Homeland Security when needed, depending on the nature, severity, magnitude, and complexity of the incident. The Group is composed of senior representatives from DHS, other federal departments and agencies, and NGOs, but the exact membership is flexible and depends on the specific incident.

The FBI's Strategic Information and Operations Center (SIOC) is the control center for all federal intelligence and law enforcement activities concerning terrorist incidents or threats. They will serve as an information clearinghouse to collect, process, and disseminate any relevant information that may be of assistance to those investigating the incident or threat. Found within the SIOC is the National Joint Terrorism Task Force whose mission is to increase the communication and cooperation among federal, state, local, and tribal agencies representing the intelligence, law enforcement, defense, diplomatic, public safety, and homeland security communities.

The role of NGOs and volunteer organizations is part of the NRP. Agencies such as the American Red Cross work with first responders, governments at all levels, and various agencies. Additionally, the role of the private sector is important and will vary based on the organization itself as well as the type of incident. The private organization may provide specialized teams or equipment. Citizen groups such as the U.S. Citizen Corps help to educate and train community volunteers to assist in emergencies. These groups include CERTS, Medical Reserve Corps, Neighborhood Watch, and Volunteers in Police Service.

The many elements of the NRP can either be partially or fully implemented, depending on the context and level of threat. The NRP supersedes the Initial National Response Plan (INRP), the Federal Response Plan (FRP), the U.S. Government Interagency Domestic Terrorism Concept of Operations Plan (CONPLAN), and the Federal Radiological Emergency Response Plan (FRERP).

Under the NRP, specific actions used to prevent incidents are essential. These include collecting, analyzing, and applying intelligence and other information; conducting investigations to determine the full nature and source of a threat; and implement countermeasures, conducting activities to prevent terrorists, terrorist weapons, and associated materials from entering into the United States.

If an incident occurs, federal, state, local, tribal, private-sector, and NGO organizations must report details of the incident using established communications channels. When the Homeland Security Operations Center (HSOC) receives the information, they will make a determination about the most appropriate response. If necessary, resources such as special teams or emergency facilities will be activated. The HSOC will also report incidents to the Secretary of Homeland Security, who then determines the need to activate components of the NRP. If the Secretary declares the activity to be an incident of national significance, federal departments and agencies will be notified. At that point, state governors or other federal agencies can request assistance from DHS.

Recovery actions need to be implemented immediately after all life-saving and property stabilization efforts are finalized and the scene of the incident is secure. Recovery actions include developing, coordinating, and implementing site-restoration plans and the reconstitution of government operations and services.

National Strategy (2007)

In 2007, The Homeland Security Council published an updated version of the 2002 National Strategy as a way to "guide, organize, and unify our nation's homeland security effort."[5] Described as a national, as opposed to a federal, strategy, the updated National Strategy combines homeland security with natural disaster preparedness. This new Strategy reflects a better understanding of the current terrorist threats that confront the United States while, at the same time, acknowledging that natural disasters can be catastrophic, and thus, have significant implications for homeland security. The aftermath of these natural disasters might result in situations that could be exploited by terrorists and others seeking to do harm.

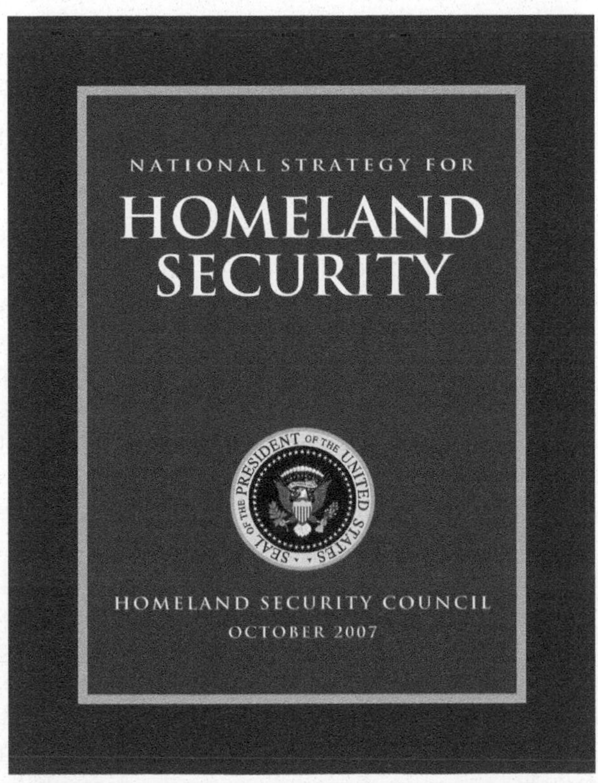

Courtesy of DHS.

In the introduction to the Strategy, President Bush acknowledged that the country continued to face the challenges related to preventing terrorist attacks and preparing for natural disasters.

Bush also expressed that the country learned from the events of Hurricane Katrina and indicated that the new Homeland Security Strategy applies the lessons learned from Katrina to make sure that America is safer, stronger, and better prepared for the future.

The 2007 National Strategy provides a framework for a national approach to protecting homeland security, as did the 2002 version. The report outlining the new strategy presents updated procedures for guiding, organizing, and unifying the country's efforts for a safe homeland. It provides four goals for the nation: Preventing and disrupting terrorist attacks; protecting the American people, our critical infrastructure, and key resources; responding to and recovering from incidents that do occur; and continuing to strengthen the basic response mechanism in order to ensure our long-term success. The report noted that terrorists can be deterred from conducting attacks if they fear potential consequences for their actions.

At the same time, the 2007 National Strategy states that the country needs to focus on natural disasters in a similar way to terrorist attacks. Events such as naturally occurring infectious diseases can pose a significant hazard to the country. Natural events such as hurricanes, earthquakes, and tornadoes, or even catastrophic accidents such as chemical spills can pose potential threats to our nation's critical infrastructure. Therefore, these events need to have the same kinds of government responses to protect the victims, provide services when needed, and rebuild the affected communities as quickly and efficiently as possible.

The new Strategy again reiterates that protecting the country is a shared responsibility among federal, state, local, and tribal governments, the private and nonprofit sectors, communities, and individual citizens. State and local governments will provide the first response to most incidents. The revised Strategy acknowledges that when an incident occurs, first responders will be local personnel. They will assess the situation and must determine the possible causes, the extent of the affected population and geographic area, and the degree of damage. After that, they must take action. Those responding must prioritize and coordinate their actions in an attempt to mitigate the consequences of the incident. They must have a consistent approach and work together effectively to deploy people, resources, and capabilities to where they are most needed. They must also anticipate any additional support that may be needed and consider requesting additional assistance if necessary. It is important that the partnerships between the federal government and state, local, and tribal governments be strengthened.

However, while most incidents can be handled at the local level, more serious events may require additional support. In those cases where state and local governments are overwhelmed, the federal government will provide additional support.

According to the updated Strategy, even as an initial response to an attack is underway, the need to begin recovery operations quickly will be necessary. This can include restoration of interrupted utility services, reestablishment of transportation routes, or the provision of food and shelter. This can come from local officials but can also be from federal officials. Long-term rebuilding efforts may take months. Community services must be restored, which will require planning and coordination from key local officials. Long-term assistance for displaced victims might be necessary. Critical infrastructures will be rebuilt.

The U.S. Congress must also take steps to protect the country. Congress should create laws to ensure that governments have the tools needed to address changing threats while protecting privacy and civil liberties, according to the new report.

National Response Framework (2008)

In 2008, a new document was generated by the federal government concerning homeland security.[6] The National Response Framework (NRF) replaced the original National Response Plan and reflected improvements in the country's ability to respond to national emergencies. The new framework is based on the previous NRP and retains much of the same content. The title was changed after some claimed the original document was not a plan but a framework for coordinated incident management. The National Response Plan was renamed to more accurately reflect the intent of the document and to encourage the continued refinement of emergency operations plans.

Like the NRP, the framework provides local, tribal, state, and federal officials with guidelines as to how they should respond to critical incidents. It presents a plan so that all responders are prepared for an emergency and know how to respond effectively should an event occur. This document attempts to create a comprehensive, national, all-hazards approach to responding to a terrorist attack or natural disaster, providing guidelines for how tribes, local government, states, the federal government, private-sector, and nongovernmental officials should respond. It is understood that the most effective response will require a unified approach in which the different levels of government provide support for the others. The framework also incorporates appropriate responses for private-sector agencies, NGOs, individuals, and households.

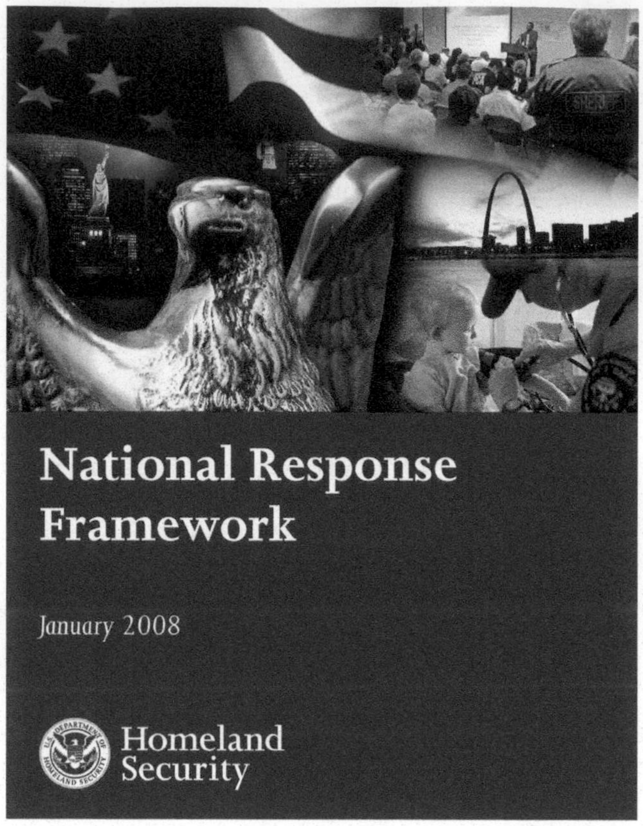

Courtesy of DHS.

The framework is supported by a NRF Resource Center, which has a website with documents to provide all emergency responders with access to the information and tools they might need to carry out their roles under the framework.[7] Any updates or changes to the framework will also be available on the website.

The NRF is built on five principles, which help to define the response actions. Taken together, these five principles of operation make up the national response doctrine. They are: Engaged partnerships (leaders at all levels must communicate and support partnerships by developing shared goals and aligning capabilities so that no one is overwhelmed in times of crisis); tiered responses (incidents must be managed at the lowest possible jurisdictional level and supported by additional capabilities when needed); scalable, flexible, and adaptable operational capabilities (as incidents change in size, scope, and complexity, the response must adapt to meet requirements); unity of effort through unified command (effective unified command is indispensable to response activities and requires a clear understanding of the roles and responsibilities of each participating organization); readiness to act (effective response requires readiness to act balanced with a clear understanding of risk). From individuals and communities to local, state, and federal governments, national response depends on the instinct and ability to act.

If needed, the federal government can provide assistance to state and local governments when responding to events. For example, the federal government can provide extra resources to an area affected by an emergency. In situations in which there may be holes in the needed services, the federal government could offer assistance. The federal government could provide an incident command structure if local and state jurisdictions are unable to do so on their own. If state or local authorities were able to reestablish their own incident command structure, the federal government could withdraw and return to its normal support role.

Private-sector organizations play a key role before, during, and after an incident. In many facets of incident response, the government works directly with private-sector groups as partners in emergency management.

One change in the new framework revolves around the term "Incident of National Significance." Previously, some people assumed that the Secretary of Homeland Security needed to declare an incident to be one of national significance before the NRP would be implemented and assistance provided. Although this was not the case, many officials continued to be confused about the term. Thus, the term was not included in the new framework.

The new framework states that the federal government provides support and resources to state and local governments when there are significant special events such as the United States hosting the Olympics. Events such as these are designated as National Special Security Events (NSSEs) by the Secretary of Homeland Security. Such events are those that may be attractive targets for terrorists because of their political, economic, symbolic, or religious significance. If an event is designated a NSSE, the lead agency responsible for coordinating the security is the U.S. Secret Service.

Another change revolves around the term, "Joint Coordination Group." Instead, the new report uses the term, "Unified Coordination Group." The JFO is led by the Unified Coordination Group, which is composed of specified senior leaders representing state and federal interests, and under certain circumstances, tribal governments, local jurisdictions, the private sector, or NGOs.

Strategic Plan (2012)

In February of 2012, the Department of Homeland Security announced a new Strategic Plan for Fiscal Years 2012 to 2016.[8] Each chapter of the report identifies missions, goals, and objectives for the department as it moves into the future (see **FIGURE 8.1**).

The first mission identified in the Plan is to prevent terrorism and enhance security in the United States. The primary goal is to prevent terrorist attacks and other threats on citizens. This will be accomplished through understanding the threat, detecting and deterring terrorist operations, and stopping the spread of violent extremism. Another goal to prevent attacks is to stop the unauthorized use of chemical, biological, radiological, and nuclear (CBRN) materials.

The objectives for DHS in this area are to control access to CBRN materials, control their movement, and protect against their use by hostile agents. DHS identified the importance of protecting critical infrastructure, leaders, and events as their third goal in the mission to prevent terrorism. Their plans to accomplish this include protecting critical infrastructure and

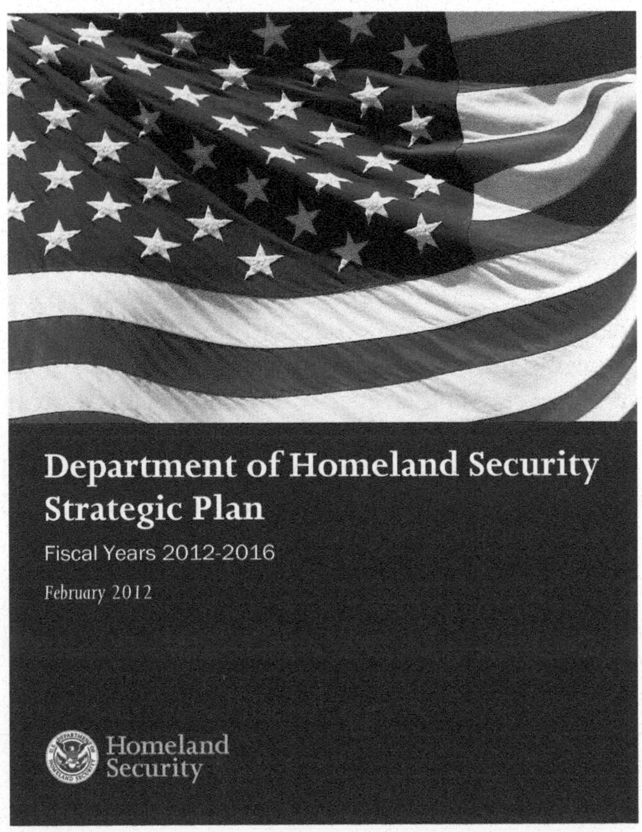

Courtesy of DHS.

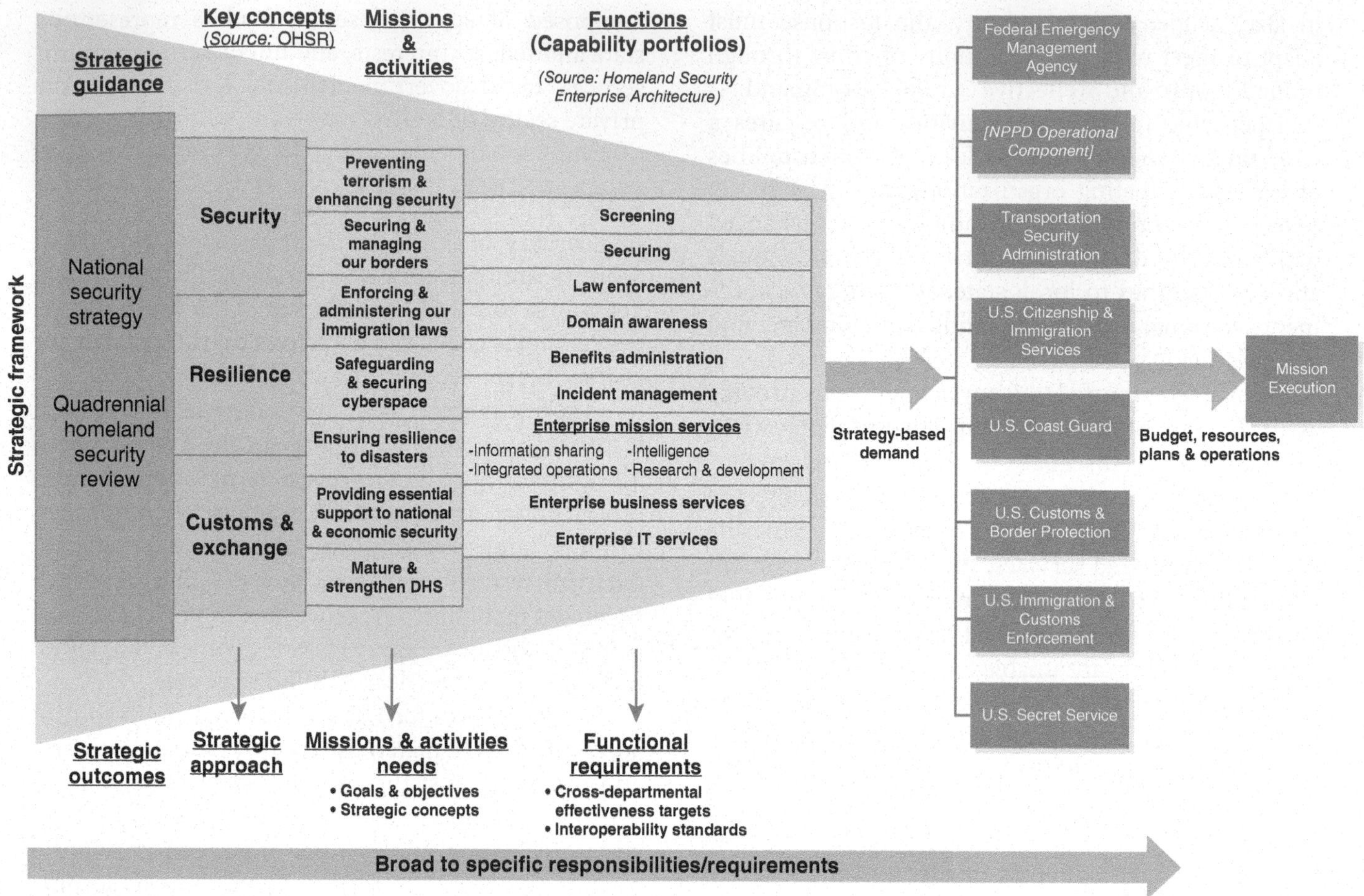

FIGURE 8.1 Department of Homeland Security Integrated Strategic Framework, 2012.

Reproduced from: Department of Homeland Security. (2012). Department of Homeland Security Strategic Plan, Fiscal Years 2012-2016.

making that infrastructure resilient to damage and adaptable to change.

The second mission identified by DHS in the 2012 plan is to secure and manage our air, land, and sea borders as a way of safeguarding trade and travel. Three goals were identified to accomplish this mission. One is to prevent the illegal flow of people and goods across the borders while at the same time allowing for the safe and efficient flow of legal trade and travel. Another goal is to build partnerships in the global market to help ensure legal global trade and transportation. The third goal is to disrupt and dismantle transnational criminal organizations and terrorist groups that traffic in illegal drugs, humans, and weapons.

The third mission in the 2012 plan is to enforce immigration laws as a way of removing criminal aliens who pose a threat to the safety of the United States. To do this, DHS plans to strengthen immigration laws and see that they are administered effectively. This means that any gaps in immigration policy are identified and corrected, and that the immigration system is simplified so that lawful immigrants can more easily integrate into American society. At the same time, DHS plans to reduce conditions that encourage unlawful immigration. Those who are found in the country illegally or who violate laws will be identified and removed.

The fourth mission identified by DHS is to safeguard and secure cyberspace. This involves federal executive branch agencies as well as privately owned infrastructure. One goal in this mission is to create a safe, secure, and resilient global cyberspace environment. By understanding the nature of cyber threats and managing the risks, malicious use of cyberspace can be limited. Another goal is to promote a general knowledge of cybersecurity and support innovative steps to increase awareness of threats and means to prevent them.

The fifth mission in the 2012 Plan is to prepare for, protect against, respond to, recover from, and mitigate a terrorist attack or natural disaster or any other large-scale emergency situation. Because it is essential to strengthen the ability of all levels of government to withstand such hazards, this was identified as the first goal. This includes reducing the vulnerabilities

Courtesy of Pete Souza/White House.

of families and individuals while also mitigating the risks to communities. DHS will work to enhance the preparedness of the country to respond to emergencies of all types. This involves strengthening the ability of agencies to respond quickly and effectively and to recover quickly.

Along with protecting the homeland, two other elements make up national security, according to the 2012 Plan, and these are national defense and economic security. In order to provide for these, DHS is involved with collecting customs revenue, maintaining the safety of maritime transportation, and conducting law enforcement activities, particularly related to preventing the exploitation of children. They also support national defense missions and support postconflict reconstruction through the Department of State.

The final section of the 2012 report looks to the future and strengthening the Department of Homeland Security, with the goal of making it more effective in the future. The report indicates that, in order to reach this goal, DHS will, among other things, enhance the management functions, increase the department's analytic capabilities and strengthen their counterintelligence capabilities, enhance information sharing, and develop more international agreements. Other plans include strengthening the workforce with training, programs for employee health, and increased workforce diversity.

Quadrennial Reports (2010, 2014)

Congress passed two federal laws, the Homeland Security Act of 2002 and the Implementing Recommendations of the 9/11 Commission Act of 2007, in which they directed the Secretary of Homeland Security to report to Congress every 4 years on the status of policies and programs designed to secure the nation from terrorism and make recommendations for improving those plans. The Secretary was asked not only to outline a security strategy that described priority mission areas for the federal government but also for state, local, tribal and territorial governments, nongovernmental organizations, and members of private agencies. There have been two such reports, called the Quadrennial Homeland Security Reviews, which provide an outline and plan for the nation's policies and plans for protecting the homeland and ensuring the rights of citizens and residents of the nation. They both provide a framework for the activities designed for the future; an analysis of needs; not only for security but also for response to natural disasters.

The first report, published in 2010, was described as the "most comprehensive assessment and analysis of homeland security to date."[9] The report acknowledges that while global communications have helped people around the world, it has also presented security challenges that affect the United States and countries around the world. The threats are constantly evolving. As new security measures are put into place, terrorists attempt to thwart those measures. Therefore, it is essential that the United States establishes a comprehensive approach to homeland security that includes three elements: Security (protecting the people and its way of life); Resiliency (the capacity for rapid recovery); and Customs and Exchange (ways to encourage lawful commerce, travel, and immigration).

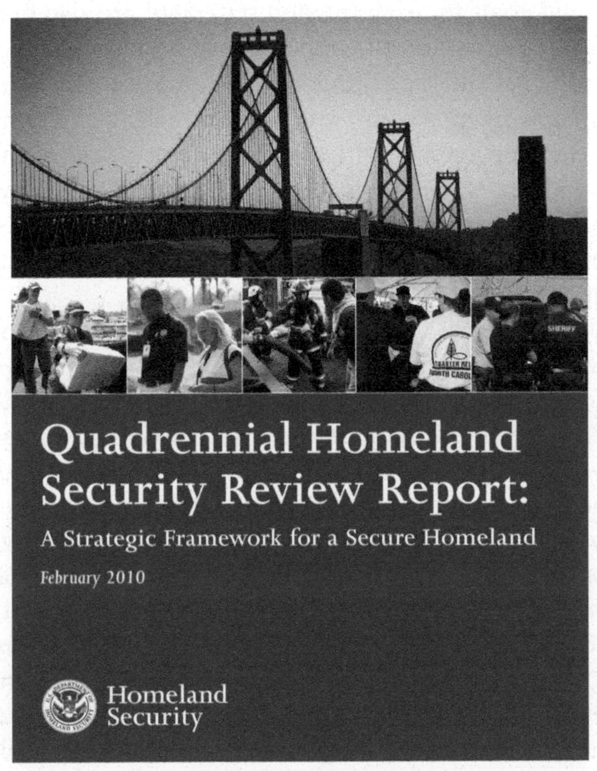

Quadrennial Homeland Security Review Report:
A Strategic Framework for a Secure Homeland
February 2010
Homeland Security

Courtesy of DHS.

TABLE 8.3 Threats and Hazards; Global Challenges and Trends

Threats and Hazards	Global Challenges and Trends
▪ High-consequence weapons of mass destruction ▪ Al Qaeda and global violent extremism ▪ High-consequence and/or wide scale cyberattacks, intrusions, disruptions, and exploitations ▪ Pandemics, major accidents, and natural hazards ▪ Illicit trafficking and related transnational crime ▪ Smaller-scale terrorism	▪ Economic and financial instability ▪ Dependence on fossil fuels and the threats of global climate change ▪ Nations unwilling to abide by international norms ▪ Sophisticated and broadly available technology ▪ Other drivers of illicit, dangerous, or uncontrolled movement of people and goods

Source: Department of Homeland Security, February 2010. Quadrennial Homeland Security Review: A Strategic Framework for a Secure Homeland: https://www.dhs.gov/sites/default/files/publications/2010-qhsr-report.pdf; p. viii.

In this report, threats and hazards to the safety of the United States and its citizens are identified, listing them as priorities for future planning. In addition, long-term global challenges and trends are noted (See **TABLE 8.3**). These are issues and concerns to nations around the world rather than just the United States, and, therefore, areas where Congress has less control over policies. Even though these trends are not based solely in the United States, they could be just as damaging if they were to occur.

A good portion of the 2010 Quadrennial Report focused on five Homeland Security Missions, as shown in **TABLE 8.4**. These establish the primary objectives for DHS, as described in Chapter 5. Individual goals for each mission statement are also presented throughout the report. Objectives for each of these goals include things such as understanding the threat, engaging communities, anticipating emerging threats, protecting critical infrastructure, preventing illegal entry, reducing demand for illegal employment, arresting/detaining/removing unauthorized foreign nationals, managing cyberthreats, and mitigating risks of disasters.

Secondary missions for DHS, as identified in the Report, include an overall improvement in the policies by "maturing and strengthening" the homeland security enterprise. This includes "enhancing shared awareness of risks and threats, building capable communities, fostering unity of effort, and fostering innovative approaches and solutions through leading-edge science and technology." The report made it clear that an essential part of strengthening homeland security was through involving state and local government agencies, families, and even individuals and maintaining effective communication among all parties. The need for increased cooperative efforts with officials from other countries was also noted.[10]

TABLE 8.4 Mission Statements for Homeland Security

Mission Statements for Homeland Security
Mission 1: Preventing Terrorism and Enhancing Security ▪ Goal 1.1: Prevent Terrorist Attacks ▪ Goal 1.2: Prevent the Unauthorized Acquisition or Use of Chemical, Biological, Radiological, and Nuclear Materials and Capabilities ▪ Goal 1.3: Manage Risks to Critical Infrastructure, Key Leadership, and Events
Mission 2: Securing and Managing Our Borders ▪ Goal 2.1: Effectively Control U.S. Air, Land, and Sea Borders ▪ Goal 2.2: Safeguard Lawful Trade and Travel ▪ Goal 2.3: Disrupt and Dismantle Transnational Criminal Organizations
Mission 3: Enforce and Administer Our Immigration Laws ▪ Goal 3.1: Strengthen and Effectively Administer the Immigration System ▪ Goal 3.2: Prevent Unlawful Immigration
Mission 4: Safeguard and Secure Cyberspace ▪ Goal 4.1: Create a Safe, Secure, and Resilient Cyber Environment ▪ Goal 4.2: Promote Cybersecurity Knowledge and Innovation
Mission 5: Ensuring Resilience to Disasters ▪ Goal 5.1: Mitigate Hazards ▪ Goal 5.2: Enhance Preparedness ▪ Goal 5.3: Ensure Effective Emergency Response ▪ Goal 5.4: Rapidly Recover

Source: Department of Homeland Security, February 2010. Quadrennial Homeland Security Review: A Strategic Framework for a Secure Homeland: https://www.dhs.gov/sites/default/files/publications/2010-qhsr-report.pdf; p. x.

2014 Quadrennial Homeland Security Review

The second Quadrennial Homeland Security Report was published in 2014. The Secretary of DHS at the time, Jeh Johnson, noted that "we will continue to adhere to the five basic homeland security missions set forth in the first Quadrennial Homeland Security Review Report, but these missions must be refined to reflect the evolving landscape of homeland security threats and hazards."[11] In this new report, five strategic priorities for DHS were identified. These included the creation of an updated posture to address the increasingly decentralized terrorist threat; a strengthened path forward for cybersecurity that acknowledges the increasing interdependencies among critical systems and networks; a homeland security strategy to manage the urgent and growing risk of biological threats and hazards; a risk segmentation approach to securing and managing flows of people and goods into and out of the United States; and a new framework for improving the efficiency and effectiveness of our mission execution through public-private partnerships.

The second report noted that threats and hazards to the nation's security continue to evolve and include groups such as al Qaida and even lone offenders. Johnson also paid attention to the dangers of cyberspace, which he described as growing significantly in recent years such that it can be used to harm both people and critical infrastructure. Natural disasters, either caused by or worsened by climate change, also pose serious threats to the U.S. Another potential threat to the nation is the ever-evolving transnational criminal organizations that continue to grow stronger and are able to carry out grave crimes.

In making new policies and laws for protecting the homeland, DHS will be guided by five principles or criteria that will help the leaders make consistent and effective policies. These are described in **TABLE 8.5**.

The report concluded by identifying "black swans," described as "potential changes in the world around us" that are not probable but would likely have a substantial effect on the country's safety and security if they did happen. They could also significantly alter a future evaluation of the security risk and priorities in the next few years. Because most people do not believe that these events will occur, they were not accounted for in the analysis for the report. However, because they could result in fundamental changes to the strategic environment, a short description of each "swan" was provided. Four possible black swans were identified in the report, as descried in **TABLE 8.6**.

TABLE 8.5 Guiding Principles

1. The Cornerstone of homeland security is preventing terrorism, but homeland security must be multithreat and all-hazard
2. Homeland security supports economic security
3. Homeland security requires a networked community
4. Homeland security relies on the use of market-driven solutions and innovation
5. Homeland security upholds privacy, civil rights, and civil liberties
6. Homeland security is national risk management

U.S. Department of Homeland Security, The 2014 Quadrennial Homeland Security Review, June 18, 2014. p. 30–32; https://www.dhs.gov/sites/default/files/publications/qhsr/2014-QHSR.pdf

2018–2022 FEMA Strategic Plan

Officials at FEMA published a Strategic Plan for 2011–2014, followed by a second edition for 2018–2022. The plans described goals and objectives for the agency. Both plans revolved around a "whole community" approach to emergency management that involved community officials and the creation of a culture of preparedness to be able to respond in the event of an emergency and become resilient.

TABLE 8.6 Potential Black Swans

- Rapid adoption of technology-driven changes to manufacturing processes, such as three-dimensional printing, fundamentally altering the importance of transnational flows of information in relation to the transnational flows of goods
- A country unexpectedly becoming a failed state, leading to consequences such as loss of control over sensitive technologies (e.g., chemical, biological, radiological, and nuclear materials) or loss of general border integrity
- A substantial increase in sophistication of hostile nonstate actors, such as a violent extremist group gaining the ability to launch a campaign of well-coordinated and highly organized attacks, conducted by interconnected but autonomous groups or individuals within the United States
- Abrupt impacts of climate change, such as drastic alterations in U.S. weather patterns and growing seasons or rapid opening of the Arctic

U.S. Department of Homeland Security, The 2014 Quadrennial Homeland Security Review, June 18, 2014. p. 29; https://www.dhs.gov/sites/default/files/publications/qhsr/2014-QHSR.pdf

FEMA officials identified three goals for 2018–2022. These were:

1. **Build a Culture of Preparedness:** The country must be prepared for emergencies, whether man-made or natural. Communities must take measures to mitigate possible damages, organize for a response, and return quickly to a state of normalcy. Planning should involve individuals, families, and communities as well as state, local, tribal, territorial, and federal governments. To do this, risks must be identified and partnerships developed so that all involved can respond quickly to a disaster.
2. **Ready the Nation for Catastrophic Disasters:** Catastrophic disasters, or those that occur with little or no warning, causing many deaths and injuries. They can, therefore, be devastating. FEMA officials must be prepared to respond quickly with recovery missions that are appropriate and successful. Communication and coordination is critical in these operations.
3. **Reduce the Complexity of FEMA:** FEMA employees must be flexible to address the diverse needs of survivors, and, at the same time, be prepared to provide assistance quickly and simply. New technology can make response easier and faster, in turn helping to increase efficiency and improve services.[11]

Department of Health and Human Services, Assistant Secretary for Preparedness and Response, Strategic Plan, 2007–2012

The Assistant Secretary for Preparedness and Response (ASPR) advises the Secretary of Health and Human Services on issues pertaining to bioterrorism or related health emergencies. ASPR has been given the task of ensuring a cohesive plan for preparing for and responding to any potential public health effects resulting from natural or man-made disasters. The report describes the importance of national health security, which "is a state in which the nation and its people are prepared for, protected from, and resilient in the face of health threats or incidents with potentially negative health consequences." In 2006, the agency prepared a strategic plan in which they identified four strategic objectives: To lead and promote strategic partnerships; to educate public health and healthcare professionals and scientists; to empower the public; and to enhance the preparedness and response infrastructure. In order to meet those objectives, the agency described three goals:

- Goal 1. Community Preparedness and Prevention
- Goal 2. Public Health Partnership
- Goal 3. Federal Response Capability

In the 2014 report, the agency described that they had made significant progress in their capacity to respond to large-scale events that could pose a serious threat to the health of those affected. In this version of the report, six goals are identified:

- Goal 1: To promote resilient communities by fostering a nation able to withstand and recover from public health emergencies: Communities must be aware of and plan for ways to protect themselves. They must be aware of potential risks, know how to get help, know their personal responsibilities, and be able to help their neighbors. ASPR helps to identify various community factors that help a community become more resilient.
- Goal 2: To strengthen leadership and capabilities within public health and medical emergency management to include prevention, preparedness, mitigation, response, and recovery: ASPR helps to train professionals so they are prepared to respond to emergencies, but they also help to train members of the public so they know how to care for themselves during an emergency. They also seek to strengthen the ability of officials to share information quickly and coordinate their responses with federal and international partners so they can share information, risk assessment, response coordination, and mutual assistance.
- Goal 3: Promote an effective medical countermeasures enterprise: The Public Health Emergency Medical Countermeasures Enterprise (PHEMCE) provides a framework for interagency coordination that provides for medical services such as vaccines, diagnostics, and nonpharmaceutical countermeasures that can be used to either protect or treat citizens if a medical emergency should occur. This requires

early detection of diseases; manufacturing and stockpiling of medical products that are needed for potential threats; the distribution and administration of medical countermeasures; and an evaluation of the effectiveness of the countermeasures provided.

- Goal 4: Lead, coordinate, and develop proactive and forward-thinking policies that support national and international public health and medical preparedness, response, and recovery capabilities In order for actions taken for public health preparedness, response, and recovery to be effective, there must be a useful policy and planning framework that results from a collaboration between state, local, and tribal governments and other partners. Each framework should provide a process that is flexible, based on evidence, ethical, and is geared toward increasing the nation's resilience to disasters. ASPR seeks to continue to improve frameworks.
- Goal 5: Improve health outcomes from disasters by strengthening the ability of our nation's health care system to effectively respond and recover In an emergency, it is essential that all health care facilities, both private and public, are able to provide care to patients, possibly with an increased demand for service health emergencies. Health care facilities that are prepared to provide efficient and effective services during normal times will be prepared to provide an effective response after a health emergency. When incidents do occur, health providers must be able to adapt to any unanticipated problems with an integrated effort that includes many aspects of the health care system. All health care providers must develop positive working partnerships that can be used prior to an emergency, but that can also be relied on after an event.
- Goal 6: Improve ASPR adaptability and resilience by maximizing workforce potential, developing leadership, and encouraging a continuous learning culture: All ASPR employees must strive to develop an organizational culture that involves all employees, attracts a talented and diverse workforce, and fosters high morale. All policies should be guided by data, evaluation, and performance measurement. The priorities of the agency should determine resource planning. This should create an effective agency with an engaged workforce.

Cybersecurity Strategy (May 15, 2018)

The Cybersecurity Strategy was created by DHS in 2018. It described the federal government's approach to protecting the nation's networks and infrastructure from criminal activity carried out through the Internet. This is a topic that receives greater attention as more systems are hacked and more citizens fall prey to cybercrimes. Major companies also fall prey to cyber criminals, losing millions of dollars. The Department's vision is described in **BOX 8.2**.

This plan is needed so the nation can prepare for a possible cyberattack on the country's computer-based infrastructure. Most Americans, both individuals and businesses, have become increasingly dependent on the Internet for their day-to-day activities. This technological development has also led to a higher risk of cybercrime activity and threats, such as terrorists, individual criminals (with malware, spyware, or ransomware), or transnational criminal groups. Because of these concerns, cybersecurity has become a topic for homeland security and, at the same time, one of the core missions of DHS.

In the Cybersecurity Strategy Report, officials at DHS identify five Cybersecurity Goals, which they define as "pillars." They include risk identification; vulnerability reduction; threat reduction; consequence mitigation; and enabling cybersecurity outcomes. Each pillar has sub-goals, as shown in **TABLE 8.7**. The Report also identifies the seven guiding principles for cybercrime. These are listed in **TABLE 8.8**. Their goal is to reduce the threats of cybercrime by preventing and disrupting criminal acts of cybercrimes. They also seek to lessen the effects of cybercrimes by implementing an effective federal response to cyberevents when they occur.

BOX 8.2 DHS Cybersecurity Vision

Vision: By 2023, the Department of Homeland Security will have improved national cybersecurity risk management by increasing security and resilience across government networks and critical infrastructure; decreasing illicit cyber activity; improving responses to cyber incidents; and fostering a more secure and reliable cyber ecosystem through a unified departmental approach, strong leadership, and close partnership with other federal and nonfederal entities.

U.S. Department of Homeland Security, Cybersecurity Strategy. May 15, 2018. https://www.dhs.gov/sites/default/files/publications/DHS-Cybersecurity-Strategy_1.pdf

TABLE 8.7 DHS Cybersecurity Goals

Pillar I–Risk Identification

Goal 1: Assess Evolving Cybersecurity Risks. We will understand the evolving national cybersecurity risk posture to inform and prioritize risk management activities.

Pillar II–Vulnerability Reduction

Goal 2: Protect Federal Government Information Systems. We will reduce vulnerabilities of federal agencies to ensure that they achieve an adequate level of cybersecurity.

Goal 3: Protect Critical Infrastructure. We will partner with key stakeholders to ensure that national cybersecurity risks are adequately managed.

Pillar III–Threat Reduction

Goal 4: Prevent and Disrupt Criminal Use of Cyberspace. We will reduce cyberthreats by countering transnational criminal organizations and sophisticated cyber criminals.

Pillar IV–Consequence Mitigation

Goal 5: Respond Effectively to Cyber Incidents. We will minimize consequences from potentially significant cyber incidents through coordinated community-wide response efforts.

Pillar V – Enable Cybersecurity Outcomes

Goal 6: Strengthen the Security and Reliability of the Cyber Ecosystem. We will support policies and activities that enable improved global cybersecurity risk management.

Goal 7: Improve Management of DHS Cybersecurity Activities. We will execute our departmental cybersecurity efforts in an integrated and prioritized way.

U.S. Department of Homeland Security, Cybersecurity Strategy. May 15, 2018. https://www.dhs.gov/sites/default/files/publications/DHS-Cybersecurity-Strategy_1.pdf

TABLE 8.8 Guiding Principles

1. Risk prioritization: The foremost responsibility of DHS is to safeguard the American people and we must prioritize our efforts to focus on systemic risks and the greatest cybersecurity threats and vulnerabilities faced by the American people and our homeland.
2. Cost-effectiveness: Cyberspace is highly complex and DHS efforts to increase cybersecurity must be continuously evaluated and reprioritized to ensure the best results for investments made.
3. Innovation and agility: Cyberspace is an evolving domain with emergent risks. Although the proliferation of technology leads to new risks, it also provides an opportunity for innovation. DHS must lead by example in researching, developing, adapting, and employing cutting-edge cybersecurity capabilities and remain agile in its efforts to keep up with evolving threats and technologies.
4. Collaboration: The growth and development of the Internet has been primarily driven by the private sector and the security of cyberspace is an inherently cross-cutting challenge. To accomplish our cybersecurity goals, we must work in a collaborative manner across our components and with other federal and nonfederal partners.
5. Global approach: Robust international engagement and collaboration is required to accomplish our national cybersecurity goals. DHS must engage internationally to manage global cyber risks, respond to worldwide incidents, and disrupt growing transnational cyber threats as well as encourage other nations and foreign entities to adopt the policies necessary to create an open, interoperable, secure, and reliable Internet.
6. National values: DHS must uphold privacy, civil rights, and civil liberties in accordance with applicable law and policy. The Department empowers our cybersecurity programs to succeed by integrating privacy protections from the outset and employing a layered approach to privacy and civil liberties oversight.

Source: U.S. Department of Homeland Security. May 15, 2018. "Cybersecurity Strategy". https://info.publicintelligence.net/DHS-CybersecurityStrategy-2018.pdf

Chapter Summary

Since 9-11, multiple plans have been developed by the federal government to coordinate the country's preparedness for, and responses to, future terrorist threats and natural disasters. They each recognize the important role that local first-responders play in controlling the harm resulting from these incidents. The coordination of activities and the sharing of information, across agencies at all levels, is key to preventing and mitigating future events. These four plans address these issues in different ways.

Review/Discussion Questions

1. What is the National Strategy, and why is it important to homeland security?
2. What is the National Response Plan, and why is it important to homeland security?
3. Why was a new National Strategy for Homeland Security written in 2007, and how does it differ from the original report?
4. What is the National Response Framework, and how does it relate to the National Response Plan?
5. What are the key missions and goals identified in the 2012 Department of Homeland Security Strategic Plan?

Additional Readings

Department of Homeland Security. (2004). National Response Plan. Available online at http://www.it.ojp.gov/fusioncenterguidelines/NRPbaseplan.pdf

Department of Homeland Security. (2007). National Strategy for Homeland Security. Available online at http://www.dhs.gov/national-strategy-homeland-security-october-2007

Department of Homeland Security. (2008). National Response Framework. Available online at http://www.fema.gov/pdf/emergency/nrf/nrf-core.pdf

Department of Homeland Security. (2012). Department of Homeland Security Strategic Plan, Fiscal Years 2012-2016. Available online at http://www.dhs.gov/xlibrary/assets/dhs-strategic-plan-fy-2012-2016.pdf

Office of Homeland Security. (2002). National Strategy for Homeland Security. Available online at https://www.dhs.gov/sites/default/files/publications/nat-strat-hls-2002

Endnotes

1. Office of Homeland Security. (2002). *National Strategy for Homeland Security*. Available online at https://www.dhs.gov/sites/default/files/publications/nat-strat-hls-2002.pdf
2. This section is based on Department of Homeland Security. (2004). National Response Plan. Retrieved online at http://www.it.ojp.gov/fusioncenterguidelines/NRPbaseplan.pdf
3. This section is based on Department of Homeland Security. (2007). National Strategy for Homeland Security. Retrieved online at http://www.dhs.gov/national-strategy-homeland-security-october-2007
4. This section is based on Department of Homeland Security. (2008). National Response Framework. Retrieved online at http://www.fema.gov/pdf/emergency/nrf/nrf-core.pdf
5. The National Response Framework Resource Center can be found at www.fema.gov/NRF
6. This section is based on Department of Homeland Security. (2012). Department of Homeland Security Strategic Plan, Fiscal Years 2012-2016. Retrieved online at http://www.dhs.gov/xlibrary/assets/dhs-strategic-plan-fy-2012-2016.pdf
7. Department of Homeland Security. (February 2010). Quadrennial Homeland Security Review: A Strategic Framework for a Secure Homeland. https://www.dhs.gov/sites/default/files/publications/2010-qhsr-report.pdf
8. Department of Homeland Security. (February 2010). 2010 Quadrennial Homeland Security Review: Executive Summary. https://www.dhs.gov/sites/default/files/publications/2010-qhsr-executive-summary.pdf
9. Department of Homeland Security. (June 2014). The 2014 Quadrennial Homeland Security Review. Retrieved at https://www.dhs.gov/sites/default/files/publications/qhsr/2014-QHSR.pdf
10. Department of Homeland Security, Federal Emergency Management Agency. (2018). 2018-2022 Strategic Plan https://www.fema.gov/strategic-plan
11. Department of Homeland Security (June 18, 2014). The 2014 Quadrennial Homeland Security Review. Retrieved at https://www.dhs.gov/sites/default/files/publications/2014-qhsr-final-508.pdf

© Steve Wood/Shutterstock

CHAPTER 9

Homeland Security Threats

CHAPTER OBJECTIVES

- Understand the different types of threats (chemical, biological, radiological, nuclear, and explosives) facing the United States
- Understand the effects of these types of weapons on humans

CHAPTER OUTLINE

During the peak of the morning rush hour on March 20, 1995, in Tokyo, Japan, five members of the Aum Shinrikyo cult carried plastic bags wrapped in newspapers into the subway system. Inside each bag was liquid sarin, a nerve agent that can cause temporary blindness, neurological damage, or even death. Once on the subway train, the cult members punctured the packets with sharpened umbrellas and then immediately left the subway. The liquid sarin leaked onto the floor, evaporated, and was inhaled by passengers. Thirteen commuters were killed and thousands of others were sickened by the attack.

One reason why the cult's actions did not kill more victims was because of the poor quality of the sarin they used. But the attack clearly demonstrated the potential dangers posed by chemical weapons that could easily be used by terrorists to injure or kill innocent people.

CBRNE

Chemical weapons like sarin, along with biological, radiological, nuclear, and explosive weapons, are referred to as **CBRNE**. These are weapons that, if used by terrorists, have the potential to cause widespread death and injury, and in some cases, mass destruction of physical facilities. The primary reason terrorist groups would use these weapons is to maximize death and destruction in an effort to bring attention to their political, ideological, or religious agenda.

The use of a CBRNE can result in both short- and long-term effects. In the short term, there can be mass death and injury to victims and destruction to buildings, infrastructure, and the environment. First responders may be overwhelmed after such an event, as could hospitals, medical facilities, and other personnel. The long-term effects may be even more harmful. A city attacked by a CBRNE may experience significant negative consequences to its economy, which could then reverberate across the country and even the world. Those who suffered injuries may have to deal with both physical and psychological effects for many years, if not a lifetime. There may also be long-term psychological effects for some who did not suffer direct harm. The effects on the environment may be long-lasting, including a community's agricultural resources, food, and water supplies. Moreover, the impact of such an event may reach farther than the immediate site. Someone may be contaminated with a biological agent and then return to their home, spreading the germ to others. This can occur with little or no warning.

It has become one goal of homeland security officials to reduce the opportunities that terrorists have for obtaining these weapons and to reduce the likelihood that they will use them against the United States. Nonetheless, communities must prepare for a potential attack and be prepared to mitigate the potential impact on critical infrastructure, the economy, and daily life.

Unfortunately, our knowledge of CBRNEs that may be used by terrorists is limited. Many of the characteristics and destructive qualities of large amounts of chemicals and biological threats are still relatively unknown by experts. To date, Americans have had little or no experience in dealing with CBRNEs or their consequences.

Following is a description of CBRNE.

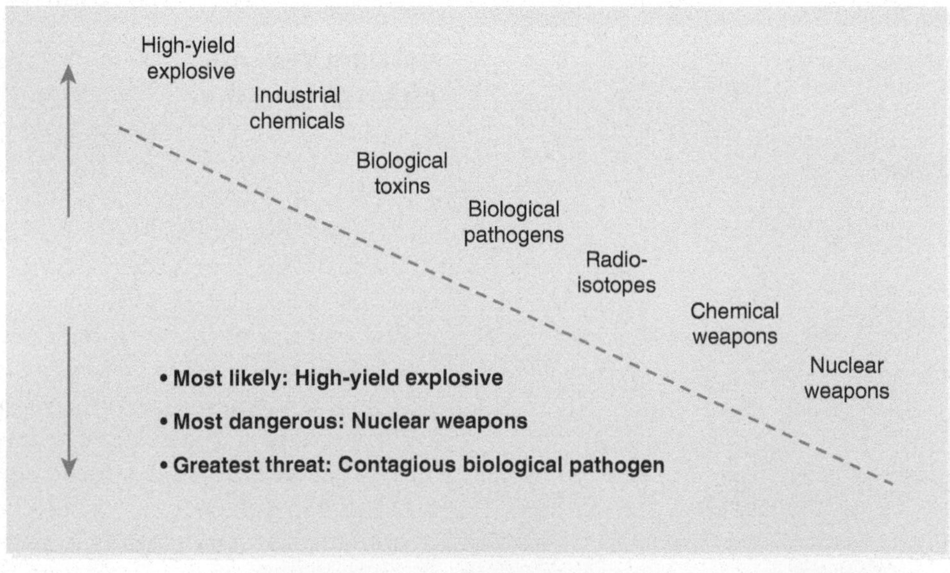

Chemical

A **chemical weapon** is a device that uses poisonous liquids, solids, gases, and vapor agents to cause death or injury to humans, animals, and plants. The exposure to the chemical can occur through inhalation, exposure of the skin or eyes, or even ingestion. Depending on the chemical involved, the concentration of the chemical, the method of transmission, and the dose received, these weapons can inflict a variety of ailments, ranging from simple discomfort to permanent injuries and death. The effects of a chemical can be immediate or they may be delayed.

Chemicals can be spread in liquid, solid (generally powdered), or gas forms. They can be released into the air by bombs (explosives) or sprayed from a vehicle. Chemicals may be left in an open container, or sent in the mail. The optimal method for mass dispersal of a chemical is a sprayer such as a crop duster. Of course, if the chemicals are released in an enclosed area such as a subway station), the effect may be much more harmful than those released in an open area. A chemical attack could also occur through product tampering or using the chemical to poison food or water supplies for a community. Another way to disperse chemicals is by using containers to hold the chemicals, then breaching those containers in some way, thereby exposing the chemical to the air.

A large-scale lethal attack would have to take place in a large, open area, which is not easy to accomplish. However, smuggling small quantities of chemical agents into a small, confined space and releasing them with a simple method would be relatively easy. Trucks, trains, and ships could easily carry large amounts of chemical materials into an area. In this case, hundreds, if not thousands, of people could be exposed.

It is thought that many potential terrorist groups have the technology and expertise needed to produce chemical weapons. Those terrorist groups with access to even modest resources could potentially produce small amounts of an effective chemical weapon. Clandestine laboratories in which the chemicals are made can be easily hidden and used to make enough chemicals to cause a significant number of deaths. There is an ongoing concern that there are still stockpiles of chemicals in arsenals left over from the Cold War that could easily be sold, stolen, or sabotaged by terrorist groups. However, any major chemical attack would require a large volume of the chemical, making it very unlikely.

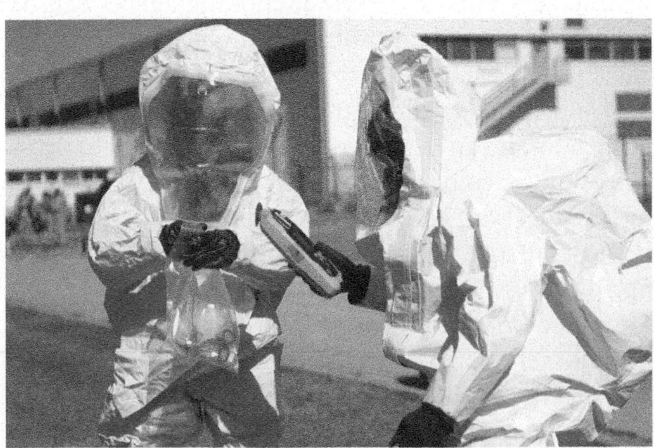

Courtesy of Jasmine Morales/US Army.

In some cases, a chemical attack is quickly and easily recognized because the effects on victims are readily evident. However, in other cases, it can be unclear to victims and responders that there has been a chemical (or even biological) attack, until further testing has occurred. Identifying the chemical used can be difficult sometimes because some evaporate quickly. Other chemical weapons may remain in the affected area long after the attack.

First responders need proper training and equipment so that they are able to respond to possible chemical attacks safely and efficiently. If not, they face potential injury or death from their exposure. They need to be trained to identify the symptoms of chemical interactions, anticipate the consequences, and be able to treat victims appropriately.

There are many chemicals that are potentially toxic to humans, animals, and plants, but not all of these chemicals can be easily made into and used as weapons. Still, there are many different chemicals that have been developed and can be used as weapons. There are seven different categories of chemicals, which are organized by their potential effects on victims. They include nerve agents, blister agents, choking/pulmonary agents, irritants, and incapacitating agents.

Nerve Agents

Nerve agents are the most dangerous chemical agents as they affect the body's nervous system. These chemicals will sometimes cause the nervous system of those who are exposed to become inactive, causing death within minutes. Nerve agents can be inhaled or absorbed by the skin or ingested through food, water, or the air.[1] The most widely known nerve agents are sarin and VX.

Sarin is a man-made nerve agent. It is a clear, colorless, and tasteless liquid with no odor in its pure form, but it can be made into a vapor to spread into the environment. Victims can be exposed by breathing air that contains sarin, but because the drug can be easily mixed with water, it can also be used to poison a community's water system. Those exposed to sarin may experience runny nose, watery eyes, eye pain, blurred vision, drooling, excessive sweating, cough, chest pains, rapid breathing, diarrhea, increased urination, confusion, drowsiness, weakness, headache, nausea, vomiting, low or high blood pressure, or even death. A person who inhaled just a small amount of sarin (.05 grams) for 1 minute would have a 50% chance of dying within 15 minutes.

VX has the texture of motor oil, making it especially dangerous as it can remain in the environment for long periods. It is odorless and tasteless and can be distributed as a liquid or as an aerosol. Early symptoms of contact with the chemical include muscular twitching, sweating, nausea, vomiting, blurred vision, or headache. A victim may also experience a shortness of breath, runny nose, chest pains, or death.[2]

It is unlikely that terrorist groups will use chemical weapons. In order to produce large quantities of chemical weapons, an industrial facility would be needed. To do this, new facilities could be built or existing plants could be converted into a facility in which chemical agents could be produced. Another obstacle to a terrorist group using a chemical is the delivery of the chemical. Transporting and dispensing a large amount of chemicals is a difficult challenge, made more so in this country in recent years with our heightened security measures.

Blister Agents

Blister agents attack the skin of those exposed, resulting in blisters and skin burns. They are chemicals that contain acid-forming compounds that must come into contact with the victims' skin in order to have an effect. If a victim comes into contact with a blister agent, it is unlikely that he or she will die, but the person will probably suffer from burns and blisters to the skin. However, if these agents are inhaled by a victim, they can be deadly. In most cases, blister agents primarily cause irritation to the lungs, eyes, and airway. The most common blister agent is mustard gas.[3]

Mustard gas (sulfur mustard) has an odor of garlic, onions, or mustard, but sometimes has no odor at all. The chemical can take the form of a gas, an oily liquid, or a solid. Mustard gas is not found naturally in the environment but must be manufactured. The chemical can be delivered through the air as a vapor. Victims can also drink it if it is in the water. The effects of mustard gas are often delayed and do not appear immediately upon ingestion. The symptoms depend on how much of the agent the victim is exposed to; exposure can lead to blistering of the skin, damage to eyes and respiratory tract, sore throat, redness and itching of the skin, swelling and tearing of the eyes, runny or bloody nose, sneezing, coughing, abdominal pain, diarrhea, fever, and nausea. Exposure to mustard gas typically is not fatal.[4]

Lewisite is another blister agent. It is a colorless liquid with an odor similar to geraniums.[5] People exposed to lewisite (or mustard-lewisite) will have an immediate reaction and may experience serious burns to the skin, burning sensations in the nasal passages, cough, shortness of breath, nausea, or vomiting. Long-term effects may include respiratory damage and damage to bone marrow and blood vessels. Those exposed to high levels may die.[6]

Blood Agents

Blood agents are chemical weapons that prevent the victim's body from using oxygen in the blood. These chemicals must come into contact with a victim's skin in order to cause a reaction. An example is hydrogen cyanide.

Hydrogen cyanide is a potentially deadly chemical that can take the form of a colorless gas; it can also be found in a crystal form. The gas may have an odor like bitter almonds, but not always. Victims of cyanide poisoning may be exposed by inhaling the drug, drinking contaminated water, eating contaminated food, or touching soil that contains cyanide. This chemical prevents the cells of the body from using oxygen, which then affects the heart and brain. Symptoms of cyanide poisoning include rapid breathing and heart rate, restlessness, dizziness, weakness, headache, nausea, and vomiting. Victims can be confused and may experience low blood pressure, slow heart rate, loss of consciousness, lung injury, respiratory failure, and death.[7]

Choking/Pulmonary Agents

Choking agents affect the respiratory system of victims by attacking the lungs and causing them to fill with fluid, which can result in suffocation. The victim can either have skin contact with the chemical or inhale it. Depending on the amount of the agent to which a victim is exposed, choking agents can be deadly. The most common choking agents are chlorine and phosgene.

Chlorine is a yellow-green gas with a strong, irritating odor. It can be converted to a liquid under pressure or under cold temperatures. A person who comes into contact with chlorine can experience irritation to the nose, throat, and eyes, and in high doses, coughing, dizziness, headaches, changes in the breathing rate, and damage to the lungs.[8]

Phosgene is a colorless gas that smells similar to new-mown hay. It can be inhaled or ingested through skin contact. The effects may be mild and delayed, causing victims to unwittingly inhale more gas over time. Effects include irritation to the skin, eyes, or respiratory tract. Victims may also experience coughing, choking, tightness in the chest, nausea, vomiting, and headache. Phosgene poisoning may cause respiratory and cardiovascular failure.[9]

Irritants

Irritants are chemicals that produce an immune response that causes irritation. In some cases, a victim's skin may never fully recover. The skin may become red, itchy, scaly, chapped, or sensitive to the touch. Respiratory irritants need to be inhaled to be most effective, but skin irritants need only be exposed to the skin. The extent of injury to victims varies depending on the type of chemical and the dose received. The symptoms include pain and swelling of skin or mucous membranes, irritation to the eyes, swelling, pain and temporary blindness, difficulty breathing, runny nose, coughing, and, in some situations, even death.

One type of irritant is pepper spray, which includes the active ingredient capsaicin, a chemical derived from the chili pepper. As the name implies, this chemical is usually sprayed but can also be put into projectiles and fired from a paintball gun. Another common irritant is tear gas, which can affect a victim through inhalation, ingestion, or contact with the skin or eyes. It can cause irritation to the skin, eyes, or respiratory system, or pulmonary edema.[10]

Incapacitating Agents

Incapacitating agents are chemicals that produce temporary physiological or mental effects or an altered state of mind. They make people unable to think clearly or cause an altered state of consciousness or even unconsciousness.[11] Two types of incapacitating agents are BZ and Agent 15.

BZ, or 3-quinuclidinyl benzilate, is an odorless chemical that is dispersed as an aerosol so that the victim may inhale it or it can be absorbed through the skin. It can remain for weeks if dispersed in moist air, and can remain in soil and water and other surfaces for long periods. BZ is highly soluble in water. While the symptoms of exposure to BZ may be immediate in some people, in others, they may not appear for several hours after contact. The effects can include blurry vision, dry mouth, rapid heartbeat, unconsciousness, delusions, hallucinations, short attention span, slurred speech, disorientation, dizziness, and/or confusion.[12]

Biological

Biological weapons (sometimes referred to as "germ weapons") are those that use a biologically derived or living microorganism, bacteria, virus, rickettsia, or fungi (any organism that causes a disease) to deliver toxins and thereby deliberately cause harm to people, animals, or crops through infections that can incapacitate or kill. A biological attack occurs when someone deliberately releases germs or other biological material for the purpose of making people sick or killing them.[13] Even a gram or less of many biological weapons can be highly lethal. Unlike chemical weapons in which a victim's reaction may be immediate, the effects of a biological weapon are not immediate. If a person is exposed to a biological weapon, there will be an incubation period before the effects are felt. During the incubation period, an exposed person may be infecting others, resulting in secondary infections.

There are two types of biological weapons. The first is pathogens, which are disease-causing organisms that often spread long after they are first released. When used, there is a potential for hundreds, if not thousands, of fatalities. However, it is difficult to deliver these agents to large numbers of people. Examples of pathogens include anthrax and smallpox. The second kind of biological weapon is a toxin, which is a poisonous substance produced by living things. Many of these weapons are lethal even in small quantities, and examples include ricin and botulinum.

Biological weapons are easier to use than nuclear material and are more dangerous than chemical weapons because they are relatively easy to produce or obtain. Biological weapons can be delivered in many ways. The most lethal method for delivering biological agents is in an aerosol form, such as a sprayer. They can also be delivered through an explosive device such as self-dispensing cluster bombs, which can destroy

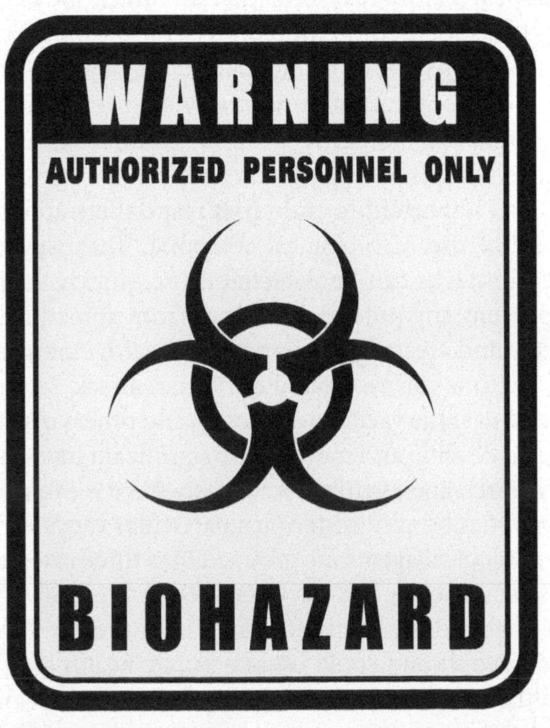

the biological agent when detonated. Food and water can also be contaminated with a biological weapon. Another way that terrorists could use biological weapons is by spreading an infectious disease through humans or animals that is not common in the United States, such as cholera, dengue, dengue hemorrhagic fever, and dengue shock syndrome. The release of biological agents could initially cause disease in one country that could easily be spread to other countries.

Infecting a municipal water supply is difficult because they are designed to filter out or kill impurities and pathogens. Most water utilities employ a combination of filtration and disinfection technologies when treating the water supply. These protections eliminate most risks from contaminated water.

Signs that a biological weapon has been used include an unusually high number of dead or dying animals, a high number of human casualties, an unusual illness for a specific region or area, a pattern of illness that is inconsistent with natural disease progression, the presence of an unusual or suspect liquid, spray, vapor, or powder, spraying devices, and unusual packages or letters.

The use of biological weapons can be difficult to recognize quickly because their consequences can take hours, days, or even weeks to emerge. With some biological agents, the incubation period may be weeks. In such a case, most people would have no idea that they had been exposed until much later because they would not exhibit symptoms. In the meantime, they could be infecting others with whom they come into contact. This means that terrorists could deploy the biological agent over a large geographic area and then disappear before it is clear that an attack took place. In attacks focused on food crops, significant destruction of crops could result that could be devastating to an entire industry, community, or region. Terrorists could use biological weapons to infect cattle and poultry, thus harming the food supply.

It is important to train first responders about the potential use of biological weapons. That way, biological attacks can be detected more quickly, helping to prevent any potential diseases from spreading too widely and creating a major public health emergency.

Victims can be treated during an attack with vaccines, but some vaccines are costly, and others may take time to develop and may require significant investment in research and testing. Sometimes, there is even a risk of fatalities by administering a particular vaccine.

Biological agents are grouped into three categories, designated A, B, and C: **Category A** are agents that can easily be disseminated over a large area and infect many people and could cause a public health catastrophe. These agents have the greatest potential for quick dissemination, and they have the highest mortality rates. Examples of diseases caused by such agents are anthrax, smallpox, plague, botulism, tularemia, and viral hemorrhagic fevers. **Category B** are also easily disseminated over a large area but have a lower mortality rate. Examples include salmonella, ricin, Q fever, typhus, and glanders. Finally, those in **Category C** are more common pathogens that could potentially be used as terrorist weapons and include hantavirus and tuberculosis. These agents are not considered to be as significant a threat as those in the other categories, but they still have the potential to cause death to the victims.

Category A Agents

One Category A agent is anthrax, which most commonly occurs in hoofed mammals but can also infect humans. This is a serious disease that can easily be used by terrorists in a biological weapon. The United States experienced several anthrax attacks in the days after 9-11, forcing many Americans to learn about the disease and its effects for the first time. A description of these attacks, sometimes referred to as "Amerithrax," is described in **BOX 9.1**.

There are several types of anthrax, depending on how the agent is introduced into the body: Skin anthrax (cutaneous) is ingested through contact with the skin; lung anthrax is ingested through inhalation;

BOX 9.1 Anthrax Attacks: Amerithrax

After 9-11, letters containing anthrax were mailed to various offices across the United States, killing five people and infecting 22 others. Letters containing anthrax spores were mailed to the offices of several news media and the offices of two Democratic U.S. Senators, Tom Daschle and Patrick Leahy. In Boca Raton, Florida, letters with anthrax were mailed to the American Media, Inc. building, which housed the offices of the *National Enquirer*, the *Sun* and other tabloid magazines. One photo editor, 63-year-old Robert Stevens, died after inhaling anthrax spores, the first to die in the attacks. A letter mailed from New Jersey was sent to news anchor Tom Brokaw at Rockefeller Studios in New York City. Days later, an employee at the *The New York Post* was diagnosed with anthrax poisoning, as was a son of an employee at *ABC News*. It is assumed that letters were sent to other media offices but may have been thrown away. Prosecutors later announced that Bruce Edwards Ivins sent the letters. Ivins was a scientist who worked at the federal government's biodefense labs. In 2008, Ivins committed suicide. Prosecutors announced that he was guilty, and on February 19, 2010, the FBI closed the investigation.

and digestive or gastrointestinal anthrax is ingested through swallowing. Cutaneous anthrax and inhalation anthrax may occur after people have handled products from infected animals or by breathing in anthrax spores from infected animal products, such as wool.[14] Gastrointestinal anthrax occurs when people eat undercooked meat from infected animals. Person-to-person spread of anthrax is rare.

The most obvious symptom of cutaneous anthrax is a small sore that develops into a blister, which then turns into a skin ulcer with a black area in the center. The symptoms of gastrointestinal anthrax include nausea, loss of appetite, bloody diarrhea, fever, and severe stomach pain, which may manifest after consumption of contaminated food.[15] Symptoms of inhalation anthrax include cold or flu symptoms such as sore throat, mild fever, and muscle aches, as well as cough, chest discomfort, shortness of breath, tiredness, and muscle aches. The symptoms of each type of anthrax typically appear within 7 days of contact.[16]

In most cases, early treatment with antibiotics can cure cutaneous anthrax. Even if untreated, 80% of people who become infected with cutaneous anthrax do not die. However, gastrointestinal anthrax is more serious; about 25 to 60% of cases results in death. Inhalation anthrax is much more severe. In 2001, about half of all cases of inhalation anthrax ended in death.[17]

Another Category A biological agent is smallpox, a serious, contagious, and sometimes fatal disease that has, at this time, no specific treatment. About 7 to 17 days after a person is infected with smallpox, he or she may suffer from fever, malaise, head and body aches, and vomiting. A rash may appear on the tongue and inside the mouth that develops into sores that break open. Later, a rash appears on the face and body that looks like small raised bumps. In recent years, the disease has become largely eradicated due to a successful worldwide vaccination program.[18]

The pneumonic plague is one more example of a Category A biological agent. This is an infectious disease caused by bacteria typically found in rodents and their fleas in many parts of the world. Infection in humans occurs when the bacteria enters the lungs. The first symptoms of infection are fever, headache, weakness, and cough. The pneumonia typically progresses between 2 and 4 days and may cause septic shock and death. Early treatment is essential.[19]

Category B Agents

Category B agents are less fatal than those categorized in the A group. One Category B biological agent is ricin. This agent is found in the form of a powder mist, or pellet, and can be dissolved in water or in a weak acid. Those coming into contact with ricin may inhale the mist or powder and be poisoned or can swallow the agent through contaminated water or food. The symptoms displayed by a victim will depend on the delivery system. If inhaled, the symptoms include coughing, tightness in the chest, difficulty breathing, nausea, and aching muscles as the victim's airways become inflamed. If ingested, the victim will suffer from internal bleeding in the stomach and intestines as well as possible vomiting and bloody diarrhea. If injected, the liver and kidneys may stop working, and the person could die from multiple organ failure.[20]

Category C Agent

One Category C Agent is hantavirus, which, if it progresses far enough, can be fatal. It is usually found in rural areas where rodents live in forests, fields, and farms. Early symptoms of hantavirus include fatigue, fever, and muscle aches. There may also be headaches, dizziness, chills, nausea, vomiting, and diarrhea. Later symptoms include coughing, shortness of breath, and fluid in the lungs.[21]

Radiological/Nuclear

Nuclear weapons are the most devastating of the various CBRNEs and, therefore, raise the most concern. Even a small nuclear weapon detonated in a major city could result in significant destruction and a high number of deaths, as well as long-term environmental damage. There are three mechanisms by which terrorists can carry out a radiological attack: Detonation of a nuclear bomb, dispersal of radiological material, or an attack on a facility housing nuclear material (power plant, research laboratory, storage site).

During a nuclear explosion, there is intense light and damaging heat. Radioactive material can contaminate the air, water, and ground for many miles. The damage will depend on the size of the weapon, which can range in size from one carried by a missile to a small portable device.

If a nuclear weapon were used by terrorists, it would cause death and damage to property in two ways. First, when the bomb detonates, there is a violent blast in which a large amount of energy is released. The initial shock wave will destroy all structures within a range of up to several miles and send debris through the air. This is followed by a heat wave close to the point of detonation. There will be high winds that accompany the shock and heat waves. An exploded nuclear device could result in a considerable amount of property damage and many people killed or injured from the blast itself.

Courtesy of National Nuclear Security Administration/Nevada Site Office.

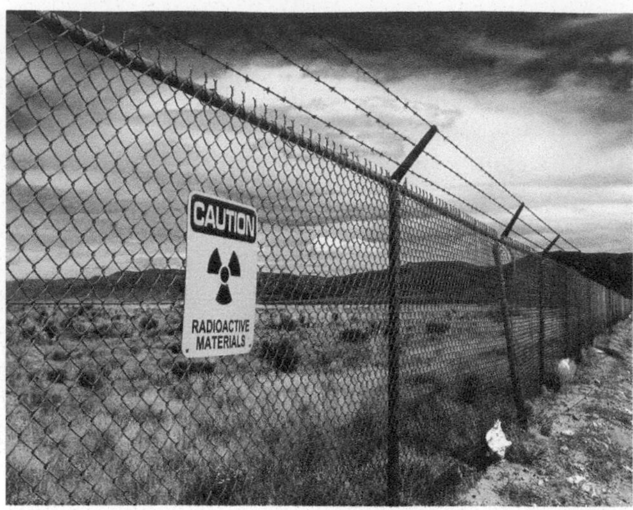

© vasakkohaline/Shutterstock.

The second means by which nuclear weapons inflict harm is through contamination or exposure to harmful radiation, which is most dangerous close to the area of detonation and can cause rapid death. However, radiation can also exist for years after the explosion.

Radiation is a form of energy that exists everywhere, and people are exposed to it every day. We are exposed through microwave ovens and x-rays. Some types of radiation have more energy than others. The radiation from these sources is so small that any adverse health effects may not be apparent for many years. Effects can be as simple as reddening of the skin or as serious as cancer and even death. However, large amounts of radiation could cause extensive death and casualties. It can also result in long-term conditions such as cancer.

Terrorists could also use these weapons against Americans by introducing radioactive material into the food or water supply. This would cause great concern and fear but would not cause much contamination or increase the danger of adverse health effects by a significant amount.

Terrorists could use explosives (such as dynamite) to scatter radioactive materials over a large area. This is called a "dirty bomb." **Dirty bombs** involve the use of a conventional explosive material that also contains radioactive material. When the explosives are detonated, the radioactive materials are dispersed into the environment. Dirty bombs are sometimes called radiological dispersion devices (RDDs), which can spread radioactive material without use of a nuclear explosion. An attack with a dirty bomb would most likely kill, injure, or sicken a great number of people. However, it is not likely that a terrorist dirty bomb would contain enough radioactive material to cause serious radiation sickness among large numbers of people.

Another way in which terrorists could spread nuclear material is by bombing or destroying a nuclear facility. An aircraft could be crashed into a nuclear power plant or a large amount of explosives could be set to detonate around the facility. There are many facilities around the country that store nuclear materials including nuclear power plants, hazardous material storage sites, medical facilities, military facilities, and industrial facilities. If these facilities were damaged, radiological materials could be released into the atmosphere. This type of attack would have essentially the same effects as a dirty bomb except the effects would, in all likelihood, be much greater. An explosion at a nuclear plant could cause the reactor core to melt down or send spent fuel waste to be released into the environment, which could then spread across a large geographic area. People at the facility would probably be contaminated with radioactive material and possibly injured as well, as would residents in the surrounding area. An attack on a nuclear power plant could result in a major release of radiation and kill tens of thousands of citizens.

Radiological weapons are also the most difficult for terrorist groups to develop. Getting highly enriched uranium or constructing the explosive lens used to construct the core of a plutonium implosion device is difficult and expensive to master. Acquiring highly enriched uranium or plutonium would require considerable technical, industrial, and financial resources.

Because of that, radiological weapons are considered the lowest threat compared with other types of weapons. However, terrorists could acquire a nuclear weapon by stealing or purchasing an existing one. Or they could gather the materials needed and construct a weapon. Some of the technologies required for production are well-known and not even state-of-the-art. Terrorists can obtain low-level radioactive materials from hospitals, construction sites, and food irradiation plants. That means that some terrorists groups could explode a small nuclear device, causing great harm. If a terrorist succeeded at making a nuclear weapon, it would more than likely be a very crude weapon; it would be large, weighing a ton or more, and would require a large amount of highly enriched uranium or plutonium. Smuggling that amount of material would be difficult.

In order to reduce the chance that nuclear material will be collected by terrorists, the Domestic Nuclear Detection Office within the Department of Homeland Security attempts to monitor the movement and smuggling of nuclear material within the United States and around the world. Many officials are concerned that the former Soviet Union could be a source of nuclear materials because many of their nuclear sites have low levels of security. After the Soviet Union collapsed, it was difficult to account for all of the nuclear weapons in that country, leading to the fear that some of these weapons could end up in the hands of terrorists. In addition, a substantial amount of radiological materials remain unaccounted for in the United States and around the world. A short description of the threat of nuclear weapons in North Korea is found in **BOX 9.2**.

Explosives

Bombs kill by the effect of the blast, by flying debris, and fires and other damage resulting from the explosion. Virtually any size terrorist group could undertake

BOX 9.2 Nuclear Weapons in North Korea

North Korea began to develop nuclear and chemical weapons programs as far back as 1954, as the Korean War was coming to an end. Officials in North Korea were fearful of an attack by Americans and sought to have a weapon that would deter such an attack. Through the late 1960s and early 1970s, the Soviets and the Chinese provided aid to North Korea so they could develop nuclear weapons. Most international officials would agree that throughout the 1980s, the North Korean nuclear weapons program grew to the point where they built a nuclear facility in Yongbyon. Today, it is alleged that North Korea has developed both biological and nuclear weapons that can be used against just about everyone. Some officials have described North Korea as one of the world's largest possessors of chemical weapons.

To maintain relationships with the North Koreans and reduce the number of nuclear and chemical weapons in that country, most governments use diplomatic measures (talks) with the North Koreans. Many summits and meetings have taken place between leaders from many countries as a way to create valid agreements to place limits on how many weapons countries can own. Some countries (and the United Nations) have resorted to economic sanctions against the North Koreans as a way to punish that country for its continued expansion of nuclear and chemical weapons. Treaties and agreements have been negotiated, including the Non-Proliferation Treaty that places a limit on the number of weapons a country may store. Countries have also agreed to allow inspectors from the International Atomic Energy Agency (IAEA) to inspect their nuclear sites to determine the extent of cooperation with agreements.

Despite all of this, the relationship between North Korea and other countries is tense. It is alleged that North Korea has missiles with nuclear warheads that can span a large portion of the globe. The threat of a nuclear attack can be daunting to many. Depending on the location of the attack and type of weapon used, a nuclear weapon has the potential to kill thousands of people. Below is a brief timeline of events detailing the evolution of North Korea's nuclear program.

1974: North Korea builds the Yongbyon Nuclear Scientific Research Center, which is later upgraded in 1979.

1985: North Korea ratifies the Non-Proliferation Treaty that will bar that country from producing nuclear weapons.

March 6, 1992: The United States imposes sanctions against various companies in North Korea for activities related to missile proliferation.

May 1992: The IAEA inspects North Korean nuclear facilities, finding evidence that North Korea has more plutonium than what was reported. When IAEA officials ask to have access to other sites; their request was denied.

Feb 9, 1993: The IAEA requests that they be allowed to inspect two sites that they suspect are storing nuclear waste. North Korea will not permit them to enter.

March 12, 1993: North Korea announces their intention to withdraw from the NPT. They also refuse to let inspectors from the IAEA to enter their nuclear sites.

July 1993: After talks between North Korea and the United States, North Korea agrees to begin consultations with the IAEA regarding future inspections of its nuclear facilities.

June 13, 1994: North Korea announces that it will withdraw from the IAEA.

August, 1994: North Korea agrees to an "Agreed Framework" with the United States under which they would put a halt to developing nuclear weapons. In return, the United States agrees to remove sanctions and provide assistance to that country.

April 1996: The United States and North Korean officials meet in Berlin for more talks.

May 1996: The United States imposes sanctions on North Korea that will ban imports or exports to firms that are considered to be "missile related."

(continues)

BOX 9.2 Nuclear Weapons in North Korea *(Continued)*

June 1997: Another round of talks between the United States and North Korea are held in New York. There are no agreements made.

April 1998: The United States imposes sanctions on North Korea after missile technology is transferred to Pakistan.

August 1998: North Korea launches a three-stage rocket, announcing that they placed a small satellite in orbit. The United States Space Command is skeptical of the announcement.

October 1, 1998: Officials from the United States and Korea meet to discuss nuclear weapons in North Korea.

March 1999: Talks continue between the United States and North Korea.

September 1999: North Korea agrees to stop testing any long-range missiles.

July 2000: A round of talks between the United States and North Korea end without any agreements.

2002: Pakistan acknowledges that North Korea has access to their nuclear technology since the 1990s.

2002: North Korea pulls out of the Agreed Framework, arguing that the United States does not uphold their end of the agreement. The United States has evidence that North Korea re-established their uranium enrichment program. North Korea claim that they had a "right" to have enrichment programs.

October 2002: The United States, Japan, and South Korea stop making shipments of oil to North Korea after Korean officials admit that they secretly developed a nuclear program.

December 2002: North Korea announces that it is reactivating its nuclear facilities in Yongbyon and force inspectors out.

January, 2003: North Korean officials announce that they are withdrawing from the Nuclear Non-Proliferation Treaty.

August 2003: A new diplomatic mission, called the Six-Party Talks, begins. This is an attempt to limit North Korea's nuclear weapons. The negotiations involve China, Japan, North Korea, South Korea, Russia and the United States. The discussions continue for years, and in 2007, North Korea pledges to abandon its nuclear programs.

2006: North Korea faces sanctions after conducting nuclear testing.

2006: North Korea refuses to admit that it is in possession of chemical weapons.

July 2006: North Korea fires seven missiles, claiming that one has the capability of reaching the United States.

October 9, 2006: North Koreans conduct an underground nuclear test. The U.N. Security Council condemns the test and imposes economic sanctions on North Korea.

March 17, 2007: As a result of the Six-Party meetings between North Korea, South Korea, Japan, Russia, China, and the United States, North Korea announces that it has agreed to close the main nuclear facility.

July 14, 2007: Inspectors from IAEA inspect the facility at Yongbyon and confirmed that it is shut down.

October 8, 2008: Inspectors from the IAEA are denied entrance into nuclear sites in North Korea.

April, 2009: North Korea launches a satellite; the Six-Party Talks end; and the North Koreans announce that they reactivated their nuclear facilities.

May 25, 2009: North Korea conduct a second underground nuclear test. On the same day, Korea launches a short range missile.

May 2010: North Korea announces that it performed nuclear fusion.

February 2012: North Korea agrees to stop any uranium enrichment at the Yongbyon Center, to halt any further nuclear weapons testing, and to permit inspectors from the IAEA to monitor Yongbyon. In return, the United States agrees to send humanitarian aid to North Korea.

April 2012: North Korea conducts a long-range missile test but it fails. In response, the United States halts food aid.

February 11, 2013: North Korea is accused of carrying out a third nuclear test after the U.S. Geological Survey discovers an "artificial quake."

March 2014: North Korea test-fires two medium-range missiles.

September 2015: North Korea confirms that Yongbyon nuclear plant is back in operation.

January 6, 2016, the U.S. Geological Survey detects an earthquake that is allegedly the product of an underground nuclear test. North Korea reports that this is actually a test of a hydrogen bomb, but officials in other countries (including the United States) question if it really was a hydrogen bomb.

March 2, 2016: The UN and other countries implement sanctions against North Korea for its nuclear testing.

September 9, 2016: North Korea carries out a fifth nuclear test. North Korean officials indicate that this test proves that they can mount a nuclear warhead to a missile.

2017: North Korea test-launches two ICBMs, one of which has the range to reach the United States.

February 18, 2017: As part of the UN sanctions on North Korea, China suspends all imports of coal from North Korea.

March 6, 2017: Four ballistic missiles are launched from North Korea. The UN and South Korea condemn the launch.

April 15, 2017: North Korea holds a massive military parade in which two intercontinental ballistic missile-sized canisters are displayed, along with submarine-launched ballistic missiles and a land-based ballistic missile.

April 16, 2017: North Korea attempts a launch of a ballistic missile but it explodes within a few seconds of the launch.

April 2017: U.S. State Department announces that North Korea will be punished with economic sanctions from China if they carry out additional tests.

July 4, 2017: North Korea launches a missile that, according to the US Pacific Command, could have reached Alaska.

July 28, 2017: North Korea launches a second ICBM that could reach the continental United States.

August 8, 2017: The Washington Post reports that the U.S. Defense Intelligence Agency notes that North Korea produced a miniaturized nuclear warhead that can be placed in a missile. They also estimate that North Korea has around 60 nuclear warheads.

September 3, 2017: North Korea announces that it has successfully tested another hydrogen bomb. The U.S. Geological Society confirms seismic activity similar to an earthquake at that time.

November 28, 2017: North Korea launches an intercontinental ballistic missile. Officials from that country announce that the missile is capable of carrying a nuclear warhead and hitting the mainland United States.

June 2018: Kim Jong Un and President Trump hold a summit in Singapore. Kim agrees to shut down a long-range rocket launch site.

January 2019: North Korean Leader Kim Jong Un meet with Chinese President Xi Jinping to discuss denuclearization.

February 2019: U.S. President Trump and North Korean leader Kim Jong Un meet in Vietnam to discuss nuclear disarmament. The talks end with no signed agreement.

March 2019: Satellite images show that North Korea is rebuilding a missile site located close to the border with China.

July 1, 2019: President Donald Trump became the first sitting president to walk into North Korea and meet with officials.

a large-bomb attack. The supplies to make bombs are readily available or can be easily bought illicitly or stolen. Specific instructions for making various **explosive weapons** are readily available on the Internet.

In the case of a bomb explosion, first responders must be able to treat multiple injuries. More than likely, there will also be considerable structural damage to buildings and facilities. First responders must also be alert to subsequent explosives that may be set to go off a short period after the first series of explosions; not an uncommon practice. In some cases, while it may initially appear that an explosion caused little harm, there may be biological or radioactive agents involved, which are unseen and unfelt by victims and first responders alike.

In 1995, the United States experienced a bomb explosion as the result of an act of domestic terrorism when Timothy McVeigh succeeded in blowing up much of the Alfred P. Murrah Building in Oklahoma City, Oklahoma. This is described in **BOX 9.3**.

BOX 9.3 The Oklahoma City Bombing

The bombing of the Alfred P. Murrah Building in Oklahoma City was a terrorist bomb attack that occurred on April 19, 1995. It was the most serious terrorist act on U.S. soil until the terrorist attacks of September 11, 2001. One hundred and sixty-eight people were killed that day, including 19 children, and over 680 people were injured. Hundreds of buildings in the surrounding area were damaged.

The person who was responsible for the bombing was Timothy McVeigh. He was assisted by Michael Fortier and Terry Nichols, both of whom helped McVeigh prepare the bomb. McVeigh was a member of the American militia movement and hated the federal government for its mishandling of the attack on the Waco complex of the Branch Davidians and the events at Ruby Ridge between militia member Randy Weaver and the federal government.

McVeigh drove an explosive-filled rental truck to a drop-off zone near a daycare center located in the building, covered up the car's Vehicle Identification Number (VIN), and returned to his home state of Kansas. As he was driving to Kansas, about 90 minutes after the explosion, McVeigh was stopped and arrested for driving without a license plate and having a concealed weapon.

McVeigh was tried in 1997 in federal court and found guilty of 11 counts of murder and conspiracy. He was executed by lethal injection on June 11, 2001. Nichols was found guilty of conspiring to build a weapon of mass destruction and of eight counts of involuntary manslaughter of federal officers. He was also found guilty on 161 counts of first-degree murder and sentenced to 161 consecutive life terms without the possibility of parole.

Fortier agreed to provide evidence to help convict McVeigh. In exchange, he received a reduced sentence. The judge sentenced him to 12 years in prison and a fine of $75,000. He served 10 and a half years before being released from prison. He currently lives in the Witness Protection Program.

© Roland IJdema/Shutterstock.

Natural Threats

Threats to homeland security not only come from man-made sources but also from natural events that come from the weather. Many natural disasters may strike at any moment, such as earthquakes. Other natural disasters may occur with some warning, or at least we will know that the conditions are there for these to occur, such as hurricanes, floods, landslides, volcanic eruptions, tornadoes, thunderstorms, and wildfires. Other events may occur over long periods of time with worsening effects, such as droughts, heatwaves, or prolonged bouts of extreme cold, as well as winter storms that continue to accumulate snow and ice. We know how to track hurricanes and how to build structures to minimize earthquake damage, but it is virtually impossible to prevent these events from occurring. However, the loss of life from these events can often be minimized through efforts such as better preparation, earlier warnings, and mandatory evacuations. The steps for emergency preparedness for natural disasters are often the same as preparing for other threats; steps such as having a family plan, especially a communication plan, as well as an emergency kit, all help people prepare for any hazardous event. It is equally true that the response to these disasters are also similar to other events such as terrorist attacks, but like each terrorist attack, each natural disaster brings its own complexities and the types of resources needed may very well be different. A drought may not cause the physical destruction of buildings like an earthquake or a hurricane may, but it can bring serious threats to human and animal life and can have compounding effects. Therefore, while nature may bring on these particular events, not man, the potential destruction that can occur should not be overlooked. A description of some natural disasters is presented in **TABLE 9.1**.

Courtesy of NESDIS/NOAA.

TABLE 9.1 Examples of Natural Threats

Threat	Definition	Area of Country	Potential Effects	Safety Precautions
Drought	A prolonged period with little or no rain	The entire country can experience periods of drought	A period without rain can harm crops and economic losses; can leave forests susceptible to fires	Practice water conservation before and during a period of drought
Earthquake	A sudden motion or shaking of the ground that results in shaking	Entire country; most often occur in states located west of the Rocky Mountains; also in the central states; California has experienced multiple earthquakes	Can cause objects to fall and structures to collapse; power, gas and water lines may be broken	Stay out of doorways; drop to the ground and cover your head; stay away from buildings and trees; do not enter an elevator; be careful of aftershocks

Floods	Overflow of bodies of water after a heavy rain or snow melting	Entire country	Rising water can cause damage to property, buildings, and farmlands, but can also cause significant deaths and injuries. They can also cause power failures	Find high land if a flood warning has been issued; do not drive through flooded streets; evacuate if told to do so
Hurricanes	Large cyclonic storm that is accompanied by high winds and large rainfall	Mostly coastal states from Texas to Maine, or Hawaii; Typically occur in summer and fall months; form over the water and move inland	Hurricanes typically result in a storm surge, which can lead to flooding and damage to property and structures; Power failures are common. Can lead to multiple casualties	Evacuate if told to do so; take shelter in an interior room; look out for flash flooding
Landslides	Falling or sliding of soil, rock, trees, and other materials	All areas of country	Loss of property and life	Move away from a landslide as quickly as possible; listen for unusual sounds such as trees breaking
Extreme Heat	2–3 days of high heat with humidity	All areas of country	Can lead to heat exhaustion and loss of life	Find an air conditioned building; avoid strenuous work during peak heat times; stay hydrated
Snowstorms	Large amounts of snow falling over a short period (several hours or a few days)	Northern states	Can lead to car accidents, a loss of power or communications	Stay indoors and be prepared for a power outage; watch for signs of hypothermia
Thunderstorm	A heavy rainstorm accompanied by lightening or hail	All areas of the country	Can cause flooding and power outages; if lightning strikes, can cause fires and result in death	Go indoors if possible; Avoid running water and use of land lines
Tornadoes	Intense cyclonic winds of 200 miles an hour	All areas of the country; prevalent in western states including Texas and Kansas	Can destroy buildings, crops, causing economic harm	Find safety indoors in a basement or storm cellar or a room with no windows; watch for flying debris
Volcanoes	An opening in the Earth's crust that emits lava and molten rock	Alaska, Hawaii, California, and Oregon	Lava can contaminate the water, spread ash through the air, and make it difficult to breath; can ruin homes and property	Evacuate if told to do so
Wildfires	Unplanned fire that burns uncontrolled	All areas of the country	Can burn homes and businesses; cause injury and deaths	Evacuate if told to do so; wear a mask to protect from inhaling ash

Source: FEMA, "Natural Threats" all-hazards.com/LGP/library/fema191_2.pdf; Department of Homeland Security, "Ready: "Plan Ahead for Disasters." https://www.ready.gov/

Chapter Summary

Threats to American homeland security come from man-made sources, such as chemical, biological, radiological, and nuclear weapons, as well as natural events. Terrorists will use the weapons that best meet their budget, expertise, target, and the resources they have available. However, the odds of a terrorist attack with a CBRNE is fairly unlikely (see **BOX 9.4**). An attack with a nuclear or radiological weapon has the potential to be the most dangerous, but they are difficult to obtain and/or manufacture. Biological and chemical weapons can be produced more easily but delivering them in such a way as to cause significant casualties is difficult. Few groups have access to these weapons or the logistical support necessary to carry out a successful attack. Nonetheless, many people are fearful that a terrorist group will use CBRNEs against U.S. citizens. It is widely understood that most terrorists have a desire to use CBRNEs against Americans.

BOX 9.4 A National Strategy for CBRNE Standards

A committee formed from the Office of the President, the Department of Homeland Security, and the Department of Commerce came together in 2011 to develop a national strategy specifically oriented toward CBRNE standards. The committee noted the following:

Emergency response teams across the nation require reliable and interoperable chemical, biological, radiological, nuclear, and explosive (CBRNE) equipment that can be used with confidence for the protection of life, health, property, and commerce. The United States government will, together with commercial and end-user communities, facilitate the development and implementation of national consensus CBRNE standards and establish an enduring capability to coordinate, prioritize, and implement those standards.

It is the vision of the National Science and Technology Council (NSTC) to establish and coordinate implementation of an integrated standards development approach that spans the full spectrum of standards, including performance, interoperability, testing and evaluation, conformity assessment, operating procedures, training, and certification. This will ensure that equipment is reliable and interoperable, and provides consistent and accurate results.

This strategy describes the elements of a standards and testing infrastructure needed to counter CBRNE threats. The subcommittee has consulted across the federal government to identify research efforts and current practices with respect to performance specifications and test methods, as well as standard development needs. The subcommittee recognizes that the CBRNE mission may only be one component of what users do each and every day. Therefore, the goals not only reflect the technical performance of the technology but also the interoperability with their suite of equipment, as well as concepts of operations involved in their deployment and the training of the users.

The following goals outline how to help achieve the vision:

GOAL 1: Establish an interagency group for CBRNE standards to promote the coordination of these standards among federal, state, local, and tribal communities.

GOAL 2: Coordinate and facilitate the development of CBRNE equipment performance standards and promote the use of standards for federal, state, local, and tribal communities.

GOAL 3: Coordinate and facilitate the development and adoption of interoperability standards for CBRNE equipment.

GOAL 4: Promote enduring CBRNE standard operating procedures for federal, state, local, and tribal use to improve national preparedness and response.

GOAL 5: Establish voluntary CBRNE training and certification standards for the federal, state, local, and tribal communities and promote policies that foster their adoption.

GOAL 6: Establish a comprehensive CBRNE equipment testing and evaluation (T&E) infrastructure and capability to support conformity assessment standards.

Reproduced from: Subcommittee on Standards. (2011). A National Strategy for CBRNE Standards. Retrieved online at https://www.hsdl.org/?abstract&did=685501

Review/Discussion Questions

1. What are CBRNEs?
2. What are the effects of chemical, biological, radiological/nuclear, and explosive weapons?
3. What are the dispersal methods for CBRNEs?
4. How likely is it that terrorists could use these weapons against the United States?

Additional Readings

Breen, C. (2012). *CBRNe, Terrorism, Medical and Major Incident Management.* New York, NY: CreateSpace.

Subcommittee on Standards. (2011). *A National Strategy for CBRNE Standards.* Retrieved online at https://www.hsdl.org/?view&did=685501

Endnotes

1. Centers for Disease Control and Prevention. (2012). *Toxic Substances Portal: Nerve Agents.* Retrieved online at http://www.atsdr.cdc.gov/toxfaqs/tf.asp?id=524&tid=93
2. Centers for Disease Control and Prevention. (2012). *Facts about VX.* Retrieved online at https://emergency.cdc.gov/agent/vx/basics/facts.asp
3. Centers for Disease Control and Prevention. (2012). *Toxic Substances Portal: Blister Agents HN-1, HN-2, HN-3, Nitrogen Mustard.* Retrieved online at http://www.atsdr.cdc.gov/substances/toxsubstance.asp?toxid=189
4. Centers for Disease Control and Prevention. (2012). *Toxic Substances Portal: Blister Agents HN-1, HN-2, HN-3, Nitrogen Mustard.* Retrieved online at http://www.atsdr.cdc.gov/substances/toxsubstance.asp?toxid=189; Centers for Disease Control and Prevention. (2012). *ToxFAQs for Blister Agents: HN-1, HN-2, HN-3 (Nitrogen Mustards).* Retrieved online at http://www.atsdr.cdc.gov/toxfaqs/tf.asp?id=921&tid=189
5. Centers for Disease Control and Prevention. (2012). *Blister Agents: Lewisite (L), Mustard-Lewisite Mixture (HL).* Retrieved online at http://www.atsdr.cdc.gov/substances/toxsubstance.asp?toxid=190
6. Centers for Disease Control and Prevention. (2012). *Toxic Substances Portal—Blister Agents Lewisite (L), Mustard-Lewisite Mixture (HL).* Retrieved online at http://www.atsdr.cdc.gov/toxfaqs/tf.asp?id=923&tid=190
7. Centers for Disease Control and Prevention. (2012). *Cyanide.* Retrieved online at http://www.atsdr.cdc.gov/substances/toxsubstance.asp?toxid=19
8. Centers for Disease Control and Prevention. (2012). *Toxic Substances Portal: Chlorine.* Retrieved online at http://www.atsdr.cdc.gov/substances/toxsubstance.asp?toxid=36; Centers for Disease Control and Prevention. (2012). *ToxFAQs for Chlorine.* Retrieved online at http://www.atsdr.cdc.gov/toxfaqs/tf.asp?id=200&tid=36
9. Centers for Disease Control and Prevention. (2012). *Toxic Substances Portal: Phosgene.* Retrieved online at http://www.atsdr.cdc.gov/MMG/MMG.asp?id=1201&tid=182
10. Centers for Disease Control and Prevention. (2012). *NIOSH Pocket Guide to Chemical Hazards.* Retrieved online at http://www.cdc.gov/niosh/npg/npgd0119.html
11. Centers for Disease Control and Prevention. (2012). *Incapacitating Agents.* Retrieved online at http://emergency.cdc.gov/agent/incapacitating/
12. Centers for Disease Control and Prevention. (2012). *Case Definition: 3-Quinuclidinyl Benzilate (BZ).* Retrieved online at http://www.bt.cdc.gov/agent/bz/casedef.aspFederal Emergency Management Agency.
13. *Biological Threats.* Retrieved online at https://www.ready.gov/Bioterrorism
14. Centers for Disease Control and Prevention. (2010). *Gastrointestinal Anthrax after an Animal-Hide Drumming Event.* Retrieved online at http://emergency.cdc.gov/agent/anthrax/faq/pelt.asp
15. Centers for Disease Control and Prevention. (2012). *Q&A: Gastrointestinal (GI) Anthrax.* Retrieved online at http://emergency.cdc.gov/agent/anthrax/gi/
16. Centers for Disease Control and Prevention. (2015). *Anthrax: Basic Information.* Retrieved online at https://www.cdc.gov/anthrax/basics/index.html
17. Centers for Disease Control and Prevention. (2015). *Questions and Answers about Anthrax.* Retrieved online at https://www.cdc.gov/anthrax/basics/index.html
18. Centers for Disease Control and Prevention. (2012). *Smallpox Basics.* Retrieved online at http://emergency.cdc.gov/agent/smallpox/disease/
19. Centers for Disease Control and Prevention. (2018). *Plague: Symptoms.* Retrieved online at https://www.cdc.gov/plague/symptoms/index.html
20. Centers for Disease Control and Prevention. (2012). *Facts about Ricin.* Retrieved online at http://emergency.cdc.gov/agent/ricin/facts.asp
21. Centers for Disease Control and Prevention. (2012). *Hantavirus.* Retrieved online at http://www.cdc.gov/hantavirus/

Courtesy of Aubrey Gemignani/NASA.

CHAPTER 10

The Homeland Security Cycle

CHAPTER OBJECTIVES

- To understand the elements of the homeland security cycle and why they are important to homeland security
- To understand the role of federal, state, local, and tribal governments in the homeland security cycle

CHAPTER OUTLINE

In May 2012, FBI agents foiled a plan by five suspected terrorists (and self-proclaimed anarchists) to destroy a bridge near Cleveland, Ohio. The plan was thwarted after an FBI informant infiltrated the group and recorded conversations in which the plot was discussed in the months before the attempted bombing. The five men were arrested by members of a Joint Terrorism Task Force who claimed that the public was never in any danger because the explosives they tried to use were provided by an undercover FBI agent and were not operable explosives.[1] Four of the men eventually pleaded guilty. Three men received sentences of 8 to 11 years in prison, and the fourth received a sentence of 6 years in prison. The last of the five men received a psychiatric evaluation, which was ruled inconclusive.

The FBI's use of a paid informant to gather intelligence on the anarchists represents the first stage in the homeland security cycle. In this stage, information is collected and analyzed as a way to prevent terrorist attacks, as was done in this case.

Other actions taken by the FBI or local law enforcement and first responders could be taken to prepare for events, should they take place. These would constitute the second stage of the homeland security cycle and could include, for example, carrying out mock drills that allow responders to "practice" their actions. The third stage of the cycle is response, which would take place right after an event. If the five suspects had been able to carry out their plot, first responders would need to react quickly and provide necessary services for any victims. The final stage, had the suspects carried out their plot, would be recovery from the event, which might include rebuilding the bridge or other actions to restore the local community.

The Homeland Security Cycle

The homeland security cycle refers to the four stages necessary to prepare for an event and to respond to it. The first two stages, **mitigation** and **preparedness**, occur before an emergency happens, whereas the final two, **response and recovery**, are the actions taken in the aftermath. Mitigation means to lessen the effects of an emergency or even prevent it from occurring, and preparedness is simply being ready for it. The third stage, response, refers to the activities that take place immediately after the event. The final stage, recovery, occurs after immediate needs are met and any dangers subside.

On the federal level, the **Federal Emergency Management Agency (FEMA)** is largely responsible for helping America with the different stages of the cycle. This is in line with their mission, which is "to lead America to prepare for, prevent, respond to, and recover from disasters." There are also state and local agencies that assist with all four stages of the cycle.

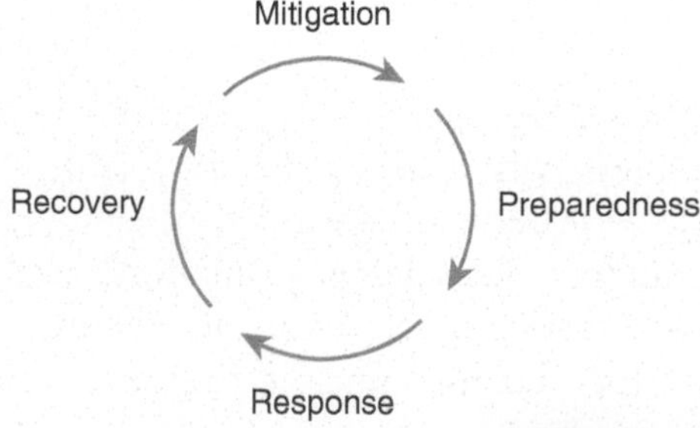

Mitigation

The term mitigation refers to the process through which attempts are made to prevent a possible emergency or to reduce the potential impact of that emergency (be it terrorist attacks, natural disasters, or man-made disasters) before it occurs. In other words, mitigation refers to those steps taken to reduce the risk of an attack or emergency, which may deter or prevent it from happening. These steps can also be thought of as any actions taken with the intent of avoiding an incident or intervening in an effort to limit the effects if an incident should occur. Mitigation also includes a level of risk management. For instance, more attention will be given to protecting the country's critical infrastructure.

The activities considered to be part of the mitigation stage are varied, but they all have the common

Courtesy of Rosanna Arias/FEMA.

goal of reducing the risks associated with potential hazards. They are the policies and actions that can be implemented as a way to reduce risk to people and property from hazardous events. These can include a range of activities such as restrictive building codes, improved surveillance of critical sites, immunizations to prevent diseases, and increased security operations.

Mitigation efforts usually address two components: The probability of an event occurring (likelihood) and the consequences of an event. When it comes to reducing the probability, it is relatively easy to implement policies that minimize the risk of a man-made attack. These can include such activities as gathering "actionable" information about terrorist activity, analyzing that intelligence, overseeing a group's communications, and various surveillance techniques. All of these activities are focused on preventing a threat from being carried out. Much of this is done by the Department of Homeland Security along with certain state and local agencies.

State and local fusion centers also collect intelligence from various agencies and organizations and analyze it in an effort to prevent terrorist actions. These centers collect and "fuse" sensitive information from many sources, including law enforcement, task forces, the National Counterterrorism Center, other fusion centers, and first responders. Today, over 70 state and local intelligence fusion centers exist, with "satellite" offices that focus on intelligence gathering and dissemination in different parts of the state.[2]

The National Strategy for Homeland Security notes that intelligence and information analysis is an integral part of the nation's effort to reduce America's vulnerabilities. They note four categories of intelligence analysis, including: (1) tactical threat analysis (analysis of a group's current and potential activities); (2) strategic analysis of the enemy (knowing the group's identities, financial and political sources of support, motivation, goals, and current and future capabilities); (3) vulnerability assessments (the consequences of a terrorist attack against specific sites or facilities); and (4) threat-vulnerability integration (mapping terrorist threats and the vulnerabilities of their potential targets).

There are numerous agencies that assist with mitigation. Within the Department of Homeland Security, a Mitigation Directorate was created as part of FEMA; its mission is to protect lives and prevent loss of property resulting from natural and man-made events. This group is responsible for implementing any risk-reduction programs for the nation that have been authorized by Congress.

FEMA has developed different courses of action for mitigation policy. One of those is the Reference Manual to Mitigate Potential Terrorist Attacks Against Buildings. This document, written for architects, engineers, and builders, provides guidelines on ways to reduce the effects of potential terrorist attacks by reducing the physical damage to buildings that can occur during an attack. Such changes will also reduce human casualties. Another is the Handbook for Rapid Visual Screening of Buildings to Evaluate Terrorism Risks (2009), and the Design Guide for Improving School Safety in Earthquakes, Floods, and High Winds (2010).

While it is impossible to implement policies that prevent a natural hazard such as a hurricane or earthquake from occurring, it is possible to reduce the impact of a natural disaster with actions taken before the event occurs. Some activities include stricter building codes, evacuation plans, building levees, and other structures. In some cases, it can simply involve educating citizens on measures they can take to reduce injury and death (e.g., first-aid techniques).

As a way to mitigate the effects of hurricanes, FEMA has created the National Hurricane Program, which conducts assessments of, and provides assistance to, state and local agencies with their own hurricane education plans. Through FEMA, experts also conduct analyses of storms to help predict the most likely effects of storm surges and high winds, help to assess shelter availability and capacity for those residents affected by the storm, and calculate evacuation times required, if needed.

Additionally, FEMA has created the National Earthquake Hazards Reduction Program. Along with the U.S. Geological Survey, FEMA conducts and supports ongoing earth science research to better understand the nature, effects, and likelihood of earthquakes.

FEMA also supports the Mitigation Grant programs to provide financial assistance to states. These grant programs include the Hazards Mitigation Grant Program, Pre-Disaster Mitigation Program, Flood Mitigation Assistance Program, Severe Repetitive Loss Grant Program, and Repetitive Flood Claims Grant Program. They also oversee the National Flood Insurance Program (NFIP), which was created by Congress as a way to mitigate future losses due to flooding. This program supports building and zoning ordinances and access to affordable, federally backed flood insurance for property owners. Grants are available for individuals, state/local governments, and federally recognized tribes.

Preparedness

The second stage of the homeland security cycle is preparedness, which has been defined by DHS as "a continuous cycle of planning, organizing, training, equipping, exercising, evaluating, and taking corrective action in an effort to ensure effective coordination during incident response,"[3] In short, it refers to those activities that help officials be prepared in the case of an emergency. It is the "state of readiness" that local, state, and federal officials must develop so they are prepared to respond to a variety of emergencies. These plans include a range of activities, programs, and systems so that officials may respond quickly and effectively at the time of a disaster. Being prepared and responding quickly to a disaster is critical for minimizing deaths, injuries, financial losses, property damage, and interruption of business activities.

FEMA has recognized the importance of preparedness and has outlined the process in its Preparedness Cycle. There are five interrelated steps in the cycle, beginning with a plan that identifies priorities and establishes roles for all stakeholders in the case of an emergency. The second stage, Organize and Equip, refers to the process by which a community ensures that they have the right personnel to respond to an event. It also means that officials have the correct equipment to enable them to react effectively. Training is the third step in the Preparedness Cycle. It is essential that first responders and their partners have the skills to perform the necessary tasks. Many opportunities for training exist including the National Training Program and FEMA Training Organizations.

The fourth step in the Cycle is Exercise. Exercises for first responders can help to prepare them for an event by identifying needed resources or weaknesses that can be addressed prior to the emergency. Through exercises, roles can be clarified and inter-agency coordination developed as needed. The National Exercise Program runs exercises nationwide, as does the National Exercise and Simulation Center.

The last stage of the Cycle is Evaluate/Improve. In this phase, officials evaluate activities during training exercises and actual events to determine how response can be improved. This can lead to additional planning and training, making the process both cyclical and interdependent.[4]

Activities related to preparedness are very closely tied to activities taken in the mitigation stage, and the distinction between them is often not clear. However, preparedness refers to actions taken to plan for the best response to an event, whereas mitigation includes all of the actions taken to minimize the scope of the event before it happens.

Many activities can be considered to be part of the preparedness stage, but they generally include developing plans and procedures to ensure that first responders are properly trained and equipped to provide assistance should an event occur. In many areas, mock exercises or drills are developed and carried out as a way to establish processes and procedures that will be used during an actual emergency. Preparedness also includes establishing (and testing or practicing, when possible) evacuation procedures from buildings, first-response training for employees (such as first aid), public education, and emergency operations centers. These are the kinds of actions that can help people survive disasters by teaching them specific procedures so that they are comfortable should they ever be needed. Whenever possible, this includes testing of all procedures before an event to ensure their effectiveness.

Preparedness also includes developing plans to coordinate all resources in a community that may be needed in an actual emergency. Every relevant agency or organization should be ready to provide a specific level of service, depending on the nature and seriousness of the incident. All organizations should ensure that they are prepared to respond to an incident and know what their specific role will be. It is crucial that all organizations and personnel who could be part of a response team are completely cognizant of their roles and responsibilities. Moreover, a comprehensive system for communication between these organizations must be established.

Some of the nation's actions to prepare for emergencies can be found in the **National Response Framework**. In this document, it is noted that a "unified national effort" is needed to prepare for a response. In the report, it is noted that all levels of government have a responsibility to develop detailed all-hazards contingency plans that clearly articulate procedures that are tailored to each jurisdiction, and should be integrated, operational, and incorporate the private-sector. The report also indicates that well-qualified teams should be assembled and provided with the equipment necessary to respond to a variety of incidents. Finally, these teams must be trained through a series of exercises that not only train individuals but

also contain a mechanism for corrective action. This is particularly important for states, as they will often be the first responders to most emergencies. Every state has established a homeland security or emergency management system, some of which are listed in **BOX 10.1**.

Preparedness also takes place on the community level. In preparation, the communities need to identify possible shelter locations for those affected by an emergency, along with food, clothing, and evacuation routes.[5] Once the potential hazards in a community are identified, officials can proceed to develop a comprehensive preparedness plan. Many communities have developed different warning systems and signals that alert citizens of dangerous weather systems. Many communities broadcast warnings through emergency radio and television broadcasts. In other areas, there are reverse 911 calls, or special sirens, or emergency workers may go door-to-door to warn people. The Emergency Alert System (EAS) is a way to warn the entire nation of a national threat or emergency on very short notice.[6]

As noted in the NRF, even "individuals, families, and households play an important role in emergency preparedness." Individuals are encouraged to reduce hazards that may exist in their own homes such as having unanchored items that may become dangerous if high winds should occur. Homes should also have emergency medical kits that can be used to help injured family members or neighbors until assistance arrives.

In order to oversee the coordinated response approach developed in the **National Response Plan**, the federal government created the **National Incident Management System (NIMS)** as a way to provide a nationwide method for federal, state, and local governments to work effectively and efficiently together to prepare for, respond to, and recover from incidents. According to NIMS, all agencies should have at least a minimal level of preparedness for communications between agencies, resource management, and command structure.

On the national level, FEMA helps states and local governments to develop preparedness plans and to be ready for an event. FEMA oversees the Homeland Security Grant Program, which helps state and local governments to develop their strategic plans.[7] For example, FEMA suggests preparing for a biological threat by ensuring that all citizens are current with required immunizations. They also suggest having extra water, a battery-powered or hand-cranked radio, and extra flashlights and batteries available in the house. A plan for contacting other family members nearby during an emergency is essential.[8]

Similar suggestions are made by FEMA in order to prepare for a chemical threat. However, in the case of a chemical attack, FEMA suggests using plastic to seal doors, windows, and vents as a way to prevent chemicals from entering the home.[9] FEMA's suggestions for preparing for a nuclear attack include having an evacuation plan, especially if you live near a potential target, which, generally speaking, includes strategic missile

BOX 10.1 State-level Agencies Preparing for Attacks

Pennsylvania Emergency Management Agency (PEMA): Helps communities and citizens mitigate against, prepare for, respond to, and recover from natural disasters, acts of terrorism, and other disasters. They provide disaster assistance to families, businesses, and communities to help them recover quickly. They provide grants to help communities develop plans for disaster preparedness and to help counties improve their response capabilities.

Tennessee Office of Safety and Homeland Security: Top priority is to protect the lives and livelihood of the citizens of the state. The state is divided into eleven districts that are able to provide teams to prevent, protect against, and respond to events.

Oklahoma Office of Homeland Security: Has identified their objectives to include preventing a terrorist attack in Oklahoma, reducing Oklahoma's vulnerability to terrorist attacks, and minimizing the damage from and response to a terrorist attack should one occur. The duties of their office are to develop and implement a comprehensive statewide homeland security strategy; to plan and implement a statewide response system; to administer the homeland security advisory system; to coordinate, apply for, and distribute federal homeland security grant funds; and to implement national homeland security plans.

New York Division of Homeland Security and Emergency Services: Divided into the Office of Emergency Management (OEM) and the Office of Counter Terrorism (OCT). OEM protects residents from environmental emergencies and man-made disasters. They help local governments identify hazards, prevent loss, plan for events, and provide training and technical support. OCT helps to prevent, protect against, and prepare for acts of terrorism. They work closely with law enforcement agencies across the state.

Data from: Louisiana Governor's Office of Homeland Security and Emergency Preparedness. (2019). Retrieved online at http://gohsep.la.gov/; Pennsylvania Emergency Management Agency. (2019). Retrieved online at http://www.pema.pa.gov/; Tennessee Office of Homeland Security. (2019). Retrieved online at http://www.tn.gov/; Oklahoma Office of Homeland Security. (2019). Retrieved online at http://www.ok.gov/homeland/About; New York Division of Homeland Security and Emergency Services. (2019). Retrieved online http://www.dhses.ny.gov/

sites, military bases, government centers (Washington, D.C., or a state capital), key transportation or communication centers, manufacturing or industrial centers, petroleum refineries, financial centers, and major ports. In order to protect from radioactive fallout, it would be necessary to take shelter in an underground area or in the middle of a large building.[10] Adequately preparing for a radioactive event, according the FEMA, requires a 2-week emergency kit with water, food, and other supplies. It is helpful to have duct tape, scissors, and plastic for covering vents, windows, and doors to prevent radioactive material from entering the building.[11]

In addition to FEMA, other federal agencies help in the planning process, such as the Centers for Disease Control and Prevention (CDC). As a way of encouraging people to be prepared for an emergency, the CDC has developed a tongue-in-cheek educational program that incites people to be prepared for a zombie apocalypse (see **FIGURE 10.1**). It is a way to reach out to new audiences and encourage them to be prepared for most any emergency. If you are prepared for a zombie attack, you will be prepared for other emergencies. It is a way to teach the importance of emergency preparedness in an entertaining way.

State and local governments also take part in strategic planning. The plans will vary depending on the jurisdiction, but most state and local governments focus on an "all-hazards" approach that includes terrorism as one hazard.[12]

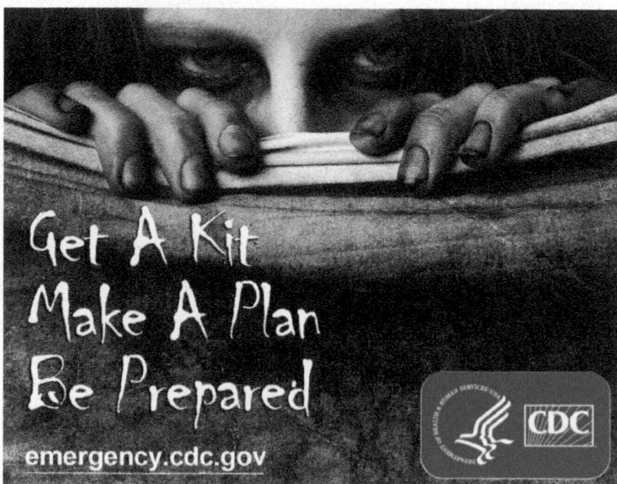

FIGURE 10.1 Preparing for a Zombie Apocalypse: The CDC is encouraging people to prepare for a zombie invasion! In case flesh-eating zombies invade, people need to have water, food, medications, tools and supplies, sanitation and hygiene, clothing and bedding, important documents, and first aid supplies to protect themselves. They will also need a plan that outlines to meet other family members, a list of emergency contacts, and an evacuation route.

U.S. Centers for Disease Control. (2011). Preparedness 101: Zombie Apocalypse. Retrieved online at http://blogs.cdc.gov/publichealthmatters/2011/05/preparedness-101-zombie-apocalypse/

Response

The third stage of the homeland security cycle is **response**, which refers to any measures taken at the onset of an emergency to save lives and protect property. These measures often require coordination between different levels of government.

There are many types of response efforts, and they will vary depending on the type and severity of the emergency. They can include issuing warnings to notify the public to take action, notifying emergency response personnel of the event, providing immediate medical assistance to victims, rescuing victims, providing traffic control, evacuating residents, or providing shelter for those who have been affected. These actions all have the goal of restoring order in the affected area in a quick and safe manner.

Response actions are generally carried out by first responders such as local police, fire, and emergency medical personnel. These officials take immediate action in order to secure the scene, maintain order, assist victims, contain any fires that have started, contain the spread of any biological or nuclear material, identify the type of chemical or biological agent used, or retrieve any bodies. Their role may be complicated because the site may be contaminated with chemical, biological, or radioactive substances. At the same time, first responders often need to collect evidence to aid in the subsequent investigation.

One critical step to responding to an event is to ensure that all response tasks are carried out, while, at the same time, ensuring that there is limited overlap. In these situations, clear Command and Control (C^2) is essential, which allows all agencies to perform their designated roles to reduce the effects of the emergency while avoiding redundant actions and the wasting of resources.[13]

In addition to fire, police, and emergency personnel, volunteer groups often respond to emergencies

Courtesy of Walt Jennings/FEMA.

and assist on the front lines. This could include groups such as the American Red Cross, the National Volunteer Organization Against Disasters, Feeding America, American Radio Relay League, or the Salvation Army. These volunteers have usually been trained to provide specific emergency response services in support of the first responders. They often work alongside local, state, and federal authorities to address the immediate needs of disaster victims by providing food, shelter, and clothing. Many of these volunteer groups are listed in more detail in **BOX 10.2**.

Other volunteer opportunities for responding to emergencies were established by the White House and The Department of Homeland Security in the months after the 9/11 attacks. When announcing these groups in 2002, President Bush called for 2 years of volunteer service from every American citizen. One of the groups is the Citizen Corps, which provided opportunities for any citizens who have a desire to make their communities safer. Presidents since Bush have maintained many of the same elements of the original Citizen Corps program including Citizen Corps Councils, Community Emergency Response Teams (CERTs), Volunteers in Police Service (VIPS), Medical Reserve, Neighborhood Watch, and Fire Corps. These groups are detailed in **BOX 10.3**.

BOX 10.2 Volunteer Groups

American Red Cross: Trains volunteers in their Disaster Action Team to assist victims in emergencies.

National Volunteer Organization Against Disasters: Founded in 1970, this group is made up of nonprofit organizations that are involved in providing assistance to communities and survivors. They provide training for their volunteers so they are acquainted with the proper procedures before the actual disaster occurs. There are national members in the organization who are responsible for coordinating volunteer efforts at the national level, while state/territory members ensure coordination efforts among organizations at the state and local level.

Feeding America (formerly America's Second Harvest): Works to provide food to survivors of disaster-affected communities. They maintain food supplies that can be distributed quickly if an emergency should occur and ensure that the food provided to victims of a disaster is safe.

American Radio Relay League: Amateur radio enthusiasts who provide emergency communications in times of emergencies or disasters to members of the community. They also provide public service announcements as needed.

Salvation Army: Has the Salvation Army Team Emergency Radio Network (SATERN) that is made up of volunteers who provide emergency communications during disasters. The organization also provides disaster relief services such as basic services, financial assistance, food and shelter, assistance with clean-up, and reconstruction efforts.

Data from: National Voluntary Organizations Active in Disaster. (2019). Retrieved online at http://www.nvoad.org; Feeding America. (2019). Retrieved online at http://feedingamerica.org; American Radio Relay League. (2019). Retrieved online at http://www.arrl.org/emergency-communications; Salvation Army. (2019). Retrieved online at http://disaster.salvationarmyusa.org/aboutus

BOX 10.3 Citizen Corps

USA Freedom Corps: Within the Executive Office of the President, it is the fifth policy council (along with Domestic, Economic, National Security, and Homeland Security) in the White House. The Corps promotes volunteerism across the nation and seeks to connect Americans to various volunteer opportunities in other federal agencies such as AmeriCorps, Peace Corps, and Senior Corps, while also encouraging citizens to find local opportunities for volunteering.

Citizen Corps: Within the DHS Office of Domestic Preparedness. Volunteers in this agency assist in the recovery process after an attack or natural disaster. As a component of USA Freedom Corps, the Citizen Corps encourages people to prepare for emergencies.

Community Emergency Response Team (CERT): CERTs are sponsored by local fire departments or emergency management groups. Volunteers are trained to help in emergencies or to provide medical assistance, crowd control, or conduct training for others. They also help to raise funds to purchase equipment. Sometimes, CERT teams go by other names, including Neighborhood Emergency Response Teams (NERT) or in the case where most of the team consists of teenagers: Teen Community Emergency Response Teams (TEEN CERT).

Fire Corps: Volunteers help local fire/EMS departments in nonemergency situations. As part of Citizens Corps, these men and women help to increase the ability of fire departments to assist and protect the community.

Medical Reserve Corps: As part of Citizen Corps, these volunteers make up a network of public health members in a community who volunteer to provide medical assistance during emergencies.

Volunteers in Police Service (VIPs): Part of Citizen Corps, this group provides support to law enforcement agencies by performing clerical tasks, assisting with search and rescue operations, or crowd control.

The National Response Plan outlines the federal government's plan for responding to an emergency. The report focused on a unified approach to managing incidents that involve many participants from all levels of government. The report notes that once an incident occurs, priorities must shift to employing resources to save lives; protect property and the environment; and preserve the social, economic, and political structure of the jurisdiction. It is essential that affected governments quickly gain and maintain situational awareness and then activate and deploy resources. After that, response actions must be coordinated as should any requests for additional support.

The federal government has many options for responding to emergencies, and there are many federal agencies that play some role in the response stage of the homeland security cycle, some of which are listed in **BOX 10.4**. In the event of a disaster, the President can

BOX 10.4 Federal Response Agencies

Integrated Hazard Information Services: Works with emergency managers, the media, private sector, and weather forecasters to inform the public about hazardous weather conditions.

Center for Domestic Preparedness Consortium: A part of FEMA, this is a partnership of several organizations that work to further counterterrorism preparedness needs for the nation's first responders. They help enhance preparedness of federal, state, local, and tribal emergency responders as a way to reduce the nation's vulnerabilities. The members include:

- Center for Domestic Preparedness: The only federally chartered training center for weapons of mass destruction
- The Energetic Materials Research and Testing Center: A research-oriented public university that specializes in training for explosives, live explosives, and incendiary devices
- National Center for Biomedical Research and Training: Training for weapons of mass destruction, counterterrorism, and high-consequence events for emergency management personnel, law enforcement, HazMat, public health, EMS, and agricultural components
- National Emergency Response and Rescue Training Center: Designs, develops, and delivers training and technical assistance for first responders
- Nevada Test Site's Counter-Terrorism Operations Support Program: Provides training for radiological/nuclear weapons; teaches first responders to detect, prepare for, prevent, respond to, and recover from acts of terrorism with weapons of mass destruction (WMDs)
- Transportation Technology Center, Inc: Provides training for first responders as well as surface transportation security, such as railroads and heavy freight transport systems
- National Disaster Preparedness Training Center at the University of Hawaii: Provides training to island communities throughout the Pacific so they are able to respond, recover, and reconstruct their communities after a catastrophe

Domestic Preparedness Office: Was originally established by the FBI in 1998 as a way to coordinate all federal efforts surrounding WMDs. The office works with other federal agencies to assist state and local first responders to respond to a WMD attack. The office was moved to the DHS in 2003.

Domestic Emergency Support Team: Was created by the Presidential Decision Directive 39 by President Clinton in June 1995; made up of many teams that can be deployed quickly from the FBI, FEMA, Department of Defense, Department of Energy, and others who respond to attacks made with WMDs. President Bush transferred it to DHS from the Justice Department in 2003.

National Disaster Medical System: Combines federal and nonfederal medical resources to establish an integrated national medical response capability that can assist first responders in times of emergency. The agency is part of the Department of Health and Human Services.

Strategic National Stockpile: Has large quantities of medicine and supplies that could be used if local supplies are exhausted as a result of an emergency. Medicine could be delivered to any state and would be free. There are enough supplies to protect people in several large cities.

Other Response Agencies: The FBI has many offices that help with response efforts. These include the Domestic Terrorism/Counterterrorism Planning Section, the Laboratory Division, and the Critical Incident Response Group. Other federal agencies play a role in response, such as the Department of Defense, Department of Energy, Department of Health and Human Services, the Environmental Protection Agency (EPA), the Department of Agriculture, and the Nuclear Regulatory Commission.

Data from: Integrated Hazard Information Services. (2019). Retrieved online at https://esrl.noaa.gov/gsd/eds/hazardservices/; Center for Domestic Preparedness Consortium. (2019). Retrieved online at https://www.ndpc.us/; Domestic Emergency Support Team. (2019). Retrieved online at https://www.fema.gov/; National Disaster Medical System. (2019). Retrieved online at https://www.phe.gov/Preparedness/responders/ndms/; Strategic National Stockpile. (2019). Retrieved online at https://www.phe.gov/about/sns

declare an emergency, which then begins the process of providing both physical and monetary assistance to those living in the affected area. This authority stems from the Disaster Relief Act of 1974, which was amended by the Stafford Disaster Relief and Emergency Assistance Act. When an emergency is declared, FEMA is given the task of coordinating federal relief efforts that may involve over 25 federal agencies and other organizations such as the American Red Cross.

FEMA has suggested ways to respond to various attacks and emergencies. For example, they suggest that during a chemical threat, people should move quickly away from the impacted area without passing through the contaminated area. If it is not possible to leave a building, they suggest closing all doors and windows and turning off the ventilation. They suggest that the room(s) be sealed with plastic sheeting and duct tape.[14]

During a nuclear blast, FEMA suggests listening for officials to make announcements about what to do: Take shelter, go to a specific place, or evacuate. If it is not possible to evacuate, they suggest finding a building made of brick or concrete to limit exposure to radioactive material. Once in the building, you should go as far below ground as possible or into the center of the structure. If possible, stay there for at least 24 hours, until radiation levels decrease. If outside, FEMA suggests taking cover behind anything that may offer protection, and lie flat on the ground, covering your head. It is important to get clean as quickly as possible, removing the outer layer of clothing, placing it in a plastic bag, and moving it far away from any people or animals.[15]

Another type of plan for responding to incidents on the federal level is NIMS. This was created after President George W. Bush called on the Secretary of Homeland Security, through Homeland Security Presidential Directive No. 5, to develop a nationally based **incident command system**. The purpose was to provide a consistent, nationwide approach for federal, state, local, and tribal governments to work together to prepare for, prevent, respond to, and recover from domestic incidents. It is a set of principles, terminology, and organizational processes that together serve as a comprehensive, standardized approach to the management of domestic incidents at all government levels. The procedures in NIMS are designed to be used to coordinate the different response actions. It is presumed that all responders will be able to share a common understanding and will be able to work together to respond effectively to an emergency.

On the local level, each township has the responsibility to provide qualified first responders who can handle a variety of emergencies. This usually includes police, firefighters, and emergency medical staff. If the emergency covers a wide region beyond their capabilities, the local leaders will rely on the state for assistance.[16] More than likely, the state and local agencies will be the first responders to an emergency. If needed, they can ask for assistance from neighboring communities or states. If the emergency is complex or requires more resources than are available, or if the costs are too high for local governments, the mayor or governor can request assistance from the federal government. The specific procedures by which a state can make an appeal to the federal government are outlined in the NRF.

If a state governor wishes, he or she can formally request that the president declare a major disaster or make an **emergency declaration**. Such a request will first be analyzed by the regional FEMA administrator, who will then make a recommendation to the national FEMA administrator. This administrator will then make a recommendation to the president, who will decide whether to declare a disaster based partly on the FEMA recommendation. If a declaration is made, the FEMA administrator will then determine which components of the NRF to activate.

Recovery

The last stage of the homeland security cycle is **recovery**, or the efforts taken to restore the infrastructure and the social and economic underpinnings of a community to a state of normalcy. This stage begins in the period immediately following a disaster and can continue for months and, in some cases, years. Recovery is a gradual process, and the health and safety of the residents must be the first concern.

With most incidents, there are both short-term recovery needs as well as long-term recovery needs. In the short term, people will need functioning transportation systems (i.e., roads), utilities, schools, medical facilities, and government buildings. Some victims will need food, shelter, and other government assistance

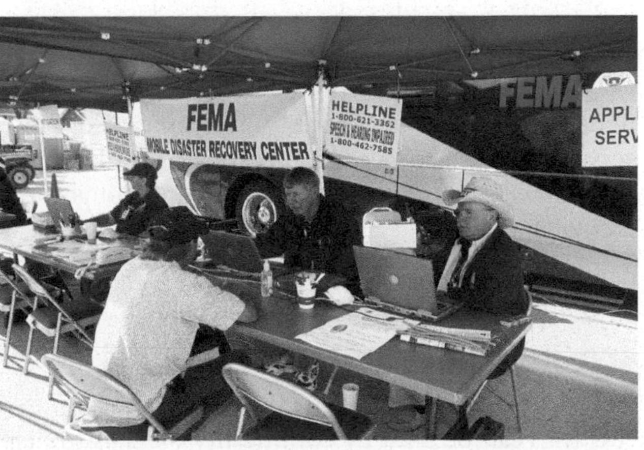

Courtesy of Greg Henshall/FEMA.

programs. The essential infrastructure will need to be repaired or maintained, such as power, communication systems, and water and sewage.

Long-term recovery may take months or even years. This will involve any actions taken to return the community to one that functions well for its citizens. Any areas that were directly affected by the incident may need to have homes or commercial buildings permanently repaired or rebuilt. Economic activity will need to be restored by resuming regular business and employment. Long-term recovery may also require emergency economic aid, accessible business loans, environmental monitoring, and long-term mental health services.

The National Response Framework addresses the need for specific policies for helping individuals and communities to recover from an emergency and return to self-sufficiency. Recovery efforts will, of course, be unique to each community, but should be overseen by a **Joint Field Office**. The JFO will do things such as coordinate assistance programs that will help individuals, households, and businesses return to normal, establish Disaster Recovery Centers, and coordinate public assistance grant programs.

The federal government plays the largest role in providing the technical and financial support for recovery. For the most part, recovery is the responsibility of FEMA. The assistance they provide to each community after a disaster will vary depending on the community and the type and severity of the emergency. The response to a hurricane, for instance, will be very different from that required from an attack that involved chemical agents.

FEMA also suggests ways to recover from different types of emergencies. For example, they recommend that after a chemical attack, it is necessary to decontaminate the area as quickly as possible in order to minimize potential health consequences. They suggest that citizens stay in a shelter until officials announce that it is safe to leave. Plus, anyone who has had any contact with a chemical agent should receive medical treatment.[17]

Effective recovery efforts may require contributions from all sectors of society. The Joint Field Office serves as the central coordination point for all levels of government, as well as private-sector and nongovernmental entities.

Threat and Hazard Identification and Risk Assessment (THIRA)

Officials at FEMA have developed a three-step process that can be used by community officials to help plan and prepare for emergencies. They called the process THIRA, or the Threat and Hazard Identification and Risk Assessment. After completing the THIRA process, officials will be able to identify the potential threats that can affect their communities, the possible impacts of these threats on their neighborhoods should they occur, and the capabilities necessary to address those needs.

There are four steps to the THIRA analysis. The first step is to identify threats and hazards. When this stage is completed, officials will have a list of threats and hazards that are specific to their community. This can include natural hazards (earthquakes, tornados, wildfires, winter storms), technological hazards (airplane crash, a release of hazardous materials, power failure, or train derailment), and incidents that are caused by human actions (biological attack, cyber incident, or school violence). Officials must also identify the likelihood of the accident occurring and the significance of the effects.

When this is completed, the THIRA analysis moves to the second stage, which is to give the threats and hazards a context. This means the conditions, time, and locations under which a threat may occur. Some communities may note that a certain threat will not affect them. For example, a person living in Ohio may not be threatened by a tsunami or volcano.

The third step for a THIRA analysis is to establish capability targets. In this stage, officials must address their capability to handle each threat identified in Step 2. A specific capability target must be developed for each threat. This helps a community define what it would take for the community to meet the challenge posed by each threat. In this stage, officials can also begin to identify their level of preparedness. They may create a list of resources available in the community that may be useful in the case of an event.

The final stage in a THIRA analysis is to apply the results. Here, officials will create a list of resources that they need to develop in order to effectively respond to an event.

There are many reasons why a community may carry out a THIRA analysis. First, it helps officials to identify what resources they have as well as possible gaps or shortfalls so these can be addressed prior to an emergency. They are able to create a long-term plan for emergencies that will help their neighborhoods return to a normal state (resiliency).

To help community officials carry out a THIRA assessment, the federal government has published the Comprehensive Preparedness Guide 201. The first edition was made available in 2012. This publication set forth the basic steps involved in a THIRA assessment, but also included the Stakeholder Preparedness Review (SPR). This was a way for community's to define their capabilities to respond to a disaster and sustain those over time. The second edition of the Preparedness Guide clarified and streamlined the THIRA process. The third edition, published in 2018, updates the THIRA and SPR procedures. When officials complete the data collection process, they will be able to identify both their capabilities and any gaps, as well as their intentions to address the gaps. In the end, the process will allow all communities to be better prepared to handle an emergency and protect the safety of its residents.

Chapter Summary

There are four stages to the homeland security cycle. They include mitigation, preparedness, response, and recovery. The first two stages revolve around activities that can be taken to lessen the chance that an event may occur, or to lessen the impact of an event. The second two stages occur after an attack or natural disaster to help citizens and communities respond and recover from the event. Activities during all four stages of the cycle may involve all levels of government, from local up to federal.

Review/Discussion Questions

1. What are the four stages to the homeland security cycle? Why are they important to homeland security?
2. What are the roles of the federal, state, local, and tribal governments in each of the stages of the homeland security cycle?
3. What role do volunteers play in the homeland security cycle?

Additional Readings

Bush, G. W. (2001). Presidential Policy Direction/PPD-8: National Preparedness. Retrieved online at http://www.dhs.gov/presidential-policy-directive-8-national-preparedness

Logan, K. G. & Ramsay, J. D. (2012). *Introduction to Homeland Security.* Boulder, CO: Westview.

Pelfrey, W. V. (2004). *Homeland Security Disciplines and the Cycle of Preparedness.* Retrieved online at http://homelandsecurityroundtable.com/wp-content/uploads/2012/07/Homeland-Security-Disciplines-and-the-Cycle-of-Preparedness.pdf

Endnotes

1. Barrett, D. (2012). "Five Charged in Plan to Bomb Ohio Bridge." *The Wall Street Journal.* Retrieved online at http://online.wsj.com/article/SB1000142405270230405030457737785161202497 4.html
2. Lahneman, W. J. (2012). Homeland Security Intelligence. In Logan, K. G. & Ramsay, J. D. *Introduction to Homeland Security*. Boulder, CO: Westview, pp. 97–124.
3. Department of Homeland Security, "Plan and Prepare for Disasters." (June 19, 2012). https://dhs.gov/plan-and-prepare-disasters
4. Center of Excellence, Homeland Security Emergency Management. (n.d). "National Preparedness Cycle. www.coehsem.com/emergency-management-cycle/
5. Federal Emergency Management Agency. (2012). *Shelter*. Retrieved online at http://www.ready.gov/shelter
6. Federal Emergency Management Agency. (2012). *Warning Systems and Signals*. Retrieved online at http://www.ready.gov/warning-systems-signals
7. Clovis, S. H., Jr. (2012). Strategic Planning. In Logan, K. G. & Ramsay, J. D. *Introduction to Homeland Security*. Boulder, CO: Westview, pp. 285–311.
8. Department of Homeland Security. (ND). *Bioterrorism*. Retrieved online at https://www.ready.gov/Bioterrorism
9. Department of Homeland Security. (ND). *Chemical Emergencies*. Retrieved online at https://www.ready.gov/chemical
10. Department of Homeland Security. (ND). *Nuclear Explosion*. Retrieved online at https://www.ready.gov/nuclear-explosion
11. Department of Homeland Security. (ND). *Radiological Dispersion Device*. Retrieved online at https://www.ready.gov/radiological-dispersion-device
12. Clovis, S. H., Jr. (2012). Strategic Planning. In Logan, K. G. & Ramsay, J. D. *Introduction to Homeland Security*. Boulder, CO: Westview, pp. 285–311.
13. Chumar, M. (2012). Public- and Private-Sector Partnerships in Homeland Security. In Logan, K. G. & Ramsay, J. D. *Introduction to Homeland Security*. Boulder, CO: Westview, pp. 47–68.
14. Department of Homeland Security. (2012). *Chemical Threats*. Retrieved online at http://www.ready.gov/chemical-threats
15. Department of Homeland Security. (2012). *Nuclear Blast*. Retrieved online at http://www.ready.gov/nuclear-blast
16. Logan, K. G. (2012). A First Look at the Department of Homeland Security. In Logan, K. G. & Ramsay, J. D. *Introduction to Homeland Security*. Boulder, CO: Westview, pp. 5–18.
17. Department of Homeland Security. (2012). *Chemical Threats*. Retrieved online at http://www.ready.gov/chemical-threats

Courtesy of Michael Rieger/FEMA News Photo

CHAPTER 11

National Incident Management System and Incident Command System

CHAPTER OBJECTIVES

- Understand the overall concept of NIMS
- Know the five components of NIMS and their purpose
- Understand the overall concept of ICS
- Recognize the 14 proven management characteristics of ICS
- Know the members of the command and general staffs in ICS

CHAPTER OUTLINE

Courtesy of Bill Koplitz/FEMA.

On August 23, 2005, Hurricane Katrina formed as a tropical storm off the coast of the Bahamas.[1] Over the next 7 days, the tropical storm grew into a catastrophic hurricane that made landfall first in Florida and then along the Gulf Coast in Mississippi, Louisiana, and Alabama, leaving a trail of heartbreaking devastation and human suffering. Katrina caused staggering physical destruction along its path, flooded the historic city of New Orleans, ultimately killed over 1,300 people, and became the most destructive natural disaster in American history.

Awakening to reports of Katrina's landfall on the Gulf Coast on the morning of Monday, August 29, American citizens watched events unfold with an initial curiosity that soon turned to concern and sorrow. The awe that viewers held for the sheer ferocity of nature was soon matched with disappointment and frustration at the seeming inability of the "government"—local, state, and federal—to respond effectively to the crisis. Hurricane Katrina and the subsequent sustained flooding of New Orleans exposed significant flaws in federal, state, and local preparedness for catastrophic events and the capacity to respond to them. Emergency plans at all levels of government, from small town plans to the 600-page National Response Plan—the federal government's plan to coordinate all of its departments and agencies and integrate them with state, local, and private-sector partners—were put to the ultimate test and came up short.

In the aftermath of Hurricane Katrina, President Bush commissioned a group to study the federal response to Hurricane Katrina and to identify what went wrong. A report was issued in 2006 that noted, among many of the lessons learned, that the National Incident Management System and the use of Incident (and Area) Command Systems was not widely developed, and therefore, because of the lack of training and exposure to these systems, the federal response (and to some degree, the state and local responses, although not the subject of the report) was inadequately prepared for the natural disaster. The recommendation was that efforts needed to be redoubled to more widely educate all responders at all levels through training and exercises in the National Incident Management System (NIMS) and the Incident Command System (ICS), the primary topics to which this chapter now turns.

National Incident Management System (NIMS)

The September 11, 2001, terrorist attacks and the 2004 and 2005 hurricane seasons highlighted the need to focus on improving emergency management, incident response capabilities, and coordination processes across the country.[2] A comprehensive, national approach, applicable to all jurisdictional levels and across functional disciplines, improves the effectiveness of emergency management/response personnel across the full spectrum of potential incidents and hazard scenarios (including, but not limited to, natural hazards, terrorist activities, and other man-made disasters). Such an approach improves coordination and cooperation between public and private agencies in a variety of emergency management and incident response activities. The National Incident Management System (NIMS) framework sets forth this comprehensive, national approach (see **TABLE 11.1**).

Incidents typically begin and end locally and are managed on a daily basis at the lowest possible geographic, organizational, and jurisdictional level. However, there are instances in which successful incident management operations depend on the involvement of multiple jurisdictions, levels of government, functional agencies, and/or emergency responder disciplines. These instances require effective and efficient coordination across this broad spectrum of organizations and activities.

NIMS uses a systematic approach to integrate the best existing processes and methods into a unified, national framework for incident management. Incident management refers to how incidents are managed across all homeland security activities, including prevention, protection, response, mitigation, and recovery.

This framework forms the basis for interoperability and compatibility that will, in turn, enable a diverse set of public and private organizations to conduct well-integrated and streamlined emergency management and incident-response operations. Emergency

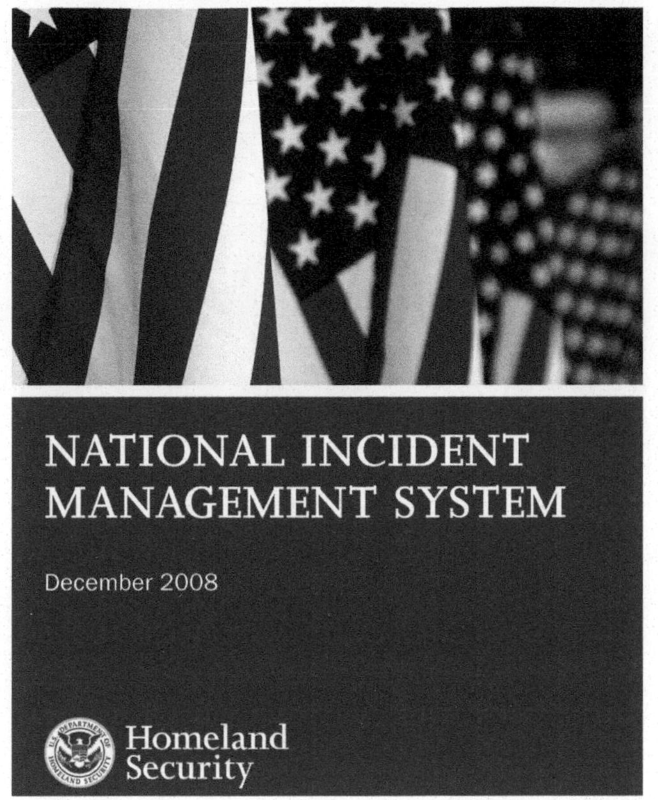

Courtesy of DHS.

management is the coordination and integration of all activities necessary to build, sustain, and improve the capability to prepare for, protect against, respond to, recover from, or mitigate against threatened or actual natural disasters, acts of terrorism, or other man-made disasters. It does this through a core set of concepts, principles, procedures, organizational processes, terminology, and standard requirements applicable to a broad community of NIMS users.

NIMS is based on the premise that utilization of a common incident management framework will give emergency management/response personnel a flexible but standardized system for emergency management and incident response activities. NIMS is flexible because the system components can be utilized to develop plans, processes, procedures, agreements, and roles for all types of incidents; it is applicable to any incident regardless of cause, size, location, or complexity. Additionally, NIMS provides an organized set of standardized operational structures, which is critical in allowing disparate organizations and agencies to work together in a predictable, coordinated manner.

The components of NIMS are adaptable to any situation, from routine, local incidents to incidents requiring the activation of interstate mutual aid to those requiring a coordinated, federal response, whether planned (e.g., major sporting or community event), predicted (e.g., hurricane) or no-notice (e.g., earthquake). This flexibility is essential for NIMS to be applicable across the full spectrum of potential incidents, including those that require multiagency, multijurisdictional (such as incidents that occur along state or international borders), and/or multidisciplinary

TABLE 11.1 Overview of the National Incident Management Framework

What NIMS Is:	What NIMS Is NOT:
A comprehensive, nationwide, systematic approach to incident management, including the Incident Command System, Multiagency Coordination Systems, and Public Information	A response plan
A set of preparedness concepts and principles for all hazards	Only applicable to certain emergency management/incident response personnel
Essential principles for a common operating picture and interoperability of communications and information management	A communications plan
Standardized resource management procedures that enable coordination among different jurisdictions or organizations	Only the Incident Command System or an organization chart
Scalable, so it may be used for all incidents (from day-to-day to large-scale)	Only used during large-scale incidents
A dynamic system that promotes ongoing management and maintenance	A static system

Data from: Department of Homeland Security. (2008). National Incident Management System. Washington, D.C.: Department of Homeland Security. Courtesy of the DHS.

coordination. Flexibility in the NIMS framework facilitates scalability of emergency management and incident response activities, and it also provides for unique implementation in specific areas around the nation.

Flexibility to manage incidents of any size requires coordination, standardization, and a common understanding among emergency management/response personnel and their affiliated organizations. NIMS provides a set of standardized organizational structures that improve integration and connectivity among jurisdictions and disciplines, starting with a common foundation of comprehensive preparedness and planning. Organizations that have adopted the common NIMS framework are able to work together, thereby fostering cohesion among the various organizations involved in all aspects of an incident. NIMS also provides and promotes common terminology, which fosters more effective communication among agencies and organizations responding to an incident.

NIMS integrates existing best practices into a consistent, nationwide, systematic approach to incident management that is applicable at all levels of government, **nongovernmental organizations (NGOs)**, and the private sector, and across functional disciplines in an all-hazards context. Five major components make up this systems approach: (1) preparedness, (2) communications and information management, (3) resource management, (4) command and management, and (5) ongoing management and maintenance.

Preparedness

NIMS provides the mechanisms for emergency management/response personnel and their affiliated organizations to work collectively by offering the necessary tools to enhance preparedness. Preparedness is achieved and maintained through a continuous cycle of planning, organizing, training, equipping, exercising, evaluating, and taking corrective action. Ongoing preparedness efforts among all those involved in emergency management and incident response activities ensure coordination during times of crisis. Moreover, preparedness facilitates efficient and effective emergency management and incident response activities.

This NIMS component describes specific measures and capabilities that emergency management/response personnel and their affiliated organizations should develop and incorporate into their overall preparedness programs to enhance the operational preparedness necessary for all-hazards emergency management and incident response activities. In developing, refining, and expanding preparedness programs and activities within their jurisdictions and/or organizations, emergency management/response personnel should leverage existing preparedness efforts and collaborative relationships to the greatest extent possible.

Courtesy of Bob McMillan/FEMA.

Communications and Information Management

Effective emergency management and incident response activities rely on flexible communications and information systems that provide a common operating picture to emergency management/response personnel and their affiliated organizations. Establishing and maintaining a common operating picture and ensuring accessibility and interoperability are the principal goals of the communications and information management component of NIMS. Properly planned, established, and applied communications enable the predictable dissemination and sharing of information with all command and support elements and, as appropriate, cooperating agencies and organizations.

Incident communications are facilitated through the development and use of a common communications plan and interoperable communications equipment, processes, standards, and architectures. During an incident, this integrated approach allows operational and support units of the various organizations to maintain communications connectivity and situational awareness. Communications and information management planning should address the incident-related policies, equipment, systems, standards, and training necessary to achieve integrated communications.

Resource Management

Emergency management and incident response activities require carefully managed resources (i.e., personnel, teams, facilities, equipment, and supplies) to meet incident needs. Utilization of the standardized resource management concepts such as typing, inventorying, organizing, and tracking will facilitate the dispatch, deployment, and recovery of resources before, during, and after an incident. Resource management should be flexible and scalable in order to support any incident and be adaptable to changes that may occur during an incident. Efficient and effective deployment of resources requires that the established resource management concepts and principles be used in all phases of emergency management and incident response.

From routine, local incidents to incidents that require a coordinated, federal response, resource management involves the coordination, oversight, and processes that provide timely and appropriate resources during an incident. Resources may support on-scene and command operations through the **Incident Command Post (ICP)** or function within the **Multiagency Coordination System (MACS)** serving at an **Emergency Operations Center (EOC)** or similar site.

As incident priorities are established, needs are identified, and resources are ordered, resource management systems are used to process the resource requests. In the initial stages of an incident, most of the resources requested are addressed locally or through mutual aid agreements and/or assistance agreements. As an incident grows in size or complexity, or if it starts on a large scale, resource needs may have to be met by other sources. In a case of competition for critical resources, MACS may be used to prioritize and coordinate resource allocation and distribution according to resource availability, needs of other incidents, and other constraints and considerations.

Command and Management

The NIMS components discussed previously—preparedness, communications and information management, and resource management—provide a framework to facilitate clear response authority, resource acquisition, and effective management during incident response. The Incident Command System (ICS), MACS, and public information are the fundamental elements of incident management. These elements provide standardization through consistent terminology and established organizational structures. Emergency management and incident response refer to the broad spectrum of activities and organizations providing effective and efficient operations, coordination, and support. Incident management, by contrast, includes directing specific incident operations; acquiring, coordinating, and delivering resources to incident sites; and sharing information about the incident with the public. Taken together, these elements of command and management are the most visible aspects of incident management, typically executed with a sense of urgency. ICS, MACS, and public information will all be described later in more detail.

Ongoing Management and Maintenance

The ongoing management and maintenance component of NIMS contains two parts or "sections": the National Integration Center (NIC) and Supporting Technologies. The NIC section of the NIMS document sets forth the responsibilities of the NIC. The Supporting Technologies section discusses principles necessary to leverage science and technology to improve capabilities and lower costs.

National Integration Center

Homeland Security Presidential Directive 5 required the Secretary of Homeland Security to establish a mechanism for ensuring the ongoing management and maintenance of NIMS, including regular consultation with other federal departments and agencies; state, tribal, and local stakeholders; NGOs; and the private sector. To this end, the Secretary established the NIC to serve as an informational assistance resource for government agencies at all levels, NGOs, and groups in the private sector that are implementing NIMS. The NIC provides strategic direction for and oversight of NIMS, supporting routine maintenance and continuous refinement of the system and its components over the long term. The NIC solicits ongoing feedback from all of its stakeholders, and revisions to NIMS and other issues can be proposed by all NIMS users (including federal, state, local, and tribal governments, as well as the private sector, NGOs, volunteer organizations, academia, nonprofit organizations, and other NIMS-related professional associations).

Additionally, the NIC administers NIMS compliance requirements, facilitates the development of guidance standards for typing and credentialing, supports NIMS training and exercises, and manages the publication of various NIMS-related materials.

Supporting Technologies

Ongoing development in the area of science and technology is integral to the continual improvement and refinement of NIMS. Strategic research and development helps to ensure that NIMS continues to be enhanced. NIMS also relies on scientifically based technical standards that support incident management. Maintaining a focus on appropriate science and technology solutions necessitate a long-term collaborative effort among NIMS partners.

To ensure the effective development of incident-management science and technology solutions, the NIC works in coordination with the DHS's Under Secretary for Science and Technology to continually assess the needs of emergency management/response personnel and their affiliated organizations.[3]

Courtesy of NOAA.

Incident Command System (ICS)

Most incidents are managed locally and are typically handled by local communications/dispatch centers and emergency management/response personnel within a single jurisdiction.[4] The majority of responses need go no further. In other instances, incidents that begin with a single response within a single jurisdiction rapidly expand to multidisciplinary, multijurisdictional levels requiring significant additional resources and operational support. The Incident Command System (ICS) provides a flexible core mechanism for coordinated and collaborative incident management, whether for incidents where additional resources are required or are provided from different organizations within a single jurisdiction or outside of the jurisdiction, or for complex incidents with national implications (such as an emerging infectious disease or a bioterrorism attack). When a single incident covers a large geographic area, multiple local emergency management and incident response agencies may be required. The responding "agencies" are defined as the governmental agencies, although in certain circumstances, NGOs and private-sector organizations may be included. Effective cross-jurisdictional coordination and communication are absolutely critical in this situation.

ICS is a widely applicable management system designed to enable effective, efficient incident management by integrating a combination of facilities, equipment, personnel, procedures, and communications operating within a common organizational structure. ICS is a fundamental form of management established in a standard format, with the purpose of enabling incident managers to identify the key concerns associated with the incident—often under urgent conditions—without sacrificing attention to any component of the command system.

ICS is used to organize on-scene operations for a broad spectrum of emergencies from small to complex incidents, both natural and man-made. The field response level is where emergency management/response personnel, under the command of an appropriate authority, carry out tactical decisions and activities in direct response to an incident or threat. Resources from federal, state, tribal, or local levels, when appropriately deployed, typically come under the command of the Incident Commander who, through the Incident Command System, determines how they will be deployed.

As a system, ICS is extremely useful: Not only does it provide an organizational structure for incident management but it also guides the process for planning, building, and adapting that structure. Using ICS for every incident or planned event helps hone and maintain skills needed for the more demanding large-scale incidents.

ICS is used by all levels of government—federal, state, tribal, and local—as well as by many NGOs and the private sector. ICS is also applicable across disciplines. It is normally structured to facilitate activities in five major functional areas: Command, operations, planning, logistics, and finance/administration. Intelligence/investigations is an optional sixth functional area, which is activated on a case-by-case basis.

Acts of biological, chemical, radiological, and nuclear terrorism may present unique challenges for the traditional ICS structure. Incidents that are not site-specific, are geographically dispersed, or evolve over longer periods of time will require extraordinary coordination among all participants—something the ICS system, if properly utilized, can provide.

Management Characteristics

When the ICS was created, it was based on 14 field-tested management characteristics, each of which applies to the current system. They are as follows:

- *Common Terminology* ICS establishes common terminology that allows diverse incident management and support organizations to work together across a wide variety of incident management functions and hazard scenarios. This common terminology covers the following:

- Organizational functions: Major functions and functional units with incident management responsibilities are named and defined. Terminology for the organizational elements is standard and consistent.
- Resource descriptions: Major resources—including personnel, facilities, and major equipment and supply items—that support incident management activities are given common names and are "typed" with respect to their capabilities to help avoid confusion and to enhance interoperability.
- Incident facilities: Common terminology is used to designate the various facilities in the vicinity of the incident area that will be used during the course of the incident.

■ *Modular Organization* The ICS organizational structure develops in a predictable and modular fashion based on the size and complexity of the incident, as well as the specifics of the hazard environment created by the incident. When needed, separate functional elements can be established, each of which may be further subdivided to enhance internal organizational management and external coordination. Responsibility for the establishment and expansion of the ICS modular organization ultimately rests with Incident Command, which bases the evolving ICS structure on the requirements of the situation. As incident complexity increases, the organization expands from the top down as additional functional responsibilities are delegated. Concurrently with structural expansion, the number of management and supervisory positions expands to address the requirements of the incident adequately.

■ *Management by Objectives* Management by objectives is communicated throughout the entire ICS organization and includes:
- Establishing incident objectives
- Developing strategies based on incident objectives
- Developing and issuing assignments, plans, procedures, and protocols
- Establishing specific, measurable tactics or tasks for various incident management functional activities, and directing efforts to accomplish them, in support of defined strategies
- Documenting results to measure performance and facilitate corrective actions

Courtesy of Robert Rose/FEMA.

■ *Incident Action Planning* Centralized, coordinated incident action planning should guide all response activities. An Incident Action Plan (IAP) provides a concise, coherent means of capturing and communicating the overall incident priorities, objectives, strategies, and tactics in the context of both operational and support activities.

Every incident must have an action plan. However, not all incidents require written plans. The need for written plans and attachments is based on the requirements of the incident and the decision of the Incident Commander (IC) or Unified Command (UC). Most initial response operations are not captured with a formal IAP. However, if an incident is likely to extend beyond one operational period, become more complex, or involve multiple jurisdictions and/or agencies, preparing a written IAP will become increasingly more important to maintain effective, efficient, and safe operations. (See **BOX 11.1**.)

BOX 11.1 Advantages of Using Unified Command

- A single set of objectives is developed for the entire incident
- A collective approach is used to develop strategies to achieve incident objectives
- Information flow and coordination are improved among all jurisdictions and agencies involved in the incident
- All agencies with responsibility for the incident have an understanding of joint priorities and restrictions
- No agency's legal authorities will be compromised or neglected
- The combined efforts of all agencies are optimized as they perform their respective assignments under a single IAP

- *Manageable Span of Control* Manageable span of control is key for effective and efficient incident management. Supervisors must be able to adequately supervise and control their subordinates, as well as communicate with and manage all resources under their supervision. The type of incident, nature of the task, hazards and safety factors, and distances between personnel and resources all influence span-of-control considerations.
- *Incident Facilities and Locations* Various types of operational support facilities are established in the vicinity of an incident, depending on its size and complexity, to accomplish a variety of activities. The Incident Commander will direct the identification and location of facilities based on the requirements of the situation. Typically, designated facilities include incident command posts, bases, camps, staging areas, mass casualty triage areas, point-of-distribution sites, and others as required.
- *Comprehensive Resource Management* Maintaining an accurate and up-to-date picture of resource utilization is a critical component of incident management and emergency response. Resources to be identified in this way include personnel, teams, equipment, supplies, and facilities available or potentially available for assignment or allocation. Effective resource management is a major component of NIMS.
- *Integrated Communications* Incident communications are facilitated through the development and use of a common communications plan and interoperable communications processes and systems. The ICS has a form (Form 205) that is available to assist in developing a common communications plan. This integrated approach links the operational and support units of the various agencies involved, which is necessary to maintain communications connectivity and discipline and to enable common situational awareness and interaction. Preparedness planning should address the equipment, systems, and protocols necessary to achieve integrated voice and data communications.
- *Establishment and Transfer of Command* The command function must be clearly established from the beginning of incident operations. The agency with primary jurisdictional authority over the incident designates the individual at the scene responsible for establishing command. If and when command is transferred, the process must include a briefing that captures all essential information for continuing safe and effective operations.
- *Chain of Command and Unity of Command* Chain of command refers to the orderly line of authority within the ranks of the incident management organization. Unity of command means that all individuals have a designated supervisor to whom they report at the scene of the incident. These principles clarify reporting relationships and eliminate the confusion caused by multiple, conflicting directives. Incident managers at all levels must be able to direct the actions of all personnel under their supervision.
- *Unified Command* In incidents involving multiple jurisdictions—a single jurisdiction with multiagency involvement, or multiple jurisdictions with multiagency involvement—**unified command** allows agencies with different legal, geographic, and functional authorities and responsibilities to work together effectively without affecting individual agency authority, responsibility, or accountability. (See **BOX 11.2**.)
- *Accountability* Effective accountability of resources at all jurisdictional levels and within individual functional areas during incident operations is essential. To that end, check-in/check-out, incident action planning, unity of command, personal responsibility, span of control, and resource tracking are the principles of accountability, which must be adhered to.
- *Dispatch/Deployment* Resources should respond only when requested or when dispatched by an appropriate authority through established resource management systems. Resources

BOX 11.2 Comparison of Single IC and UC

Single Incident Commander: The IC is solely responsible (within the confines of his or her authority) for establishing incident objectives and strategies. The IC is directly responsible for ensuring that all functional area activities are directed toward accomplishment of the overall strategy.

Unified Command: The individuals designated by their jurisdictional or organizational authorities (or by departments within a single jurisdiction) must jointly determine objectives, strategies, plans, resource allocations, and priorities, and work together to execute integrated incident operations and maximize the use of assigned resources.

BOX 11.3 Primary Functions of the Incident Commander (or Unified Commander)

- Have clear authority and know agency policy
- Ensure incident safety
- Establish the ICP
- Set priorities and determine incident objectives and strategies to be followed
- Establish ICS organization needed to manage the incident
- Approve the IAP
- Coordinate command and general staff activities
- Approve resource requests and use of volunteers and auxiliary personnel
- Order demobilization as needed
- Ensure that after-action reports are completed
- Authorize information release to the media

not requested must refrain from spontaneous deployment to avoid overburdening the recipient and compounding accountability challenges.

- *Information and Intelligence Management* The incident management organization must establish a process for gathering, analyzing, assessing, sharing, and managing incident-related information and intelligence. This is usually done by the operations section (see following text) or it can become its own section if ordered by the Incident Commander. (See **BOX 11.3**.)

Incident Command and Command Staff

Incident Command (IC) is responsible for overall management of the incident. Overall management includes command staff assignments required to support the command function. The command and general staffs are typically located at the Incident Command Post (ICP).

The incident command function may be conducted in two general ways. The first is through a single incident commander. When an incident occurs within a single jurisdiction and there is no jurisdictional or functional agency overlap, a single IC should be designated with overall incident management responsibility by the appropriate jurisdictional authority. In some cases where incident management crosses jurisdictional and/or functional agency boundaries, a single IC may be designated, if agreed upon. The designated IC will develop the incident objectives on which subsequent incident action planning will be based.

The second way that incident command may function is through a Unified Command (UC). UC is an important element in multijurisdictional or multiagency incident management. It provides guidelines to enable agencies with different legal, geographic, and functional responsibilities to coordinate, plan, and interact effectively. As a team effort, UC allows all agencies with jurisdictional authority or functional responsibility for the incident to jointly provide management direction through a common set of incident objectives and strategies and a single IAP. Each participating agency maintains its authority, responsibility, and accountability.

Command Staff

In an incident command organization, the **command staff** typically includes a public information officer, a safety officer, and a liaison officer, who all report directly to the IC/UC and may have assistants as necessary (see **FIGURE 11.1**). Additional positions may be required, depending on the nature, scope, complexity, and location(s) of the incident(s), or according to specific requirements established by the IC/UC. The following are the duties and functions of the various command staff members:

1. *Public Information Officer* The public information officer is responsible for interfacing with the public and media and/or with other agencies with incident-related information requirements. The public information officer gathers, verifies, coordinates, and disseminates accurate, accessible, and timely information on the incident's cause, size, and current situation; resources committed; and other matters of general interest for both internal and external audiences. The public information officer may also perform a key public information-monitoring role. (See **BOX 11.4**.) Whether the command structure is single or unified, only one public information officer should be designated per incident. Assistants may be assigned from other involved agencies, departments, or organizations. The IC/UC must approve the release of all incident-related information.
2. *Safety Officer* The safety officer monitors incident operations and advises the IC/UC on all matters relating to operational safety, including the health and safety of emergency responder personnel.

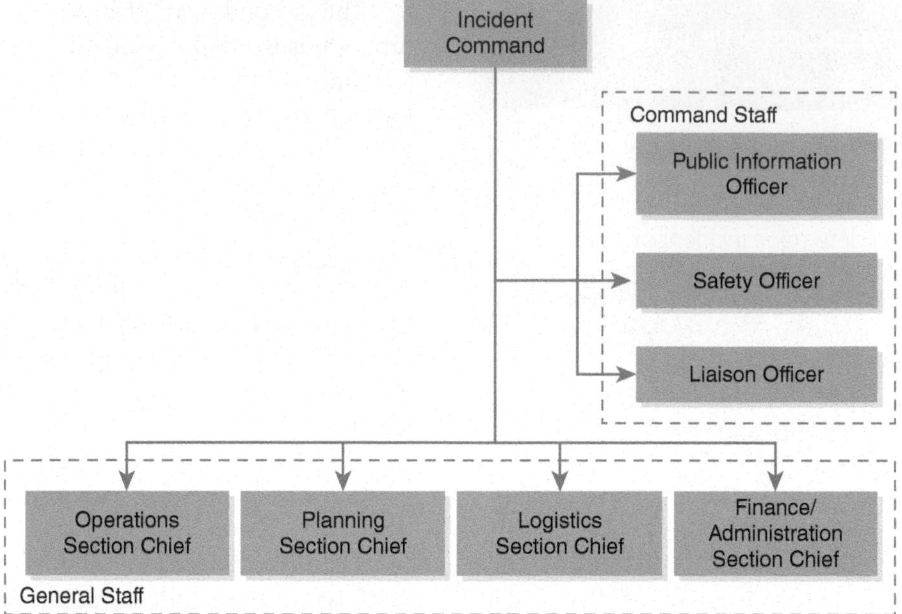

FIGURE 11.1 Incident Command System: Command Staff and General Staff.

Reproduced from: Department of Homeland Security. (2008). National Incident Management System. Washington, D.C.: Department of Homeland Security. Courtesy of the DHS.

The ultimate responsibility for the safe conduct of incident management operations rests with the IC/UC and supervisors at all levels of incident management. The safety officer is, in turn, responsible to the IC/UC for the systems and procedures necessary to ensure ongoing assessment of hazardous environments, including the incident safety plan, coordination of multiagency safety efforts, and implementation of measures to promote emergency responder safety, as well as the general safety of incident operations. The safety officer has immediate authority to stop and/or prevent unsafe acts during incident operations. It is important to note that the agencies, organizations, or jurisdictions that contribute to joint safety management efforts do not lose their individual identities or responsibility for their own programs, policies, and personnel. Rather, each contributes to the overall effort to protect all responder personnel involved in incident operations. (See **BOX 11.5**.)

3. *Liaison Officer* The liaison officer is Incident Command's point of contact for representatives of other governmental

BOX 11.4 Primary Functions of the Public Information Officer

- Determine, according to direction from IC, any limits on information release
- Develop accurate, accessible, and timely information for use in press/media briefing
- Obtain the IC's approval of news releases
- Conduct periodic media briefings
- Arrange for tours and other interviews or briefings that may be required
- Monitor and forward media information that may be useful to incident planning
- Maintain current information summaries and/or displays on the incident
- Make information about the incident available to incident personnel
- Participate in planning meetings
- Implement methods to monitor rumor control

BOX 11.5 Primary Functions of the Safety Officer

- Identify and mitigate hazardous situations
- Create a safety plan
- Ensure that safety messages and briefings are made
- Exercise emergency authority to stop and prevent unsafe acts
- Review the IAP for safety implications
- Assign assistants qualified to evaluate special hazards
- Initiate preliminary investigation of accidents within the incident area
- Review and approve the medical plan
- Participate in planning meetings to address anticipated hazards associated with future operations

BOX 11.6 Primary Functions of the Liaison Officer

- Act as a point of contact for agency representatives
- Maintain a list of assisting and cooperating agencies and agency representatives
- Assist in setting up and coordinating interagency contacts
- Monitor incident operations to identify current or potential interorganizational problems
- Participate in planning meetings, provide current resource status, including limitations and capabilities of agency resources
- Provide agency-specific demobilization information and requirements

agencies, NGOs, and the private sector (with no jurisdiction or legal authority) to provide input on their agency's policies, resource availability, and other incident-related matters. Under either a single IC or a UC structure, representatives from assisting agencies and organizations coordinate through the liaison officer. Agency and organizational representatives assigned to an incident must have the authority to speak for their parent agencies or organizations on all matters, following appropriate consultations with their agency leadership. Assistants and personnel from other agencies or organizations, public or private, involved in incident management activities may be assigned to the liaison officer to facilitate coordination. (See **BOX 11.6**.)

4. *Additional Command Staff* Additional command staff positions may also be necessary, depending on the nature and location(s) of the incident(s) or specific requirements established by Incident Command. For example, a legal counsel might be assigned to the planning section as a technical specialist or directly to the command staff to advise incident command on legal matters, such as emergency proclamations, the legality of evacuation and quarantine orders, and legal rights and restrictions pertaining to media access. Similarly, a medical advisor might be designated to provide advice and recommendations to incident command about medical and mental health services, mass casualty, acute care, vector control, epidemiology, or mass prophylaxis considerations, particularly in response to a bioterrorism incident. In addition, a special needs advisor might be designated to provide expertise regarding communication, transportation, supervision, and essential services for diverse populations in the affected area.

General Staff

The **general staff** is responsible for the functional aspects of the incident command structure. The general staff typically consists of the operations, planning, logistics, and finance/administration section chiefs. The section chiefs may have one or more deputies assigned, with the assignment of deputies from other agencies encouraged in the case of multijurisdictional incidents (see **FIGURE 11.2** as an example of how an Incident Command General Staff may be created). The functional sections are discussed more fully next.

1. *Operations Section* This section is responsible for all tactical activities focused on reducing the immediate hazard, saving lives and property, establishing situational control, and restoring normal operations. Lifesaving and responder safety will always be the highest priorities and the first objectives in the IAP. (See **BOX 11.7** and **FIGURE 11.3**.)
2. *Planning Section* The planning section collects, evaluates, and disseminates incident situation information and

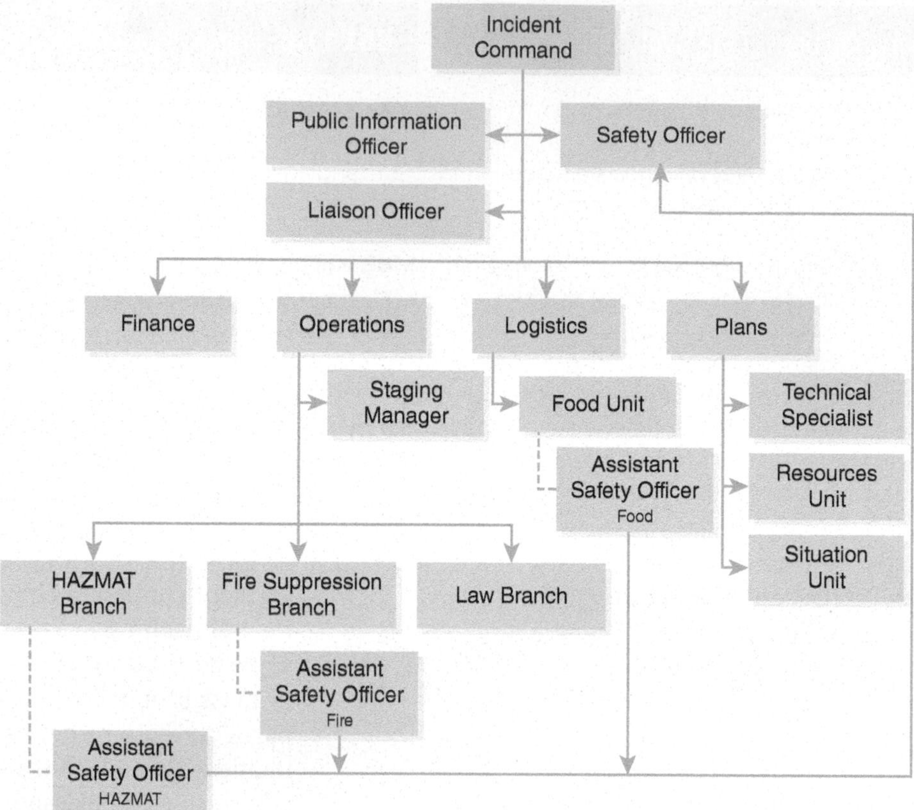

FIGURE 11.2 Example of a More Developed Incident Command Staff.

Reproduced from: Department of Homeland Security. (2008). National Incident Management System. Washington, D.C.: Department of Homeland Security. Courtesy of the DHS.

intelligence to the IC/UC and incident management personnel. This section then prepares status reports, displays situation information, maintains the status of resources assigned to the incident, and prepares and documents the IAP, based on operations section input and guidance from the IC/UC. (See **BOX 11.8**.)

BOX 11.7 Primary Functions of the Operations Section Chief

- Ensure safety of tactical operations
- Manage tactical operations
- Develop operations portions of the IAP
- Supervise execution of operations portions of the IAP
- Request additional resources to support tactical operations
- Approve release of resources from active operational assignments
- Make or approve expedient changes to the IAP
- Maintain close contact with the IC, subordinate operations personnel, and other agencies involved in the incident

BOX 11.8 Primary Functions of the Planning Section Chief

- Collect and manage all incident-relevant operational data
- Supervise preparation of the IAP
- Provide input to the IC and operations in preparing the IAP
- Incorporate traffic, medical, and communications plans and other supporting material into the IAP
- Conduct/facilitate planning meetings
- Reassign out-of-service personnel within the ICS organization already on scene, as appropriate
- Compile and display incident status information
- Establish information requirements and reporting schedules for units (e.g., Resources Unit, Situation Unit)
- Determine the need for specialized resources
- Assemble and disassemble task forces and strike teams not assigned to operations
- Establish specialized data collection systems as necessary (e.g., weather)
- Assemble information on alternative strategies
- Provide periodic predictions on incident potential
- Report significant changes in incident status
- Oversee preparation of the demobilization plan

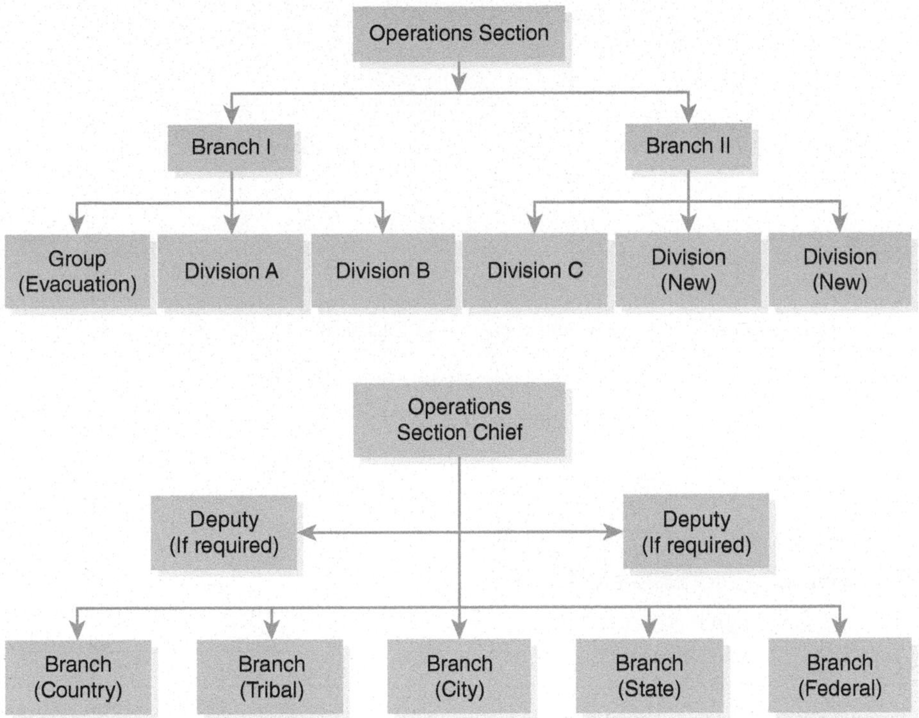

FIGURE 11.3 Operations Section Organized by Geography or Multiple Jurisdictions.

Reproduced from: Department of Homeland Security. (2008). National Incident Management System. Washington, D.C.: Department of Homeland Security. Courtesy of the DHS.

3. *Logistics Section* The logistics section is responsible for all service support requirements needed to facilitate effective and efficient incident management, including ordering resources from off-incident locations (see **FIGURE 11.4** as an example).

   This section also provides facilities, security (e.g., of the incident command facilities and personnel), transportation, supplies, equipment maintenance and fuel, food services, communications and information technology support, and emergency responder medical services (including inoculations), as required. (See **BOX 11.9.**)
4. *Finance/Administration Section* A finance/administration section is established when the incident management activities require on-scene or incident-specific finance and other administrative support services. Some of the functions that fall within the scope of this section are recording personnel time, maintaining vendor contracts, administering compensation and claims, and conducting an overall cost analysis for the incident. If a separate section is established, close coordination with the planning section and logistics section are essential so that operational records can be reconciled with financial documents. The finance/administration section is a critical part of ICS in large, complex incidents involving significant funding originating from multiple sources. (See **BOX 11.10.**)

BOX 11.9 Primary Functions of the Logistics Section Chief

- Provide all facilities, transportation, communications, supplies, equipment maintenance and fueling, food, and medical services for incident personnel, as well as all off-incident resources
- Manage all incident logistics
- Provide logistics input to the IAP
- Brief logistics staff as needed
- Identify anticipated and known incident service and support requirements
- Request additional resources as needed
- Ensure and oversee development of traffic, medical, and communications plans as required
- Oversee demobilization of logistics section and associated resources

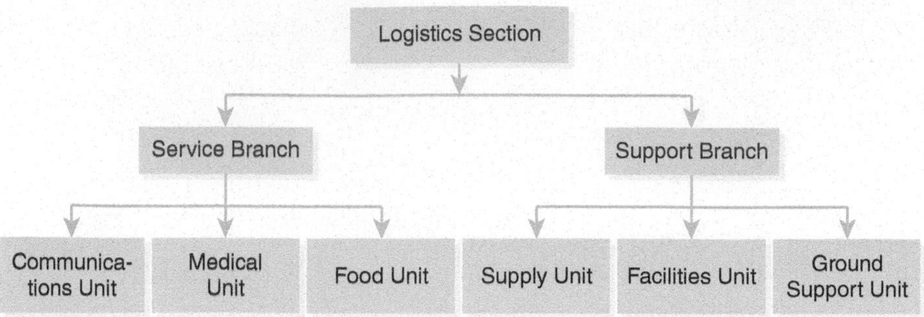

FIGURE 11.4 Logistics Section.

Reproduced from: Department of Homeland Security. (2008). National Incident Management System. Washington, D.C.: Department of Homeland Security. Courtesy of the DHS.

BOX 11.10 Primary Functions of the Finance/Administration Section Chief

- Manage all financial aspects of an incident
- Provide financial and cost analysis information as requested
- Ensure that compensation and claims functions are being addressed relative to the incident
- Gather pertinent information from briefings with responsible agencies
- Develop an operational plan for the finance/administration section and fill section supply and support needs
- Determine the need to set up and operate an incident commissary
- Meet with assisting and cooperating agency representatives as needed
- Maintain daily contact with agency(s) headquarters on financial matters
- Ensure that personnel time records are completed accurately and transmitted to home agencies
- Ensure that all obligation documents initiated at the incident are properly prepared and completed
- Brief agency administrative personnel on all incident-related financial issues needing attention or follow-up
- Provide input to the IAP

Additional Management Structures

The incident command structure also allows for the system to continue working when the incident becomes complex: For instance, if there are multiple incidents handled by a single incident command (incident complex) or if there are multiple incident commands handling one incident (area command). There are also those events requiring the resources of not only multiple local agencies but state and federal resources as well (multiagency coordination system). Descriptions of these additional structures or processes (as in the multiagency coordination system) follow:

1. *Incident Complex* An incident complex refers to two or more individual incidents located in the same general area assigned to a single IC or UC. When an incident complex is established over several individual incidents, the general guideline is that the previously identified incidents become branches within the operations section of the Incident Management Team (IMT). This provides greater potential for future expansion, if required. Each branch thus has the increased flexibility to establish divisions or groups. Additionally, because divisions and groups may already have been established at each of the incidents, the same basic structure can be propagated. If any of the incidents within a complex has the potential to become a large-scale incident, it is best to establish it as a separate incident with its own ICS organization.
2. *Area Command* Area command is an organization to oversee the management of multiple incidents handled individually by separate ICS organizations or to oversee the management of a very large or evolving incident engaging multiple incident management teams. An agency administrator/executive or other public official with jurisdictional responsibility for the incident usually makes the decision to establish an area command. An area command is activated only if necessary, depending on the complexity of the incident and incident management span-of-control considerations. Area commands are particularly relevant to incidents

that are typically not site-specific, are not immediately identifiable, are geographically dispersed, and evolve over longer periods of time (e.g., public health emergencies, earthquakes, tornadoes, civil disturbances, etc.).

3. *Multiagency Coordination Systems*
Multiagency coordination is a *process* that allows all levels of government and all disciplines to work together more efficiently and effectively. Multiagency coordination occurs across the different disciplines involved in incident management, across jurisdictional lines, or across levels of government.

Multiagency coordination can and does occur on a regular basis whenever personnel from different agencies interact in such activities as preparedness, prevention, response, recovery, and mitigation. Often, cooperating agencies develop a MACS to better define how they will work together in order to work more efficiently; however, multiagency coordination can take place without established protocols. MACS may be put in motion regardless of the location, personnel titles, or organizational structure. MACS include planning and coordinating resources and other support for planned, notice, or no-notice events. MACS define business practices, standard operating procedures, processes, and protocols by which participating agencies will coordinate their interactions. Integral elements of MACS are dispatch procedures and protocols, the incident command structure, and the coordination and support activities taking place within an activated emergency operation center. Fundamentally, MACS provides support, coordination, and assistance with policy-level decisions to the ICS structure managing an incident.

Written agreements allow agencies within the system to conduct activities using established rules, which are often self-defined by the participating organizations. A fully implemented MACS is critical for seamless multiagency coordination activities and essential to the success and safety of the response whenever more than one jurisdictional agency responds. Moreover, the use of MACS is one of the fundamental components of command and management within NIMS, as it promotes the scalability and flexibility necessary for a coordinated response.[5]

The Effectiveness of ICS

Although the Incident Command System (ICS) had been around since the early 1970s, it did not become a part of the National Incident Management System until after 9/11. It was incorporated largely because it was a system already in existence and because, according to Jensen and Thompson (2016), those in "the emergency management practitioner community had widely heralded the potential benefits of the ICS."[6] As a result, the Department of Homeland Security became the Incident Command System's greatest supporter.[7] The question that remains is whether the ICS is an effective management system when it comes to all-hazard disasters. While many praise the system for its flexible system designed to rapidly adapt to any size incident, it has its critics, such as Waugh (2009), who once remarked, "such systems, by their very nature, are inflexible, slow, and cumbersome and would be much less adaptable in task environments characterized by uncertainty and rapid change."[8] Naturally, after having invested so much time in implementing and teaching both NIMS and ICS (and after an entire chapter in this book was dedicated to the topic), one does have to wonder what the research tells us? Is the ICS effective?

There is a small but growing body of empirical literature related to the implementation and effectiveness of the ICS.[9] Jensen and Thompson reviewed the literature and found that much of the literature is descriptive in nature, typically describing the successful implementation of ICS, but they do not test the effectiveness of the system. Other articles either did not report any original findings or they were only tangentially related to the ICS, usually only by assessing some aspect of the system, such as the methods of training on ICS. Their ultimate focus was the studies that assessed the effectiveness of ICS when it was responding to a hazard event. These studies included the use of ICS during a wildland fire,[10] an outbreak of SARS (Severe Acute Respiratory Syndrome),[11] Hurricane Rita,[12] and mudslides in Taiwan.[13] Two studies looked at the effectiveness of ICS in multiple events.[14]

A conclusion of some of these studies echoed that which was found in the After Action Report from the response to Hurricane Katrina, and that is, unless everyone is trained and there is "buy-in" to the ICS system, its effectiveness will be challenged from the very beginning.[15] In order for any hope of ICS to be effective in a disaster event, all of the agencies involved in forming the ICS response must be trained, knowledgeable on the system, and believe that it is the right method to employ. In those cases where training, knowledge and buy-in varies, the effectiveness of ICS is sure to vary as well.

The last finding extends to another conclusion found among these empirical studies and that is in the implementation of ICS, despite being a uniform system, it does not show a lot of uniformity in its execution. For instance, the study involving Hurricane Rita found that some Emergency Operation Centers used ICS, while others did not, and for those EOCs that did implement ICS, it was found to have varied greatly based on the people involved, their knowledge of ICS, and any past experience in using ICS. Those authors concluded, "ICS, as currently designed and trained, does not generalize well to all types of organizations."[16] This again, may suggest variations in the training, knowledge, experience, and buy-in to the ICS system, creating the variation in its implementation.[17]

In addition, one of the multiincident evaluations, which assessed FEMA's Urban Search and Rescue Task Forces, also found similar unevenness in the implementation of ICS but did find that some of ICS methods proved effective, such as the incident briefings. Moynihan (2009), noted that "ICS fostered learning by establishing predictable flows of information and learning forums to consider this information," and that adopting ICS "also helped to curb strategic uncertainty by reducing the autonomy of member agencies and providing some basic guarantee that members were part of a collective effort."[18] So, while ICS may show wide variation in its implementation, it does feature some elements that prove successful in bringing people together and getting them to communicate, working toward an effective response to a disaster. This does not guarantee effectiveness in the disaster's response but may contribute to those things necessary to reach an effective conclusion to the incident.

Several of the studies did reach the conclusion that the employment of ICS had, in fact, proved successful. Bigley and Roberts, in their study of the use of ICS in response to wildland fires, concluded that "the ICS approach may represent an especially viable organizational solution."[19] Likewise, Tsai and colleagues found that in the response to the SARS outbreak, the use of ICS proved effective.

Despite the variation in the studies, recommendations for the implementation of ICS can be drawn from these few studies. First, it is possible for ICS to be effective, but what may be critical is ensuring that everyone is trained in ICS; has a working knowledge of the system; can gain experience, whether through actual incidents or training simulations; and, perhaps most important, that everyone buys into the system. This, indeed, may be the system's greatest hurdle. Once that is achieved, using the ICS mechanisms of command, control, and communication to facilitate participation in the response may very well lead to an effective outcome. It is clear that not only is there a need for casting a wider net in training but there is also a need for more empirical research in the use of the ICS.

Chapter Summary

In the aftermath of the September 11, 2001, attacks, the federal government created a National Response Plan that set into motion the National Incident Management System (NIMS) and the Incident Command System (ICS). When Hurricane Katrina struck New Orleans, the National Response Plan was tested and found to be highly deficient, in part because it was not widely implemented and many of those at various levels of government had not been trained on either system. In the aftermath of Hurricane Katrina, NIMS has become the method by which the nation at all levels coordinates the preparations and response throughout the homeland security cycle, and ICS is the means by which local first responders react to all incidents and are then supported by other agencies at all levels of government. Empirical research suggests that ICS can be effective as a response to disasters, but there is a need for all participants to be trained, knowledgeable, and to have bought into the system.

Review/Discussion Questions

1. Explain how the National Incident Management System fits into the homeland security apparatus.
2. What are the five components of NIMS? Explain each in detail.
3. The ICS is said to be based on 14 previously time-tested management characteristics. Name five of these and describe each in detail.
4. Describe the makeup of the ICS, paying special attention to the command staff and the general staff.
5. The Incident Command System (ICS) has become the centerpiece of how agencies respond to terrorist incidents and major disasters. According to the research, how effective has it been?

Additional Readings

Department of Homeland Security. (2013). *National Incident Management System*. Retrieved online at http://www.fema.gov/national-incident-management-system

Department of Homeland Security. (2013). *Incident Command System*. Retrieved online at http://www.fema.gov/incident-command-system

Jensen, J. & Thompson, S. (2016). "The Incident Command System: A Literature Review." *Disasters, 40*(1), 158–182.

Walsh, D. W., Hank, T. C., Miller, G. T., Callsen, C. E., Jr., Cilluffo, F. J., & Maniscalco, P. M. (2005). *National Incident Management System: Principles and Practice*. Sudbury, MA: Jones and Bartlett Publishers.

Endnotes

1. Department of Homeland Security. (2006). *The Federal Response to Hurricane Katrina: Lessons Learned*. Washington, D.C.: U.S. Department of Homeland Security.
2. Department of Homeland Security. (2008). *National Incident Management System*. Washington, D.C.: U.S. Department of Homeland Security.
3. Department of Homeland Security. (2013). *National Incident Management System*. Retrieved online at https://publicintelligence.net/dhs-nims-intel-guide/
4. This section is based on Department of Homeland Security. (2008). *National Incident Management System*. Washington, DC: U.S. Department of Homeland Security.
5. Department of Homeland Security. (2017). *Incident Command System*. 3rd edition. Retrieved online at https://www.fema.gov/media-library-data/1508151197225-ced8c60378c3936adb92c1a3ee6f6564/FINAL_NIMS_2017.pdf
6. Jensen, J. & Thompson, S. (2016). "The Incident Command System: A Literature Review." *Disasters, 40*, 158–182, p. 160; See also Buck, D., Trainor, J. & Aguirre, B. (2006). "A critical evaluation of the Incident Command System and NIMS." *Journal of Homeland Security and Emergency Management, 3*, 1–27; Tierney, K., Lindell, M. & Perry, R. (2001). *Facing the Unexpected: Disaster Preparedness and Response in the United States*. Washington, D.C.: Joseph Henry Press; Wenger, D. E., Quarantelli, E., & Dynes, R. (1990). "Is the Incident Command System a plan for all seasons and emergency situations?" *Hazard Monthly, 10 (March)*, 8–12.
7. Department of Homeland Security. (2013). *National Incident Management System*. Retrieved online at http://www.fema.gov/national-incident-management-system
8. Waugh, W. (2009). "Mechanisms for collaboration in emergency management: ICS, NIMS, and the problem with command and control." In *The Collaborative Public Manager: New Ideas for the Twenty-first Century*, R. O'Leary and L. Bingham (eds.). Washington, D.C.: Georgetown University Press, 157–175, p. 171.
9. Jensen, J. & Thompson, S. (2016). "The Incident Command System: A Literature Review." *Disasters, 40*, 158–182.
10. Bigley, G. & Roberts, K. (2001). "The Incident Command System: high reliability organizing for complex and volatile Tasks." *Academy of Management Journal, 44*, 1281–1299.
11. Tsai, M. C., Arnold, J. L., Chuang, C. C., Chi, C. H., Liu, C. C., & Yang, Y. J. (2005). "Implementation of the Hospital Emergency Incident Command System during an outbreak of Severe Acute Respiratory Syndrome (SARS) at a hospital in Taiwan, ROC." *Journal of Emergency Medicine, 28*(2), 185–196.
12. Lutz, L. & Lindell, M. (2008). "Incident Command System as a response model within emergency operations centers during Hurricane Rita." *Journal of Contingencies and Crisis Management, 16*(3), 122–134.
13. Lam, C., Lin, M. R., Tsai, S. H., & Chiu, W. T. (2010). "A pilot study of citizens' opinions on the Incident Command System in Taiwan." *Disasters, 34*(2), 447–469.
14. Buck, D., Trainor, J. & Aguirre, B. (2006). "A critical evaluation of the Incident Command System and NIMS." *Journal of Homeland Security and Emergency Management, 3*, 1–27; Moynihan, D. (2009). "The network governance of crisis response: case studies of incident command systems." *Journal of Public Administration Research and Theory, 19*, 895–915.
15. Office of Homeland Security. (2006). The Federal Response to Hurricane Katrina: Lessons Learned. Washington, D.C.: U.S. GPO.
16. Lutz, L. & Lindell, M. (2008). "Incident Command System as a response model within emergency operations centers during Hurricane Rita." *Journal of Contingencies and Crisis Management, 16*, 122–134, p. 132.
17. Bigley, G. & Roberts, K. (2001). "The Incident Command System: high reliability organizing for complex and volatile Tasks." *Academy of Management Journal, 44*, 1281–1299.
18. Moynihan, D. (2009). "The network governance of crisis response: case studies of incident command systems." *Journal of Public Administration Research and Theory, 19*, 895–915, p. 196.
19. Bigley, G. & Roberts, K. (2001). "The Incident Command System: high reliability organizing for complex and volatile Tasks." *Academy of Management Journal, 44*, 1281–1299, p. 1296.

CHAPTER 12

Political Responses to Homeland Security

CHAPTER OBJECTIVES

- To help the reader have better knowledge of presidential responses to terrorism
- To help the reader become more informed about the legislation passed by Congress to deter terrorism or help the country respond to an emergency event such as terrorism or a natural disaster

CHAPTER OUTLINE

Najibullah Zazi was a legal U.S. resident from Afghanistan living in Denver, Colorado. On September 9, 2009, Zazi drove from his home in Denver, Colorado, to New York City with plans to detonate explosives on the New York City subway during rush hour. After being told by a local imam that he was being watched by law enforcement, Zazi aborted his plans and flew back to Denver, where he was arrested days later by the FBI. He was charged on September 24, 2009, with one count of conspiring with others to use weapons of mass destruction, including bombs or other explosives. On February 22, 2010, Zazi pled guilty to conspiring to use weapons of mass destruction, conspiring to commit murder in a foreign country, and providing material support to a terrorist organization. Zazi faces a possible life sentence without the possibility of parole for the first two counts and an additional sentence of 15 years for the third count.[1]

U.S. officials point to the Zazi case as evidence that the expanded surveillance powers given to law enforcement after 9-11 allowed officials to disrupt a possible terrorist plot against the United States. Authorities first noticed Zazi's suspicious behavior when he traveled to Pakistan, where they caught him talking on his cell phone about chemicals. After that, the FBI agents from the Denver field office were on his trail. The ability of law enforcement to search business records and use roving wiretaps allowed officials to connect Zazi with al Qaeda and the plot to use explosives in the subway, potentially causing death and injuries to citizens and destruction of property.[2]

Political Responses

Immediately after the attacks of September 2001, there was a great public outcry for the president and Congress to pass new laws that would allow law enforcement to investigate the terrorists and to take action against them as a way to deter future acts. The president responded by issuing 24 Homeland Security Presidential Directives (HSPDs) and announced National Security Presidential Directives (NSPDs) on homeland security. Congress also reacted. Between the time of the attacks and January 11 of 2002, 98% of the official business in the House of Representatives and 97% of that in the Senate was related to preventing and investigating terrorism. During that time, over 450 counterterrorist resolutions were passed, compared with 1,300 in the entire U.S. legislative history.[3] It is clear that as a result of public concern about terrorism, there have been many presidential actions and new laws passed by Congress designed to help keep U.S. citizens safe from future terrorist activity.

Courtesy of Tina Hager/White House.

Presidential Action

Within days of the attacks, President Bush took action by issuing numerous **executive orders**, presidential directives on homeland security (**Homeland Security Presidential Directives [HSPDs]**), and **National Security Presidential Directives (NSPDs)** on homeland security. Executive orders are regulations or instructions from the executive office geared toward governing policy. One type of executive order is a Presidential Directive, which is given by a president with the advice and consent of an executive-level agency or department. All executive orders are checked by Congress through their budget authority.[4] NSPDs are directives used to transmit decisions on national security matters. Many of them govern homeland security policy (see **TABLE 12.1**). Although none of these actions create new legislation, per se, they still have the force of law.

One example of presidential activity in homeland security is HSPD-20 / NSPD 51, which deals with the continuity of the federal government in the event of a catastrophic emergency. It describes the need for a cooperative effort among the executive, legislative, and judicial branches of the federal government, coordinated by the president, which will take the place of the nation's regular government if terrorists attack government structures.

In Homeland Security Presidential Directive 3 (HSPD-3), a Homeland Security Advisory System was established as a way to provide information about the risk of a possible terrorist act. In this directive, the president announced a color-coded warning system to indicate the nation's alert level. For example, yellow meant an "elevated or significant" risk of an attack and orange indicated a "high" risk of a terrorist attack.

TABLE 12.1 Examples of President Bush's NSPDs on Homeland Security

National Security Presidential Directive No.	Title	Year of Issue
NSPD 9	Defeating the Terrorist Threat to the United States	2001
NSPD 21	Support for Inspections in Iraq	2002
NSPD 26	Intelligence Priorities	2003
NSPD 33	Biodefense for the 21st Century	2004
NSPD 36	U.S. Government Operations in Iraq	2004
NSPD 37	Relating to Support of Iraqi Government	2004
NSPD 38	National Strategy to Secure Cyberspace	2004
NSPD 46	U.S. Strategy and Policy in the War on Terror	2006
NSPD 47	National Strategy for Aviation Security	2006
NSPD 51	National Continuity Policy	2007
NSPD 59	Biometrics for Identification and Screening to Enhance National Security	2008

Homeland Security Presidential Directive 5 (HSPD-5) was announced by President Bush on February 28, 2003. The goal of the directive was to increase the ability of the United States to manage emergencies more effectively. The president ordered that there be a single, comprehensive national incident management system and that all levels of government be involved in it. To do this, the president asked the Secretary of Homeland Security to establish the National Incident Management System (NIMS) as a means to organize the response for possible attacks.[5]

President Bush called for federal initiatives to protect critical infrastructure and described the role of the private sector in that process in HSPD-7.[6] He established a national policy for federal departments and agencies to identify and prioritize critical infrastructure and key resources and to protect these from terrorist attacks.

In HSPD-8, President Bush gave the DHS the task of creating a national preparedness system and policies to strengthen all-hazard preparedness capabilities for domestic terrorist attacks, major disasters, and other emergencies. This was modified and updated by President Obama in 2011.

In the National Security Presidential Directive 47 (NSPD 47), along with the Homeland Security Presidential Directive-16 (HSPD-16), President Bush requested that a National Strategy for Aviation Security be created to protect the airlines from terrorist activity.

Courtesy of Jocelyn Augustino/FEMA.

Executive Order 13340 was an interpretation of the Geneva Conventions concerning detention and interrogation. Through this executive order, prohibitions against abuse and torture could be removed for certain members of al Qaeda, the Taliban, and other groups that the CIA considered to be "unlawful enemy combatants" or who were thought to have information that could be used to detect or prevent terrorist attacks. Because of this action, the CIA was then allowed to detain and interrogate prisoners.

Homeland Security Information Sharing was the focus of Executive Order 13311, along with Executive Order 13356, titled, Strengthening the Sharing of Terrorism Information to Protect Americans. Together, these presidential actions allowed federal agencies to share information concerning potential terrorists and terrorist activities.

President Bush's Homeland Security Advisory Council and Senior Advisory Committee for Homeland Security were established with Executive Order 13260. These groups served as advisors to the president before the Department of Homeland Security was created. Executive Order 13407, the Public Alert and Warning System (along with Homeland Security Presidential Directive #3), established the color-coded warning system used to advise the public of terrorist threat levels.

President Obama

Like President Bush, President Obama has also addressed issues surrounding homeland security. His executive orders relating to homeland security are listed in **TABLE 12.2**.

President Trump

Since becoming the president in 2017, much of President Trump's policies for homeland security revolve around illegal immigration. In his first 2 years in office, he has issued numerous Executive Orders regarding the need to limit the entry of certain people into the United States, especially terrorists or others who seek to harm residents. One of his first acts as president was to issue Executive Order 13767, which

TABLE 12.2 President Obama's Executive Orders Relating to Homeland Security

Executive Order	Description
Executive Order 13491	Ensuring Lawful Interrogations—January 22, 2009: Revoked an earlier Executive Order (13440) from the Bush Administration. Specifies that detainees should be treated humanely and not subjected to violence or torture.
Executive Order 13492	Review and disposition of individuals detained at the Guantanamo Bay Naval Base and closure of detention facilities—January 22, 2009.
Executive Order 13493	Review of Detention Policy Options—January 22, 2009: Created a Special Interagency Task Force on detainee disposition to identify options for detaining individuals captured or detained in connection with counterterrorism operations.
Executive Order 13526	Classified National Security Information—December 29, 2009: Defines what information may be considered "classified" and under what circumstances.
Executive Order 13527	Establishing Federal Capability for the Timely Provision of Medical Countermeasures Following a Biological Attack—December 30, 2009: Made it a policy to plan and prepare for provision of medical countermeasures in the event of a biological attack.
Executive Order 13539	President's Council of Advisors on Science and Technology—April 21, 2010: Created the President's Council of Advisors on Science and Technology to, among other things, advise the president on policy concerning national and homeland security.
Executive Order 13456	Optimizing the Security of Biological Select Agents and Toxins in the United States—July 2, 2010: To ensure that biological agents shall be secured in a manner appropriate to minimize the risk of misuse, theft, loss, and accidental release.
Executive Order 13549	Classified National Security Information Program for State, Local, Tribal, and Private Sector Entities—August 18, 2010: Created a Classified National Security Information program to safeguard and govern access to classified national security information shared by the federal government with state, local, tribal, and private sector entities.
Executive Order 13553	Blocking Property of Certain Persons with Respect to Serious Human Rights Abuses by the Government of Iran and Taking Certain Other Actions—September 28, 2010: Prevented property in the United States from being transferred to an official of Iran's government, or a person who ordered or directed the commission of serious human rights abuses against people in Iran.

Executive Order 13558	Export Enforcement Coordination Center—November 9, 2010: Ordered the creation of an interagency Federal Export Enforcement Coordination Center that would share information about detection, prevention, disruption, investigation, and prosecution of activities that may threaten national security.
Executive Order 13567	Periodic Review of Individuals Detained at Guantanamo Bay Naval Station Pursuant to the Authorization for Use of Military Force—March 7, 2010: Ordered a review of certain detainees being held at the Guantanamo Bay facility.
Executive Order 13584	Developing an Integrated Strategic Counterterrorism Communications Initiative and Establishing a Temporary Organization to Support Certain Government-Wide Communications Activities Directed Abroad—September 9, 2011: To reinforce communications efforts about counterterrorism efforts directed to audiences outside of the United States and targeted against violent and terrorist organizations.
Executive Order 13587	Structural Reforms to Improve the Security of Classified Networks and the Responsible Sharing and Safeguarding of Classified Information—October 7, 2011: Ordered reforms to ensure that sharing of information on computer networks is protected for privacy and civil liberties.
Executive Order 13597	Establishing a Visa and Foreign Visitor Processing Goals and the Task Force on Travel and Competitiveness—January 19, 2012: Ordered the Department of Homeland Security to maintain a process for coordinating and implementing proposals to enhance and expedite travel to, and arrival into, the United States by foreign nationals.

was geared toward improving immigration policies and building a physical wall on the Southern border between the United States and Mexico. He also sought new policies that would permit U.S. officials to deport illegal aliens more quickly than in the past. A portion of this Executive Order is presented in **TABLE 12.3**.

A few days later, in Executive Order 13768 (Enhancing Public Safety in the Interior of the United States (January 25, 2017), President Trump again focused on removing illegal aliens from the country swiftly. He not only asked all agencies to use any lawful methods to do this but also proclaimed that any state, local, or tribal agency that did not make efforts to remove illegal immigrants would not receive any funds from the federal government. Trump also included a provision to provide support to any victims of crimes that were carried out by illegal aliens while in the country. Certain immigrants were prioritized for removal, including those who had committed a criminal offense or had been charged with one, or who pose a risk to national security. To be able to carry this out, Trump sought to hire additional border patrol agents. A section of this executive order is presented in **TABLE 12.4**.

TABLE 12.3 Executive Order 13767: Border Security and Immigration Enforcement Improvements (January 25, 2017)

Executive Order	Description
Executive Order 13767	"It is the policy of the executive branch to (a) secure the southern border of the United States through the immediate construction of a physical wall on the southern border, monitored and supported by adequate personnel as to prevent illegal immigration, drug and human trafficking and acts of terrorism; (b) detain individuals apprehended on suspicion of violating Federal or State law, including Federal immigration law, pending further proceedings regarding these violations; (c) expedite determinations of apprehended individuals' claims of eligibility to remain in the United States; (d) remove promptly those individuals whose legal claims to remain in the United States have been lawfully rejected, after any appropriate civil or criminal sanctions have been imposed; and (e) cooperate fully with States and local law enforcement in enacting Federal-State partnerships to enforce Federal immigration priorities, as well as State monitoring and detention programs that are consistent with Federal law and do not undermine Federal immigration priorities."

Source: Trump, Donald J. Executive Order 13767—Border Security and Immigration Enforcement Improvements Online by Gerhard Peters and Woolley, John T. The American Presidency Project. Retrieved from https://www.presidency.ucsb.edu/node/322155

TABLE 12.4 Executive Order 13768, Enhancing Public Safety in the Interior of the United States (January 25, 2017)

Executive Order	Description
Executive Order 13768	***Sec. 2. Policy.*** It is the policy of the executive branch to: (a) Ensure the faithful execution of the immigration laws of the United States, including the INA, against all removable aliens, consistent with Article II, Section 3 of the United States Constitution and section 3331 of title 5, United States Code; (b) Make use of all available systems and resources to ensure the efficient and faithful execution of the immigration laws of the United States; (c) Ensure that jurisdictions that fail to comply with applicable Federal law do not receive Federal funds, except as mandated by law; (d) Ensure that aliens ordered removed from the United States are promptly removed; and (e) Support victims, and the families of victims, of crimes committed by removable aliens. ***Sec. 5. Enforcement Priorities.*** In executing faithfully the immigration laws of the United States, the Secretary of Homeland Security shall prioritize for removal those aliens described by the Congress . . . as well as removable aliens who: (a) Have been convicted of any criminal offense; (b) Have been charged with any criminal offense, where such charge has not been resolved; (c) Have committed acts that constitute a chargeable criminal offense; (d) Have engaged in fraud or willful misrepresentation in connection with any official matter or application before a governmental agency; (e) Have abused any program related to receipt of public benefits; (f) Are subject to a final order of removal, but who have not complied with their legal obligation to depart the United States; or (g) In the judgment of an immigration officer, otherwise pose a risk to public safety or national security.

Source: Trump, Donald J. Executive Order 13768—Enhancing Public Safety in the Interior of the United States Online by Gerhard Peters and Woolley, John T. The American Presidency Project. Retrieved from https://www.presidency.ucsb.edu/node/322157

Two days after that, President Trump issued a third executive order, but this time, focusing particularly on preventing terrorists from entering the country. In Executive Order 13768, he sought to suspend issuing visas to people from selected countries. Trump sought more limits on immigration in Executive Order 13769, as shown in **TABLE 12.5**.

A similar executive order was issued in March, 2017, called Protecting the Nation From Foreign Terrorist Entry Into the United States (#13780). Here, the president claimed that it would be detrimental to the safety of the United States to allow unrestricted entry of people from the countries of Iran, Libya, Somalia, Sudan, Syria, and Yemen. He suspended entry of people from these countries. The list of countries could expand on the advice of the Secretary of Homeland Security. A portion of this executive order is shown in **TABLE 12.6**.

In addition to limiting immigration, President Trump also sought to strengthen the country's cybersecurity. In Executive Order 13800, he ordered federal agencies to implement risk management procedures that were geared toward limiting unauthorized access, use, disruption, or destruction of information stored on the Internet. Each agency was

TABLE 12.5 Executive Order 13769: Protecting the Nation From Foreign Terrorist Entry into the United States (Jan 27, 2017)

Executive Disorder	Description
Executive Order 13769	***Sec. 2. Policy.*** It is the policy of the United States to protect its citizens from foreign nationals who intend to commit terrorist attacks in the United States; and to prevent the admission of foreign nationals who intend to exploit United States immigration laws for malevolent purposes.

Source: Trump, Donald J. Executive Order 13769—Protecting the Nation From Foreign Terrorist Entry Into the United States Online by Gerhard Peters and Woolley, John T. The American Presidency Project. Retrieved from https://www.presidency.ucsb.edu/node/322204

TABLE 12.6 Executive Order 13780—Protecting the Nation From Foreign Terrorist Entry Into the United States March 6, 2017

Executive Order	Description
Executive Order 13780	**Sec. 2.** *Temporary Suspension of Entry for Nationals of Countries of Particular Concern During Review Period*... to ensure the proper review and maximum utilization of available resources for the screening and vetting of foreign nationals, to ensure that adequate standards are established to prevent infiltration by foreign terrorists, and in light of the national security concerns referenced in section 1 of this order, I hereby proclaim... that the unrestricted entry into the United States of nationals of Iran, Libya, Somalia, Sudan, Syria, and Yemen would be detrimental to the interests of the United States. I, therefore, direct that the entry into the United States of nationals of those six countries be suspended for 90 days from the effective date of this order, subject to the limitations, waivers, and exceptions set forth in sections 3 and 12 of this order. (f) At any point after the submission of the list described in subsection (e) of this section, the Secretary of Homeland Security, in consultation with the Secretary of State and the Attorney General, may submit to the President the names of any additional countries recommended for similar treatment, as well as the names of any countries that they recommend should be removed from the scope of a proclamation described in subsection (e) of this section.

Source: Trump, Donald J. Executive Order 13780—Protecting the Nation From Foreign Terrorist Entry Into the United States Online by Gerhard Peters and Woolley, John T. The American Presidency Project. Retrieved from https://www.presidency.ucsb.edu/node/326308

asked to file a report with DHS that reviewed potential risks but also methods to mitigate those risks. There must also be a regular process for reassessing the risk and developing new plans to address them. Additionally, the critical infrastructure that has the highest risk of attack and that, if attacked, would result in catastrophic effects to the public, would receive additional federal support.

Another key part of this Executive Order focused on the nation's cybersecurity. The president sought to have a viable Internet for the future so he ordered federal agencies to design strategic options for deterring cybercrimes. He also sought to increase international cooperation and education on cybersecurity. Portions of this Executive Order are shown in **TABLE 12.7**.

Congressional Action

Congress has passed many new laws related to terrorism since September of 2011. The most recognized was titled the Uniting and Strengthening America by Providing Appropriate Tools Required to Intercept and Obstruct Terrorism, more commonly known as the **USA PATRIOT Act.**

Immediately following the terrorist attacks of 9-11, President Bush and Attorney General John Ashcroft asked Congress for new laws that would increase the ability of law enforcement to gather intelligence related to terrorism. They requested that Congress pass a bill that gave law enforcement the ability to use roving wiretaps, nationwide search warrants, wider electronic access, Internet disclosure, immigrant detention, consolidated appeals, foreign wiretap evidence, define the term "terrorist," and tougher penalties for convicted terrorists.[7] The proposed bill that emerged was the USA PATRIOT Act. The intent of the PATRIOT Act was to grant law enforcement officials more authority to investigate and prosecute those who were responsible for the terrorist attacks on America and to protect the country from future attacks.

At first, both Republican and Democratic members of Congress were hesitant to support the bill because of concerns related to privacy and civil liberties. They were apprehensive about proposals allowing government officials to track emails and other electronic communications, and if law enforcement should be permitted to "watch over the shoulders" of computer users. They claimed that some provisions were too vague and sweeping, and, therefore, could be abused by law enforcement.

But other members supported the proposal. The FBI and other law enforcement groups argued it was necessary for them to have more advanced technology to help infiltrate terrorist cells and prevent future attacks.[8] The Bush administration pushed hard for their proposal, and eventually, both the House and Senate agreed to the bill.[9] President Bush signed the antiterrorism legislation into law (HR 3162 / PL 107-56) on October 26, 2001.

The final bill contained 10 titles and over 1,000 sections. It addressed issues such as intelligence, investigations, controlled substances, and financial transactions (see **TABLE 12.8**). It contained much of

TABLE 12.7 Executive Order 13800—Strengthening the Cybersecurity of Federal Networks and Critical Infrastructure (May 11, 2017)

Executive Order	Description
Executive Order 13800	***Sec. 1. Cybersecurity of Federal Networks.*** (c) *Risk Management:* (i) Agency heads will be held accountable by the president for implementing risk management measures commensurate with the risk and magnitude of the harm that would result from unauthorized access, use, disclosure, disruption, modification, or destruction of IT and data. ***Sec. 2. Cybersecurity of Critical Infrastructure.*** (b) *Support to Critical Infrastructure at Greatest Risk.* The Secretary of Homeland Security, in coordination with the Secretary of Defense, the Attorney General, the Director of National Intelligence, the Director of the Federal Bureau of Investigation, the heads of appropriate sector-specific agencies . . . shall: (i) identify authorities and capabilities that agencies could employ to support the cybersecurity efforts of critical infrastructure entities identified . . . to be at greatest risk of attacks that could reasonably result in catastrophic regional or national effects on public health or safety, economic security, or national security (section 9 entities); (ii) engage section 9 entities and solicit input as appropriate to evaluate whether and how the authorities and capabilities . . . might be employed to support cybersecurity risk management efforts and any obstacles to doing so; ***Sec. 3. Cybersecurity for the Nation.*** (a) *Policy.* To ensure that the Internet remains valuable for future generations, it is the policy of the executive branch to promote an open, interoperable, reliable, and secure Internet that fosters efficiency, innovation, communication, and economic prosperity, while respecting privacy and guarding against disruption, fraud, and theft. Further, the United States seeks to support the growth and sustainment of a workforce that is skilled in cybersecurity and related fields as the foundation for achieving our objectives in cyberspace. (b) *Deterrence and Protection.* Within 90 days of the date of this order, the Secretary of State, the Secretary of the Treasury, the Secretary of Defense, the Attorney General, the Secretary of Commerce, the Secretary of **Homeland Security**, and the United States Trade Representative, in coordination with the Director of National Intelligence, shall jointly submit a report to the President, through the Assistant to the President for National Security Affairs and the Assistant to the President for Homeland Security and Counterterrorism, on the Nation's strategic options for deterring adversaries and better protecting the American people from cyber threats.

Source: Trump, Donald J. May 11, 2017. "Executive Order 13800—Strengthening the Cybersecurity of Federal Networks and Critical Infrastructure". The American Presidency Project. Retrieved from https://www.presidency.ucsb.edu/documents/executive-order-13800-strengthening-the-cybersecurity-federal-networks-and-critical

TABLE 12.8 Intelligence Law Provisions

Focal Area	What the Law Changed
Director of National Intelligence	Created a Director of National Intelligence (DNI) to be the head of the U.S. intelligence community who would serve as the principal adviser to the president, the National Security Council, and the Homeland Security Council.
Information Sharing	The DNI would establish a system to share information among agencies, which included purchasing necessary technology to allow for easy communication.
Improving Analysis and Coordination	Created the National Intelligence Council and the National Counterterrorism Center as part of the DNI Office to analyze intelligence on international terrorism and counterterrorism. Also created the National Counter-Proliferation Center to analyze intelligence on the proliferation of weapons of mass destruction.

Civil Liberties	Established the Civil Liberties Protection Office to ensure that the civil liberties of U.S. citizens were protected.
Other Intelligence Changes	The DNI would develop educational materials and linguistic training for the intelligence community to improve their ability to gather information on terrorists and interpret intercepted communications. The law required the DNI to ensure that the intelligence community would monitor unclassified information on national security threats, establish a National Intelligence Reserve Corps composed of former intelligence employees who could be called to work during a national emergency; and mandated the CIA to develop a more effective foreign language program and to hire agents with more diverse backgrounds, including Arab or Middle-Eastern.
Transportation Security	The Secretary of DHS would create a national strategy to improve transportation security and create a recovery plan in the case of an attack. The Secretary would also begin biometric screening systems at airports that would include methods such as retinal or iris scanning, fingerprints, or face recognition. The TSA would test a "no fly" list. Employees of airports, airlines, and security services would also have to undergo screening. The TSA was required to create a plan for screening all passengers and their luggage for explosives. The TSA would have to make it easier for air marshals to protect their anonymity. New screening of passengers and crew members on cruise ships would be created.
Border Security and Immigration	DHS would add 2,000 border patrol agents every year from 2006 to 2010 and 800 new immigration investigators; it would provide 40,000 new beds in detention facilities to house illegal aliens; it was authorized to use unmanned planes and other technologies to patrol the border; expanded the number of U.S. immigration officers in foreign airports; created a new visa and passport security program; created a Human Smuggling and Trafficking Center; barred any foreign national from entering the U.S. who had committed torture or other atrocities abroad.
Terrorism Prevention	The law amended the Foreign Intelligence Surveillance Act (FISA) to allow the FBI to conduct surveillance on a single terrorist, otherwise known as a "lone wolf"; terrorist suspects would be denied bail and held in jail until trial, unless they could prove they were not flight risks or a danger to society; made it a crime to provide support (money, lodging, advice, training) to anyone involved in a potential terrorist act; made it a crime to use the mail to carry out an attack with a weapon of mass destruction; expanded criminal penalties for production, possession, and use of radiological explosive devices, or "dirty bombs."
Financial Provisions	Authorized $35.5 million to support the Financial Crimes Enforcement Network to fund a program designed to analyze data from financial institutions; required the Treasury Department to create a national strategy for combating money laundering; authorized the Bureau of Engraving and Printing to print foreign currency and other sensitive documents of foreign governments as a way to test anti-counterfeiting measures.
Foreign Policy Provisions	Declared that the United States should help Pakistan control its territorial borders and waived restrictions on foreign assistance to Pakistan through fiscal 2006; authorized funds for assisting Afghanistan in fiscal 2005 and 2006; reiterated U.S. support of the U.N. Human Rights Commission; declared that the United States would work toward creating a "Middle East Free Trade Area."
Homeland Security	Authorized mutual aid between local governments and regional authorities in the Washington area that could be used by regional or local authorities to share emergency services or resources in responding to a terrorist attack, which included provisions aimed at improving emergency communications systems; called for a greater emphasis on providing grants to high-threat areas while guaranteeing a minimum to all states; authorized a study to determine if DHS could develop a homeland security warning system to disseminate information; expanded the duties of the counter-narcotics office to allow the director to serve on the Joint Terrorism Task Force; created an Office of Geospatial Management in DHS to coordinate mapping, satellite analysis, and other geographic technologies.

Data from: "Details of the Intelligence Overhaul Law." In *CQ Almanac 2004*, 60th ed., 11-9-11-13. Washington, DC: Congressional Quarterly, 2005. Retrieved from http://library.cqpress.com/cqalmanac/cqal04-836-24353-1084612

what Attorney General Ashcroft and President Bush requested, including authority for the government to obtain nationwide search warrants and roving wiretaps to conduct secret searches of suspects' property, and to detain immigrants indefinitely if they were viewed as national security threats. It also strengthened money-laundering laws and removed the statute of limitations on some terrorism crimes. It modified or amended over a dozen existing federal statutes and greatly expanded the powers of the executive branch of government and law enforcement officials. Some of the most controversial provisions (i.e., wiretaps) were set to expire on December 31, 2005.

In 2003, only 18 months after the PATRIOT Act was passed, the President and some members of Congress sought to give law enforcement more tools for investigating suspected terrorists. However, some members preferred to take back some provisions of the original law that they believed could infringe on civil liberties. Because of the controversy, Congress could not agree to revise the act. But they did expand the FBI's ability to access financial records when investigating suspected terrorists with another new bill (under a law reauthorizing intelligence programs for fiscal 2004).[10]

Many of the controversial provisions in the original PATRIOT Act were to be phased out in December of 2005. At that time, President Bush and the Republicans in Congress sought to make the surveillance provisions of the original law permanent and give law enforcement additional powers. But other members of Congress sought increased protections for civil liberties as well as establishment of additional time limits on some of the more contentious parts of the act. Congress compromised by supporting a bill (HR 3199 / PL 109-177) that gave the FBI power to seek "roving wiretaps" and get access to business records. The bill also included a 4-year extension of a provision in the intelligence law (PL 108-458) that allowed law enforcement to seek warrants against "lone-wolf" terrorists who were acting alone and not associated with a foreign power.[11]

Courtesy of Barry Bahler/DHS.

The law made 14 provisions of the original PATRIOT Act permanent. The law:

- Allowed law enforcement to use wiretaps and other surveillance techniques to investigate suspected acts of terrorism such as computer fraud
- Allowed law enforcement to share information on matters of national security
- Made it easier to issue orders for *pen register* and *trap-and-trace devices* that could be used to track telephone calls and Internet communications
- Extended the length of time for the use of wiretaps and search warrants from 90 days to 120 days, with possible extensions of up to 1 year
- Allowed officials to use search warrants to get access to voice mail
- Permitted Internet providers to disclose customer records to law enforcement in emergency situations
- Allowed law enforcement to intercept electronic communications if the owner of a computer system believed someone was hacking into his system from the outside
- Allowed federal judges with jurisdiction over a particular investigation to issue search warrants for electronic evidence stored anywhere in the country
- Provided for civil suits against unlawful disclosure of information obtained through the law's wiretapping authority, while giving immunity to those who assist in the carrying out of investigations under the law

The new law also added some additional safeguards to the legislation, including provisions to:

- Require the FBI director or deputy to sign off on applications for court orders for library, bookstore, firearm sales, tax return, and educational and medical records
- Allow those ordered to turn over business records, credit reports, or telephone records under a National Security Letter (a letter from a U.S. government agency that demands information without a search warrant because it is related to national security) to contact an attorney and challenge the order in court
- Require the government to notify the subject of a "sneak and peek" search (conducted secretly without notifying the subject of the search) within 30 days, with a possible extension

- Require that investigators seeking a roving wiretap order identify the specific target or evidence they seek, and that they notify the court within 10 days after beginning surveillance of any new phone[12]

In 2009, the USA PATRIOT Act was scheduled for reauthorization again. This time, Congress extended the three expiring sections of the PATRIOT Act. The first of the three provisions, for "business records," gave the FBI the authority to get a court order for "any tangible thing," such as a list of books someone was reading, or even blood or DNA. This could have happened when officials claimed that they would need such evidence as part of an investigation. The second provision, for "roving wiretaps," provided investigators with the authority to obtain court orders to track terrorism suspects who used various types of communication methods such as multiple telephones, cellular phones, or Internet connections. The third was the "lone wolf" provision, which allowed investigators to seek warrants from the Foreign Intelligence Surveillance Court to spy on suspected terrorists who were not connected with a foreign power or other recognized organization.[13]

President Obama supported the reauthorization with as few changes as possible. The American Civil Liberties Union and some members of Congress argued that the laws gave the FBI powers that directly contravened the Fourth Amendment's protections against unreasonable search and seizure.[14]

In 2011, the USA PATRIOT Act faced renewal again. In S 990 (PL 112-14), the PATRIOT Sunsets Extension Act of 2011, the original law was once again extended, this time until 2015. Provisions concerning roving electronic surveillance orders and requests for business records and other tangible things were extended. The "lone wolf" provision was extended until June 1, 2015.

The USA PATRIOT Act expired on June 1, 2015. The next day, members of Congress passed the USA Freedom Act that included many of the same provisions of the original act and renewed them until 2019. One change with the new law was a limit placed on the ability of the National Security Agency to gather mass data from phone companies. In the new law, the phone companies will keep track of the information and provide it to the agency on a case-by-case basis, and only with the approval of the FISA court.

107th Congress (2001–02)

In addition to the PATRIOT Act, Congress passed other terrorist-related bills in the 107th Congress. One law was the Aviation Security Act (S 1447 / HR 2951 / PL 107-71). This act created the TSA and defined its responsibilities. Additionally, the new law made passenger screening at airports a responsibility of the federal government; prior to this, passenger security was the responsibility of the airlines.

After the anthrax attacks on members of Congress, a proposal was made that would direct the Secretary of Health and Human Services to further develop and implement a coordinated and comprehensive strategy to prepare and respond to a possible bioterrorism attack or other public health emergency. This was called the Public Health Security and Bioterrorism Preparedness and Response Act of 2002 (HR 3448 / PL 107-188). The act called for close coordination with the states. Moreover, Congress passed an appropriations bill that provided $2.5 billion for the purchase of vaccines and antibiotics to be used during a bioterrorism attack.[15]

The Enhanced Border Security and Visa Entry Reform Act (HR 3525 / PL 107-173) was a bill to increase the number of Immigration and Naturalization Service (INS) investigators and inspectors by 200 full-time employees above the number authorized by the PATRIOT Act. It also directed U.S. law enforcement groups to share alien admissibility- and deportation-related information with the INS.

Two bills dealt with ports and port security during this session. One of those was S 1214 (PL 107-777), the Maritime Transportation Security Act of 2002. This bill directed the Secretary of Transportation to identify those vessel types and U.S. port facilities that pose a high risk of being involved in a transportation security incident. The Secretary would then need to prepare a national Maritime Transportation Security Plan for deterring and responding to a possible security incident at U.S. ports.

The second bill that dealt with port security was S 1215 (PL 107-295), which was passed to increase security at U.S. ports. For the first time, a comprehensive antiterrorism plan would be developed for the nation's 361 commercial seaports. It also expanded the role played by the Coast Guard in port security following any attacks (see **BOX 12.1**).

The Terrorism Risk Insurance Act (TRIA) of 2002 (PL 107-297) was intended to help stabilize the commercial property and casualty insurance markets after the attacks in September of 2001. In the time after the attacks, the insurance industry was in disorder because of the extreme number of claims made by those who lost loved ones, were injured, or who suffered property damage. Insurers claimed that they would no longer offer terrorism insurance unless the federal government agreed to share the risk. Without terrorism

BOX 12.1 Provisions of the Port Security Act

- Required the Coast Guard to conduct assessments of U.S. ports, vessels, and other facilities such as nuclear power plants or chemical facilities that could be vulnerable to terrorist attack. These reports will be used to develop local and national security plans, as well as customized plans for specific facilities and vessels identified as vulnerable.
- Created local security advisory committees at every port to coordinate planning between law enforcement, intelligence agencies, the Customs Service, Coast Guard, immigration, port authorities, shipping companies, and port workers.
- Directed the Coast Guard to establish teams that could be deployed quickly in the event of a terrorist threat or criminal action.
- Authorized, armed Coast Guard personnel to act as "sea marshals" to board incoming vessels to prevent or respond to acts of terrorism.
- Created a new grant program to assist ports in upgrading port security.
- Authorized $15 million a year for research and development of technologies to assist the Customs Service in targeting suspicious cargo and detecting explosives, chemical and biological agents, and nuclear materials.
- Asked the Transportation Department to develop and issue a new national transportation security card that would allow eligible port workers, merchant mariners, and truck drivers to work in "secure" areas of ports and other transportation facilities.
- Required the Coast Guard to assess security measures at foreign ports and authorized them to stop vessels from entering U.S. ports if they came from a foreign port that failed to meet security standards.
- Required the Transportation Department to develop and maintain an antiterrorism cargo identification, tracking, and screening system for containerized cargo shipped through U.S. ports. It also required the department to develop standards for container seals and locks as well as a system to detect tampering.
- Required the Transportation Department to establish a program to collect and analyze information concerning any vessel operating in U.S. waters.

Reproduced from: "Law Calls for Tighter Port Security" In *CQ Almanac 2002*, 58th ed., 19-5-19-7. Washington, DC: *Congressional Quarterly*, 2003. http://library.cqpress.com/cqalmanac/cqal02-236-10372-664261

insurance coverage, mortgages for big projects would have been too costly for builders. Congress agreed to provide help to the industry and passed legislation that mandated that insurers must provide coverage against terrorist acts but made the federal government responsible for 90% of claims above $15 billion. The government's responsibility topped out at $100 billion.[16] The law provided for a 3-year program that would give private insurance companies a transition period in which they could develop pricing and risk models.

President Bush supported the legislation, saying, "The Terrorism Risk Insurance Act will provide coverage for catastrophic losses from potential terrorist attacks. Should terrorists strike America again, we have a system in place to address financial losses and get our economy back on its feet as quickly as possible. With this new law, builders and investors can begin construction in real estate projects that have been stalled for too long and get our hardhats back to work."[17]

108th Congress (2003–04)

After the 9/11 Commission reported on the failure of U.S. intelligence to detect and deter the terrorist attacks, it was clear that the government needed to improve the cooperation between intelligence agencies so that intelligence would be more effectively shared. Congress sent President Bush a bill to overhaul and reorganize the U.S. intelligence community. The new law (PL 108-458) created the position of Director of National Intelligence (DNI) who would serve as head of the U.S. intelligence community, as well as the principal adviser to the president, the National Security Council, and the Homeland Security Council. The director would be appointed by the president and require confirmation by the Senate. The director would ensure that all federal agencies, the Joint Chiefs, and relevant committees of Congress had access to all necessary information. The DNI would have access to all national intelligence that had been acquired by any federal department. The bill also authorized additional Border Patrol agents, created uniform security clearance procedures, and included provisions related to transportation security and efforts to combat money laundering and terrorist financing.

In addition to changes in the intelligence agencies, Congress also passed the Identity Theft Penalty Enhancement Act (HR 1731 / PL 108-275) that established new penalties for stealing someone's identity. It also altered the existing identity theft prohibition to include acts of domestic terrorism.

Another effort by Congress in this session was Project Bioshield (S 15 / PL 108-276). This refers to the Bush administration's initiative to permit the government to develop and stockpile vaccines and medications to be used in the case of a bioterrorism attack. The bill authorized the Secretary of Health and Human Services to conduct research regarding countermeasures such as a drug; biological product; or other device that could be used to treat, identify, or prevent harm from any biological, chemical, radiological, or nuclear weapon.[18]

The Terrorism Insurance bill passed in the earlier session (PL 107-297) was set to expire in 2005. Insurers and the real estate industry won a 2-year extension through December 31, 2007 (PL 109-144), which also raised the insurers' threshold to $50 million in 2006 and $100 million in 2007.[19]

109th Congress (2005–06)

In the 109th Congress, the members worked on changes to immigration and illegal entry of aliens and terrorists. One bill that they passed was the Secure Fence Act (HR 6061 / PL 109-367). This new law directed the Secretary of DHS to take actions to achieve more effective border surveillance through better use of personnel and technology, including physical infrastructure enhancements as a way to prevent unlawful border entry. The bill also facilitated border protection by U.S. Customs and Border Protection by adding additional checkpoints.

In another bill (HR 5441 / PL 109-295), Congress passed a $34.8 billion fiscal spending bill that included $1.8 billion in funds for border security. Most of the emergency funding—$1.2 billion—was intended for the construction of fencing along the U.S.–Mexico border. This was described as a physical and "virtual" barrier, using sensors and cameras in remote areas.

The Secretary of Energy was instructed to increase the safety and security of nuclear facilities from deliberate attacks in the Energy Policy Act (HR 6 / PL 109-190). In this new law, Congress mandated the Secretary to analyze the security of existing nuclear power plants and to consider the viability of a private security force for defending nuclear plants from possible threats. Another provision in this bill established the Task Force on Radiation Source Protection and Security that would evaluate the security of radiation sources from potential terrorist threats. It would also require that anyone given unescorted access to facilities must have a criminal history and fingerprint check.

The Coast Guard and Maritime Transportation Act (HR 889 / PL 109-204) authorized the Secretary of Transportation, during an act of terrorism, to order the Coast Guard Ready Reserve members to active duty. The Act also directed the Coast Guard Commandant to report on the potential costs and effectiveness of developing technology that could identify inbound vessels and their cargo for any possible threats to national security before they reach U.S. ports.

Congress passed a bill aimed at security in U.S. ports, and President Bush signed it on October 13 (HR 4954 / PL 109-347). In it, Congress authorized over $2 billion over 5 years for port and container security programs. It required the 22 largest U.S. ports to scan all incoming containers for radiation, established protocols to resume trade in the event of a catastrophic incident that suspended trade, and offered new benefits for trusted shipping companies. The effectiveness of each port's security plans would be verified at least twice a year including at least one unannounced inspection. Other provisions established a network of Interagency Operational Centers at appropriate seaports and created a program to train port security officers, law enforcement, and the private sector to prepare for and respond to port security incidents.[20]

110th Congress (2007–08)

During the 110th Congress, the members passed the Court Security Improvement Act of 2007 (HR 660 / PL 110-177). The law required the U.S. Marshals Service to consult with the Judicial Conference regarding security requirements for the courts. It also provided additional funds to hire new deputy U.S. Marshals to provide security for the courts, and prohibited possession of dangerous weapons in federal courts.

The Terrorism Risk Insurance Program Reauthorization Act of 2007 (HR 2761 / PL 110-160) passed Congress in this session. The law reauthorized the Terrorism Risk Insurance Act for 7 years. It redefined an act of terrorism to eliminate the requirement that the individual or individuals committing a terrorist act be acting on behalf of any foreign person or foreign interest. The new program required insurance firms that sold commercial property and casualty insurance to offer clients insurance coverage for damages caused by foreign terrorist attacks. The government would pay 90% of claims arising from a terrorist attack once insurers' aggregate losses exceeded a certain threshold, beginning at $15 billion and rising annually after that. The government's responsibility was capped at $100 billion per year. President Bush signed it into law on December 26, 2007.[21]

The safety of transportation was the focus of one bill during this session, called The Railroad Safety Enhancement Act of 2008 (HR 2095 / PL 110-432). The bill authorized appropriations for railroad safety by requiring the Federal Railroad Administration to make safety in railroad transportation the highest priority and to develop a long-term strategy for improving railroad safety.

Congress passed legislation (HR 556 / PL 110-49) to revise the process for reviewing foreign investments that might affect U.S. national security. The law made the Committee on Foreign Investment in the U.S. (CFIUS) permanent. The committee would review investments to determine if there were any national security implications of any transaction that might result in foreign control of a company engaged in interstate commerce. CFIUS was also required to complete an investigation if a review found that the transaction threatened to impair national security, if the transaction involved a company owned by a foreign government, or if it involved critical infrastructure and national security concerns. The committee would notify Congress on any investigation, as well as submit an annual report.[22]

After the 9/11 Commission released its report in 2004, Congress passed an overhaul of the U.S. intelligence community (PL 108-458). It created a new director of national intelligence to oversee intelligence agencies, authorized additional Border Patrol agents, created uniform security clearance procedures, and included provisions related to transportation security, efforts to combat money laundering, and terrorist financing. But this law did not include all of the commission's recommendations. During the 110th Session, Congress passed a bill (HR 1) that made the remaining recommendations law. The bill required that federal grants for first responders be distributed based on risk, expanded the scrutiny of cargo for nuclear devices, and created a new grant program to improve emergency communications among agencies.[23] President Bush signed the bill on August 5, 2007 (PL 110-53). More details of the bill are listed in **BOX 12.2**.

After Bush's policy of surveillance on Americans without a court order became public, there was public outcry for legislation to ban such activity. However, the administration submitted a proposal for a new law, arguing that it was necessary for the government to conduct counterterrorism-related electronic surveillance and have the right to spy without warrants on foreign-to-foreign communications that passed through the United States. In response, Congress passed a bill to loosen rules for electronic surveillance (S 1927 / PL 110-56).

111th Congress (2009–2010)

In the 111th Session, Congress passed a bill to permit the Commissioner of U.S. Customs and Border Protection to convert an employee serving overseas on a

BOX 12.2 Provisions of the Homeland Security Bill

Grant distribution: Changed the distribution of the homeland security grant programs by reducing the minimum amounts guaranteed for each state and requiring that the rest of the money be distributed on the basis of risk.

Intelligence budget: Required the government to disclose the total amount appropriated each year for intelligence programs.

Cargo screening: Required all U.S.-bound seaborne cargo containers loaded in foreign ports to be scanned.

Aviation security: Required that, within 3 years of enactment, all air cargo placed on passenger aircraft must be screened.

Surface transportation: Authorized $4 billion over 4 years for rail, transit, and bus security grant programs; also required the development of risk assessments and security plans, set training requirements for workers, and extended whistleblower protections to transit employees.

Emergency communications: Established a grant program to improve the interoperability of state and local emergency communications.

Civil liberties: The Privacy and Civil Liberties Oversight Board was made an independent agency in the executive branch.

Liability shield: Provided immunity from civil lawsuits in federal, state, and local courts for individuals who, in good faith, reported suspicious activities relating to passenger safety. Officials who responded to their warning also received immunity.

Visa waivers: Expanded the visa-waiver program, under which nationals of certain allied countries could enter the country for short periods without visas.

Nonproliferation: Repealed limits on the aid that could be given to former Soviet states for nuclear nonproliferation and anti-terrorism activities.

limited appointment to a permanent appointment if he or she proves successful in that capacity. The bill was called the U.S. Customs and Border Protection Agents Employment Act (HR 1517/ PL 111-252).

In the Pre-disaster Hazard Mitigation Act of 2010, Congress agreed to increase the amount of money guaranteed to each state under the pre-disaster hazard mitigation program (HR 1746 / PL 111-351). This would allow states to help prevent and prepare for possible terrorist attacks in their local jurisdictions.

Congress also agreed to expand the food safety activities of the Secretary of Health and Human Services. Under the new law, records related to food would be inspected more often, there would be improvements to guarantee the safety of imported food, and there would be more capacity to detect and respond to food safety problems. The name of this bill was the FDA Food Safety Modernization Act (HR 2751 / PL 111-353).

Another example of action taken by Congress to keep the public safe was HR 3360 / PL 111-207, titled the Cruise Vessel Security and Safety Act. In this law, minimum training standards were set and new certification required for passenger vessel security personnel and law enforcement officials focused on the prevention, detection, evidence preservation, and reporting of criminal activities in the international maritime environment.

112th Congress (2011–2012)

Multiple new laws were passed by Congress in the 112th session regarding homeland security. One of those was public law 112-205, passed in December of 2012, known as the Maime Zapata Border Enforcement Security Task Force A. When this bill was passed, it created BEST units that would increase cooperation among federal, state, local, tribal, and foreign law enforcement agencies to increase border security and homeland security. It also increased the dissemination of information among all of these agencies.

Public Law 112-77 was the Disaster Relief Appropriations Act. When Congress passed this law, it provided appropriation for the Disaster Relief Fund found in FEMA. The money would be used to help repair damage that resulted from major disasters.

113th Congress (2012–2013)

One bill pertaining to homeland security that became law during the 113th Congress was HR 2952 (PL 113-246), or the Cybersecurity Workforce Assessment Act. When this was passed, the secretary at DHS was required to conduct an assessment of the cybersecurity workforce within DHS (i.e., vacancies or training), and develop a strategy to address these needs. In the end, the goal was to increase the ability of DHS to protect the nation's cybersecurity and respond effectively if an attack should occur.

Another bill passed by Congress during this session was S 2519 (PL 113-282), called the National Cybersecurity Protection Act. This law created a National Cybersecurity and Communications Integration Center to oversee the protection of critical infrastructure and cybersecurity. The Center would share information with relevant stakeholders on risks, incidents, and analysis of attacks. They will also provide technical assistance and recommendations if needed.

PL 113-254 is another bill passed by Congress, which was referred to as the Protecting and Securing Chemical Facilities from Terrorist Attacks of 2014. This law re-established the Chemical Facility Anti-Terrorism Standards program, and authorized it for 4 years. All chemical facilities were required to submit information regarding their security risk and measures that they were taking to protect the facility from an attack. DHS would be authorized to approve the plan or suggest alternatives, if needed.

Before the end of the session, Congress approved S 1353 (PL 113-274), or the Cybersecurity Enhancement Act. This law required the development of new standards and procedures to reduce cyber risks to the country's critical infrastructure. The standards would be the result of input from experts, owners, operators, industry, and other relevant stakeholders. The standards would identify, assess, and manage potential risks and then develop ways to mitigate impacts on businesses and individuals. In addition, the bill required the development of a federal strategic plan for increased cybersecurity.

114th Congress (2015–2016)

Members of the 114th Congress gave support to PL 114-29, the Department of Homeland Security Interoperable Communications Act. This law was a plan to achieve and maintain communications among the different agencies located within DHS. This includes information on daily communications, planned events, and emergencies.

Another example of a law passed by the 114th Congress was S 1915 (PL 114-268), or the First Responder anthrax Preparedness Act. The Congress sought a pilot program to provide anthrax vaccines to first responders who may find themselves exposed to anthrax if an attack should occur. Doses of the vaccine would be those that were housed at the strategic national stockpile, which are close to expiring.

As a result of PL 114-143, the Integrated Public Alert and Warning System Modernization Act, FEMA would be provided with funds to ensure that, under certain circumstances, all federal agencies, state, local, and tribal governments could alert citizens of natural disasters, acts of terrorism, or other man-made disasters.

115th Congress (2017–18)

During the 114th Congress, members passed HR 227 (PL 115-400), the Vehicular Terrorism Prevention Act that would help DHS assess the activities it undertakes to help first responders react to threats of vehicular terrorism.

Another bill, HR 7213, the Countering Weapons of Mass Destruction Act (PL 115-387) directed DHS to establish a new office called the Countering Weapons of Mass Destruction office. The office was tasked with coordinating a strategy to detect weapons and then protect people from importing, possessing, storing, transporting, developing, or using chemical, biological, radiological, or nuclear weapons.

A bill called Securing our Agriculture and Food Act (HR 1328/PL 115-43) mandated the DHS to coordinate efforts to defend the food, agriculture and veterinary systems in the U.S. against acts of terrorism.

Public Law 115-278 (HR 3359) was the Cybersecurity and Infrastructure Security Agency Act that renamed an agency within DHS from the National Protection and Programs Directorate to the Cybersecurity and Infrastructure Security Agency (CISA). This agency would be the primary agency responsible for defending the country's infrastructure against physical or cyberattacks. The agency would be composed of three divisions: Cybersecurity, Infrastructure Security, and Emergency Communications.

State Action

After the 9-11 terrorist attacks on New York and Washington, the federal government launched new agencies and policies to help the government prepare for, and respond to, future terrorist activities and natural disasters. State governments did the same. State officials realized that their agencies were most likely to be the first to respond to an emergency and, therefore, had to be prepared to manage the immediate response. In the time since the 9-11 attacks, every state has reviewed their existing emergency response plans and either developed new agencies and policies or updated and modified existing ones to prepare officials and citizens for what may lie ahead.

It is fundamental that cities prepare for emergencies because they are most at risk to be targeted in an attack. To date, terrorist attacks have been an urban phenomenon and they have been highly localized events. Local governments are likely to be the first on the scene of an emergency and, therefore, in charge of managing the essential services such as police, fire, medical, and other emergency service personnel.[24] Additionally, cities have the fiscal duty to pay for these services. This all means that they must be ready for all types of urgent situations.

Knowing this, state and local governments have developed and implemented their own security plans. They assigned police to protect any critical infrastructure that may be the target of an attack; bought new equipment; and trained their fire, police, and medical communities. However, Congress provided only limited funds for these activities, putting this burden primarily on the states. Many states find it difficult to fund such programs. To make matters worse, while Bush created the Homeland Security Council in the Executive Office, there were no representatives from state or local governments on it.[25] The lack of cooperation between the state and federal government when it came to homeland security quickly became readily apparent.

Consequently, it became evident that it was essential to establish a new approach to intergovernmental cooperation in homeland security and that existing gaps in the provision of services by federal, state, and local agencies had to be filled in a more coordinated fashion. The tasks related to emergency response now had to be interconnected between the federal, state, and local governments in order to provide a comprehensive response in a way that had not been done before. It was now essential that all states coordinate their activities with other agencies within the state, in other states, and the federal government. This required that changes be made in the way that governments were organized, how agencies communicated with others, and the funding structure.

Many changes were made and since then, there have been improvements to intergovernmental relations (IGR) surrounding homeland security activities. The federal government is now providing more grant money to states and allowing them to develop response plans, purchase equipment, and provide necessary training. In the PATRIOT Act, the Office of Domestic Preparedness was given the duty of overseeing grants to state and local governments that would help fund training for, and plan responses to, terrorist acts. Two of those grants were the State Homeland Security Grant Program (SHSGP) and the Urban Area Security Initiative (UASI).[26] In the beginning, there were problems in getting the money to the state and local governments, but issues were addressed and the funds found their way to the states.[27]

With the additional funds, states continue to develop new ways to respond to emergencies. The particular response plans developed by each state will vary, depending on the characteristics of the state. In Florida, for example, Governor Jeb Bush took only 1 month after the 9-11 attacks to prepare an Executive Order that created seven regional domestic security task forces that were placed under the Florida Department of Law Enforcement. It is now their responsibility to "coordinate responses to terrorist incidents, endure proper training for state and local personnel, and collect and disseminate terrorist intelligence."[28] The task forces are composed of police chiefs, health officials, state and local government officials, and executives from private agencies. The task forces answer to the State Emergency Response Team.[29]

Courtesy of Barry Bahler/DHS, Office of Public Affairs.

In New York, officials created the New York State Division of Homeland Security and Emergency Services in 2010. Composed of five offices, it is geared toward improving the state's response to a terrorist attack or natural disaster. They provide training and disseminate information as a way to improve readiness, response, and recovery capabilities of state officials, and provide assistance to federal grants. They also provide direct assistance to the public through weather, travel, fire, and safety alerts, as well as safety information. It also makes it easy for citizens to report suspected terrorist activities through their website.

Other states have developed various agency structures, a few of which are outlined in **BOX 12.3**.

BOX 12.3 Examples of State Homeland Security Agencies

New York State Division of Homeland Security and Emergency Services

The responsibilities for this agency were divided into four offices:

1. Office of Counter Terrorism (OCT): Created as part of a merger that resulted in the Division of Homeland Security and Emergency Services; OCT supports initiatives by federal, state, local, tribal, and private sector agencies to prevent, protect against, and prepare for acts of terrorism. While OCT is not a law enforcement agency itself, the agents work closely with law enforcement to help mitigate and respond to threats.
2. Office of Emergency Management: Coordinates activities of all states to respond to both natural and man-made disasters and emergencies to protect citizens and businesses. They also provide training and exercises to first responders so they are ready for an event.
3. Fire Prevention and Control: Has many responsibilities to keep people in the state safe. The agency's main goal is delivery of essential fire and life safety protection to all people who live in the state. They investigate fires; conduct inspections; and provide training to first responders and emergency responders. They also administer the Emergency Services Revolving Loan Program. The program provides additional funds to fire departments for needed firefighting equipment, rescue vehicles, or personal protective equipment.
4. Office of Interoperable and Emergency Communications: Responsible for the effective interoperable and emergency communications training in the case of an event.

(continues)

BOX 12.3 Examples of State Homeland Security Agencies *(Continued)*

Nebraska Emergency Management Agency

This office was given the task of "reducing the vulnerabilities of the people in Nebraska from the damage, injury, and loss of life and property resulting from natural, technological, or man-made disasters and emergencies." They have four units:

1. Preparedness: This includes planning, the continuity of government plan(s), grants, state emergency operations plan, NIMS, and citizen corps.
2. Operations: Includes the Governor's Emergency Fund to help local governments recover from a disaster and training and exercises to help officials prepare for an event.
3. Technical Hazards: Contains the Radiological Emergency Preparedness unit that prepares for a radiological emergency and the State Emergency Response Commission.
4. Recovery: Offices here include the state's Hazard Mitigation Program and information on response and recovery plans.

Maine Emergency Management Agency

In Maine, the Emergency Management Agency (MEMA) is tasked with homeland security and terrorism-related incidents and natural disasters. The agency is housed within the Department of Defense, Veterans and Emergency Management. The Commissioner of the Agency is also the Adjutant General of the Maine National Guard and the Governor's official Homeland Security Advisor. MEMA coordinates activities in the state such as training, equipment, and planning; provides technical assistance and grant funding to state and local agencies; and coordinates with the Maine Intelligence Analysis Center or the fusion center to provide information to interested parties. The Homeland Security Advisory Council, established in 2005, advises the governor on all matters related to homeland security. Additionally, it coordinates homeland security planning and citizen preparedness.

Chapter Summary

Since 9-11, the president and Congress have taken action to keep Americans safe. Both President Bush and President Obama have issued multiple executive orders and presidential directives that have impacted the U.S. policy toward terrorism and homeland security in some way. Members of Congress have also passed numerous pieces of legislation geared toward limiting terrorist acts and/or helping communities respond quickly to an emergency event. In the end, all of these political actions are responses to the 9-11 attack and are attempts to prevent another similar attack.

Review/Discussion Questions

1. What have President Bush and President Obama done in response to the threat of terrorism?
2. Since 9-11, what laws have been passed by Congress to deter terrorism or help the country respond to an emergency event such as terrorism or a natural disaster?
3. What are some elements of the USA PATRIOT Act?

Additional Readings

Kettle, D. F. (2007). *System Under Stress: Homeland Security and American Politics.* 2nd ed. Washington, D.C.: CQ Press.

Logan, G. & Ramsay, J. D. (2012). *Introduction to Homeland Security.* Boulder, CO: Westview.

Sylves, R. (2008). *Disaster Policy and Politics: Emergency Management and Homeland Security.* Washington, D.C.: CQ Press.

Endnotes

1. Afghan People by Century: 21st-Century Afghan People, Najibullah Zazi. Books LLC, 14th Oct 2010.
2. Austin, J. (2010). "'Patriot Act' Gets Short-Term Renewal." *CQ Almanac 2009*, 65th ed. Retrieved online at http://library.cqpress.com/xsite/document.php?id=cqal09-1183-595452251457&from=cqalmanac&type=query&num=Patriot+Act%E2%80%99+Gets+Short-Term+Renewal&
3. Christie, K. (2008). *America's War on Terrorism.* Lewiston, NY: Edwin Mellen Press, p. 109.
4. Bentley, E. (2012). "Homeland Security Law and Policy." In Logan, K. G. & Ramsay, J. D. *Introduction to Homeland Security.* Boulder, CO: Westview, pp. 19–45.
5. Chumar, M. (2012). "Public- and Private-Sector Partnerships in Homeland Security." In Logan, K. G. & Ramsay, J. D. *Introduction to Homeland Security.* Boulder, CO: Westview, pp. 47–68.
6. Chumar, M. (2012). "Public- and Private-Sector Partnerships in Homeland Security." In Logan, K. G. & Ramsay, J. D. *Introduction to Homeland Security.* Boulder, CO: Westview, pp. 47–68.
7. CQ Almanac. (2002). "Anti-Terror Bill Zooms Into Law." *CQ Almanac* 2001, 57th ed. Retrieved online at http://library.cqpress.com/
8. CQ Almanac. (2002). "Anti-Terror Bill Zooms Into Law." *CQ Almanac* 2001, 57th ed. Retrieved online at http://library.cqpress.com/
9. CQ Almanac. (2002). "Anti-Terror Bill Zooms Into Law." *CQ Almanac* 2001, 57th ed. Retrieved online at http://library.cqpress.com/
10. CQ Almanac. (2003). "Congress Re-Examines Patriot Act." *CQ Almanac* 2003, 59th ed. Retrieved online at http://library.cqpress.com/
11. CQ Almanac. (2006). "Disputes Delay Reauthorization of Anti-Terrorism Act Provisions." *CQ Almanac 2005*, 61st ed. Retrieved online at http://library.cqpress.com/
12. CQ Almanac. (2006). "Disputes Delay Reauthorization of Anti-Terrorism Act Provisions." *CQ Almanac 2005*, 61st ed. Retrieved online at http://library.cqpress.com/
13. CQ Almanac. (2010). "'Patriot Act' Gets Short-term Renewal." *CQ Almanac 2009*, 65th ed. Retrieved online at http://library.cqpress.com/xsite/search.php?source=cql&action=newsearch&product=all&products%5B%5D=&fulltext=Patriot+Act%E2%80%99+Gets+Short-term+Renewal&x=15&y=15
14. CQ Almanac. (2010). "'Patriot Act' Gets Short-term Renewal." *CQ Almanac 2009*, 65th ed. Retrieved online at http://library.cqpress.com/cqalmanac/cqal09-1183-59545-2251457
15. CQ Almanac. (2001). "Bio-Terrorism Bill Founders." *CQ Almanac 2001*, 57th ed. Retrieved online at http://library.cqpress.com/cqalmanac/cqal01-106-6374-328201
16. CQ Almanac. (2001). "Bio-Terrorism Bill Founders." *CQ Almanac 2001*, 57th ed. Retrieved online at http://library.cqpress.com/cqalmanac/cqal01-106-6374-328201
17. Bush, George W. (2002, November 26). Remarks on Signing the Terrorism Risk Insurance Act of 2002. The American Presidency Project https://www.presidency.ucsb.edu/node/215960
18. CQ Almanac. (2004). "Bioshield Funding Decision Delayed." *CQ Almanac 2003*, 59th ed. Retrieved online at http://library.cqpress.com/cqalmanac/cqal03-835-24327-1083669
19. CQ Almanac. (2005). "Terrorism Insurance Extension Dies." *CQ Almanac 2004*, 60th ed. Retrieved online at http://library.cqpress.com/cqalmanac/cqal04-836-24362-1085047
20. CQ Almanac. (2007). "Ports Debate Focuses on Screening." *CQ Almanac 2006*, 62nd ed. Retrieved online at http://library.cqpress.com/cqalmanac/cqal06-1421202
21. CQ Almanac. (2008). "TRIA Extension Backs Up Insurers." *CQ Almanac 2007*, 63rd ed. Retrieved online at http://library.cqpress.com/cqalmanac/cqal07-1006-44908-2047783
22. CQ Almanac. (2008). "Bipartisan CFIUS Overhaul Calls for Tighter Review of Foreign Investment." *CQ Almanac 2007*, 63rd ed. Retrieved online at http://library.cqpress.com/cqalmanac/cqal07-1006-44916-2048037
23. CQ Almanac. (2008). "Sept. 11 Recommendations Enacted, Making Good on Democrats' Pledge." *CQ Almanac 2007*, 63rd ed. Retrieved online at http://library.cqpress.com/cqalmanac/cqal07-1006-44905-2047715
24. Chenoweth, E. & Clarke, S. E. (2010). "All Terrorism is Local: Resources, Nested Institutions and Governance for Urban Homeland Security in the American Federal System." *Political Research Quarterly*, *64*, 495–507.
25. Krane, D. (2002). "The State of American Federalism, 2001–2002: Resilience in Response to Crisis." *Publius: The Journal of Federalism*, *32*, 1–21.
26. Eisinger, P. (2006). "Imperfect Federalism: The Intergovernmental Partnership for Homeland Security." *Public Administration Review*, *66*, 537–545; Chenoweth, E. & Clarke, S. E. (2010). "All Terrorism is Local: Resources, Nested Institutions and Governance for Urban Homeland Security in the American Federal System." *Political Research Quarterly*, *64*, 495–507.
27. Eisinger, P. (2006). "Imperfect Federalism: The Intergovernmental Partnership for Homeland Security." *Public Administration Review*, *66*, 537–545.
28. Caruson, K. & MacManus, S. A. (2006). "Mandates and Management Challenges in the Trenches: An Intergovernmental Perspective on Homeland Security." *Public Administration Review*, *66*: 522–536.
29. Caruson, K. & MacManus, S. A. (2006). "Mandates and Management Challenges in the Trenches: An Intergovernmental Perspective on Homeland Security." *Public Administration Review*, *66*: 522–536.

CHAPTER 13

Legal Responses to Homeland Security

CHAPTER OBJECTIVES

- Understand the balance between civil rights and the need to collect intelligence
- Understand the objections civil rights advocates have about the USA PATRIOT Act
- Understand the Supreme Court's reactions to U.S. policies toward detainees

CHAPTER OUTLINE

© J Pat Carter/AP/Shutterstock.

Jose Padilla was born in Brooklyn, New York. As a young adult, he adopted the practice of Islam and traveled extensively in the Middle East. Upon returning to the United States after one trip from Pakistan, Padilla was arrested at Chicago's O'Hare airport as he exited the plane. Law enforcement suspected him of being involved in a terrorist plot, alleging that Padilla conspired with senior al Qaeda members to build and detonate a radioactive "dirty bomb." Padilla claimed that his actions were simply a ploy to escape from Pakistan and return to the United States.

Although Padilla was not engaged in any threatening activity at the time of his arrest, the government held him as an unlawful **enemy combatant** without providing him with the opportunity to defend himself against the charges. He was detained in Chicago, where he appeared before a district court and had a public defender appointed to represent him. Subsequently, he was transferred to a naval brig in Charleston, South Carolina. The only evidence against him was a short, written statement by a U.S. government agent. Padilla was not allowed to have contact with an attorney, his family, or any nonmilitary personnel for 18 months.

Padilla's legal treatment was questioned by some civil rights leaders. They argued that Padilla was denied his due process rights granted to U.S. citizens in the Constitution, which were designed to protect American citizens from unlawful arrest and jailing. These rights include the right to representation in court, the right of accused persons to know the evidence against them, and the right to confront their accusers. Civil rights leaders questioned if American citizens could be held indefinitely without a trial simply because the government believed them to be dangerous.

The case was appealed to the Supreme Court, and, in November 2005, the justices decided that, as an American citizen, Padilla was entitled to due process. Padilla either had to be formally charged or released. In essence, the justices declared that American citizens accused of any crime, including terrorism, are entitled to due process, including the right to defend themselves in court and to be given a timely trial.[1]

Padilla's legal rights as a U.S. citizen against improper treatment by the government are granted to him through the Constitution. Immediately after 9-11, many people were detained for offenses related to terrorism, some allegedly unfairly. There are estimates that nearly 15,000 people were detained worldwide since 9-11, the majority of whom were held without being charged or tried.[2]

© JMiks/Shutterstock.

When U.S. citizens are charged or tried illegally, it is said that their civil and human rights have been violated. The term "civil liberties" refers to the individual freedoms that people have under a system of law. They are the rights granted by law to citizens that protect them from unfair treatment by the government. A related term is "human rights," which are the basic rights that all people should have, but are not necessarily guaranteed by law. They are the rights that most people agree should be given to all people, regardless of their citizenship. These rights include such things as safe food, water, and shelter, along with the right not to be physically abused or punished cruelly.

In the United States, the civil rights granted to all citizens are outlined in the Constitution, specifically in the Bill of Rights, or the first 10 amendments to the Constitution. The amendments most often used to challenge government anti-terrorist activities are the First, Fourth, Fifth, Sixth, Seventh, and Eighth Amendments, which relate to free speech, illegal search and seizure, and the conduct of criminal trials. These limit the power of government while protecting the rights and freedoms of citizens, which are listed in **TABLE 13.1**.

While the Constitution and Bill of Rights provide legal limits on government actions against citizens, it is limited in the sense that the Constitution also allows the government to act in certain ways during times of emergency. In other words, the government is constitutionally granted the power to carry out actions that would be prohibited during times when no emergency exists. Unfortunately, there is no clear understanding of what constitutes an "emergency." After 9-11, the Bush Administration used this clause to carry out certain actions that some regarded as unconstitutional, arguing that terrorism is not a continuing emergency.

TABLE 13.1 Rights Guaranteed Under Bill of Rights

Amendment	Description
First Amendment	Freedom of Speech, Press, Religion, Assembly, and Petition. The government cannot interfere with a person's right to practice any religion they choose. Citizens have the right to speak freely, assemble in groups, and make their voices heard.
Fourth Amendment	Protection against Search and Seizure. Citizens' bodies, houses, papers, and property cannot be searched or seized by the government without evidence of wrongdoing. A court must issue a warrant to conduct a search, which then must include the specific place to be searched and the evidence being collected.
Fifth Amendment	Protection against Illegal Prosecutions. A person can be tried for a crime after a grand jury determines that there is evidence that the person may have committed that offense. However, during times of war or public danger, there are exceptions. The Amendment also allows those accused of crimes to refuse to make statements that could incriminate themselves in a court of law. Moreover, no one's life, liberty, or property can be taken without a proper trial. The Fifth Amendment also prevents a person from being put on trial twice for the same offense and guarantees due process of law.
Sixth Amendment	Right to a Speedy and Public Trial. The Sixth Amendment states that in all criminal cases, those accused of a crime have the right to a speedy and public trial by an impartial jury. Additionally, a person accused of a crime has the right to be informed of the charges against him or her. The accused person also has the right to see the witnesses who are providing evidence against him or her, to have witnesses speak in his or her favor, and to have the assistance of competent legal representation.
Seventh Amendment	Right to a Trial by Jury. This amendment guarantees that someone accused of a crime can be tried by a jury in a court of law.
Eighth Amendment	Excessive Bail, Cruel and Unusual Punishment. Under the Eighth Amendment, judges cannot impose unusually large bail on a defendant, and cruel and unusual punishments cannot be applied to those convicted of crimes.
Fourteenth Amendment	Addresses rights of citizenship and equal protection under the law. Suspects cannot lose their rights except by due process of law.

The problem of how to balance national security objectives (and provide for safety and security from terrorism) while at the same time protecting civil liberties remains a significant problem for U.S. officials in the time after 9-11.[3] The United States and other liberal democracies often point out that the rights of citizens and minorities in their societies are protected. After 9-11, some would argue that the United States created an imbalance in this area.[4] This concern—of the erosion of civil liberties—was highlighted with the USA PATRIOT Act.

USA PATRIOT Act

Objections

The USA PATRIOT Act was passed immediately after 9-11 as a way to provide law enforcement with added powers to track down and punish those responsible for the attacks and to protect the United States against any similar act from occurring in the future. The act gave the Department of Justice, and law enforcement agencies such as the FBI, new and significantly broader investigatory authority. These new powers were very controversial, and opponents argued that they violated Americans' civil rights and allowed law enforcement to encroach upon the civil liberties of citizens.[5]

Objectors say the law violates the First, Fourth, Fifth, Sixth, and Eighth Amendments. Opponents claim that the powers granted to law enforcement are simply too wide-ranging and will erase the protections granted by the Constitution and may affect the freedom of its citizens. They also argue that U.S. citizens are given the right to be free from having their government infringe upon those freedoms that are guaranteed in the Constitution and Bill of Rights.

One simple objection concerned the new definition of "domestic terrorism," which was expanded to include nonviolent crimes such as computer fraud and leaks of intelligence agents' identities. This revised definition allowed law enforcement to use surveillance against a greater number of citizens, and some argue that this new definition discourages political dissent because it includes activities of unpopular political organizations within the United States.[6] They argue that enforcement agencies should not be allowed to interfere with citizens who choose to engage in political associations, even if they are unpopular.

To make matters worse, the ability of law enforcement to use surveillance against citizens (i.e., watching and listening to people, usually without their knowledge) was made easier by passage of the PATRIOT Act. Now, law enforcement can carry out electronic surveillance on more forms of communication. Restrictions on placing wiretaps on telephones were lessened so that police could monitor the private conversations of individuals who are suspected of criminal activity, even without probable cause. Law enforcement was also given the right to track and intercept other types of communication such as email for both law enforcement and intelligence purposes. Police could pursue suspected computer hackers without warrants.

Surveillance tactics by police were further expanded by changes to the Foreign Intelligence Surveillance Act (FISA), a law that lowered standards for courts to approve surveillance of foreign intelligence gathering. Under this law, the standards for approval of a criminal wiretap are far less strict than in a criminal case. The PATRIOT Act amended FISA so that surveillance requests do not have to establish that surveillance is for intelligence-gathering for national security reasons. Instead, all that is now required is that surveillance is needed for a "significant" purpose. This makes it easier for officials to get around limits on permissible domestic surveillance. The concern, obviously, is that the government might use its newly expanded powers without sufficient discretion.[7]

Some of the wiretaps that police can now use are called "roving wiretaps." This means that a wiretap targeted to a particular person would not be confined to a single computer or telephone. Instead, the wiretap could "rove" wherever the target goes.

The roving wiretaps are of great concern to some. Before the Act, a pen register/trap order was only valid in the district in which it was obtained. A pen register is an electronic device that records all of the numbers being called from a specific phone and the trap order allows the government to capture this information. That meant if a suspect moved to a different district, law enforcement would have to obtain another pen/trap order from this second district. Under the PATRIOT Act, once a pen/trap order is obtained, it is valid throughout the United States. This violates the Fourth Amendment's requirement that a warrant specify the place to be searched and evidence to be seized.[8]

In addition to phone conversations, law enforcement was given easier access to an individual's personal financial, credit, educational, medical, and other records. Federal agents can now browse those records, or even library records, without first showing evidence of a crime.[9]

If law enforcement believes that national security is jeopardized, the law allows federal agents to secretly enter people's homes and offices and search and remove people's possessions, read and photograph letters and documents, and read and copy files on computers without a warrant or prior notification. If the search is conducted, it is legal for the government to keep that search secret (called a gag order). This is called a "sneak and peek" search.

Objectors point to the Fourth Amendment, which forbids searches of homes and property (including personal records) without a warrant based on evidence that a person is involved in a specific crime. "Sneak and peak" searches allow the FBI to evade the requirement that probable cause be shown before a warrant is issued to search a home or place of business. Instead, if the FBI believes that information might provide some intelligence and help an investigation, it can search for evidence and seize it. In short, the FBI can spy on Americans who no court has determined have done anything wrong. Opponents argue that law enforcement should only gather intelligence when there is a clear reason to suspect criminal activity.

Another concern with the PATRIOT Act stemmed from provisions requiring phone companies and Internet service providers to turn over customer records to law enforcement. If required to do so, the companies would be forbidden from telling their customers of their actions. While the government argued that such secrecy is necessary so as not to alert potential terrorists, opponents argued that the gag orders related to searches violate the First Amendment, which guarantees people's right to free speech. In addition, objectors point out that in "typical" criminal cases, a court gives law enforcement agents a warrant that gives them permission to monitor the activities of a specific person for a limited time period, and when the investigation is over the person must be told that the surveillance occurred.

The PATRIOT Act has provisions that allow the government to oversee bank records with more ease, making some people uncomfortable. The government argued that this was necessary in order to curtail financing of terrorism, because if terrorists do not have access to financial resources, they are unable to carry out future attacks. The PATRIOT Act imposes new bookkeeping requirements on financial institutions. It gives the Secretary of the Treasury increased regulatory powers to combat corruption of U.S. financial institutions involved in foreign money-laundering activities. Federal law enforcement can now interact with banking regulators and have the power to arrest suspects outside of U.S. borders if an individual is suspected of financing terrorism and conducting money laundering.

The law also has new provisions concerning immigration, seeking to tighten security at the borders, closing them off to terrorists. Other provisions serve to detain and expel terrorists who may already be in the country. Authorities can detain and even prosecute non-U.S. citizens suspected of being involved in hostile activities against the United States. The law revised immigration laws to expand the categories of who could be deported based upon a possible connection with terrorist activity, and reduced the procedural protections surrounding their deportation.[10] Any immigrants who were "certified" as posing a threat to national security would be detained without bond pending deportation proceedings. In those cases where the country would not accept the alien, detention could become indefinite.[11] To protect the border, the new law increased border patrols and monitoring of foreigners within the United States.

The law makes it easier for law enforcement to share sensitive intelligence on Americans with other law enforcement, immigration officers, and intelligence agencies such as the CIA. Any government law enforcement officer or attorney can share the contents of intercepted communications or from a "sneak and peak" operation with other federal officers, including the CIA.[12] The Regional Information Sharing System (RISS) can now be used to share intelligence with ease, whereas prior to the PATRIOT Act, RISS was only used in criminal investigations.

Traditionally, law enforcement agents investigate and collect evidence on a specific crime that has already been committed. But under the PATRIOT Act, the government's surveillance activities are not necessarily intended to catch specific terrorists. They are scanning huge amounts of computerized records and other information as a way to look for patterns that may indicate terrorist activity. This is called data mining.

Support

Supporters of the PATRIOT Act claimed that these provisions were necessary to allow law enforcement to find evidence that a person is engaged in terrorist activity against the U.S. Police agents argued that the new provisions for increasing intelligence would allow them to track terrorists who use modern technology to plan and carry out their crimes. In the end, supporters argued that the PATRIOT Act would increase the federal law enforcement's ability to respond to terrorism.

Critics understand the need to keep some information secret, such as the identity of agents who are working undercover within a terrorist organization. However, there is a big concern when the press's access to government officials and information is restricted. This makes it very hard for the public to know if the government's activities are legal.

While there are certain instances when the intelligence community should share info with the criminal justice community, Congress gives these agencies and others too much power to share intelligence without judicial review.

Other Concerns

There are other concerns about government policies passed after 9-11. Two of these are the "No-Fly Watch List" and the "Automatic Selectee" list maintained by the U.S. government. These lists can restrict a person's ability to travel by air. Any person whose name appears on the No-Fly list is not permitted to board airplanes at all, whereas those on the Automatic Selectee list are identified for closer scrutiny when passing through airport security.

The reason for having these lists is clear: To stop any terrorists who may be attempting to board an airplane with the intent to harm others. These lists also make it more difficult for terrorists' to travel to another location to carry out an act of terrorism.

However, the data supplied by U.S. intelligence agencies is often incomplete and/or inaccurate. Many travelers have the same name as a terrorist on the list and have been incorrectly identified as being potential terrorists. In September of 2006, the Congressional Research Service (CRS) issued a report that the data supplied by the intelligence agencies included numerous incorrect entries and a lot of outdated information. In May 2012, an 18-month-old girl was "flagged" as being on the No Fly List and she and her parents were taken off of a flight.[13]

The No-Fly list has about 20,000 names on it, including the names of about 500 Americans. It is maintained by the FBI's Terrorist Screening Center. In 2010, the ACLU filed a suit with the U.S. District Court in Portland, Oregon, for 15 plaintiffs who were all U.S. citizens and Muslims. The plaintiffs claim that the government refuses to explain why their names are on the list.[14]

In the past, the No-Fly Watch List has been challenged in the courts. The ACLU has questioned the legality of the No-Fly Watch List and has gone to court to try to stop the use of such lists, claiming that the collection and sharing of information on citizens who are not under investigation for a specific crime is forbidden by the Bill of Rights.

Another concern revolves around a proposed national DNA database. The Department of Justice is considering a plan to add a DNA database to the FBI's existing crime-related database. When this database is operational, DNA would be collected from: those people arrested as being a suspect in the War on Terror; anyone arrested and accused of committing a federal crime (even if they are not found guilty); and, people accused of entering the country illegally or those who stay longer in the country than their visas allow.

While supporters of the database argue that it will make it easier for law enforcement to track potential terrorists, to stop illegal aliens from entering the U.S., and to help solve crimes committed by illegal aliens, opponents argue that collecting DNA from people who are not convicted of offenses violates their civil liberties. They argue that the database will not prevent crimes because DNA is collected after the crime has been committed and cannot be used to stop crimes from occurring. They also argue that a database like this would be ineffective because it is simply too difficult to analyze the DNA of such a large number of people.

Executive Power

After 9-11, President Bush and Vice President Cheney felt that the president and the executive branch had the power to designate certain terrorists as enemy combatants, allowing for their trial in special military courts. Along those same lines, they also argued that the president has the authority to ask federal law enforcement and other national security intelligence agencies to listen to telephone calls that originate in the United States but are directed to suspected terrorists in foreign countries. President Bush and the U.S. Attorney General developed new policies that allowed law enforcement to rely only on reasonable suspicion as a standard for launching an investigation. The FBI was able to search for indicators of illegal activity by monitoring chat rooms and attending political rallies or religious events as a way to identify possible threats. Local FBI offices were permitted to begin inquiries based on their own information. In doing these things, Bush and Cheney were making decisions without congressional oversight—in essence, expanding the power of the executive office.

Critics of this approach argue that increasing executive power to counterterrorism is abuse of executive power. As presidential and police power increase, citizen protections have been decreasing. During times of emergency, police are allowed more intrusions into people's behavior, but were the events of September 11 a time of emergency?

USA Freedom Act

The PATRIOT Act expired on June 1, 2015, and the next day the members of Congress passed a new bill, the USA Freedom Act, which stands for the Uniting and Strengthening America by Fulfilling Rights and Ending Eavesdropping, Dragnet-collection and

Online Monitoring Act. The bill limited the ability of the National Security Agency (and other intelligence groups) from bulk collection of data on U.S. citizens. Instead of getting bulk collections of data, agencies must now ask for information on a specific agency or entity. In addition, it gives private companies more opportunities to inform the public about how many requests they get for information from the FISA court, and how often they have provided that information to an agency.

Critics of the new bill claim that the government is still able to collect bulk information on citizens through phone companies. Instead of being collected by the NSA or the FBI, the phone companies will collect the data and provide it to the intelligence organizations, if requested. In order for the NSA or FBI to collect the information, they must file a request with the FISA court. If there is an emergency, the U.S. Attorney General may require that the records be produced without a court order. In that case, the Attorney General must reasonably determine that the situation requires that the information be produced; that a factual basis exists to issue the order; he informs the FISA judge of the decision; and the Attorney General makes an application to the FISA judge within 7 days after approval of the transfer of information. Once the necessary information is obtained, the collection of data must stop.

The Freedom Act also made changes to the Trap and Trace devices. An agent requesting the use of a trap and trace device or pen registers must include a specific period of time for which the device will be used when requesting permission from a FISA court. Moreover, the new law requires that a specific geographic region be specified. Tighter privacy procedures must be used to collect, retain and use private information of a U.S. citizen through the use of a trap and trace device or a pen register. The new law will permit the use of roving wiretaps through December, 2019.

Guantanamo Bay

Anyone suspected of carrying out, or engaging in, terrorist actions have been labeled by the U.S. government as an "unlawful enemy combatant." Since 9-11, the United States has often placed those individuals in custody in Iraq or Afghanistan. They are interrogated with the hope that any intelligence gathered will help prevent new terrorist attacks.

Some detainees are held at a detention camp and naval base in **Guantanamo Bay**, Cuba. Because Guantanamo Bay is not a part of the U.S. mainland, it is more difficult for the press and other Americans to follow events or hold protests there. The majority of those being detained at Guantanamo Bay were captured abroad. Some of the detainees are members of al Qaeda and were involved in active plots against Americans. But not all of the detainees are members of a terrorist group. Instead, they may be loose associates of terrorists, such as friends or family members of supporters of terrorist groups.

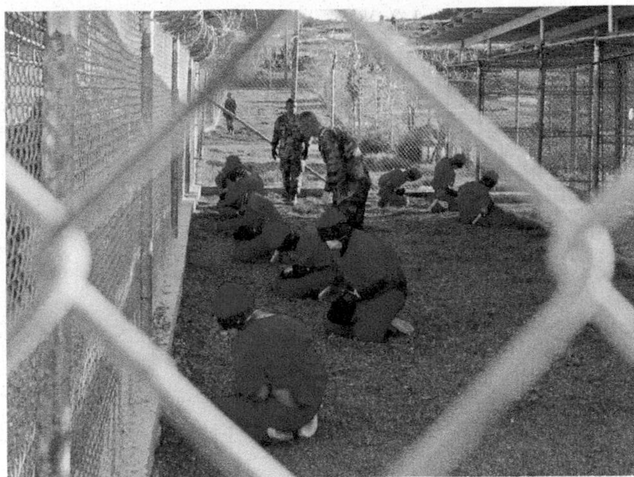

Courtesy of Shane T. McCoy/U.S. Navy.

Many human rights issues have come to the forefront because of the actions taken by the government against suspected terrorists held at Guantanamo Bay. Detainees can be held at Guantanamo Bay for years without access to legal protection. Conditions for detainees at the Guantanamo Bay camp are reportedly harsh. Those prisoners who have been released later reported that detainees were tortured and abused. Another controversial question surrounded the right of detainees to file a writ of habeas corpus. The president is allowed to suspend habeas corpus in times of national emergency—but, again, what exactly constitutes an emergency?

President Bush declared that his administration had the right to detain those individuals who were suspected of terrorist acts. He argued that the detainees at Guantanamo are enemy combatants, not prisoners of war, so they are not entitled to certain rights under the Geneva Conventions. The definition, then, was trying to separate out the difference between lawful combatants (prisoners of war) versus unlawful combatants (dubbed enemy combatants). Bush declared that the detainees are not entitled to protections described in the Geneva Conventions because they are not members of any specific entity that abides by the agreement, and thus the protections are not relevant. Bush also said that if the prisoners were to be tried for their actions, it would be in military courts that provide fewer human rights and civil liberty protections than criminal courts in the United States.

One argument that has been made to justify suspending civil rights of detainees is that terrorism is a crime unlike any other, and one terrorist can do enormous harm; therefore, different standards and a different legal approach should apply.

Human rights advocates seek to change policy so that detainees are treated humanely, including given the right to be tried in court within a reasonable time after their arrest. Some human rights advocates question if the Geneva Conventions should apply to those detainees being held at Guantanamo Bay. The term "Geneva Conventions" refers to four international treaties signed in Geneva, Switzerland, and that detail, among other things, the way enemy soldiers and prisoners of war must be treated by those holding them. The documents outlaw the use of torture, require that prisoners be fed and treated humanely, and that prisoners be tried and sentenced by a court. Moreover, because Guantanamo is on foreign soil (although leased from Cuba since 1903), the detainees are beyond the reach of U.S. law.[15]

There are many possible violations of civil rights in military courts as opposed to criminal courts in the United States. In a civilian criminal case, a defendant is entitled to review all of the evidence against him or her. In military courts, officers acting as judges can consider evidence that is not released to the accused individual. This affects the ability of the accused to build a defense. Second, in typical criminal court hearings, any evidence obtained by use of torture is not admissible. In military courts, this rule does not apply; instead, that evidence would be admitted. Third, in a civilian proceeding, if a prisoner is found not guilty, he or she must be released. In military hearings, the government may choose to detain a prisoner after a hearing, even if the court does not find the defendant guilty.

In June of 2006, the U.S. Supreme Court ruled against President Bush when they decided that trying detainees in military courts would be a violation of both U.S. law and the Geneva Conventions.

This meant that the detainees had to be tried in U.S. courts. In response, Bush convinced Congress to pass the Military Commissions Act of 2006. The law allowed detainees to be tried by a special military commission called military tribunals. These tribunals allow secret or classified information to be used against the detainees. In essence, the act returned power to the President to decide the fate of the detainees.

Many U.S. citizens favor detention without arrest and military tribunals for suspected terrorists, even if it includes denying the civil rights to accused terrorists. On the other hand, civil libertarians tend to support providing constitutional protections to suspected terrorists, including trials in civilian courts and dismantling detention facilities like Guantanamo Bay. For more on legal issues surrounding homeland security.

When he became president, Barack Obama vowed to reverse many of the Bush administration policies. Just after taking office, Obama worked to close the facility at Guantanamo Bay and tried to have five suspects involved in the September 11 attacks moved to New York City for a civilian trial. The president also asked the Department of Justice to look for a new detention facility within the United States. Opposition immediately arose on the grounds that the terrorists would use the publicity surrounding the trials as a stage. In the end, the Obama administration reversed its decision. It also continued many of the security measures originally started in the Bush administration, such as monitoring communications.

President Trump assured his supporters that he would keep Guantanamo open and that he would "load it up with some bad dudes."[16] He also promised to "bring back waterboarding." He said, "Don't tell me it doesn't work—torture works," and "If it doesn't work, they deserve it anyway, for what they're doing to us."[17] Trump made his thoughts on detaining terrorists clear in Executive Order 13823 in which he revoked Obama's closure of Guantano Bay and ordered the continued detention of detainees as a way to protect the country from further acts of terrorism (see **TABLE 13.2**).

There are allegedly around 40 people held in Guantanamo, all Muslim men. Some claim that many of them have been tortured, and many of them were cleared for transfer many years ago.

TABLE 13.2 Executive Order 13823—Protecting America Through Lawful Detention of Terrorists (January 30, 2018)

Executive Order	Description
Executive Order 13823	***Section 1. Findings.*** (a) Consistent with long-standing law of war principles and applicable law, the United States may detain certain persons captured in connection with an armed conflict for the duration of the conflict. (b) Following the terrorist attacks of September 11, 2001, the 2001 Authorization for Use of Military Force (AUMF) and other authorities authorized the United States to detain certain persons who were a part of or substantially supported al-Qa'ida, the Taliban, or associated forces engaged in hostilities against the United States or its coalition partners. Today, the United States remains engaged in an armed conflict with al-Qa'ida, the Taliban, and associated forces, including with the Islamic State of Iraq and Syria. (c) The detention operations at the U.S. Naval Station Guantánamo Bay are legal, safe, humane, and conducted consistent with United States and international law. (d) Those operations are continuing given that a number of the remaining individuals at the detention facility are being prosecuted in military commissions, while others must be detained to protect against continuing, significant threats to the security of the United States, as determined by periodic reviews. (e) Given that some of the current detainee population represent the most difficult and dangerous cases from among those historically detained at the facility, there is significant reason for concern regarding their reengagement in hostilities should they have the opportunity. ***Sec. 2. Status of Detention Facilities at U.S. Naval Station Guantánamo Bay.*** (a) Section 3 of Executive Order 13492 of January 22, 2009 (Review and Disposition of Individuals Detained at the Guantánamo Bay Naval Base and Closure of Detention Facilities), ordering the closure of detention facilities at U.S. Naval Station Guantánamo Bay, is hereby revoked. (b) Detention operations at U.S. Naval Station Guantánamo Bay shall continue to be conducted consistent with all applicable United States and international law, including the Detainee Treatment Act of 2005. (c) In addition, the United States may transport additional detainees to U.S. Naval Station Guantánamo Bay when lawful and necessary to protect the Nation.

Trump, Donald J. Executive Order 13823—Protecting America Through Lawful Detention of Terrorists Online by Gerhard Peters and Woolley, John T. The American Presidency Project. Retrieved from https://www.presidency.ucsb.edu/node/331780

Civil Liberties

Police

Police are at the forefront of the battle against terrorism. Their behavior determines whether civil liberties are protected or whether they are abused. Police are responsible for collecting information, which can be personal information that may have no relation to a criminal offense. Their attempts to gather intelligence may alter the expectations that citizens have about law enforcement. This new role changes the focus of police work, which can interfere with the traditional role of fighting crime.

After 9-11, local, state, and federal government began to share information like never before. State and local law enforcement agencies and the FBI created Joint Terrorism Task Forces. There were also Anti-Terrorism Task Forces created within the nation's U.S. Attorneys' offices; this name changed to Anti-Terrorist Assistance Coordinators in 2003.

Under the Fourth Amendment, law enforcement cannot collect information without reasonable suspicion. Citizens' civil liberties may be at risk if law enforcement collects that information illegally.

Courts

In January of 2003, The American Library Association issued a resolution stating that some sections of the PATRIOT Act violated the constitutional and privacy rights of library patrons. They announced that they were opposed to any use of governmental power to suppress the free and open exchange of knowledge and information, and encouraged U.S. librarians to support free and open access to information. They considered sections of the act to be a danger to the constitutional and privacy rights of library users.[18]

Some Supreme Court decisions have reversed White House policies that have served to expand executive authority since 2001. In June of 2004, the Court made two decisions that allowed enemy combatants the right to contest their arrests. In April of 2006, the Court decided that U.S. citizens who were arrested in the United States could not be tried outside the U.S. criminal court system. Then, in June of 2006, the Court declared that the military tribunal system that had been established at Guantanamo Bay was illegal because it did not have the approval of Congress and did not follow the Geneva Conventions. As a result, charges against two enemy combatants were dropped based on the June 2006 Supreme Court decision.

In *Hamdi v. Rumsfeld* (542 US 507, 2004), the Supreme Court justices clarified the status of 21-year-old American citizen Yaser Hamdi. Hamdi was captured by American forces while fighting for the Taliban in Afghanistan in the fall of 2001. He was held for over 2 years without access to the courts. He was initially detained at Guantanamo Bay where administration officials labeled him as an "enemy combatant" even though they could not provide any evidence that Hamdi had any links to terrorists. Because he was an American, he was moved to the naval brig in Norfolk, Virginia. Because he was deemed an "enemy combatant," he was not entitled to legal representation. Furthermore, he could be held for an indefinite period of time without charges being filed. If a lawyer was present, all conversations had to be recorded, a violation of the Fourth Amendment. The Court held that Hamdi's detention was proper, and the United States could continue to detain him. But it also held that Hamdi, as a U.S. citizen, had the due process right to challenge the government's justification for his detention (to challenge his status as an enemy combatant) before a neutral decision-maker.[19]

In *Rasul v. Bush* (542 US 466, 2004), a majority of the justices on the Supreme Court held that the detainees at Guantanamo Bay who are not U.S. citizens have the right to file habeas corpus petitions in federal court to challenge the legality of their detention. They held that the foreign nationals (non-U.S. citizens) were wrongfully imprisoned. This had to do with four British and Australian citizens who were captured by the American military in Pakistan and Afghanistan. The men were held in Guantanamo Bay. Their families filed for a writ of habeas corpus to have their detention declared unconstitutional. The government claimed that since the men were not U.S. citizens, the federal courts did not have jurisdiction to hear the case.

Together, the *Rasul* and *Hamdi* cases determined that detainees on American soil or being held in American facilities must be given the chance to contest the legality of their detention.

The Supreme Court addressed the legality of military commissions set up by the Bush administration in *Hamdan v. Rumsfeld* (548 US 557, 2006). Salim Ahmed Hamdan, a citizen of Yemen, served as a bodyguard and chauffeur for Osama bin Laden and was captured by Afghani forces. He was turned over to the United States and sent to Guantanamo Bay, where he was charged with conspiracy to commit terrorism and tried before a military tribunal. Hamdan then filed a petition for a writ of habeas corpus in a federal district court, arguing that the military commission that had been convened to try him was illegal because it did not provide him with the civil rights protections required under the Geneva Conventions. Supreme Court justices decided that the military commissions that the Bush Administration set up to try detainees being held at Guantanamo could not proceed because they did not follow the Geneva Conventions. Furthermore, the President did not have the authority to set up the special military commissions without oversight by Congress. Because of this, the commissions were deemed illegal.[20]

In another ruling the same day as *Hamdan v. Rumsfeld*, the Court decided in a 5-4 ruling that the Jose Padilla case was filed in the wrong jurisdiction and against the wrong defendant. They sidestepped the constitutional issues of the Padilla case. In *Rumsfeld v. Padilla* (542 US 426, 2004), the court addressed the Padilla case (described previously). Padilla was a U.S. citizen who had been labeled an "enemy combatant" in the war on terror. Unlike Hamdi or Hamdan, Padilla was arrested on U.S. soil rather than overseas. In the case, attorneys for Padilla asked whether the defendant had the right to contest the legality of his detention in a federal court.

All three of these cases illustrated the question of individual rights versus government power. The decisions in these cases dealt the Bush administration a major blow in its belief that the executive branch wielded enough power to bypass constitutional rights and liberties. The Court decided that the executive branch could not hold foreign-born prisoners at Guantanamo Bay indefinitely without access to the American judicial system and the rights of due process.

Boumediene v. Bush (553 US 723, 2008) involved Lakhdar Boumediene, a naturalized citizen of Bosnia and Herzegovenia, who was being held in Guantanamo Bay. He was accused of being involved in a plot to attack the U.S. embassy. While in Guantanamo Bay, Boumediene filed a petition for a writ of habeas corpus. The Supreme Court found in favor of the detainees. They declared that those detained in Guantanamo Bay had a right to habeas corpus and that the Military Commissions Act was an unconstitutional suspension of that right.[21]

In January of 2010, The Supreme Court gave its first ruling against the provision in the PATRIOT Act

TABLE 13.3 The Legal Complexity of Cybersecurity

In order to understand the legal complexity of homeland security, the topic of cybersecurity was selected as an example of how previous laws may impact current-day issues. The following list is based on a congressional report that assessed all of the federal laws that may be related to the issue of cybersecurity in the United States.

- Posse Comitatus Act of 1879
- Antitrust Laws and Section 5 of the Federal Trade Commission Act
- National Institute of Standards and Technology Act
- Federal Power Act
- Communications Act of 1934
- National Security Act of 1947
- U.S. Information and Educational Exchange Act of 1948 (Smith–Mundt Act)
- State Department Basic Authorities Act of 1956
- Freedom of Information Act (FOIA)
- Omnibus Crime Control and Safe Streets Act of 1968
- Racketeer Influenced and Corrupt Organizations Act (RICO)
- Federal Advisory Committee Act (FACA)
- Privacy Act of 1974
- Counterfeit Access Device and Computer Fraud and Abuse Act of 1984
- Electronic Communications Privacy Act of 1986 (ECPA)
- Department of Defense Appropriations Act, 1987
- High Performance Computing Act of 1991
- Communications Assistance for Law Enforcement Act of 1994 (CALEA)
- Communications Decency Act of 1996
- Clinger-Cohen Act (Information Technology Management Reform Act) of 1996
- Identity Theft and Assumption Deterrence Act of 1998
- Homeland Security Act of 2002 (HSA)
- Federal Information Security Management Act of 2002 (FISMA)
- Terrorism Risk Insurance Act of 2002
- Cyber Security Research and Development Act, 2002
- E-Government Act of 2002
- Identity Theft Penalty Enhancement Act
- Intelligence Reform and Terrorism Prevention Act of 2004 (IRTPA)

that prohibits providing material support to any group labeled a terrorist organization and attached a possible 15-year sentence. In other words, the PATRIOT Act made it a crime to provide support, including humanitarian aid, literature, and political advocacy, to a "terrorist group." In *Holder v. Humanitarian Law Project* (561 US 1, 2010), the justices decided that the provisions prohibiting material support were not vague and did not violate freedom of speech.[22]

In *Ashcroft v. Al-Kidd* (563 US 731, 2011), the Supreme Court ruled against a former star college football player from the University of Idaho who, while in college, converted to Islam. As he was boarding a flight to Saudi Arabia, he was arrested and held as a material witness in a terrorism probe for 16 days. He was never charged with a crime and ultimately released from custody. Al-Kidd claimed that he was mistreated while in custody. He claimed he was strip-searched, shackled, interrogated like a terrorist, and held with hardened criminals. He brought a suit against Attorney General John Ashcroft because he was detained on suspicion of supporting terrorists even though there was no evidence to charge him with a crime.

The justices found in an 8-0 decision that the Attorney General could not be personally sued in the case. They said there was no violation of the Constitution. Additionally, Justice Scalia concluded that Ashcroft was entitled to qualified immunity because he did not violate clearly established law. For more on the legal complexities involving many homeland security activities, see **TABLE 13.3**.

Chapter Summary

After 9-11, the government had to figure out how to balance the need to obtain information and intelligence with the need to protect law-abiding citizens from being treated unfairly. They had to find a balance in policies that preserve citizens' civil liberties and allow people to feel secure from unjustified attacks by the government while at the same time being protected from terrorists.

Review/Discussion Questions

1. What are the rights guaranteed to U.S. citizens by the Bill of Rights?
2. What are some objections held by civil rights advocates against the PATRIOT Act?
3. What has the Supreme Court decided concerning the U.S. government's actions toward detainees?

Additional Readings

Alperen, M. J. (2011). *Foundations of Homeland Security: Law and Policy.* Hoboken, NJ: John Wiley & Sons, Inc.

Brasch, W. (2005). *America's Unpatriotic Acts.* New York, NY: Peter Lang.

Christie, K. (2008). *America's War on Terrorism.* Lewiston, NY: Edwin Mellen Press.

Whitley, J. D. & Zusman, L. K. (2009). *Homeland Security: Legal and Policy Issues.* Washington, DC: American Bar Association.

Endnotes

1. Brasch, W. (2005). *America's Unpatriotic Acts.* New York, NY: Peter Lang.
2. Christie, K. (2008). *America's War on Terrorism.* Lewiston, NY: Edwin Mellen Press, p. 121.
3. Davis, D. W. & Silver, B. D. (2004). "Civil Liberties vs. Security: Public Opinion in the Context of the Terrorist Attacks on America." *American Journal of Political Science, 48*, 28–46.
4. Christie, K. (2008). *America's War on Terrorism.* Lewiston, NY: Edwin Mellen Press.
5. McAdams, A. J. (2005). "Internet Surveillance after September 11: Is the United States Becoming Great Britain?" *Comparative Politics, 37*, 479–498.
6. Rackow, S. H. (2002). "How the USA Patriot Act will Permit Governmental Infringement Upon the Privacy of Americans in the Name of 'Intelligence' Investigations." *University of Pennsylvania Law Review, 150*, 1651–1696.
7. Henderson, N. C. (2002). "The Patriot Act's Impact on the Government's Ability to Conduct Electronic Surveillance of Ongoing Domestic Communications." *Duke Law Journal, 52*, 179–209.
8. McAdams, A. J. (2005). "Internet Surveillance after September 11: Is the United States Becoming Great Britain?" *Comparative Politics, 37*, 479–498.
9. Sinnar, S. (2003). "Patriotic or Unconstitutional? The Mandatory Detention of Aliens Under the USA Patriot Act." *Stanford Law Review, 55*, 1419–1456.
10. Henderson, N. C. (2002). "The Patriot Act's Impact on the Government's Ability to Conduct Electronic Surveillance of Ongoing Domestic Communications." *Duke Law Journal, 52*, 179–209.
11. Pfeiffer, E. (2012). 18-month-old Baby Pulled from Flight, Parents Interviewed by TSA. *Yahoo! News.* Retrieved Online at https://news.yahoo.com/blogs/sideshow/18-month-old-baby-pulled-flight-parents-interviewed-175521187
12. Springer, D. (2012). Muslims, ACLU Challenge the Government's No-fly List. *Foxnews.com.* Retrieved online at https://www.foxnews.com/politics/muslims-aclu-challenge-the-governments-no-fly-list
13. Bruck, C. (August 1, 2006) Why Obama has Failed to Close Guantánamo" The New Yorker. https://www.newyorker.com/magazine/2016/08/01/why-obama-has-failed-to-close-guantanamo.
14. American Library Association. (2003). Resolution on the USA Patriot Act and Related Measures That Infringe on the Rights of Library Users. Retrieved online at http://www.ala.org/Template.cfm?Section=ifresolutions&Template=/ContentManagement/ContentDisplay.cfm&ContentID=11891.
15. Hamilton, M. (2004). "The Supreme Court's Terrorism Cases: What They Held, and Why They Are Important." *FindLaw/Legal Commentary.* Retrieved online at http://writ.news.findlaw.com/hamilton/20040701.html.
16. The Oyez Project. (2012). *Hamdan v. Rumsfeld.* The Oyez Project. Retrieved online at http://www.oyez.org/cases/2000-2009/2005/2005_05_184.
17. Center for Constitutional Rights. (2010). Supreme Court Ruling Criminalizes Speech in Material Support Law Case. Retrieved online at https://ccrjustice.org/home/press-center/press-releases/supreme-court-ruling-criminalizes-speech-material-support-law-case
18. American Library Association. (2003). Resolution on the USA Patriot Act and Related Measures That Infringe on the Rights of Library Users. Retrieved online at http://www.ala.org/Template.cfm?Section=ifresolutions&Template=/ContentManagement/ContentDisplay.cfm&ContentID=11891.
19. Hamilton, M. (2004). "The Supreme Court's Terrorism Cases: What They Held, and Why They Are Important." FindLaw/Legal Commentary. Retrieved online at http://writ.news.findlaw.com/hamilton/20040701.html; Brasch, W. (2005). America's Unpatriotic Acts. New York, NY: Peter Lang.
20. The Oyez Project. (2012). Hamdan v. Rumsfeld. The Oyez Project. Retrieved online at http://www.oyez.org/cases/2000-2009/2005/2005_05_184.
21. The Oyez Project. (2012). Boumediene v. Bush. The Oyez Project. Retrieved online at http://www.oyez.org/cases/2000-2009/2007/2007_06_1195
22. Humanitarian Law Project. (2012). Supreme Court Ruling Criminalizes Speech in Material Support Law Case. Retrieved online at http://hlp.home.igc.org/

Courtesy of Barry Bahler/DHS

CHAPTER 14

Homeland Security Communication and Technology Issues

CHAPTER OBJECTIVES

- To understand the role of communications and communications technology in homeland security and to identify some of the major programs dealing with homeland security communications
- To identify different types of cyber threats and attacks and understand the importance of cyberterrorism in homeland security
- To understand the role of technology in the context of homeland security, both as a benefit to homeland security professionals as well as a potential threat to homeland security

CHAPTER OUTLINE

HOMELAND SECURITY AND COMMUNICATIONS

CYBERSECURITY

- Cyberterrorism
- Problem with Cybersecurity in America
- Cyber Defense

TECHNOLOGY AND HOMELAND SECURITY

- HSARPA
- Support to the Homeland Security Enterprise and First Responders Group

CHAPTER SUMMARY

Courtesy of Adam DuBrowa/FEMA.

One of the identifiable elements of modern society is technology.[1] No matter the field or in what area of the country, computers, tablets, and cell phones have become virtually ubiquitous. As of mid-2012, there were more cell phones than people in the United States—and that number has continued to grow.[2] Along with providing convenience, however, these technologies, and especially those linked to (and sometimes running) our infrastructure, also provide targets for potential enemies.[3] Further exacerbating the threat is the fact that many of the systems have developed independently from one another, with agencies adopting communications platforms that work well for them, but not across jurisdictions or agencies.[4] This fact was perhaps made most clear on September 11, when the communication systems at the World Trade Center were overwhelmed and miscommunication among agencies was a significant problem.[5] At the same time, technology is providing homeland security professionals with additional tools to protect the homeland in both the "cyber world" as well as the physical world. The double-edged sword of technology is something that is essential for understanding the modern elements of homeland security.

This chapter examines these pressing problems of technology and vulnerability—as well as addressing what the homeland security apparatus is doing to prevent technology-based problems in the future. The chapter is divided into three parts, the first examining communication issues in homeland security and the policies and organizations that have arisen to address these issues. The second section deals with cyberthreats in the context of homeland security and how these threats are being combatted. Finally, in the third section, general issues of technology and homeland security are addressed, focusing on the state and local levels.

Homeland Security and Communications

One of the most significant problems facing homeland security post 9-11 was the issue of operational communications between and among agencies. According to the *9/11 Commission Report*,

> The inability to communicate was a critical element at the World Trade Center, Pentagon, and Somerset County, Pennsylvania, crash sites, where multiple agencies and multiple jurisdictions responded. The occurrence of this problem at three very different sites is strong evidence that compatible and adequate communications among public safety organizations at the local, state, and federal levels remains an important problem.[6]

While the original identification of the problem is now over 15 years old, and some progress has been made, there is still no comprehensive solution to the issue of communications within a homeland security context.[7] Elements of a communications plan have been included in significant legislation like the Intelligence Reform and Terrorism Prevention Act of 2004 (IRTPA), but with the requirements for a comprehensive broadband solution to communications issues costing tens of billions of dollars over the next several decades,[8] political will for a solution has been somewhat lacking.[9] Provisions in the IRTPA include the mandate that communications systems be interoperable and that there be a system in place that allows for emergency communications across all levels of government, but there was little in terms of specific guidance for how these goals should be accomplished.[10]

In response to the requirements for emergency communications during a homeland security incident, as well as problems experienced during 9-11 and Hurricane Katrina, the Department of Homeland Security in 2007 created the Cybersecurity and Infrastructure Security Agency (CISA)'s Office of Emergency Communications (OEC) within the Emergency Communications Division, which is responsible for partnering with communications stakeholders at all levels of government to improve emergency capabilities. In order to successfully carry out this mission, the Division is responsible for various elements of emergency communications coordination including:

- *Policy and Planning*: Responsible for the coordination of strategy and policy for the OEC, including development of communications protocols in line with the requirements of the IRTPA. Additionally, they provide research and position papers on policy issues affecting communications and direct special projects focusing on elements of emergency communications.[11]
- *Public Safety and National Security and Emergency Preparedness Partnership (NS/EP)*: Responsible for partnerships across all levels of government and internationally as well as with the private sector, focusing on issues of national security and public safety from an emergency communications perspective.[12]
- *Technical Assistance*: Responsible for handling requests for technical assistance from the states (and other levels of government) as well as national-priority technical assistance.[13]
- *Regional Coordination*: Responsible for building collaboration among partners at the regional level, through the coordination by regional coordinators, to achieve operability and interoperability in emergency communications.[14]
- *Architecture and Advanced Technology*: Responsible for technical analyses and assessments of new technology in homeland security-related functions.[15]
- *Communications Portfolio Management (CPM)*: Responsible for managing priority telecommunications services including several specific programs (mentioned next).[16]

As part of the 2010 National Security Strategy, the president mandated that the United States must, as part of its national security response, prevent disruptions to critical communications.[17] Pursuant to that strategy, President Obama issued Executive Order 13618, which changed the way the federal government operated in terms of emergency communications. Among the ways it changed these operations was by abolishing the National Communications System and establishing a National Security/Emergency Preparedness Communications Executive Committee (CEC), responsible for program management through the Communications Portfolio Branch, mentioned previously. This branch is specifically responsible for managing several programs fundamental to communications during times of national crisis.[18]

Specifically, programs were developed to assist the government in times of national security, like the **Government Emergency Telecommunications Service (GETS) program** (see **BOX 14.1**), which keeps call completion rates high on land lines for national security and emergency planning officials during emergencies[19] and the TSP program, which allows NS/EP organizations to get priority for telecommunications services during national emergencies—even on private networks.[20] This has caused some controversy, with some critics complaining that the new executive order allows for a government takeover of private communications during a national emergency.[21] Other programs, like FirstNet, are on private networks and some agencies have been reluctant to participate.

Recent activity has focused on the necessity for the government to secure bandwidth for use by officials during times of emergency. This is a difficult and expensive proposition because, along with the important interoperability issues that the Communications Division currently faces, there is the additional challenge of having to manage change into the future. This requires anticipating new technological developments and making sound policy that allows for emergency access when necessary.[22]

In addition to coordinating at the federal level, the Communications Division has also mandated states and territories to develop and submit Statewide Communication Interoperability Plans (SCIPs), which both examine current interoperability issues as well as plan for future development of better emergency communications across jurisdictions.[23] These plans have helped jurisdictions progress in their interoperability goals, but there still remain significant hurdles to overcome at all levels of government.

Communications is one of many important elements that affect homeland security and it is an area in which we have made significant strides over the past decade, although problems still remain. From the policy recommendations of the *9/11 Commission Report* to the recent executive order from the president, the communications strategy of DHS has changed in important ways designed to help ensure that emergency communications are interoperable and secure, today and well into the future. While there has been controversy over some of the policies implemented, the changes represent an important step in addressing an issue essential to both homeland security and emergency management.

BOX 14.1 The Government Emergency Telecommunications Service (GETS)

With an increasing reliance on telecommunications technology comes an increased risk during times of emergency if the system goes down or becomes otherwise unusable. One of the primary dangers is that phone lines get overloaded and calls do not connect. This is particularly problematic when the individuals trying to use the phone system are national security or emergency planning personnel. GETS is designed to circumvent this problem by providing priority access to those individuals with appropriate designations. The program is directed by the White House but administered as part of the National Communications System in the Office of Cybersecurity and Communications Division, National Protection, and Programs Directorate in the Department of Homeland Security.

The Need for GETS

New technology like broadband communications, fiber optic networks, and high-speed digital switching has changed the way we communicate. This increase in technology also leads to increased vulnerabilities in the system. Major events, such as natural disasters and terrorist attacks, and even minor events like power outages and cables being cut, have demonstrated that entire regions of the telecommunications system can be disrupted. Back-up systems, although present, cannot always cope with the increased traffic during disasters. The necessity for uninterrupted communications among homeland security professionals during these times of increased traffic is obvious, and GETS provides a system to supply that need.

How GETS Works

During an emergency, phone lines are sometimes overwhelmed by the number of calls being placed. This, in turn, makes communications difficult for emergency management professionals. The GETS program is activated by the White House during these emergencies to accommodate those individuals with a particular need to communicate. These personnel are given an access number and pin, which they use to gain priority routing through the telephone system, leading to a much lower number of dropped or incomplete calls. The system works by providing priority processing through the Public Switched Telephone Network (PSTN), which gives access to approved individuals using either land lines or cell phones.

Conclusion

GETS is one of several programs in place to enhance the communications capability of emergency management and homeland security professionals during a crisis. By utilizing a private system to prioritize relevant calls, GETS ensures that telecommunications among those who need it most will not be interrupted. The program has met with success thus far; however, given the increase in technology, new systems will likely need to be developed or the current systems will need to continue to evolve.

Data from: Department of Homeland Security. (n.d.). GETS program information. Retrieved from http://gets.ncs.gov/program_info.html on March 13, 2013.

Cybersecurity

Many areas of homeland security are influenced by technology, either through methods of detection and threat elimination as in the case of counterterrorism or through new threats from adversaries wanting to damage the United States. **Cyberattacks**, and more specifically, **cyberterrorism**, are one of the most technology-reliant threats—and potentially one of the most damaging if carried out on a large scale successfully. Cyberattacks are, however, not a *new* threat, with the link between computer technology and national security dating from at least 1991, when it was mentioned in a report by the National Academy of Sciences.[24]

Cybersecurity involves a broad set of issues, dealing with national security threats from other nations, subnational actors (like terrorist organizations), and even private organizations and individuals.[25] This makes defining it a difficult proposition, and attempts have used both the effects of the attack (how much and the type of damage done) as well as the motivation for the attack (e.g., economic versus political). There is some agreement on the fact that three somewhat different cyber threats exist: cyberattacks (which is the broadest category, in which the others fit), **cybercrime** (which is criminal activity carried out through computing) and cyberterrorism, discussed next. A fourth category, cyber warfare, relies on the identity of those carrying out the attack—specifically a nation-state—in order to meet its definitional criteria. In general, all cyberattacks are uses of malicious computer code meant to disrupt the normal processing or logic of the target system or to steal information from the target system.[26] Of these types of attacks, cyberterrorism gets the most media attention.

Cyberterrorism

Given the general definitional problems arising around terrorism and cybersecurity, cyberterrorism is even more difficult to define.[27,28] Take, for instance, the case of a country that hires a terrorist organization to carry out an attack against a privately held critical infrastructure. The line between warfare, crime, and terrorism is difficult to draw under such a circumstance, and the scenario is not unlikely.[29] Definitions of cyberterrorism, therefore, are contentious among academics and practitioners. In fact, the government does not officially define cyberterrorism at all, although different agencies have adopted differing definitions to help scope day-to-day operations. Two of these definitions, one from the FBI and the other from the National Infrastructure Protection Center (NIPC), both rely on elements of political motivation, violence, and destruction of property as key elements of cyberterrorism.[30] Dorothy Denning, in the influential book *Networks and Netwars*, defines the term as "... politically motivated hacking operations intended to cause grave harm such as loss of life or severe economic damage."[31]

Although the threat was identified over 20 years ago, the threat of cyberterrorism has still not been realized in any broad sense; however, concern is growing.[32] Former FBI Director Robert Mueller stated, "terrorists increasingly use the Internet to communicate, conduct operational planning, proselytize, recruit, train, and to obtain logistical and financial support. That is a growing and increasing concern for us."[33] In fact, some use of cybercrime to support ongoing terrorist activity seems to be an important element in the definition of cyberterrorism. For example, in at least one case, through an email, an Internet user was directed to a fake eBay site in which she entered her financial information, which helped finance a terrorist cell planning physical attacks in both Europe and the Middle East (see **BOX 14.2**).[34]

Though it has not yet happened, physical damage through malicious computer use is a possibility. A 2007 test conducted by researchers in conjunction with DHS and the Department of Energy demonstrated the ability of hackers to get into an energy plant's information systems and cause a generator to self-destruct.[35] Similar threats have been popularized by the mass media,[36] although there is disagreement on how close terrorists are to being able to conduct these types of attacks successfully.[37,38]

The general consensus, insofar as one has developed, suggests that while terrorists likely lack the capability to conduct these attacks, there is the

BOX 14.2 2018 Cybersecurity Strategy

In 2009, under the direction of the White House, a comprehensive policy review was undertaken to examine the effectiveness of the nation's cybersecurity policies. The review of these policies was not positive. The final document pointed out several issues with the nation's cybersecurity, including its vulnerability to attack and the government's current inability to secure the digital infrastructure of the United States. The review specifically stated,

> The architecture of the nation's digital infrastructure, based largely on the Internet, is not secure or resilient. Without major advances in the security of these systems or significant change in how they are constructed or operated, it is doubtful that the United States can protect itself from the growing threat of cybercrime and state-sponsored intrusions and operations.

However, in pointing out these deficiencies, the review also suggested a way forward—government working with the private sector to enhance the security of cyberspace and America's digital interests.

Since that 2009 report, advances have been made in the nation's cybersecurity. Notably, the recent 2018 National Cybersecurity Strategy spends a significant amount of time detailing how to continue many of the advances made under previous administrations within the four pillars laid out in the strategy.[39]

The Need

The United States, like other developed nations, is increasingly reliant on network technology in nearly all aspects of its operations. From the day-to-day carrying out of government tasks to issues of fundamental importance to homeland security, the government is not immune to risks via bad actors attacking it through its network infrastructure. Additionally, the threat to homeland security goes well beyond state actors attempting to hack government systems—although, as in the case of the 2017 DHS hack, that remains a significant issue—but also extends to private organizations and actors working to disrupt industries or individual companies that are essential to the economy or to the nation's security in a different way.

(continues)

BOX 14.2 2018 Cybersecurity Strategy *(Continued)*

DHS Cybersecurity Strategy

DHS periodically puts together a cybersecurity strategy to deal with threats to the nation's homeland security from cyberspace. The most recent strategy was released on May 15, 2018, by the Trump Administration. It is organized across five "Pillars" and includes seven goals:

- Pillar I – Risk Identification
  - Goal 1: Assess Evolving Cybersecurity Risks
- Pillar II – Vulnerability Reduction
  - Goal 2: Protect Federal Government Information Systems
  - Goal 3: Protect Critical Infrastructure
- Pillar III – Threat Reduction
  - Goal 4: Prevent and Disrupt Criminal Use of Cyberspace
- Pillar IV – Consequence Mitigation
  - Goal 5: Respond Effectively to Cyber Incidents
- Pillar V – Enable Cybersecurity Outcomes
  - Goal 6: Strengthen the Security and Reliability of the Cyber Ecosystem
  - Goal 7: Improve Management of DHS Cybersecurity Activities

These pillars and goals form the basis of DHS cybersecurity operations for the next 5 years. They are loosely based on the risk management principles offered by DHS to other entities to help reduce their risk for cyberattacks and other incidents, both from cyberspace and in the physical world.

Conclusion

While the nation's current ability to defend against cyberattack is low, the defense of our digital infrastructure is improving. The Cybersecurity Strategy establishes significant steps that can be undertaken to enhance the government's ability to engage in cyber defense. These steps are only an outline for comprehensive cybersecurity, and many of the details are significant, if vague. The way these details are addressed in policy will determine how secure our nation's digital infrastructure is in the future, and given the growing importance of the Internet and related technologies, may be some of the most important security policies developed.

Data from: The White House. (2018). U.S. Department of Homeland Security Cybersecurity Strategy. Retrieved from https://www.dhs.gov/sites/default/files/publications/DHS-Cybersecurity-Strategy_1.pdf

possibility that they will contract with countries or organizations that do.[40] Indeed, as with terrorists using cybercrime to raise funds, they may also be working with hackers to exploit vulnerabilities in software that the government relies on to either maintain critical infrastructure or communications. In the latter case, it is believed that, should there be a large physical attack, communications could be disrupted to amplify the effects of the attack.[41]

Problem with Cybersecurity in America

The Internet and associated technologies represent the nation's "nervous system," and without these technologies, the government and economy could not function. As such, the digital infrastructure has been designated by DHS as one of the areas of critical infrastructure (see chapter on "Antiterrorism and Counterterrorism"). One of the problems with defending the nation's cyber interests is the fact that most of the country's digital infrastructure is privately owned by both American and international companies. Furthermore, the security management of cyberspace is distributed over a wide array of federal departments and agencies, making coordination of cyberdefense difficult.

Exacerbating the problem is the fact that digital threats have already manifested as actual attacks of the country or damaging the ability of the military to defend the nation. One example of this is the recent Equifax attacks. In these attacks, digital thieves stole the credit information—including Social Security numbers and driver's license numbers–from over 143 million individuals. Making the attack worse, people do not "opt in" to credit report checking, so many of those exposed in the attack would not know they were compromised, and unless negligence can be proven, there is little they can do by way of recouping any losses that eventually accrue from the breach.[42]

Digital criminals have stolen hundreds of millions of dollars, and nation-states have captured sensitive military data and intellectual property. The increase in these digital intrusions may only be precursors to even more damaging cyberattacks, including the potential for crippling the communications systems of either financial networks or even elements of the national security apparatus.

Cyber Defense

In the context of homeland security, then, it is important that the threat of cyberattacks is dealt with, despite the scant agreement on the definitions involved. Increasing the complexity of the problem of defense is the fact that cyberterrorism is not limited to the realms of homeland security or national security specifically. So, as with other areas of homeland security (counterterrorism specifically), there are several agencies involved in the activities surrounding cyberdefense. Chief among these are DHS, the Department of Defense, the FBI, and the NSA.

Department of Homeland Security

DHS's role in the realm of cyber defense is largely focused on preparation and mitigation in the event of a cyberattack. The Cyber Security Division (CSD), housed under the Cybersecurity and Infrastructure Security Agency (CISA), is responsible for the coordination of relevant agencies in the wake of cyberterrorism and has several programs in place to assess the vulnerabilities of the nation's critical infrastructure. They describe their mission as:

> The Cybersecurity and Infrastructure Security Agency's (CISA) Cybersecurity Division leads efforts to protect the federal ".gov" domain of civilian government networks and to collaborate with the private sector - the ".com" domain - to increase the security of critical networks. This occurs through four primary functions.
>
> - The National Cybersecurity and Communications Integration Center
> - Stakeholder Engagement and Cyber Infrastructure Resilience
> - Federal Network Resilience
> - Network Security Deployment
>
> CISA's National Cybersecurity and Communications Integration Center's (NCCIC) is the Nation's flagship cyber defense, incident response, and operational integration center. Since 2009, the NCCIC has served as a national hub for cyber and communications information, technical expertise, and operational integration, and by operating our 24/7 situational awareness, analysis, and incident response center.[43]

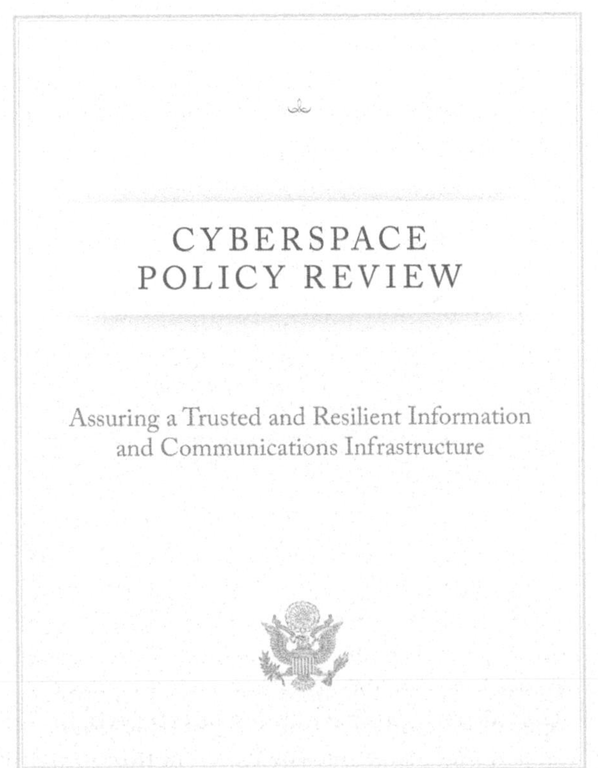

CYBERSPACE
POLICY REVIEW
Assuring a Trusted and Resilient Information
and Communications Infrastructure

Courtesy of the White House.

Another component of DHS's role in the context of cybersecurity is the Computer Emergency Readiness Team (US-CERT), tasked specifically with the security of government cyber operations and collaboration among state and local partners as well as those operating in the private sector. Under the auspices of this program, security alerts are distributed to relevant partners and responses are developed to assist with defense and resiliency. Additionally, US-CERT is tasked with the management of information-sharing across all partners.

Department of Defense

In addition to the DHS coordination efforts, the Department of Defense (DOD) is also responsible for cybersecurity issues, although its role tends to be more offensive than DHS's role.[44] While much of what the DOD engages in, in terms of cyber warfare, remains classified, the *Department of Defense Strategy for Operating in Cyberspace* makes it clear that the department views cyber issues as a natural outgrowth of its regular military mission:

> Though the networks and systems that make up cyberspace are man-made, often privately owned, and primarily civilian in use, treating cyberspace as a domain is a critical

> organizing concept for DOD's national security missions. This allows DOD to organize, train, and equip for cyberspace as we do in air, land, maritime, and space to support national security interests.[45]

In light of this, and the specific vulnerabilities that DOD faces due to their own reliance on computer networks to conduct operations, the military established the **Cyber Command (USCYBERCOM)**.[46] USCYBERCOM is specifically tasked with managing risk within DOD networks and making sure that those networks are resilient in case of an attack, working with other agencies and organizations to ensure coordinated response to any attacks that occur, and to develop and deploy innovative capabilities in terms of the cyber-defensive environment.[47]

Uniquely, USCYBERCOM is co-located in the National Security Agency (NSA), and the director of the NSA is also the commander of USCYBERCOM, underlying the importance of coordination across agencies, without which missions can easily fail.[48] This relationship also highlights the importance that intelligence, the NSA's specialty, plays in the realm of cybersecurity.

National Security Agency

The NSA, in addition to housing USCYBERCOM, has an important role to play in the context of cyber defense. The agency is responsible for gathering intelligence from electronic signals, including computer networks, and responds directly to tasking from any executive agency, including both DOD and DHS.[49] Importantly, there are restrictions on the ability of the NSA to gather information on U.S. persons, as a way of safeguarding citizens' privacy.

Courtesy of the White House.

Like the DOD, much of what the NSA does with regard to cybersecurity is classified. The NSA does monitor suspect websites and occasionally renders them inaccessible.[50] Additionally, the NSA is a co-sponsor (with DHS) of the National Centers of Academic Excellence in Information Assurance Education, which allows colleges and universities to apply for a designation as a center of excellence, providing their students access to scholarships in related areas.[51]

Central Intelligence Agency

The Central Intelligence Agency's role in cyberdefense is somewhat limited relative to homeland security. It is primarily responsible for identifying and evaluating foreign threats to domestic computer systems. Specifically, the Information Operations Center at the CIA has conducted a series of exercises to determine the nation's vulnerability to cyberattacks from both state and nonstate actors.[52] The results of these exercises have been helpful in identifying potential vulnerabilities and logistical issues, including the problem of coordination, as much of the nation's cyber infrastructure is controlled by private organizations.[53]

Federal Bureau of Investigation

The role of the Federal Bureau of Investigation (FBI), as it relates to cyberattacks, is limited primarily to issues dealing with cybercrime and terrorism. The FBI deals with computer intrusion issues related to crime within its Cyber Division. The FBI's Deputy Assistant Director, Cyber Division, said this regarding the FBI's cyber capability:

> The FBI is expanding our efforts to address the rapidly growing cyber threat as it relates to both terrorism and national security. The number of individuals and groups with the ability to use computers for illegal, harmful, and possibly devastating purposes is on the rise. We are particularly concerned about terrorists and state actors wishing to exploit vulnerabilities in U.S. systems and networks. . . . The FBI has a division dedicated to combating cybercrime and cyberterrorism. We are committed to identifying and neutralizing those individuals or groups that illegally access computer systems, spread malicious code, support terrorist or state-sponsored computer operations, and steal trade secrets that present an economic and security threat to the United States (see **BOX 14.3**).[54]

BOX 14.3 Office of Personnel Management Data Breach

In 2015, the Office of Personnel Management (OPM), an independent agency in the federal government of the United States, suffered a massive data breach. The initial breach, termed X1, was thought to include 4 million individuals' information, but by the end of the investigation, it was discovered that there was at least one additional breach (X2) and over 21 million individuals were affected. While not the largest breach of information in recent years, the OPM data breach was both unique and important because of the facts that it was background check information stolen and the perpetrator was a nation-state with which the United States is not allied.

The Information

While OPM provides a variety of tasks, one of the most important is the maintenance of information related to security background checks for government employees. The SF-86, which among other documents, is the document most closely associated with gaining a clearance within the government, allows an individual to see classified information. As such, the form contains information on a variety of topics, including previous places of residence, former roommates, foreign contacts, as well as identifiable information like Social Security numbers. Additionally, and perhaps even more problematically, the information stolen—outside of the SF-86—included information on biometrics, including fingerprint information.

The depth and breadth of the breach did not go without notice from the oversight elements in Congress. Specifically, the Committee on Oversight and Government Reforms had this to say in the executive summary of their investigation of the breach:

> The government of the United States of America has never before been more vulnerable to cyberattacks. No agency appears safe. In recent data breaches, hackers took information from the United States Postal Service; the State Department, the Nuclear Regulatory Commission; the Internal Revenue Service; and even the White House.
>
> None of these breaches though compare to the data breaches at the Office of Personnel Management (OPM). In what appears to be a coordinated campaign to collect information about government employees, attackers exfiltrated personnel files of 4.2 million former and current government employees and security clearance background investigation information on 21.5 million individuals.[55]

Rationale

One of the more disturbing pieces of the breach is the fact that it is widely suspected that the Chinese were behind it. Although there is no public, definitive proof available, there is wide speculation by members of the defense community that the breach was carried out by government agents for the Chinese. The information could be used in a variety of ways, including to help "social engineering" projects to extract other information from those affected by the attack. Additionally, because of the wide-ranging nature of the information stolen, it is possible that some of it could be used to impersonate American personnel in a variety of circumstances, which could have a set of negative outcomes ranging from ruining the credit of a given individual of importance to blackmail for national security secrets.

Significance

In addition to the singular impact that the OPM data breach could have on national security, the loss of data also has a broader significance. It represents both the power of information contained in online systems and the danger of inadequate protection of that information. The OPM breach represents the larger possibilities of what can be done by a malicious party, be it an individual or foreign government, if data provided to the government is not secure. This not only falls under the responsibility of DHS, but as the intertwining of public and private systems continues unabated, will increasingly fall to private companies. Given the recent "hacks" at places like Sony and Target, it remains to be seen how effective any protection regime can be against a determined adversary.

Source: Committee on House Oversight and Government Reform, U.S. House of Representatives, 114th Congress. 2016. "The OPM Data Breach: How the Government Jeopardized Our National Security for More than A Generation". Retrieved from https://www.scribd.com/document/323265444/the-opm-data-breach-how-the-government-jeopardized-our-national-security-for-more-than-a-generation.

Cybersecurity, although not a new realm of homeland security, is increasing in importance. Despite the difficulties in defining exactly what constitutes a cyber issue for homeland security, there is consensus that it poses a potential risk in a variety of areas including potentially critical infrastructure. While DHS is the lead agency in some respects, the response to cyberattacks is governmentwide, with responsibility falling to a variety of federal agencies. While the advent of a major cyberattack that, by itself, causes casualties is slim, the threat of a cyberattack in conjunction with other terrorist-related activities seem higher. In any event, the threat to our homeland security is significant enough that cybersecurity is clearly an area that cannot be ignored.

Additionally, as Box 14.3 shows, the direct threat is only one of the risks in the cyber realm. Individual data breaches can provide access to information by which individuals in important positions can be compromised and forced to give additional information, and others can be targeted as potential sources for intelligence through methods like "catfishing" or other forms of social engineering.

© Charles Krupa/AP/Shutterstock.

Technology and Homeland Security

While homeland security has suffered threats resulting from the increasing amount of technology in society, it is clear that technology also presents opportunities to better safeguard the homeland.[56] From the advent of DHS, technological solutions to the problem of homeland security have been part of the overall department mission.[57] The Homeland Security Act of 2002 mandated that a counterpart to the Defense Department's Advanced Research Projects Agency (DARPA) be created in a homeland security context.[58] **The Homeland Security Advanced Research Projects Agency (HSARPA)**, housed within DHS's Directorate of Science and Technology, is responsible for the development of advanced technology for the protection of the nation's critical infrastructure and other important elements of homeland security.[59] HSARPA is, however, not the only technologically directed program within DHS, as other elements, such as the First Responder's Group (FRG), also have technologically relevant missions.[60]

HSARPA

HSARPA is the agency responsible for developing some of the most technologically advanced elements of homeland security. As part of their mission, HSARPA works directly with many of the lead stakeholders in homeland security, such as the Secret Service, bomb squads, transportation authorities and others, to develop technological solutions to real-world problems that these organizations face. HSARPA itself has several areas of focus, housed within divisions in DHS:

- Borders and Maritime Security Division
- Chemical and Biological Defense Division
- Cyber Security Division
- Explosives Division
- Program Executive Office Unmanned Aerial Systems
- Apex Technology Engines
- Integrated Product Team

Each of these divisions is tasked with identifying gaps in the areas of need most relevant to the practitioners where technological solutions will have the most impact.[61] One example of these projects is the recently developed Imaging System for Immersive Surveillance system, a 360-degree camera with high resolution, which was developed under the Science and Technology Infrastructure and Geophysical Division for assistance with surveillance at public events.[62] Other, similar programs exist within each of HSARPA's areas (see **BOX 14.4**).

Support to the Homeland Security Enterprise and First Responders Group

In addition to the advanced research projects provided by HSARPA, a second high-technology group exists within the Directorate of Science and Technology. The Support to the Homeland Security Enterprise and First Responders Group (FRG) is tasked with the goals of making first responders safer as well as increasing the operational capacity of first responders through the adoption of technology that makes elements such as communication easier and more reliable.[63] Unlike HSARPA; however, the mission of the FRG is not to develop new technologies, but rather, to assist with the deployment of existing technologies. The FRG accomplishes its mission through three divisions: the **National Urban Security Technology Laboratory (NUSTL)**, Office for Interoperability and Compatibility (OIC), and the R-Tech (TCR).[64]

BOX 14.4 Ground-Penetrating Radar to Detect Tunnels—HSARPA in Action

One of the challenges facing the U.S. Border Patrol is the increasing use of tunnels by smugglers on the United States/Mexico border. While the tunnels have always been a problem, the number has gone up dramatically in recent years, with over 60% of the tunnels discovered being found in the past 7 years. These represent a significant threat to the homeland security of the United States, not only because of the drugs and illegal immigrants who are normally brought across the border but also because of the potential to use these tunnels to smuggle terrorists or WMDs into the country.

The Homeland Security Advanced Research Projects Agency (HSARPA) is working in conjunction with Lockheed Martin Advanced Technology Laboratories to develop technology to help the Border Patrol identify the location of these tunnels so they can be blocked. This is difficult because many of the tunnels are in urban areas and can begin and end in buildings or behind structures, making it difficult to detect them from the air, the approach originally suggested. Instead, HSARPA is pursuing ground-penetrating radar technology, which can help map the tunnels from above ground.

How It Works

The radar system will be attached to a vehicle and pulled across areas where there may be tunnels. Electromagnetic waves from the radar can be used to construct complete pictures of what appears underground. Tunnels will show up as red, yellow, and aquamarine dots against a neutral background, making identification of these threats relatively simple.

The technology being used for tunnel detection is already field tested in the sense that engineers already use ground-penetrating radar for a variety of purposes. However, these uses tend to be confined to finding cables and other underground elements relatively near the surface. The tunnels being used for illegal activity frequently are dug much deeper, which requires a technological redevelopment by HSARPA and Lockheed Martin. The new radar will use frequencies much lower than those currently being used, allowing for additional depth of detection.

Conclusion

Technologies like the tunnel-detecting radar represent the utility of HSARPA for homeland security. Not only does it make it possible to detect and possibly deter threats from adversaries, but it also represents a successful collaboration between the public and private sector to improve homeland security. Projects like this one also demonstrate the importance of primary research, which can propel the next generation of homeland security technologies.

Data from: Department of Homeland Security. (2009). Tunnel-vision. Retrieved from http://www.dhs.gov/tunnel-vision on March 13, 2013.

The NUSTL is focused, as its name suggests, on the adoption of technology primarily for urban environments. Housed in New York City, the NUSTL serves as the technological authority for promoting and integrating useful technologies for end-users in homeland security—primarily first responders.[65] Additionally, the NUSTL conducts test programs and evaluations of new, homeland security-relevant technologies for first responders, while applying their knowledge of the first-responder environment for integration of these technologies. Further, the FRG plays a significant role in developing and establishing operations standards for homeland security equipment and technology.[66]

The OIC, on the other hand, is focused directly on the problems mentioned previously in this chapter. Specifically, they help with communications interoperability and operations for first responders.[67] This mission is particularly difficult, and particularly relevant, because the current first-responder landscape consists of over 60,000 state and local public safety agencies that have some homeland security responsibility. The OIC mission is to make communications among these agencies as seamless as possible, and they accomplish this mission through the development of technologies and standards for communications equipment and processes.[68]

The TCR is focused on a different mission than either the OIC or the NUSTL. It has the mission of deploying technologies that are field-ready for first responders operating in the homeland security environment. It is a rapid-deployment program, with the goal of meeting 80% of requirements that fill an operational gap 12 to 15 months after that gap has been identified. The program received requests from active first responders rather than through an internal process of identification, ensuring that the technologies delivered meet the specific needs of those in the field.[69]

Although technology represents a "double-edged sword," it is clear that DHS is relying on significant technological advancement and standardization to help in its mission. The goals of the Science and Technology Directorate, particularly in reference to HSARPA and the FRG, are essential given the ubiquity

Courtesy of DHS.

of technology across all critical domains. The technology developed by HSARPA implemented through the HRG provides first responders at all levels with solutions that they need to help fulfill their own respective homeland security missions.[70] As it has been from the advent of DHS, technology will continue to be an essential part of defending the homeland.

Chapter Summary

Issues in communications and cyber defense are increasing in importance across the homeland security domain. With the increasing use of the Internet, and the use of networked systems for controlling much of our everyday lives, the risk of a cyberattack (of whatever type) has steadily increased. Additionally, and perhaps unsurprisingly, there has been an increase in the nexus of cybercrime and terrorist organizations. Meanwhile, communications issues identified after 9-11, although improved, still are not resolved. True interoperability and compatibility across the nation's 60,000 agencies remains somewhat distant.

However, even with the problems technology can present, it is clear that it can also provide solutions. The advent and promulgation of new technologies by organizations in homeland security such as HSARPA and the FRG have assisted first responders at all levels of government. Developments such as new surveillance options as well as communications equipment and explosive detection technology have assisted in helping secure the homeland from attack. Additional technologies being developed will most likely also assist in combating terrorism and aiding emergency response efforts.

In any event, technology is likely to remain both a focal point for future threats, particularly in cyberspace, and a method by which those threats can be neutralized. DHS and related agencies have devoted significant resources to studying the threat as well as developing appropriate responses.

Review/Discussion Questions

1. What role does communications technology play in homeland security, and what problems were identified by the 9/11 Commission as issues?
2. How many cyberattacks have there been that have physically damaged infrastructure in the United States? Does it represent a significant threat?
3. What are the problems with defining cyberterrorism? How might that affect homeland security operations?
4. What do you think the role of HSARPA should be with regard to homeland security technology, and why is this role important?
5. Is there a good way to divide cyberdefense issues between the Department of Defense and the Department of Homeland Security? How might these jurisdictions be defined?

Additional Readings

Arquilla, J. & Ronfeldt, D. (Eds.). *Networks and Netwar.* Santa Monica, CA: Rand.

The White House. (2009). *Cyberspace Policy Review.* Retrieved from http://www.dhs.gov/sites/default/files/publications/Cyberspace_Policy_Review_final_0.pdf on March 13, 2013.

Endnotes

1. Misa, T. J., Brey, P., & Feenberg, A. (Eds.) (2004). *Modernity and Technology*. Boston, MA: MIT Press.
2. Wireless Quick Facts. (2013). Retrieved from http://www.ctia.org/advocacy/research/index.cfm/aid/10323.
3. Panetta, L. (2013). *Remarks by Secretary Panetta at Georgetown University, Washington, D.C.* Retrieved from https://archive.defense.gov/speeches/speech.aspx?speechid=1747.
4. Jenkins, W. O. (2006). "Collaboration Over Adaptation: The Case for Interoperable Communications in Homeland Security." *Public Administration Review, 66*, 319–321.
5. National Commission on Terrorist Attacks Upon the United States. (2004). *The 9/11 Commission Report: Final Report of the National Commission on Terrorist Attacks Upon the United States (Authorized Ed.).* New York: W.W. Norton & Company, Inc.
6. National Commission on Terrorist Attacks Upon the United States. (2004). *The 9/11 Commission Report: Final Report of the National Commission on Terrorist Attacks Upon the United States (Authorized Ed.).* New York: W.W. Norton & Company, Inc.
7. Collins S. (2011). *Ten Years after 9/11: Improving Emergency Communications*. 112–403: Ten Years After 9/11 – 2011, Hearings Before the Committee on Homeland Security and Governmental Affairs, United States Senate, One Hundred Twelfth Congress. Retrieved from https://www.hsdl.org/?view&did=733983.
8. Moore, L. K. (2012). *The First Responder Network (FirstNet) and Next-Generation Communications for Public Safety: Issues for Congress* (CRS report No. R42543). Retrieved from http://www.fas.org/sgp/crs/homesec/R42543.pdf.
9. Moore, L. K. (2005). *Public Safety, Communications: Policy, Proposals, Legislation and Progress* (CRS report No. RL32594). Retrieved from http://www.fas.org/sgp/crs/homesec/R41842.pdf.
10. Intelligence Reform and Terrorism Prevention Act of 2004. Pub. L. No. 108–458, §7303, 118 Stat. 3638.
11. Department of Homeland Security. *Emergency Communications Policy and Planning*. Retrieved from http://www.dhs.gov/oec-policy-and-planning-branch.
12. Department of Homeland Security. *Public Safety and National Security/Emergency Preparedness (NS/EP) Partnerships*. Retrieved from http://www.dhs.gov/node/6018/.
13. Department of Homeland Security. *Office of Emergency Communications Technical Assistance Program*. Retrieved on May 16, 2019 from http://www.dhs.gov/office-emergency-communications-technical-assistance-program.
14. Department of Homeland Security. *OEC Regional Coordination Program*. Retrieved from http://www.dhs.gov/oec-regional-coordination-program.
15. Department of Homeland Security. (2016). Office of Emergency Communications Architecture and Advanced Technology Support. Retrieved from https://www.dhs.gov/oec-architecture-and-advanced-technology-support
16. Department of Homeland Security. *OEC Communications Portfolio Management Branch*. Retrieved from http://www.dhs.gov/oec-communications-portfolio-management-branch.
17. Office of the President (2010). *National Security Strategy*. Washington, DC: GPO.
18. Reese, S. (2012). *National Security and Emergency Preparedness Communications: A Summary of Executive Order 13618* (CRS report No. R24740). Retrieved from http://www.fas.org/sgp/crs/homesec/R42740.pdf.
19. Department of Homeland Security. White House Gives Homeland Security Control of All Communications Systems." (13 July 2012). RT.com. Retrieved from http://rt.com/usa/news/white-house-systems-order-142/
20. Department of Homeland Security (2019). *About TSP*. Retrieved from http://tsp.ncs.gov/.
21. "White House Gives Homeland Security Control of all Communications Systems." (13 July 2012). RT.com. Retrieved from http://rt.com/usa/news/white-house-systems-order-142/.
22. Moore, L. K. (2012). *The First Responder Network and Next-generation Communications for Public Safety: Issues for Congress* (CRS report No. R42543). Retrieved from http://www.fas.org/sgp/crs/homesec/R42543.pdf.
23. Department of Homeland Security (2019). *Statewide Communication Interoperability Plans*. Retrieved from https://www.dhs.gov/cisa/statewide-communication-interoperability-plans.
24. Cavelty, M. D. (2007). "Cyber-terror—Looming Threat or Phantom Menace? The Framing of the US Cyber-threat Debate." *Journal of Information Technology & Politics, 4*, 19–36.
25. Rollins, J. & Wilson, C. (2007). Terrorist Capabilities for Cyberattack: Overview and Policy Issues (CRS report No. RL33123. Retrieved from https://fas.org/sgp/crs/terror/RL33123.pdf
26. Wilson, C. (2008). *Botnets, Cybercrime and Cyberterrorism: Vulnerabilities and Policy Issues for Congress* (CRS report No. RL32114). Retrieved from http://www.fas.org/sgp/crs/homesec/RL32114.pdf.
27. Cavelty, M. D. (2007). "Cyber-terror—Looming Threat or Phantom Menace? The Framing of the US Cyber-threat Debate." *Journal of Information Technology & Politics, 4*, 19–36.
28. Wilson, C. (2008). *Botnets, Cybercrime and Cyberterrorism: Vulnerabilities and Policy Issues for Congress* (CRS Report No. RL32114). Retrieved from http://www.fas.org/sgp/crs/terror/RL32114.pdf.
29. Weimann, G. (2008). "Cyber-terrorism: Are We Barking up the Wrong Tree?" *Harvard Asia Pacific Review, 9*, 41–46.
30. Centre of Excellence Defense Against Terrorism, ed. (2008). NATO science for peace and security series. Sub-series E: Human and societal dynamics, ISSN 1874-6276.
31. Denning, D. (2001). "Activism, Hactivism, and Cyberterrorism: The Internet as a Tool for Influencing Foreign Policy." In Arquilla, J., and Ronfeldt, D. (eds.). *Networks and Netwar*. Santa Monica, CA: Rand.
32. Weimann, G. (2008). "Cyber-terrorism: Are We Barking up the Wrong Tree?" *Harvard Asia Pacific Review, 9*, 41–46.
33. *Current and Projected National Security Threats to the United States*, 110 Cong. S. Hrg. 110-835. (2007). (Robert Mueller).
34. Krebs, B. (6 July 2007). "Three Worked the Web to Help Terrorists." *The Washington Post Online*. Retrieved from http://www.washingtonpost.com/wp-dyn/content/article/2007/07/05/AR2007070501945.html.
35. Meserve, J. (2013). *Sources: Staged Cyber Attack Reveals Vulnerability in Power Grid*. Retrieved from http://www.cnn.com/2007/US/09/26/power.at.risk/
36. Wilson, C. (2008). *Botnets, Cybercrime and Cyberterrorism: Vulnerabilities and Policy Issues for Congress* (CRS report No. RL32114). Retrieved from Retrieved from http://www.fas.org/sgp/crs/terror/RL32114.pdf

37. Wilson, C. (2005). *Computer Attacks and Cyber Terrorism: Vulnerabilities and Issues for Congress* (CRS report No. RL32114). Retrieved https://digital.library.unt.edu/ark:/67531/metacrs6315/m1/1/high_res_d/RL32114_2005Apr01.pdf
38. Cavelty, M. D. (2007). "Cyber-terror—Looming Threat or Phantom Menace? The Framing of the US Cyber-threat Debate." *Journal of Information Technology & Politics, 4*, 19-36.
39. The White House (2018). National Cyber Strategy. Retrieved on 23 March 22, 2019 from https://www.whitehouse.gov/wp-content/uploads/2018/09/National-Cyber-Strategy.pdf.
40. *Cybersecurity: Preventing Terrorist Attacks and Protecting Privacy in Cyber-space*, 111 Cong. S. Hrg. 111-664. (2007). (Steven Chabinsky).
41. Wilson, C. (2003). *Computer Attacks and Cyber Terrorism: Vulnerabilities and Issues for Congress* (CRS report No. RL32114). Retrieved from https://opencrs.com/document/RL32114/2003-10-17/.
42. Bernard, T. S., Hsu, T., Perlroth, N., & Leiber, R. (2017). Equifax Says Cyberattack May Have Affected 143 Million in the U.S. *The New York Times*. Retrieved on 23 March 2019 from https://www.nytimes.com/2017/09/07/business/equifax-cyberattack.html.
43. Department of Homeland Security. *Cyber Security Division*. Retrieved from https://www.dhs.gov/cisa/cybersecurity-division
44. Gjelten, T. (2013). *Pentagon Goes on the Offensive Against Cyberattacks*. Retrieved from http://www.npr.org/2013/02/11/171677247/pentagon-goes-on-the-offensive-against-cyber-attacks.
45. Department of Defense. (2011). *Department of Defense Strategy for Operating in Cyberspace*. Retrieved from https://csrc.nist.gov/CSRC/media/Projects/ISPAB/documents/DOD-Strategy-for-Operating-in-Cyberspace.pdf
46. Department of Defense. (2011). *Department of Defense Strategy for Operating in Cyberspace*. Retrieved from https://csrc.nist.gov/CSRC/media/Projects/ISPAB/documents/DOD-Strategy-for-Operating-in-Cyberspace.pdf
47. Department of Defense. (2011). *Department of Defense Strategy for Operating in Cyberspace*. Retrieved from http://www.defense.gov/news/d20110714cyber.pdf.
48. Nakashima, E. (19 March 2010). "Dismantling of Saudi-CIA Web Site Illustrates Clearer Need for Cyberwar Policies." *Washington Post Online*. Retrieved from http://www.washingtonpost.com/wp-dyn/content/article/2010/03/18/AR2010031805464_pf.html
49. National Security Agency. *Signals Intelligence*. Retrieved from https://www.nsa.gov/what-we-do/signals-intelligence
50. Nakashima, E. (19 March 2010). "Dismantling of Saudi-CIA Web Site Illustrates Clearer Need for Cyberwar Policies." *Washington Post Online*. Retrieved from http://www.washingtonpost.com/wp-dyn/content/article/2010/03/18/AR2010031805464.html?sid=ST2010031901063
51. National Security Agency. *National Centers for Academic Excellence*. Retrieved from https://www.nsa.gov/resources/students-educators/centers-academic-excellence/
52. Bridis, T. (26 May 2005). "'Silent Horizon' War Games Wrap Up for the CIA." *USA Today*. Retrieved from http://usatoday30.usatoday.com/tech/news/techpolicy/2005-05-26-cia-wargames_x.htm.
53. Rollins, J. & Wilson, C. (2007). Terrorist Capabilities for Cyberattack: Overview and Policy Issues (CRS report No. RL33123. Retrieved from https://fas.org/sgp/crs/terror/RL33123.pdf
54. *Hearing on Cyberterrorism*, 108 Cong. (2004). (Keith Lourdeau). Retrieved from http://www.fbi.gov/news/testimony/hearing-on-cyber-terrorism.
55. Committee on House Oversight and Government Reform, U.S. House of Representatives, 114th Congress. (2016). The OPM Data Breach: How the Government Jeopardized Our National Security for More than A Generation. Retrieved from https://www.scribd.com/document/323265444/the-opm-data-breach-how-the-government-jeopardized-our-national-security-for-more-than-a-generation.
56. George Washington University Homeland Security Police Institute. (2008). *Technology in Homeland Security: A Double-edged Sword*. Retrieved from https://cchs.gwu.edu/technology-homeland-security-double-edged-sword.
57. Homeland Security Presidential Directive 7: Critical Infrastructure Identification, Prioritization, and Protection. Retrieved from http://www.dhs.gov/homeland-security-presidential-directive-7#1.
58. Homeland Security Act of 2002, Pub. L. No. 107-296 § 307, 116 Stat. 2135.
59. Department of Homeland Security. *Science and Technology Directorate Homeland Security Advanced Research Projects Agency*. Retrieved from http://www.dhs.gov/st-hsarpa.
60. Department of Homeland Security. *Science and Technology Directorate Support to the Homeland Security Enterprise and First Responders Group*. Retrieved from http://www.dhs.gov/st-frg.
61. Department of Homeland Security. *Science and Technology Directorate Homeland Security Advanced Research Projects Agency*. Retrieved from http://www.dhs.gov/st-hsarpa.
62. Department of Homeland Security. ISIS: *New Video Camera Sees It All*. Retrieved from http://www.dhs.gov/isis-new-video-camera-sees-it-all/.
63. Department of Homeland Security. *Science and Technology Directorate Support to the Homeland Security Enterprise and First Responders Group*. Retrieved from http://www.dhs.gov/st-frg.
64. Department of Homeland Security. *Science and Technology Directorate Support to the Homeland Security Enterprise and First Responders Group*. Retrieved from http://www.dhs.gov/st-frg.
65. Department of Homeland Security. *National Urban Security Technology Laboratory: Strategic Plan 2009-2013*. Retrieved from http://www.dhs.gov/xlibrary/assets/st_dhs_nustl_strategic_plan.pdf.
66. Department of Homeland Security. *Science and Technology Directorate Support to the Homeland Security Enterprise and First Responders Group*. Retrieved from http://www.dhs.gov/st-frg.
67. Department of Homeland Security. *Science and Technology Directorate Office for Interoperability and Compatibility*. Retrieved from https://www.dhs.gov/st-oic.
68. National Public Safety Communications Council. *Office for Interoperability and Compatibility (OIC)*. Retrieved from http://www.npstc.org/oic.jsp.
69. Department of Homeland Security. *Science and Technology Directorate Technology Clearinghouse / R-tech*. Retrieved from http://www.dhs.gov/st-tcr
70. Department of Homeland Security (2019). *First Responder Technologies*. Retrieved on July 13, 2019 from https://www.dhs.gov/science-and-technology/first-responder-technologies#.

CHAPTER 15

Domain Security and the Future of Homeland Security

CHAPTER OBJECTIVES

- To understand the importance of domain security, particularly airline security, port security, and border security
- To understand the role TSA plays in airline security and its additional oversight responsibilities in reference to other elements of domain security
- To identify the roles of the U.S. Border Patrol and Immigration and Customs Enforcement in terms of border security
- To understand the challenges faced by homeland security in the future

CHAPTER OUTLINE

SEA, LAND, AIR—AND CYBERSPACE

AVIATION SECURITY

Commercial Passenger Aviation

All Cargo Aircraft and General Aviation Security

MARITIME SECURITY

OTHER TRANSPORTATION SECTORS

BORDER SECURITY

Immigration

Criminal Networks

(continues)

The flight attendants did not notice the large man, at least 6′4″ and 200 lbs, as he got on the plane.[1] He had an aisle seat, 29C, near the back of the Boeing 767 that was on its way from Paris's Charles De Gaulle Airport to Miami International Airport in Florida. Perhaps like many of the passengers, the man was jittery—after all, the 9-11 attacks on the World Trade Center and the Pentagon had only happened about 3 months before.[2] The man, assumed to be on his way to a vacation, carried no luggage.[3]

As the flight took off and the attendants offered refreshments to the passengers, the man declined them all, including water—unusual for someone on a 10-hour transcontinental flight. One flight attendant tried to speak to the man in French, but he indicated that he spoke English. This piqued her curiosity, and she joked with the man about being on a diet, but her suspicions persisted. When asked where he was from, the man replied that he was from Sri Lanka, which the attendant didn't believe.[4]

Just after the 2-hour mark, the point at which it would be impossible for the plane to return to Paris,[5] some passengers complained of a smell of smoke in the cabin. Looking around, the attendant saw the man attempting to light a match. She reminded him that smoking on the flight was not allowed, and the man promised not to attempt it again. However, a few minutes later, she came by the man's seat again and found him bent over, apparently hiding something. Believing he was smoking a cigarette, she pulled him up after asking him what he was doing, and at that point, saw that he was attempting to light another match—but this time, there was a shoe in his lap with what seemed like a fuse sticking out.[6]

Once the attendant realized what was happening, she tried to stop him, although he pushed her to the floor. With the help of other passengers, the flight crew subdued the man, and, using plastic handcuffs, seat belt extenders, and other items, made sure he was immobile. A doctor on board the flight administered Valium to the man to keep him calm.[7]

The man was Richard Reid, the now infamous "shoe bomber" and an al Qaeda operative.[8]

While this act of heroism is deservedly celebrated as an instance of those in transportation thwarting a terrorist attack, the attempted bombing highlights one of the major issues that the homeland security community is still attempting to address today. While we place a premium on security in air transportation, the passenger system is designed for efficiency and convenience for the passengers—not to be perfectly secure.[9] At the time of Richard Reid's attempted attack, shoes—and other items that still make it through security without being completely inspected—could conceal weapons or bombs used against aircraft.[10] Importantly, other essential systems in the United States share a similar vulnerability—our shipping systems, immigrations systems, and our ports were all originally developed as commercial enterprises, making their security especially problematic.

Sea, Land, Air—and Cyberspace

Homeland security is challenging, in part, because of the variety of environments that the United States has to protect.[11] The challenges from adversaries are not limited to air transportation—what most people think of post-September 11. Instead, homeland security in America deals with a variety of environments and threats, from protecting our land borders from a diverse range of actors (e.g., illegal immigrants and transnational criminals),[12] to protection of our maritime interests,[13] securing our airways for our public and cargo, and protecting the government and critical infrastructure from cyberattacks.

This chapter is focused around these four environments—air, land, sea, and cyberspace—as each represents some of the most pressing threats to homeland security today. The section dealing with aviation and transportation security specifically examines the issues of passenger transportation and cargo shipping by air and land in the United States, while the following section focuses on **border security** and immigration issues. The third section examines maritime issues, particularly focusing on port security. The fourth section examines issues unique to cyberspace. Finally, this chapter examines the future of homeland security, examining the potential of future threats and what an appropriate response to these threats might be.

Although these sections are addressed individually, it is important to remember that they are not individual issues. Port security, for instance, is not simply a matter of **maritime security** but also it involves significant elements of the air-transport system in the United States, particularly cargo and individuals coming from abroad. Similarly, border security is not an issue confined only to the southern United States/Mexico border, although many of the most significant threats from a homeland security perspective do come from that area.

In short, domain security is a challenging, multi-faceted area of homeland security with a variety of overlapping issues. Without securing each, the security of the other areas is jeopardized, and given the economic impact of each domain, it is essential that they all remain as protected as possible.

Aviation Security

While there have been many security changes in the post-9-11 homeland security environment, perhaps none of these changes are as familiar to most Americans as the changes to air security procedures. The additional requirements of taking off shoes,[14] instituted after the Richard Reid attempt, as well as the limitation on the amount of liquid-per-bottle, enforced after the failed "Operation Bojinka" plot was discovered,[15] have been widely mentioned in the press and ridiculed by some.[16] These, mostly reactive, changes are only the public face of a large series of security changes that have taken place in aviation security post-9-11, the most important of which is the development of the **Transportation Security Administration (TSA)**.

The TSA was created by virtue of the Aviation and Transportation Security Act of 2001,[17] passed just

Courtesy of DHS.

2 months after the September 11 attacks. The agency was moved from the Department of Transportation and folded into the Department of Homeland Security upon the latter's creation in 2003.[18] As of 2010, the agency had approximately 52,000 employees and a budget of about \$7.66 billion.[19] The TSA has a wide range of responsibilities related to homeland security and transportation, the most visible of which is the screening of all passengers and baggage for commercial flights originating in the United States. In addition to the security obligations for commercial flights, the TSA's aviation responsibilities include the security of recreational aviation and primary responsibility for the security of air-freight and cargo (see **BOX 15.1**).[20]

TSA, in its role as the organization primarily responsible for airline security, has had several statutory mandates placed upon it. Chief among these is the mandate to screen all passengers and cargo placed on passenger aircraft, particularly those aircraft coming to the United States from outside of the country, as well as eventually screening 100% of the shipments on all-cargo aircraft, although TSA has argued that a risk-based screening process is more effective.[21] In addition, the TSA is responsible for the development and deployment of new technologies and procedures for screening passengers.[22] Interestingly, the TSA is also required to examine the possibility of privatizing airport screening operations through the Screening Partnership Program[23] and manage the security of large, general-aviation aircraft. In their aviation security role, the TSA has been responsible for some of the more controversial processes that have been put in place since September 11, 2001. These include the new, arguably more invasive, screening procedures at airport checkpoints[24] as well as the use of the consolidated terrorist watch list, against which TSA checks all passengers who have an American destination.[25]

BOX 15.1 Passenger Screening Technology

There are few who dispute the need for the Transportation Security Administration (TSA) to physically screen passengers for dangerous items. There has been, however, much debate about appropriate methods of screening and screening technologies. TSA has made revisions in its screening policy to try and adapt to these complaints, with particular modifications to screening policy focused on children under the age of 12 and passengers over the age of 75. In addition to these changes, and partially as a response to complaints about invasive pat-downs by TSA employees, the agency has developed new, advanced imaging technologies to assist with passenger screening.

Screening Technologies

TSA began testing advanced screening methods beginning in 2007 and had deployed some units by 2008. Two types of technology are being used to screen passengers in the new, more advanced systems. Millimeter wave and backscatter technologies allow for fast and complete scans of individuals, allowing TSA to identify contraband items quickly and effectively. The new technologies are, however, not without detractors. Many individuals are concerned about the potential long-term effects of the x-rays used in the process and the sometimes detailed images that can result from the backscatter machines, in particular.

General Acceptance

Despite the controversy surrounding these technologies, there seems to be a general consensus on their use. According to the TSA, more than 99% of passengers choose the new screening process over the alternative screening procedures offered by the TSA. Also, a *CBS* poll suggests that a high percentage of Americans support the use of advanced imaging technology at airports. There is also some evidence to suggest that passengers with particular issues, such as knee replacements and other medical devices that would set off a regular metal detector, may prefer the newer technologies.

Conclusion

While the technology used in TSA's new, advanced imaging systems is controversial, there seems to be a general acceptance of the technology as necessary. The adoption of any new screening technology is likely to be controversial, as there are changes in the way passengers interact with the airport security system. Privacy issues notwithstanding, the new imaging technologies tend to be faster and provide for a more secure environment in the commercial passenger airline system.

Data from: Transportation Security Administration. (2013). *Advanced imaging technology (AIT)*; Wald, M.L. (2010). Cancer risks debated for type of x-ray scan. The New York Times.

Commercial Passenger Aviation

The TSA carries out its aviation security mission in what it describes as a "layered approach."[26] The layers identified by the TSA begin with an appropriate collection of intelligence on potential threats and range through every layer of the aviation process and end with passengers as the last line of defense, as occurred on 9-11 on United Flight 93 (see Prologue).[27] The first layer is tied to compliance with the International Civil Aviation Organization—established to govern international aviation security standards. Perhaps the most significant aspect of the next layer is the screening processes, which involves the checking of names against the terrorist watch list maintained by the Terrorist Screening Center[28] and the physical screening of passengers considered "high risk."[29] The third layer involves the physical screening of passengers and their baggage, as well as the procedures developed to keep dangerous items off planes. The final layer involves stopping attacks in progress during flights, through on-board security (U.S. Air Marshals), armed pilots, and, as a last resort, the crew and passengers themselves.[30]

All Cargo Aircraft and General Aviation Security

While TSA obviously gets attention for its work on commercial passenger aviation, the organization is also responsible for the security of both commercial shipping and general aviation.[31] These two areas represent a significant percentage of the aircraft in the air at any given time, and perhaps more importantly, represent at least 25% of the commercial value of the aviation industry.[32] Unlike commercial passenger aviation, however, general aviation aircraft do not necessarily have to file flight plans, and until fairly recently, those traveling on these aircraft did not go through a significant vetting process.[33]

In addition to their aviation responsibilities and in conjunction with state and local partners, TSA is also responsible for the security of the nation's railway systems and other transportation networks, although the bulk of their operations are focused in the aviation arena with state, local, and private organizations taking larger roles in the other transportation sectors.

Maritime Security

The attacks on September 11, 2001, while focused on commercial aviation, suggested vulnerabilities in all modes of transportation. Since 9-11, port security has been highlighted as one of the areas of importance for dealing with terrorist threats of a number of types including smuggling of terrorist personnel, weapons of mass destruction, or other types of dangerous material into the country. These threats, however, not only extend to the movement of arms or personnel but also include the ports themselves as a target, as much of the nation's commercial activity originates in ports. The *9/11 Commission Report* stated,

> While commercial aviation remains a possible target, terrorists may turn their attention to other modes. Opportunities to do harm are as great, or greater, in maritime and surface transportation. Initiatives to secure shipping containers have just begun.[34]

The threat of attack is complicated by the nature of port systems, as well as the number of organizations involved in both port security and managing the commercial activity of the ports.[35] The U.S. maritime port system includes more than 300 sea and river ports and has more than 3,700 cargo and passenger terminals. Additionally, there are more than 1,000 harbor channels spread along the country's vast coastlines. The scope of the commercial activity in these ports is enormous. The top 50 ports in the United States account for 90% of all cargo tonnage, and 25 U.S. ports account for 98% of all container shipments. Ships carry approximately 80% of world trade by volume, and the United States is the world's leading maritime trading nation, responsible for 20% of the worldwide shipping volume.[36]

There are a range of threat scenarios that have been identified in a maritime context. The smuggling scenario, mentioned previously, is one of the more benign, with other scenarios including using a ship as a collision weapon,[37] using a ship to cause a massive in-port explosion, or causing an offshore discharge of oil and fire. While some of these offer the possibility of high levels of civilian casualties, much of the danger also stems from the loss of commercial activity that these attacks could entail.[38]

There are a number of federal agencies involved in port security. The Coast Guard, Bureau of Customs and Border Protection, the TSA, and all DHS agencies have some responsibility, and other organizations such as the Maritime Administration, the Department of State, and the Department of Defense also have significant roles.[39] Each of these agencies has a specific role to play in the overlapping system of port security in the United Sates, and each plays a significant role in the security of maritime activity.[40]

The U.S. Coast Guard (USCG) is the principal agency in charge of maritime homeland security and operates under the auspices of the Department of Homeland Security.[41] Rolled into the department in 2003, the USCG is responsible for boarding, inspecting, and evaluating the threat of any commercial ships entering the territorial waters of the United States and for countering threats at U.S. ports.[42] In addition to their general homeland security responsibilities, the USCG has developed the concept of maritime domain awareness, which assists in giving a more complete picture of the maritime threat environment.

The Bureau of Customs and Border Protection (CBP) has a different role in maritime homeland security. It is responsible for inspecting cargo and containers that commercial ships bring into U.S. ports. Additionally, the CBP inspects crew manifests and cruise-ship passenger lists from any foreign port.[43] This combines the functions previously performed by two separate agencies, U.S. Customs Service and Immigration and Naturalization Service, which were combined into the CBP after the advent of DHS. CBP has several initiatives related to maritime homeland security, including the Container Security Initiative (CSI)[44] and the Customs-Trade Partnership Against Terrorism (C-TPAT).[45] These are designed to expand the United States' "zone of security" to foreign ports so that a container's cargo can be verified through pre-screening before ever making it to the shores of the United States.[46]

The TSA also has a significant maritime security role, although it is not as large as its aviation role, as it is not the lead agency. The TSA has maritime security responsibility for, among other things, tracking containers through ports for security purposes and creating a transportation worker identification system—DHS's Transportation Worker Identification Credential system, which will help ensure that those employed by ports are not threats to U.S. homeland security.[47] The TSA works in conjunction with the FBI in some cases to assess whether individuals working at port authorities around the nation appear on the terrorism watch list.

In addition to those agencies having a role at the federal, state, and in particular local level, port authorities also have important responsibilities for maritime homeland security. Port authorities, responsible for managing day-to-day operations at ports, have to work very closely with those agencies responsible for maritime homeland security. In the

BOX 15.2 The *Limburg* Attack

On October 6, 2002, the double-hull oil tanker *Limburg* was attacked in the Gulf of Aden off of the Yemeni coast. The tanker was carrying 400,000 gallons of oil when it was attacked by a small vessel, killing one crew member, injuring 12 others, and rupturing both of the ship's hulls. Ninety-thousand gallons of oil leaked into the gulf from the breach caused by the attack. Although originally denying that the blast was the result of an attack, Yemeni officials eventually acknowledged that the ship was attacked after French investigators found traces of TNT in the *Limburg's* hull. The attack was similar to the suicide bombing of the *USS Cole* in a Yemeni harbor in 2000 that killed 17 Americans.

The Threat

The *Limburg* attack, like the attack on the *USS Cole* before it, represents a significant threat to the maritime security interests of the United States. While neither attack was enough to sink the ships, the fact that a small boat can be used to attack a much larger ship and do significant damage is a problem for all larger ships. Even the differences in the attacks suggest the scope of the threat. While the *USS Cole* was in port, the *Limburg* was on the move when it was attacked.

Aftermath

Although the attack was not against American interests, the United States has been involved in pursuing the terrorists who were responsible for the attack, in part because at least one of the terrorists was also involved in the bombing of the *USS Cole* and was an al Qaeda operative. In August of 2012, the United States launched drone attacks against eight terrorists driving in the Hawra district in Yemen. One of the terrorists who was killed was Khaled Batis, the mastermind of the *Limburg* attack, who had escaped from a Yemeni prison in 2011. Abdul Mun'im Salim al Fatahani, another terrorist involved in the plot against the *Limburg*, was killed in a drone attack in January of 2012.

Conclusion

The attack on the *Limburg* represents the manifestation of one of the most significant maritime threats facing American interests. In many ways, it represents the *best*-case scenario, as the vessel did not sink, and there was no accompanying fire. If a similar attack were carried out in a port, the resulting issues—fire, casualties, damage to the facility—could be much greater. In addition, aside from the specific threat that the *Limburg* attack demonstrated, it also points to greater maritime threats, such as the hijacking of a liquefied petroleum gas tanker for use as a weapon of mass destruction.

Data from: BBC News. (2002). Yemen ship attack was terrorism; Roggio, B. (2012). *US drone strike kills AQAP operative involved in Limburg tanker attack*. The Long War Journal. Public Multimedia Inc.

event of an incident at a port, the first responders are local port authority fire and police agencies.[48] Additionally, given the fact that the vast majority of maritime activity is commercial, there is substantial cooperation required on the part of commercial organizations who engage in maritime trade.

While port security is probably the most directly relevant area of maritime homeland security, there are other significant elements that come into play in a maritime environment. The risk to ships that are not actually in port is significant, particularly container ships and oil tankers, as they are slow-moving and vulnerable to attack by smaller, faster vessels, particularly when at anchor in a harbor or coming into port.[49] This scenario is particularly frightening considering that attempts have already been made, such as the attack on the French oil tanker *Limberg* in 2002 (see **BOX 15.2**).[50] Furthermore, ships are at risk for piracy, which some believe has a significant fundraising link to terrorism.

Maritime crimes are also problematic from a homeland security perspective. Like piracy, these activities can be used to finance terrorist activities. Additionally, the threat of smuggling individuals in through the cargo system is a significant vulnerability, considering the tremendous amount of cargo passing through U.S. ports.[51]

Maritime homeland security issues are some of the most significant facing the nation. Given the economic importance of the country's ports, and the unique vulnerabilities that they represent, protecting these assets is one of the most important elements of a homeland security strategy. Furthermore, given the complex nature of a port and its consistent contact with international trade, maritime homeland security requires a great deal more cooperation, from locally to internationally, than perhaps any other area contained within homeland security. The primary responsible agencies, the USCG, CBP, and the TSA, all have large-scale programs to address this complex area of homeland security.

Other Transportation Sectors

While airline security understandably has been the primary focus of transportation security since 9-11, other methods of transportation are also vulnerable to attack. Notably, the rail system in the United States, particularly subways in major cities, carries about five times as many passengers as airlines do on a given day. This high volume of passenger traffic makes it a particularly significant potential target for terrorists.[52]

The daily volume of passengers also makes individual-level screening a virtual impossibility.[53] The focus of transit security has, therefore, been risk mitigation and consequence management in the event of an attack. Combined with a large grant program to assist rail systems to improve their security, these efforts have helped make the system more secure.

The problem with busing systems dwarfs the threat to the rail transportation system. Even more passengers use public busing systems or private passenger buses than use commuter rails. Up to 19 million people a day (during the week) utilize the nation's busing systems. Some efforts have been made to help secure these systems, primarily in the form of increased surveillance at stations and on buses, but the system remains vulnerable to a variety of potential attacks.[54]

Border Security

Border security has long been an issue for the United States. Well before 9-11, the country faced a variety of problems threatening its security stemming from the border domain, and laws were made to exclude individuals who were perceived as affecting national security. Anarchists, communists, and terrorists have all been excluded from immigrating at different points in our history. Smuggling, too, has a long history on the border, with laws in place at least since the Prohibition Era of the 1920s and early 1930s meant to stop contraband from coming into the country.[55]

However, like port and maritime security, border security is a complex issue. There is an increasing diversity of threats emerging at the border, from illegal smuggled goods and persons[56] to spill-over violence from drug cartels, and managing these risks is a difficult problem for DHS as legitimate trade needs to continue efficiently while the threats to security are stopped.[57] Border risks are, by and large, linked to the flow of goods and people across the border and any item (or individual) crossing the border without appropriate permission represents a potential threat to U.S. security.[58]

More specifically, DHS's border security mission has three primary foci. The first, unauthorized migration, is perhaps the largest-scale problem. The second, criminal networks, is also important, particularly with regard to the contraband that those networks attempt to bring into the country. Finally, potential terrorists represent a third threat to border security, primarily in illegal attempts at immigration.[59] There is also, obviously, overlap among these three threats as well. The complete border security picture is outlined in **FIGURE 15.1.**

Transnational terrorist activity, especially post 9-11, is one of the major security concerns that deal with border issues. The difficulty of carrying out the border control mission in a terrorist context was summed up well by the *9/11 Commission Report*:

> When Doris Meissner became INS [Immigration and Naturalization Service—now part of Customs and Border Patrol] Commissioner in 1993, she found an agency seriously hampered by outdated technology and insufficient human resources. Border Patrol agents were still using manual typewriters; inspectors at ports of entry were using a paper watch list; and the asylum and other benefit systems did not effectively deter fraudulent applications.[60]

The primary concern regarding borders is the illegal movement of terrorists into the country. This is statutorily prohibited by the Immigration and Nationality Act,[61] but not surprisingly, there have been documented instances of terrorists attempting to cross the border at legal points of entry.[62] Additionally, smuggling of contraband that is helpful to terrorists such as weapons of mass destruction (WMDs) remains a threat as well, especially considering the failure of DHS to actively screen all cargo coming into the United States over land borders, particularly cargo carried by trucks.[63]

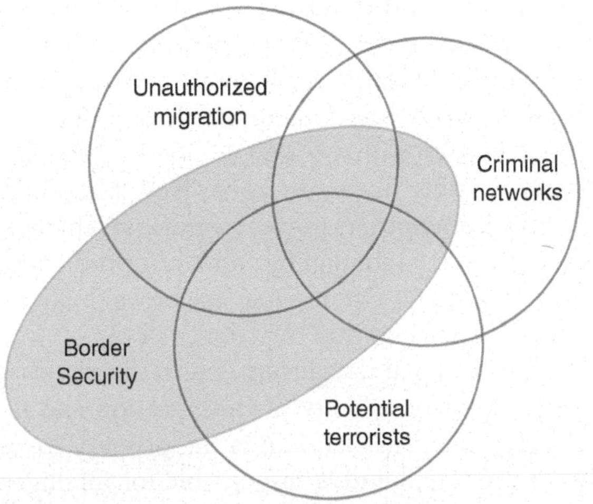

FIGURE 15.1 Border Threats and DHS Mission.

Reproduced from: Peterman, D.R., Elias, B., and Frittelli, J. (2011). *Border Security: Understanding Threats at U.S. Borders* (CRS No. R42969), p. 4. Retrieved from www.fas.org/sgp/crs/homesec/R42969.pdf.

Immigration

As with terrorists, the INA prohibits the movements of certain people into the country; specifically, those with particular health concerns, those who raise foreign policy concerns, and those who are likely to become a public charge, are prohibited from entering the country.[64] Most important, though, are those aliens who simply migrate without proper vetting or authorization. While most likely moving simply for better economic opportunity, those individuals, because they are unknown, pose a potential threat to homeland security.

This is, of course, not to equate illegal immigrants with terrorists. The motivations of the two groups differ dramatically, and the threat that the former poses is usually negligible. However, because there is no simple way to separate out those undocumented immigrants who are here simply to seek a better life from those who wish to do the country harm, illegal immigration remains a significant homeland security problem.

There are two agencies responsible for immigration in a homeland security context. The CBP is responsible for securing the borders, both checkpoints where individuals can cross borders legally as well as patrols where individuals may cross illegally (although the patrols are carried out by the U.S. Border Patrol, a component of CBP).[65] This is made difficult by the sheer scope of the problem. CBP, in addition to its charge of dealing with illegal immigrants, is also responsible for stopping terrorists (as mentioned previously), preventing illegal contraband from entering the country (including drugs), as well as protecting the country's agriculture system from harmful pests and diseases.[66]

Complicating the issue further is the geographic size of the U.S. borders. The country's northern border with Canada is over 5,000 miles long and covers a range of ecosystems, including mountains and forests, as well as urban border crossings.[67] The United States' southern border with Mexico is about 2,000 miles long and includes Texas, Arizona, New Mexico, and California. Both borders present significant challenges with illegal entry, smuggling, and criminal activity, making it virtually impossible to prevent all such instances from occurring.[68]

When someone dangerous enters the country, it becomes the responsibility of Immigration and Customs Enforcement (ICE). ICE is the primary investigative arm of DHS and is responsible for intelligence and investigation of terrorists who have entered the country, criminal migrants, and any illicit material that has crossed the borders into the U.S. used for

Courtesy of James Tourtellotte/DHS.

support of criminal or terrorist activities. Unlike CBP, which is limited to border activities, ICE is responsible for investigations throughout the United States pertaining to immigration and customs violations.[69]

Criminal Networks

Criminal networks, particularly along the southern border of the United States, represent one of the larger challenges to U.S. homeland security. Transnational criminal gangs, like Mara Salvatrucha (MS-13), represent a threat because of their connection to specific criminal activity, such as smuggling weapons, drugs, and even individuals across the border.[70] There is also significant danger presented by drug cartels which, even aside from their smuggling activities, pose a threat because of the violence that occurs between cartels and with law enforcement that sometimes spills across the border into the United States (see **BOX 15.3**).[71]

There is also an additional concern that comes when terrorism and criminal networks meet. While it is unlikely that a criminal network would seek to carry out an act of terrorism for its own purposes, there is much concern that they could do so if they were paid for their activity.

Although border security and immigration—particularly in the areas of criminal networks, terrorist activity, and illegal immigration—present significant dangers respectively, it is perhaps most concerning where these threats overlap. The cooperation between criminal networks and terrorist organizations to smuggle terrorists, or weapons to be used by terrorists, into the country is one of a number of challenging threat scenarios that has to be addressed by DHS. However, given the size of the borders of the United States and the volume of traffic that legally comes across these borders, the scope of this problem makes it difficult

BOX 15.3 The Border Debate

Background

There has been a significant amount of debate, and quite a bit of misinformation, regarding the nation's border security in recent years. Much of this has centered around construction of "a wall" at the border, much popularized by President Donald Trump during his 2016 campaign. Said by its supporters to be a deterrent to those thinking of crossing as well as a literal barrier to those who actually attempt to cross, it is said by detractors to be an unnecessary expenditure for border security when there are declining numbers of migrants attempting to cross the border in recent years—particularly across the Mexican border.

"The Wall" Itself

In addition to the difficulties over whether a wall is necessary, there has also been extensive debate about what constitutes a wall. Initially, President Trump indicated that the wall would be a continuous physical barrier from California to Texas. More recently, discussion has moved to a border barrier that would be erected in certain strategic locations, with much of the work done in other locations through increasing surveillance technologies.

Migration

Amid the debate regarding the wall has been an increase in the number of migrant "caravans" from parts of Central America and the Caribbean. These are largely composed of men, women, and children who wish to claim asylum in the United States because of threats to their safety within their home countries from gangs or political parties. While numerically large in terms of numbers of individuals (sometimes, at their outsets, in the thousands), they do not generally represent a very large portion of those seeking to come into the United States, even on the day they arrive. The related problem of people smuggling, particularly by "cayotes" transporting individuals illegally across the Mexican border, however, is a grave danger to the migrants themselves and, given the clandestine nature of the entry, appeals to those individuals who are not seeking asylum.

Conclusion

While this debate is ongoing, there is much agreement that, while the border between the United States and Mexico is increasingly secure, more can and should be done in terms of border security. Whether this constitutes a wall, or simply an increase in manpower and technology, the debate will likely continue into the foreseeable future.

to implement. CBP and ICE are the agencies with primary responsibility for combatting these threats, although there are additional federal resources being brought to bear on the problem. With political change such as immigration reform now possible, it is difficult to know whether the security situation on the border will change and how.

Cyberspace

While issues of land, sea, and air are obviously essential to the nation's homeland security, one area that has gained, and will increasingly gain, in importance is cyberspace. Cyberspace can be conceptualized as the linkages between all networked technologies, and as technology continues to develop, can be thought to underlie many (if not all) areas of homeland security, including the other areas of domain security.

Given the digital nature of cyberspace, and the fact that anyone can gain access, it is extremely difficult to secure—and will likely never be a domain that does not pose significant threats to homeland security. Additionally, with the increasing importance of the Internet of Things (IoT), new vulnerabilities appear within cyberspace as networks of devices from cameras to refrigerators continue to grow. Further still, the number of threat actors in the environment is also growing, with everyone from nation states to "script kiddies" (beginner hackers) able to potentially take advantage of vulnerability in various networks' security.

Across the Enterprise

One of the challenges with securing cyberspace is that it's not located in any one particular agency's purview. So, while there are agencies that take the lead in certain areas of securing cyberspace, and indeed DHS is the primary agency responsible for the cyber-domain in the government, there are small units within many organizations in the government that are responsible for their own areas of cybersecurity.

One particularly good example of this is the role that ICE plays in cybersecurity. Homeland Security Investigations (HSI) is an office within ICE that houses what is known as the Cyber Crimes Center (C3). C3 is responsible for a variety of types of investigations within ICE, all of which revolve around using the Internet to commit crimes. Investigations can range from digital theft of intellectual property to illicit e-commerce but involve transnational borders being crossed within the context of the crimes being committed.

In addition to general cross-border crimes, C3 also engages in investigations into child exploitation. These cases often revolve around the Internet, either through children being pictured in digital content shared online or through individuals who buy tickets to travel abroad to exploit children. Both of these crimes, as well as other crimes involving the exploitation of children, are the responsibility of the Child Exploitation Investigations Unit (CEIU) in C3. They also provide support to a variety of other agencies whose jurisdictions bring them into contact with individuals who may be using the Internet to exploit children.

Another DHS agency that has an arm focused on cyberspace is the United States Secret Service (USSS). The USSS, while using some of the same tools as ICE, has a different focus congruent with the agencies' general focus on financial crimes. USSS maintains the Electronic Crimes Task Force (ECTF), which investigates crimes like bank fraud, cyber intrusion, and other computer-related crimes. These investigations can span the DHS enterprise and often focus on long-term investigations.

DHS's involvement in cyberspace is not limited to investigations, however. DHS also has responsibility (as mentioned in Chapter 3), for securing networks relied upon by the federal government. To that end, the Network Security Deployment (NSD) division, which is responsible for the National Cybersecurity Protection System. This system is designed to provide data and a set of capabilities to prevent and mitigate intrusions into federal networks and provides a "center of excellence" for both public and private network security.

Private Infrastructure

One of the key challenges in securing cyberspace is the fact that many of the problems are geared toward private networks. This means that government has little involvement beyond general policies before an incident occurs. Hacks of Sony, Target, and others have demonstrated that the vulnerabilities in private networks can have significant public effects. If a large financial institution, for instance, fell victim to a significant attack, which locked up their data using ransomware, it could be a significant market event and negatively impact the nation's homeland security.

In order to combat this, DHS has created the National Cybersecurity and Communications Integration Center (NCCIC). The NCCIC is the primary hub for information sharing between the public and private sector for cybersecurity incidents. While the focus on cyber-events is new, the NCCIC has a historic pedigree going back to the 1960s in efforts to deal with disruptions in communications technology which can be seen in **FIGURE 15.2**.

Future of Homeland Security

One of the most difficult challenges of homeland security is the fact that the environment in which homeland security professionals operate is not static.[72] The threat environment changes on a regular basis due to a variety of circumstances, the vast majority of which are totally outside of the control of the homeland security community. Three things, in particular, can affect the homeland security threat environment—as well as the potential responses that homeland security professionals can provide in the event of an incident. These three areas are international threats, domestic threats, and the political climate in which decisions on how to address threats are (or are not) made.

International Threats

As one of the primary missions of homeland security deals with terrorism, and much of the terrorist threat is determined by factors outside of the United States, it is essential to understand the international environment.[73] Unfortunately, as is often the case, the international context is quite dynamic, making threats to homeland security difficult to pin down.

This, perhaps, has never been truer than now. The international political context has changed dramatically in the past 10 years, with the occurrence of the Arab Spring,[74] the replacement of the leadership in Libya,[75] the current civil war in Syria, and Russia's seeming reemergence; many of these are countries with some previous connection to terrorism or historic adversaries of the United States. Additionally, North Korea, and perhaps Iran, have developed capacities that could be used to aid terrorists, particularly

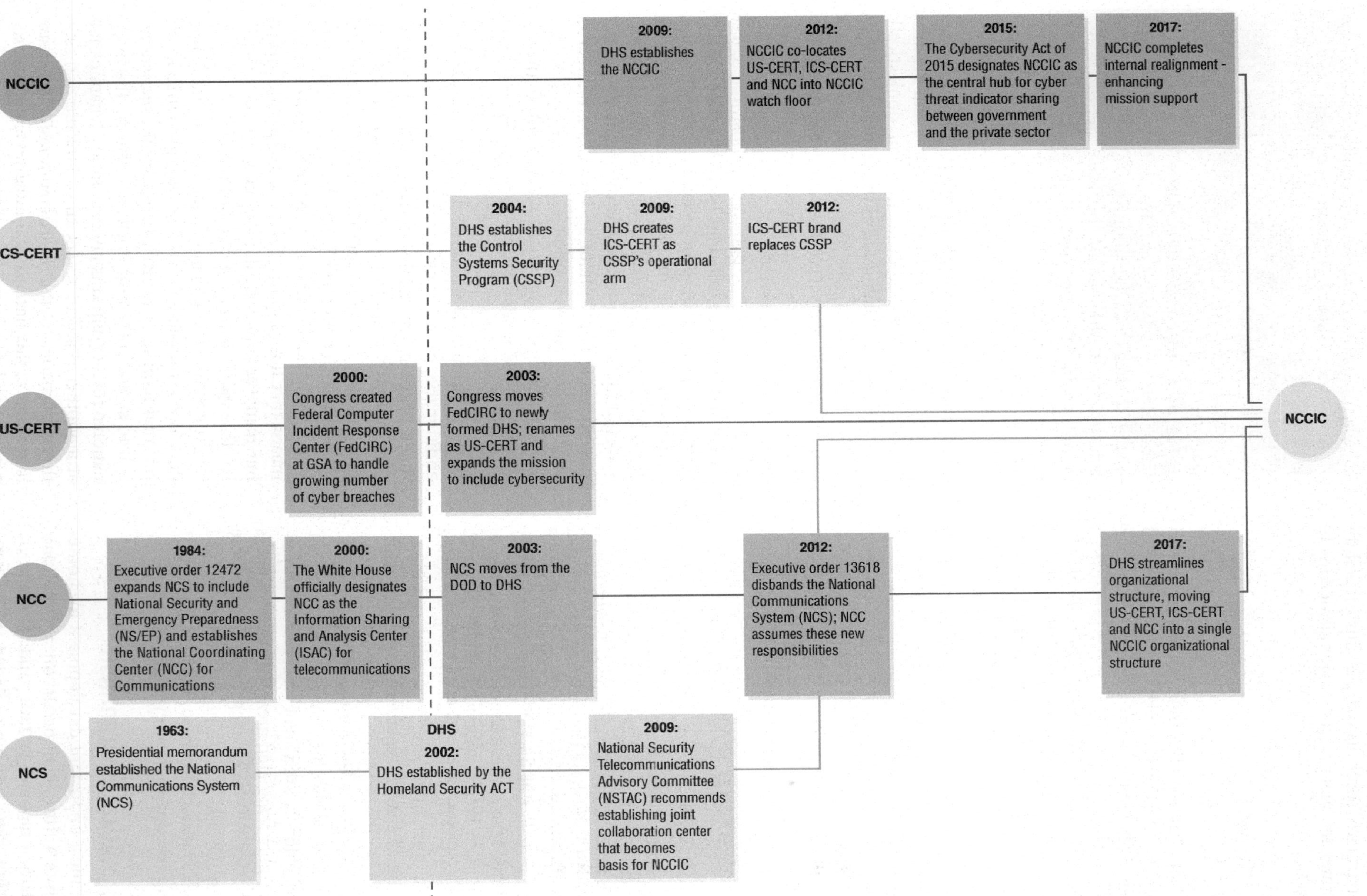

FIGURE 15.2 NCCIC Timeline.

Although the development of the NCCIC is ongoing, an April 2018 GAO report[76] cited the fact that the organization had yet to develop sufficient metrics to understand its own effectiveness. This means that, while there seem to be improvements in how DHS has been handling cyberspace more broadly, there remain a number of challenges for them to address moving forward.

https://www.dhs.gov/national-cybersecurity-and-communications-integration-center.

if those countries continue to feel threatened by increasing international pressure, generally led by the United States.

Domestic Threats

Like the international threat context, it is unclear where the domestic security situation lies at the moment. While the United States is undoubtedly more secure than before the September 11 attacks, there remain significant domestic terrorism threats, primarily in the guise of right-wing and racist terrorist activity and eco-terrorism.[77] However, these threats are, in part, determined by political issues. Immigration reform, for instance, has the potential to impact nativist organizations in the United States that might pose a potential threat.[78] In addition, the increasing focus on income inequality may stimulate activity among certain left-wing political organizations.

And vulnerabilities remain throughout the homeland security system. As discussed previously, there is a persistent threat to port security and our land borders are not 100% secure—and we are uncertain of how unsecure cyberspace remains. All of these factors make threat prediction quite difficult.[79]

Natural Disasters

As with terrorist activity, there is much uncertainty when it comes to natural disasters. Aside from the fact that there is little ability for advanced prediction of many of these threats, there is increasing concern that natural disasters are getting worse because of global climate change (see **BOX 15.4**).[80] Super-storm Sandy and Hurricaine Maria, are examples of the types of disasters that many believe we must be better prepared for in the future. While it has been long contested whether storms are increasing in number and intensity due to climate change, regardless, natural disasters will always pose a threat to our homeland security.[81]

Not only are major storms becoming more frequent but other weather conditions such as droughts, flooding, and wildfires are also of great concern,[82] particularly in highly populated areas.[83] First responders at the local level will be bearing the brunt of these weather systems, and it is unlikely that there will be many additional changes to support those first responders in reacting to these events.

Courtesy of U.S. Air Force photo/Master Sgt. Mark C. Olsen.

Changing Political Environment

Perhaps the most important development for homeland security's future will occur on the political front. While September 11, 2001, and then shortly afterward, Hurricane Katrina provided the political motivation necessary to institute the significant changes that led to the current homeland security system, there has not been an event domestically approaching the magnitude of those incidents since. While, on one level, this may represent a success of our homeland security system, it also means that there is little impetus to provide additional resources or support for that system.

Anthony Downs, a political scientist, referenced this idea in what was called the Issue Attention Cycle.[84] This was adapted by a homeland security theorist Christopher Bellavita in 2005 and he suggested that there was difficulty in dealing with homeland security issues in the long term because the public would lose interest over time without an increasing number of events to keep their attention.[85]

Equally important to the future of homeland security in the United States are domestic issues that have little immediate relevance to the topic of security. In brief, the current economic climate is one in which additional appropriations for security are not easily made, without the driving force of another significant event. In fact, along with other scheduled cuts, the sequester that went into effect in 2013 includes $4 billion in cuts to DHS.[86] Some of this has been avoided, but the threat of sequestration remains. This means that not only is DHS itself suffering cutbacks but many state and local agencies are also suffering because their grants have come to an end.[87]

The future of homeland security is difficult to predict. There are many moving pieces, and much of the risk that homeland security seeks to mitigate is difficult to assess in the best of circumstances. The international threat context is perhaps more dynamic than at any other point in recent time, and the domestic threat, particularly with regard to domestic terrorism, is in a state of flux because of the changing political situation. Similarly, the effects of global climate change

BOX 15.4 Climate Change and Homeland Security

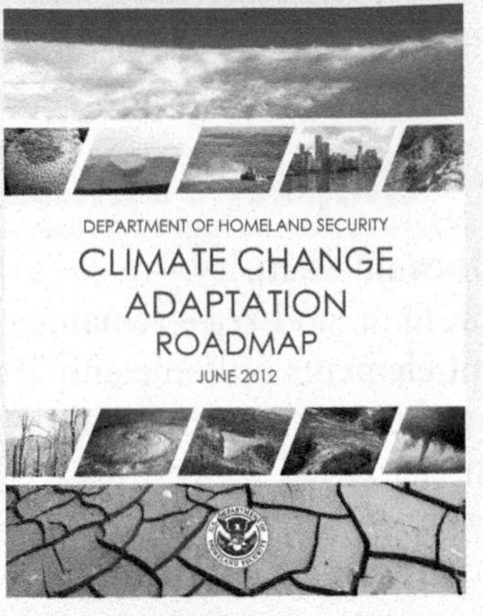

Courtesy of DHS.

Global climate change is a scientific fact and is increasingly being recognized as a national and homeland security threat. Among the impacts that climate change can have is an increase in the number of significant weather events and the severity of the events when they do occur. This fact, in turn, demonstrates why climate change is an increasingly relevant problem for homeland security. In 2010, both the *Quadrennial Defense Review* and the *National Security Strategy for the United States* recognized global climate change as a potential threat to national security.

The Threat

The threat from global climate change is relatively complex. While unlikely to directly generate conflict by itself, climate change can act as an "accelerant" of instability and can indirectly tax defense agencies because they may have to support civil authorities for disaster relief. There is also a more direct threat from climate change. As stated in the *Quadrennial Defense Review*, "in 2008, the National Intelligence Council judged that more than 30 U.S. military installations were already facing elevated levels of risk from rising sea levels." In its report, *Climate Change Adaptation Roadmap*, DHS suggests that the threat from climate change is particularly relevant to the organization, as it deals with the federal emergency management aspects of climate change.

The Response

As a direct response to the challenges posed by climate change to national and homeland security, President Obama issued Executive Order 13514, charging the Interagency Climate Change Adaptation Task Force, made up of members of over 20 government agencies, with finding solutions to the challenges presented by climate change. The 2011 report produced by the task force, *Progress Report of the Interagency Climate Change Adaptation Task Force*, identifies several areas in which the government can make significant progress in combating the effects of climate change. These include:

- Integrating adaptation into federal government planning and activities
- Building resilience to climate change in communities
- Improving accessibility and coordination of science for decision-making
- Developing strategies to safeguard natural resources in a changing climate
- Enhancing efforts to lead and support international adaptation

This framework represents the tangible elements of a plan for coping with climate change at the federal level. One of the major recognitions of the task force, however, is that the majority of response to climate change will happen at the local level, so one of the primary responsibilities of the federal government is supporting local agencies.

Conclusion

With the inclusion of climate change as a significant element of the *Quadrennial Defense Review, Climate Change Adaptation Roadmap*, and *National Security Strategy*, the federal government is recognizing the fact that climate change presents significant dangers to the security of the United States. This recognition is most important in terms of homeland security, as any of the effects mentioned by the documents are likely to impact territories within the United States. Additionally, the increasing scientific recognition of severe weather events as a consequence of global climate change illustrates the increasing importance of this topic to homeland security.

More recently however, particularly with the acendency of the Trump administration, climate change has taken a back seat to other homeland security concerns. Specifically, while still mentioning "changing climate" in their strategic documents, Trump administration officials have re-emphasized the fight against religious terrorism and have downplayed the effects of climate change on homeland security. While what this means in practice remains to be seen, it is clear that with the lower priority climate change now has, it will play less of a role in homeland security preparedness.

remain to be seen, although it appears that there will be an increasing number of severe weather events in the coming years.

Perhaps most important is the domestic political situation with regard to homeland security, which, as September 11 recedes in memory, may result in less money and political influence to support the homeland security system. This issue is exacerbated by continuing economic and social problems facing the country. Because of these many factors, it is unclear what the future holds for homeland security in the United States. Barring another catastrophic attack or disaster on American soil, the future of homeland security remains an open question.

Chapter Summary

Domain security—or securing the environments of air, land, and sea—remains one of the most important elements of homeland security. With issues ranging from air passenger transport to port security, the threats faced by this area of homeland security are complex, and solutions require high levels of interaction among homeland security agencies. Moreover, these areas represent some of the largest segments of the U.S. economy, making them desirable targets for terrorists and criminals.

While 9-11 understandably focused the United States on air passenger safety, other elements of domain security are also essential for the overall security of the country. The nexus of immigration, crime, and terrorism on the border represents one of the most significant threats to the homeland. Additionally, protecting the nation's ports is one of the most difficult aspects of homeland security generally and domain security specifically. With high numbers of targets and successful attacks taking place in the past, maritime security is still a significant issue in homeland security. This is not to mention the only partially solved issues of rail and other commuter transportation systems in the United States.

Addressing these issues is the mission of several elements of DHS. The TSA is responsible for air cargo and passenger safety, as well as significant elements in other parts of domain security like the verification of transportation workers. The USCG is responsible for securing ports and maritime security while CBP secures the borders. ICE, as the investigative arm of DHS, examines cases of smuggling, terrorism, and other activities in the interior of the country. All of these agencies, along with other agencies outside of DHS, like the FBI, must coordinate their efforts in the major areas of domain security in order to fulfill their individual missions.

This is all made more complicated by the changing nature of homeland security threats. Internationally, the system has changed dramatically in recent years, and much of the current threat situation remains unknown. Domestically, the threat situation is also in flux, with the political landscape changing rapidly and influencing radicalized groups within the United States. Other issues, such as global climate change, may also have an unforeseen impact on homeland security in the United States as the number of natural disasters seems to be increasing and severe weather events getting worse when they do occur. Moreover, the growth and expansion of technology outside of computers to everyday objects may also impact security in profound but not yet understood ways.

However, despite all of these issues, what makes the future of homeland security most challenging to predict is the national political situation. With no catastrophic terrorist events or natural disasters occurring in the past 10 years—with the possible exception of Hurricane Maria in Puerto Rico—much of what brought homeland security to the forefront is receding in the public's mind. This, combined with the slow economic recovery from the 2008 financial crisis and the potential effects of government-wide budget cuts, means that homeland security will be vying for increasingly scarce resources.

Whatever changes happen to homeland security, however, it will remain an essential part of the security apparatus of the United States and will continue to be so for the foreseeable future.

Review/Discussion Questions

1. What role does the Transportation Security Administration play in the country's aviation system? What other roles does it play across other types of transportation?
2. Border security has been an issue in the United States for a long time. What elements of border security are most important and why?
3. What is the difference between the roles of the U.S. Border Patrol and Immigration and Customs Enforcement?
4. What future threats to homeland security are the most important? Why?
5. What role might climate change play in the future of homeland security in the United States?
6. What is the primary challenge regarding cybersecurity in the United States? Why?

Additional Readings

Department of Homeland Security. (2010). *Quadrennial Homeland Security Review.* Retrieved from http://www.dhs.gov/xlibrary/assets/qhsr_report.pdf

Elias, B., Peterman, D. R., & Frittelli, J. (2016). *Transportation Security: Issues for Congress.* Retrieved from http://www.fas.org/sgp/crs/homesec/RL33512.pdf

Endnotes

1. Booth, C. T. (2002). "The Flight Attendants. Courage in the Air." *Time*. Retrieved from http://www.time.com/time/magazine/article/0,9171,1003224-2,00.html.
2. Fenton, B. & Ball, I. (2001). "Bomb on Flight 63." *The Telegraph*. Retrieved from http://www.telegraph.co.uk/news/worldnews/northamerica/usa/1366231/Bomb-on-Flight-63.html.
3. Booth, C. T. (2002). "The Flight Attendants. Courage in the Air." *Time*. Retrieved from http://www.time.com/time/magazine/article/0,9171,1003224-2,00.html
4. Booth, C. T. (2002). "The Flight Attendants. Courage in the Air." *Time*. Retrieved from http://www.time.com/time/magazine/article/0,9171,1003224-2,00.html
5. Fenton, B. & Ball, I. (2001). "Bomb on Flight 63." *The Telegraph*. Retrieved from http://www.telegraph.co.uk/news/worldnews/northamerica/usa/1366231/Bomb-on-Flight-63.html
6. Booth, C. T. (2002). "The Flight Attendants. Courage in the Air." *Time*. Retrieved from http://www.time.com/time/magazine/article/0,9171,1003224-2,00.html
7. Booth, C. T. (2002). "The Flight Attendants. Courage in the Air." *Time*. Retrieved from http://www.time.com/time/magazine/article/0,9171,1003224-2,00.html
8. Ressa, M. (2003). "Sources: Reid is al Qaeda Operative." Retrieved from http://www.cnn.com/2003/WORLD/asiapcf/southeast/01/30/reid.alqaeda/.
9. Elias, B., Peterman, D. R., & Frittelli, J. (2016). *Transportation Security: Issues for Congress.* Retrieved from http://www.fas.org/sgp/crs/homesec/RL33512.pdf
10. Department of Homeland Security. (2011). *Congressional Budget Justification 2011.* Retrieved from http://www.dhs.gov/xlibrary/assets/dhs_congressional_budget_justification_fy2011.pdf.
11. Elias, B., Peterman, D. R., & Frittelli, J. (2016). *Transportation Security: Issues for Congress.* Retrieved from http://www.fas.org/sgp/crs/homesec/RL33512.pdf
12. Department of Homeland Security. (2012). *Border Security Overview.* Retrieved from http://www.dhs.gov/border-security-overview.
13. Frittelli, J. F. (2005). *Port and Maritime Security: Background and Issues for Congress* (CRS No. RL31733). Retrieved from http://www.fas.org/sgp/crs/homesec/RL31733.pdf.
14. Transportation Security Administration. (2013). *Need for Removal of Shoes at Checkpoint.* Retrieved from https://www.tsa.gov/news/statements/2013/01/07/need-removal-shoes-checkpoint
15. Elias, B. (2010). *Screening and Securing Air Cargo: Background and Issues for Congress* (CRS No. R41515). Retrieved from http://www.fas.org/sgp/crs/homesec/R41515.pdf.
16. Barro, J. (2012). "The TSA's Fake Liquid Rule." *Forbes*. Retrieved from https://www.forbes.com/sites/joshbarro/2012/05/02/the-tsas-fake-liquids-rule/#4f1a2fc414df.
17. Aviation and Transportation Security Act of 2001, Public Law 107-71, 115 Stat. 597 (2001).
18. Office of the Inspector General. (n.d.). *Transportation Security Administration.* Retrieved from https://www.oig.dot.gov/agency/transportation-security-administration
19. Haddal, C. C. (2010). *Border Security: Key Agencies and Their Missions* (CRS No. RS21899). Retrieved from http://www.fas.org/sgp/crs/homesec/RS21899.pdf.
20. Elias, B. (2010). *Screening and Securing Air Cargo: Background and Issues for Congress* (CRS No. R41515). Retrieved from http://www.fas.org/sgp/crs/homesec/R41515.pdf
21. Elias, B. (2010). *Screening and Securing Air Cargo: Background and Issues for Congress* (CRS No. R41515). Retrieved from http://www.fas.org/sgp/crs/homesec/R41515.pdf
22. Elias, B., Peterman, D. R., & Frittelli, J. (2016). *Transportation Security: Issues for Congress.* Retrieved from http://www.fas.org/sgp/crs/homesec/RL33512.pdf
23. Transportation Security Administration. (n.d.). *Screening Partnership Program.* Retrieved from https://www.tsa.gov/for-industry/screening-partnerships
24. Rosen, J. (2010). "The TSA is Invasive, Annoying—and Unconstitutional." *The Washington Post Online.* Retrieved from http://www.washingtonpost.com/wp-dyn/content/article/2010/11/26/AR2010112604290.html.
25. Krouse, W. J. & Elias, B. (2009). *Terrorist Watchlist Checks and Air Passenger Screening.* Retrieved from http://www.fas.org/sgp/crs/homesec/RL33645.pdf
26. Transportation Security Administration. (n.d.). *Layers of Security.* Retrieved from http://www.tsa.gov/about-tsa/layers-security
27. Transportation Security Administration. (n.d.). *Layers of Security.* Retrieved from http://www.tsa.gov/about-tsa/layers-security
28. Krouse, W. J. & Elias, B. (2009). *Terrorist Watchlist Checks and Air Passenger Screening.* Retrieved from http://www.fas.org/sgp/crs/homesec/RL33645.pdf.
29. Elias, B., Peterman, D. R., & Frittelli, J. (2016). *Transportation Security: Issues for Congress.* Retrieved from http://www.fas.org/sgp/crs/homesec/RL33512.pdf
30. Transportation Security Administration. (n.d.). *Layers of Security.* Retrieved from https://www.tsa.gov/blog/2017/08/01/inside-look-tsa-layers-security
31. Aviation and Transportation Security Act of 2001, Public Law 107-71, 115 Stat. 597 (2001).
32. Elias, B. (2007). *Air Cargo Security* (CRS No. RL32022). Retrieved from http://www.fas.org/sgp/crs/homesec/RL32022.pdf.
33. Sauter, M. & Carafano, J. J. (2012). *Homeland Security* (2nd ed.). New York, NY: McGraw Hill.
34. National Commission on Terrorist Attacks Upon the United States. (2004). *The 9/11 Commission Report: Final Report of the National Commission on Terrorist Attacks Upon the United States* (Authorized Ed.). New York: W.W. Norton & Company, Inc.

35. United States Department of Transportation. (1999). *An Assessment of U.S. Marine Transportation Systems.* Retrieved from https://www.maritime.dot.gov/sites/marad.dot.gov/files/docs/resources/2386/assessmntoftheusmts-rpttocongrsep1999combined.pdf
36. Department of Homeland Security. (2005). *National Plan to Achieve Maritime Domain Awareness.* Retrieved from http://www.dhs.gov/xlibrary/assets/HSPD_MDAPlan.pdf.
37. Department of Homeland Security. (2005). *National Plan to Achieve Maritime Domain Awareness for the National Strategy for Maritime Security.* Retrieved from http://www.dhs.gov/xlibrary/assets/HSPD_MDAPlan.pdf.
38. Fritelli, J. F. (2005). *Port and Maritime Security: Background and Issues for Congress* (CRS No. RL31733). Retrieved from http://www.fas.org/sgp/crs/homesec/RL31733.pdf.
39. Fritelli, J. F. (2005). *Port and Maritime Security: Background and Issues for Congress* (CRS No. RL31733). Retrieved from http://www.fas.org/sgp/crs/homesec/RL31733.pdf
40. Homeland Security Act of 2002, Public Law 107-296, 116 Stat. 2137 (2002).
41. O'Rourke, R. (2007). *Homeland Security: Coast Guard Operations—Background and Issues for Congress.* Retrieved from http://congressionalresearch.com/RS21125/document.php?study=Homeland+Security+Coast+Guard+Operations+-+Background+and+Issues+for+Congress.
42. Fritelli, J. F. (2005). *Port and Maritime Security: Background and Issues for Congress* (CRS No. RL31733). Retrieved from http://www.fas.org/sgp/crs/homesec/RL31733.pdf
43. Customs and Border Protection. (2019). *CSI: Container Security Initiative.* Retrieved from https://www.cbp.gov/border-security/ports-entry/cargo-security/csi/csi-brief
44. Customs and Border Protection. (2019). *CSI: Container Security Initiative.* Retrieved from https://www.cbp.gov/border-security/ports-entry/cargo-security/csi/csi-brief
45. Department of Homeland Security. (2018). *DHS/CBP/PIA – 013 Customs-Trade Partnership Against Terrorism (C-TPAT).* Retrieved from https://www.dhs.gov/publication/customs-trade-partnership-against-terrorism-c-tpat.
46. Peterman, D. R., Elias, B., & Frittelli, J. (2011). *Transportation Security: Issues for Congress* (CRS No. RL33512). Retrieved from http://www.fas.org/sgp/crs/homesec/RL33512.pdf
47. Department of Homeland Security. (n.d.). *TWIC.* Retrieved from https://www.tsa.gov/for-industry/twic
48. Port of Houston. (n.d.). *Port Security and Public Safety.* Retrieved from https://porthouston.com/port-security/
49. Fritelli, J. F. (2005). *Port and Maritime Security: Background and Issues for Congress* (CRS No. RL31733). Retrieved from http://www.fas.org/sgp/crs/homesec/RL31733.pdf
50. Global Security. (n.d.). "Limberg Oil Tanker Attacked." Retrieved from http://www.globalsecurity.org/security/profiles/limburg_oil_tanker_attacked.htm.
51. Bakir, N. O. (2007). A Brief Analysis of Threats and Vulnerabilities in the Maritime Domain. Retrieved from http://citeseerx.ist.psu.edu/viewdoc/download?doi=10.1.1.660.995&rep=rep1&type=pdf
52. Government Accountability Office. (2007). *Critical Infrastructure: Challenges Remain in Protecting Key Sectors.* Retrieved from http://www.gao.gov/assets/120/115905.pdf.
53. Elias, B., Peterman, D. R., & Frittelli, J. (2016). Transportation Security: Issues for Congress. Retrieved from http://www.fas.org/sgp/crs/homesec/RL33512.pdf
54. Elias, B., Peterman, D. R., & Frittelli, J. (2016). *Transportation Security: Issues for Congress.* Retrieved from http://www.fas.org/sgp/crs/homesec/RL33512.pdf
55. Rosenblum, M. R., Bjelopera, J. P., & Finklea, K. M. (2013). *Border Security: Understanding Threats at U.S. Borders* (CRS No. R42969). Retrieved from http://www.fas.org/sgp/crs/homesec/R42969.pdf.
56. Donna Bucella. (2012). Border Security Threats to the Homeland: DHS' Response to Innovative Tactics and Techniques. 113 Cong. Retrieved from https://www.hsdl.org/?view&did=743058
57. Customs and Border Protection. (2019). *CBP.* Retrieved from http://www.cbp.gov/xp/cgov/about/
58. Rosenblum, M. R., Bjelopera, J. P., & Finklea, K. M. (2013). *Border Security: Understanding Threats at U.S. Borders* (CRS No. R42969). Retrieved from http://www.fas.org/sgp/crs/homesec/R42969.pdf
59. Rosenblum, M. R., Bjelopera, J. P., & Finklea, K. M. (2013). *Border Security: Understanding Threats at U.S. Borders* (CRS No. R42969). Retrieved from http://www.fas.org/sgp/crs/homesec/R42969.pdf
60. National Commission on Terrorist Attacks Upon the United States. (2004). *The 9/11 Commission Report: Final Report of the National Commission on Terrorist Attacks Upon the United States* (Authorized Ed.). New York: W.W. Norton & Company, Inc.
61. Immigration and Nationality Act § 12, 8 USC 12 (2012).
62. Anti-Defamation League. (2004). *Canada and Terrorism.* Retrieved from https://web.archive.org/web/20160312203130/http://archive.adl.org/terror/tu/tu_0401_canada.html
63. Rosenblum, M. R., Bjelopera, J. P., & Finklea, K. M. (2013). *Border Security: Understanding Threats at U.S. Borders* (CRS No. R42969). Retrieved from http://www.fas.org/sgp/crs/homesec/R42969.pdf
64. Immigration and Nationality Act § 12, 8 USC 12 (2012).
65. Department of Homeland Security. (n.d.). *Border Security Overview.* Retrieved from http://www.dhs.gov/border-security-overview.
66. Haddal, C. C. (2010). *Border Security: Key Agencies and Their Missions* (CRS No. RS21899). Retrieved from http://www.fas.org/sgp/crs/homesec/RS21899.pdf.
67. United States Census Bureau. (2011). *U.S., Canada and Mexico Border Lengths.* Retrieved from https://www2.census.gov/library/publications/2010/compendia/statab/130ed/tables/11s0359.pdf
68. Rosenblum, M. R., Bjelopera, J. P., & Finklea, K. M. (2013). *Border Security: Understanding Threats at U.S. Borders* (CRS No. R42969). Retrieved from http://www.fas.org/sgp/crs/homesec/R42969.pdf
69. Haddal, C. C. (2010). *Border Security: Key Agencies and Their Missions* (CRS No. RS21899). Retrieved from http://www.fas.org/sgp/crs/homesec/RS21899.pdf
70. Federal Bureau of Investigation. (2008). *MS-13 Threat: A National Assessment.* Retrieved from http://www.fbi.gov/news/stories/2008/january/ms13_011408.
71. Archibold, R. C. (2009). "Mexican Drug Cartel Violence Spills Over, Alarming U.S." *New York Times Online.* Retrieved from http://www.nytimes.com/2009/0323/us/23border.html?pagewanted=all&_r=0.
72. U. S. Government Accountability Office. (2018). DHS Needs to Enhance Efforts to Improve and Promote the Security of Federal and Private-Sector Networks. Published: Apr 24, 2018.

Publicly Released: Apr 24, 2018. Retrieved from https://www.gao.gov/products/GAO-18-520T.

73. Department of Homeland Security. (2010). *Quadrennial Homeland Security Review Report.* (2010). Retrieved from http://www.dhs.gov/xlibrary/assets/qhsr_report.pdf.
74. Building Secure Partnerships in Travel Commerce and Trade with the Asia-Pacific Region. 112th Cong. (2012) (Mark Koumans).
75. The National Conterterrorism Center. Office of the Director of National Intelligence. We lead the way in analyzing, understanding, and responding to the terrorist threat. Retrieved from http://www.nctc.gov/press_room/speeches/dnctc_testimony_before_hpsci_111006.pdf
76. Hauslohner, A. (2011). "Gaddafi's Abandoned Arsenals Raise Libya's Terror Threat." *Time.* Retrieved from http://www.time.com/time/world/article/0,8599,2092333,00.html.
77. Federal Bureau of Investigation. (2012). *Testimony.* Retrieved from http://www.fbi.gov/news/testimony/the-domestic-terrorism-threat.
78. Federal Bureau of Investigation. (2012). *Testimony.* Retrieved from http://www.fbi.gov/news/testimony/the-domestic-terrorism-threat
79. Department of Homeland Security. (2010). *Quadrennial Homeland Security Review.* Retrieved from http://www.dhs.gov/xlibrary/assets/qhsr_report.pdf
80. Rice, D. S. (2012). "Report: Climate Change Behind Rise in Weather Disasters." *USA Today.* Retrieved from http://www.usatoday.com/story/weather/2012/10/10/weather-disasters-climate-change-munich-re-report/1622845/.
81. Broder, J. M. (2009). "Climate Change Seen as Threat to U.S. Security." *The New York Times.* Retrieved from https://www.nytimes.com/2009/08/09/science/earth/09climate.html
82. Intergovernmental Panel on Climate Change. (2012). *Managing the Risks of Extreme Events and Disasters to Advance Climate Change Adaptation.* Retrieved from https://www.nytimes.com/2009/08/09/science/earth/09climate.html
83. Cornish, A. (2012). "Climate Change May Spark More Wildfires in Future." *National Public Radio.* Retrieved from http://www.npr.org/2012/06/13/154959089/climate-change-may-spark-more-wildfires-in-future.
84. Downs, A. (1972). "Up and Down with Ecology: The 'Issue Attention' Cycle." *National Affairs 28*, 38–50.
85. Bellavita, C. (2005). "Changing Homeland Security: The Issue Attention Cycle." *Homeland Security Affairs, 1*, 1–4.
86. Office of Management and Budget. (2013). *OMB Report Pursuant to the Sequestration Transparency Act of 2012.* Retrieved from https://obamawhitehouse.archives.gov/sites/default/files/omb/assets/legislative_reports/stareport.pdf
87. Department of Homeland Security. (2012). *DHS Announces Grant Guidance for Fiscal Year (FY) 2012 Preparedness Grants.* Retrieved from http://www.dhs.gov/news/2012/02/17/dhs-announces-grant-guidance-fiscal-year-fy-2012-preparedness-grants.

Glossary

A

Anti-terrorism the defensive aspects of protection from terrorism and can range from academic study to "target-hardening"

B

Biological weapon weapons that use a biologically derived or living microorganism, bacteria, virus, rickettsia, or fungi to deliberately harm people, animals, or crops through infections that can incapacitate or kill

Border patrol a patrol sent to keep watch over an area along a country's border.

Border security protecting the land borders of the United States from illegal movement

C

Category A biological weapon agents that can easily be disseminated over a large area and infect many people and could cause a public health catastrophe

Category B biological weapon agents that are easily disseminated over a large area but have a lower mortality rate

Category C biological weapon common pathogens that could potentially be used as terrorist weapons

CBRNE Chemical, Biological, Radiological, Nuclear, and Explosive weapons

Chemical weapon a device that uses poisonous liquids, solids, gases, and vapor agents to cause death or injury to humans, animals, and plants

Civil defense an effort to protect the citizens of the United States from a military attack

Command staff Incident Command's staff that provides information, liaison, and safety services for the entire Incident Command and reports directly to the Incident Commander

Counter-terrorism all offensive activities dedicated to tracking and eradicating terrorists both domestically and internationally

Critical infrastructure key resources Critical infrastructure protection is comprised of the activities meant to prevent, deter, neutralize, or mitigate the effects of a terrorist attack on the nation's critical infrastructure

Customs and Border Protection (CBP) the mission of CBP is to keep terrorists and their weapons out of the United States. It also has a responsibility for securing and facilitating trade and travel while enforcing U.S. regulations, including immigration and drug laws.

Cyber attack any type of attack on America carried out through computing

Cyber crime criminal activity carried out through computing

Cybersecurity measures taken to protect computers against criminal or unauthorized use of electronic data

Cyberspace the virtual environment in which communication over computer networks occurs.

Cyber-terrorism an attack that is conducted for terroristic purposes against the United States and is carried out through computing

D

Department of Homeland Security a federal cabinet-level agency created in 2002 by taking various pre-existing agencies and placing them under one federal bureaucracy charged with protecting America's homeland

Dirty bomb a device that involves the use of conventional explosive material that also contains radioactive material

Domain security securing the environments of air, land, and sea

Domestic terrorism the use of violence and intimidation in the pursuit of political aims committed by those from within one's own state/country

E

Emergency declaration declarations to trigger aid that protects property, public health, and safety and lessens or averts the threat of an incident becoming a catastrophic event

Emergency management the preparation for and the carrying out of all emergency functions, other than functions for which military forces are primarily responsible, to minimize injury and repair damage resulting from emergencies or disasters caused by enemy attack, sabotage or other hostile action, by fire, flood, earthquake, storm or other natural causes, or by technological or man-made catastrophes

Emergency operations center (EOC) a central command and control facility for carrying out emergency management

Enemy combatant historically, it meant someone fighting against the United States military, but the Bush Administration used the term to mean someone who fighting the United States unlawfully and therefore did not have the protections of the Geneva Convention as a soldier fighting for a country

Executive order a presidential order that directs the executive branch or a specific agency within the executive branch to take some form of action

Explosive weapon conventional weapons that have explosive properties

F

FEMA the Federal Emergency Management Agency is the agency within the Department of Homeland Security responsible for responding to catastrophes and issuing a disaster and/or emergency declaration, thereby allowing them to provide monetary assistance

Fusion centers an information sharing center created by the U.S. Department of Homeland Security and the Department of Justice to assist state and local law enforcement

G

General staff This staff focuses the key functions of incident command, operations, planning, logistics, and finance/administration and reports directly to the Incident Commander

GETS Government Emergency Telecommunications Service designed to ensure calls go through when a national emergency creates a congested phone line system

Guantanamo Bay a bay located in Cuba that the U.S. acquired in the 1960s, that was converted into a U. S. military prison in 2002

H

Hazard a danger or risk

Homeland security 1) an effort to prevent, mitigate, respond, and recover from natural and man-made disasters, including terrorist attacks; 2) a department within the Federal Government focused on prevention, mitigation, responding to and recovering from both natural and man-made disasters

Homeland security areas of emphasis various ways of perceiving homeland security as detailed by Homeland Security expert Christopher Bellavita

Homeland security concepts fundamental aspects of homeland security that are common to all responses whether they are natural disasters or terrorist attacks, such as preparedness

Homeland security enterprise the collective efforts and shared responsibilities of federal, state, local, tribal, territorial, nongovernmental, and private-sector partners—as well as individuals, families, and communities—to maintain critical homeland security capabilities

Homeland security goals those key tasks that must be accomplished in order for the homeland security mission to be accomplished

Homeland security mission those key items that must be achieved in order for the homeland to be secure and the homeland security strategy implemented

Homeland security policing the local police role in protecting the homeland

Homeland Security Presidential Directives presidential executive orders that are focused on Homeland Security and advise the federal bureaucracy on administrative requirements the president wants implemented

Homeland security strategy the overarching plan for dealing with all hazards that focuses on shared goals and responsibilities for protecting and defending the homeland

HSARPA the Homeland Security Advanced Research Projects Agency, which is focused on providing security for critical infrastructure in the U.S.

I

Immigration and Customs Enforcement (ICE) federal organization whose primary mission is to promote homeland security and public safety through the criminal and civil enforcement of federal laws governing border control, customs, trade, and immigration.

Incident Command Post (ICP) the physical location of the Incident Commander and his or her staff

Incident command system the Incident Command System (ICS) is a standardized, on-scene, all-hazards incident management approach

Intelligence community a group of government agencies and organizations that carry out intelligence activities for the United States government; headed by the Director of Central Intelligence

International terrorism the use of violence and intimidation in the pursuit of political aims committed by those from outside of one's own state/country

J

Joint field office when an incident is of such severity, magnitude, and/or complexity that it requires coordinated

Federal assistance, the Secretary of Homeland Security, in coordination with other Federal departments and agencies, initiates actions to respond to and recover from the incident, including the establishment of the Joint Field Office to provide the Incident Commander Federal Resources

Joint Terrorism Task Force a partnership between various American law enforcement agencies that is charged with taking action against terrorism

M

Maritime security protecting the coastal waters of the United States from illegal movement

Mission areas designated areas that are supervised by experienced personnel whose goal is to avoid, prevent, or stop a threatened or actual act of terrorism.

Mitigation the effort to reduce loss of life and property by lessening the impact of disasters

Multiagency Coordination System(s) (MACS) a process that allows all levels of government and all disciplines to work together more efficiently and effectively; coordination occurs across the different disciplines involved in incident management, across jurisdictional lines or across levels of government

N

National Counterterrorism Center (NCTC) U.S. government agency that integrates the national counterterrorism (CT) effort by combining foreign and domestic CT information, providing terrorism analysis, sharing information with partners across the CT enterprise, and driving whole-of-government action to secure national CT objectives.

National Incident Management System the National Incident Management System (NIMS) identifies concepts and principles that answer how to manage emergencies from preparedness to recovery regardless of their cause, size, location or complexity

National Infrastructure Protection Plan provides a unifying framework that integrates a range of efforts designed to enhance the safety of our nation's critical infrastructure

National-level Intelligence Agency government agency responsible for the collection, analysis, and exploitation of information in support of law enforcement, national security, military, and foreign policy objectives.

National Response Framework part of the National Strategy for Homeland Security which provides the guiding principles enabling all levels of domestic response partners to prepare for and provide a unified national response to disasters and emergencies

National Response Plan the National Response Plan (NRP) is an all-discipline, all-hazards plan that establishes a single, comprehensive framework for the management of domestic incidents; it provides the structure and mechanisms for the coordination of federal support to state, local, and tribal incident managers and for exercising direct federal authorities and responsibilities (replaced by the broader National Response Framework)

National Security Presidential Directives similar to an executive order, these directives are focused on directing the various agencies in the executive branch focused on matters concerning national security

National Strategy for Homeland Security a strategic document which guides, organizes, and unifies our Nation's homeland security efforts

Natural disaster an event that occurs in nature, not caused by humans, that affects the environment and results in financial and/or human loss

Nongovernmental organizations (NGOs) legally constituted corporations by people that operate independently from any form of government, such as the American Red Cross

Nuclear weapon an explosive device that derives its destructive force from nuclear reactions, either fission or a combination of fission and fusion

NUSTL National Urban Security Technology Laboratory focused on providing security for large cities and metropolitan areas

O

Office of Homeland Security the office inside of the White House (executive branch) led by former Governor Tom Ridge, charged with securing the homeland, and which served as the nucleus for the Department of Homeland Security

P

Phishing the fraudulent practice of sending emails pretending to be from reputable companies in order to induce individuals to reveal personal information, such as passwords and credit card numbers.

Preparedness a continuous cycle of planning, organizing, training, equipping, exercising, evaluating, and taking corrective action in an effort to ensure effective coordination during incident response

R

Recovery the efforts taken to restore the infrastructure and the social and economic underpinnings of a community to a state of normalcy

Response any measures taken at the onset of an emergence to save lives and protect property

Risk the possibility of loss or injury

S

Security community a region in which a large-scale use of violence has become very unlikely or even unthinkable. The concept of a security community is related to a group of states that enjoys relations of dependable expectations of peace.

Social engineering manipulating people psychologically into performing actions or divulging confidential information.

T

Technocrime also referred to as cybercrime; a type of white collar crime most always resulting in some sort of financial gain.

Transportation Security Administration the federal department under Homeland Security responsible for transportation security in the U.S.

U

Unified command (UC) a structure that brings together the "Incident Commanders" of all major organizations involved in the incident in order to coordinate an effective response while at the same time carrying out their own jurisdictional responsibilities

USA PATRIOT Act a ten-letter acronym for federal legislation formally titled Uniting and Strengthening America by Providing Appropriate Tools Required to Intercept and Obstruct Terrorism Act of 2001; an act of Congress passed in 2001, six weeks after the 9-11 terrorist attacks, that gave new tools to investigate potential terroristic threats in the United States

USCYBERCOM U.S. Cyber Command is specifically tasked with managing risk within DOD networks and making sure those networks are resilient in case of an attack

Index

Note: Page numbers followed by *b* , *f* , and *t* indicate material in boxes, figures, and tables, respectively.

D

I

O

P

U

V

W

Z